Into the Storm

Into the Storm

A Study in Command

TOM CLANCY

with

General Fred Franks, Jr. (Ret.)

G. P. PUTNAM'S SONS
NEW YORK

G. P. PUTNAM'S SONS
Publishers Since 1838
a member of
Penguin Putnam Inc.
200 Madison Avenue
New York, NY 10016

All maps C. P. Commanders, Inc., by Laura Alpher

Library of Congress Cataloging-in-Publication Data

Clancy, Tom, date.
Into the storm : a study in command / Tom Clancy,
with Fred Franks, Jr.
p.   cm.
ISBN 0-399-14236-3
1. Franks, Fred.   2. Persian Gulf War, 1991—United
States. 3. Persian Gulf War, 1991—Biography.
I. Franks, Fred.   II. Title.
DS79.724.U6F7324   1997   96-38068 CIP
956.7044'2—dc21

Printed in the United States of America
1   3   5   7   9   10   8   6   4   2

This book is printed on acid-free paper. ∞

Book design by Deborah Kerner

THIS BOOK IS DEDICATED TO:

THE VETERANS OF
THE DESERT STORM VII CORPS JAYHAWKS
AND THEIR FAMILIES.

THE BLACKHORSE TROOPERS
OF THE 11TH ACR.

THE MEN AND WOMEN OF AMERICA'S ARMY,
WHO DO THEIR DUTY EVERY DAY,
WHO BEAR THE WOUNDS OF WARS PAST,
AND WHO DIED IN SERVICE TO OUR COUNTRY.

CONTENTS

Introduction

THE QUIET LION

HEROES RARELY LOOK THE PART. THE FIRST HOLDER OF THE MEDAL OF Honor I met looked more like a retired accountant than John Wayne, and when I introduced General Fred Franks to a physician friend, the latter remarked that he was a dead ringer for the professor of pediatrics at Cornell University Medical School. And that's really the basis on which we first met. In 1991, I knew a young lad named Kyle who was afflicted with a rare and deadly form of cancer. A friend of mine, Major General Bill Stofft, was heading over to the Persian Gulf after the conclusion of hostilities. There was a senior officer over there, I'd heard, who'd lost a leg in Vietnam. My little buddy had just endured the surgical removal of his leg, and I asked Bill if he might approach this officer and ask him to write a brief letter of encouragement to Kyle, then at Memorial Sloan-Kettering Cancer Center in New York. The officer, I learned from General Stofft, was Fred Franks, then a lieutenant general, and commander of VII Corps. Bill delivered the request, and Lieutenant General Franks responded at once, calling it a privilege. He wrote a warm letter to my friend, and copied it to me with a cover note thanking me for making him aware of my friend and his affliction. That, really, is the bond between us.

Soon thereafter, Fred received another star and a new post as commanding general of the U.S. Army's Training and Doctrine Command (TRADOC) at Fort Monroe in the Virginia Tidewater, a plum job whose mission it is to look into the future and prepare for it, and it was there that we met for the first time. The first order of business was to thank him for his gracious solicitude to my little friend. He waved it off, thanking me again for the opportunity to look after a child, and really that's most of what I needed to learn about this gentleman.

Fred is a man of modest size and words—on the rare occasions when he swears, even that is quiet. There's an engaging shyness to this general officer. Don't be fooled. He's one of the undramatic people who gets the job done and moves on without fanfare to the next mission, leaving accomplishment in his wake.

Soldiers are not what we most often see portrayed on the screen. The best of them, the ones who ascend to generals' stars, are thoughtful students of their profession, scholarly commentators on history, and gifted observers of human psychology. The profession of arms is every bit as broad and deep as medicine or law. Like physicians, officers must know their subject in every detail, for they deal in the currency of life and death, and some mistakes can never be corrected. Like attorneys, they must plan everything in exquisite detail, because in some arenas you have but one chance to get it right.

The sheer intellectual complexity of command is something few have discussed with anything approaching accuracy. In preparing to move his VII Corps across the desert, Fred first of all had to consider the major pieces: U.S. 1st and 3rd Armored Divisions, the renowned 1st Infantry Division (Mechanized), the 1st Cavalry Division, U.K. 1st Armored Division, U.S. 2nd Armored Cavalry Regiment, and three separate artillery brigades. Those units alone account for nearly 100,000 soldiers, each of whom was assigned to a vehicle. Toss in the "loggies," the logistical troops whose unsung but vital job was to keep the "shooters" equipped with everything from diesel fuel to computer chips.

Okay, now imagine that you have to plan the rush hour for a city of, oh, say, 1 million, deciding how each worker gets home; that you have to account for every single one of them, from point of origin to destination, and that everyone has to arrive home at exactly the right time.

Oh, that's not all: Fred had to plan seven different options for his move. So you also must allow for seven different combinations of closed streets, road work, and broken bridges, while still allowing every commuter to make it home at the proper time.

By the way, if you mess this little job up, human lives will be lost.

Sounds easy? We haven't even gotten to the really hard part yet. People will be trying to kill the commuters—organized, trained people, with weapons—and you also must minimize that little hazard.

And yet, in a way, this *was* the easy part. Just to get to that point Fred Franks and his colleagues—men like Creighton Abrams, Ed Burba, Bill DePuy, Colin Powell, Butch Saint, Norm Schwarzkopf, Pete Taylor, Carl Vuono, and so many others—had to fix an Army that in their younger days as lieutenants and captains had been broken by poor political leadership and public antipathy. Fred lost part of a leg in Vietnam. His colleagues were all hurt in one way or another, and the Army nearly lost its soul, while America lost her confidence as a nation. As a major with 1.5 legs, lying in a bed in Valley Forge, he had to conquer pain and heartache, to wonder if he had a career before him at all, and wonder also if his country gave a damn about him and his fellow amputees.

Remember just how dark those days were? The Army was on its back, its NCO corps bled nearly to death in Vietnam, drugs rampant throughout the institution, and morale so low that on more than one post, officers entered barracks only with an armed escort.

Fred was one of the men who had to make good all that others had conspired to destroy. Like the Army of the 1970s, he had to learn to walk all over again. As he had to repair the wounds in his heart, so the Army had to restore its confidence. All these things did happen, however, because Fred and men like him never lost faith in their country or their own ideals.

How great was their task? Looking back from today's perspective, it is more frightening, perhaps, than it was at the time, but the magnitude of the accomplishment can be measured simply: America won the Cold War because she and her allies were too strong to lose. That happened only because Fred Franks and his wounded but proud band of brothers made her so, and that only after healing themselves. I started meeting these men in 1988, and that's when the idea for this book really began. The public image of the Army is most often that of the cinema, and that is generally an infantry squad, because a movie can show only so much. By the same token, the heaviest firepower the Army has—tanks and artillery, which do most of the killing on the modern battlefield—has been largely ignored. And so the image we have of the military is not so much false as limited. That's a lesson I learned at Fort Irwin, California, on a cold January morning. Having had the taste, I had to learn more, and I was fortunate in finding a superb collection of teachers.

Any army is a vast community of people more than a collection of their awesome tools. It may seem grotesque to call war-fighting an art, but war-fighting is more than anything else the leadership of people, and handling people is the most demanding of human arts, all the more so when the currency is life and death. More than that, in a nation's military, you find the nation itself, all of its qualities, whether good or bad, distilled to an odd sort of purity. Our Army has traveled in a single lifetime down a strange and crooked road, from the triumph of World War II through the embarrassment of Korea, through peacekeeping and holding the line in Europe, through tragedy and waste in Vietnam, through near total collapse thereafter, through a long and wrenching process of reconstitution, then again to dominance on the sands of Iraq and Kuwait.

It's a story I could hardly tell by myself, and it's a story for more than one book. From Fred Franks I learned the story of the United States Army, so grievously wounded in Vietnam. Though the viewpoints and perspectives are mine, much of the story is his, and in certain chapters I have felt it only fitting that he tell it in his own words. Other aspects of America's recovery and dominance will come from others in future books, and I hope the reader will come to grasp just how much was done, and how much is owed. There were plenty of infantry squads, and tank crews, and cannoneers, and loggies, all wearing their nation's colors. All of them were trained, supported, and led by the professionals who kept the faith.

And so the man and the army that advanced across sand and rock were ready for their task, their memories of Vietnam never far from their minds, and the lessons of that experience in their hands. The army America deployed to the Persian Gulf might well have been the finest in all of history, equipped with the best weapons, trained in the most realistic fashion, and led by men who'd learned the hard way why you have to get it done right the first time. We all saw the results on TV.

It's been my honor to get to know this man. A man of iron and letters—he's taught poetry at the university level—Fred Franks symbolizes our army as well as any man could.

—TOM CLANCY

1

THE DAY BEFORE

After the evening briefing and a brief talk to his staff and the liaison officers from subordinate units, Fred Franks went back to his sleeping shelter.

In his talk, Franks was emotional about the soldiers and hard-nosed about the task ahead. The staff was quiet and serious. Most listened quietly, and there was a lot of eye contact. When he finished, they all hollered a big "JAY-HAWK"—VII Corps's nickname—and that was it. He left the tent.

Then he was alone with his thoughts. Before he got some rest he wanted to go over some things about the operation ahead and reflect on the events of this day.

There was one thought that would not leave him. "Don't worry, General, we trust you." A soldier in 3rd Armored Division had said that to him on 15 February during one of his many visits to VII Corps units. Now, how am I going to fulfill that trust? he asked himself. It was what the soldiers were thinking—he knew that—and he wanted to be worthy.

During Vietnam, that bond between the soldiers and the country's leaders in Washington had been shattered. It was an open wound. Fred Franks wanted to be one of the commanders who could heal that wound, who could rebuild that trust. It was a powerful, consuming thought on this eve of battle, one that never left him, ever.

★ The next day was G-Day, the beginning of the ground attack to liberate Kuwait of Iraqi forces. The Coalition plan was for the U.S. Marines and the Saudis to attack at 0400, 200 kilometers to the east of VII Corps, while the light forces of U.S. XVIII Corps—the 82nd Airborne Division and the 101st Airborne (Air Assault) Division—and the French would attack 100 kilometers to the west. And then the heavy forces—VII Corps, the armored units of XVIII Corps, and the JFCN (the Arab Joint Forces Command North, an Egyptian Corps and a Syrian division)—would attack on G+1, the day after the next, at BMNT (the beginning of morning nautical twilight, or first light), or 0538 GPS local time (they used global positioning systems to give exact time).

What Franks didn't know then was that this night was going to turn out to be the eve of his own VII Corps attack. When he learned of this change of plans the next day, it was to be for him one of the two greatest surprises of the war.

As far as he knew, the plan and the attack times were set, and he was considering nothing different. Nobody had mentioned the possibility of going early, not Third Army, CENTCOM,* John Yeosock (the Third Army commander, and Franks's immediate superior), or Norm Schwarzkopf. They had hashed out the timing time and again. As far as he knew, they had settled it. The Marines and the Saudis would go into Kuwait and fix Iraqi forces there, and then the heavy forces would go after the RGFC—the Republican Guards Forces Command. VII Corps, the Egyptian Corps, and the heavy part of XVIII Corps were scheduled to attack on G+1 at BMNT.

As he sat there in the silence of his sleeping shelter—an expando van on the back of a five-ton truck—he checked his cigar supply. It was still holding up. Then he lit one as he began to go over in his mind the posture for the attack the day after tomorrow. He had no map, but by now they had been over the plan so many times he had it almost committed to memory. As was his practice, he used the Army's basic problem-solving method and one he himself had taught many times, which went by the acronym METT-T (Mission, Enemy, Terrain, Troops available to you, and Time).

MISSION

The mission was simple: to destroy the RGFC in the VII Corps zone (the corps area of operations) and be prepared to defend northern Kuwait.

ENEMY

The situation was the same as it had been for the past several weeks. The Iraqis had essentially stayed in place, which was not surprising, considering the punishment they would take from the air if they tried any major force repositioning. As far as Fred Franks was concerned, that was just fine. The coalition had them where they wanted them.

Directly in front of VII Corps across the border was the Iraqi VII Corps.

---

*Third Army was Franks's next higher command, while CENTCOM (Central Command) was the overall U.S. Joint Command (Army, Navy, Air Force, and Marines) in the Gulf. CENTCOM was commanded by General H. Norman Schwarzkopf.

Their defense consisted of five infantry divisions, side by side, east to west, and one mechanized division behind them in depth. That defensive line started about twenty kilometers north of the border, with a complex obstacle system of mines, trenches, and defensive bunkers, thicker in the east and less so in the west. In the west, they had left an opening of about forty kilometers, where their defense line curved to the north and west, in order to prevent an envelopment. In military terms, this is called "refusing the flank." The width of their defending infantry divisions was about twenty-five kilometers each, with a total depth of twenty to thirty kilometers.

The VII Corps plan was for the 1st Infantry Division to penetrate one of these divisions in a breach mission, while an enveloping force, consisting of the 2nd Armored Cavalry Regiment, the 1st Armored Division, and the 3rd Armored Division, would simultaneously sweep around the Iraqi flank and attack toward the RGFC. The British 1st Armored Division would meanwhile pass through the 1st INF (infantry) breach, once that was secured, and attack toward the east, to prevent Iraqi forces from threatening the VII Corps flank.

A big disagreement ahead of time had concerned the estimated width and depth of Iraqi frontline division sectors. U.S. intelligence thought the sectors were twenty-five kilometers wide and not so deep; the British thought the Iraqi division sectors were a more narrow fifteen kilometers and deeper. The British were correct, as it turned out, except that the division sectors got wider the farther west you went. That was of significant consequence later, as the British attack hit the command posts of the Iraqi frontline divisions rather than passing to their rear.

Behind the Iraqi VII Corps, the Republican Guards, Iraq's best, had not moved, either. There were six RGFC divisions, three armored/mechanized and three infantry (each Guards division had three brigades), with the closest of these about 150 kilometers from the VII Corps's line of departure. Though at this point, all six were in the VII Corps zone of attack, from the start Franks's intent was to aim VII Corps at the three Guards armored/mechanized divisions (Tawalkana, Medina, and Hammurabi). They knew about where these heavy divisions were, as well as the locations of the three RGFC infantry divisions.

Because air had been able to fix the RGFC strategically (the Iraqis knew that if they tried any major moves, they'd get hit hard), there had not been any apparent major force repositioning since the air campaign had started on 17 January. But air had not completely immobilized the RGFC. The Guards were able to move up to brigade-sized units locally in tactical repositioning, and they had done so frequently. Since immediate intelligence about these changes in position was not available to VII Corps, they would know only approximately where the RGFC brigades were located at any given time.

In other words, that meant that the Iraqi armored forces retained tactical freedom of movement and could move from twenty-five to fifty kilometers to adjust their positions. Thus, attacking units would not know for sure what was just beyond visual range. It would therefore be up to attacking troops to fix the enemy tactically, and then to destroy them. That distinction would dictate Franks's tactics and those of his subordinate unit commanders as they approached RGFC locations. It was likely that attacking units would be involved in a great many "meeting engagements."*

As he pictured in his mind the layout of Iraqi forces, Franks turned his attention to some of the number designations of Iraqi brigades and divisions. They had been the subject of many discussions among intelligence staffs—was it the 12th Division over here, and the 52nd Division over there, or the other way around? These were interesting discussions, and important historically to get the record straight, yet for the purposes of the upcoming attack, he did not think such matters had any practical consequence. Getting unit designations right is valuable for history books, but what he really needed to know was how many divisions and brigades there were, and where they were located. And he had a very good idea of that.

Turning his thoughts back to the Iraqi VII Corps, Franks pictured their five infantry divisions forward on line, behind a barrier system that was less complex moving west from the Wadi al Batin. (The Wadi is an ancient, dry river valley, angling south and west out of Iraq into Saudi Arabia. Along the way, the Wadi defines the western boundary between Kuwait and Iraq.) The division numbers from east to west were the 27th; 25th; 31st; 48th; and 26th. The tactical reserve, located behind the 25th and 31st divisions at a depth of fifty to seventy-five kilometers, was the 12th Armored—actually the 52nd (it was one of the unit designations they'd gotten wrong). Again, it didn't really matter to Franks whether it was numbered the 52nd or the 152nd. It did matter that there was an Iraqi mechanized division that could move; if it could move, it could interdict his logistics or otherwise get in the way of his attacking force. In order to make sure that didn't happen, he had assigned to the British the mission of defeating that division.

The Iraqi VII Corps's westernmost division, the 26th, had two brigades forward in the defensive line. In order to refuse that western flank, they had an

---

*A meeting engagement is a tactical action in which a force that is usually moving "meets" or otherwise runs into an enemy force that is also usually moving, but which could also be stationary. Normally, this is a surprise encounter, even though you know the enemy is out there somewhere. The faster-reacting force usually wins. It takes a lot of practice for units to absorb the initial surprise and continue to act faster than the enemy and in a way that brings combat power to bear. It is a tough tactical maneuver, and indeed a commander obviously would prefer to know in advance where the enemy is so he can think ahead about his mode of attack.

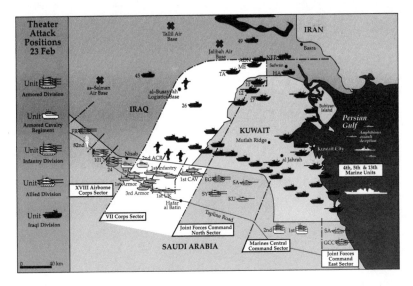

The forces arrayed by the Coalition spread from the Persian Gulf to approximately 600 kilometers inland. VII Corps's mission was to destroy the Republican Guard in their sector of attack.

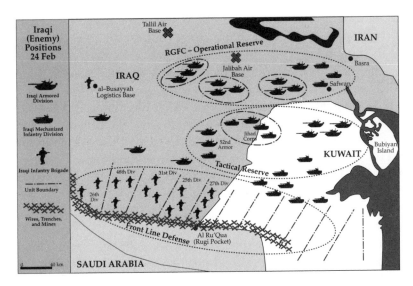

The Iraqi defenses were arrayed in three belts. The frontline consisted primarily of infantry units defending behind a massive obstacle belt of minefields, trenches, and wire. The tactical reserve was poised to reinforce wherever the front lines were breached. The operational reserve—the Republican Guards and other units—defended the southern approaches into Iraq and were capable of counterattacking the Coalition force.

infantry brigade in depth, stretching perhaps fifty kilometers to the rear of the defensive line. It was this 26th Division that the 1st Infantry Division, the Big Red One, would penetrate in their breach mission and that the enveloping force would overrun.

The Iraqi VII Corps had assigned their artillery to frontline divisions and to their subordinate brigades located with those units. Other artillery retained under their corps control was positioned to support the frontline divisions. Total gun count along that initial Iraqi VII Corps defense before the air attacks began was approximately 400 to 500, with over half that in range of the 1st INF breach.

Though Franks was relatively sure about what they were facing in Iraqi VII Corps, he was less sure of the organization of their deep forces and how they would fight. He knew the Guards were their best and most loyal forces. They also were the best equipped, mostly with Russian-made T-72s, BMPs, and self-propelled artillery. In the Iran-Iraq War, they had done well. In the invasion of Kuwait, they had moved and fought efficiently. Even though air had hit them hard, there wasn't much doubt that the RGFC would fight.

Franks's key question, then, was what the Republican Guards would attempt to do when or if they discovered the attack. Defend? Maneuver toward VII Corps units to meet their attack? Attempt to escape up Highway 8 to Baghdad? (Highway 8 was the main route on the south side of the Euphrates between Basra and Baghdad.) Retreat toward Basra? Franks's aim was to fix them where they were, or surprise them before they could move.

There were other Iraqi heavy divisions in the corps's zone as well, the 10th and 12th Armored divisions, formed into what he discovered later was the "Jihad Corps." What would these intermediate forces do? In addition, another heavy division, the 17th, was located near the RGFC, but was not in the VII Corps zone. The presence of these formations and their subordination to the Guards would make a difference in how the Iraqi high command chose to fight VII Corps. Not counting the three RGFC infantry divisions, that gave the Iraqis a six-division theater reserve, three RGFC heavy divisions and three other armored divisions.

As he played all this in his mind's eye, he also considered something else: the location of the Iraqi army was only one piece of the intelligence picture. The other piece was how strong were they? What was their ability to fight? Even at this point, he was not very confident that he knew the answers to that.

In his zone of attack were two very different-type forces. Except for their mechanized infantry reserve, the Iraqi VII Corps consisted of five frontline conscript infantry divisions, fixed in a World War I–type defensive arrangement. VII Corps had had some combat against these units over the previous two weeks, and prisoners and deserters had been taken. After these Iraqi soldiers had been questioned about their dispositions, strength, unit identification, and morale, Franks and his commanders had gotten a pretty clear picture of the Iraqi VII Corps. The infantry divisions were brittle and would easily crack at the first hard, sustained ground attack. They'd been hurt badly by U.S. air, Apache, and artillery attacks, and by the desertion of some of their own leadership. The conclusion was that they were between 50 and 75 percent strength. They did not have much fight left in them.

But Franks had no such clear picture of the RGFC, or of the other Iraqi armored/mechanized formations. Prewar air campaign objectives had called for the reduction of RGFC strength by 50 percent by the time the ground war started. Theater had selected that number based on an analysis of friendly and enemy force ratios. If that figure was achieved, they'd thought, VII Corps would have enough combat power available to finish the destruction in direct ground combat.

As it happened, none of the ground commanders had participated in setting this objective. And when they had learned of it, most had thought it would not be achievable unless the attacks went on a long time.

The real problem was not the specific objective (whether 50 percent or whatever). The problem was that there was no reliable method for determining if the objective had actually been achieved. There was no way of knowing, in fact, if they were even close. Precise bomb-damage assessment (BDA) was difficult. It was relatively easy to figure damage done to a fixed target such as a bridge or an aircraft shelter by a precision-guided weapon, but damage against mobile armored units by dumb bombs or 30-mm cannons from 10,000 feet and higher—now, that was harder.

So VII Corps estimates of Iraqi RGFC strength remained quite conservative. Though in the plans they had briefed they had assumed the stated objective of 50 percent, they always hedged their bets. Their own estimate was that Guards and other Iraqi armored/mechanized units would be closer to 75 percent when VII Corps hit them. Corps also thought that, unlike the front-line infantry divisions, the Guards would fight, and not run away or desert.

As Franks weighed these numbers, he became aware that the real art was to assess enemy fighting capabilities, competence, and willingness to fight. Locating them and determining numbers was the easy part. It was almost scientific. It was this other part that was the art. You wanted neither to overestimate nor underestimate the enemy.

Fred Franks's experience in Vietnam had influenced him on this matter. If he erred, he wanted to err on the side of overestimating the enemy. He wanted to be sure that, this time, the results would be different.

★ In the final analysis, Franks knew that he had a decent intelligence picture for Iraqi unit locations but a poor picture of RGFC strength, fighting capability, and competence.

He was aware again that he had to come to a conclusion. He would also need to predict and influence their tactical maneuver. Would VII Corps be able to keep them fixed where they were and surprise them in the size and direction of the attack? Would they come toward his advancing units? Would they attempt to go up Highway 8? Would they attempt to escape out of the theater? And he also knew he would have to decide all that about twenty-four hours after the VII Corps attack at first light on 25 February.

TERRAIN

From his perspective as corps commander, Franks had not spent a lot of time examining terrain. In Europe it had been vital to determine key terrain—the pieces of ground that dominate an area—and to look very closely at avenues of approach—the areas that allowed rapid movement by large formations in the direction in which you or the enemy wanted to go. They had examined the cross-country traffic ability—the capability of the terrain to allow heavy armored movement—and looked at roads, bridges, airfields, towns, and cities, and at how they might influence operations and logistics.

Not much of that mattered here. This was desert. Fighting here was like naval surface warfare on the open ocean. Here they could essentially take their fleet anywhere, and in almost any formation they wanted. Now smaller units in the corps had to be concerned with the normal rises and drops in the desert as they attacked. They also had to be aware that in some places—especially in 1st AD sector—the sand was softer than in others (and thus less trafficable for heavy armor), and that in some places there were narrow defiles.

So that they could have the best available intel about such areas, a Special Forces night flight had been sent forward into the VII Corps zone to look over the terrain. When the flight had determined that the terrain would hold anything Franks wanted it to, he'd figured he could maneuver his fleet anywhere. So could the Iraqis, he realized. But as it turned out, they anchored their fleet with short chains. Since they had no confidence in cross-desert maneuver (and they did not have access to GPS receivers), the Iraqis mainly stuck to their roads.

In fact, weather turned out to be a bigger factor. Severe local sandstorms, called *shamals*, hid VII Corps attacks from Iraqis, but also limited some use of Apaches, and troops had to fight through cold night temperatures and torrential rains.

TROOPS

The VII Corps situation was excellent. The plan was sound and well understood by all units; they had rehearsed and war-gamed it. The Corps was at full strength, and the equipment availability of major combat assets such as tanks and Bradleys was at 97 percent. That was better than in the Corps's best Cold War days in Germany as part of NATO.

The commanders were ready, and the teamwork among them was tight. It was a talented team. Franks's major maneuver commanders were Major General Tom Rhame, 1st Infantry Division; Major General Ron Griffith, 1st Armored Division; Major General Paul "Butch" Funk, 3rd Armored Division; Major General Rupert Smith, 1st (U.K.) Armored Division; Colonel Don Holder, 2nd Armored Cavalry Regiment; and Colonel Johnnie Hitt, 11th Aviation Brigade. Brigadier General John Tilelli commanded the 1st Cavalry Division, which was to be released to CENTCOM as theater reserve the next day. The corps artillery commander was Brigadier General Creighton Abrams; and Brigadier General Bob McFarlin was the commander of the Corps's almost 27,000-soldier Support Command.

The troops were mentally ready, and they were trained to a razor's edge. During the weeks before combat, they had trained hard to adapt their tactics to the desert and to practice their tasks. They also had been in combat against Iraqis. During the two weeks prior to the attack, Franks had wanted some actual fighting in order to get his forces mentally ready to fight, as well as to conduct feints to deceive the Iraqis as to the actual point of attack, and to destroy artillery in range of the breach site. As a result, the artillery and aviation of every major maneuver unit in VII Corps had by now participated in a combat action against Iraqi frontline units.

TIME

The timing of the attack was clear. They would attack the day after tomorrow at G+1 at BMNT.

Franks's best commander's estimate was that the whole operation would take about eight days: two days to get through non-Guards Iraqi forces and the 150 to 200 kilometers to the Guards themselves, four days to destroy the Guards, and two days for consolidation. The Third Army estimate had been two weeks for the ground offensive and another four for consolidation.

★ That was the METT-T situation facing Fred Franks as he sat in his sleeping shelter, gazing out the opening to the now-quiet life of the main command post.

It was a very familiar scene. It was the Army's practice to use three command posts, called the "tactical," "main," and "rear" posts, depending on their closeness to the enemy. The close—or immediate—battle was led using the tactical command post as a base of operations; the rear post directed all the logistics or combat service support of the unit; and the main command post kept track of the immediate fight and the deeper fight beyond that one, and planned the battles to be fought in the future. At the main command post, all three command activities were normally fully coordinated, as was air support. The main command post was also the link to higher headquarters, both for operational matters as well as for intelligence—all downlink terminals were located there, which brought direct theater or national intelligence system "feed" to the unit.

Franks pictured the main CP in front of him—essentially, a large campsite with tents and truck vans. The area of the CP covered about 500 meters in diameter and perhaps a kilometer in circumference. The entire area was behind a circular, ten-foot-high berm of sand shoved up by Corps engineers. About ten feet outside the berm was triple-strand concertina barbed wire arranged triple-thick and piled in tightly tangled coils. At regular intervals around this berm were six-by-six-foot bunkers, with up to two feet of overhead cover. These were manned by armed soldiers with communication to a central post commanded by the HQ battalion commander.

There was only one entrance to the command post area. To get in, you had to identify yourself to military police, who would pull the temporary sliding wire barrier out of the way, and then you had to drive down a serpentine course past high mounds of sand. Only a few vehicles were permitted inside, and these were directed to a parking area just inside the entrance. There all personnel would dismount and walk to wherever they needed to go. To allow much vehicle traffic inside the CP was to stir up so much sand that it was harmful to the equipment, plus it wasn't safe at night with no lights, and it made life unbearable for the troops. Most vehicles parked outside, and their occupants walked to their destination. Troops manning the entrance could spot vehicles approaching from a long distance.

Inside the perimeter, the truck vans were arranged according to their individual function: Staff elements were located close to other staff elements with whom they needed to coordinate. For example, intelligence and operations were always next to each other, and Air Force air, corps artillery, and Army aviation stayed close together.

These truck vans were what the U.S. Army called "expando vans," like Franks's own sleeping shelter. They were five-ton trucks with a steel enclosure on the back. When the vehicle was stationary, this could be "expanded" by about two feet on each side, thus increasing the work area. The inside of these vans took on various physical configurations depending on their function. Inside dimensions were about twenty by fifteen feet, and they were prewired, so that when you stopped you could plug in cables and have lights. In other words, they were essentially portable offices.

At the main CP were about a thousand soldiers and perhaps two hundred vehicles. Because of the time needed to install long-haul communications for both intelligence and command, and because of the network of cables and wires that had to be hooked up to provide electronic networking capability between these vans, it was not very physically agile.

The picture of a high-tech CP Franks's unit was not. Patton or Bradley would have been right at home here. They used paper maps with hand-drawn symbols on acetate coverings to depict boundaries, phase lines, and objectives, the usual control measures for a corps. They used line-of-sight radios and longer-haul comms that were the equivalent of radio telephones to reach Riyadh or the United States. They used commercial fax machines to transmit hard copies of small papers. For larger acetate overlays, they drew them one at a time and sent them via land or air courier to subordinate units. They had computers for analysis, word processing, and especially intelligence. But in the end, the central focus of all the friendly and enemy information was a paper map posted by hand, not a large-screen computer monitor. It was around that map that they held their discussions, and where Franks made whatever decisions he made in the CP and where he gave guidance.

During the war, Franks would not stay in the main CP, but in the smaller, more mobile TAC CP closer to the fight. He wanted to be up front, where he'd have a more precise feel for the battle.

In Riyadh as well, the battle was tracked on paper maps. In order for information about friendly and enemy units to be accurately and timely posted on those maps, the staff had to rely on voice phone calls and written situation reports that were hours old. In such a setup, where there was no automatic and simultaneous electronic updating of these common situational displays, you had a built-in prescription for misunderstanding.

EARLIER THAT DAY

Franks let his attention stray back over the events of the day, and especially his visits to the units.

He had gone all around the corps talking to commanders, looking soldiers in the eye, shaking their hands, banging them on the back, handing out VII Corps coins, saying a few words, such as "good to go," "good luck," "trust your leaders, we've got a great scheme of maneuver here," "the Iraqis will never know what hit them." And he had called out a "JAYHAWK" or two.

He wanted to show confidence and to get a sense of the electricity going through the units. And he found to be true what he had reported to Secretary Cheney and General Powell on 9 February in the final briefing in Riyadh: "VII Corps is ready to fight." Soldiers were all pumped up. There was some of the usual "kick their ass" type of thing, "the Iraqis are messing with the wrong guys." Soldier-to-soldier chatter.

For the most part, the troops and leaders were going about their work with an air of quiet professionalism. They were doing small things that count, such as cleaning weapons, checking fuel, checking oil in their vehicles, and doing a little maintenance on their vehicles.

During his visits with commanders that day, Franks had talked about some of the pieces of the attack maneuver. Though by this time they had been over the basic maneuver many times, he wanted to review some of the details again. For example, he wanted to look over the coordination between the 1st Armored Division coming up on the left of the 2nd Cavalry. That is, he wanted to review how the 2nd Cavalry, which was initially covering—in front of—both the 1st AD and 3rd AD, would uncover the 1st AD—get out from in front of them—so that 1st AD could dash forward to al-Busayyah, which was their initial objective (called Objective Purple), about 140 kilometers from the attack start point.

He had also talked to Major General Gene Daniel, his deputy, about the task force headquarters that Daniel would head up at the breach. Since the 1st Infantry Division, the British, the Corps logistics elements, two Corps artillery brigades, and perhaps the 1st Cavalry Division had to pass through the breach, he needed a commander there who could make sure that process went without letup, and who could make the necessary adjustments on the spot. (The 1st Cavalry Division was the theater reserve; it was expected—but not certain—that this division would be added to the VII Corps attack.)

And he went to visit the 1st CAV again. His intention had been to attend the memorial service for two soldiers killed on 20 February during division actions in the Ruqi Pocket,* but because of GPS navigation problems (not that unusual in a helicopter), he hadn't arrived at the division until the service was over. However, he was still able to stay around and talk to the troops and commanders. It had been an emotional moment, visiting soldiers who had just

---

*In order to lure the Iraqis into believing that the main American attack was coming due north up the Wadi al Batin axis rather than further west, Franks and his planners had devised a deception scheme that had the division operating in the Ruqi Pocket of the Wadi al Batin. (The Ruqi Pocket was at the tricorner area where the borders of Iraq, Kuwait, and Saudi joined. This area lay at the eastern edge of the VII Corps zone of operations.) Here the 1st CAV had conducted a skillful series of feints and demonstrations against Iraqi forces. During their operation they had captured 1,800 Iraqi prisoners.

lost friends in combat. He knew well that death in combat is sudden and usually unexpected, even though you know it will happen. And he was reminded again of the inner steel required of soldiers and leaders. Soldiers were speaking in soft tones about the action. While they were clearly touched by the loss of their buddies, they were not about to back off. They were ready to go again.

He drew two lessons from the firsthand accounts he heard of the action that morning: First, the 1st CAV was able to strike back hard with a combination of ground maneuver, artillery, and air and severely punish the Iraqis. Second, the Iraqis could deliver heavy and accurate fires if you happened to drive into their predetermined defensive area.

At the 1st Infantry Division, he visited Colonel Bert Maggart's first brigade. Maggart, his commanders, and his brigade staff gave him a thorough briefing on their attack plans in their TAC command post (three M577s parked side by side with canvas extensions off the back to form a small twenty-five-by-thirty-foot work area). They needed no notes or references. They had been over it many times before. Their soldiers were keyed up, ready to go; plans for the attack were set and rehearsed; soldiers had confidence in their leaders and their ability to accomplish the mission. You could see it in their eyes. You could hear it in their voices. Because there had been lots of predictions about the timing of the attack, the troops were getting a little impatient with all the fits and starts. By now they wanted to get into it and finish it and go home.

He found the same attitude in both the 3rd and the 1st Armored Divisions. "We're trained, we know what to do," troopers told him again and again. And he, too, was saying the same thing again and again: "We're ready, we're tough, we're trained. Just look out for each other, follow your leaders, and know what the hell you're doing." He got quick status reports from both division commanders.

At the 1st Armored Division, the spirit of one unit especially touched him, and he spent the better part of an hour with them. They were a Bradley platoon, the 1st Platoon, Company C, 1st Battalion, 7th Infantry, 3rd Brigade, 3rd Infantry Division. They called themselves "Raiders" and their motto was "Get some." The platoon leader was First Lieutenant Doug Morse, and the platoon sergeant was Staff Sergeant Jamie Narramore. They were ready and tough and not without a sense of humor. They had composed a song and sang it for him, a profane description of how tough they were and what they were about to do to the Iraqis. He wasn't sure how they had done it, but they had put every cussword he knew in there. "Thanks for not court-martialing us," Sergeant Narramore told him afterward. They had even gotten him to sign his name on a Bradley for good luck, and Franks and the twenty-eight platoon members had posed for a team picture. After the war, just before they got on the plane to go home, Franks and the Raiders had a mini-reunion; they told him some war stories. They had not had anyone wounded or killed in the action. He still has the Raiders picture on his wall at home.

Some of the leaders were going through last-minute rock drills when he visited. In a "rock drill," leaders go out in the sand and mark out a piece of ground with white engineer tape to make a scaled replica of their actual anticipated battle area. Then, using rocks as unit icons, they move the rocks to show how they plan to move their units in relationship to one another, the terrain, and the enemy.

Based on what he'd seen in Vietnam, the troops were in about the right frame of mind and keyed up properly. In Vietnam, another generation of American soldiers had gone across half the world to do what their country had asked; and tactically they'd done it as well as any other generation of American combat soldiers could. But this time it was going to end differently. They all would see to that.

REFLECTIONS

Franks was proud of his VII Corps team. After looking back over the day's visits, he thought again about trust—and made a quick inventory of what he needed to do to fulfill that trust.

He had gone over his "commander's intent" with his commanders a number of times. This is the concise expression of how you visualize the operation, and it is always written by the commander personally. In the absence of specific orders, it could be used as operating guidelines. By now he thought it was clear and well understood. It read,

> *I intend to conduct a swift series of attacks to destroy RGFC and minimize our own casualties. Speed, tempo, and a coordinated air/land campaign are key. I want Iraqi forces to move so that we can attack them throughout the depth of their formations by fire, maneuver, and air. The first phases of our operation will be deliberate and rehearsed, the latter will be more METT-T dependent. We will conduct a deliberate breach with precision and synchronization, resulting from precise targeting and continuous rehearsals. Once through the breach, I intend to defeat forces to the east rapidly, with one division as economy of force, and to pass three divisions and ACR as point of main effort to the west of that action, to destroy RGFC in a fast-moving battle with zones of action and agile forces attacking by fire, maneuver, and air. CSS must keep up, because I intend no pauses. We must strike hard and continually and finish rapidly.*

Franks then turned his attention to a specific skill: the ability to picture operations in his head, and to judge time/distance factors to get the right units in the right combination at the right place at the right time. Franks called this "orchestrating" the battle. How would we do? How would his commanders?

The Army had given Franks lots of opportunities to practice and develop this skill, from platoon leader to corps commander. That training and some excellent mentors had a lot to do with the honing of his ability, as had the crucible of Vietnam. But it was not only a matter of practice and experience; it also had to do with the way the brain worked—with imagination.

All he knew was that somehow he could see a battle clearly in his head, relate the physical and soldier pieces together, and figure how long it would take a division, for example, to turn three brigades ninety degrees, or to mark twenty-four lanes of a minefield breach, or to close an artillery brigade on a moving division, or to close three divisions on a common objective.

Some commanders were better than others at orchestrating a battle. For some it was a learned skill; for others it came more easily. For the conduct of battle they were about to wage, it was indispensable. But Franks felt all his commanders had it. He had had the opportunity to make his own judgments about all of them during their time together these past few months.

At Third Army he trusted John Yeosock. Even though he had not commanded a corps, Yeosock understood all this, as did his G-3, Brigadier General Steve Arnold. Senior to them, Franks was not quite sure. He was never sure, especially at CENTCOM in the basement of the MOD building in Riyadh, how VII Corps maneuvers would be interpreted. As it happened, the perception there of what it would take to maneuver this large, multidivision, 146,000-soldier armored corps in a coordinated attack of over 200 kilometers was very different from how it was on the scene in Iraq and Kuwait. This difference in perception would lead to controversies later.

Allied to this last issue was a communications matter that did not concern him then—CENTCOM HQ's picture of both the enemy and friendly situation. In light of later events, he realized it should have.

Would their picture be the same as his own? Would his main command post (itself many kilometers from his location and the battle) be able to track the battle close enough to keep Third Army informed and to accurately write the required daily commander's situation reports? And then would this information get passed accurately to CENTCOM? Would J-3 (CENTCOM operations) even pay attention to what a single corps was doing? Or would that get rolled up in a big picture? Would CENTCOM be aware of the normal time-info lag of ground operations reports and situational displays? And then would they ask for an update before making decisions critical to ground ops?

Where would Franks's higher commanders choose to locate themselves during the conduct of the ground war? Would they come forward into Iraq, where he would be in order to get a firsthand feel for the fight? And, finally, should he talk to Schwarzkopf during the war? Or should he communicate primarily with his immediate commander, John Yeosock?

He was confident that his subordinates at VII Corps's main command post would get the communication job done. They were a smart, talented, skilled group. They would certainly report the correct picture of VII Corps's actions to Third Army.

★ Possible use of chemical and biological weapons was a big concern, however. Had they gotten to all the Iraqi artillery capable of reaching the 1st Infantry Division in the breach or the follow-on units passing through the breach? They had no way of completely knowing. No other issue made Franks feel so much anger at the Iraqi leadership as their possible use of chemical or biological warfare.

VII Corps was face-to-face with the possibility that the Iraqis would use one or both. They had them. They had used them on their own people and against Iran. There was nothing in their behavior or battle tendencies that indicated they would do anything different this time. Franks truly expected it.

The VII Corps commanders and soldiers were not intimidated by any of this, however. For a long time, they had trained in chemical protective gear in NATO and U.S. training exercises, fully expecting the Warsaw Pact to use chemicals. It had all seemed so abstract then, though. They would endure these periods of time in masks and chemical suits, shouting in squeaky voices through their masks to be heard on the radio, sweating even in the winter inside the charcoal suits, fumbling as they tried to lace up the damned rubber booties someone had designed to go over their regular boots, wearing the monster rubber gloves, and laboring to look through gun sights with a protective mask on. They had made it work through disciplined training. They had done it so much it had become routine and a source of confidence, as long as they had the right gear. They had gotten that taken care of a few days before. They had protective measures. They also had antidotes. They were ready.

Biological warfare was a different matter. Franks was not so sure about this. They had had very little training against biological agents in Germany and were mostly unfamiliar with the agents, even though some of them, such as anthrax, botulism, and salmonella, were commonly known sicknesses. The problem with biological warfare is that the biological agents have a delayed effect, which makes detection of the source difficult. It's hard to find evidence of who did it—and thus retaliation is difficult. They had all taken a crash course on Iraqi delivery means, though. The VII Corps NBC officer, Colonel Bob Thornton, and G-2 (Intelligence) Colonel John Davidson were helpful in getting whatever information was available. Franks wanted to stop a lot of rumors and bad information going around. He did not want the troops intimidated by Iraqi biological warfare capability. Of all the capabilities possessed by the Iraqis, it was the one that concerned him the most, right up to the end of the war.

⭐ He also was aware of some other things that night—larger issues beyond the actual conduct of their mission.

To Fred Franks, and to most of his soldiers and leaders, what they were about to do was their duty, pure and simple. They were professionals sent to skillfully use force as an instrument of their government (and of the U.N.), to compel a foreign belligerent to do what a U.N. resolution had ordered them to do. They knew how to do that. But this was not a jihad for them. This was neither total war, nor a war to save civilization, nor a war to stop madmen from trying to enslave the greater part of the world. The mission was clear: to liberate a nation and drive an invader out in an area of vital interests. It was use of force to gain specific strategic objectives at the least cost to their own side—then go home. This would affect Franks's selection of tactics; he thought it would be irresponsible of him and of VII Corps to pay an unlimited price in the lives of their soldiers for a limited objective. Vietnam had taught them all that.

Perhaps SfC Ed Felder of Company D, 1st Battalion, 37th Armor, 1st Armored Division had said it best: "Nobody wants to go to war, but we train for it every day. That's what we get paid to do. We're professionals." And PFC Bruce Huggins, a tank mechanic of that battalion's headquarters company, said, "They asked for our help and we're going to give them that help and we'll free that country. We'll do our job, go home, and carry on with life."

The end result was never in doubt. They would win. For him as a major commander it was a matter of selection of method and one that would come at least cost to soldiers for the mission assigned. There would be individual acts of heroism, as there always were. But for senior commanders, Franks saw nothing particularly heroic in what they were about to do. He had said right from the start, "We'll go do what we have to do and talk about it later." This was in the mode of Korea, Vietnam, and Panama. It was not a crusade.

That distinction comes hard for Americans. In our own history, more often than not, we have fought "crusades" or used force for national survival: the Revolution, the War of 1812, the Civil War, World Wars I and II. Not only do Americans have less experience with the other kind of war, but they tend as a matter of national character not to be warlike—even though America's sons and daughters make the best warriors when called upon.

The other factor that stayed with Franks was Vietnam. In the hospital at

Valley Forge, where he had had his leg amputated, he had made a pledge to his fellow amputees and to his fellow Vietnam veterans: "Never again." Never again would young men and women come away from a battlefield on which they were asked to risk their lives without gaining their objectives, without having those objectives thought to be worth the effort, without an agreement ahead of time that the tactical methods needed to achieve strategic objectives were acceptable for the military to use, and without a word of thanks to those who went when it was all over.

Fred Franks was not in charge of all that; but he was in a position to satisfy himself as a commander that all these mistakes would not be repeated. That conviction burned hot in him, like a blue flame. Vietnam was never far from him throughout Desert Shield and Desert Storm. Now, that was a crusade, at least for Fred Franks.

Another factor he got out of Vietnam was a respect for war and its costs, and for what it takes to win. When you're on the battlefield, you get into fights, either deliberately or in surprise meeting engagements with the enemy, and they got into a lot of those in Vietnam. Franks believed that you had to make it an unfair fight as rapidly as you could. You wanted to get all the advantages on your side, and to win the tactical engagement as rapidly as possible and at least cost to your soldiers. That meant a lot of firepower. It also usually meant moving into a positional advantage and bringing brutal amounts of fire to bear on the enemy, until they called it quits and ran away, or you destroyed their capability to continue, and controlled the area. And that was the end of it.

In Vietnam, "If the enemy fired at us with a single AK-47 round, we pounded them with all we had. We put as much firepower back on them as we had, so much firepower that they wished they hadn't started something."

That influenced his thoughts on Iraq. Different commanders might do things in different ways, but Franks's way was, "When we came into contact in the area of main attack, then it was going to be with a big fist. We were going to hammer the Iraqis relentlessly with that fist until we finished them. We were going to sustain the momentum of that attack until we were through with what we came there to do."

So the idea of "fair fight" had no meaning for Franks in this context. It seemed totally insane to give the enemy some sporting chance to win.

"If you have to fight," Franks liked to say, "then 100 to nothing is about the right score for the battlefield. Twenty-four to twenty-one may be okay in the NFL on Sunday afternoon, but not on the battlefield.

"My inclination in tactics is to maneuver our force to bring so much combat power to bear on the other force that we will get them backpedaling. I want to get them on the ropes and keep them there. Then, when we've got them down, we'll finish them. We're going to finish them.

"If we have to fight, then we were going to go for the jugular, not the capillaries.

"But once we are winning our battles, we've got to link those successful battles in some pattern or direction, so they add up to mean something bigger. They have to end up accomplishing your strategic aims. That is why you are fighting those battles. And that is why the troops who are risking it all to win those battles trust that the generals and Secretaries of Defense and Presidents know what they are doing, and will make all that sweat and blood count for something."

From what Franks and his commanders had seen so far, the command climate was far different from the one in Vietnam. They could feel the steel in the will, from the President and the Secretary of Defense through General Powell, to the theater. It was solid.

⋆   Finally he was at peace with himself, as much as any commander could be on the eve of battle. His troops and leaders were ready. They had worked like hell to get to where they were, and most units had had the minimum two weeks' training he thought necessary. Soldiers were confident in themselves, their equipment, one another, and their leaders. Franks had known that would come because of the training in Saudi Arabia and the team-building they had worked on since the start of the mission to deploy on 8 November. They had become the VII Corps team so necessary for success in combat.

On 21 February, Sam Donaldson of ABC News came to visit VII Corps. Franks escorted him to the 2nd ACR and 1st AD. While at 1st AD, Donaldson talked to members of an M1A1 tank company commanded by Captain Dana Pittard. Franks was never more proud of his soldiers than he was when he heard them talk of the mission and of one another. Specialist Shawn Freeney, a mechanic in Headquarters Company, 1st Battalion, 37th Armor, said, "It lets you know that, when it comes down to it, you're around family. All of us here are family—right here is my family."

They had prepared the way you would for a big game. They had emphasized skills in fundamentals and teamwork. They had gone through situation drills against possible game situations. They had gotten their "batting practice" under close-to-game conditions and they had had some scrimmages.

But where Franks knew the sports analogy stopped was game time. War is different. Ground combat is physically tough, uncompromising, and final. The enemy can be as close as a few meters or thousands of meters. There you deal in the ultimate reality—life and death. There is no home-and-home scheduling. There is no next year. When it's over, it's over; the memories and results are frozen in time for a lifetime. For some soldiers, there would be no more lifetime after this. Fred Franks knew that, and so did they.

Franks thought again of his soldiers and leaders. "Have I prepared them well enough for this mission? I think so. Did we have a workable plan? Yes. Have we thought of everything? Probably not. Have we ignored anything major? I don't think so. Are the troops ready? Yes. They know what to do, they're motivated by the right things, and they want to get this going and get it finished so they can go home. Not a complicated set of emotions. Soldiers and units go at two speeds, all-ahead full or stop. There can be no half-stepping, especially for a mounted attack. We're ready."

He recalled then something Captain Dana Pittard had said to Sam Donaldson: "My biggest fear, of course, is making sure I don't do something wrong that would cost somebody's life or something else. There's no fear on the personal side." He also recalled the old saying that generals can lose battles and campaigns, but only the soldiers can win. He believed that. He also believed that if he got them and their commanders to the right place at the right time in the right combination, in battle after battle, they would take it from there and win.

★ His thoughts turned to Denise, his wife of thirty-one years, and to their daughter, Margie, and her family. They were all a close family; they'd been through a lot together. Denise was now busy at home in Germany with family support work. For the first time in the history of the U.S. Army, they had taken units already deployed in one theater (with families), deployed to another, and left their families overseas.

Someone had asked Denise if she was "going home"—that is, leaving Stuttgart and returning to the United States. "I am home," she replied. Though they could have returned to the States, most families stayed right there. In doing that, they were breaking new ground, adapting to new realities. And Denise was providing leadership and moral strength in her own quiet and forceful way. She was showing her own form of courage . . . just as were all the other family members in Germany. They were answering the call. Their favorite song was "From a Distance."

Franks remembered all that he, Denise, and Margie had been through during and after Vietnam. And he remembered the hospital recovery of almost twenty-one months.

Before he'd left for the Gulf, he had promised Denise he'd come back "whole" from this operation, but with a smile, she'd reminded him that that was no longer possible. They hadn't been able to phone each other often while he was on duty in the Gulf. The one phone call they'd had to this point in January was tense and full of feeling.

In Bad Kissingen, Germany, Margie, also now an Army spouse, had her own family of two boys and her husband, Greg. Greg was a captain in the Blackhorse. At that moment, he was S-3 of the 2nd Squadron, 11th ACR, or "Battle 3," the same job Franks had had in Vietnam. Now Margie's dad was at war again. Denise had sent him a tape recording of the family, and he would listen to it to hear the sounds of their voices. Family was real close, just like his VII Corps family. They both inspired him.

After pulling his tanker suit pant leg over the top so he did not have to remove the boot, Franks unstrapped his prosthetic leg. He set it where he could reach it in the dark, then pulled the sleeping bag over him, said a prayer for his troops and that he would have the wisdom to do what was right, and slept soundly.

2

DUTY

MAJOR FRED FRANKS FOUGHT IN VIETNAM WITH THE 11TH ARMORED Cavalry Regiment, the "Blackhorse," from August 1969, when he arrived, to May 1970, when he was severely wounded during the Cambodian invasion. He had previously served with the Blackhorse in Germany for almost three and a half years, from March 1960 to July 1963, and he was glad to be back in his old outfit. He was a cavalry officer; he knew cavalry; cavalry was his home. And the Blackhorse was his regiment.

Like so many Americans before him, Franks got off the plane with his fellow soldiers at Long Binh, Vietnam, ready to do his duty. He had flown over in a stretch DC-8 out of Travis Air Force Base, just north of San Francisco. Just the day before, he had said good-bye to Denise and Margie at the Philadelphia International Airport and flown to San Francisco. His kid brother, Farrell, had driven them to the airport, and his mother and dad met them there to say good-bye. It was a quick forty-eight-hour transition from what soldiers called "the world" to a combat zone.

The first thing that hit him getting off the plane was the unmistakable smell. It was a combination of the heat, the smoke in the air from burning wood, and who knew what else. But he would never forget it.

Fighter aircraft were parked close by. He heard sounds of jet fighters taking off and flying overhead, as well as the unmistakable Vietnam sound of UH-1 "Huey" helicopter rotor blades slapping in the air. He was intent on taking in as much as he could, right away, as he thought back on how he'd gotten there.

After graduating from West Point in 1959, Franks had asked for and was commissioned into armor. He was a "tanker," and yet he saw himself as more than that. Though tanks are the centerpiece of cavalry—they give it its punch—cavalry goes beyond tanks. Armored cavalry is the first team; it has a command freedom, an esprit, an ethos. In the cavalry, small units operate a combination of potent weapons systems (in the Army, this is called "combined arms") that give them the capability to move fast and hit hard. On the battlefield, these units operate under decentralized leadership in missions that are out in front of everyone else.

First, though, Franks had to go through some fundamentals: a basic armor course at Fort Knox, then Ranger and airborne schools at Fort Benning. Chest deep on patrol in the dark waters of the Florida swamps and then in the numbing cold of the Dahlonega, in the Georgia hills, Franks learned a lot about himself and combat. It was the best individual peacetime training he ever got in the Army.

Franks did his apprentice work in armored cavalry along the Iron Curtain between Czechoslovakia and West Germany during a time that included the 1961 Berlin crisis and the 1962 Cuban missile crisis. In the crucible of daily life as a young troop leader in the Blackhorse, he learned from the officers and noncommissioned officers the tough, hard skills of small-unit tactical leadership. Combat veterans of World War II and Korea drilled them on combat cavalry fundamentals and taught them tribal wisdom through war stories during the long nights at the border camps along the Czech border. Like so many others, he developed his tactical skills by doing his job day to day in the field, by listening, working hard, and by making damn-fool mistakes, and being allowed to get back up and learn from them.

For his first fifteen months in the Blackhorse, Franks was a lieutenant leader of the smallest combined-arms unit in the U.S. Army, an armored cavalry platoon of scouts, tanks, mechanized infantry, and a self-propelled mortar. From there he was the squadron's support platoon leader, responsible for leading truck resupply of the squadron. For the next eight months, he was executive officer (second in command) of a cavalry troop. Then he commanded Troop I.

When he headed to Vietnam, it was the Blackhorse he intended to belong to—but he almost didn't make it. By the time Franks got to Vietnam, the beginnings of the U.S. drawdown had screwed up the individual replacement system so badly that all orders were canceled, and new replacements were sequestered upon arrival to await new orders. He was instructed not to call anyone. No way, Franks thought, I've got to get to a phone. He got through to a sergeant at the Blackhorse unit at Long Binh. "Wait right there, don't go anywhere else, we'll be over to get you. We knew you were coming."

The next morning, true to the sergeant's word, the Blackhorse sent a vehicle over and picked him up. "Major Franks? Come with me, sir. Your orders are all cut and we're ready to go." When Franks saw that rearing black horse patch on the soldier's shoulder, he felt as though he had seen a family member. Actually, he had.

In 1969, the Blackhorse was one of four cavalry regiments on active duty in the Army. The others, 2nd, 3rd, and 14th, were in Germany. The Blackhorse had been withdrawn from Germany in the summer of 1964 and stationed at Fort Meade, Maryland. When the big U.S. buildup in Vietnam began in 1965, it soon became apparent that an armored cavalry regiment would be a valuable asset in the war, and the 11th ACR was deployed to Vietnam, arriving in 1966. It immediately established itself as a tough combat regiment, successfully completing a wide variety of missions on many different terrains. Soon it had inflicted heavy punishment on the Viet Cong and the NVA, the North Vietnamese Army.

The Army is a competitive organization, but Franks was a competitive man. When he joined the 11th ACR in Vietnam, he had not yet met a wall that could stop him. If there was a hurdle to leap—physical, psychological, or intellectual—he leapt it. If he failed the first time, he worked and trained until he made it over. He was an athlete; he was used to intense training and to hard drills. And he was used to the payoff that hard training gave him. Though at five-eight, he couldn't be called physically impressive, he was a talented baseball player who'd reached a career batting average of better than .300 on the West Point baseball team, and been team captain. There's a good chance he would have succeeded as a professional ballplayer. He was tempted. In 1961, the choice confronted him: to be a soldier or a baseball player. Franks chose soldier.

There was also in him a finely tuned, well-developed mind, and in 1964, the Army sent him to Columbia University to study for an M.A. in English. Afterward, he was scheduled to teach at West Point. It was a two-year course at a high-ranking school, but characteristically, he pushed it. He finished the degree in a year, in the belief that he would be sent to Vietnam for the second year, and then to West Point following that. Somehow a bureaucratic foul-up put a stop to that: "If we've set you up for two years of study," he was told, "you have to put yourself through two years of study." And it turned out he couldn't go to Vietnam in 1965 after all. Daunted, yet still pushing hard, he continued at Columbia and completed most of the course work for a Ph.D. Then he went on, as planned, to West Point, where, on a teacher's schedule, he had the opportunity to finish up his days at a reasonable hour and perhaps spend real time with Denise and Margie (like most young Army officers, he'd been away more often than he was home).

Don't count on it. He did get to spend more time with them, but he also hit the books and completed his Ph.D. orals, while carrying a full teaching load and taking on the job of assistant varsity baseball coach for the fall and spring. On top of that, he took a correspondence course from Fort Sill to keep his nuclear weapons proficiency current, a necessary skill for officers in the 1960s.

★ Serious American involvement in the Vietnam War began in 1962. By the late 1960s, U.S. forces had grown to over half a million, and with that increase came a number of plans and programs for victory. Though not all of them were ill conceived, even the best needed time for successful completion, and some came too late. The United States was out of time. By the late summer of 1969, strong antiwar feelings in the States, brought about primarily by the ever-increasing American casualties, had caused President Nixon to begin a general withdrawal. At the same time, he hoped to give the South Vietnamese government some chance at survival. The program was called Vietnamization. Its aim was to turn more and more of the ground war over to the South Vietnamese, while the United States simultaneously provided air and logistics assistance and began to withdraw its own combat troops. Operations were launched to attempt to buy time for the South Vietnamese, such as the continuation of the "secret" bombings of Cambodia, then the invasion of Cambodia in May 1970. Others would follow.

In August 1969, the regimental command post of the Blackhorse was at the village of Quan Loi. Quan Loi was just east of the market town of An Loc, forty kilometers from the Cambodian border and about a forty-five-minute helicopter ride or a four-hour armed convoy trip from Long Binh. A C-130-capable airstrip was also at Quan Loi, and the regiment's air cavalry troop operated out of there. The 11th Cavalry rear base was at Long Binh, near Saigon, the largest U.S. Army logistics facility in Vietnam.

The regiment was commanded at the time by Colonel Jimmie Leach, an experienced and aggressive cavalry commander. A World War II tanker, Leach had commanded a tank company in General Creighton Abrams's 37th Tank Battalion in the 4th Armored Division.

One of the regiment's missions was to keep open the major road from Lai Khe, in the south, through An Loc, to Loc Ninh to the north. To do this required a daily mine sweep of the road, plus active reconnaissance of the area to either side of it. All three of the regiment's squadrons and the air cavalry troop were engaged in this operation. The Blackhorse at the time was under the operational control of the Big Red One, the 1st Infantry Division, whose headquarters were at Lai Khe. Other missions involved direct attack on NVA units when they were found and fixed, and area reconnaissance of the entire area to keep the NVA out. Meanwhile, as part of the consolidation that was one of the first consequences of Vietnamization, the 1st Infantry had been given orders to begin to redeploy back to the United States. As part of that redeployment, they would give up some of their rear base camps around Long Binh and Di An, and the Blackhorse rear base was moved from Xuan Loc, their home from the time they came to Vietnam, to Long Binh. Some residual 2nd Squadron elements were to move to Di An.

When Franks reported for duty, Leach assigned him to 2nd Squadron, but ordered him back south to Xuan Loc to help clear up some problems and to plan the rear base move to Di An. Franks knew he had a lot to learn in a short period of time.

Franks was what the troops called a "fanoogie," abbreviated as FNG and standing for "f'ing new guy." It was a way for veterans to set themselves apart from the newcomers and to tell the new guys that they had lots to learn and some rites of passage to go through. There was an official way to do it, too—the Army sent all newcomers through a five-day course in-country to indoctrinate them in the ways of the unit and combat techniques and the enemy. Unfortunately, those courses were at Long Binh and Franks was at Xuan Loc, some distance away. He needed a substitute crash course fast.

The course he needed was right under his nose at Xuan Loc. Franks had always felt new leaders and commanders should spend a lot of time listening, and not a lot of time sounding off: When you join a new unit, you find mostly soldiers and leaders who want to belong to a great outfit. They want you to succeed. They want you to be able to lead and command them well. Give them a chance to tell you early on how they think they can help you do that. It had worked for him in the Blackhorse before. Gain the soldiers' confidence and respect by treating them the same way you want to be treated. Earn your way on the team in a hurry and learn while you are doing it. The first few weeks are when you learn the ropes and you also make a first impression, and, like it or not, as soon as you get there, you are being sized up by the soldiers, your peers, and your superiors. They will put you through both formal and informal rites of passage to see what you are made of. You just have to be ready to rise to the challenge.

So Franks wanted to spend as much time as possible with the soldiers, because it was the best way to read himself into this new situation. Many of the NCOs there in 2nd Squadron had seen considerable action in the past months. All he had to do was ask. Franks was able to draw out of them information about the country and terrain, the enemy, and about small-unit fighting techniques and tactics. He also had the opportunity to spend time with Captain Claude "Keyes" Hudson, who had been commanding the 2nd Squadron rear base, had recently been a cavalry troop commander, and was soon to go home. Hudson turned out to be a walking repository of lessons learned, and Franks pumped him for more information. Franks knew how to fight troops and the squadron. What he did not know were the actual tactical methods that worked here, in this terrain, against this enemy. Keyes and the NCOs gave him an introduction to Vietnam and to the Blackhorse he could not have gotten anywhere else.

That was lucky, because what Franks had gotten back in the States hadn't been any help. Before he left, he had been sent to Fort Knox for a standard "refresher course," whose aim was to bring officers up to speed for service in Vietnam. Franks couldn't believe what he found. They were teaching World War II in Central Europe, and using an old series of radios no longer in service in Vietnam. After a few days, he'd stopped going to class and sought out Vietnam veterans, especially Blackhorse veterans, for information. It was invaluable, and a far sight better.

Then he got a break. Lieutenant Colonel Jim Aarstaat wanted him to come forward to Quan Loi to become the 2nd Squadron S-3 (in charge of plans and operations) when the current squadron S-3, Major John Gilbreath, went on R and R. Though the job was officially temporary, it looked likely to become permanent. When Gilbreath returned, he would probably become the squadron XO (second in command) and Franks would remain S-3.

To Franks, this was the best job you could have as a major in the Blackhorse. In the U.S. Army, majors do not command; the closest they could get to the action was as a battalion or squadron S-3. It was the first team. To be a major S-3 in an elite outfit like the Blackhorse was a real honor, and the toughest, most challenging combat job an armor major could find.

But it sure happened fast. John Gilbreath was about twenty kilometers west of Quan Loi operating out of a small firebase. Franks asked Gilbreath when he was going on R and R. He said tomorrow. They had a short transition meeting about the squadron mission and how it was conducting operations, then Gilbreath took him up on a reconnaissance flight over the area. It was fast and low, and the only place for him to ride was on the floor in the back of the OH-6 helicopter as Gilbreath pointed out the terrain, the enemy routes, and recent battle sites. And that was it. He was the S-3 of the squadron. He'd been in Vietnam for all of two weeks. Years later, Franks would remember those two weeks as he thought about how much time VII Corps needed to prepare for combat in Saudi Arabia.

Meanwhile, all this was not unfamiliar. The organization was basically the same as in Germany. The enemy was different, but it was apparent that the squadron operated just as he would expect it to. The cavalry troops, including the air cavalry troop, would find and fix the enemy. Then, while air and artillery isolated them on the battlefield, sealed off the enemy retreat, and simultaneously pounded the enemy with fires, the big fist of the tank company would maneuver against them, along with the cavalry troops. The job of the S-3—under the commander—was to orchestrate it all and bring all the weapons into the fight simultaneously.

As a young officer in a cavalry troop, you pick up an enormous amount of experience doing these things. You're involved in operations where a large number of actions are going on simultaneously, almost all of them out of your sight. You need a creative imagination. You have to know what's going on by listening to reports on the radio. You see some of it. You hear most of it. You picture it in your mind. One action in the woods. Another over by the river. Another near the town. Maybe some indirect fire behind the woods. Maybe some attack helicopters between the woods and the town. And maybe some close air support coming in along the river. Quick decisions are required, often without seeing it all except in your head. You have to figure time/distance factors. Can a unit reinforce in time? Can they beat the enemy to the punch? All of these actions are happening simultaneously, and all of them happening, much of the time, under conditions of stress and fatigue, in all kinds of weather, and with casualties. And so as a cavalry officer, you grow to be proficient at juggling half a dozen or so thoughts simultaneously in your head, picturing actions in your mind's eye, and constantly making judgments about when to act and when to remain silent and let things go on.

Because he had had so much practice at this kind of "battle orchestration" during his time in Germany with the Blackhorse, Franks had no doubt that he could do what he had to as S-3 in Vietnam. It was a matter of adapting quickly to the techniques to be used in *this* terrain against *this* enemy, and at the squadron level, instead of the smaller cavalry troop.

And he knew he better get it right from the start, because there were a lot of soldiers depending on it. They had every right to expect him to know what he was doing, and if he did not measure up, they had every right to get someone else.

When he took over as 2nd Squadron S-3, this is what Fred Franks had to deal with:

An armored cavalry squadron in Vietnam normally consisted of a headquarters, with about 200 troops; three lettered cavalry troops (2nd Squadron troops were E, F, and G), each with better than 130 men; a tank company of seventeen M48A3 tanks and about 85 troops; and a howitzer battery of six 155-mm artillery pieces, with about 125 troops. Later, the 2nd Squadron would get two eight-inch howitzers, with about forty troops, and a platoon of 40-mm antiaircraft pieces, which was an attached unit that went with the squadron. A combat engineer platoon from the regiment's 919th Engineer Company also went with them. At that time, the cavalry troops did not have tanks, but instead vehicles known as ACAVs, Armored Cavalry Assault Vehicles (M113s), which were lightly armored tracked vehicles armed with machine guns. The squadron also had a section of four helicopters to be used for command and control of squadron operations. There were two UH-1 "Hueys" and two OH-6 "Loaches." Normally, the squadron commander used the UH-1s, and the S-3 used the OH-6s. There were crews for each aircraft and they flew alternate days, while the commander and S-3 flew every day. The regiment also had an aviation troop with Cobra attack helicopters and OH-6 scout helicopters. These normally flew in support of daily squadron operations or worked independently at the regimental commander's directions. The Cobras were called "red" teams, and the scouts were "white" teams (cavalry colors are red and white). When they worked in pairs (one Cobra and one Loach), they were called "pink" teams.

The job of the S-3 was to plan the operations and run the nerve center of the squadron. Under the commander's guidance, the S-3 would devise a plan that would ensure that the elements of the squadron combat power—artillery, engineers, tanks, scouts, cavalry troops, and air—were all tied together in some coherent way to do what the commander wanted done to defeat the enemy at least cost to the squadron. At the forward command post, the commander and S-3 would work out of three M577 command post tracked vehicles. They each also had their own command tracked vehicle, M113 ACAVs.

The command post of a cavalry squadron is small and informal. It was—and is—organized like this: below the executive officer was a staff—S-1, S-2, S-3, and S-4 (S is for "staff"). The -1 handled personnel; the -2 handled intelligence; the -3 handled plans and operations; and the -4 handled logistics. Normally, the S-3 was the senior of these four and coordinated with them. The 2nd Squadron of the 11th ACR in Vietnam was set up so that the personnel and logistics elements, and the XO, normally stayed at the base camp (at Quan Loi at that time), while the operational element (S-2 and S-3) was out ranging as far as fifty kilometers from there. Lieutenant Colonel Aarstaat would choose where to be to command if a fight broke out. There was a fight nearly every day.

By August 1969, the enemy was now no longer the Viet Cong, but North Vietnamese regulars. The Tet Offensive of 1968, which has usually been perceived as a disaster for U.S. forces, was actually a catastrophe for the Viet Cong. Tet virtually destroyed the Viet Cong as an operational force. Afterward, the North Vietnamese Army took over military operations in the south. The few Viet Cong that were left might have laid mines or involved themselves with other minor actions, but any serious engagements involving 2nd Squadron were always with the North Vietnamese. This was army in the field against army in the field, at least for the Blackhorse. The NVA were excellent light infantry and they were hard to find and fix, but they were not guerrillas.

When Fred Franks took over as S-3, the 2nd Squadron part of the regimental mission was to keep open the highway—actually, a two-lane dirt road—from An Loc to Lai Khe, a distance of about thirty kilometers. The regiment used the road for its own supply to An Loc from Long Binh, but civilian traffic also needed it. To establish that the South Vietnamese government was in control of the area, the free flow of normal civilian traffic had to be restored. By this time, the Blackhorse and the 1st Infantry Division, along with some

ARVN units, had established good control over the area. The threat of mines remained, but the probability of ambushes by NVA units was low. Second Squadron's mission was to keep it that way by aggressive reconnaissance to the west of the road out to distances of twenty to thirty kilometers. There they would intercept any NVA units moving in the direction of the road.

In late August, 2nd Squadron operated out of a firebase approximately twenty kilometers from An Loc and ten kilometers west of the highway. The operational element of the main command post (the S-2 and S-3) was there, along with the tank company and artillery battery. At night, and in the location where they had been operating, the cavalry troops set up a tight laager for self-protection.

During the day, the squadron aviation could fly over the convoys and be available if a fight broke out. When convoys were not operating (there was normally one per day), the squadron was engaged in aggressive reconnaissance in troop-sized operational areas to the west of the road, where they looked for the enemy and frequently found him. The threat from ground attack at the time was so low that the cavalry troops were not involved in protecting the convoys. But artillery locations were spaced in mutually supporting positions along the road. The squadron commander or S-3 would fly over the convoy, and could deal with the enemy with fires available from the artillery along the route, or from close air support or helicopter attack aviation.

It was during this time that Franks received his baptism by fire. This is how he remembers it:

> "What's that?" I asked my pilot, as there was a pop-pop sound and green tracers zinged past the OH-6 helicopter.
>
> "We're taking fire," he said, turning the Loach quickly out of the area.
>
> I suspected as much.
>
> That was my first experience of being directly shot at in combat. It would not be the last. You always wonder how you will react. It got my attention. I felt the normal fear rising to take control, and I was instantly more aware. My senses were on super-alert. In an instant, though, you get on top of the fear, put it aside, and try to focus on what you know you must do. I found I could do that. That did not make me unique, but it was reassuring to pass that first test. I also did not feel as though the fire would hit us. Somehow, a sort of calm came over me, and I found I was able to think, and otherwise do my duty and hang in there. There would be many more of these on the ground and in the air. My reaction was always the same, right up until I was wounded the second time. One night in Germany, I had asked Captain Herm Winans, our squadron S-2 and a decorated Korean War veteran, "What's it like to be shot at?" He told me, "The

first time is the worst, and after five seconds you are all veterans. Don't worry about it. Your training will kick in." A bit of old-soldier wisdom in a nightly chat at our border camp along the Czech–West German border. He was right.

A few days later, an ARVN infantry unit walked by mistake into an area near our firebase where our engineers had put out a field of mines and booby traps. They went off. We got them on the radio and had them freeze in place, then went to get them out via the safe lanes. I saw my first battle casualty as a leg with the boot still on it, separated from the ARVN soldier who had been killed. You never get used to seeing casualties, even though you know they are part of combat. There would be more. You feel every one.

During this period of almost three weeks, the 2nd Squadron had a number of engagements with the NVA, ranging from a single enemy rocket fired into their firebase to an NVA company–size attack against one of the cavalry troops. In the course of these operations, Franks would do all the things an S-3 of a cavalry squadron would do in combat: call in and adjust artillery fire, call in air strikes, maneuver forces on the ground, and in a battle, orchestrate all the fire and movement simultaneously over a single and tightly disciplined radio frequency. No U.S. soldiers were lost to enemy action. Although he was not yet a seasoned combat veteran, he was a changed soldier from the one of three weeks before.

In early September, Lieutenant Colonel Grail Brookshire replaced Aarstaat as squadron commander, and officially made Fred Franks the 2nd Squadron S-3 (and Gilbreath the XO). For all he had learned, however, Franks knew he had a long way to go. He also was aware that he had to execute while he grew in combat experience. He did not want his growth to be at the expense of the soldiers. Over the next nine months of combat, he would form some very definitive thoughts about how to win at least cost to his soldiers. Some were confirmations of things he'd developed from previous experience in training, education, and command. Some were a direct result of seeing what worked in combat. They were both parts of being a soldier—matters of the mind and matters of the heart. For soldiering involves much thinking and intense problem solving, but it is also an intensely passionate profession, because in command, in order to do your duty, you put in harm's way that which you have come to love so much—your soldiers (as Michael Shaara said so well in his Civil War novel, *The Killer Angels*).

Fred Franks knew what made units great in peacetime training. He was now to see what made a unit great in combat. And he was to learn that they were the same.

The Mind of a Commander*

Many parts make up a commander—many attitudes, skills, experiences, and convictions. Some of these are fundamental and eternal—duty, honor, country, courage, integrity, loyalty, patriotism. Others are more particular and personal; they grow and develop over time. The particular constellation of attitudes, skills, experiences, and convictions that Fred Franks brought to 2nd Squadron, and which grew and developed during his months in Vietnam, later characterized his performance as a commander, up to and including his command of VII Corps in Desert Storm. You don't understand Fred Franks unless you understand these.

Let's start with the blindingly obvious. When you fight in combat, you don't fight halfway. Fighting is for keeps. When you play ball, you walk away from the game. You lose today, you play again tomorrow. But in combat the stakes are final. It can bring about the deaths of people you've worked with, are responsible for, and care about, or your own death. You don't get second chances. This means, as I've already indicated Fred Franks is fond of saying, when you win, you don't want to win close. You don't want drama. You want to win 100–0, not 24–23. In other words, there's no room for sloppiness. And there's no room for lapses in alertness. It means that when you're a soldier, you want not just a small edge over your enemy, but as large an edge as you can get. Thus, where you can, you want to work your units into situations where the difference between winning and losing, or between life and death, does not hang on acts of extreme courage—or on Medal of Honor–winning bravery. It may come to that and the mission might demand it, but you try to work it so those actions add to the edge. For a soldier, ordinary courage should be more than enough (and ordinary courage is not at all *easy!*). Ordinary courage means doing what you're supposed to be doing as well as you can; and it means not letting down those who depend on you. Acts of ordinary courage sometimes require extraordinary measures . . . but that's another story.

What gives them the edge they need? Here are the ways, as Franks came to know them:

Soldiers

Franks was to confirm what he already knew: It all starts with the soldiers themselves. It is their training and courage, and the quality of their noncommissioned officer and officer small-unit leadership, that win.

*The following ideas—as well as most of the other more "conceptual" or "philosophical" portions of this chapter—do not actually represent Fred Franks's understanding of his experiences while he was in Vietnam. Rather, and more accurately, they represent the distillation of a lifetime of experiences. In Vietnam, this understanding was in seed and green shoot form. But it was there.

In those early days of combat, Franks quickly saw that the real heroes of Vietnam were the soldiers who by and large had been drafted and who had come to Vietnam to do what our country had asked them to do. In the 2nd Squadron Franks found a tight-knit team who were fiercely proud of the unit and who looked out for one another. They lived out of their vehicles for months on end, fighting from them, living in them. Day after day they would go on their missions, looking for the enemy and on most days finding him. By late August 1969, they had been at it constantly for almost six months. Franks wanted to be part of that team.

He also began to see something else.

By this time, Vietnam had gotten personal for most in the ranks as well as for the thousands of next of kin of those killed in action, wounded, missing in action, or POWs. Many had already served there, some more than once. Some of Franks's West Point class of 1959 had been killed in action, one from his cadet company. In the spring of 1969, two friends of Franks were killed in action a week apart. (One of his pilots in the 2nd Squadron, it turned out, had been flying the helicopter the day one of those friends had been killed; he and Franks would talk about it.) And so when Franks went to Vietnam in the summer of 1969, he did so as a professional, but the war quickly became part of his soul.

Combat Power

There are four main ingredients of combat power:

- **FIREPOWER:** Using everything available to you at the right place and time.
- **PROTECTION:** *Preserving* your force for use at the right time.
- **COMMAND AND LEADERSHIP:** The battlefield is a chaotic place. If your side is less mired in chaos than your enemy's, if your force is more agile and can respond more quickly to changing events, you have a big edge. You do that through vision and sensing. If you can see your own units and the enemy better than your enemy can see you, then he is, relatively speaking, more entangled in confusion and chaos. You also have to see in your mind's eye what you cannot see physically. You have to know where and how to get the right information to form that vision.
- **MANEUVER:** If you can move around the battlefield faster than your enemy in the right combination of units, you effectively increase your own numbers and increase the number of directions from which you can hit the enemy. This is how you gain and maintain the initiative and win.

Combat Discipline

Combat discipline is not the same as parade-ground discipline. The latter has its uses—though these don't figure high in the greater scheme of things. On the other hand, without combat discipline, you lose. Combat discipline means maintaining weapons and maintaining vehicles. It means doing what is right even when no one is watching. It means following orders. It means staying put and fighting if that is the mission, even though the odds may not look good. It means applying lots of violence with focused firepower on the enemy, but when the engagement is over, being able to shut it off. And it means staying alert and on edge, and looking out for one another.

Noncommissioned officers and leaders and commanders need to know how to keep the edge that comes from combat discipline, especially during lulls between combat actions. If units don't engage in a combat action at least once every three or four days, their effectiveness falls off very rapidly. Units and leaders cannot get complacent. Complacency is a fatal disease. With that in mind, Brookshire and Franks would spend much of their time going out and around, visiting units, listening to the troops, talking to the troop commanders (and the troop commanders and noncommissioned officers would, of course, be doing the same thing), making sure the troops were using battle lulls to clean their weapons, keep their ammo clean, maintain their vehicles, and attend to some personal hygiene (not easy, living out of a combat vehicle).

Focus

Focus is equal parts concentration and awareness. Ground combat is relentless, both physically and mentally. You live and fight from your vehicles, no letup, no rear areas, nothing but day after day of looking for the enemy. If you give in to exhaustion, you grow careless or overconfident, and then you become a hazard not only to yourself but, if you are a leader, even more so to your soldiers.

Before a planned battle, you get focused, no matter how tired you are. It requires every ounce of energy you can generate but you have no choice, and you must stay that way the entire action. In combat, time passes differently. Sometimes it seems like slow motion—actual combat time always seems longer than it really is—but you can't let up, ever.

When that planned battle begins, however, you sense the newness of it all, because each battle is different, and that is a help. It adds to the normal alertness, no matter how tired you are. During the battle, your senses come alive. They are supercharged. You see more, hear more, sense more. You fight to keep them under control. Your intuition lights up. Combat veterans call it a "sixth sense." Once, after midnight in War Zone C, the squadron firebase came under intense rocket and direct fire attack. Franks was asleep on a cot when it started. Rather than stand up, he rolled off his cot and crawled out. When he looked the next day at the sides of the shelter, they were riddled with shrapnel and bullet holes. Standing up would have been sure death. He could not explain why he had not stood up.

In battle, thought processes that might usually take longer take place in your head in nanoseconds. Your senses and brain are working overtime, stimulated by the action and your own sense of responsibility to the mission and your troops. But if you are tired going in, once that battle stimulus is removed, leaders and units crash. Breaking the momentum of an attack and then starting tired units back again is almost impossible.

If you are a senior commander, you are intensely focused on the present—on the immediate fight in front of you. But at the same time you try to remain detached enough that you can forecast and anticipate the next fight, and the one after that. The more senior you are, the more future you have to create.

If you constantly stay focused, you usually can outthink the enemy. You can run him out of options as you simultaneously outfight him. That's how you win.

Loyalty to Friends

Our friend W. E. B. Griffin has called this attitude, correctly, the Brotherhood of War. Yes, soldiers fight for their country. Yes, love of country is right in there among their own deepest-held beliefs—along with love of family and love of God. But when it comes down to it, soldiers in combat actually fight for their friends who are side by side with them in the fight . . . for the other members of their tank crew, for the rest of their squad. In a good unit, each soldier feels a boundless, unquestioned loyalty to the others. He does his best not to bring bad things to the others. He feels enormous peer pressure to pull his own weight in a fight. And he will sometimes reach impossible heights of bravery looking out for the others. In January 1970, near Bu Dop, for example, Captain Carl Marshall landed his Cobra amid enemy fire one morning at the beginning of a huge battle in order to rescue a fellow pilot who had been shot down in his scout Loach and was about to be captured by the NVA. Franks was in his own Loach adjusting artillery fire into the trees to keep the NVA away while beginning to maneuver ground troops, and he saw it all. He saw Marshall land, open the canopy of his Cobra, and with his cannon firing into the trees lift off and rescue his fellow aviator.

The commander's goal, not always achieved, is to create the conditions that will endow the whole unit with that feeling, and the behavior that follows from it. If the brotherhood feeling is working at a high level—in, say, a regiment—then you really have the power that can give you the decisive edge over your enemy.

Loyalty to troops—the Brotherhood of Warriors—has always been a powerful force in Fred Franks's own life and in his deepest convictions as a commander. He has always identified more directly with the soldiers than with the institutional hierarchy.

"To lead is to serve," he likes to say. "The spotlight should be on the led and not the leader.

"In battle, character counts in leaders and soldiers as much as brains. Stuff like courage, mental and physical toughness, and integrity really count. Yet competence is also important for leaders, because I believe soldiers have every right to expect their leaders to know what they are doing. Leaders must also share the danger, the pain, and also the pride that the troops feel. Leaders need to be up front in combat. They need to be where the soldiers are."

To Franks there is always unimaginable nobility about young Americans who are willing to risk it all for the sake of accomplishing what their country has asked them to do. That implies an almost blind trust on their part that their leaders have the stomach to see it through and will do that at the least cost to those inside the actual flames of combat. It implies that before the commitment to battle is made, the leaders have reached the reasonable conclusion that the objectives are worth the cost. It also implies that the tactical methods to be used will accomplish the strategic objectives. And it implies, finally, that after the battle is over, no matter what the outcome, they will acknowledge and recognize the sacrifice of those who carry in their bodies and their souls the living record of battle, a record that lasts far longer than the individual lives of soldiers or leaders. If leaders trust that soldiers are willing to give up their lives, or parts of their bodies, in order to accomplish their aims, then soldiers have a right to expect that their sacrifice will be worth it and remembered.

When, not long before the attack into Iraq, that soldier came up to General Franks and said, "Don't worry, General, we trust you," that remark touched deep within Fred Franks's inner core; it captured exactly what he had hoped the soldiers felt, and exactly what he had hoped that he himself was providing for them. And the highest praise that came to him after the victory was from a sergeant in the 2nd ACR. "You generals didn't do too bad this time," he said.

The question of loyalty affected Franks in another way.

Many of his professional generation were affected personally by Vietnam but kept it to themselves, and it perhaps did not affect their performance of duties later. Some might even say after Desert Storm and Provide Comfort that Vietnam had not affected them in the Gulf. That was not to be so for Franks. There was not a single day during Desert Shield and Desert Storm that he did not remember Vietnam and the fellow soldiers of his generation. Vietnam and the broken trust. Vietnam and the courage of the soldiers taking fire both on the battlefield and at home in America. It was a national tragedy of the 1970s. Being in the hospital with those soldiers hurt badly by war and seeing the pain caused them by those who linked them to the cause of the war left Franks identifying more with these young soldiers than perhaps with some of his own generation of professionals who were untouched by that personal experience. It was to make a difference the rest of his life.

Building a Team

Combat units are teams. They are in fact teams of teams: squads, platoons, troops, squadrons, and on up to higher teams such as divisions and corps.

To build his team, the commander watches over three elements: He makes sure that the team members share—and *work* toward—common goals (in particular, the commander's intent). He listens (to know what is actually going on). And he makes himself aware of the chemistry both within the team and between it and other teams. He allows differences unless they fracture teamwork.

Squadron commanders normally changed their troop commanders every six months. Fox Troop was due for a change in March. In due course, Brookshire pulled Captain Max Bailey out of Troop F and put in a captain who had been the squadron S-4 (logistics). Immediately, Brookshire and Franks sensed a change in the personality of the unit. That was to be expected. But this was not a welcome change. They were now a little less aggressive in the fight, less coordinated when an action started. They weren't as quick and crisp as before. The teamwork among the troops, and between Troop F and the artillery battery, was breaking down. It wasn't that the new captain was incompetent, but the chemistry was wrong—and something had to be done to make it right.

Though Brookshire had probably already made up his mind, he asked Franks for his thoughts.

"I don't think you have a choice," he said. "Soldiers deserve the best leadership we can provide. The guy in Troop F is a good guy, and he knows the job. It just isn't working. You can stay with him for another couple of months, but I don't think it's going to work, and we're going to end up with somebody getting hurt and maybe killed in the process. So my recommendation is for you to pull him out without prejudice, send him to another unit, and put Bailey back in command of the troop."

That is what Brookshire did. The chemistry of the unit demanded it. The captain was sent to command a mechanized infantry company in another division, where he had a fine combat record, and Troop F's teamwork was once again crisp.

The Human Dimension

The commander has to know how his soldiers are fighting in combat. He has to be aware of the momentum of his units, and of their reactions to success or failure. He has to know how much they have left in them, and how much peak effort they can still put out—during all the stress, intensity, and exhaustion of combat.

In November, the squadron was given the mission of opening the road between the towns of Loc Ninh and Bu Dop, about thirty kilometers away. It was a slow job: the road had been closed for some time and was full of mines, and the jungle had grown over it. By December, they were halfway there. Meanwhile, part of the mission involved flying in a task force to secure Bu Dop. This task force was commanded by Major Jim Bradin, and its mounted element was Max Bailey's Fox Troop, plus Troop B from 1st Squadron.

Though Franks's duty was on the road, and not in Bu Dop, he kept an eye and an ear aimed in their direction—just as he kept an eye and ear aimed at all the units of 2nd Squadron. He wanted to make sure they were OK; if trouble broke out, he could offer help fast.

One day, Franks was in his helicopter listening in: Fox Troop was in a fight. They'd run into an ambush in a rubber plantation. In early August, Echo Troop had fallen into a situation very like this one—NVA regulars dug in, in bunkers—and had come out of that fight with over half the troop as casualties. The action had left deep scars. And now Fox Troop was in a similar stiff fight against a major force in an area the NVA had owned for years. The stakes were high. Things could go very badly, the way they had with Echo Troop. Or they could badly hurt the enemy, and even break the back of NVA forces around Bu Dop. As it happened, Max Bailey was away on R and R, so the executive officer, Lieutenant John Barbeau, was commanding the troop.

Franks called Bradin. "Can I help?"

"Hell, yes, you can help. I can't get a helicopter to get up in the air to go over there to run the fight. Can you come over and do that?"

This was unusual: taking charge of a fight for someone else in his area of operations. But Franks called Brookshire, and he OK'd it. It was an unselfish thing for Bradin to do. He was thinking only of what was best for the mission and the soldiers.

It took five minutes at top speed to reach Fox Troop. Then he flew over the area, watching the firing back and forth at close quarters (no more than fifty to one hundred meters), getting a sense of the engagement. The NVA were firing at his Loach, too, but he accepted that. It wasn't the first time.

Meanwhile, he did what he needed to do to help: he brought in artillery and attack helicopters to seal off the area, while the troop continued the fight on the ground. He switched to the troop radio frequency and immediately heard the sharp exchanges so characteristic of commanders in a stiff fight. Meanwhile, Bradin had sent another cavalry unit, Troop B, to join the fight.

Things were going well until a call came from Barbeau saying that they had some casualties.

"OK," Franks told him, "evacuate your wounded, establish an LZ, and finish the fight. I'll call a medevac in." In other words, his intent was for a security element to go out with the wounded, nothing more than that.

But the troop had had more casualties and wounded than Franks knew—four soldiers KIA and twenty wounded, almost 50 percent of what they had gone in with—and instead Barbeau pulled the whole troop out of the engagement area. That made sense, but . . .

That lets Troop B in there and the fight not finished, Franks thought. They had the NVA trapped, right where they wanted them, had paid a big price, and now needed to finish them. Plus, Franks wanted Troop F to own the area for which they had fought so well, and not to be out of there as though the NVA had run them out.

So Franks landed his Loach and said to the commander, "You, me, and this cavalry troop, we're going back in there. Leave some security here to evacuate the wounded, then mount up and let's go." And then he got into the commander's track with Barbeau and they moved back up and secured the area with Troop B and made sure the NVA weren't capable of attacking again.

He was taking a chance on Troop F at that moment, but he knew them as a unit and how tough they were. Barbeau and Troop F were all heroes that day. Hurt as they were, they went back in and finished the battle. The NVA never again threatened Bu Dop until after the Blackhorse left.

Know the Enemy

This is not just knowledge learned from reports and briefings. This is knowledge gained from action, from contact with the enemy. It's fingertips-to-gut knowledge. Once you have this kind of knowledge, you begin to see vulnerabilities in the enemy, and then you can take the fight to the enemy and hit him hard.

Brookshire, Franks, and 2nd Squadron came to know the NVA well, in day-in, day-out actions. They respected them, and so did everyone else in the Blackhorse.

The NVA were tough, well-drilled, well-armed light infantry. That is to say, their usual armament was individual weapons—AK-47s, machine guns, RPGs (rocket-propelled grenades, something like World War II bazookas), and small mortars. On occasion they used heavier 107-mm and 122-mm rockets, but usually only when staging an attack on a fixed site, such as a firebase. They were tightly disciplined in their individual actions, movements, and use of fire, and they were highly motivated, rarely surrendering or leaving dead or wounded. When you captured them, NVA prisoners would talk, but they knew only what they themselves were supposed to do, and not much more. Nevertheless, interrogation of prisoners often obtained vital information, especially if it could be done *right now*, as soon as they were taken. Because NVA communications were poor, when they left a base camp to move out on an operation, they had a hard time making adjustments. They did what they'd been ordered to do, come hell or high water. Though short-term adjustments came hard, over the longer term they adapted both their strategies and their tactics to suit changing situations. They were smart and they adapted. So did 2nd Squadron.

The NVA were elusive infantry who had a remarkable ability to move around without being detected. Over time the squadron credited them with the capability, perhaps too much, to operate at night.

This was not true, as they discovered in War Zone C.

After 2nd Squadron completed the job of opening the road to Bu Dop in early February, they were moved to War Zone C on an interdiction mission. War Zone C, 100 kilometers to the north and west of Saigon and south of an area of Cambodia called the Fishhook, was essentially uninhabited—no commerce, no civilians, only the NVA and the Blackhorse. There, the mission was not to keep roads open but to keep NVA regulars and supplies away from the air base at Bien Hoa, Loc Ninh, and the populated area around Saigon. The squadron had that mission until the invasion of Cambodia in May 1970.

Though Agent Orange had been heavily used in War Zone C, the effects were intermittent. There were bare patches that left the jungle looking as if it had been hit by winter, and there were large areas of dense rain forest. But on the whole, despite the defoliants, the forests of War Zone C were higher and denser than what the squadron had experienced up to then—triple canopy rather than single canopy. The NVA were transporting their people and supplies through this labyrinth on bicycles along a network of jungle trails and often using flashlights to do it at night.

Time and again after fights and B-52 strikes, American soldiers discovered flashlights on dead and captured NVA. Nobody made very much of this until, all of a sudden, it hit someone that they carried flashlights because they couldn't *see* at night, not nearly as well as Americans. Because of their diet—fish and rice, few fresh vegetables—they were practically blind in the dark. At night in thick jungle, they could hardly see the trails with their flashlights, much less navigate. The only reason they operated at night was that operating during the day was even more dangerous. In other words, the NVA didn't own the night. They were vulnerable.

When that point grew clear, one of the officers had an inspiration. His name was Captain Sewall Menzel, and he came up with a way to lay an ambush for the NVA without exposing American troops. When the North Vietnamese came down a trail, one of them would hit a trip wire; behind him, preset claymore mines and other weapons would go off, killing nearly everyone on the trail. They had tried it earlier with some success. It would work much better in War Zone C.

Soon, 2nd Squadron troops were setting "trap lines," as they called them, along assigned trails. Each of the cavalry troops had an assigned area and their "trap lines" to set and check daily. Before long, these automatic ambushes had succeeded in cutting way back on the amount of men and supplies coming through.

When you really *know* the enemy, you can see his weaknesses and hit him hard.

Prepare Soldiers to Fight
Doing this has both immediate and long-term aspects.

Long-term preparation for combat is *absolutely* the most crucial component of keeping soldiers at a combat edge. The word for long-term preparation is training. Franks later liked to quote Rommel, who said, "The best form of welfare for the troops is first-class training."

If you don't have much experience with today's Army, there's a good chance you have misconceptions about how soldiers spend their working life. The tendency is to think of Army life as dull but predictable: you have to work your way, as best you can, around a large, unresponsive bureaucracy. In truth, there's more than a little bit of all that, but none of this is the true Army.

Soldiers and leaders in the U.S. Army spend the better part of their lives training for war, and training hard. American soldiers train like Olympic athletes—but with this difference: they train their bodies to perform at the highest pitch, but they also train their minds to work at the same high pitch. In combat, the mental edge is as important as the physical. You also have to know how to handle your weapons. You have to know how to run and maintain your vehicles. And you have to know how to do all that in consort with other vehicles . . . in a team, with other teams. And that means you have to think, not only about what's going on now, in your own immediate situation, but also in relation to several other situations that depend on you. And at the same time, you have to think about how each of these situations is changing, and likely to change, over the course of the next few minutes, or hours . . . or for longer periods for higher commanders. Finally, you have to be able to predict or judge or intuit or guess how your enemy is going to be acting and reacting to all these situations, then decide on a course of action that gives your units the edge they need.

This kind of thinking is thinking at a very high level.

Fred Franks has always had a passion for units skilled in combat fundamentals, a carryover from playing lots of sports. He particularly valued accurate firepower, for being able to hit what you aim at. It is his conviction that most battles and engagements are won by units with weapons skills. Maneuver is important, as is knowing how to maneuver, but in the final crunch, it's the unit's fighting capability in terms of toughness and their weapons skills that wins in a fight.

How do you train for toughness and weapons skills? By drills and exercises. By setting up a qualification course for vehicles such as tanks. And then by practice and more practice to reach combat standards. You push your unit's edge as far as you can. Then you push it farther than that.

Units need intensive training—if they can get it—even in combat zones.

After Grail Brookshire took command as 2nd Squadron commander from Jim Aarstaat early in September, the squadron completed its move to Di An. There they were to exchange most of their M113s for newer Sheridan light tanks. And there they also drew 81-mm mortars in exchange for their 4.2 in weapons (the 81-mm mortar could shoot closer in to its own position, a capability Brookshire wanted).

At Di An, in addition to receiving new weapons, the squadron would undergo a CMMI (Command Maintenance Management Inspection), an administrative procedure that looked into how the squadron's maintenance program was going. The new weapons were an important addition to the squadron. The CMMI was a bureaucratic joke.

"For Christ's sake," Franks said to himself when the inspectors made their appearance in their crisp, spiffy rear area uniforms, "the squadron's in the middle of a combat theater, and here come these rear area guys with clipboards checking us out like we're at Fort Knox with nothing better to do."

There were too many scenes like this:

"Hey, look here," a CMMI officer laments, adding up check marks on his clipboard. "These vehicles have *holes* in them."

"Shit, sir, they got hit by RPGs," a soldier answers, with barely concealed disgust. "That happens when you fight."

Franks knew the CMMI threatened to take the squadron's focus off needed combat training. They did not let it happen. They kept their eye on the ball. It was a great lesson. Franks would later remember this as he kept focused on the training and preparation for war amid all the distractions of VII Corps's deployment to Saudi Arabia.

Despite the CMMI, the standdown for maintenance came at a good time for the unit. Most vehicles the squadron was keeping needed to be fitted out with new tracks or otherwise repaired and brought up to speed. This time also gave Brookshire a chance to get to know the squadron and for them to get to know him. More important, they needed a rest. They had been on line in operations for more than six months without a break.

It wasn't a holiday. Brookshire wanted discipline, combat discipline. He wanted a training program, to institute maintenance procedures that would work in combat, and to stress teamwork. He also wanted to get the squadron provisioned with all the right equipment, and to replace what was lost to combat actions. Weapons needed to be fixed or replaced, and fire control on tracked vehicles corrected. They needed spare parts, and they needed to load up on ammunition. While all this was going on, Brookshire was everywhere looking into everything, and he expected Franks as the S-3 and Gilbreath as the executive officer to be doing the same thing. It was a break from combat, but a busy time for the squadron.

Meanwhile, they took in the new Sheridans, and on the whole, they were glad to have them.

The Sheridan light tank was an innovative, and in many ways a flawed, machine (its official title was Armored Airborne Reconnaissance Assault Vehicle, or AARAV). Originally designed to be dropped by parachute, for use by airborne units (the 82nd Airborne is phasing out Sheridans, but used them effectively in Panama in 1989), the Sheridan was fitted with aluminum armor and an aluminum frame. It had a decent powerplant, which made it quick and agile (much better than the M113 in that regard); and because it was light, it didn't normally bog down in the often soft terrain of Vietnam. Soldiers also welcomed the big weapon it carried, a 152-mm cannon (the tank commander had, additionally, a .50-caliber machine gun). From this you could fire either an antipersonnel flechette round, a HEAT round, or even a Shillelagh antitank missile. The flechette round is packed like a shotgun shell with three-inch-long darts that are propelled to a velocity comparable to the muzzle velocity of a bullet. HEAT rounds (High Explosive Anti-Tank) were used for bunker busting. They were not actually used against tanks, since in those days the U.S. Army did not see NVA tanks. Shillelaghs were not used in Vietnam.

On the other hand, the Sheridan came with serious drawbacks. Its aluminum underside offered little protection against mines. The remedy for this problem, three- or four-inch belly armor bolted underneath, meant that the Sheridan could no longer be air-dropped. The aluminum armor on the front and sides didn't offer a lot of protection, either. This made the Sheridan especially vulnerable to NVA RPGs. Worse, the Sheridan's cannon used what is called combustible-case ammunition (This was the Army's first attempt at combustible-case ammunition. Though there were problems with it, the Army continued to correct these problems. The 120-mm combustible-case ammunition on the M1A1 works very well.) During that time, all too often, when you were firing a number of rounds in a short time period—as in a fight— still-burning residue from incompletely consumed rounds would often stay in the chamber, and you'd get a premature detonation. You don't want to be inside a Sheridan when that happens.

Still, for all that, the Sheridan was an improvement over the older M113s, and the troops welcomed them. Meanwhile, they had to learn how to use them. They had to learn to drive, load, shoot, and maintain them, and the vehicle commanders had to be taught how to command them.

When the Sheridans arrived, Brookshire asked Franks to draw up the new equipment training program—a job very like the one he would have on a larger scale twenty years later as brigadier general in Grafenwohr for the Seventh Army Training Command in Europe. There he put together the new equipment training programs for the M1 tanks, Bradley fighting vehicles, and MLRSs (Multiple-Launch Rocket Systems), then newly arriving in Europe. In Di An, the job was smaller, but more immediately pressing. Second Squadron would be taking the Sheridans into combat in only a few weeks.

For the training program, they had some help. The Army sent a team along with the Sheridans to teach the squadron's crews about the vehicle— about how to drive it, how to operate the turret, and about maintenance (both in the shop and at crew level). But it was Franks's responsibility to train the crews how to fight with the Sheridan and to determine whether they were combat ready. He wanted to create a rite of passage.

Under Franks's direction, the noncommissioned officers of the squadron built a crew qualification course near Di An, where crews would have to pass a series of tough, realistic exercises with strict standards. On the course, Sheridan crews would fire at a number of situational targets, that is, standard silhouette targets that replicated the kinds of situations they were likely to face in combat. There also were a few hard targets—damaged vehicles were used for that purpose. For these exercises, live ammunition was used and tank crew examiners rode along in the vehicles when they were shooting to score and critique the crews. If the crews didn't pass, they shot again until they did. At the end of the training, there was a graduation course. When they passed that, they were certified ready for combat.

It was a good program, and it paid off. When 2nd Squadron crews completed Fred Franks's training program, they were ready to fight with the new vehicles, and to fight with them in units.

ACTION

In early October, the squadron was sent to Loc Ninh, about thirty kilometers north of An Loc, with a mission much like their earlier operation in August, to secure both the road to An Loc—Highway 14—and the area around Loc Ninh.

Loc Ninh was a village of close to fifteen hundred people (three or four thousand people lived in An Loc, which was the market town and commercial center for the district). Around and about Loc Ninh were farms and rice paddies, and a small logging industry operated in the forests nearby. The road was the only access for the local people to their markets, and the Army needed the highway for military convoys to resupply 2nd Squadron. The North Vietnamese and the Viet Cong tried to close the road by laying mines and setting up ambushes. There were quite a few NVA around Loc Ninh, and Franks and the squadron saw constant action, sometimes two or three times a day.

Just as on the road to An Loc, the squadron set up a fire support base for the tank company, the artillery battery, and the forward command post element. (Franks named the base "Marge," after his daughter.) From there, the cavalry troops would fan out in their own areas of operation, searching for the enemy. When the cavalry troops found NVA units, they'd call in artillery and, if necessary, the tank company, and usually air. The artillery battery and air would fix the enemy in one place, while the cavalry troops and, as needed, the big fist of the tanks moved in and destroyed or captured them.

Franks or Brookshire, meanwhile, would be in a helicopter. Whoever was in the air at the time the fight started would organize it. He'd isolate the enemy, call in artillery, call in TAC air and attack helicopters, and maneuver the ground troops and help them navigate. The other would be in the firebase—in the command M577s and on the radio a short distance away or with the troops. Rarely would they both be on the ground. Usually they could do more for the troops if one of them was in the air, as most of the action involved only one of the cavalry troops. The helos were based in Quan Loi.

Although Franks spent some time on the ground to get a feel for what the fights looked like from there, most of the time he was in the helicopter eight or ten hours a day. In between operations, he and the troop commanders talked together a lot, so Franks knew how best to help them in their operations when he was in the helicopter.

The OH-6 was a great scout helicopter. Its power-to-weight ratio and general aerodynamics made it an extremely agile machine, immediately responsive and capable of tight maneuvers over the top of the jungle close to the ground. It was crash-worthy because of the small passenger bubble and high skids. However, as a command aircraft it was marginal because of the weak radios. For the times when the helicopter FM radio broke, which happened frequently, Franks took along an infantry portable radio, stuffed it next to his seat, and stuck the receiver next to his ear, pushing the handset if he wanted to talk. In addition to FM, it had both VHF and UHF radios, which Franks used mainly to talk to attack helos and close air support. The helo radios were activated by pressing a button on the floor by his foot. Talking on three radios with two different activation devices, plus looking at the ground and his map, and keeping his wits in a fight while sometimes getting ground fire was a challenge, to say the least. Though he considered that minor compared to the troops banging around in their ACAVs and Sheridans all day through jungle. . . .

They called it "busting jungle," where armored vehicles literally made a road through the forest by knocking down trees. Except for drivers, troops rode on the outside of their vehicles most of the time. It was cooler, and safer—paradoxically. If you were hit by an RPG, you were better off outside than inside. If you had to get inside fast, you could do that. Sometimes they hit bamboo thickets so strong, the M113s would be thrown back (when bamboo grows thick, it grows *thick!*). Sometimes they hit trees full of large biting red ants that would rain down on the troops. They'd have to stop and strip out of their fatigues and beat the ants off. Sometimes tree limbs would break off and come crashing down on top of the vehicles, or worse, on one of the soldiers. Some of these caused serious injury.

Every evening, after the day's operations were finished, Franks and Brookshire talked about the operations coming up the next day. They'd look at the mission and the enemy, and then at various hypothetical solutions to mission problems: What if they do this? Can we do that? After they had a good idea of how they wanted the operation to run, they would war-game it. Once they were satisfied, Brookshire would say, "OK, that's what we're going to do. Get the word out to the troops." Either Brookshire or Franks would call the troops on the secure radio and explain the operations to them. Though there'd be an entry in the squadron log, the bulk of squadron communications was oral. It was all talked through.

Few actions involved more than an individual cavalry troop, and rarely required the whole squadron to take part. There also were small-unit patrols and ambushes to stop the NVA and Viet Cong from mining Highway 14. Later, on the mission to Bu Dop, two infantry companies from 1st CAV Division were attached to the squadron. They kept the NVA away from the road-clearing operation. Franks was almost constantly executing coordination of ground units, both mounted and dismounted, artillery, attack aviation, and air strikes. He was confident that Brookshire trusted him to handle all that; he valued the trust. Brookshire often left him to orchestrate actions, without interfering.

Later, just after Christmas, Brookshire had to rush back to the States on an emergency leave. While he was away, Franks commanded the forward elements of the squadron. During that time, he took the squadron the rest of the way into Bu Dop.

They both had a lot of help. The troop commanders were first rate. Ross Johnson, then Fred Kyle in Troop E, Max Bailey in Troop F, Paul Dickenson, then Sewall Menzell in Troop G. The tanks (H Company) were commanded by Bob Hurt, Malcolm Gilchrest, then Miles Sisson. The artillery (HOW Battery) was under George Fisher, then Dick Trageman. Senior NCOs also were outstanding. The command sergeant major in the 2nd Squadron was Ray Burkett, a highly respected and veteran CSM. Burkett was wounded in early April 1970 and had his left arm amputated. Second Squadron was a sharp, tight team.

Franks had particular help from his own team, both on the ground and in the air.

On the ground, in the S-3 shop, were Master Sergeant Bob Bolan and his assistant, Sergeant First Class Tommy Jones. In the air, Franks's pilots were Chief Warrant Officers John Malette and Doug Farfel; his crew chiefs were Specialists John Lamonia and "Polack" Terzala. It was a tight team—a combat family. Bolan left a large impression on Franks. A wise veteran, he ran the S-3 shop like clockwork, and was on his fourth combat tour in Vietnam. He was killed in action as the squadron command sergeant major in July 1970.

COMMAND STYLE

Commanders have different command styles. If you spend any significant amount of time around Army people, you're going to encounter no little commentary about these differences. There is no right way to command, no template out of which commanders are stamped. Some commanders—to point out the more visible of differences—are loud, physically dominant extroverts; others are quieter, more soft-spoken, more given to indirection. Such opposites can be equally effective as commanders.

Grail Brookshire was a soldier's soldier, six foot one, 180 pounds, and sharp featured. When he spoke, his voice was clear and loud. When he reinforced a point, he was usually profane. Before taking over 2nd Squadron, he had been the regimental S-3, and knew the regiment's operations. At 2nd Squadron, he was technically skillful, and very aggressive: he took the fight to the enemy. Brookshire had a special affinity for tactics and a finely tuned sense for a fight. And he was always at the right place to conduct it. Simultaneously orchestrating ground maneuver elements, artillery, Army air, and Air Force air came naturally to him. (This "coming naturally" was a result of long study and practice.) As a complement to his tactical skills, he knew soldiers, what made them tick and what would inspire them to push their own edge. He believed in tight discipline and technical competence. But he also liked to stay out with front-line troops, working with them and sharing their hardships. And Brookshire liked to communicate with his subordinates. He liked to talk with them, to ask and take their opinions. He was a master at creating and building team-work in a combat unit.

Franks and Brookshire took to each other as soon as they met. Their leadership styles and personal styles instantly meshed. Though Franks and Brookshire had never worked together until 2nd Squadron, it wasn't long before they built under fire a close working relationship. This grew into a close friendship, based on shared hardships and dangers, and shared concern for soldiers, this in spite of very different personal styles. Brookshire was boisterous, profane, and very direct. Franks was more quiet and soft-spoken, with a deep inner intensity, but also direct and profane when the situation called for it. They talked long and often, exchanging ideas about how to conduct a fight. And they both smoked cigars, a habit Franks had begun in the 11th Cavalry as a platoon leader. Together they developed a natural and comfortable working groove. Before long, it all became natural and instinctive.

On 7 December there was a regimental change of command, when Colonel Donn Starry took command of the 11th ACR from Colonel Jimmie Leach.* Though he and Franks did not then know each other, the relationship that developed between them turned out to be as lasting as the one between Franks and Brookshire. For one thing, in May, in Cambodia, Donn Starry saved Franks's life. And later, back home in the States, they would work together again.

Most commanders are intelligent people. Not all of these intelligent people are smart commanders. That is to say, not all of these people make the best decisions for their commands.

Out of these intelligent people, most are readers (usually of history and military history); most also, these days, have earned advanced, professional degrees (I've met three-star lieutenant generals with Ph.D.'s); and some few are intellectuals. These will make a contribution during their career to the way the Army thinks about itself and its missions, both strategic and tactical. Donn Starry was one of the Army intellectuals, and so, it turned out, was Fred Franks. The relationship between Fred Franks and Donn Starry that began in

---

*After Vietnam, Leach became armor branch chief at the Army's Personnel Command in charge of assignments of all armor officers. While there, he saw to it that battle-wounded soldiers who wanted to remain in the Army were given the opportunity to do so. More than anyone else, Jimmie Leach helped Franks stay on active duty. Franks would never forget this. It was the cavalry family looking after its own.

the jungles near the Cambodian border would continue on into TRADOC. Part, at least, of the contribution Franks was eventually to make to the Army built upon the foundation that Donn Starry had constructed in the 1970s and 1980s, when he commanded first the Armor Center at Fort Knox and then TRADOC, the Training and Doctrine Command.

Starry's command methods inspired fierce loyalty in his subordinates. He always talked to and listened to soldiers and subordinate commanders. He also led from out front. He shared the dangers.

From the beginning, you never doubted that he was in charge. You always knew he was there and aware of what you were doing. He would monitor your combat actions on the radio, but usually broke in only when you needed something or when he could help in some way. He would meet you almost every day at your location. He didn't send for people to come see him; he'd go to them. When there was an action, he liked to stay with the lead squadron, and not in the rear at his command post, but otherwise, he left you pretty much to run your own show. As long as you were operating within his intent, he didn't intrude much into your business.

Starry encouraged and demanded initiative. He valued those commanders and others who could "orchestrate" a battle. You came to realize that non-judgmental listening and focused questioning were major facets of his command technique. (Listening to your subordinates, without jumping in with comments, observations, or directives, is a good way to find out what is *actually* going on in a unit.) Starry certainly had a very good idea what he wanted done, but he would lead people to find that on their own, as though they themselves had discovered it. He would do that by asking questions and pointing out relevant facts and issues. If his subordinates still missed seeing what he saw—if they needed, say, to add an element to a plan—he would ask a question that would indicate that . . . or, if it came to that, he would interrupt and directly make himself clear. Otherwise, he'd listen. He was a commander's commander.

Starry also valued noncommissioned officers. He and his Command Sergeant, Major Don Horn, were inseparable. Horn was a wise senior NCO, with a lot of combat and soldier tactical savvy. When Horn had something to say on one of Starry's visits, Franks listened.

★   Fred Franks has always been a sensible, creative, intelligent leader. He always thinks ahead. You have to think ahead if you're going to fight at the highest pitch of violence at the least cost to your troops. But *that's* not the *entire* Fred Franks.

Sometimes your intuitive sense lets you go on instinct and get lucky in combat, and you have to leave room for that. But you have to pick your spots.

North of An Loc, and in War Zone C, he and his crew used to set the Loach down near recently bombed NVA bunkers or B-52 strikes in order to obtain accurate BDAs or to pick up POWs or captured documents from squadron troops on the ground. The Air Force liked accurate BDAs; they showed how well they were doing their job. Getting BDAs on the ground was the only way to ensure accuracy; but doing that was a little mad. On the other hand, in exchange for accurate BDAs, the Air Force took special care of 2nd Squadron when they needed TAC air. Young Major Franks thought that was worth the risk. But it was not risk free. Franks and his crew would go down four times in their Loach, twice from enemy fire.

The first day they were in War Zone C, he was flying observation in his Loach along the border with Cambodia when he spotted North Vietnamese earthen bunkers. He called in air. Some Cobras dived in, and the North Vietnamese scattered. Then Franks noticed a pair of rucksacks on the ground, apparently dropped in a clearing near one of the bunkers, now deserted. The NVA infantry that had manned it were at the moment running for their lives toward the Cambodian border, a short distance away. On the chance that the rucksacks might contain valuable intelligence, and ignoring the strong possibility that they were booby-trapped or that the NVA were still around, he wanted to land and get them. Because they were all in it together, Franks asked John Mallette, who was flying the helicopter, and John Lamonia, his crew chief, if they'd be willing to go down to pick them up. They agreed it was worth the risk.

The Loach set down and, with Franks covering him, and Captain Carl Marshall circling close above in his Cobra gunship, Lamonia raced out and snatched the two rucksacks. After Lamonia returned to the Loach, an NVA soldier appeared, refused to surrender, and tore off toward other NVA bunkers that were visible through the trees. Since Franks and his crew didn't know what this soldier was planning to do or if anyone was in the bunkers, and since they wanted to get the hell out of there, Lamonia dropped the NVA soldier with his M-60 machine gun and suppressed the enemy in the bunkers. *Then* they got the hell out of there.

The snatch proved valuable. One of the rucksacks contained a detailed map showing infiltration and resupply routes through War Zone C, as well as unit identification. This map was immensely useful to 2nd Squadron and allowed them to set numerous ambushes along those trails.

Later the next day, Brigadier General George Casey, the assistant division commander of the 1st Cavalry Division, on one of his many visits to the regiment, visited Franks, Mallette, and Lamonia in an informal ceremony. "Franks," he said, "I don't know whether to court-martial you for stupidity or pin a medal on all of you for what you did out there. I guess because it turned out OK, I'll pin a medal on you all. That's the spirit of the cavalry we want. That's what the cavalry's all about—out in front."

★ Two months later, at the end of April, the Blackhorse was out in front again. They were going into Cambodia. Second Squadron would lead.

3

CAMBODIA

GOING INTO CAMBODIA MADE SENSE. IF VIETNAMIZATION WAS TO WORK, then the United States had to buy time for the South Vietnamese, so they could grow stronger and take over the war. General Creighton Abrams, MACV commander, planned the spoiling attack into Cambodia to give them that time. The NVA sanctuary there had to be destroyed—up to now, it had been off limits—the enormous stores of arms and supplies and all the other NVA infrastructure near the border had to be captured or eliminated; and the NVA themselves had to killed or taken prisoner, or else pushed back and kept back.

When Brookshire learned they were to go in, he and Franks put a plan together in less than forty-eight hours—*far* less time than the weeks it took to plan VII Corps's attack into Iraq twenty years later. There were other differences.

The squadron had about 900 soldiers and maybe 200 vehicles in a zone about fifteen kilometers wide. VII Corps had 146,000 soldiers and close to 50,000 vehicles in a sector 120 kilometers wide and over 250 kilometers deep. Both missions were force-oriented, with terrain as a guide, and for both, the mission was to destroy the enemy in zone. In Iraq, however, they had better intelligence about specific enemy locations—Franks does not recall any intelligence that was accurate in pinning down enemy locations in Cambodia, except around Snoul. But they knew their enemy well when they went into Cambodia. They had fought him for a long time. Their enemy knew them as well. It was not like that in Iraq at the beginning.

The squadron mission was straightforward: 2nd Squadron would lead the 11th Cavalry units, as part of Task Force Shoemaker, and formed of units of the 1st CAV Division and the 11th ACR. They would attack into the Fishhook (just north of War Zone C) and move quickly to Cambodian Highway 7, and on the third day, the plan was to attack up the highway to the town of Snoul, a rubber plantation town and provincial capital of a size and importance comparable to An Loc, on the Vietnamese side of the border. Along the way they would seek out and destroy North Vietnamese supplies and units, and especially the large cache that was thought to be near Snoul. Intelligence additionally believed that a major NVA headquarters was located in the area.

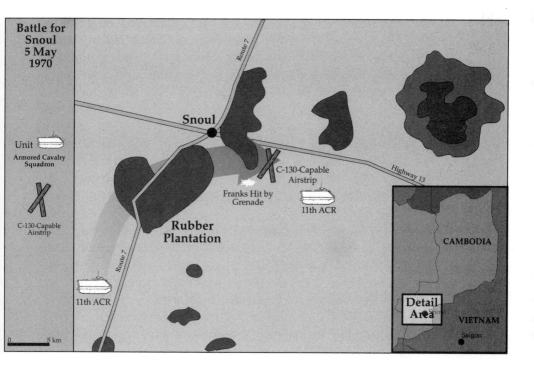

Battle for
Snoul
5 May
1970

Unit

Armored Cavalry
Squadron

C-130-Capable
Airstrip

0   5 km

Route 7

Snoul

C-130-Capable
Airstrip

Franks Hit by
Grenade

11th ACR

Rubber
Plantation

Route 7

11th ACR

Highway 13

CAMBODIA

Detail
Area

Snoul

VIETNAM

Saigon

In technical Army talk, this was to be a tactical reconnaissance in force, with some meeting engagements toward a specific terrain and enemy at some distance, all within the larger operational framework of a spoiling attack. By contrast, the mission in War Zone C had been a security and interdict operation over a specific piece of terrain. In War Zone C, the mission was similar to the 11th CAV's role in Germany facing the Warsaw Pact: to screen the border and barrier interdiction, a traditional cavalry operation. The operation into Cambodia was no less traditional: to penetrate quick and hard.

The territory between War Zone C and Snoul was a mixture of grassy savanna-like lowlands and somewhat higher ridgelines of iron-rich, clayey soil along which the rubber plantations were situated. One of these ridges ran from Snoul through Loc Ninh to An Loc. Highway 7 ran along another extension of this ridge. The tactical problem was this: if you wanted to attack toward Snoul, you couldn't move through the savannas; they were too boggy. You had to follow the ridgeline, and thus were forced into a predictable corridor where setting up defenses and ambushes was much easier for the North Vietnamese.

The other planning problems were more immediate. War Zone C was vastly different from the part of Cambodia they were entering. War Zone C was mostly empty of people, and except for the areas defoliated by Agent Orange, it was heavily covered by tall, triple-canopy rain forest. In Cambodia, once the squadron reached Highway 7, they would run into a large number of civilians and all the infrastructure of civilian life: villages, poles and wires for phones and electricity, trucks, cars, buses, bicycles, normal commerce— none of which they had seen much since they were near An Loc or Loc Ninh. For the past weeks, they had been operating under rules of engagement that did not take into account the presence of civilians. Cambodia was different. As it happened, Cambodian civilians proved to be naturally friendly and helpful to Americans. The North Vietnamese had been there for some time now, and the Cambodians seemed glad to see our soldiers coming in and running the NVA out.

Logistics was going to have to involve helicopters. The regiment had many gas- and diesel-guzzling vehicles to be fed. Fuel and supply trucks could come up from C on a few roads and trails, but it made more sense to bring in most of what they needed by air. Typically, the squadron would operate during the day and draw up into semi-defensive laagers at night. Helicopters would bring in large fuel bladders and drop these down near the laagers. The tanks and other vehicles would then line up to refuel just like at a filling station. There was never a scarcity of fuel during the Cambodian invasion.

With these elements under control, the rest of the planning was relatively straightforward. Devising an operation for a squadron does not take long, and they were a veteran team. It was a matter of asking and answering questions such as "How are we going to attack? What kind of alignment are we getting into? How do we arrange the corridors for moving the squadron from their interdiction mission in C to their attack positions for driving into Cambodia?" And: "Will our fire support keep up with us? Or will we outrun it?" On the plus side, they would have far more indirect fires available than they were used to, both from artillery and from TAC air. They even got some naval air, flying off carriers. In consequence, Franks had to devote serious planning to managing the amount of close air support available.

On April 30, just south of the Cambodian border, Brookshire called in the troop commanders to brief them about the structure of the mission and the tactics of their attack across the border. It was a simple scheme of maneuver. They would initially go in column, then spread the three cavalry troops across the sector, each with its own zone, to move toward Highway 7. Once there, they would advance on the road, with cavalry troops on either side of the road heading toward Snoul. When they got to Snoul, they would decide how to attack from there. Second Squadron, with Brookshire commanding and Franks as S-3, was the lead squadron.

By then, all the troop commanders were veterans. The squadron's string of tactical successes had driven morale high and confidence even higher. They were good, and the troops knew it. So did the NVA, Franks suspected. By this time, he had been the S-3 for more than eight months. Brookshire had stayed in command longer than the normal six months' tour. Some of the troop commanders also had been there longer than the normal six months. Starry encouraged that. Franks suspected it was because he disagreed with the six-month-and-out policy for commanders and others in key positions, because it broke the teamwork so necessary in combat. Their senior NCOs were strong. Teamwork in the squadron was almost automatic, without a lot of talk. The squadron command radio frequency was incredibly crisp and free of any useless chatter. Everyone realized the importance in battle of a disciplined radio frequency. Franks had never felt as close to any organization or group of soldiers as he was then. It was real family.

It was also intensely personal by that time. His driver, Specialist Ray Williams, had been killed in action on April 8 while going back to help a fellow soldier, CSM Burkett. Franks had written in a letter to Denise, "The real blow of the whole action was that my driver was killed. . . ." Burkett lost an arm. Earlier in the month, First Sergeant Willie Johnson of Troop F also had been killed in action.

During the squadron's final preparations, Donn Starry showed up at the squadron command post and announced that he wanted to go in with them—the lead squadron—and that he needed a vehicle. They found him a command ACAV. But the vehicle they found for him immediately threw a track, so he had to get off that and climb aboard Fred Franks's vehicle. Franks stayed in his ACAV the first two days of the operation.

On 1 May, at 0730, they moved into Cambodia through a marsh they called the Pig Path. Because the weather had been dry recently, the marsh didn't prove to be as difficult a passage as the leaders thought. In fact, the skies remained clear throughout the Cambodia operation.

During the next four days, there were several heated incidents, but they did not make major contact with the enemy until they reached Snoul. The NVA, knocked off balance by the invasion, were not eager to make a stand until they could pull themselves together. Time and again on the way to Snoul, troops came across abandoned NVA positions and caches. The attack had yielded sizable results toward its spoiling attack objective.

Second Squadron pushed on, rapidly improvising crossings over bridges the NVA had destroyed, until they reached the neighborhood of Snoul. On the evening of 4 May, they were in a laager five kilometers from the town. It was clear that evening that the NVA had stopped running. Snoul was for them a vital supply area and force concentration. They would make their stand there. They'd fight there, no matter what it cost them.

SNOUL

The next morning, 5 May, Major Franks and Lieutenant Colonel Brookshire were hunched over a map, planning the attack they would launch in less than an hour. They knew they were in for some serious action. They were going to fight at least one NVA regiment, maybe two. The enemy knew the territory, they were expecting Americans, and they'd had time to prepare. The first days in Cambodia had gone relatively smoothly, with running actions and hasty attacks. This day called for more detailed orders and a full squadron attack.

As they huddled over the map, these questions remained in the back of their minds: "How do we find the enemy? How do we smoke them out? How do we hit them the way we want to hit them, and not let them hit us the way they want to hit us?"

They would put 2nd Squadron into what the Army calls a reconnaissance in force. When they located the enemy, they would isolate and fix them in position with air and artillery, then maneuver the ground units in for the kill. As always, they would use maximum force and try to win at the least cost.

If they were lucky, they would be able to interrogate some captured NVA, to learn from them the locations of the enemy forces. If they were to lessen the chances of harming civilians and damaging Snoul—if they were to increase their own chances for success while minimizing their own losses—it was absolutely critical to find an NVA prisoner who would talk.

They looked at their options: To attack directly into town up Route 7? Or to maneuver through the rubber plantation toward the plantation airstrip?

A large number of refugees were fleeing Snoul. The locals weren't blind to what was going on around them. They knew that luck would more likely flow to those out of town when the Blackhorse arrived than those who stayed at home. Some of these civilians reported the NVA were setting up an ambush in the rubber trees along the highway—bringing back memories of other ambushes in other rubber plantations: Echo Troop in August, Fox Troop near Bu Dop.

Attacking into an ambush had little appeal to Fred Franks and Grail Brookshire. They did not want to get tangled up with enemy RPGs and small arms on the road with little room to maneuver. The civilians were friendly, even helpful. They wanted the NVA out more than the Americans did. All that came down to: "If we can stay out of Snoul, we will."

"What do you think, Three?" Brookshire asked Franks. "Three" was Franks's radio call sign.*

---

*The following dialogue was reported by James P. Sterba in "Scraps of Paper from Vietnam," The New York Times Magazine, 18 October 1970.

"Intel plus some locals say some NVA are waiting for us up Highway 7 in the rubber," Franks answered. "I recommend we go around them to the east and approach the airfield and their major positions from the south."

"I agree. Get the commanders huddled over here ASAP."

Brookshire gave the order quickly. He was precise and direct about what he wanted done, as always. There was no doubt who was to do what.

"When we get there, four-six [our tank company] and three-six [Troop G] will break out and start down this way. And I don't think that going down the redball [Highway 7] is necessarily the way we want to go. Work your way through the rubber [trees]. One-six [Troop E], you'll start here and move on up into the town. . . .

"Now if you take fire, return it. . . .

"This is a reconnaissance in force to find out what's in there and also, if possible, to take the town—without destroying it . . . and when you take fire, shoot. Try to avoid shooting into crowds of civilians. . . .

"Now, if we can get around these f'ers, we might have them bottled up down in this end of the rubber. They figure us to come right up Highway 7. Villagers between here and there told us they have broken the highway, and they undoubtedly have. We'll have to find a way around it. We can always come up through the rubber through this draw.

"Three, I'll be on the ground with Blackhorse 6 [Colonel Starry] with the lead troop. You get airborne."

"Wilco."

In Southeast Asia, rubber plantation towns all look pretty much alike. Because it was a provincial capital on a major crossroads, Snoul was a little larger than some. But aside from that, if you've seen An Loc, you've seen Snoul. If you've seen Snoul, you've seen Loc Ninh—the same red, clayey soil; the same ranks of rubber trees at various stages of growth; the same manor house, with surrounding veranda, and maybe a pool; the same grassy airstrip nearby, so the French managers could fly over to Phnom Penh or Saigon for business or shopping. Rubber trees grow moderately high, up to fifty feet or so, and the mature ones are fifteen or eighteen inches wide at the base. So you couldn't easily bull your way through a rubber plantation with tanks. On the other hand, the ranks of rubber trees were wide enough to create lanes Sheridans and ACAVs could pass through. Maneuvering through the rubber was bold, but it was not impossible, and they hoped it would catch the NVA by surprise.

Once they committed to that action, Franks knew, it was essential that they keep moving without interruption to sustain the momentum of the attack. Once they showed their hand and turned east, that would be apparent to the NVA. So there could be no poking around to give them time to adjust. Surprise lasts only as long as it takes the enemy to adjust. Tactically, you have to continue to give the enemy more and more situations to adjust to, thus maintaining and keeping the initiative and, at the same time, keeping him off balance.

For the record, the halt on the night of the fourth did not count as an interruption of momentum. As long as they had the option of going either up Highway 7 or east toward the airfield, the enemy had no way to adjust until 2nd Squadron had committed to one way or the other. In other words, the elements of momentum and surprise were completely under 2nd Squadron's control.

There was one other advantage to taking the airfield. The airstrip at Snoul was long enough to handle C-130s, and C-130s could bring in far more supplies than the trucks driving overland or the helicopters coming in from An Loc. They also could base their attack helicopters out of there, rather than have them go through the long turnaround at An Loc.

In that event, the choice of the airport over the town was the right one. The NVA were dug in around the strip, and they'd placed three 12.7-mm antiaircraft machine guns in doughnut-shaped gun pits on the southern end of the runway. It seems they expected the Americans to make an air assault on the airfield by elements of the 1st Cavalry Division, followed by linkup with the Blackhorse. So they set up their ambush on Highway 7 to stop the Blackhorse, and they placed their antiaircraft on the south side of the airstrip to face the direction of approach of the American air-assault helicopters.

When the Americans came in on the ground, they weren't ready for that. Meanwhile, the American helicopters that were in the air stayed low and far enough to the east to avoid giving away the ground attack.

★ Warrant Officer John Mallette and Specialist Terzala were Fred Franks's crew that morning. Mallette already had the Loach running when Franks stepped up to board it. Before he climbed in, Terzala grabbed him. "Major," he said, "today you need to wear your chicken plate. You are not getting on this helo until you put it on."

Franks didn't usually wear the chicken plate, but he took Terzala's advice and put it on.

The chicken plate was a steel vest that protected the chest and back from shrapnel and direct-fire weapons such as the AK-47. Because it was hot and heavy (when you wore it, you were even more bent over after a day of flying), the chicken plate wasn't always worn. But in the helicopter, Franks and his crews had come to trust and look out for one another, and Terzala knew that they were going into a situation that was likely to be more heated than normal. No sense messing around with fate.

They took off.

On the OH-6, you sit side by side, with the Plexiglas bubble in front of you. The pilot, Mallette, was in the right-hand seat; Fred Franks was in the left; and Terzala, the crew chief/gunner, was in the back, sitting on the floor, with an M-60 machine gun cradled in his lap. Mallette was as skillful a Loach pilot as you're likely to find; he and Franks had been together for nearly ten straight months of tough flying. They'd taken some hits, but had avoided most. Franks trusted his life with John Mallette and Terzala, without question.

Whap!

They were hung up on a telephone wire. It was stretched across the front of the bubble, just at eye level.

Helicopters striking wires happens on occasion. And it is frequently fatal, especially when your ship is just taking off and full of fuel. If you're a pilot, you try to look where you're going—obviously. But wires are thin and hard to see against a background of trees. And in their case, they had been operating for several weeks in an area where there weren't any wires to worry about. Now here they were, hanging thirty feet in the air, with a phone wire ready to slip one way or the other, up or down their bubble. If it slipped up, it would likely tangle around the rotor head, and down they would go . . . almost instantly to be engulfed in quick, consuming flames. If it slipped down, it would likely hit the skids, catch, and they would flip over. Down they would go into quick, consuming flames.

"Oh, shit!" Franks blurted out.

Mallette put the Loach into full power. The wire slipped down. Caught in the skids. Franks braced himself for the Loach to pitch over.

The line snapped.

And they lurched up toward the sky.

Moments later, the Loach peeled off toward the east to take up station just above the canopy top, ready to help Brookshire and the squadron navigate through the lanes of rubber trees. They stayed low so as to avoid hostile fire, and also to keep out of sight of the NVA so that they would not give away their advancing troop positions.

Franks didn't have much time to reflect on their good luck. He had a mission to continue. M48s, Sheridans, and ACAVs were already in the rubber. But he did have time to think, "That's it for us today. We've had our close call. Everything from here on out will be OK."

A few minutes later, Franks's Loach was over the airstrip, while H Company (the tanks) and Troop G were maneuvering toward the strip on the ground. Troop E, together with Brookshire and Starry in their command tracks, was less than a kilometer away, and also approaching. Off to the west, up on a little rise, was the town of Snoul.

If they wanted a meeting engagement, they had it.

Meanwhile, staring at Franks's Loach was a North Vietnamese manning a .51-caliber AA weapon, his shoulder against the stock, and ammunition clearly fed into it. If he had had it pointed up toward the Loach and pulled the trigger, he would have blown them out of the sky. But luck was with them a second time that morning. When the Loach appeared, the crew was frantically trying to depress the weapon so that they could fire at the unexpected oncoming armor.

The squadron had achieved the element of surprise. Now they had to maintain the momentum surprise had created and keep the NVA off balance. Now more than ever, speed was crucial. The squadron was committed. They had to move quickly. Franks's immediate job was staring him in the face. There were two NVA down there with that AA gun. Normally the antiaircraft people were aware of the disposition of the rest of their forces, because they all would be mutually supporting. So if one of them could provide useful information about further defensive NVA locations, that would refine the intel picture, help the squadron keep up its momentum—and save American lives. There were also a lot of civilians in the area. If they could better pinpoint the NVA, they could then avoid civilian damage and civilian casualties.

When Franks wanted to mark a position where they had taken fire for gunships or TAC air to attack, he would drop a smoke grenade nearby and talk the fires in. They had devised a scheme where they would pull the pin from a smoke grenade, then shove the grenade back inside the cardboard canister it was packaged in. The only thing holding the handle was pressure inside the canister. That way, you could kick the canister out of the Loach when the enemy fired. The grenade would then come free of the canister, ignite, and smoke the area you wanted to mark while you were getting the hell out of there and calling in fire.

Franks kicked a grenade free to mark the AA, and then got on the radio to Brookshire. "Battle Six, this is Three. NVA .51-cal by the smoke."

"Roger, Three."

Brookshire ordered Troop E, commanded by Captain Fred Kyle, plus parts of H Company, commanded by Captain Miles Sisson, to move quickly to capture the position and get ready to continue the attack around the Snoul airstrip (used by the rubber plantation owners, but not that day). Brookshire and the squadron command section was with Troop E, as was Colonel Donn Starry.

Since nobody else was around, Starry grabbed his M-16, some NCOs, and soldiers and charged up toward the gun pit. A moment later, they'd captured the gun and two of the crew, and they were unloading the weapon. But two men from the crew made a run for it—the lieutenant and a soldier—and dived into a bunker a few meters away . . . really just a hole in the ground covered by logs and grassy sod. They probably slept there, or kept ammo there; no one ever found out.

While that was going on, Franks's Loach set down, and he jumped out to see what info they could pull out of the prisoners. Mallette and Terzala stayed behind in the OH-6, with the engine running, so that they could lift back up fast with whatever new intel they had. Franks, moving fast, didn't grab his steel pot or the CAR 15 he carried in the Loach, though he did have his .45-cal pistol on his belt. And he was wearing the chicken plate. He didn't have much time. By then the unit was pretty exposed to the NVA. The enemy knew there wasn't going to be an air assault and that the squadron had slipped their ambush. They would adjust to this new situation. But how fast? Franks knew they would not run away, but would move to a different position and set up again for them there. So the surprise they were working with now was rapidly fading. He hurried over to the pit.

The squadron had a Vietnamese interpreter and scout (they called them Kit Carsons; this one they'd nicknamed "Rocky") who was trying to coax information out of the NVA who didn't dive into the bunker. No luck; the men kept silent. Then the Kit Carson went over to the bunker and tried to talk the other two out. In Vietnam, they would have called in once for their surrender, paused a few seconds for a response, and then blown the bunker. Here was different. They badly needed the intel these men could give them.

Franks, by this time convinced the NVA weren't going to do him any good, was on his way back to the helicopter. "Hey, Major," someone called, "we got two more in a bunker over here."

So Franks changed his mind about taking off. He pulled out his pistol and raced over to the bunker. When he got there, the Kit Carson was crouched over the hole, trying to get the NVA to surrender.

"Let's dig them out," Franks called out. "Let's get him out of there." And he started pulling and dragging at the logs over the bunker to try to open it up. He wanted that intel. Battle is full of split-second judgments, and that was a big one for Franks. The NVA threw a Chicom grenade that he never saw.

Colonel Starry was just then talking to Sergeant Major Horn, the regimental command sergeant major. As he did so, he glanced over at Franks. Out of the corner of his eye, Starry noticed the NVA grenade lying in front of the bunker, fuse lit, next to Franks. It was called a potato masher, because that's what it looked like. They were made by the Chicoms, but they were based on the old German designs everyone has seen in World War II movies—tin cans with handles stuck in them and a cord out the bottom. You pull the cord and that lights the fuse . . . maybe half the time. This time it lit. Starry could see it burning.

Five or six thoughts ran through his head, all in the moment he stood there watching, for the space of a breath or two, paralyzed.

And Starry thought, Oh, Jesus, what about Fred? If somebody doesn't do something about Fred, he's going to get hurt bad.

So Starry burst into motion. He actually dove into Franks . . . trying to knock him out of the way of the blast.

There was an ice-white flash. Then a harsh, head-filling, bone-jarring crack.

The next thing Donn Starry remembered is that he was backed up against his command track. The next thing Fred Franks remembered, he was lying flat on the ground. He was knocked unconscious by the blast.

"Jesus . . . oh, my God . . . The major, the major's hit. . . . Get down. There's another one in there. . . . The colonel's hit. . . . What'd he throw? . . . Grenade . . . Is that son of a—still in there? Yeah . . . *get a frag* . . . Get a god-damn frag. We'll blow that bastard outa there. . . .

"One-six [Troop E] has got contact, heavy shit. Where's that other f'er? I'll kill that bastard. Man, the major's really f'ed up. . . . The major's the worst."*

Franks's left foot was a total mess; it was as though some giant had taken a monstrous boulder and smashed it into the foot and leg. When he regained consciousness, the pain was intense. There was also head pain, hard ringing in the ears, and stinging pains in his hand, arm, and side. He moved his head from side to side and simultaneously pulled clumps of ground and grass up, as though that would ease the pain. He said nothing. Then he lifted his eyes and saw the soldiers standing around him. Their faces, and his own pain, told him all he needed to know.

A medic gave him a shot of morphine, and that gave him a little ease.

Seven Americans had been standing around when the grenade blew. All of them suffered frag wounds, though none was as bad as Franks's.

Contrary to his own orders, Donn Starry hadn't worn his chicken plate that day. If he had, he would have only been scratched. Fred Franks's chicken plate saved his life, thanks to Terzala. It was in shreds. As it was, Starry got ten or fifteen holes of various sizes in his face and down the front part of his body. The worst of these was in the stomach; a frag had taken a long strip of flesh out of there. Though there was a lot of blood, this was basically a surface wound, and he was able to walk around on his own after he'd had a chance to pull himself together.

Meanwhile, Master Sergeant Bob Bolan, acting squadron command sergeant major, who had been Franks's operations sergeant and a great coach for him when he had been new to Vietnam, took his .45-caliber pistol and directed the action that destroyed the bunker and killed the two NVA soldiers.

*Dialogue again as reported by James P. Sterba.

Specialists Gus Christian and Dave Kravick in E-18, a Sheridan, were there, providing cover. MSG Bolan was himself killed in action in July 1970 and remains to this day one of Franks's personal heroes.

"Medevac on the way!"

They set up an LZ with colored smoke. But it turned out the medevac wasn't the first ship down. Colonel Starry's command-and-control Huey came in ahead of it.

Somebody helped Colonel Starry aboard. Then others lifted in Fred Franks's litter. He was feeling dry in the mouth, from the morphine. And he would fade in and out, from the pain in his crushed foot and from the drug. The other troops who were hit in the incident also were aboard.

One of the other AA positions was still operating. When Starry's Huey took off, it put serious fire in their direction. With tracers flaming close . . . erupting all around them . . . the pilot took the ship down low, skimming over treetops. As out of it as he was by then, Franks could hear the popping sounds from the AA.

It was less than fifteen minutes after the grenade blew.

★ Later that day, the battle that started near the airstrip expanded and intensified. Though they tried to avoid it, the Blackhorse had to take the fight into the town of Snoul. When it was all over, they had dealt the NVA a defeat, but at the cost of serious collateral damage to the town. If they had managed to obtain the intel Fred Franks wanted from the NVA at the AA site, all that might have been avoided.

Thirty minutes after Franks was lifted out of Snoul, he was at the aid station at Quan Loi, near the 11th ACR base camp. The aid station was a triage area. They decided which of the wounded they could fix up there and which had to be medevaced back to Long Binh. Franks was clearly evacuation material.

When the doctor at Quan Loi looked him over, Franks asked him, "Am I going to lose my foot?"

"Nah," he said. "You'll be OK. Don't worry about it."

They always underestimate combat wounds. . . .

A medevac took him to the 93rd Evacuation Hospital at Long Binh. When he arrived, they rushed him into surgery. And during the next two days, he was in surgery again, more than once. How many operations he had then, he doesn't know. He was pretty much out of it during that time.

He asked a doctor at Long Binh: "Doc, am I going to lose my foot?"

"Nah," he said. "Six months and you'll be up and around doing duty."

On 7 May, they flew him to Camp Zama Hospital in Japan. He was there for a week.

He asked a doctor at Zama, Dr. Jeff Malke, "Doc, am I going to lose my foot?"

"You don't want to hear this," Malke answered, "but six months from now, you're going to decide you'd be better off without that foot. But you're probably going to have to go through a battle to decide that yourself. You're not going to get around well on that leg. Major, that is just not a good-looking leg and foot."

Dr. Malke was a wise man, but Fred Franks did not want to hear such wisdom just then.

He said to himself, The hell with that. He doesn't know what he's talking about. I'm going to beat this thing. I haven't met a hurdle yet I can't get over.

It was not, in truth, a good-looking leg and foot. The entire ankle was shattered, dislocated. The bones of the ankle and foot were splintered or crushed, and part of the lower leg had serious damage.

The war was over for Franks. Little did he realize that his, and the Army's, biggest battles lay ahead.

★ Fred Franks tells what happened next.

4

VALLEY FORGE

2408 CLEVELAND AVENUE, WEST LAWN, PENNSYLVANIA.

That's where I grew up.

My family moved there in the fall of 1946, right after Boston lost the World Series to St. Louis. I was nine. Housing was scarce in 1946, and my dad was lucky to find the place. It was what was called a double home, a two-family house, and it had been built in the twenties. There were no sidewalks out front, and to the rear of the house were open fields where people still hunted for small game. A baseball diamond was across the street next to the double railroad tracks of the Reading Railroad. It was there and on other athletic fields around Berks County that I learned about competition and teamwork.

It was a great place to grow up. Even though the Army sent Denise and me all over the world, that part of Pennsylvania is still home to us. In that neighborhood, my sister, Frances, my brother, Farrell, and I grew up with a spirit of togetherness—my mother and dad saw to that. And it is where I first met Denise in 1949, right after she moved into the school district and took the seat in front of me in homeroom in Wilson High School. We learned values at home from our family and had them strengthened in that community in school, in church, in sports, and with our friends and their families.

It was a modest, mostly blue-collar community. People worked hard, many in the factories of the Textile Machine Works or the Berkshire Knitting Mills in nearby Wyomissing. Homes were small, but clean, and well kept inside and out. There was pride there, and humility. Hard work was the ethic. Earn your way to the top, then when you get there, be modest, don't get a big head.

In the summer of 1969, after I got orders to Vietnam, Denise, our daughter, Margie, and I moved into the old homestead at 2408. The house had been vacant since Mom and Dad had moved to Endwell, New York, in 1968, following my dad's promotion to a senior management position with the Endicott Johnson Shoe Corporation. I had just finished three years at West Point as an instructor in the English Department and as assistant varsity baseball coach. I felt good that Margie and Denise would be home while I was gone, and that Margie would go to the same grade school in West Wyomissing that Frances, Farrell, and I had attended many years earlier. Some of the same teachers were still there. And Denise's parents, Eva and Harry, lived less than a half mile away, in the house where Denise grew up. Most of our relations were within fifty miles. Just as when we had both grown up, the three us were surrounded by family and friends.

In late July 1969, as I kissed Denise and Margie good-bye in the Philadelphia airport, I was off to war, but I was happy that my family was in good hands.

It was to that house that I would return on Christmas 1970 to decide whether to have my left leg amputated.

VALLEY FORGE GENERAL HOSPITAL

Valley Forge General Hospital, just outside Phoenixville, Pennsylvania, is forty-five minutes by medevac helicopter from the hospital at Fort Dix, New Jersey. I had spent the night there after a long, C-141 medevac trip from Camp Zama hospital in Japan. It was the Army's policy to place long-term-care soldiers as close to home as possible, and Phoenixville was about an hour's drive for Denise each way, mostly on two-lane roads. On 18 May 1970, the helicopter landed on the asphalt Maltese Cross landing pad at Valley Forge.

Though it was great to be back in the U.S.A., I was beginning to grow concerned about my leg. Since I'd been wounded on 5 May, I had undergone surgery in a string of hospitals. Each time, the doctors had been less and less optimistic.

On the night before I came to Valley Forge, I had an emotional reunion with Denise and Margie, who had driven the three hours from our home to Fort Dix with our friend Betsy Hassler. It was a reunion not much different, I suspect, from those many of my fellow soldiers experienced when they returned home wounded from Vietnam. At first Margie was not permitted to come to my room, but a sergeant snuck her up the back stairs. Sergeants just know sometimes.

When we were all together, few words passed. We hugged each other and did not talk about the obvious. By now, some of the wounds on my hand, arm, back, and both legs were healing, although there were still bandages and stitches. But there was still some concern about my ear, which had been damaged by the grenade, and my smashed lower left leg. If Denise had any thoughts about my condition, she never let on, although she told me later the wounds were more extensive than official communications had indicated. We tried to put a positive face on it all.

Valley Forge General Hospital was a World War II–type hospital, with two stories, a wood frame, and a sprawling design. (Most of these facilities have since been torn down or used for other purposes; Valley Forge was closed in the late 1970s.) There was a central nurses' station, with long wings reaching out on each side, and a corridor connecting them all. The wards were open, with four to six beds on each side, for a total of eight to twelve per section, and three sections per wing. A few private and semi-private rooms were sandwiched in between the nurses' station and the wings. With four wings per ward, on two floors, each ward had a total patient population of 150 to 200, and the total patient census at the hospital at that time was somewhere around 1,400 or 1,500. The military installation included the hospital itself, plus other activities supporting it, such as the troop barracks, gymnasium, chapel, small PX and commissary, service club, and even an officer and NCO club. There was also a nine-hole golf course. Later, an amputee instructor gave some of us instruction there on how to play golf as an amputee. The facility was not large, but covered maybe 200 acres, including the golf course. The orthopedic ward—3A and 3B—held approximately 300 soldiers, all male. We actually had more patients (about 400) than we had beds. The hospital got around that by putting about 100 people on convalescent leave at any one time. The hospital was full.

Valley Forge was a general hospital, in which every kind of medical problem was treated. There were psychiatric patients, an entire ward devoted to amputees, and an orthopedic ward devoted to non-amputees.

I was admitted to Ward 3A/B, the non-amputee orthopedic ward. We had a lot of badly hurt soldiers there, a lot of them much worse off than I was. At first I was in a room by myself, but later shared one with a warrant officer aviator named Tom Merhline. Though Tom had severe abdominal wounds and couldn't get out of bed, he was a tough guy and fought his battle day after day. I admired his courage.

As for me, the next several months, I ran up against a wall I could not get over no matter how hard I tried.

DECEMBER 1970

After more than six months in the hospital, I knew I had to make a decision about the leg. I talked about my choices a few days before Christmas with Dr. Phil Deffer, the chief of orthopedics at Valley Forge.

"So, Doctor, what are my options?"

"You have two," he said. "First, we can continue to work on your foot and ankle to try to stop the infection and help you walk better. We'll leave you with something that looks like a foot. Chances are you'll be able to walk a few blocks without too much pain, but you might have some continued bone infection."

"What's the other one?"

"Amputate your left leg below the knee and hope we got high enough so there is no residual infection. We'll probably have to leave the end of your leg open for some time, to be sure there is no infection in the remaining bone. No guarantees."

"What about staying in the Army?"

"There's no way to do that and keep your leg. The Army does allow amputees to remain on active duty. But that depends on your motivation and the medical board recommendation."

"That's it?"

"That's it."

"Okay, Dr. Deffer. Tough choice, but that's what I needed to know. I'm going to talk about it over Christmas with my wife and daughter.

"The choices are clear to me."

Nothing had worked.

CHRISTMAS 1970

I do not like to think much anymore about the six months that had just passed. I was in a real losing streak and did not seem able to do anything about it. I was losing not only physically, but in other, less visible ways.

Multiple operations at many hospitals up to and including Valley Forge had failed to halt the infection or ease the constant pain. For the first eight weeks after I arrived, it had been surgery every week to debride the wound. In July, they'd stopped operating to try to get me to walk. We tried it all. I got a special shoe to keep weight off what was left of the ankle and foot. Then we tried a brace above and below the knee to take more weight off the ankle. Physical therapy was twice a day, but I was walking with a thirty-degree list. I continued to lose weight. During those six months, my weight dropped from a normal 165 down to less than 130. The only thing that worked was a skin graft to the side of my leg to replace a large area of lost skin, but even that took three attempts.

The days were long but the nights were longer. I was running temperatures almost every night, followed by night sweats. They checked for malaria and everything else likely, but they found nothing except the leg wound and the resulting infection. The cultures from my leg were not good, and I had received four or five pints of blood because of blood loss during surgery. Meanwhile, the multiple surgery had taken more of the bones away. Even with all that, my ankle remained dislocated, and I could barely move my toes. I had maybe ten to twelve degrees of motion in the ankle.

By now I could change my own bandage, which was necessary because of the constant drainage from the wound. I did that about twice a day. It was ugly. I had been on pain medication for almost eight straight months, every four to six hours. I would watch the clock, waiting for the time to pass between medications. Try as I may, I just flat could not walk straight or put much weight on that foot and ankle. I even tried to kill an ant on the sidewalk but could not put down enough pressure to do that.

I was losing the physical battle—and another one as well. I was rapidly becoming someone different. I was absorbed in myself and this wound and my inability to overcome it. I could not concentrate for long periods of time. I raged, but did not know at what or whom. Anger would erupt for no apparent reason. The events of 5 May 1970 ran like a video in my mind, often starting at times I least expected. That instant replay was a source of great mental anguish, and played itself over and over again, always the same. And I second-guessed myself without letup: Why? I would ask. Why didn't you do something different? Then, Why me? Why did this have to happen to me? Then the guilt: Why am I alive and all those other soldiers were killed in action? Why me?

I had to do something. I was in free fall. I knew I had some steel in me. I had to find it, grab hold, and start back. My battle was a lot like that of many others from that generation. Some would never make it back.

The doctors and medical staff at Valley Forge had done all they could. It was up to me. It was my choice.

I was home on convalescent leave. I had Denise, who was both my wife and my best friend. She had been my daily companion in the hospital ever since I had come to Valley Forge in the middle of May 1970. Many times she was just there after I'd come out of surgery and was not very coherent. Always there. A squeeze of the hand, a kiss, talk, and listen. Trying to help, but puzzled by this man who had gone off to war almost a year ago and was now in another battle. "I'll get by," I had inscribed in her wedding band when we were married. The rest of that song goes, "as long as I have you." How true that turned out to be.

Denise had her own battles. She had given birth to our second child in May 1966, a son who had died shortly after birth and whom we had buried in the cemetery at West Point. Denise knew about pain. For her there would be more. She knew the difference between pity and compassion. My friend.

Our daughter, Margie, was now nine years old and also part of this battle. We would write stories together. I'd write a sentence, then she would add a sentence, and so on until we had a made-up story. Our favorite was about whales. She was, and is, a strong girl, and our future.

And then there were my fellow soldiers at Valley Forge.

During physical training sessions, I saw men who were amputees move around with a lot more agility and a lot better attitude than I had. Many of them had wounds far worse than mine. I was far from being the only one in a fight. We all were; many had much bigger battles than I did. We helped one another. I was fortunate to have so much help. Not everyone there had my good fortune.

Denise said she was ready to help in any way she could, but she agreed with me. I needed to do something.

It was a tough Christmas.

We did what we could to make Christmas the usual joyful time it has always been in our family. Denise even bought me a La-Z-Boy chair, black like Blackhorse, with a raise-up footrest so I could keep my foot elevated. She did it, she said, because when a wounded combat veteran talks to visitors, he should sit up with some pride—when I'd been home on convalescent leave, my practice had been to lie down on the couch with my leg elevated. She was trying to help me save my dignity, but I did not get it at the time. I was too absorbed in myself.

I would sit looking at that foot and ankle. Was I giving in too soon? Should I fight it some more? Maybe some other kind of treatment was possible. More second-guessing. It was a tough Christmas, all right, not only for me, but for Denise and Margie as well. I was not much fun to be around.

As I look back on it now, it amazes me how much my world had shrunk and how absorbed I was in myself. It happened, and I didn't even notice, but I'm sure others did. I know Denise did, but she kept holding out a hand to pull me out or to shock me into an awareness of where I was.

One day, she arranged for us to go bowling with lifelong friends Carl and Betsy Hassler to a place called Colonial Acres on Route 222 just outside Shillington. I would stand at the foul line and, without any steps, roll the ball down the alley. We used to like to bowl together, but this was no fun at all. I was thirty-four years old and had been a decent athlete. And here I was, standing at the foul line, struggling to roll the ball from there: not exactly the image of self I'd had in mind for the rest of my life. I got the message.

It was that Christmas that I reached the bottom.

It was up to me.

VALLEY FORGE GENERAL HOSPITAL
JANUARY 1971

"Doctor, I've made the choice. I want you to amputate my leg."

The surgery took place later in January, the morning after the Super Bowl. I watched the game from my bed in Ward 3B the night before. The morning of the surgery, just for the hell of it, with my cane, I struggled on the leg I was about to have amputated down the hall to the common latrine to shave. Then I came back and they wheeled me to surgery. I would not look back.

It was my choice. I had to win this battle and get on with my life. I had to be thankful for what I had rather than what I did not have, to focus on that and drive on. Life would not be the same. It never is.

Following surgery, Denise was waiting for me in my room. She said nothing, but she squeezed my hand. We both knew what was going on inside. Looking down the length of the bed and seeing only one peak at the end in the sheet was a shock. It was gone. No looking back. No second-guessing. Time to get on with my life, one day at a time.

And that is what it was. One day at a time.

Within days, I started to feel better. My appetite returned. The pain was still there, but it was a different pain, the consequence of the open end of my leg. Changing the dressing was not my favorite time of day. We had a female Army medic who called herself "Charlie"; Charlie had such gentle hands that we all asked for her for those dressing changes.

Due to the gross infection, they had to leave the end of my leg open until they were sure there was no residual bone infection. When I asked how long that might take, they told me it could take months. It turned out to take nine. They initially had me in traction to keep the skin flap pulled down over the end of my stump. Later, when I went home on convalescent leave, Denise and I hooked the contraption up to the bedroom doorknob to give the necessary tension. I had to stay in that for three or four hours a day for the first six weeks. I also had the usual phantom pains amputees get—the sensations that my foot was still there. They never completely go away.

A few weeks after surgery, they fitted me with a pylon—a temporary plaster of Paris prosthesis made to go over my stump to lessen swelling and to get me vertical and bearing weight. I was anxious to walk and start moving again. I wanted to get on with my life. I was feeling better physically and now had a goal: to get moving. I could get on top of this, maybe even stay in the Army.

As I looked back on it, the difference in my thinking before and after the operation was that of night and day. It's okay, I was able to say to myself. I've got to go on now. I'm going to get well physically. I've got a mission in life. I've got to pass from here. I've been like a fool with my family. I've got to focus, get back up off the deck swinging. I've been down long enough. It felt good to be able to fight back.

Valley Forge itself had long traditions for our country, of course, and the courage and sacrifices of the patriots of the Continental Army, who in 1778 had rebuilt themselves into a tough army, were not lost on me. Nor were the battles my fellow soldiers in the hospital were going through. I drew strength from them. It is hard to overstate the courage of the young Americans there in the amputee ward, people such as Angel Cruz, Jim Dehlin, "Big" John, Mike Stekoviak, and Dave, who went back to being a ski instructor as a below-the-knee amputee. They were all heroes, and they inspired me.

We all go through Valley Forge experiences in our lives. At that time, I thought Denise and I might have to rebuild the relationship that had so dramatically changed during the two years from July 1969 until March 1971. Denise had been doing everything, running the home and raising our daughter on her own. We had to get back to doing that together, to rebuild our life based on where we were, not where we had been. We began to make that happen.

I also talked to others. One whose influence was great was retired Colonel Red Reeder, an old friend and former assistant baseball coach at West Point. Wounded five days after D-Day on Utah Beach commanding the 12th Infantry Regiment in the 4th Infantry Division, he had had his leg amputated below the knee. At that time, he could not remain on active duty. Among the things Red told me was how Mrs. Anna Rosenberg, Assistant Secretary of Defense in the 1950s under George Marshall, had changed U.S. military regulations to permit amputees and others with disabilities to remain on active duty. Red actively encouraged me to stay in the Army, and he gave me a book to read, *Reach for the Sky*, the story of Douglas "Tin Legs" Bader of the U.K., who had lost both legs in an airplane accident in 1929, but went on to fly Spitfires in the Battle for Britain in 1940. I met Bader in London some years later.

Colonel Jimmie Leach, one of my 11th ACR commanders in Vietnam, came by one day, and so did John "Mac" MacClennon, who had been an Air Force forward air controller in Vietnam (and is now in the Connecticut National Guard). His call sign was Niles 06. One day in Vietnam, Mac had gone out and flown with me, and I damned near got him killed. Most days I was in the OH-6 talking to him on the radio while he flew in his FAC fixed-wing aircraft. One day, though, I put him in the backseat in my helicopter while I was directing an air strike; I wanted him to see firsthand what we did. Did he ever! Despite that, though, Mac and I still exchange correspondence (he came all the way down to Fort Myer for my retirement in November 1994). Jim Sutherland, my assistant S-3 in Vietnam, also came to see me. One day he was riding in my helicopter when we got hit on one of our rotor blades by ground fire. He had been asking to go along, so the day I said OK was the day I damned near got him killed, too! And Grail Brookshire came with his whole family. The brotherhood of combat.

And one day there was a letter from General Omar Bradley. Though I did not know him at all, he'd been told about my case by Red Reeder. The day the letter came, I had been away from the house. When I drove up to the curb and got out of the car, Margie ran up and said, "Daddy, you got a letter with five stars on it!"

"You've got to be mistaken," I said.

"No," she said. "See, here it is." That was Bradley's letter.

As I began to put on weight and grow stronger, my opportunities for convalescent leave increased, and I was able to spend more time at home. At first I could not walk on my leg because of the open wound. That period lasted the better part of two months. I would wear the pylon for short periods of time. The rest of the time I'd use the metal "Canadian walker" crutches with my pant leg pinned up. Soon, at a civilian prosthetic place on Thirty-third Street in Philadelphia, where the Army had contracted for that work, I was fitted with my first prosthesis. It was a strange experience standing up in that plastic leg for the first time and taking a few steps. I had to learn how to walk all over again.

We had physical therapy twice a day. Depending on where we were in rehabilitation, we would go through various range-of-motion and strength exercises. After my leg was amputated, it was for me a matter of hip-strengthening exercises, upper-leg strengthening, and upper-body exercises. But mainly it was a matter of walking, of learning how to do that all over again.

The PT ward was an open hospital bay, roughly thirty by seventy feet. In there was the usual array of PT gear for orthopedic patients. There were also excellent PT specialists, men and women soldiers trained to help their fellow soldiers. The chief was Lieutenant Colonel Mary Matthews, who happened to be the sister of our neighbor at Fort Benning, Jack Matthews, whom I had met when Jack and I had been students at the Infantry Officer Advanced Course from 1963 to 1964. Not that that got me any favors with Mary, or Colonel Matthews, as I called her then. She was another case of tough compassion, and a skilled leader.

For amputees to practice walking, two vertical mirrors, each about six feet by two feet, were placed facing each other at a distance of maybe thirty feet. Each mirror had a string running vertically down the middle. The drill for amputees was to walk in between these mirrors, lining yourself up so you split the mirror, using the string as a guide. To get your gait right, there was a piano metronome. So you would walk and walk and walk by the hour in between these two mirrors to the ticktock of the metronome. With enough practice, you would walk straight and with an even gait without even thinking about it. It was drill, pure and simple. With most amputees, if they discipline themselves to get it right when they first learn to walk, they will continue to do well later. I was determined to get it right. I knew drill and the importance of technique from playing a lot of sports. There were also stairs for us to go up and down. First we used a railing, and then we did without. We used to joke that when we could walk, talk, and chew gum at the same time, we were ready to go on convalescent leave. That was not far from the truth.

Dr. Phil Deffer, the chief of orthopedics (he went on to retire as a brigadier general), was a great blend of tough compassion and skilled doctoring. He was well aware that there was not only a physical but a mental and emotional part to the healing. He knew that there were stages, and that in one of those stages, the patient had to stop feeling sorry for himself and learn to do things for himself. So he pushed us to help one another out, and he made sure that the staff did not do everything for us. In other words: open the doors for yourself, even on crutches. You had to go to physical training every day, to dress your own wounds after nurses showed you how to do it, to walk and stay out of wheelchairs, to get out on your own two feet or prosthesis and get around. And in that hospital, with its long connected passageways, it was a long way from one place to the other. I'm sure there were elevators, but I never remember using one.

I would also be remiss if I didn't mention Jim Herndon, the doctor I came to know best, who performed my amputation and final stump revision. He also did my medical board, and it was he who recommended I be retained on active duty. I owe him a great deal. He was a favorite with the troops.

As time went on, I was permitted more and more convalescent leave to go home, which was good for both body and soul. When I was out of the hospital, I had to get around on my own, even though the bottom of my stump was still open and not ready for long, steady use. So on leave I managed that, sometimes on crutches, sometimes with one crutch or a cane, and sometimes solo.

Our goal at home was to restore some normalcy to our lives. We would do things together as a family, either around the house or in the local area. Margie and I continued our story writing together, and I helped her with schoolwork, a practice Denise had been taking care of alone during most of the past two years. We also got together with our close friends, the Hasslers, for family activities, and we even managed a short vacation to the Jersey shore.

But 1971 was not a great year for our family. We learned Denise was pregnant, and though this was a moment of great joy and hope for us, we had concerns, too. Since Denise had given birth to our second child prematurely in 1966 and he had died shortly after birth, we went to a local civilian doctor in West Reading for advice. He advised some procedures to ensure Denise could carry the baby to full term, and he also advised her to have a cesarean section. In August 1971, he judged she had reached full term, so he admitted her to the Reading Hospital and performed the C-section procedure. Meanwhile, Denise, Margie, and I had completely prepared my old bedroom at 2408 Cleveland Avenue for our new baby.

It was not to be.

Our baby was born on 25 August 1971. We named him Frederick Carl (after Carl Hassler). Denise saw Frederick Carl once right after he was born. He weighed a little less than six pounds. Almost immediately after his birth, we both were told he was having trouble breathing. Not long after that, they had him in an incubator. He had the same condition the Kennedys' baby had died of, they told us, hyaline membrane disease, and the next three days would be critically important. If Frederick could make it past three days, he would be OK. They never again brought our son to Denise. Because she was not permitted out of bed, she had to hear news and descriptions of our son from Margie and me.

For two long days and nights, we prayed together.

· Early in the morning of 27 August at around 0500, I got a call that I should come to the hospital right away. Margie had been staying at Denise's parents' home in West Lawn. I drove the three miles to the hospital down a largely deserted Penn Avenue. All I managed to think about was Denise and our son and to keep praying, "Please, God, spare our son. Your will be done."

I went to newborn emergency care. Our son was fighting for his life in the incubator, unable to take in enough oxygen to sustain his life. Denise knew what was happening; she wanted desperately to see her son. It was not to be. Frederick Carl died that morning, three days after he was born. It had been Denise's fourth pregnancy.

The loss was devastating.

I did not know what to do for Denise, except to be with her, as she had with me. Margie took it hard, too. There were a lot of tears; she kept asking why, and kept wanting to be with Denise.

We took apart the bedroom at 2408 Cleveland Avenue. I had seen courage on the battlefield. Now, at home, I was to see it in my wife, in another way. We decided to bury Frederick with his brother in the cemetery at West Point; we held a graveside ceremony there. My dad went with me, as did Pastor Bill Fryer from our Lutheran church in West Lawn, the same church where Denise and I had been confirmed.

Now we had two sons at West Point, both in the cemetery.

Later, in 1972, Denise would undergo an operation to remove fibroid tumors at Bethesda Naval Hospital. Because the doctor suspected cancer, they performed a total hysterectomy. There was no cancer, and there would be no more children. She was thirty-six at the time.

★ You gain wisdom and strength through enduring pain, or else you die as a person. No one seeks out pain, but it finds most of us. That year, the one before, and the one to follow, it found us often. But we would fight back. It is not getting knocked down, but the getting back up and going on that counts. So Denise, Margie, and I resolved to fight our way out of this dark time, to reach inside and grab hold of the steel we knew was there and go on. We would be thankful for what we had and not what we did not have. We would not look back. We would live life every day. We would not mortgage the present for the future.

We would learn these things, and later would try to help others learn them. But that was later. At the time, we were just fighting back with all we had, and barely making it.

THE HOT BLUE FLAME

More happened to me than just the personal recovery. There was a change inside as well as outside, and the change inside proved to me far more important and lasting. The physical recovery, it turned out, was the easy part. I was also slowly undergoing a change in my outlook on life, and that was much harder. Much of that change came out of what my family and I were going through. But much of it also had to do with my other family—the soldiers who were the Army.

I was beginning to see my fellow soldiers at Valley Forge and Vietnam in a way I had not been able to before my leg was amputated.

Now that I was able to go on convalescent leave and get around on my own, I took a volunteer job in the hospital. I began to teach soldiers, preparing them to take their high school GEDs or helping them with other schoolwork. During this time, I began to notice some things going on at Valley Forge that affected me deeply.

The soldiers at Valley Forge did their best to encourage each other. That support had been there for me before the amputation as much as it was still there afterward. There was a lot of chatter and banter and good-natured kidding. Most of the other wounded soldiers were considerably younger than I was. They called me the "Major." "Hey, Major," they'd call out, "you old guys heal slow. You're gonna be around here a lot longer than we are." I was one of them. We were a family there.

There was amputee humor, too, which helped. Stories of guys hollering "shark" when they came out of the surf, of presents of foot powder to double amputees, of drinking beer out of prosthesis sockets, of wheelchair races and contests. And there were also the endless critiques of our walking during PT.

But there was pain as well. An amputee died in an apartment fire in Phoenixville; he was alone and could not get to his legs fast enough. Another died in a single-car accident while he was on convalescent leave. Mostly the pain was about dealing with rejection and the internal emotional pain of adjustment to the new physical reality and the new self-image.

For some, there was rejection by families who could not adjust to these new realities, or broken engagements by fiancées. There was the self-image adjustment. Up to that point in our lives, most of us at Valley Forge had gotten a lot of our identity from what we had been able to do physically. Physical identity is a big thing for soldiers. Small-unit proficiency in the combat branches of armor, infantry, and artillery is very demanding, and strength, endurance, and raw physical courage count a great deal. If it had not been for whatever happened to bring us to Valley Forge, we would have gone on in life doing physical things to earn our living and to make our way. Now most of that ability was gone. That was the tough adjustment. The hospital tried to help, with social services counselors, VA counselors, counselors from the Disabled American Veterans. The professional staff encouraged amputees to help themselves and to help each other: no elevators, open your own doors, no wheelchairs unless absolutely necessary. They arranged sports, wheelchair basketball, amputee skiing, and amputee golf instruction.

All that worked in our tight amputee family unit there at Valley Forge, but sooner or later we all had to deal with the adjustments to life and try to go on. I was fortunate. I had family, and a profession that might take me back. Some had neither.

Worst of all was the perception in the United States that what the troops had done was all for nothing. The war in Vietnam was going badly. Americans were sick of it, and were losing faith in the nation's commitments there. The tragic consequence of it all was loss of faith in the warriors.

Making the transition back into that society was going to be hard enough, but this rejection would double the difficulty.

Not long after the amputation, I was in the lobby of a shoe store in Reading, Pennsylvania. I was on crutches with my pant leg pinned up. A woman approached me and asked, "How were you hurt?" And I told the story: I was wounded in combat action in Cambodia and my leg was amputated. "What a waste," she said, with pity on her face. "You did all that for nothing. You and all those boys did all that for nothing. What a waste."

All the amputees had stories like that. They all got the same question, and they all got the kinds of responses I got. It wasn't exactly what we wanted to hear. Wounds in combat action against an enemy on the battlefield were a badge of honor, or so I guess we thought. It began to seem to me that something was horribly wrong.

Though in time most of them learned to handle those situations, still, the overall adjustment was hard and ripped at my heart when I heard the stories. Some of them made up tales, rather than say they were wounded in combat. Made up stories! "Well, I was hurt in an explosion in a paint factory." Or, "I was hurt in a car crash." Or they would just avoid the question entirely . . . because none of them wanted to deal with the terrible reality that they had gone away to a distant country to do what their country had asked them to do, and then they had been rejected by their fellow Americans when they came home. It was not supposed to be like this. These were sons of the World War II generation. They'd heard all about those experiences. So when they'd been drafted, they'd gone, just as their fathers had gone twenty-plus years before. Their country needed them. They went, pure and simple. That's the way Americans did it. Now this. Why? What the hell was going on here?

Americans couldn't separate the war from the warriors.

The soldiers couldn't help it that the leaders had fouled up the strategy and adopted tactics that did not accomplish their strategic objective. The soldiers had gone out and done what they were asked to do. They were point men and stepped on a mine, or got wounded in an ambush or a firefight. Why blame them?

I kept asking myself, Why? Why in the hell blame them? Where are all the leaders now, telling these soldiers thanks, telling these soldiers that their sacrifice was worth it? During all of my time at Valley Forge, only one officer above the rank of colonel, General Bruce Clarke, visited those young soldiers to let them know their country was grateful. I never saw any elected officials. Maybe others came when I was on convalescent leave, but I never heard about it. None.

The leaders abandoned the warriors. I could never forgive that betrayal of trust.

Volunteer organizations did come around, God bless them, people from the Red Cross and the Salvation Army, from the local community, people of all ages and from as far away as Pottsville. The Salvation Army came every Monday night for *Monday Night Football* and brought snacks and sandwiches and young people to visit with the troops. There were sports figures, tickets to the Philadelphia 76ers and Philadelphia Eagles games, and a few entertainers. They were all a big hit with the troops, and much appreciated. They cared.

But there were no leaders to tell them what they badly needed to hear from them alone: "Thank you, your country's grateful." These soldiers had trusted those leaders. Where were they now? I was a graduate of West Point and truly believed in duty, honor, and country. So did these soldiers. Were we all fools for believing in those things? *No*, I wanted to shout. It cannot be so.

Among the amputees, I was the senior officer. There were a few captains, but most of the other patients were junior enlisted soldiers. When I was with the soldiers, at parties or just sitting around, some of them would pour out their stories to me, because I was the "Major." I was the old man, I was part of the establishment, I was supposed to be able to help. But as time passed, I was one of them. We were brothers. And what they said choked me up. It broke my heart. I vowed then I would do something about it. It lit in me a flame of commitment to soldiers that went far beyond any I had felt before. It was an inner rage that only the restoration of trust could calm.

Though I was helpless to make up for the absence of senior leaders, as the months went by, I grew ever more determined to do something more for those soldiers than they were getting. I wanted to help, somehow, to make it clear to them that their lives—and their loss—had some meaning. I wanted a ful-fillment of their sacrifice. I wanted to make sure, if our country ever went to war again, if young men and women ever had to go answer duty's call, it wouldn't end up this way.

For all of my own personal loss, I knew—after the amputation—that I was going to be just fine. Though I was aware that I had to adjust to a permanent change right down there at the core of my self, and that what I had given up would never come back, I had my own family. I was a professional soldier. The Army might not take me back—there was a question about that—but I had an identity that would survive everything I had suffered over the past months. But what about these other young men?

And so there was lit what I still call the "Hot Blue Flame." I had a burn-ing resolve to do what I could, in whatever my circle of responsibility, to see to it that soldiers never again found themselves in a situation where trust was fractured. That Blue Flame resolve has stayed with me since then. I felt it in Desert Storm. I still feel it.

Many of us go through serious life changes. Though the popular impres-sion has it that such changes have to be both religious and sudden—an over-whelming flash in the night sweeps you out of consciousness and you wake up a changed person—that is not always the case. I have nothing against ex-periences like these. People go through them. But most conversions are slower. They take more time. And not all conversions are even religious. A conversion often results from a severe setback overcome, or from wisdom gained out of pain. So it was with us.

Without so much as a real awareness, I passed through a conversion ex-perience at Valley Forge. It was not religious, though I consider myself a reli-gious man, and it didn't hit me suddenly. It took years. I and my family had a severe setback in our lives, and we overcame it and then pressed on toward new missions.

After Valley Forge I was not, on the surface, a very different man. I was still confident, assertive, and willing to take risks physically; I still worked hard at professional excellence; I was still sensitive to other people; and I cared deeply about other soldiers and liked to be around them. If anything, most of these qualities intensified. I think my inner intensity, my drive, actually increased.

But now I was also a much wiser man, with a changed perspective about life. I now had a never-before-experienced inner peace and a new passion for excellence, and for the trust between leader and led. It gave me the inner steel to grab onto when I needed it, to fend off external criticisms and hostility in the face of what I knew to be right. After Valley Forge, I was a man with what you could almost call a crusade, a calling, a burning desire to do something about the terrible betrayal and tragedy that had been thrust upon my fellow soldiers. I was not alone in this among my professional peers, but I determined to see it through.

The wisdom and peace that came from those experiences were not only about soldiers. They manifested themselves in other ways . . . in, for instance, my relationship with Denise and Margie, and in the way I would establish policies and deal with military families in the future.

In the military, it often happens that a professional soldier will deny his (or her) family, give up time with them—holidays, vacations, evenings, weekends—normally for the often-unexpected call of duty. The military is a demanding and sometimes cruel profession that exacts a toll on families, all in the name of duty and service. Too often, the present gets mortgaged for the future. You tell yourself, "Well, I'll have time for that later in life, after I retire. For the time being, I have to work hard, and maybe the family has to pay the price." Most of the time, duty leaves you little choice.

Now I came to the realization that the present is the *only* time you have. You have to focus on the present, on what you have, and not on the past and its gains or losses, or on the future, and what you don't have. You get *there* successfully only by taking care of the present. You don't ignore the future, but you enjoy the day-to-day more, and you enjoy the people you love now, rather than putting that off. You have to live life now and build on what you have every day. I began to realize I was not powerless in this tension between the demands of duty and family considerations. I could do something about it in our lives, and within my circle of responsibility I could help others cope better by establishing policies that helped.

I looked at soldiers, at leaders and commanders, and at units a bit differently. Ever since that time, when I have had occasion to build a team, I am much more aware of soldiers who in their life experiences and in their military experiences have suffered severe setbacks. Out of my own family experience, and out of Valley Forge, I've learned that those who get knocked down and get back up to fight are the really tough ones. People who sail through life without knowing any adversities are suspect. You never know how they are going to react when something hits them. This is especially true on the battlefield. You don't want people responsible for soldiers' lives who could go to pieces when the trauma of their first setback hits them. You want the ones you know will come back out swinging. The same is true for units. You train and build units so that they can come back hard, confident they can take the ups and downs and still win. You have to allow for all this without sacrificing excellence in performance. It's never easy, but I had a much better insight into how to do that now.

★ In the spring of 1971, I began to give serious consideration to returning to active duty. It wasn't easy—then or now—for someone with an otherwise disqualifying physical condition to stay in the military, but it was possible, if the medical and physical evaluation board reports were positive enough, if your motivation was strong enough, and if the Army wanted you badly enough. A few senior officers at that time helped—Colonel Jimmie Leach, for instance, was very instrumental in persuading the Army medical department to listen to soldiers who were wounded and wanted to stay on active duty.

I started making phone calls, talking with others. There was a possibility that I would be offered a permanent position teaching at West Point, but I turned that down. I wanted to stay in the mainstream of the Army. I wanted to play on the armor/cavalry team. I wanted no favors, only a chance to compete.

I did consider other possibilities because, like all of us there, I did not know how it would all turn out. I sent a letter to the Ford Foundation with my résumé, asking if I could contribute in some way to that public service organization. I investigated the possibility of attending the Wharton Business School at the University of Pennsylvania. But then I came to the realization that all I ever really wanted to do was be a soldier. I had to pursue that for all I was worth. I had this burning passion now and a developing wisdom about myself and the Army that I wanted desperately to give a chance. I wanted to serve again.

Fortunately for me and a few others there at Valley Forge, the Army would give us that chance.

★ I was discharged from Valley Forge in January 1972, after a stump revision operation in September 1971, two unsuccessful operations on my left ear earlier in the year, and the loss of our son in August. I reported to the Armed Forces Staff College as a student in early February 1972, ready for duty after an almost two-year absence from the line.

Dr. James Herndon had written on my medical board report, 22 July 1971, "He is highly motivated and desires to remain on active duty in the Army. At the present time he has recently been accepted to attend the Armed Forces Staff College, and when his stump has been revised, he will do so." In December 1971, Dr. Vernon Tolo made an addendum to that medical board: "Recommendations remain the same as on the original board dictation." On 12 January 1972, I sent in my formal application to continue on active duty. On a form dated 4 February 1972, I received the permission I had asked for: "The request for continuance on active duty is approved."

★ As it turned out, our Army as an institution also was seriously wounded in Vietnam. The trust between the Army and the country was fractured. Over the next twenty years, the U.S. Army and I went through many changes; we both got to and fought Desert Storm, and that trust was rebuilt.

I did not look back, except to remember my fellow amputees and to promise to myself to keep the faith with them.

The Army would give me that opportunity.

WASHINGTON, D.C.
8 JUNE 1991

"This one was for all of you, too."

"We know. Today we felt better than we have in a long time."

After the 4.2 miles down Constitution Avenue and the enormous outpouring of emotion from our fellow Americans, there was one place I wanted to go. Denise and I had been there before. The quiet place. The Vietnam Veterans Memorial. The names of friends, relatives, fellow soldiers; gone, never forgotten, never far away. This one was for you, too. The silence there. The memories of heroes who did what our country asked.

Now there were more names. Not for the Vietnam Memorial, because that now belongs to another time, but new names, families. After the parade, they wanted to talk. "Did you know my son?" There are always new names and new memories after combat. Combat is for keeps and the memories are forever. But this time it would also be different.

Unit guidons had been placed on the Ellipse as rallying points for combat veterans of those units and family members. Soldiers of VII Corps were quietly talking with families, proud, confident, full of thanks for a nation and a city who would honor them so. They had done their duty and done it with valor and sacrifice just like the generation whose names were on the Wall down the street.

But this time it was different. The American people and their Army were united. It was not like before.

I remembered the words of that 3rd Armored Division soldier in the days before we attacked into Iraq: "Don't worry, General, we trust you."

Trust reunited.

I had seen both now. I had seen the painful no-thanks return from Vietnam and the silence and pain at the Wall down the street, now this. It was difficult to absorb it all. I felt somehow guilty, because I had had the chance to experience all this, while many of that generation had not. Yet I also felt a great pride in my fellow soldiers of this generation who had won a great victory. I had kept my promise to them and to my fellow Vietnam veterans. Our Army had come full circle. So had I.

How did all this happen? How did we both get from 1971 to 1991?

5

THE REBIRTH OF THE ARMY

FOUNDED BY THE CONTINENTAL CONGRESS IN 1775, THE U.S. ARMY IS older than the country it serves. It is and always has been an army of the people, and over the course of our nation's history, it has probably reflected American society more than any other uniformed service. As a consequence, it is the service that has most frequently felt the nation's mood swings concerning foreign military ventures. Such ventures have rarely sat well with the American public, or with their representatives in Congress, and because of that, and the nature of American geography, Congress has historically had little patience for a large standing peacetime Army, preferring early on to rest secure behind our ocean boundaries, and later to rely on the technology of the Navy and Air Force.

In the early 1970s, neither the United States nor the Army was in good shape. You can blame the condition of both on the outcome of the war in Vietnam, and you won't be wrong, but there were deeper causes. Fortunately, the Army's leaders were willing to face up to them.

What was happening? What did they see?

By 1972, most U.S. ground forces were out of Vietnam, and the war had been turned over to the ARVN, though with support from U.S. logistics and airpower.

No matter what you may have heard, however, when our Army left Vietnam, they had not lost.

Before they left, U.S. Army tactical forces had performed superbly. They were victorious in every tactical engagement, some at considerable cost in soldiers, and technical and tactical innovations, such as air assault and attack helicopters, had proved successful. The NVA had to wait until some time after the departure of U.S. ground forces before they dared to start major operations in the south, and even longer before they risked undertaking a major invasion of the south with mechanized forces and tanks. Yet, even then, U.S. airpower was still assisting ARVN forces.

And then the air support stopped.

When that happened, U.S. military professionals, especially those in the Army, felt that the long, terrible sacrifice by young Americans had been betrayed. Just as bad was the loss of national honor: we abandoned an ally we had pledged to assist. The professionals would never forget that.

There was little support for the war on the home front, and it was reflected in attitudes toward the military. It was a bad idea to wear the uniform off post or base. Protests at the Pentagon became news clichés, and when National Guard troops were called out to keep protesters in check, feelings against the military intensified even further.

Meanwhile, the whole society was passing through a major upheaval: polarization of whites and blacks, testing of authority, insensitivity to minorities, drug problems, the sexual revolution. The Army was not immune; as drug use and racial tensions divided America, so, too, did they divide the U.S. Army.

An Army has a spirit, an identity, an image. Part of it comes from its own institutional personality and traditions; part from the people from whom it springs. In the 1970s, the U.S. Army's public image was in ruin, its spirit in danger of being broken, its identity in danger of being lost.

A prime example could be found not in Vietnam or the United States, but in Europe, where the Army faced its greatest challenge, in the Warsaw Pact. How ready was the Army, as part of NATO, to stop a Warsaw Pact armored sweep aimed at Western Europe?

Not very.

The years of fighting in Vietnam had drawn Europe-based forces down to unacceptable strengths. Worse, the insatiable appetite for personnel had stripped our forces of officer leadership, and almost destroyed the Army's professional noncommissioned officer corps, long the backbone of the Army. A series of hasty training programs to fill depleted ranks had left the Army with NCOs who all too often were poorly trained in basic leadership techniques. Because the NCO is the first-line leader in the Army, the one person primarily responsible for the basic individual soldier skills on which every successful operation depends, training and discipline suffered. In some cases, it went to hell.

In Europe, many in the Army were on drugs, mostly hashish, but some were on heroin. There was racial violence in the barracks, which sometimes spilled over into the streets. Gangs ran some barracks. Leaders—officers or noncommissioned officers—were physically attacked. The chain of command in units struggled day to day simply to maintain good order and discipline.

It was not an Army that expected to win, or was ready to win.

Equally serious, while the Warsaw Pact had strengthened their forces during the previous ten years, U.S. Army capabilities had steadily declined. While fighting in Vietnam, the Army had missed a whole equipment modernization cycle. Many Army units would have been expected to fight with equipment from the early 1960s, with no prospect for change anytime soon.

Just as important, though less immediately visible, the Army war-fighting doctrine—the ideas with which it fights—had not undergone a serious examination since World War II.

And finally, Army leaders realized—with shock—that the U.S. Army was not prepared to fight and win in a mechanized battlefield that had the speed and lethality of the 1973 Mideast War. A whole generation of leaders had seen Army unpreparedness in World War II and Korea, and knew its cost in the lives of soldiers. The thought of unpreparedness haunted the U.S. military perhaps more than it did any other major power. It would be hard to underestimate the sense of urgency with which such feelings drove the Army reforms of the 1970s and 1980s.

Meanwhile, in 1973, the draft law expired, which meant that from then on, the armed services would have to exist as an all-volunteer force. The initial results were almost entirely predictable. It was difficult to find true volunteers, and of those who joined up, all too many were not high-quality recruits. Too many were at the lower ranges of intelligence, and some of them came in only after they were given the choice of prison or military service. All that made an already deteriorating discipline situation worse.

Some professionals left the Army then. They'd had enough of an Army gutted by Vietnam, indiscipline, low morale, and betrayal. Others left involuntarily, as the Army rapidly drew down from its peak strength during Vietnam. But many stayed. They stayed because they wanted to be soldiers, because they wanted to be part of the solution, because they saw an Army never defeated on the battlefield struggling for its very existence as a viable force, and they wanted to help in these times of trouble. They stayed because the Army was wounded and needed help; you do not abandon a wounded buddy on the battlefield. They stayed because it was their duty. They were in for the long haul. It wasn't always easy or fair, but they knew that sometime, someplace in the future, the nation would need her Army to go fight and win, and it had better be ready.

Senior Army leadership knew all this when they took a look around their institution in the early 1970s. That they did not like what they saw goes without saying. And so they set out to change it.

There was much work to be done.

MISSION AND FOCUS

To begin with, in order to rebuild the Army, it was not enough to publish directives and policies. The entire Army had to internalize the need to remake itself, and do it so pervasively that all its members felt the same urgency. In

order to renew its focus, the Army needed to renew its sense of its mission—
or rather, it needed to understand what exactly its mission was.

An Army's mission is to win wars on the ground. But what did that actually mean for the U.S. Army in the early 1970s? And what would the Army
have to do then to accomplish it?

The answers were provided for them by Secretary of Defense James
Schlesinger, Army Chief of Staff Creighton Abrams, and Secretary of the
Army Bo Calloway.

James Schlesinger was sworn in as Secretary of Defense in July 1973, after
spending several years at the Rand Corporation, one of the premier strategic
and military think tanks. In those years, the United States had tended to rely
more on nuclear weapons than on conventional forces for the defense of Central Europe. Schlesinger's experience at Rand had left him with the conviction that the United States needed to turn that balance around. There was
an urgent need, in his words, "for a stalwart conventional defense in Europe,"
a need that was not likely to be met immediately, given the "dreadful" condition of the U.S. Army at the time. He had in fact seen a growing indication
that the Europeans had given up on American forces in Europe. Because of
the drawdown of our forces there to support Vietnam, the Europeans had concluded that our army in Europe lacked credibility.

That situation had to stop, and stop soon. Thus, as a first order of business, Schlesinger determined to "rebuild deterrence" in our conventional
forces in order to fight and win in Europe. That was his answer: Focus on Europe. Focus on stopping the Warsaw Pact, if it decided to start something.
Focus on winning a war there, if we were called upon to fight one.

In Creighton Abrams and Bo Calloway, Schlesinger found effective partners.

Abrams became Army Chief in October 1972, well aware that the Army
needed to intensify the work begun by his predecessor, General William Westmoreland, to remake itself in the wake of Vietnam. Abrams had just come from
four years as the senior U.S. commander in Vietnam; he knew the Army in
the field. He also had a justly deserved reputation as a soldier's general; he
was not given to airs or to spit and polish, but to hard, tough soldiering and
aggressive actions on the battlefield. Abrams had also been arguably the
Army's most celebrated and successful tactical small-unit commander in
World War II in Europe. He brought with him a spark, a steady hand, and impeccable integrity. When General Abrams talked about the Army to the public or to Congress, he did it with a candor and with an emotion born of
genuine love.

General Abrams was to repeat his theme over and over again: "You've got to know what influences me. We have paid, and paid, and paid again in blood and sacrifice for our unpreparedness. I don't want war, but I am appalled at the human cost that we've paid because we wouldn't prepare to fight."

Together, Abrams, Schlesinger, and Calloway made the case to Congress for necessary resources. The national security interests in Europe were simply too high, they argued; the Europeans' regard for U.S. credibility was too low. Something had to be done *now*. They began to get their money.

Part of that money went for manpower levels. The Army needed to operate with steady and predictable force levels, and needed to know it would have those levels for enough time to rebuild a credible force without having to argue for them each budget year. In a since-famous "handshake" agreement, the Army got that. Schlesinger told Abrams, "I am prepared to freeze your manpower at 785,000," enough to set the total Army on a course that in the 1980s would reach to sixteen active and twelve National Guard divisions (it would remain at that level until after Desert Storm). This gave Abrams and the Army what it needed to blend together the active forces and Reserve components (National Guard and Army Reserves) into what came to be known as the Total Army Concept. Never again would the active forces be called upon to fight a war alone. The Reserve component—the force closest to the everyday fabric of American life, to the American people—would be fighting right along with them.

QUALITY

To rebuild the Army, however, meant finding the right people. Though it can't do without them, the Army is not weapons, or machines, or vehicles, or organizations, but is the quality of the personnel. The Army needed people who could train with all the fire, intelligence, and intensity of world-class athletes to fight on a battlefield that was more lethal and fast-moving than the leaders of World War II or Korea could possibly have imagined.

In rebuilding this foundation, the Army got off to a rocky start, yet to its credit, it did not wait for directives, nor did it get defensive and try to excuse its actions. The Army attacked its problems.

In the fall of 1968, as the Vietnam War had worn on, Army Chief Westmoreland commissioned a study to see if an all-volunteer Army could offset the growing morale and discipline problems. In the early 1970s, the Army leadership was already moving toward what they considered the inevitable ending of the draft. In 1971, to make service life more attractive to young Americans, they began Project VOLAR. It was a huge experiment, and it touched every facet of the Army's daily life, from haircuts to pass and leave policies, to reveille formations, to beer in barracks and mess halls, to the establishment of enlisted men's councils to give soldiers some say in the chain of command. In 1971, VOLAR adopted a slogan: The Army Wants to Join You. Barracks were even painted pastel colors.

In the main, the experiment didn't work. To attract young Americans, the Army had let itself slide into practices that could only fail. You can't have a "touchy-feely" Army.

In making Army life "nicer," VOLAR compromised some of the Army's basic principles of discipline; it began to resemble a social club where everything was up for discussion. Something was very wrong if the Army had to compromise its basic identity in order to attract volunteers. The enlisted men's councils, for instance, did not so much give ordinary soldiers a voice in the halls of power as they undercut the legitimate chain of command. Unit commanders were predictably unenthusiastic about this and other "reforms."

The Army Wants to Join You . . . ?

"God, I just want to vomit," General Bruce Palmer, then Army vice chief of staff, announced when he heard that slogan.

It was not that they did not need good ideas to make service life more attractive, or that the Army culture did not need adjustment. It was just that those adjustments had to be made while simultaneously maintaining the good order and discipline necessary for the exacting duties of soldiers in combat. It was simply a case of too much too soon. The Army culture in the field was just not ready for such sweeping changes in such short order.

But some good came of all this tension. The professional Army learned quickly how to make necessary adjustments in discipline and equal opportunity without compromising readiness. And senior-level policy makers learned that overly directive and restrictive policies from Washington were likely to be met with failure in the field. The VOLAR experiment, though itself a failure, turned out to be a useful time of growth for the Army as an institution, and better prepared it for the time when the all-volunteer Army became law in 1972.

The Army moved on:

• It established major equal-opportunity policies, including workshops, mandatory classes on prevention of sexual harassment, and ethnic sensitivity sessions to alert leaders to expected language and behavior.

• It established a zero-tolerance policy on drugs, with regular urinalysis drug testing. More and more soldiers came into the Army motivated and drug free—and these soldiers did not want to be around soldiers who used drugs. Peer pressure began to move soldier culture in a positive direction.

• Similar programs were instituted for alcohol abuse, and alcohol was no longer glamorized.

• Women were actively recruited, and in 1980, for the first time, women graduated from West Point.

• Weight-control programs were started. Passing physical-fitness tests became a part of officer and NCO fitness reports.

All these programs together created a winning and proud climate in the Army. Now soldiers not only felt like winners, they wanted you out of their outfit if you didn't feel the same way.

One hurdle still remained in the quality of the volunteers. The aim was relatively simple in concept, though hard to implement in practice: the smarter the better. On the new battlefield, you were going to need not just physical strength, but knowledge, resourcefulness, mental agility, and leadership. For its volunteer force, the Army's initial goal was 70 percent high school graduates. By 1974, Army recruiting was up to 55 percent high school graduates, but that still was not enough. Something was needed.

That something was Max Thurman.

Major General Max Thurman assumed command of the Recruiting Command in the summer of 1979. From his previous position on the Army staff, he'd come to three conclusions: First, the Army was having a hard time recruiting high school graduates. Second, the Army had a lot to offer to young people graduating from high school, if only they could get the word. And third, young Americans wanted to be challenged.

The Army is a big organization, he reasoned, a melting pot, like the nation it serves. Quality people joined up and stayed for many different motives, some of them utilitarian, some closer to the heart and soul:

You feel you're a winner if you're on a winning team, he thought, if you feel you're living in a climate where you can truly realize all of your potential. Here was the Army: a place of equal opportunity for everyone—men, women, white, black, Hispanic. There were opportunities to work with new, high-tech weapons systems; opportunities for better pay; and incentives, such as help for higher education. Why not broadcast them to the world?

Before assuming command, Thurman had done his homework. He'd gotten himself a tailor-made course in modern advertising and recruiting techniques from the Army's advertising agency. Soon after that, Recruiting Command adopted a new advertising campaign, whose touchstone was a new slogan: Be All That You Can Be (a far cry from the 1970s' The Army Wants to Join You). It worked. Young Americans began to see what the Army could offer. And they joined up. By Desert Storm, the percentage of high school graduates numbered in the high nineties, and many in the NCO corps had college diplomas. (Thurman went on to four-star general as Army vice chief, TRADOC commander, then led the Panama operation in December 1989.)

Another thing that helped Thurman was what was happening in the world at large. A large part of a winning attitude comes out of the way you compare yourself to your opponents. If you know in your heart he is going to beat you— in a game, in a contest, in a fight, or in a war—there isn't much room for a winning attitude.

During the 1970s, we all saw the Soviets as "ten feet tall"—not without reason: the Soviets maintained a huge, modern, and (apparently) high-tech army. By 1980, the Soviets had a tank inventory of about 48,000; the United States had 10,700. Although there was never a U.S. Army intent to match the Soviets tank for tank as long as our tanks were qualitatively better than theirs, Army leaders were understandably worried when the Soviets fielded the T-64 and then the T-72 with 125-mm cannon, while part of the U.S. Army tank inventory included improved M60 series tanks and some tanks still equipped with 90-mm guns.

But then, in 1979, the Soviets invaded Afghanistan, and almost immediately proved themselves to be mortal. While their initial strike was quick and impressive, their ability to follow up and adapt to the terrain and tactics of the Afghan resistance turned out to be glaringly ineffective. Before long, it began to look as though the huge Soviet war machine could be beaten.

TRAINING

With the realization of the speed and lethality of the modern mounted battlefield came the deeper realization of what it would take to fight and win on such a battlefield. If it was going to win the first battle of the next war, the U.S. Army had to develop better training standards and performance levels.

Training for war is what an Army does in peacetime. How it does that, with what rigor, against what standards, and with what realism all determine how well it is prepared to fight and win the nation's wars. It was against that set of criteria that the Army began a revolution in training and leader development that touched every aspect of the way the Army prepared for war. If you fight the first battle unprepared, you pay for learning with the lives of American soldiers. Army leaders were determined to create conditions of training that replicated actual battle conditions as closely as possible. If you "lost" there, you learned better how to win in combat.

Because most Army leaders see themselves as trainers and have strong opinions about methods, they realized that the Army had to standardize its approach to training; it had to agree on tasks, conditions, and standards, from the individual all the way up to the corps. It had to publish those standards and stick to them, and hold leaders accountable for reaching them.

It began with TRADOC and FORSCOM.

TRADOC AND FORSCOM

On 30 June 1973, the U.S. Army's Continental Army Command ceased to exist. In its place the Army established two new commands, TRADOC, the Training and Doctrine Command, with headquarters at historic Fort Monroe, Virginia, and FORSCOM, Forces Command, with headquarters at Fort McPherson, Georgia.

The two major areas of responsibility set out for TRADOC were to operate the Army's institutional school system of training and education and to ensure that the Army was prepared to fight and win the next war. It was responsible for establishing uniform training standards throughout the Army, from individuals to units, and it was to operate the Army's considerable school system, including basic training of new recruits. It was also to look to the future, so that the Army would never again be caught unawares of the changing nature of war. TRADOC would establish requirements for material and organizations to fight that next war, and it would also write the operational doctrine for the employment of Army forces as part of a joint team. For the first time, the Army had a major command responsible for integrating doctrine, training, leader development, organization design, and material requirements. As a result, soldiers and units could now modernize and change much more rapidly and effectively.

This new and revolutionary organizational concept has since been copied by many armies of the world.

General Bill DePuy, the first TRADOC commander, was by background and temperament the right choice to get the new command. He was arguably the Army's preeminent tactician, a man of genuine intellect and a pragmatic soldier. By his own drive and intelligence, DePuy touched virtually every aspect of the Army's recovery, and he profoundly influenced those who carried his work on into the 1980s, following his retirement in 1977.

When DePuy took over TRADOC, he got off to a fast start. He set to work to root the Army in a set of training standards from individual soldiers to divisions; he revitalized the school system; and later, after seeing the results of the 1973 Mideast War, set about writing an operational doctrine for the Army, the first of a revitalized FM 100-5 series that focused on how to fight and win outnumbered in Central Europe. It fell to DePuy and to TRADOC to give substance to the Army's restated mission and focus. Just stating it was not enough. Much work had to be done.

Even before he assumed command of TRADOC, General DePuy outlined his vision of the future Army. "It seems to me," he said in a talk at Fort Polk on 7 June 1973, "that we all have to be aware of the fact that we are probably going to be members of an entirely different kind of an Army than we have belonged to for the last few years. . . . Wars will tend to be like the Suez attack of the British and French, and are very likely to be turned off by the world politicians as quickly as possible. And it means, therefore, that the most likely thing that any of you guys will be involved in will be something short, violent, and important. . . ." That means "we have to be better than" the Army of Europe in the 1950s and 1960s "by quite a large margin."

General Walter "Dutch" Kerwin assumed command of FORSCOM the same day DePuy took command of TRADOC.

FORSCOM had responsibility for the training readiness of all U.S. Army units stationed in the United States, as well as for training the Reserve component—the U.S. Army Reserve (the federal force) and the Army National Guard (who in peacetime are under command of state governors). To FORSCOM and its leaders fell the less visible but vitally important role of improving combat readiness while incorporating the new "volunteers" into units and solving the Army's discipline problems. Additionally, FORSCOM began to implement the Army's new Total Army Concept.

"Dutch" Kerwin was perfect for getting this task moving. A World War II combat veteran of North Africa and Europe, he had also commanded a division in the Germany-based U.S. Army. In Vietnam, he had been General Abrams's chief of staff, and had commanded II Field Force. He was a senior officer of impeccable integrity, with a firm yet compassionate way with soldiers and leaders. Kerwin knew winners and how to build winning teams, and he was to typify all those leaders, both NCO and officer, who held the Army's units together in the field and slowly began to turn them around.

THE 1973 MIDEAST WAR

If the Army needed help in heightening its sense of urgency to rebuild itself, it got it when the eighteen-day war broke out in the Middle East in October 1973. This short war shocked Army leaders into a new awareness of the speed and lethality of the modern battlefield and the density of tank-killing systems. During those eighteen days, more tanks were lost than what the U.S. Army in Europe had in its whole tank inventory.

The Yom Kippur War was a surrogate for what the Army expected to face in Central Europe should a war break out against the Soviets. On the one side were forces organized and equipped like the Soviets, and operating according to the Soviet echelonment doctrine of attack. On the other side was a force with a large quantity of American equipment.

But it wasn't just numbers that disturbed the Army leaders, it was the quality of equipment. The T-62 Soviet-built tank (used by the Syrians and the Egyptians) had a 115-mm smoothbore tank cannon fully capable of defeating U.S. tanks, with a 50 percent probability of hit and kill at 1,500 meters. Worse, many reserve U.S. tanks had only 90-mm cannons. Moreover, antitank guided missiles were killing tanks at ranges in excess of 3,000 meters. And artillery had doubled in lethality and increased in range by about 60 percent since World War II.

Quick to seize on these points, General Bill DePuy sent a team to Israel to gather lessons, and the Israelis generously shared the things they'd learned with the U.S. Army (they even sent a number of captured T-62 tanks to the U.S. Army for examination). This contact opened a continuing dialogue with the Israel Defense Forces (IDF), which greatly benefited the U.S. Army's preparations for fighting on the new battlefield.

From General DePuy and TRADOC's many briefings and studies, two concepts came out of the lessons of the Yom Kippur War. These concepts became rallying cries:

- "Fight outnumbered and win."
- "Win the first battle of the next war."

These drove the Army's thinking, training, and equipping throughout the Cold War, and they were the basis for much of what happened in Desert Storm.

THE TRAINING BEGINS

The training revolution started during the years from 1971 to 1975, and though it was the work of many people, it was principally sparked by Bill DePuy and Paul Gorman.

Gorman was an innovator, a soldier with a highly fertile mind and a passion for training. Gorman had been General DePuy's G-3 when DePuy had commanded the Big Red One in Vietnam, and it was DePuy who arranged to have then–Brigadier General Gorman assigned to the Infantry School as assistant commandant.

There Gorman headed the Board for Dynamic Training, and later what became known as the Combined Arms Training Board (CATB), established by Westmoreland in 1971. At CATB, a systems approach to training and what would be called Tactical Engagement Simulation (TES) were developed.

Working with scientists at Florida State University, the CATB developed a system whereby every major function on the battlefield could be broken into discrete tasks.

First, you made a front-end analysis to determine what tasks had to be performed by individuals and by teams in the company, then you determined the standards of performance that had to be executed to ensure the mission was successful. The list of individual tasks were then arranged according to the skill levels of soldiers, and these were put into books called *Soldiers' Manuals*. Soldiers could then study these manuals, and NCOs could teach from them. Next came what was called a "skill qualification test," which required each soldier to demonstrate proficiency once a year in his or her specialty.

Unit tasks, meanwhile, were put into booklets called ARTEPs (Training and Evaluation Plans—an evaluative list of tasks). ARTEPs permitted commanders to judge better and more systematically their units' ability to accomplish particular battlefield unit tasks.

TES was simply train as you fight. It was a system of shoot-back simulations that replicated the battlefield with great fidelity, and its concept was both eye-opening and (after the fact) blindingly obvious: If you survived your first combat engagements, you would go on to perform at much higher levels. This was shown to be true of both individuals and units. The Navy created their Top Gun School in the late 1960s, after they realized they needed to train their pilots through their "first fights" before they had their real first fights in the skies over North Vietnam, and the Army decided to build a similar school for land warfare.

What Gorman wanted to do with TES was to develop simulations that would allow an opposing force to maneuver and "shoot back" in training. Such a system would objectively score target hits and kills in training fire with opposing forces. The problem was that Gorman didn't have the technology for it. Right now, units fired blanks at each other, and an "umpire," or neutral observer assigned to the exercise, judged who won or lost and by how much.

That all ended when Gorman came upon the technology eventually called MILES—Multiple Integrated Laser Targeting System. It was an eye-safe laser beam that used the normal sights on a weapon, and it allowed units and individuals to "fire" at each other and to "hit" without danger to either side. All individuals and equipment had receivers, and when a laser hit your receiver, you either heard a loud ring or a light went on signaling a "kill."

Meanwhile at Fort Benning in CATB, Gorman and his group proposed a revision of tasks to make them more relevant and so that they could better meet standards. This came to be called "performance-oriented training," which meant that training was no longer conducted according to some arbitrary time criterion. Rather, you kept at it until standards were met. This was as simple as it was profound: You stayed at it until you got it right. In April 1975, the Army officially changed its training regulations, and from then on, performance-oriented training was the law. It also laid the basis for the evaluation system of the ARTEP. Army training would never be the same again.

With this kind of training, soldiers and units would become veterans before they actually went into combat. To complete that vision, the Army more than ever needed a world-class national training facility that included rigorous practice battlefields with large-unit live fire.

★ Other training innovations came out of practical experience in the field, and some of them had long-term consequences.

Early in 1976, Lieutenant General Donn Starry assumed command of U.S. Army V Corps in Germany. (Starry, of course, had been one of the 11th ACR commanders at the time Fred Franks served with the Blackhorse in Vietnam.) He was immediately faced with two especially daunting challenges: In V Corps, he found a unit that doubted its ability to fight and win against the combined armies of the Warsaw Pact (a serious overmatch, at least in numbers). And the U.S. V Corps was essentially all that stood in the way of a rapid Warsaw Pact thrust over the short 120 kilometers to Frankfurt, the industrial and financial capital of West Germany.

Deeply troubled by all this, Starry went to work to fix it. His aim was to restore confidence to his corps by showing them how they could fight and win there, even outnumbered.

Starry came to V Corps from TRADOC, where he had been one of the principal authors of the soon-to-be-published 1976 FM 100-5. He put this new doctrine to use immediately. Using videotapes, he pointed out that the avenue of approach that ran from the West German city of Fulda to Frankfurt had to be hugely tempting to Warsaw Pact planners, and that it was vital to deter such an attack. Starry's presentations called attention to what was forever after referred to as the "Fulda Gap."

But Starry did more than talk. He instituted an innovative, mission-focused training program that related the specific tasks of training to the specific tasks needed to accomplish a wartime mission. And he started what he and the Army came to call "terrain walks": Once every three months he required all commanders and leaders to go out on the actual ground where they anticipated they would fight. There they would explain in detail to their next-higher commander just how they intended to conduct the fight. (Starry and all his subordinate commanders personally attended these sessions.) Afterward, they were required to construct "battle books." In these, commanders detailed unit and weapon positions, how they intended to manage the flow of battle, and how their actions fit the overall corps plan.

Starry's training methods, and his terrain walks, proved so effective that they were used in all of Europe up to the end of the Cold War. And they went a long way toward restoring confidence to V Corps and other U.S. units in Germany.

★ By the 1980s, the Army was infused with the objectives leaders had begun articulating in the previous decade: Fight and win the first battle of the next war. Fight outnumbered and win. Fight a "come-as-you-are war"—a war with a short preparation and warning time. Train the way you fight.

Unit training facilities were being constructed or modified to re-create with great fidelity the modern highly lethal battlefield. Principal among these was the new National Training Center at Fort Irwin, in California's Mojave Desert.

Three components were needed to make the NTC work:

• A professional opposing force (OPFOR). Its full-time mission was to emulate in maneuver, in war fighting, and in doctrine the most likely enemy of the U.S. Army. In the 1980s, that enemy was the Soviets. Hence the OPFOR at the NTC became the Red Army, down to the last uniform detail.

• A core of maneuver experts to accompany the Blue (training unit) and to help and advise them as they learned by doing. The Army called these experts observer controllers (OCs).

• A system to promote learning.

At the heart of the learning system was the AAR, or After-Action Review.

After a training event, the OC led a small seminar for participants during which they could discover for themselves what they needed to do—improve commander and unit performance. Generally, AAR seminars used the following framework: What was the unit trying to do? What actually happened? And why the difference? The aim of an AAR was not to blame or judge, and AARs required active participation by all attendees, both commanders and subordinates. Subordinates had the freedom to bring up issues that reflected both favorably and unfavorably on their commander's decisions and actions. Commanders opened up and analyzed their own performance. All of it was based on the objective data furnished by MILES and by the observing and recording instruments that covered the entire maneuver area.

It required a significant cultural adjustment for commanders to let themselves be openly questioned by subordinates in the presence of video cameras and to overcome the feeling that the NTC experience was training, not an official report card. Many militaries around the world still cannot get over those hurdles. Though it took a while, the U.S. Army did make that adjustment, and in fact, the AAR process led to significant and positive behavioral changes more than any other training innovation. After training and the AAR process, commanders and leaders at all levels have become less arrogant and more willing to listen . . . without sacrificing bold acts and decisions. AARs have reduced the aura of expected infallibility around commanders, without absolving them of ultimate responsibility or taking away their will to win.

It's no surprise that the AAR method has spread throughout the Army. In fact, it's now required after every event where performance can be improved.

✭ During the 1980s, the Army began to systematically exploit computer simulations in training. For individual weapons crews, for instance, the Army developed conduct-of-fire trainers. In realistically configured crew stations, using computer simulations of the actual fire control in their vehicles and computer-simulated scenarios, crews would engage computer-simulated targets. Following its development by the Advanced Research Projects Agency (ARPA), the Army began a program called SIMNET, or simulations networking. Whole units were placed in simulators and linked in a live scenario. Units drove around and fought, and commanders controlled them, just as they would have done on the ground. AARs were conducted. In time, over linked networks, it was possible to do all this simultaneously, with units separated geographically.

Other training improvements went forward, as well. For instance, firing ranges all over the Army needed to be modernized to replicate the tasks, conditions, and standards of combat. At Grafenwohr, Germany, a program was begun to put in stationary and moving targetry. Such a system could be varied through software adjustments to allow units to fire according to consistent standards but with tasks varied to resemble wartime situations more closely. Range-firing standards were revised upward, for example, to require individual tanks to kill up to five enemy tanks by themselves. Firing ranges at Fort Hood and other installations in the United States underwent similar modernization.

Thus, with a combination of simulations using computer-assisted scenarios, actual live training using simulated enemy targets on ranges, and force on force using MILES, the U.S. Army gained combat experience without having to fight a war. This generation of leaders was realizing and carrying on the early visions of DePuy and Gorman.

As far as I'm concerned, the most interesting battlefield simulation is in the Battle Command Training Program (BCTP) for division and corps commanders, which was developed at Fort Leavenworth in 1986–87. BCTP did for those commanders what the NTC did for smaller units—but all in simulation. The idea for BCTP came from Lieutenant General Jerry Bartlett, commandant of the U.S. Army Command and General Staff College. Fred Franks was the deputy commandant at the time, and together they named the program, and Franks selected Colonel Dave Blodgett to give the idea form and substance. In 1987, General Carl Vuono made the program part of the Army's combat training centers.

Here is Fred Franks describing a BCTP WARFIGHTER exercise in Germany just before he left command of the 1st Armored Division to command VII Corps:

> In the Army's Battle Command Training Program for divisions and corps, there are three distinct phases. The first is a weeklong seminar, where commanders and staffs solve tactical problems and record the solution in operations order format in a classroom environment on a ten- to twelve-hour-a-day schedule. You do this at a deliberately slow pace, so you can perfect your command and staff problem-solving apparatus.
>
> Sometime after that, you go through the second phase of the BCTP, which is a practice WARFIGHTER, with an opposing force. There you take your command apparatus out into the field with their normal vehicles and communications setup (you use the same radios and other communications devices you would use in combat). Then a computer simulation translates actions and orders into unit icons on screens, and when units make contact with the enemy, the computer has a set of algorithms and formulae that solve the battle outcome and sets up new problems.
>
> Units do this practice for themselves. It allows you to make the transition from the seminar to the actual war-fighting environment, and it also allows your people to practice interfacing orders with computer simulations.
>
> In the third phase, you go through your actual WARFIGHTER. This time you have a professional opposing force (housed at Fort Leavenworth), and they play whatever opposing force you want them to play, but they do it electronically, from Fort Leavenworth. It's beamed to your particular location—Germany, Korea, somewhere in the United States. The exercise is free play to be decided on the skill of the Blue side (the training unit) or the OPFOR.
>
> You also get a team of observer-controllers (also permanently stationed at Fort Leavenworth but who travel to your location). They take notes, teach your staff, and conduct the AARs. When the observer-controller's team arrives, they are assigned to various places around your unit, some to the staff, some to subordinate units.
>
> And finally, you get a senior observer-controller. The senior OC is a retired three- or four-star general, who has commanded at your echelon. He watches the whole process, advises the OCs, and mentors the division or corps commander.

Senior observer-controllers were an invention of Army Chief Carl Vuono. Vuono wanted the best mentors he could get for his division and corps commanders, people who had credibility with serving division and corps commanders. So senior OCs tend to have a lot of wisdom, based on their long time of service, their understanding of the doctrine, their command of the echelons they're observing, and on going around the army as senior OCs for various units. Over a period of a year or two, they build up a lot of savvy about what commanders and staff should and should not do.

Our initial seminar in the 1st Armored Division was held at Fort Leavenworth in March 1989. General Dick Cavazos was the senior observer-controller assigned to our exercise. During the course of that week, as we were going through commander and staff problem solving and decision making, he was there giving us advice and assistance—both to my staff and to me personally.

Dick Cavazos is a veteran of the Korean War. He was a company commander there; a battalion commander in Vietnam; a division commander of the 9th Infantry Division at Fort Lewis, Washington; and a corps commander, of III Corps at Fort Hood, Texas. He retired as a four-star general, commander of FORSCOM. He is a very wise and experienced field commander. Additionally, Dick loves soldiers . . . he has an intuitive feel for them, genuinely from the heart, so he's a great observer of human behavior and interaction. At the same time, he's very skilled in analyzing problem-solving techniques and an expert tactician. He knows how to get the most combat power on the battlefield at a particular point in time. In terms of temperament, in his feel for the mind and the heart of being a soldier, in his feel for the battlefield, I personally identify with him in my own approach to commanding units and leading soldiers in battle.

So General Cavazos and I hit it off right away.

Almost immediately, he spotted a few things in my own problem-solving and decision-making techniques that were causing some friction between me and the division staff. The way I like to work with my staff is to ask a lot of questions, open things up, and choose a course of action that presents the most options for a given mission. Sometimes that takes time. This didn't always sit well with my staff, and Dick Cavazos noticed. He led some back-and-forth discussion in an AAR.

"What we discovered was this. What your commander is trying to do is generate options continually as the battle moves on. He doesn't want to run out of options. What you've got to do is to keep giving them to him so the commander always has a viable option to use against an enemy move. So don't be bothered by your commander asking you a lot of questions, by driving you to come up with additional alternatives. What he's trying to do is think his way through the situation, just like you're trying to do. He's problem-solving, just like you are. Commanders just don't passively sit around and wait for the staff to solve the problems.

"Next," he went on, "most savvy tactical commanders wait until the last minute to decide something. Why is that? Well, that gets back to what you are trying to do. That gets back to this: you want to stay out ahead of the enemy. That means you don't want to decide too far in advance what you're going to do. If you do that, by the time you execute, the situation may have changed, and you may have another option available to you. On the other hand, you don't want to wait so long to decide that your unit can't execute.

"Well, this drives the staff nuts. Why? They've got a lot of details to attend to, so they want the commander to decide very early. So they're always pushing the commander to decide so they can get their work done. So if they don't understand why the commander is doing what he's doing, then they're going to look at their commander as indecisive. In fact, he isn't indecisive at all. What he's looking for is the right intuitive moment to decide to act. Then he executes very forcefully without looking back."

Before Dick Cavazos led us through this discussion to these conclusions, I had not been able to articulate it, either to myself or to my staff, with anything like this clarity. Now, as a senior tactical commander, he had really let me see myself in a mirror.

So after I took in what we had all discussed, I told myself, Yes, that's true, that's exactly what I do, that's the way I've been at squadron, regiment, and now as a division commander. I was starting to see tension between me and the staff, most of whom I had long known or personally chosen. Now I understood. Actually, it's normal senior tactical commander behavior.

General Cavazos, then, was the first person to open up for me why commanders tend to wait till the last possible minute to decide what they're going to do. That had been my tendency, anyway, almost intuitively, and it had been successful. And now he was explaining me to myself, as it were. He saw me as I had not been able to see myself, and he reinforced for me what had been up to then inexplicable intuitive commander behavior.

Before this exercise, I had not really known Dick Cavazos. But here, our meetings and subsequent work together in other exercises turned into a deep friendship.

That seminar at Fort Leavenworth was a very valuable week.

After that, we went on to train for WARFIGHTER, and then, in July of '89, about a month before I moved on to command VII Corps, we ran the actual WARFIGHTER exercise. The exercise was very instructive as well. What it did was prove to me yet again that planning is not fighting.

In the Battle Command Training Program, you normally set up your command posts out in the field, with all the vehicles and communication gear. And you also have your subordinate colonel-level commands—that is, the commanders of your four maneuver brigades, your DISCOM (division support command), and your DIVARTY (division artillery). You are essentially in your wartime setup, except that all your troops are not out there with all their equipment.

At brigade, division, and corps, the U.S. Army normally operates with three command posts, as was discussed briefly in the opening chapter: a small tactical command post forward, a main command post, which is much larger, and a rear command post, which deals mainly with logistics. Normally, your assistant division commander for maneuver goes forward to the tactical command post, where he controls the fight that's right up against you—what is called the close fight. Your assistant division commander for support, another brigadier general, is at the rear command post. There he coordinates all the support—the logistics—for the fight, watches over the security of the division rear area against enemy special forces teams, and controls real estate, so two units do not try to occupy the same ground. The division commander normally operates from the main command post or main nerve center. From there, he can synchronize the close fight, the support functions, and also the deep fight, the second-echelon fight as far deep as the division can go.

When this WARFIGHTER started, I followed doctrine and started out at the main command post, but soon I found that the decision-making agility in our division was too slow with me there. By staying at the command post, I didn't have enough of an intuitive feel of the fight. Now, I'm not comfortable doing that anyway. I don't like to stay so far removed from the actual fight and let someone else do it. But I hadn't commanded a division before in a fight, so I said, "Okay, I'll start out doing what you're supposed to do."

So what happened? The opposing force began to break through us. As BCTP adjusted the exercise, I made an adjustment to the way I commanded.

We restarted it.

"This time," I said, "I'm going to be out where I know I belong, out at the tactical command post, and moving around." From then on, we were very successful. And I never forgot that. It was a great lesson: What I had done during the first day of the exercise was to abandon my intuitive sense of what I ought to do as a commander. Instead, I'd followed what the doctrine expected me to do and stayed in the main command post.

I remembered that lesson during Desert Storm—and did not stay at the main command post.

As a matter of fact, we were not particularly dispersed during the BCTP, so I could move around in a wheeled vehicle. Because of the confines of the local training area, everything was fairly close together. If it had been an active operation, I would probably have had to get in a helicopter, the way I did in Desert Storm.

The main thing was that I wanted to get my subordinate commanders' sense of what was happening, and then give them my own sense and tell them what I wanted them to do in the next twelve to twenty-four hours. When I was there with them, I could look them in the eye and see if they understood what I wanted. That way, there could be no ambiguity in orders. There is an old saying: If an order can be misunderstood, it will be.

There were other benefits: First, I could try ideas out on my commanders. If I was thinking of doing something different, I could give them a heads-up and get their reaction to it.

Second, at the division tactical command post, you get the best, the freshest, information. By the time information moved from the units in contact, through their headquarters and the tactical command post, and then back to the main command post, it was hours out of date. So when I was at the tactical CP, and not visiting commanders, I was able to get a better view of the tactical situation and to make better, quicker decisions.

Third, senior commanders really get to make only a few key decisions during the fight. What you want to do, then, is to inform yourself so that you can determine the best time to make those decisions. By being forward, talking to my subordinate commanders, and being with the troops, seeing and sensing the fight, I better informed myself.

By being up front, you gain immediacy. But you also gain something else: Soldiers are getting hurt, wounded, killed in action. Commanders shouldn't be staying in their command post. They should be out and around the soldiers, where they can be feeling the pain and the pride, and where they can understand the whole human dimension of the battle. That way of operating has practical, tactical consequences. It will better inform commanders' intuition about what to do; it will suggest alternative courses of action that will accomplish their mission at least cost to their troops.

And so that's what I found myself doing on both the practice battlefield and the real battlefield. And so it turned out that in this BCTP we were very successful in the end and defeated the OPFOR.

Early on in this fight, in this scenario, we had to make the following decisions. We had to determine which way the major enemy force was coming; how we were going to win the counterfire fight (that is, defeat the enemy's artillery); and where and when we were going to commit the division reserve to stop the enemy attack and regain the initiative. To do all this, you have to read the battle quickly. Tactics during battle is a series of adjustments to stay ahead of the enemy.

In the BCTP, after I moved up front, I read the battle quickly, then saw the enemy forces coming, and we committed our reserves, stopped the enemy cold, and began a series of counterattacks against them.

That BCTP exercise capped an intense period of command experience in the 1st Armored Division. Franks and his division chain of command had been the umpires for the annual two-week fall 1988 REFORGER exercise of V Corps vs. VII Corps. There he had seen two corps in action, made tactical judgments as the senior umpire with his commanders and staff, and observed General Butch Saint command an Army Group. He would also gain experience in commanding the division both at Hohenfels in their own training maneuver exercises, and in their training exercises on their actual wartime terrain near the German border. The 1st Armored Division was also undergoing force modernization, receiving new M1A1 tanks, Bradleys, and Apaches. Because of his strong belief in the importance of fundamental skills, Franks trained as an individual tank commander with a tank crew and successfully went through the annual M1A1 tank crew qualification exercises at Grafenwohr to ensure that, as an armored division commander, he could command a tank. It was a tight combat-ready team in "Old Ironsides" (the 1st AD nickname). Franks was seeing for himself how far he and the Army had come since the early 1970s.

BIG FIVE

None of this could have been possible, of course, without the right equipment—and that was another major element in the rebirth of the Army.

In 1972, even before the '73 Mideast War, the Army was already aware of its urgent need for new and better fighting equipment. Under the leadership of General DePuy, then the Assistant Vice Chief of Staff of the Army, the Army adopted an approach with Congress and the Department of Defense that communicated this urgent need in a focused and disciplined way. They called this program the "Big Five," for the five new systems the Army could hardly live without: a new tank, an infantry fighting vehicle, an attack helicopter, a utility helicopter, and an air defense system. These would become the M1 Abrams, the Bradley, the Apache, the Blackhawk, and the Patriot. With the help of the

1973 Mideast War and James Schlesinger's continuing focus on restoring credibility to U.S. conventional defense in Central Europe, all five systems were approved.

Though today these systems have shown themselves to be hugely successful, none of them went through the acquisition process without serious debate, downright skepticism, and opposition inside the government and out. (Critics have been hard to find since Desert Storm.)

Let's look briefly at three of the five—the Apache, the Bradley, and the Abrams.*

—During Vietnam, the U.S. Army pioneered the concept of air assault and attack helicopters. There, because its air assault capability added a third maneuver dimension, the 1st Cavalry Division proved a superb tactical success. Likewise, rocket-firing helicopter gunships, and later the Cobra, proved equally effective. Later still, the Army attached TOW (Tube-launched, Optically tracked, Wire-guided antitank) missiles to both the Cobra and the UH-1 (Huey). These proved effective against NVA tanks and other targets during the Easter offensive of 1972.

From the beginning, the Army had wished to build an attack helicopter equipped with a combination of rockets, antitank missiles, and cannon; and so was launched the Cheyenne program. The Cheyenne was designed for speed, but costs escalated and a prototype crashed, and so the program was terminated.

The Army still wanted an attack helicopter, though—a helicopter capable of day and night and adverse-weather operations against enemy armor and other hardened targets, and so the Apache program was launched.

The Apache was to be a true attack helicopter, able to fight in close direct fire battles or to go deep into the enemy rear. Its design emphasized the ability to fly at low level, sort out its targets, and launch weapons from long range, outside the enemy's antiaircraft range. At the same time, Apaches made no compromise in the areas of sensors, weapons, agility, and survivability. The airframe structure, for instance, is designed to take a 20-g crash without killing the crew, and the fuel tanks are self-sealing and crash-resistant.

Apaches were fielded in the mid-1980s, and they quickly proved themselves to be the main battle tanks of the Army's air fleet at both division and corps.

—The Bradley is a well-armed armored fighting vehicle, designed to permit infantry to fight mounted or, in another role, to drop its rear ramp and let the infantry fight dismounted in small teams, while supporting them with fire as necessary. It can also provide scouting for cavalry units, and infantry sup-

---

*For a more complete description of all these systems, see my Armored Cav: A Guided Tour of an Armored Cavalry Regiment.

port for armored units on the battlefield. It's not designed to take the kind of heavy punishment a tank can, nor is it designed to deliver the kind of heavy blows a tank can deliver (though its punch is in no way *light*—with TOW missiles and a 25-mm cannon). Its versatility, however, clearly complements the tank-infantry team to produce a potent battlefield combination.

Like Apache, Bradley was created out of the failure of another program—this one called MICV (Mechanized Infantry Carrier Vehicle), which was designed to accompany M1 Abrams tanks into battle. It was not a wonderful piece of equipment. The one-man turret was inadequate, and the vehicle was as high as an early World War II tank, making it a vulnerable target. In early 1975, after the TRADOC studies of the 1973 Mideast War, General DePuy recommended killing the MICV. In his view, it wouldn't survive on the modern battlefield.

Out of the ashes of the MICV, the Bradley program was born. Like MICV, Bradley had doubters, and it would continue to have doubters right up to the attack on Desert Storm: "It's underpowered. The transmission doesn't work. The turret is too complex. The vehicle is not survivable." And on and on.

In the end, it worked superbly.

—The Abrams was likewise built on the ashes of failed programs (the U.S.-German MBT-70, and then the U.S. MBT-80). The Abrams likewise took its share of criticism, which in the end was not justified. Not only is designing a tank no small matter, but the United States had not built a completely new tank since the late 1940s. In tank design there are always trade-offs between survivability, mobility, and firepower. You have to lose something; you can't have it all. Large, heavily armored tanks with large cannons weigh a lot. That means they tend to be slow, they break bridges, and they can't get through underpasses. A tank like that isn't useful. Very quick light tanks without enough firepower to engage enemy armor and enough armor protection to survive are equally useless. So judgments have to be made in order to hit the right balance. How do you design a twenty-ton turret with fire-control equipment so precise it will allow gunners to track moving targets day and night and hit what they aim at, yet so rugged it can be used for days at a time without having to be taken to a shop for repairs? You also have to consider costs and maintenance. How many miles will your tank go between major failures of components?

The Abrams was a controversial machine, with a new and untried turbine powerplant, new armor, new electronics, and a new interior turret design. It was a tribute to American engineering that it took only eight years from the written requirements in 1972 to bring the first tank off the production line. Along the way came the questions and criticisms. Some worried about weight.

Some worried about dust and sand getting into the turbine engine. Some worried about survivability. Some wondered if the new interior turret design would really work.

In the end, it turned out to be the world's best main battle tank. If you went out onto a used tank lot, where all the world's best tanks were lined up for sale, the Abrams would be the one you'd pick. Its 1,500-horsepower turbine engine will drive it across a battlefield at speeds in excess of forty miles an hour; it has great dash speed, accelerating to twenty mph in less than ten seconds; and it will do it *quietly.* (Some early opponents in NATO exercises called M1s "the Whispering Death.") The M1A1 that VII Corps took into Iraq carried a 120-mm smoothbore cannon as well as a .50-caliber and two 7.62-mm machine guns.

Crew protection is superb. Primary armor protection for the M1 comes from its Chobham armor (named after the British research facility in Chobham, England). The M1 is also equipped with an automatic fire-detection/suppression system, and the M1A1 additionally has an atmospheric overpressure system to allow the crew to survive and fight on a battlefield contaminated with toxic chemicals, biological agents, or nuclear fallout.

In Desert Storm, M1A1s killed many Iraqi tanks. "When I went into Kuwait, I had thirty-nine tanks," a captured Iraqi battalion commander reported. "After six weeks of air bombardment, I had thirty-two left. After twenty minutes in action against M1s, I had none."

By the end of the 1970s, the Army in Europe had grown weary of staring down the superior Soviet equipment from their lightly armed M551 Sheridan light tanks and their 1950s-technology M60-series tanks. All that changed by the early 1980s, when the Army started to field the Big Five. They were a shot in the arm for the confidence of the Army in Europe.

DOCTRINE

Not only was it necessary to have new tools and new training, but it was crucial to learn a whole new way to fight. The ideas with which an army fights are only slightly less important than the ideas for which it fights. Doctrine is a statement of how the Army intends to fight. It gives the Army a common language and a common reference point that allows shorthand professional communication. It's not a dogma; it's a guideline, a statement of principles that should prove helpful in solving battlefield problems. But the solutions themselves will be dictated by the specifics of the situation. For an Army with a degree of complexity caused by the lethality and speed of modern battle, such a common work plan is invaluable.

In July 1976, the U.S. Army published its remarkable document FM 100-5. This manual was the Army's capstone doctrine statement. You could call it the Army's Philosophy of War.

The '76 FM 100-5 came largely out of studies of the '73 Mideast War by General DePuy and his colleagues at TRADOC; its focus was on how the U.S. Army must fight to win on the modern battlefield; and it was written largely by a small group of senior officers under General DePuy's direction, including then–Major Generals Donn Starry and Paul Gorman. The book differed from earlier general manuals in that it was designed as a primer to inform the Army about how to understand the modern battlefield and how to fight and win when outnumbered on that battlefield. The book was meant not only to inform and instruct, but to restore confidence.

As an instructional manual the new FM 100-5 was widely applied—the Army quickly internalized the changed battlefield it now confronted—but as a how-to-fight manual, it was widely misread. Because its chief focus was on what it called "Active Defense," many leaders discounted it. They thought the approach was too "defensive"—too passive—but it was no such thing. A careful reading in the context of its times shows that it was in fact a very clear expression of what the U.S. Army could actually do at that time in order to get itself ready to fight and win. Later advances on this early doctrine would go a long, long way in the direction of attack. Meanwhile, however, a start had to be made with what was then available and possible.

✯ When Donn Starry commanded V Corps in Germany, even as he implemented FM 100-5 and rebuilt warrior confidence in the unit, one thing still bothered him: Warsaw Pact army doctrine called for attack in waves. They'd hit you, and then hit you again and again, with fresh echelons of troops. Starry was not convinced he could be successful with an outnumbered force if the Warsaw Pact continued to introduce fresh echelons of troops into the fight. This issue had been on his mind ever since he himself had stood on the Golan Heights with Israeli Major General Musa Peled just after the 1973 Mideast War. There he'd listened to Peled's accounts of the IDF's fight against the Soviet echelonment tactics used by the Syrians. The IDF had won outnumbered on the Golan by attacking deep with air and 175-mm artillery, and then by maneuvering Peled's own division deep during the last days of the war.

Starry had long been convinced that, like the IDF, the U.S. Army had to think deep, and now that he was V Corps commander facing a possible echelon attack in a real mission, he was even more convinced. But Starry was also a pragmatist. He was fully aware that the Army could absorb only so many new ideas at any one time, and it was just about to be hit by the new doctrine of active defense. So he put off his thoughts until later.

In the summer of 1977, Starry succeeded DePuy as TRADOC commander. He was still deeply concerned about Warsaw Pact echelonment tactics and the enormous disparity in numbers. If something wasn't done about them, and if war broke out, sooner or later the sheer weight of numbers would prevail. In the end, he knew, the Army's Active Defense doctrine came down to attrition warfare, and in attrition warfare, numbers do count.

Starry's idea was to reintroduce a battle in depth: to extend the battlefield deep on the enemy's side of the forward line of contact, to attack follow-on echelons, and to break up the enemy's momentum and disrupt his ability to bring his mass to bear. To do all this required intelligence and deep targeting, and it required the orchestration of this fight with the principal deep-attack assets available to the USAF.

TRADOC presented Starry with the opportunity to implement this idea.

Starting with Starry's germ, over the next four years TRADOC developed what became known as AirLand Battle. Actual doctrine creation was a team effort involving two principal doctrine authors at the Army's Command and General Staff College, Colonels Huba Wass de Czege and Don Holder, both of whom worked directly for Lieutenant General Bill Richardson. Wass de Czege and Holder wrote a doctrinal book that built on the strengths of the 1976 edition, while adding both depth and maneuver, and ideas about gaining the initiative and going over to the attack. The idea was to win, and not just to stop the enemy advance.

At first, Starry called this idea the "extended battlefield." Later, it was "deep battle," and finally AirLand Battle.

★ In 1982, Colonel Fred Franks was given command of his old regiment, the 11th ACR, Blackhorse, which was now stationed in Germany in the Fulda Gap. There he was to have his first opportunity to command a large tactical unit. That meant that he was also a military community commander—essentially the mayor of a city of about 10,000 soldiers, civilians, and family members.

As commander of the 11th ACR, he wanted to introduce the new AirLand Battle doctrine—which the Army was about to publish in August—to teach it not only to the regiment, but also to the V Corps covering force, which consisted of about 10,000 soldiers from various units in the corps that had been put under his operational control to fight the initial battles and break up the momentum of a Warsaw Pact attack toward Frankfurt through the Fulda Gap.

Franks's corps commander during his two years with the Blackhorse was Lieutenant General Paul (Bo) Williams, a skilled and understanding commander who saw the vital importance of linking the Blackhorse's mission success (as covering force) to his overall corps success. Williams's G-3 was also a cavalryman, Colonel Tom Tait, who was a big help in the continuing work to strengthen the covering-force fight. He and Bo Williams were receptive to Franks's continuing arguments, taken in large part from the AirLand Battle doctrine that Franks himself had helped work on at TRADOC—that they had to begin to win immediately, especially in light of the growing capabilities provided by the new equipment that was becoming available. Franks believed, in fact, that early success in the covering force might even provide a basis for early limited counterattacks in NATO territory, which would break up the massed momentum of the other side before it really got started.

In 1983, Franks had a chance to put these ideas into practice at a RE-FORGER exercise.

REFORGER (REturn of FORces to GERmany) was a method of rapidly reinforcing U.S. units stationed in the central region of NATO. In times of crisis, troops would fly in from the United States, link up with equipment already stored in Europe, and—if they had to—go to war. In order to demonstrate U.S. political resolve, as well as to actually exercise the concept, there was a REFORGER exercise each year.

The '83 REFORGER involved V Corps units in Germany and units coming from the States. Though the exercise was to be held on the actual Fulda Gap terrain, it was set back some distance from the border. In it, the 3rd Armored Division was to be the Blue, or friendly, force against the opposing Orange force. The 11th Cavalry was not listed to be part of the exercise.

Fred Franks takes up the story:

> I went to Lieutenant General Bo Williams and asked if we could take part in the exercise so that we could get training on the terrain and work for the first time with our new M1 tanks. After a certain amount of persuading, he agreed to allow us to participate, but only for the first week of the two-week exercise; we would operate in front of the 3rd Armored Division as a covering force, and only with three of our four squadrons plus two battalion-sized task forces from 3rd AD.
>
> Some is better than none. So I chose my 1st and 3rd ground squadrons and my aviation squadron.
>
> During that week, the Orange force was to cross the "border" and attack the 3rd AD. For the limited time we had, I wanted to do something bold. I wanted to attack with our M1-equipped squadron (we had only one at the time) as soon as the opposing force moved toward us, so as to surprise them and break up their momentum of attack.
>
> After I went to the assistant division commander, Brigadier General Tom Griffin, and explained what I had in mind, he agreed to support this. But he told me he knew there would be controversy. Some on the other side

were going to claim we were "not playing by the rules, since we were supposed to be on the defense." In my judgment, that was the whole point. When the opposing force attacks, they'll expect to find us defending and backing up. So we should attack early in a preemptive strike and surprise them. In the confusion that followed, we could exploit with additional air and ground attacks, and maybe stop their attack before it got started.

We anticipated that the opposing force attack would come at first light.

To create deception, we decided to lead the opposing force to believe our M1 squadron was in our northern sector, when in fact we had them hidden in the center, waiting for the moment to attack. Thus, we sent a few M1s to the northern sector and made sure they were clearly visible to the other side on the evening before the attack. Then we played M1 noise over loudspeakers all along that sector, while we pulled the actual tanks out, loaded them on heavy equipment transports, and then moved them the seventy to eighty kilometers to the south to rejoin the rest of their unit.

The other piece of my plan was to make a sack for the other side to fall into. Our center squadron was to be the bottom of the sack, so to speak. In other words, I ordered them to defend and then to give way some, so we could draw the enemy after them. Once they were inside, we would attack with the fast-moving M1s. Meanwhile, during the night before the attack, I ordered my aviation squadron (with their newly developed night-flying skills) to give me a clear picture of the posture of the opposing force. I wanted to hit them just after they moved against us.

We were ready. We had rehearsed this, so we all knew what we were doing. I had a great team of commanders and soldiers who could pull this off. And in Tom Griffin I had a senior commander who trusted us and was not afraid to go out on a limb and risk a decision for us.

At 0715 the first morning, I advised Tom that conditions were right. Our aviation had reported that the opposing forces had concentrated a large force in the area we wanted to attack. These looked to be second-echelon units to be used later in the day, after the initial attack was successful. Meanwhile, our middle squadron (the 3rd Squadron of the 11th, commanded by then–Lieutenant Colonel Stan Cherrie, who was to be my G-3 on Desert Storm) had reported that the opposing force had attacked. They could hold, but not for long. Our M1 squadron (1st Squadron of the 11th, commanded by then–Lieutenant Colonel John Abrams, now a lieutenant general and V Corps commander in Germany) had reported they were ready (I had them on an immediate attack readiness posture).

My operations officer, Major Skip Bacevich (later my G-3 in the 1st Armored Division and later still commander of the 11th Cavalry in a rapid deployment to Kuwait in June 1991), was with me in our two M113 com-

mand vehicles on a hill overlooking the attack area. The weather was clear. Perfect! But if we waited much longer, the opposing force would break through my middle squadron and I'd have to use my M1 squadron to stop that. I wanted to attack and seize the initiative, just as our doctrine recommends. So did Tom Griffin. He gave us the approval. I ordered John and the aviation squadron to attack.

The attack was a success. We completely surprised the opposing force and caused such confusion that the exercise had to be stopped while forces got untangled and reset to begin again.

That whole experience was a lesson for us all. I'll never forget it. We had the right people, the right doctrine, the right equipment, a bold plan, and a commander who knew what we were doing and who trusted and supported us. It was magic. I was learning how to be a senior tactical commander.

And Fred Franks was proving the efficacy of AirLand Battle in the toughest kind of trial short of war.

★ Succeeding Starry at TRADOC was General Glen Otis. Otis had been the Army's operations deputy at the Department of the Army and was thoroughly familiar with the evolving doctrine. Drawing on studies coming out of the Army's War College, Otis was taken with the idea of addressing three levels of war: strategic, operational, and tactical. Strategy was beyond the scope of Army doctrine, but a lot could be done with the operational level. At that level, tactical battles were not discrete, unconnected events. Rather, they needed to be so woven together that they achieved a campaign objective, and thereby gained the overall strategic aim of a military operation.

The missing strategic link in Vietnam was the operational level of war. Year after year, tactical battles were won by U.S. and allied forces, but in the absence of an operational plan, these never added up to gaining the overall strategic objective.

Otis included the three levels in the new FM 100-5, and Otis's successor at TRADOC, Bill Richardson, directed expansion of the operational doctrine.

Meanwhile, while at Fort Leavenworth as deputy commandant of the Army's Command and General Staff College, Lieutenant General Bob Ris-Cassi assigned Franks direction of the project to revise the Army's 1982 FM 100-5 that, while retaining AirLand Battle, included this expanded discussion, which it described as the "design and conduct of major operations and campaigns." Such design would be called "operational art"—the thinking that translated strategic aims into effective military campaigns. The book was approved and published in May 1986, and because operational art and design was a new thought for the U.S. Army, the doctrine was accompanied by a briefing put together by Colonel Rick Sinnreich, director of the School for Advanced Military Studies (SAMS), that would explain it to the U.S. Army and our allies. In Desert Storm, this 1986 book would serve as the U.S. Army's basic doctrine and directly influence the design of major operations.

✭ Training and doctrine flow—or at least they should flow—out of the same source. Doctrine gives you mission and focus. Training gives you the skills to carry out your mission.

In the spring of 1988, before he assumed command of the 1st AD, Fred Franks had the opportunity to visit Eastern Europe to observe a Warsaw Pact military exercise as part of the observer exchanges of the Conference on Security and Cooperation in Europe (CSCE). This visit gave him a unique opportunity to see for himself the training and doctrine of his potential enemy in operation.

This was the first time he had been behind the Iron Curtain to have a look for himself. Though he had patrolled it as a platoon leader, troop commander, and regimental commander during two previous tours in Europe, for the first time he was driving through the checkpoints, then down to Prague, and on up to the training exercise north of the capital. He spent a week in the field visiting a Soviet armored division and watching them go through training exercises. He took a lot of pictures, talked to Soviet officers, talked to observers from other countries, and saw at first hand the capabilities and limitations of a Soviet armored division.

The visit to Czechoslovakia confirmed all he'd always imagined about them: The Soviets' doctrine emphasized tight control. Everything had to go according to a timetable; nobody did anything on his own.

Franks visited a Czech mechanized infantry unit in a dug-in defensive position, and saw a Soviet unit in a similar position and a Soviet tank unit, equipped with T-72s. They were permitted to take pictures of it and of the troops and their positions, and also observed one of their second-echelon units moving up; they stopped on the side of the road and got out to talk to them. From all this, he got a decent insight into their mentality, leadership, equipment capabilities, approach to training, and approach to wartime situations. They were technically competent. Their field craft was quite good—digging holes, camouflage, movement of vehicles. But everything was very rehearsed. On their major maneuver range, you could see well-worn trails in the snow where unit after unit had done the same thing over the same ground. If anything unexpected happened, or if any radical change was required by some unexpected actions, that would be very disruptive to them.

Their training was very rote, very set-piece. They did this, then they did that. There were no real opposing forces—or thinking enemy, in what the U.S. Army calls free-play exercises. Our training exercises were dynamic; things are allowed to happen unexpectedly. We demanded of commanders that they deviate from the plan, because the enemy has a mind of his own. But here in Czechoslovakia, it looked as if they were going through a series of tightly scripted one-act plays. They'd move from Point A to Point B and then stop and get into positions.

Here are a couple of anecdotes. The experience could have been insightful had we fought them.

A Soviet major general had been escorting Franks and his colleagues around a tank firing range. It was very cold, and it started to snow. As it happened, he finished his tour and presentation about twenty minutes early.

Did they move Franks and his colleagues out to the buses waiting for them and get them to the next scheduled event? No. They didn't have that kind of flexibility. So there they stood in a blinding snowstorm, waiting for the appointed time when they could load the buses and move to their next station.

At the next station, they observed what the Soviets called a live fire exercise. Franks sat in warm bleachers that were covered, fully enclosed, with glass in front. Underneath were latrines with running water. It was like a sports stadium box for maybe two hundred people, obviously used time after time for VIPs and officers. And the range in front was full of ruts and tank trails, so you could see that they'd performed this exercise time after time. They'd bring their officers in, sit them down in the bleachers, and then carefully explain how a tank battalion supported by Hind helicopters would attack a position. We would call this a demonstration. They called it training.

All of this confirmed the wisdom of the United States' own doctrine: Before the Soviets gained mass and velocity to produce the momentum of their attack, the West needed to hit them early and hard and often while they were still getting themselves together and trying to organize their great numbers on limited terrain. The West had to add to the normal confusion, to hit their command posts while they were dealing with the early disruptions. Since nobody would exercise initiative—they were not allowed to—without their command posts they'd be lost.

Franks came away from there with two impressions:

One, they weren't supermen. In fact, our ideas about how to fight them, as written into doctrine, were exactly correct.

And two, with each side visiting the other, something had to give. They would observe our new modern equipment and superb soldiers and NCOs, and they couldn't help but realize that our soldiers were capable of things they could not even imagine.

But that wasn't really the important thing . . . showing off or learning how to fight each other. The important thing was that better understanding had to take place. They would see us. We would see them. We'd get to know each other better. And we'd open up little by little. And with that happening, the confrontation simply had to go away eventually. Franks didn't know when or how, but as a result of that visit, he was convinced the Cold War couldn't go on forever. That was the real aim of the visit.

Soviet and Iraqi doctrine and practice, he reflected later, had many similarities. Although they had equipment from South Africa, Brazil, France, and elsewhere (even from the United States), the Iraqis were equipped mainly with Warsaw Pact equipment. And although, in a curious way, their military was organized more on Western lines (into corps, divisions, and brigades) than on Soviet Warsaw Pact lines (into armies, divisions, and regiments), and although some of their tactics looked more Western than Soviet, in their actual behavior and in the way they laid out their defense and anticipated fighting a defensive battle, their behavior was profoundly Warsaw Pact. The Iraqis exercised very tight control. Everything they did was very, very rote. Every little thing had to go according to plan.

That meant that if you happened to do exactly what they predicted you would do, and at a place where they predicted you were going to do it, then they could hurt you. They had a lot of firepower. They had excellent artillery weapons. On the other hand, if you did something unexpected—such as time of attack, or speed of attack, or the location of the attack—and caused them to alter the rote pattern that they had anticipated, they had difficulty adjusting.

In other words, what Franks saw in 1988 in Czechoslovakia, he saw again with the Iraqis in Desert Storm. He saw the strength of our doctrine and the weakness of theirs.

(The Iraqi army was different from Warsaw Pact countries in one major respect, however: in the brutal way they treated their own soldiers and the savage treatment of their own citizens. That was pure Iraqi.)

★ During the 1980s, while the Army continued to deter Soviet aggression as part of NATO, it fought small wars in Grenada and Panama. And late in 1989, the Cold War ended. The Soviet empire had started the sag toward its final collapse.

Army leaders looking around at the beginning of the decade could not have easily imagined the incredible events at decade's end. To win the war, the Army had prepared to fight for the better part of two generations. To do it without firing a shot . . . you can't beat that for success.

LEADER TRAINING

There was one final ingredient to the rebirth of the Army.

From the days of Baron von Steuben during the American Revolutionary War, the NCO has been the "backbone of the Army." It is the sergeant who is responsible for the individual training of the soldier, who leads the soldiers in small units under the command of officers, who is closest to the soldiers, enforces good order and discipline, and provides the example of what soldiers should be to the junior enlisteds.

Let's make a kind of syllogism: Because Vietnam gutted the NCO corps, many small units went to hell. Ergo, it was necessary to fix the NCO corps. Thus, very early on in the rebirth process, Army leaders decided to change the way noncommissioned officers were trained and educated.

In 1969, Army Chief General William Westmoreland, having seen first-hand what Vietnam was doing to the NCO corps, directed General Ralph Haines, then his vice chief, to look into the whole situation and devise a solution. The "Haines Board" recommended that, throughout their careers, NCOs attend a series of progressive and sequential leader development schools designed to develop their leadership skills at each step in their advancement. Such a system was already in place for officers. Now NCOs would have a similar system—called NCOES, or noncommissioned officer education system.

How does the Army grow good NCO leaders? Before becoming sergeants, people showing leadership potential during their first three years in the Army attend a Primary Leader Development Course, or PLDC. Following promotion to sergeant and after serving for a few years, but before promotion to the next grade, NCOs attend the Basic Noncommissioned Officer Course (BNCOC), which is designed for small-unit leaders, such as squad leaders or tank commanders, and devoted to skills necessary to those positions. Following more years of practical experience, NCOs return to the Advanced Noncommissioned Officer Course (ANCOC) to help them make the transition from single-team leader to multi-team leader. By this time, an NCO will have perhaps ten to twelve years of service. Following successful performance of those duties and after demonstrating increased potential, NCOs attend a course designed to assist them in becoming first sergeants, or the senior NCO in a company organization ranging from seventy to two hundred soldiers. Finally, NCOs with senior leadership potential attend the nine-month Sergeants Major Academy at Fort Bliss, Texas, to prepare them for the most senior NCO positions—from command sergeant major of battalions to sergeant major of the Army. In the mid-1980s, the Army linked successful graduation from these schools to promotion.

This leader development system for NCOs saw its fulfillment on the battlefields of Desert Storm. By 1991, most of the senior NCOs of combat battalions had entered the Army in the mid-1970s and had had the opportunity to attend most of the NCOES courses. Meanwhile, all of the more junior NCOs had had the opportunity to attend these schools as they grew in rank and responsibilities. Their collective performance, and that of their soldiers in Desert Storm, was a direct effect of the long-sustained commitment to excellence of the U.S. Army's NCOES begun almost twenty years earlier. No other army in the world has such a system.

★ There were also major changes in the ways officers were educated.

From studies in the late 1970s, observations of commander and staff performances in NATO and at the new NTC, and renewed emphasis in doctrine on the operational level of war, Army leaders concluded that improvements had to be made in the way officers were developed.

In the middle 1970s the Army had adopted a central selection board process to pick its lieutenant colonel– and colonel-level commanders. Then, in the early 1980s, a pre-command course was created for those officers, which brought them up to date with the rapidly modernizing Army in the field, and gave them instruction and war-gaming practice (by way of simulations) on their new level of command. The course itself was two to three weeks of instruction and hands-on training in new equipment at the officers' basic branch school (armor, infantry, artillery, etc.), followed by two weeks of instruction in combined arms and issues of command at Fort Leavenworth.

For captains, the Army took a bolder step, by establishing a combined-arms services and staff school (the Army called it CAS3). Though it was begun as a pilot in 1983, the school wasn't fully operational until it moved into a new, specially designed classroom building built in the fall of 1986. CAS3 was to be attended by all Army captains sometime during their sixth to tenth year of service. Seminar groups of twelve to fifteen students from all disciplines in the Army were led through an intense nine-week course by an ex–battalion commander. There they learned how to solve tactical problems and how to manage a variety of tactical communications, including writing orders. CAS3 immediately produced results in significantly improved staff skills for the student graduates (and for the faculty as well—many of whom went on to senior-level command).

As CAS3 was getting off the ground, it became apparent that a second-year course was needed at Fort Leavenworth for selected students to study the complexities of the operational level of war with much more intellectual rigor than had been possible in the Army's educational system before. This need turned into the School for Advanced Military Studies (SAMS). Begun in a small converted gymnasium, the school opened with twelve students in

1983–84, and expanded to its current level of fifty-two students by 1985–86. SAMS was, and is, a highly selective operation, with an intensive entrance examination, including interviews. It initially drew only Army student volunteers from the graduates of the one-year Command and General Staff College course, but eventually USAF and USMC students also came out of that course. The curriculum is as rigorous as any graduate-level program in the United States (SAMS is certified to grant master's degrees in military arts and sciences by the Middle States Accreditation Board), and its graduates have gone on to distinguish themselves as operational-level planners in every major U.S. contingency operation from the late 1980s until today. Some of these gained publicity in Desert Storm as the "Jedi Knights," who crafted the basic CENTCOM plan used to liberate Kuwait.

This explosion of energy at Fort Leavenworth transformed the Army's Command and General Staff College. Long a training ground for future commanders and staff officers, CAS3, SAMS, and pre-command courses made it truly a university for the tactical and operational level of land warfare.

The entire atmosphere was transformed: Officers from captain to lieutenant general now came to study at Leavenworth, while officers from almost 100 different countries attended the regular course. Authority to grant the MMAS injected a graduate-school rigor into the second-year program. Creation of a combat studies institute attracted civilian faculty with broad academic credentials in the history of military art. Army leadership now looked to Fort Leavenworth for studies of future scenarios, which were then taken to senior-level leader seminars. The Battle Command Training Program also brought division and corps commanders and their staffs to Fort Leavenworth, and a Center for Lessons Learned was created to capture valuable training and war insights. In time, Fort Leavenworth became the symbol of the intellectual heart and soul of the tactical field army. Guest speakers and other visitors enriched the quality of the intellectual environment. Leaders from Congress, media, academia, and militaries around the world came for discussions and exchanges. Just as Fort Leavenworth had once been a frontier to the future of the American West on the banks of the Missouri, so now had it become a frontier to the Army's future.

RUNNING HARD

By the middle 1980s, the Army had more than turned the corner. It was running hard. The Grenada invasion, for instance, though demonstrating some difficulties in joint operations, was a success for the Army, and it showed how far it had come from the doldrums of the 1970s. The Army had reason to feel good about itself, and could point to an operational success as proof.

Meanwhile, the Army came to realize it might have to face situations where armor/mechanized forces (what it calls "heavy" forces) might not be as effective as "lighter," pure infantry forces. And so Army Secretary Jack Marsh and Army Chief John Wickham directed the creation of two light infantry divisions, to add to its sixteen current divisions. In order to do this without increasing the manpower authorizations of the active force, it turned again to the "round-out" concept, where National Guard brigades were folded into active-duty divisions, to "round" them out to full strength.

These divisions were to be truly "light"—in the spirit of the "light" troops who had stormed the redoubts at Yorktown in our Revolution. They would depend not so much on firepower as on stealth, infiltration, speed of movement through difficult terrain, tough physical conditioning, field craft, and relentless drills on the fundamentals of small-unit soldiering. It was in the latter where they excelled.

The Army also upgraded its special operating forces (SOF), expanding the Rangers to a regiment of three battalions. These would be the elite among elites—fit volunteers, trained to a razor's edge and beyond, to operate in small units behind the lines. As an elite force, they were given ample training budgets, stable personnel policies (less rotation in and out than normal units), their pick of volunteers, and leaders and commanders who were already experienced company commanders.

The Army's ambitious fielding of two light infantry divisions was a success. Schools for "light fighters" were established. Bold commanders such as Major General Ed Burba in the 7th Division at Fort Ord, California, would seize on the light fighter concept and transform their new divisions to operational reality in short order. Because light infantry soldiers drilled and trained hard on fundamentals of fitness and basic infantry close-combat skill, it wasn't long before they became a world-class fighting force. Their proficiency and zeal for combat fundamentals soon infected the Army—an unexpected bonus that has lasted. Convinced that light fighters needed an NTC-like facility to train to realistic battlefield conditions, General Richardson successfully pushed hard for a Joint Readiness Training Center. The JRTC was opened in 1986 in temporary facilities at Fort Chaffee, Arkansas. Later it was moved permanently to Fort Polk, Louisiana.

At Fort Hood, Texas, General Bob Shoemaker, then Lieutenant General Dick Cavazos after him, as III Corps Commander, formed training units to teach the Army how to employ the new Apache to attack deep and en masse. Resisting those who would parcel the Apaches out in small units throughout the tactical Army (reminiscent of the "penny packaging" of tanks in the 1920s), they became strong advocates of aviation brigades to add a new maneuver and deep firepower dimension to the tactical Army.

At Fort Hood, in 1985, a young Lieutenant General Crosbie "Butch" Saint assumed command of III Corps. Saint had previously commanded the 11th Armored Cavalry in Fulda, Germany, had been deputy commandant of the CGSC during the formulation of AirLand Battle, had recently commanded the 1st Armored Division in Germany, and was soon to become well known in the Army as an advocate of mobile armored warfare. III Corps's new mission in Northern Army Group in NATO was to attack to restore the territorial integrity of Germany after an initial Warsaw Pact attack. In order to accomplish this mission, Saint set out to utilize the corps's significant additional combat power and to create what he called a "mobile armored corps." III Corps drilled and practiced attacks, made long unit moves and attacked from the march, worked on the logistics of refueling on the move, and even published a tactical handbook to supplement the existing doctrine and further lay out the tactics. By now, they had Apaches in the brigade organization and employed them deep and massed.

Saint's ideas influenced a generation. In 1990, as the commander of U.S. forces in Germany at the end of the Cold War, he put the whole of U.S. Army Europe on the same tactical training regimen he'd started with III Corps.

GOLDWATER-NICHOLS

Never has national security legislation brought such sweeping—and wise—changes to the U.S. military as the Goldwater-Nichols National Security Act of 1986. It transformed the relationship of the service departments to the Joint Staff; it promoted operational "jointness" by legislating service for officers on joint assignments; and it streamlined the command authority from the President and Secretary of Defense to the Unified Commanders worldwide.

Goldwater-Nichols essentially removed the service departments from operational matters. Under the law, they still had their budget authorities, but now, under Title 10, their sole responsibility was to man, equip, and train forces, which would then be provided to the unified CINCs (commanders in chief) worldwide for employment in missions assigned by the President and the Secretary of Defense. The Joint Staff now no longer answered to the collective body of the Joint Chiefs, but only to the chairman of the Joint Chiefs of Staff (JCS) and the Secretary of Defense. This simplified staff procedures and did away with the need to gain all service agreement on operational matters. In other words, before offering military advice to the President or Secretary of Defense, the Chairman JCS no longer required the total agreement of the service chiefs. Though the service chiefs were still senior advisers on national strategy, they were no longer involved in the day-to-day operational role. Meanwhile, because they were now free of individual service involvement, the authority of the Unified Commanders in areas around the world was significantly strengthened.

Joint education was to be required of all officers; all service schools were now to have a joint war-fighting curriculum approved and accredited by the Joint Staff; prior to promotion to flag rank, officers were required to serve in joint assignments; and those who qualified as CINCs would have to serve in a joint assignment as a flag officer.

Goldwater-Nichols was not an unqualified success. Though it gave the Secretary of Defense, the Chairman JCS, and the Joint Staff full authority to make the strategic analysis that would force decisions and trade-offs between service priorities, budget authority was left within service departments (so they could take care of their Title 10 responsibilities), and that invited bureaucratic maneuvering and interservice rivalry. Each service wanted to gain a larger share of the defense budget. That is still the case ten years and three JCS Chairmen later.

Goldwater-Nichols was an enormous adjustment for each service department, including the Army. Fortunately, and to its lasting benefit, in the summer of 1987 the Army chose as its new chief an officer uniquely suited for this transitional period, General Carl E. Vuono.

THE VUONO YEARS

General Carl Vuono came to be Army Chief as a man long immersed in the Army renaissance. He had not only lived it, he had increasingly helped to form some of its most important policies. He continued to do both as Army Chief.

In the late 1970s, Vuono had served General Starry as his chief for combat developments, and in that position, he had seen to it that the Army fielded the Big Five in a way that integrated training, organizational design, and equipment fielding so as to gain combat power in the shortest possible time. As commander of the 8th Infantry Division, he had stamped on that unit his own training beliefs and modernization plans, which would become a model for the rest of the Army. At Fort Leavenworth, from 1983 to 1985, as deputy TRADOC commander, he had completed the work on the new Army of excellence and had seen the establishment of SAMS and CAS3. From 1985 to 1986, as Army operations deputy for General Wickham, he had assisted General Bill Richardson in establishing the Joint Readiness Center at Fort Chaffee, Arkansas, and later at Fort Polk, Louisiana. As TRADOC commander, he had published the first senior leadership doctrine manuals and committed to the establishment of the BCTP for division and corps commanders. He was uniquely qualified to be Army Chief.

Soon after he took over that position, Vuono laid out a vision for the Army.

At its core is what he called a "trained and ready Army" (exactly what the Goldwater-Nichols Act envisioned the service departments should have). He charged the Army with keeping its eye on balancing investments and energies among six imperatives: training, force modernization, war-winning doctrine, quality soldiers, "leader development" (his term), and force structure—with the right mix of heavy, light, and special operating forces to fulfill missions of the CINCs.

Each of these six imperatives was important, but it was in training and leader development that Vuono was to leave his greatest legacy.

Vuono was long convinced that if leaders successfully grew other leaders, then that was their finest gift to succeeding Army generations—thus "leader development." Such development was a commander's responsibility, not a staff responsibility of the Department of the Army Chief for Personnel. It had to be related to the way the Army fought. Thus, he wanted leader development institutionalized at the Army's senior tactical war-fighting school at Fort Leavenworth. As we have already seen, that came to be embedded in a three-level approach: formal Army schooling, each level featuring standards that officers had to pass before they could move along to the next stage in their career; practical experience serving in units at various levels of responsibility, including the rigorous experiences of the NTC, JRTC, and BCTP; and self-development through private study, reading, and learning from others.

Vuono's chief training focus was in a rigorous combat simulation system—hands-on performance-oriented training. Believing that all training short of war was simulation, he had the Army combine computer-assisted simulations and live field maneuvers to give leaders and combat staffs the rigors of simulated combat. For the first time in the Army's history, every commander—from the individual tank commander on his crew-qualification Table VIII to the corps commander on his BCTP WARFIGHTER exercise—had to undergo a rigorous and stressful combat exercise. Every exercise was externally evaluated and followed by a series of AARs. Everyone had to perform to standard.

Vuono also had training practices codified into training doctrine. Long a believer that mission focus for wartime missions should drive training, he set out to write it into a manual, which was called FM 25-100.

FM 25-100 coined the term Mission-Essential Task List (METL). METL is a simple concept. A commander examines the wartime mission the theater commander has assigned him and from it determines the tasks necessary for its execution. Thus: Mission-Essential Tasks. Then he has his unit train for these tasks, which are then broken down further by echelon of command, down to individual tasks for soldiers. When FM 25-100 was in preparation, Vuono conducted a series of senior leader training conferences throughout the Army, personally involving other commanders in the composition of the manual. When that one was finished, he set about to produce a second manual, called FM 25-101, which was to provide further details for lower tactical echelons. Together, these standardized the Army's approach to training in schools and on the field.

As the end of the Cold War approached, Vuono set down three essential tasks for the Army during the transition years to a new strategic era:

• To win the wars the Army was called on to fight;
• To maintain readiness in the force not associated with those operations (remembering the deplorable state of readiness of our forces in Europe as they were systematically drawn down to fight in Vietnam);
• And to remain balanced in the six imperatives as the Army reshaped itself from its Cold War strength of over 1 million active and Reserve component strength to new levels.

GENERATIONS

Continuity of focus has been indispensable to the Army's recovery from Vietnam—a focus on training and readiness and the warrior spirit, while maintaining the ability to adapt as the strategic environment and resource availability changed. Such continuity was the consequence of the experience of four generations of leaders, each generation passing the torch to the next.

In the words of General Carl Vuono, the Army "cannot afford a generation that does not have that focus." Every Army generation must "bring along a cadre of people who feel as strongly" about mission focus and staying trained and ready. For Vuono and all the generations of Army leaders, there could be no compromise.

The first generation was that of World War II combat leaders, with Korean War combat experience. These men were the commanders of divisions and higher echelons in Vietnam: Westmoreland, Abrams, Weyand, DePuy, Kerwin, Davison, Kroesen.

The second generation's entire service was in the Cold War. They either had combat experience in Korea; or they'd commanded at battalion or brigade level in Vietnam; and they'd been brigade, division, or corps commanders in the 1970s: Rogers, Meyer, Wickham, Starry, Otis, Cavazos, Richardson, Brown, Keith, Shoemaker, Gorman.

The third generation did command battalions in Vietnam, and had colonel-level command in the 1970s: Vuono, Thurman, Merritt, Lindsay, and Grange.

The fourth generation had Vietnam combat experience at company-grade and junior-field-grade levels; and in the Army of the 1970s, they had battalion-level command, from which vantage point they could see firsthand the Army's low points. These men would witness the end of the Cold War, as well as the Army's successes in Just Cause and Desert Storm: Powell, Sullivan, Reimer, Saint, Stiner, RisCassi, Burba, Franks, Joulwan, Luck, Griffith, Peay, Tilelli.

Continuity in focus and leadership from those who "grew up right" was vital to Army work from the early 1970s to Desert Storm. Neither the U.S. Army nor the nation could afford a "generation gap."

These four generations of soldiers and civilians were motivated by a sense of duty and commitment to the nation. There were no quick fixes. Success was not assured. It was not the result of a single piece of legislation. There were ups and downs, successes and reversals, tensions and disagreements. Factions argued for their positions, and sometimes went too far in one direction, and the right solution had to be found through experimentation. Yet all these were only arguments over ways to reach the ends. The ends were always the same: a combat-ready Army ready to win the first battle of the next war.

And in the end, it got done. That it did so was the result of quality people, vision, hard work, and perseverance in the face of resistance and obstacles—the very same characteristics that win on the battlefield. It was a successful partnership among the Congress, the Army, the Executive Branch, and the American people. It was a good-news story for America.

FRED FRANKS—1972–1989

As the Army was starting its road back, so was Fred Franks—from the depths of Valley Forge to the desert victory in southwest Asia. It took him to schools, to staff work, and to commands where he was given every opportunity to compete and to learn and grow. He was to take his place with his peers among the fourth generation, which had had the opportunity to "grow up right," though for Franks personally there would be an added challenge.

—At the Armed Forces Staff College in Norfolk, Virginia, after he left Valley Forge in 1972, Franks learned joint warfare—the combining under one mission and focus of elements of more than one military service; for example, units from the Army, Navy, and Air Force.

There he would also learn for the first time how readily he was accepted back into the family of the military. There was no mention of his amputee condition; instead he was accepted for what he could do. He coached a slow-pitch softball team and played himself, played volleyball as well, and threw himself into a rigorous regimen of physical conditioning, pushing himself to see if he could still compete. There he would also hear from his Navy and Air Force classmates of their Vietnam battles in the air over North Vietnam and the courage that took. It would heighten his own feelings for those who had served in Vietnam.

—From the time he left the Armed Forces Staff College until June 1975, Franks was on the staff at the Department of the Army and then was military assistant to three Army undersecretaries. While he was on the Department of the Army staff, he worked again for General Donn Starry, and he met Colonel Dick Cavazos for the first time. Both assignments gave him a great appreciation for the enormous challenges involved in rebuilding the Army. From there came command of a cavalry squadron in the 3rd ACR in June 1975. That tour was the true turning point for Franks. That the U.S. Army would take the risk to allow him to command a cavalry squadron only heightened his commitment. When he left that post a year and a half later, he would say, "I felt whole again as a man and as a soldier. The soldiers and leaders on the field in front of me were responsible for that. We had been through a lot together and I had grown as a leader. I knew that with their help I had passed my own test as an armored cavalry commander. I would be forever grateful and would never forget our service together and that close cavalry brotherhood."

Late in 1976, six months before he attended the National War College, Franks took part in what was called the Tank Force Management Group. The concept behind it was simple: though the numbers of the U.S. armor force are small, their contributions on the battlefield are huge. But at that time, the armor force needed a lot of work in order to realize that potential. The TFMG's mission was to focus its attention in an armor context on areas such as doctrine, training, material improvements, and soldier quality. In other words, the group was a microcosm for the work the entire Army was trying to do after the sharp lessons of the 1973 Mideast War.

At the TFMG, Franks came to his first realization about how far the Army needed to go before it could actually fight and win on the kind of battlefield it had seen in the Mideast. If the armor—the Army's heaviest punch—needed the intensive effort he and the others were putting in at TFMG, what kind of shape was the rest of the Army in?

Later, during the 1977–78 school year, he studied strategic and national security issues with students from the other services and from civilian agencies of the government at the National War College at Fort McNair in Washington, D.C. That year included intense studies of the Middle East, such as a trip in which he personally saw the 1973 battlefields with both Israeli and Egyptian escorts.

In the summer of 1978, Franks began his first stint at TRADOC, under General Starry and then under General Otis. He was there for over three years, working to develop his, and the Army's, ideas about current and future land warfare (with the emphasis on maneuver warfare). There was—additionally—a practical side: during his first eighteen months at TRADOC, he directed an office under Major General Carl Vuono that wrote requirements for future weapons systems, watched over systems already in development to make sure they got through all their decision gates on the way to procurement, and made sure the Army was able to rapidly assimilate these new and improved weapons systems in a way that increased combat power. Again, the mix of ideas and practice that so characterized his Army career. Here also was another splendid window for viewing the Army's rebirth.

From the other side of the desk (from 1985 to 1987), now–Major General Franks was deputy commandant of the Command and General Staff College (CGSC) at Fort Leavenworth. As deputy commandant, Franks not only ran the college on a day-to-day basis but set long-term policy goals. It was like being chancellor and president all rolled into one.

He was glad to be there, for it was both the intellectual center for tactical thought and a great crossroads of the Army. He liked to teach and to throw ideas around in discussions about the profession of arms: ideas about command, war fighting, maneuver, fighting deep, team building, soldiers . . . ideas that have appeared in many guises throughout this book.

At West Point and afterward, he did the normal professional reading and liked to experiment with new ideas and innovations. He realized how much personal study and reading it took to be a serious, professional soldier, and was further inspired by the examples of soldiers such as Creighton Abrams, Bill DePuy, and Donn Starry. These men linked hard-nosed, professional soldiering with forward-looking ideas; and, so armed, they helped to begin to lead the Army back from Vietnam.

Later, when Franks commanded the 11th ACR, General Bo Williams paid him a compliment that has stayed with him since: "You're a soldier with ideas," Williams told him, "but you're also a very practical soldier, who always figures out how to execute the ideas before you raise them."

On Christmas Eve, 1986, while Franks was deputy commandant of CGSC, he learned that he was to be appointed the first J7 on the Joint Staff. The Goldwater-Nichols Act required generals to have joint-duty experience before they could become a CINC or serve as a general in a joint assignment. Since Franks was what was called a "joint-duty lacker," he needed such an assignment. He was not, however, thrilled to take this new job. Now at age fifty, he was, in fact, devastated to leave CGSC in the middle of the school year to be going to a staff assignment in the Pentagon.

But of course he went, because that's what soldiers do.

As J7, his official title was director of operational plans and interoperability. That meant that he and his new staff were responsible for the worldwide war plans of all the Unified Commands and for promoting improved interoperability among all the uniformed services. Or, more simply, his job was to make sure that in their joint missions, the Army, Navy, Air Force, and Marines worked well together. . . . Not easy. It was three months after enactment of Goldwater-Nichols, and the climate was hostile. The services did not like what was happening to their authority, and Franks was a junior major general on a three-star staff who was trying to start up a new agency.

At that time, there was no joint doctrine, joint doctrine program, or joint requirements system. There also was no lessons-learned system—to learn from mistakes so that corrective action could be taken next time. There was a joint exercise program, but it had no basis in mission tasks. In other words, there was no system for analyzing worldwide missions, then determining joint tasks, and then setting up an exercise program to practice those tasks.

In other words, his goal was to form a kind of joint equivalent of the Army's TRADOC.

That didn't happen completely, but Franks and his staff did have some successes—coming up, for example, with a means to analyze joint Mission-Essential Tasks, which became the basis for the yearly joint exercise programs; beginning a joint doctrine program; and publishing the first joint doctrine. They also helped General Bob Herres establish the Joint Requirements Oversight Council to better define new systems requirements that fit more than one service.

In the spring of 1988, General Vuono managed to get a waiver for Franks that asserted he was now "joint qualified" and so rescued Franks from what should have been a three-year tour of duty. Franks was now to assume command of the 1st Armored Division in the middle of July, and a year later he would become a lieutenant general commander of VII Corps. It was in that position that he would encounter the greatest challenge of his life.

If we can begin to understand what he and the Army went through in the deserts of Iraq and Kuwait from 24 to 28 February 1991, however, we will first have to understand one thing.

If Fred Franks can be said to have a single focus, it's armored cavalry . . . *always* the cavalry: maneuver, not just force, but moving force, hitting from sometimes unexpected directions. He has spent a lifetime growing and developing his knowledge and skills in maneuver warfare, and that is what brought him through Desert Storm. And that is what we come to now: the art of maneuver warfare.

6

MANEUVER WARFARE

Maneuver warfare is all about moving powerful mounted formations to gain an advantage over an enemy force to defeat or destroy them. How that is done has undergone significant evolution in the twentieth century, up to and including Desert Storm. It will continue to evolve. The thoughts that follow represent the distillation of the experience and wisdom about maneuver warfare and mobile armored formations that Fred Franks has spent the better part of a professional lifetime acquiring:

★ South of Chancellorsville, Virginia, predawn, 2 May 1862, at a planning meeting between General Robert E. Lee and General Thomas "Stonewall" Jackson:

"What do you propose to do?" Lee asked.

"Go around here."

"What do you propose to make the movement with?"

"With my whole corps."

"And what will you leave me?"

"The divisions of McLaws and Anderson."

"Well, go on," Lee said.

Lee's "Well, go on" set off as grand a maneuver as has taken place in the history of the U.S. military. At a little after 0700 that same morning, Stonewall Jackson began moving his corps of almost 32,000 soldiers and over 100 artillery pieces twelve miles along the covered route of Furnace Road to Brock Road across the front of two Union corps. His movement would put his corps on both sides of the Old Orange Turnpike, facing east in a position of great advantage to attack into the now-exposed west flank of the Union XI Corps, who were facing generally south. Jackson's attack at a little after 1700 that afternoon caught the Union XI Corps completely by surprise and set off a chain of events that led four days later to Union general Joseph Hooker's quitting the field and moving his numerically superior army back north.

Normally, a tactical envelopment requires both a fixing force and an enveloping force. The fixing force holds the enemy in place while the other force maneuvers and envelops the enemy. In this case, Lee was left to fix Hooker with McLaws's and Anderson's divisions, while Jackson commanded the enveloping force.

In the history of warfare, the two warring sides have always tried to gain such positional advantage over each other. The reason is quite simple. Hit the other side from an unexpected direction with enough strength that he cannot recover, and you will soon own the initiative and then the battlefield.

Battle is chaos on a grand scale, with chance occurring continually. What you are trying to do as a commander is keep the enemy in this chaos, while operating with some sense of order and cohesion on your own side. You try to place your soldiers in an advantageous position where they can physically outfight the enemy. But in placing them in such an advantageous position, you are also outthinking the enemy commander—as Lee and Jackson outthought Hooker at Chancellorsville. You are trying to give the enemy more problems to solve in a given time than he and his organization can possibly handle. You are trying to run him out of options, and thus force him to fight you on your terms. Then you physically defeat or destroy him.

Combat is the application of physical force. Yet brute force applied directly against brute force is usually not the most effective application of physical force, and will soon wear down the attacker to the point where he cannot continue. Consequently, the aim of commanders is to maneuver and thereby gain positional advantage that puts the enemy into chaos and keeps him there by repeated blows until he quits or you own the area.

Thus, it is not only forms of mobility that make successful maneuver warfare. It is using whatever form of mobility is available to move forces to positions of advantage. From there you can then overwhelm the enemy with a series of repeated blows. Forms of mobility are important only as they move the attacker to those positions of advantage, and as they give the attacker relative advantage over the defender.

HISTORY

Evolution of Mounted Warfare

There have been many means of movement to these positions of advantage. Each of these has been adapted continually to remain useful, or else it has been discarded. For example, excellent training, discipline, and physical conditioning of soldiers on foot have given them a relative advantage over their battlefield enemies in many historical situations, and even today on some terrain.

Recent history is full of examples of the advantages gained in maneuver. In May 1940, German attacks into France across the Meuse River and on to the Atlantic coast allowed German armored forces to swiftly position themselves between major elements of the the Allied forces, forcing evacuation of British forces from Dunkirk and creating the opportunity to defeat the now-outnumbered French forces to the south. In 1941–42, Rommel's repeated flank attacks to the south of British Eighth Army defenses in the Western Desert led to the continued collapse of British positions almost up to Alexandria, Egypt. The maneuver of the Japanese fleet to a position north of Hawaii to attack Pearl Harbor on 7 December 1941 is another example. Yet the Japanese inability to follow up their initial success gave no staying power to the initial chaos caused by the attack. In September 1950, MacArthur's landing of U.S. X Corps at Inchon, Korea, put a major allied force well behind the North Korean forces and astride their logistics routes, and sped the destruction of that army in the field. Later, in the Vietnam War, refusal by our own government to permit land, sea, and air forces to maneuver to positions to cut off the flow of men and material from North Vietnam to South Vietnam lengthened that conflict and led ultimately to loss of South Vietnam by its physical occupation from the North. In October 1973, the Israeli crossing of the Suez to position a major force to operate well inside Egypt was a key factor in ending the brief but lethal war Israel fought with Egypt and Syria. Simultaneous air assault and airborne maneuvers by elements of XVIII Corps on the night of 20 December 1989 put them in positions to rapidly isolate and physically defeat Panamanian forces in less than forty-eight hours. These examples point to various forms of movement, foot-mobile infantry, tanks, ships, and aircraft, employed on land, sea, or air to gain positional advantage over the defender.

Forms of ground mobility have gone through several changes. The horse and the various formations of what we know as cavalry once gave skilled commanders a shock effect to the immediate battle, as horse-mounted soldiers swiftly attacked less mobile formations. These commanders soon found cavalry also useful for longer-range operations and missions, such as positioning in the enemy rear, then attacking his homeland. One notable example was Colonel B. H. Grierson's cavalry raid from La Grange, Tennessee, through Mississippi, to Baton Rouge, Louisiana, from 17 April to 2 May 1863, during the American Civil War. (This was the Grierson who went on to command the 10th Cavalry, Buffalo Soldiers, in campaigns in the Southwest following the Civil War.) With 1,700 troopers of 6th and 7th Illinois and 2nd Iowa Cavalry, Grierson's deep-attacking force, according to *Harper's Pictorial History of the Civil War*, "in sixteen days traversed 800 miles of hostile territory, destroying railroad bridges, transportation, commissary stores, paroling a large number of prisoners, and destroying 3,000 stand of arms, at a cost of only twenty-seven men."

The arrival of rapid-firing rifles, machine guns, and more powerful, longer-range, accurate artillery soon called into question these horse-mobile formations in the increasingly deadly killing grounds of the close-combat battle. The idea of gaining a positional advantage, and the disruption it could bring to the coherence of an enemy formation, still had wide appeal, but the mobility to accomplish this was compromised, and then stopped, by the deadly fires of machine guns and artillery. Hence the stalemates of World War I. Not many battles of position. Just battles of brute force against brute force, hurling masses of men at each other in an attempt to break the firepower stranglehold of the other side. The cost in casualties, simply to gain and control even minor pieces of the enemy's real estate, became unacceptable. The result was the incredible human cost of World War I—8 million dead.

Military thinkers, especially in Britain, Germany, and Russia, looked for ways to restore maneuver to a battlefield that had evolved to gridlock.

What to do? The solution lay in developing mobile protected firepower, and then organizing these capabilities into formations that could operate with speed and combat efficiency on a battlefield dominated by defensive firepower. This became possible because of technology already available and in use during the early twentieth century, marking a convenient convergence of military war-fighting ideas and available technology.

Major technology available at the time included the internal-combustion engine, caterpillar-type tracked laying vehicles, wireless radios, and the airplane. The internal-combustion engine led, of course, to a transition from horse-drawn or steam-driven mobility in the civilian sector to power provided by these new engines to a wheeled base for mobility. Heavier vehicles that had to travel over unimproved ground, such as farmland and construction sites, soon turned to machines known as caterpillar crawlers or tracked laying vehicles. Though earlier versions of these caterpillar vehicles had been steam driven, new possibilities arose with the internal-combustion engine. Around 1908, it was demonstrated that a heavy vehicle could be mounted on two oval "tracks." Connecting these tracks to the power output of the internal-combustion engine propelled the vehicle over the ground. The vehicle crawled like a caterpillar, or rather the tracks were laid out on the ground for the vehicle to ride over.

Enter the tank, an effective combination of protection for the crew, mobility to move relatively quickly about the battlefield, and sufficient firepower to destroy enemy machines like theirs.

Unfortunately, early tanks did not work as well as their developers intended. Significant technical problems plagued their early designs, especially during World War I. Not the least of these were difficulties with crew-machine interaction (what modern-day designers call ergonomics) and a reliable track and suspension system.

It was a case where the ideas endured long enough for the the technology to catch up. This is not always so, but it was in this case.

Back on the battlefield, now with tanks roaming over it, another piece had to be added, to prevent more chaos. That piece was voice communications. In an attack on the enemy, in order to permit some semblance of continuing organizational coherence, soldiers in tanks needed a means to talk to other tanks. Without such voice communications, it would prove difficult to impossible to keep coherent hundreds of noisy, tracked vehicles moving at various speeds over broken ground. At best, major formations of armored vehicles would have to rely on visual signals in order to remain grouped together, and would have to stop frequently to dismount and talk among themselves to change or adjust orders. Lacking the coherence gained from some kind of fast, dependable communication, the attacker would not be able to physically mass firepower when needed, or to change direction or type of maneuver.

By the late 1920s, wireless radios capable of line-of-sight transmission would permit individual tank commanders to communicate with each other and with their larger unit commanders. Such a breakthrough would allow control of attacking formations without the continuing need to halt, dismount, and communicate. Continuous operations would now be possible, as would the ability to adjust tactics rapidly, while retaining relative order and coherence of attacking formations.

Other wider-ranging possibilities soon became apparent to military theorists. For instance, they quickly saw that indirect fire support could come from longer-range artillery units in formations positioned to the rear of the immediate battle area. Target information transmissions from frontline mounted tankers would allow these units to deliver volumes of accurate and deadly fire in support of tank attacks.

Meanwhile, airpower advocates were discovering that the third dimension of airspace could provide external combat support. They recognized that the skies above the battlefield provided a positional advantage and an attack direction that could produce effects similar to cavalry, both in close-in battles and deeper in the enemy's rear. Observers on the ground looking at enemy targets could pass on the enemy location to aviators via radio. The aviators would then attack the enemy from the air, and further introduce chaos to the enemy. This concept was first used with devastating battlefield effect by the Germans with their Stukas, from 1939 to 1942, and later by Allied forces, notably U.S. ground and air forces of Third Army and 19th Air Force in 1944–45.

Theories

Three breakthrough war-fighting ideas significantly influenced the early design and experiments with mounted armored formations in the 1920s and 1930s.

• The first has become known as all arms or combined arms. According to all-arms theory, all combat, combat support, and combat service support functions should be mounted and be immediately available to the mounted commander. This would create a self-contained mobile force, with its own tanks, infantry, artillery, engineers, signal, and logistics (such as trucks for fuel, ammunition, food, and spare parts). Such an all-arms approach allowed the mounted commander to devise a variety of combinations of forces from within his own basic organization. Using these, he could exploit opportunities in changing battle situations without the need to constantly stop and reorganize. Skilled commanders could then conduct operations at a tempo of attack that brought them to positions where they presented the enemy with more situations than he could possibly handle in a given time and space. In this way, the initiative lost in the firepower-dominated battlefields of World War I was regained.

• The second of these theories held that mounted formations would attack dismounted or less mobile units, break through their front lines, then operate in their rear, destroying artillery, command posts, and logistics. Using the metaphor of a small penetrating stream that swiftly swelled into a flood, British theorist B. H. Liddell Hart named this theory the "expanding torrent." According to Hart's theory, the penetrating tank attack would have the effect of first destroying the initial line and eventually of collapsing the front. . . .

Some later critics questioned whether Hart's theory was truly innovative, or whether it was merely an adaptation of the infiltration tactics adopted by both sides to break the deadly trench warfare grip on opposing forces mainly on the western front. In fact, many theories, and many tactics, were tried by military professionals to break this grip. By war's end, they had used every technology available at the time—not only armored forces, infiltration tactics, and air, but also, of course, chemical warfare. Original or not, theories such as Hart's became important for the inspiration they gave to later experiments in restoring the maneuver option. Hart was one of many such theorists, albeit one of the more prolific, readable, and influential writers. Other practitioners worked less noticeably in field experiments with the same goal.

• Third: In battle, it was now considered possible to fight both close and deep. This concept of a battlefield of much greater depth was proposed by Russian theorists, notably Tuchachevsky, in the 1930s. (It must be noted that many ideas were being rapidly exchanged between theorists in England, Russia, and Germany at this time.) Tuchachevsky theorized that it was possible with operational maneuver groups and air to create a zone of attack where you would simultaneously fight close and deep in the enemy rear, unlike during World War I, where units slugged it out along a line. "Our technical equipment," he wrote in 1937, "enables us to put pressure on the enemy not only directly on the line of the front, but also to break through his disposition and attack to the full depth of the battle formation."

Such theories would ironically see their greatest advocates in the early to mid-1980s in the U.S. Army's AirLand Battle doctrine, designed to defeat the military descendants of Tuchachevsky, the Warsaw Pact.

Few new theories advance without hindrance, and such was the case with these. There were many arguments against all of them. Indeed, the arguments particularly held back newer ideas from finding a place in the U.S. Army. In the United States, the Tank Corps of World War I was disbanded, and the National Defense Act of 1920 assigned tanks to the infantry. The doctrine that the tank "is designed to assist the advance of the infantry and the tank service is a branch of the infantry" lasted until 1930. Even as late as 1930, the newly appointed Army Chief of Staff, General Douglas MacArthur, would continue assigning tanks to assist various existing military branches, rather than use them in ways that would be truly militarily useful. In his own words, "The infantry will give attention to machines to increase the striking power of the infantry against strongly held positions." Liddell Hart, always impatient with the propensity among much of the military to lock itself into the status quo, would write about such attitudes, "The most difficult thing with a military mind is not getting a new idea in, it is getting the old idea out."

In defense of the U.S. Army, we should point out that during the Depression, it had a strength of only a little over 100,000 men, it had little money for research and development, it thought as the nation did that another major war was not in its immediate future, and it was anyhow busy with CCC projects and assisting in maintaining federal law and order. (Today we call these last "Operations Other Than War.") The cavalry at Fort Riley even wanted to keep its horses. In other words, the context of the times did not help leaders look much to the future.

Meanwhile, land battles in Europe and Africa saw increasing application of new tank and other mechanized technologies employed in battlefield tactics derived from the three war-fighting theories. Spectacularly, the German Wehrmacht stunned the world with their lightning "blitzkrieg" attacks into Poland in 1939, France in 1940, and Russia in 1941. And Rommel's brilliant flanking maneuvers in North Africa in 1941–42 stunned the world yet again.

The Wehrmacht's expert use of both battle in depth and all arms—including air, rapid penetration, and envelopment using mounted forces—not only came as a great surprise to the defenders, it also restored maneuver to the European battlefield lost in World War I. Later, in 1943, British and Soviet formations would apply similar methods and score successes against the same Wehrmacht in both North Africa and Russia. The U.S. Army came to adopt these new theories late, and as a consequence suffered a serious defeat against German forces at Kasserine Pass in Tunisia in February 1943. Learning and adapting swiftly, however, by 1944–45, U.S. armor forces under Patton and others in France and Germany were as expert practitioners of maneuver warfare as any in World War II.

Unlike the Germans, the U.S. Army did not form armored corps or armored armies. They relied instead on the basic division formation for armored forces. Two or more armored divisions could be found in corps during World War II, but at no time did U.S. planners form a totally armored corps for a deep thrust as envisioned by the interwar theorists, choosing short tactical thrusts instead. Even so, U.S. forces were all to a certain extent mobile, given the availability of truck transport.

The large-scale armor successes in World War II, together with the continuing influence of the leaders of armored maneuver formations, would cause maneuver theories and their application in equipment and formations to dominate thinking up through the 1960s and into the early 1970s. Swift battlefield victories by Israel, first in 1956 and then again in 1967, reinforced these ideas.

Transition

Many new maneuver war-fighting ideas and theories were advanced and tried following World War II, mostly experiments with forms of movement and organizational changes. Some methods developed in World War II continued. In Korea, for instance, maneuver played a large role, as troops came from the sea at Inchon in an amphibious assault. U.S. forces were mainly foot and truck mobile north, and tanks mainly supported infantry in up to battalion-sized formations, since the terrain did not permit major mounted maneuver.

In 1956, the U.S. Army experimented with and then adopted what was called the "pentomic" division, a radically new organizational design to allow freedom of action and maneuver options on what was anticipated as a nuclear battlefield. This doctrine was abandoned in1962 for a return to more evolutionary methods of combining all arms in a division, while retaining the maneuver option.

Mounted soldiers and units played a big role in U.S. tactical victories in Vietnam. The largest ground-mounted unit in that war was the 11th ACR,

Blackhorse, which was skillfully employed over a large area of operations in a wide variety of typical mounted missions to inflict heavy losses on Viet Cong and North Vietnamese units. It was not only able to reposition quickly to continually gain positional advantage over North Vietnamese units, it also had a large firepower advantage when finding and fixing enemy forces in the battles that followed.

The most significant innovation in warfare of that generation was initiated in that war, with the introduction by the U.S. Army of army aviation as a maneuver element. First, with experiments at Fort Benning, then later in combat in Vietnam with the 1st Cavalry Division, the U.S. Army pioneered air assault and the use of the third dimension in ground maneuver warfare. The creation of some pioneer theorists and tacticians in the 1950s and early 1960s, air assault and attack aviation led to new thinking and new dimensions of maneuver warfare that the U.S. Army would practice with newer technology during Desert Storm.

The 1967 war in the Middle East demonstrated once again the deadly linkage of tank forces with tactical air when combined in a series of mutually supporting actions.

Yet even as all these events were playing out, and as both NATO and the Warsaw Pact fielded more powerful and capable mounted forces through the early to mid-1960s, a change was taking place that threatened the continued existence of maneuver on the battlefield.

The change most clearly made its presence felt not in Europe, but in the 1973 war in the Mideast.

On the Jewish holy day of Yom Kippur, 1973, Egyptian and Syrian forces made surprise attacks into Sinai and the Golan with new weapons and new combinations of forces. The introduction in a big way of the SAGGAR missile, combined with an effective air defense umbrella, allowed attacking Egyptian and Syrian forces to gain a series of initial advantages, and in the case of the Egyptians, to inflict heavy losses on some counterattacking Israeli units. For the first time, this broke the Israeli air-ground team. The Israelis fought outnumbered on defense, and after heavy losses themselves but heavier losses on the attackers, they won engagements to go on the counterattack.

The U.S. Army took a very hard look at that war. Fighting outnumbered, and winning, was easy for that Army to identify with, considering its own situation in Central Europe.

The first and hardest lesson of the two-week '73 war was the threat to hard-won battlefield maneuverability. Tanks no longer restored the mobility lost with the demise of horse cavalry. Though the Israelis managed to restore maneuver during the war's closing days, initially, the war pitted brute force against brute force. Forces of roughly equal mobility and firepower faced each other. On the war's first day, with three divisions forward and two to follow, close to 1,000 Syrian tanks attacked Israeli positions on the Golan. A comparable number of Egyptian tanks in the Sinai attacked in formations similarly echeloned, with divisions stacked one behind the other. This echelonment permitted successive waves of mounted forces to hurl themselves at defenders, and then to wear them down and fracture the integrity of the defense. The Arab forces battered themselves against Israeli defenders much as World War I infantry formations did—with the same high cost of people and material on both sides. In both the Golan and Sinai, these attrition tactics, using waves of attacking armor, came dangerously close to breaking Israeli forces. It was only late in the two-week war that Israeli formations were able to stop advancing threat forces and have sufficient combat power to maneuver to positions of advantage on the west bank of the Suez and toward Damascus, east of the Golan.

Gone was Hart's expanding torrent. Instead of the light, speedy breakthrough formations envisioned in the 1920s, attacking softer targets in the enemy rear and shattering the less mobile front lines, mounted forces were now like harvesting machines in a Kansas wheat field. Formations defending front lines in 1973 had as much mobility and firepower as the mounted attacker. Although attacking formations were still capable of sweeping deep to attack vulnerable enemy capabilities there, it was apparent they must also now be principally designed and used as the forces to close with and destroy an equally powerful defending enemy force.

Forces roughly equal in firepower and mobility had been opposing each other since the early 1940s in the deserts of North Africa and on the plains of Russia, but now this was also true on virtually every terrain suitable for large mechanized formations.

Meanwhile, foot-mobile infantry was also still required, as World War II in the Pacific, Korea, and Vietnam clearly demonstrated. (To restore maneuver in Vietnam to foot-mobile infantry, U.S. Army thinkers, most notably Generals Howze and Kinnard, introduced the air cavalry and air assault formations mentioned earlier.) Even so, where mounted formations could be employed, they ruled the battle areas. It was, however, proving to be a perilous rule, for close combat of every kind had become increasingly lethal. The firepower invented to offset the mobility advantages seen in World War II— principally the antitank guided missile, attack helicopters, and tactical air with precision munitions—saw to that. Mobility and hence maneuver were once again threatened by increasingly lethal firepower.

Faced with this challenge, maneuver theorists were still able to employ all arms and depth, but with the added realization that mounted formations now had to become the principal destructive agents on the battlefield. To fill this expanded role, mounted units now required considerable firepower of their own to be able to sustain themselves in increasingly high-tempo, high-lethality battles. This increase came mainly in the following areas: air defense, deep fires (the ability to strike far into the enemy rear), some redundancy of capabilities (the ability to absorb casualties and still go on), and the ability to sustain themselves with supplies such as fuel and ammunition in those high-tempo, high-lethality battles.

U.S. Army AirLand Battle Doctrine

In the late 1970s and early 1980s, U.S. Army theorists, notably General Donn Starry, returned depth to the battlefield, but added to it.

From his studies of the '73 war, Starry had seen that the only way to counteract the density of both Syrian and Egyptian mounted attacks was to fight them close and deep at the same time. In order to defend against the echelonment doctrine of Soviet and Soviet-style forces (such as Syria and Egypt), Starry considered it necessary to bring depth back to U.S. Army doctrine. Like Syria and Egypt in '73, Soviet forces used waves of attacking echelons to ultimately overwhelm a defender by attrition at the point of attack. If the defender did not attack follow-on echelons at the same time he defended against attacking echelons, he would soon be overwhelmed. By separating the echelons and stopping the momentum of the attack, while destroying valuable or irreplaceable battle assets deep in the enemy rear, the combination of close and deep attacks would first slow down and then defeat echeloned attacks.

In Starry's view, depth meant both delivery of firepower from aerial platforms and artillery and ability of maneuver forces to occupy and control key areas by attacking vital enemy capabilities in deep ground assaults. In other words, mounted forces needed to be able to move quickly into the enemy rear (like the Israelis in their crossing of the Suez and in their armored counterattack out of the Golan toward Damascus). But in addition, they also needed to be able to target and attack deep in the enemy's rear with fires and their own attack aviation. In consequence, a mounted commander now had to see in much greater depth the battle space assigned to him to accomplish his mission.

In this effort to rethink depth, Starry was assisted by Colonels Huba Wass de Czege and Don Holder, who, as mentioned before, not only developed more fully than ever before the concept of depth, but also expanded on the important tenet of initiative, so vital to an American army, and especially to one that anticipated fighting outnumbered.

Starry and others to follow him at TRADOC, notably General Glen Otis and General Bill Richardson, gave these thoughts life in U.S. Army doctrine and capabilities. The name they gave these theories was AirLand Battle. Though the concepts included under the AirLand Battle rubric were first introduced by Starry in the U.S. Army's doctrine FM 100-5 in 1982, they were the product of study and analysis he and others had been doing since 1973.

Operational Art

One other idea resurrected from the past the U.S. Army called "operational art." In essence, successful battles and engagements had to be linked together in both time and space in the design of a campaign to achieve a larger operational objective. Achievement of that operational objective would lead to gaining the overall theater strategic objective and victory. Such theory had been routinely practiced in World War II. In other words, to achieve the theater result in Western Europe in 1944–45 of unconditional surrender, it was necessary to secure the lodgment in Normandy, conduct a breakout from there, cross the Rhine, and then finally defeat remaining German forces in their homeland from the west as Russian forces advanced from the east. Those series of major battles would together achieve the overall theater objective of German defeat.

U.S. Army writers began writing about operational art at the U.S. Army War College at Carlisle, Pennsylvania, in the early 1980s. Brigadier General Don Morelli, then chief of doctrine at TRADOC, and General Glen Otis, TRADOC commander, included the idea in the 1982 version of FM 100-5. Building on that beginning, General Bill Richardson and Lieutenant General Carl Vuono, and later Lieutenant General Bob RisCassi, expanded on those thoughts, making "operational art" a major change to the revised FM 100-5 in 1986.

After some debate on the level of command that could best handle this new doctrine on the tactical battlefields anticipated, the U.S. Army settled on the corps. The corps was selected because it was the Army's largest tactical formation that was self-contained; it had the necessary all-arms and support requirements to operate independently, and the redundancy to sustain longer-duration campaigns. Therefore, the U.S. Army corps would be self-contained and have two to five divisions in it for maneuver. It was to be different from World War II corps in that it would have its own logistics organization. Where it was necessary in NATO to employ multiple corps, NATO army groups would also practice the operational art. In that arena, corps would design a series of battles and engagements necessary to be won to achieve the operational objective assigned by the army group.

During the Cold War, it was not anticipated that the U.S. Army would fight in multicorps campaigns outside NATO. Hence there were no provisions for

U.S.-only headquarters capable of commanding two or more U.S. corps. These decisions to abandon the field army were made by Army leadership well before AirLand Battle doctrine, and were driven by NATO considerations, yet were essentially revalidated in the 1982 and 1986 versions of the U.S. Army's doctrine. Thus, in the fall of 1990, there were no provisions for a U.S.-only field army or army group headquarters.

Though the Army ran into initial problems in theater because of these last issues, AirLand Battle and operational art dominated the thinking and organization of U.S. mounted forces in Desert Storm: All arms, destructive effects on the enemy, battles in depth both by fires and maneuver, and the linkage of these battles to achieve the campaign result.

ORGANIZATION

Role of the Corps

The corps bridges the strategic and the tactical levels of war. Using land, sea, and air forces, strategy decides the overall campaign objective. The operational level then devises a campaign plan of a linked series of battles and engagements that, when fought and won, will together achieve the strategic objective. The tactical level fights these battles and engagements successfully to achieve the operational results that in turn achieve the strategic objective. The corps participates in the design of the campaign and directly conducts the tactical operations to gain the campaign objectives.

The corps is the largest land formation in the U.S. Army. It is built with a mix of units that provides the commander a wide range of options. These options derive from the variety of combinations of units that he can put together to accomplish a given mission against a given enemy on a particular piece of terrain.

A mounted corps is a team of teams. The U.S. Army calls these teams echelons of command. They begin with the smallest entity, normally an individual vehicle and its crew, then build into echelons of command such as platoons (four to six vehicles), companies (four to six platoons), battalions (four to six companies), brigades (four to six battalions), divisions (six or more brigades), and a corps (two to five divisions, with up to eight to ten non-division brigades and a cavalry regiment). At each of those echelons is an officer chain of command, with a commander and subordinates, and a noncommissioned officer network that normally places a noncommissioned officer directly subordinate to each officer. It additionally places an NCO in direct command of individual crews and sections where there is no officer. The U.S. Army uses noncommissioned officers more extensively than any other army in the world, a

1st Armored Division "Wedge"

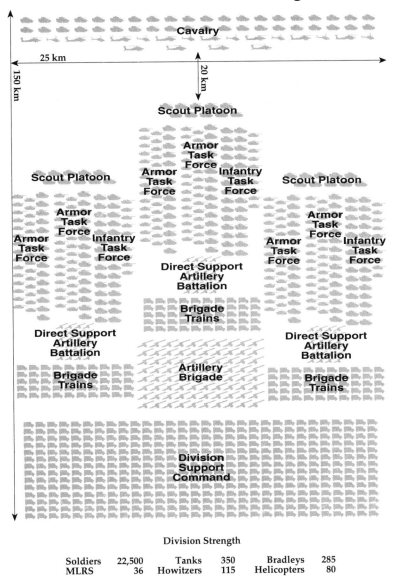

Division Strength

Soldiers	22,500	Tanks	350	Bradleys	285	
MLRS	36	Howitzers	115	Helicopters	80	

This diagram, while not accurately portraying the space between units, all the support vehicles required, or the distances between vehicles in combat, gives an indication of the type of ground equipment in a rolling armored division and the amount of combat power in this force. During Desert Storm, General Franks controlled five of these types of combat units, plus additional combat, combat-support, and combat-service-support units.

proven practice going all the way back to the Revolutionary War. It is why the NCO corps is often called the "backbone of the Army."

Each division in the corps is a carefully balanced combined-arms organization consisting of combat capabilities, direct combat-support capabilities, and logistics or combat service support, and is also a team of teams. The cavalry regiment has a similar organization. Each of the other non-division units in the corps is likewise a team of teams, with its own ability to support itself for short duration. But none of these is a balanced combined-arms organization. Rather they are single-function organizations of artillery, engineer, aviation, signal, intelligence, military police, medical, etc.

Even though all corps are different, they do have common organizational characteristics. Normally for a mounted corps, this mix of units will consist of from two to five armored and mechanized infantry divisions, usually eight to ten various non-division brigade-size units, and include armored cavalry and aviation, an artillery command of varying numbers of types of brigades, and a support command that will vary widely in terms of numbers and types of units for logistics support, depending on the theater of operation.

Tailoring a Corps

From this common organizational base, corps normally are tailored for a specific geographic theater of operations against a specific enemy. They are each tailored for their mission and anticipated use and they train for that specific purpose.

To accomplish this tailoring, the numbers and types of complete teams—or major command echelons to be included in the corps—are determined by examination of the factors of METT-T (or Mission, Enemy, Terrain, Troops available, and Time to accomplish the mission). Commanders look at these factors and compile the right mix of combat units (armored divisions, cavalry regiment, air defense, aviation brigade, artillery, and engineer), combat-support units (military police, military intelligence, and signal), and combat-service-support units (personnel, finance, medical, transportation, maintenance, supply, etc.) to give the widest range of options or combinations to accomplish anticipated missions.

Depending on the results of a particular METT-T analysis, the mix of units in a corps and their training will vary considerably. For example, a corps in Korea, given a mission there in that terrain, will be configured with units specially trained to conduct operations against the possible enemy there and on that terrain. It might have a mix of infantry, armor, and artillery quite different from a corps configured to fight on the deserts of the Persian Gulf region. During the Cold War, V and VII Corps in Germany were configured with units to operate in a NATO army group, in a relatively advanced civilian infrastructure of roads, railroads, and communications, on terrain that offered few restrictions to armored movement, and against the Warsaw Pact modernized armor formations. During Desert Storm, VII Corps was built sequentially as it arrived in the theater unit by unit, tailoring it for that theater and the mission there. Only approximately 42,000 of the VII Corps's 146,000 soldiers of Desert Storm had been in the NATO VII Corps. VII Corps was complete in theater only at the end of the first week in February, two weeks before the ground attack. It was only in the final move to attack positions on 14 to 16 February that Fred Franks had the one and only opportunity to train and maneuver that corps as a corps in the conduct of what would be a complex maneuver a week later to destroy the Republican Guards Forces Command.

Most differences between corps will be in the type of combat units involved (tank, infantry, artillery), support required (communications, engineers, etc.), and logistics (trucks, fuel, ammunition, medical, etc.). Each of these different corps will train according to its specific mission. That will include practicing with various combinations of units to ensure they can operate together.

Working with this basic mix of units, the commander then decides how to array them in time, space, and distance to focus combat power continually on the enemy in a moving zone about 150 kilometers wide and 175 kilometers deep. (The width and depth are functions of the terrain over which you are operating and the enemy forces you face—sometimes you are more condensed and sometimes you can expand even farther.) In other words, you begin with a basic mix of units in the corps that gives you the widest range of options against a particular enemy on a piece of terrain. It is then the commander's job to use effectively the power available to him by arranging those units in such a way that the right combination of units will be at the right place at the right time. And he will either keep them that way or will change the combination as needed to suit changing situations during the series of battles he chooses to fight to accomplish the campaign objective.

A commander also has to look at some inescapable physical realities. For example, each of the close to 1,600 tanks in VII Corps in Desert Storm was capable of firing a projectile at more than a kilometer a second over a range in excess of 3.5 kilometers and destroying whatever it hit. So on a relatively flat desert in confined space, you want to ensure that each of these 1,600 units is pointed in the right direction. Otherwise some of the fire, inadvertently, might not be directed at the enemy but at your own troops. In the desert, for example, on a corps front 150 kilometers wide with all 1,600 tanks on line (not a high probability), you would have a tank every 100 meters. Direction of attack and spacing between units become especially important in such a confined space.

Other inescapable physical realities involve continued support of such a large, moving organization. In VII Corps on Desert Storm, there were almost 50,000 vehicles and close to 800 helicopters, and some 20 fixed-wing two-engine intelligence-gathering aircraft. They needed fuel. Daily fuel consumption was about 2.5 million gallons of diesel for ground vehicles and about half that much aviation fuel for aircraft. With their turbine engines switched on, tanks use the same amount of fuel, moving or stopped. The rule of thumb was to refuel tanks every eight hours. After one refueling, the fuel trucks accompanying units would have to travel to a resupply point, fill up with fuel, then return to their units. Meanwhile, while the fuel trucks were resupplying, their units were moving away in the opposite direction from the resupply run. In medium to heavy enemy contact, the corps used about 2,500 tons of ammunition a day. Normally, tanks and other direct-fire systems carried enough ammunition to last them several days, so they did not need immediate resupply. On the other hand, artillery and mortars firing at a much higher rate required resupply from accompanying trucks. These would then have to make the same resupply runs as the fuel trucks. Some corps units also needed places to operate from—airfields, forward operating bases (for helicopters), staging areas (for logistics support, etc.). This required some real estate management and some need for roads (even in the desert), and priorities had to be established for use of those areas and roads.

PRINCIPLES OF APPLICATION

Orders and Intent

Since, as stated earlier, battle is chaos on a grand scale, with chance intervening continually, you try to create chaos for the enemy by giving him more situations than he can handle in a given time frame and to keep him in that state. At the same time you must keep a certain amount of control and focus on your own operation.

To create and instill this sense of order to their own side, commanders use "intent" and "orders." They then rely first on the disciplined translation and then on the execution of these by each echelon in their organization. In other words, at each succeeding echelon of command—corps, division, brigade, battalion, company—that commander must understand what the next higher commander ordered, then figure out what his echelon must do to accomplish his part in the overall mission. The idea here is not to stifle initiative in subordinate echelons, but to ensure unity of effort in the entire organization and maximum use of available combat power.

To attain this unity of effort through intent and orders, there is communication, both written and oral. After communication, interpretation and problem solving follow, at each echelon of command, to determine what has to be done at that echelon. During this process, commanders allow room for their subordinates to exercise initiative and to operate with the freedom to adjust to local conditions (in those cases where these local adjustments don't also require adjustments by the whole organization). This need to adjust to local conditions is both the reason why there are so many command echelons and why U.S. Army doctrine demands that each of these exercise local initiative. All this takes time. If orders are not clear, or if they are constantly changing, it takes more time.

In VII Corps, Fred Franks's order as corps commander had to be received by division commanders. Once it was received, each of them had to understand and then decide what they needed to do to comply with it. Then they would translate Franks's order both into their own words and into terms that fit their particular situation. As soon as this was done, they would pass the order to their subordinate echelons. This process would be repeated at each echelon until all members of the corps had their orders.

A commander's "intent" is quite simply his vision of how he sees the operation working out. It is his concise expression of the means, of the end, of the main effort, and of the risks he is prepared to take. Because of its importance in putting the commander's personal stamp on the operation, commanders usually write the intent themselves. Often in battle, if a commander's intent is well understood, subordinate commanders can continue to operate even in the absence of written orders or when communications break down. Late on 27 February 1991, Lieutenant Colonel Bob Wilson and the 1st Squadron, 4th Cavalry, in the 1st INF Division lost communications with his higher headquarters. But because Wilson understood division's and corps' intent of earlier that morning, he and his squadron continued to attack east across Highway 8 between Basra and Kuwait City, where they captured large numbers of prisoners.

An "order" takes that intent and lays out the complete written set of instructions for the entire operation. It is a formal publication that is normally written by the staff using decisions by the commander that contains the commander's intent, a more detailed concept of the operation, and a detailed list of instructions to each of the subordinate echelons, which they in turn use to do their own plan. The order normally has a number of annexes that detail how the combat-support and combat-service-support units will harmonize their operations according to the commander's intent. Characteristically, it is long.

The organization of an order in the U.S. Army follows a five-paragraph organization originated at the turn of the twentieth century. These five paragraphs are:

1. enemy situation, friendly situation, and attachments and detachments in terms of organizations of the major unit;
2. mission;
3. operations—including a concept for the major unit, a concept for maneuver, a concept for fires to include a whole fires annex, a detailed list of tasks to subordinate units, and a list of major coordinating instructions;
4. logistics;
5. command and signal (i.e., the command arrangements), including key radio frequencies for command radio nets and succession of command in case of death or evacuation of the commander.

Annexes will include details of intelligence, engineer, signal, airspace command and control, air defense, logistics, and any other special considerations, such as psychological operations, special operating forces, and deception operations. A complete corps order might total 200 or more pages, complete with graphic drawings and overlays to depict unit boundaries, phase lines, and objective areas used as control measures to ensure coherence of the operation. At more senior tactical echelons, such as brigade, division, and corps, it is also the practice in the U.S. Army to include a matrix—called a "synchronization matrix"—that seeks to synchronize all major activities with battlefield events and time.

In order to achieve focused energy, each subordinate plan must be in harmony with the plan of the next higher echelon. General Bill DePuy used to call such harmonized plans "nested concepts." In U.S. Army doctrine, enough variance is permitted, even demanded, at each subordinate echelon so that commanders can exercise their own initiative as situations develop in their area of operations. Yet, in order to achieve the necessary cohesion in the chaos that is land battle, this initiative must always be exercised within the overall intent of the higher headquarters. Determining how much leeway to allow subordinate echelons is a matter of command judgment, and it is influenced by many factors, including the complexity of the mission, the size of the operating area, and the personality and capabilities of subordinate commanders. Nonetheless, to take full advantage of the leadership and talent available in soldiers and leaders, and thus reach full combat potential, initiative is required and demanded in U.S. Army doctrine.

When VII Corps received an order from its next higher echelon (Third Army in Desert Storm), the corps would make its own analysis and devise its own plan, then issue that plan to the corps as an order in the format described above. This process would have to be repeated seven times to reach a tank crew in one of the divisions in VII Corps. All this, of course, takes time. The rule of thumb in the Army is that you should use one-third of the available time yourself and allow your subordinates to use the other two-thirds. This gives your subordinates time to figure out their own actions (which can be rather complex in and of themselves: a division has about 8,000 vehicles and in Desert Storm had up to 22,000 soldiers), to issue their own orders to their echelons (normally in writing and with sketches and map diagrams), to do some war gaming and other preliminary testing to ensure the plan will work, and then to conduct some rehearsals to ensure that all commanders understand what is expected of them and their organizations. Sometimes these rehearsals suggest changes to the plan.

In a corps the size of VII Corps, the rule of thumb is that this entire process takes as much as seventy-two hours to travel from the commander down to, say, a tank crew. In other words, from the time Franks got his orders from his own next higher echelon (in Desert Storm, Third Army), the orders process was done seven times before that tank crew started moving toward its new objective.

In an attempt to remove as much chance of misunderstanding as possible, this communications process of intent and orders has been refined over the years. Military terms are used, each with a specific meaning, and maps and other graphic symbols are also used, each with its own specific meaning. In spite of this, normal human dynamics, chance occurrences, and enemy actions lead to misinterpretations, and these are often exacerbated by dynamics of fatigue, physical danger, and on occasion by personality and character distortions. In his great classic, *On War*, the German theorist Clausewitz called the cumulative effect of all this "friction." Such "friction" is quite simply a code word for everything that gets in the way of perfect understanding and perfect execution. Some elements of friction are physical and external, such as effects of weather on soldiers and material, cold, heat, sandstorms, light, or lack of it. Others are human, such as fatigue, imprecise language and thus misinterpretation, personality traits of various commanders, etc. Some others are due purely to the kinds of chance events that inevitably occur when so many people and machines operate in confined spaces: map-reading errors, wrong turns, breakdown of key equipment, unexpected enemy actions, etc. Commanders try to be aware of all of these and to minimize their effects.

Since the entire process of battle command—problem solving, dissemination of the solution, and actual physical execution—tends to take a long time, commanders are always looking for ways to reduce that time. They also look to minimize friction, in order to ensure that their own organization can make necessary battle adjustments faster than the enemy. Franks and his commanders worked and drilled this hard in VII Corps.

Battle is always two-sided. As you are working on your problem, your enemy is working on the same problem you are and has his own solution. Thus, while you want to begin with a basic plan or idea of what you want to get done, you always have to tell yourself that plans are never static. Your enemy—and friction—will see to that. That is why plans frequently change after contact with the enemy is made.

After that, you are literally in a fight. In battle, you and the enemy are each constantly looking for the edge to win. You are each looking to gain the initiative. Often it is the side that can adjust most rapidly that will eventually gain the initiative and go on to win. You and your commanders try to outthink the enemy commanders, and thus give your troops all the advantages to outfight the enemy. You try to give him more problems to solve in a given time than he and his organization can possibly handle. You try to run him out of options, break the coherence of his operation, and thus force him to fight you on your terms. Then you physically defeat or destroy him.

Senior commanders must therefore decide far enough in advance of a planned action for their subordinate echelons to do their own problem solving, communicate the solution, and execute it. One of the greatest skills of senior commanders is the ability to forecast. The more senior you are, the farther into the future you have to force yourself to look. You must be able to see beyond what others see. You must be involved in the present to know what is going on, but you must also discipline yourself to leave those actions for your subordinates to handle while you forecast the next battle, and the one after that. And at the same time, you must see that all of these battles are linked in purpose. Then you must decide—leaving sufficient time for subordinates to react both intellectually and physically.

—Intellectually, so they can do their own problem solving and communication to their organizations;

—Physically, so they can get the right combination at the right place at the right time, and with soldiers and units motivated and fit for battle.

Smart commanders share their thoughts. They think "out loud." In the Army, there are terms, and even procedures, for this. For instance, commanders can give subordinates a "heads-up"—"this is what I am thinking of doing"—to put their subordinates into their own head space. A "heads-up" requires no action. They can also issue a "warning order," which does require action. A "warning order" is a shorthand but official communication that tells a subordinate, "I will order your unit to do the following; I'll send the formal, more detailed order shortly."

Once they have forecast and decided, senior commanders must resist the temptation to tinker at the margin of orders they've issued. Tinkering will only contradict and confuse the process. (An emergency caused by an unexpected opportunity or an unexpected enemy action requiring immediate action to preserve the force will of course require a change in orders.) Orders issued are difficult to impossible to retrieve, especially when units and leaders are tired and in physical danger. So decide, make it stick, and leave it alone.

Yet adjustments are necessary, so commanders can and do plan ahead to give themselves and their subordinates choices during changeable situations. For example, if the enemy stands still, you do one thing. If he retreats before you, you do another. If he moves toward you, you do something else. If he tries to maneuver around you, you do still something else. In such cases, you want to be able to make adjustments without going through an entire seventy-two-hour cycle. These adjustments frequently resemble the "audibles" used in football. When a quarterback looks over the defense and sees a situation that's different from what he anticipated when he called the original play, he can call an "audible"—a play from a previously rehearsed list of possibilities. Commanders also develop "plays" to call in certain anticipated future situations. The formal name for these in doctrine is "branches and sequels." (Branches are variances off the original plan; sequels are follow-on actions to continue the original plan.) In VII Corps in Desert Storm, the branches and sequels were called FRAGPLANs. These FRAGPLANs were each contingent on a future battlefield situation. You forecast the future. If it looks like this, you adjust to do this. Meanwhile, each of your echelons will also have developed its own set of FRAGPLANs for execution when or if you call one of yours. No forecast will ever be perfect, so at best some minor adjustments are normally required.

Missions

Missions for a mounted corps are normally either terrain or force oriented. The corps will take certain actions principally to occupy or defend terrain, or else they will take other actions principally to defeat or destroy enemy forces. These types of missions are not mutually exclusive, but they are fundamentally different. In NATO, for example, VII Corps had the mission of defending NATO territory. To do that they had to defeat any enemy force that came into their area . . . and maybe even attack to throw such a force out. But the main aim was preservation of territory. Defeat or destruction of the enemy force was a means to that end. Theoretically, if no enemy had come into their area, they could have gone elsewhere to help someone else. In the offense, terrain orientation means that you want possession of what is called key terrain. If you have key terrain and deny it to the enemy, that will contribute to the defeat of the enemy by giving you positions of advantage. Many times, of course, the enemy has the same appreciation of key terrain that you do and will do his best to occupy it or fight you for it. In that case, you'll have to attack that enemy force in order to occupy or otherwise control the ground.

Korea was a good example of terrain orientation on the 38th Parallel. After Chinese intervention and the beginnings of armistice talks, UN forces attacked to gain ground that would put them on or above the 38th Parallel and thus restore the original Korean status quo. In the Gulf War, XVIII Corps had a terrain orientation to interdict Highway 8, in order to prevent Iraqi forces from reinforcing from Baghdad or escaping the Kuwaiti theater to Baghdad. Their mission was to get to Highway 8 fast. Enemy forces were a target only as they got in the way of interdicting Highway 8. Since in fact few enemy forces stood in their way, and since their terrain orientation gave them a fixed geographic spot to reach, measuring how fast they traveled from their start point to Highway 8 made eminent sense.

Force orientation is another matter. In a force-oriented mission your essential task is to aim your force at the enemy force in a posture and in a direction that allows you to accomplish your mission at least cost to your troops. Except that it must be negotiated to get to the enemy, terrain is not of much consequence. Sometimes that is a real problem, requiring considerable effort in the use of bridges and limited road networks, and in bad weather. A mission to conduct a force-oriented attack is time- and space-independent until the commander assigns an area within which to conduct the mission and then adds time or distance constraints if they are required. Though you will have to cover space in order to close with and defeat or destroy the enemy force you are aiming at, your orientation does not directly depend on how fast you go or on the physical distances you cover. In other words, unless your mission requires specific time parameters, you focus on the enemy and operate at the speed and over the distances that allow you to defeat or destroy him. A further priority is to retain physical cohesion and protection of your own force, so that when you strike the enemy you do it with all the advantages to your side. Normally, the enemy force is either stationary in known locations or capable of moving. Thus you are not quite sure where they will be when you reach them.

Because of the greater number of variables involved, aiming your own moving force at a moving enemy force, and hitting it, is the height of skill required in maneuver warfare. Some sports analogies—such as open field tackling or blocking on a screen pass—come to mind. But with a corps you are not talking about a few players on either side but about tens of thousands of vehicles and aircraft. Not only must each of these change direction and speed, but—to generate focused combat power—each of them must also remain in the right physical relationship to the others. Since battles and engagements in land warfare are usually decided by destruction of the enemy, it is vital for you to maneuver the various parts of your force to positions where they can either do that or threaten to do it, and thus cause the enemy to quit or go away. So where you position your tanks, artillery, intelligence collectors, and logistics all determines how much physical combat power or firepower you will be able to focus on the enemy. Thus, even as the two forces are in motion relative to each other, you are looking hard at the capability of your own forces and their disposition, while judging the capability and disposition of enemy forces. Because there is no fixed target to aim your force at when the enemy is moving, after you find him, you try to fix him. The art in this is to make your final commitment to a direction of attack and an organization of your forces that will hit the enemy at a time and place that will result in fixing him at a relative disadvantage, or so that the enemy cannot adjust to your attack in your chosen configuration and direction. Then your troops outfight him and you win.

The success of a force-oriented mission is achieved by the defeat or destruction of the enemy force, as measured against your own losses, within the time you are given, if that is a criterion. The success of a terrain-oriented mission is judged by the occupation of the ground, again within whatever time you are given, if that is a criterion. When comparing unit performance to the sole standard of the amount of ground covered in a given period, the unit with a force-oriented mission will always come out second best.

A mounted corps moving and aimed at a moving enemy force can put itself into any number of configurations on the ground. When you are certain the enemy will be at a place and time and in a known configuration, you can commit your own forces early to the exact attack formation you want and leave them that way. When the enemy is less predictable and has a few options still available to him, then you want to move initially in a balanced formation, and commit to your final attack scheme as late as possible. You want your own forces to be able to execute, but you don't want to give your enemy time to react. That is a matter of judgment and a—much misunderstood—art form that takes much skill, brains, intuition, and practice to develop well. It is the essence of senior-level tactical decision making. To commit to an attack maneuver prematurely is to give the enemy time to react. To commit too late is to prevent your own forces from accomplishing the maneuver.

Principles

A commander will also pay attention to traditional military principles.

The principles of war—so called—were derived late in the nineteenth century, but they are still applicable today. They usually characterize any successful operation. They are:

- *Mass*—physical and firepower concentration on the decisive point;
- *Maneuver*—ability to gain position advantage over the enemy;

- *Surprise*—gaining advantage by achieving the unexpected in time, location, numbers, technology, or tactics;
- *Security*—protection of your own force from the enemy and from other factors, such as accidents and sickness;
- *Simplicity*—making operations as concise and precise as possible;
- *Objective*—focus on what is important while avoiding distractions;
- *Offensive*—gaining and maintaining the initiative over the enemy, usually by attacking;
- *Economy of force*—using smaller forces—"economizing"—where possible, in order to leave larger forces for the main effort; and
- *Unity of command*—one commander in charge of each major operation.

During Desert Storm as VII Corps commander, Fred Franks constantly checked his own thinking against these rules to see if he was violating any of them. (Violating them is OK and even called for at times, but you must consciously know you are doing it and why.)

Other principles a commander must consider are the elements of combat power: firepower, maneuver, leadership, and protection. And he must understand further that combat power is situational, relative, and reversible. In other words, you can bring your own combat power to bear on the enemy and enjoy an advantage, but you have to be aware that the advantage is not absolute, does not last forever (the enemy can react and usually does), and depends on a particular situation and a particular enemy force. Situations can change rapidly to your disadvantage. The German surprise attack in the Ardennes in World War II was immediately successful, but after the Allies adjusted to the surprise, they inflicted a crushing defeat on attacking German forces. To put this another way, war will always involve risk and hazard.

In this connection, Field Marshal Erwin Rommel, one of the masters of maneuver warfare and battle command, liked to make a distinction between taking risks and taking gambles: With a risk, if it doesn't work, you have the means to recover from it. With a gamble, if it doesn't work, you do not. You hazard the entire force. Normally, to succeed you must take risks. On occasion you have to make a gamble. Because of the extreme difficulty of the maneuver, Franks's decision during Desert Storm to turn VII Corps east ninety degrees and attack at night with three divisions on line was a risk. But the greater risk was to allow the Iraqi defense more time and to fail to use superior U.S. night-fighting capabilities. His decision the first night to halt major ground offensive movement, on the other hand, was a gamble. If the Iraqis discovered it, they could have attacked with chemicals or positioned the RGFC more skillfully to defend against the VII Corps attack and caused more casualties. The greater gamble was getting the corps strung out, causing piecemeal commitment against RGFC units 100 kilometers away. After balancing the vulnerabilities, Franks made his decision. No choices for commanders in war are free of degrees of risk or gamble. Often you must choose between difficult or even bad alternatives.

✭ Just as in any profession, military professionals use precise terms for economy and precision of language. A few of these terms are worth mentioning.

• *Center of gravity* is a term first used by Clausewitz to designate the source or characteristic from which the enemy derives his power and which should be your aim in your attack. General Schwarzkopf rightly named the RGFC as the center of gravity in the Kuwaiti theater of operations, because the Republican Guards represented the power that permitted the Iraqis to continue to occupy Kuwait and threaten them in the future.

• *Culminating point* is the limit reached by an attacking force beyond which it is without power to continue or to defend itself in the face of a determined enemy attack. At its culminating point, an attacking force is literally "exhausted." At El Alamein in 1942, Rommel's Afrika Korps had gone past its culminating point.

At the start of an attack, you are at the peak of your power or strength. You know that in time you will be weakened by your own physical actions and by what the enemy does. The art of command is to husband that strength for the right time and the right place. You want to conduct your attack in such a way that you do not spend all your energy before you reach the decisive point. You want to stay at sustained hitting power for as long as you can. If your main objective is at some distance from your starting point, then you want to pace your maneuver toward your objective so that when you reach it, you will be able to sustain your hitting power long enough to finish the enemy. The ability to do that is a function of both physical and human factors, and commanders must pay attention to both.

• *Deliberate attacks* are conducted when you need time to get your forces arrayed and the possibility of surprising the enemy is low.

• *Hasty attacks* are normally conducted when it is better to attack than to wait—when waiting longer would give the enemy a better chance to defend. In Desert Storm, except for the breach, which was a deliberate attack, VII Corps units conducted mainly hasty attacks.

• *Pursuit* is a form of tactical offense. You conduct a pursuit when all or most enemy resistance is broken, the enemy is attempting to flee the battlefield, and you want to prevent his escape. Since Desert Storm, there has been a hot controversy over whether VII Corps was in pursuit or attack during the first three days of the battle (24 to 27 February). The evidence shows that they were in attack until 27 February, when much of the Iraqi resistance was broken. But most of at least two divisions in VII Corps (1st and 3rd Armored) were in hasty attacks right up to the cease-fire.

Maneuver Theories

In attack problem solving—bringing his corps to the right place at the right time in the right combination of units, with his soldiers in the right condition—a corps commander must try to see (in his mind's eye or on a map) the current situation (his own and the enemy's), envision what the future situation must look like to accomplish his mission, then figure out how to move from one state to the other at least cost to his troops, communicate that in clear, precise, concise language and by sketches on maps, and finally command the physical execution of the maneuver. In short, attacking requires what the U.S. Army Infantry School taught Fred Franks a long time ago: "Find, fix, and finish the enemy." Conducting an attack has an intellectual or continuing problem-solving dimension as well as physical and human dimensions.

Successful attack problem solving is a combination of art, science, and years of education, training, and experience. VII Corps had more than fifteen major subordinate units, each with from 500 to 8,000 vehicles. With that many moving parts, there are many opportunities for chance and friction to interfere with plans. Orchestrating such a massively complex organization through even the simplest of maneuvers (the VII Corps attack maneuver in Desert Storm was anything but simple) involves both constant problem solving and raw brute-force physical execution. Knowing how and when to execute the maneuver involves picturing all those moving parts in your mind and having the latest intelligence on the enemy. Then all of your units need skill, hard physical work, teamwork, and discipline, in order to execute the maneuver, in both daylight and darkness.

A mounted corps uses as its instruments of destruction its armored and mechanized divisions with their carefully put-together punch of tanks, infantry fighting vehicles, artillery, and attack aviation. They are the heavyweights. The commander works out how to put the maximum of that power onto the enemy in the shortest possible time. He uses the rest of the corps to reinforce his heavyweight punch. That is the physical. The human dimension rests with his soldiers. They alone bring this awesome physical combat power to its full potential. What is the human dimension? It is the quality of their training and the competence of their small-unit leadership. It is their courage and toughness. It is their motivation to accomplish the mission. It is also their mental and physical state. To the extent you can, you want your soldiers and leaders in such a mental and physical state when they hit the enemy that they are relatively fresh and can sustain the momentum of their attack until the enemy is destroyed.

When the enemy fights back and a battle ensues, adjustments are necessary. That is the essence of fighting. In the midst of these demands, soldiers and small-unit leaders must keep their heads and execute. Leaders must very quickly decide whether to stay the course or adjust. In the face of all this, all soldiers need physical toughness, perseverance, and an iron will. It is a matter of the mind and of the human spirit. Commanders have to influence both.

The forms of maneuver available to the corps to attack an enemy force are well known:

• *Penetration*—normally an attack on a very narrow front by a concentrated force to rupture an opening in a set enemy defense;

• *Infiltration*—normally passing through small friendly units by stealth into the enemy's rear, then turning on the enemy from there;

• *Envelopment, either single or double*—taking your force around one end or both ends of an enemy formation and then either attacking the enemy from the side or bypassing him to reach other objectives;

• *Turning movement*—a movement around the end of an enemy defense designed to force the enemy to turn out of his defense to face you from a different direction; and

• *Frontal attack*—usually the most costly maneuver; in a frontal attack, you attack directly into a prepared enemy position, normally seeking to defeat it by weight of numbers and firepower.

In a particular attack, the corps might be in one form of maneuver and the divisions of the corps in another. When VII Corps turned ninety degrees east early on 26 February 1991, the corps itself was executing a turning movement, while the divisions of the corps were executing an envelopment.

Selection of one of these forms of maneuver also involves command preference. "If called on to fight, my preference has always been for use of overwhelming force," Franks says. "My combat experience in Vietnam and in thousands of training exercises has convinced me to crush the enemy force and not sting him. In Desert Storm, I did not want to poke at him with separate fingers; I wanted to smash him with a fist (we even named one of our phase lines "smash"). I've said this before. I'll say it again: Get the enemy down and then finish him off. Get him by the throat and don't let go until he is finished. Go for the jugular, not the capillaries. . . . That thinking influenced my selection of tactics and maneuver options."

Depth

Depth of the battle space is a vital element on any modern battlefield. As weapons gain longer reach and become increasingly lethal, formations on land are tending to grow smaller and more dispersed. A similar process has gone on in the air and at sea. It's doubtful that we'll ever see again anything like the massed air and sea armadas of World War II. The developments on the ground allow an army commander to use more and more of the battle space to focus his combat power simultaneously on more and more of a given enemy force. Such capabilities require a senior tactical commander to look ahead in time two to three days, and in distance normally 150 to 200 kilometers.

He must, in short, consider the battle space in depth. During the Cold War, the echelonment doctrine of Soviet and Soviet-style forces—waves of attacking echelons that ultimately overwhelm a defender by attrition at the point of attack—made it necessary to consider depth. If the defender did not attack follow-on echelons at the same time he was defending against attacking echelons, he would soon be overwhelmed. Even after the collapse of the Warsaw Pact, a corps commander in today's battlefield environment must see the battle space given him to accomplish his mission as three dimensional. It has width, depth, and airspace above it. Within that bounded area, the corps decides where, when, and in what priority to continually apply its own combat power (as well as that temporarily available from air- and sea-based forces) to accomplish the mission it has been given.

To gain intelligence of the enemy forces in this depth, the corps has available to it its own intelligence-gathering capabilities in a military intelligence brigade. The corps further depends on the intelligence-gathering assets available to the theater command and those available at the national level.

The corps also receives help in conducting operations in depth from the theater in the form of theater attack air assets. Normally a corps commander will be able to select targets or enemy capabilities he wants destroyed deep in his operational area (up to the forward boundary of his battle space, or about 150 kilometers). Though this was the doctrine in NATO, it was not the practice in Desert Storm; and that greatly influenced how VII Corps and XVIII Corps could shape the battles they were fighting into the depth of the enemy's formations.

Another area for theater help is in logistics. Normally, theater assets are used to rapidly replenish supplies consumed by an attacking corps. In Desert Storm, this was especially critical in the area of fuel. The theater corps logistics support connection worked well.

Meanwhile, in the attack, the idea is to give the enemy no rest. You want to create a moving 150-kilometer-wide and 175-kilometer-deep killing zone

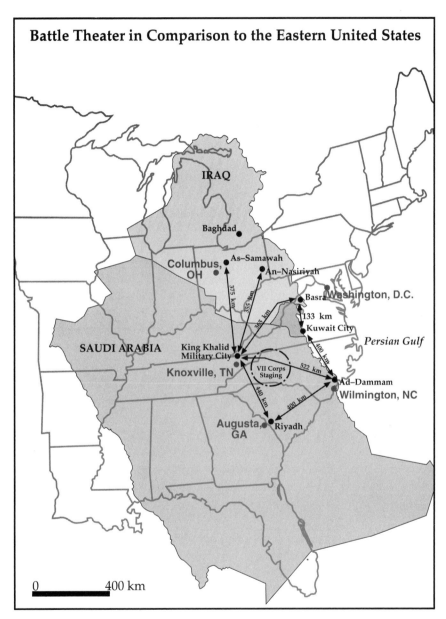

Battle Theater in Comparison to the Eastern United States

IRAQ

Baghdad

As–Samawah

Columbus, OH

An–Nasiriyah

375 km

355 km

Basra

Washington, D.C.

365 km

133 km

Kuwait City

SAUDI ARABIA

King Khalid Military City

400 km

Persian Gulf

Knoxville, TN

VII Corps Staging

522 km

Ad–Dammam

Wilmington, NC

440 km

400 km

Augusta, GA

Riyadh

0   400 km

Time and distance are important to any commander, and these factors held some particular challenges in the deserts of Saudi Arabia and Iraq. The map of southwest Asia superimposed over a portion of the eastern United States gives the distance challenges facing General Franks and his commanders in commanding, maneuvering, and resupplying VII Corps while simultaneously keeping Third Army and CENTCOM aware of the disposition of the corps.

in which he can neither hide nor survive. To create this, depth of the corps battle space is normally divided between the divisions and the corps. Divisions will usually fight to a depth of about 30 to 40 kilometers in front of their forward-most units. Beyond that and out to a depth of 150 to 200 kilometers, the corps will normally fight simultaneously with the divisions, mainly with fires. The killing zone of the attacking divisions dominates the terrain and the enemy. It is all-inclusive. Beyond this 30-to-40-kilometer killing zone, the destruction is more selective, because the attacking assets are usually limited to air, attack helicopters, and long-range Army tactical missiles. With those attacking assets, corps normally go after targets and enemy capabilities that, if taken out, will leave the enemy weakened for the advancing divisions, or take apart the enemy's coherence and cause chaos. Some of these targets might well be the enemy's command centers, his long-range artillery, his logistics and supplies, and his reserves (to keep them out of the division's fight and to severely attrit them).

In some circumstances, the corps commander might see an opportunity to break through with a ground formation and send them deep into the enemy's rear. Such an action can severely disrupt the enemy, for a ground force has not only destructive power but staying power. That is (unlike air, which has limited staying-power effect and eventually goes away), it stays and controls the area it is in, thus denying it to the enemy. In Desert Storm, for example, XVIII Corps positioned the 101st Airborne Division (Air Assault) on Highway 8, thus blocking early any hope of RGFC retreat toward Baghdad. When to do this and when not to is a major decision for the corps commander and involves both combat power and the capability to continually support such a deep attacking force.

Allocating airspace boundaries above the landmass is also important, so that all air assets can be used simultaneously. For example, the corps wants to be able to operate its own helicopter fleet (up to 800 in VII Corps), while allowing centrally controlled fixed-wing assets to attack targets simultaneously within the same battle space. In Desert Storm, an airspace boundary of 1,000 feet was agreed to; that is, VII Corps could fly its helicopters wherever and whenever they wanted, as long as they stayed below 1,000 feet. This did not prove to be a problem, as air forces flew combat missions normally at 10,000 feet or above.

Formation Alignments
With only passing regard to VII Corps maneuver during its eighty-nine-hour attack in Desert Storm, let us look at a hypothetical situation in which a mounted corps moves to contact an enemy force that is also moving. Imagine, for example, a three-division corps moving toward an enemy force that is

itself moving toward the corps. Each formation has the mission to defeat the other. Perhaps 200 kilometers initially separate the forces. One might also assume air forces are in parity, that is, the air battle at the moment gives no advantage to either side.

The friendly commander's first priority in this situation will be to designate a point of main effort. Let us imagine that the corps sees an enemy vulnerability and a terrain avenue of movement that will allow a swift attack against the enemy's key reserve units (that is, the reserves he is saving for his own main effort). The friendly commander then designates that operation as his main effort. This designation signals that it is that particular operation that must receive the full support of the corps, and that if the operation is successful, the corps will accomplish its mission. The friendly corps commander designates this part of the operation as his main effort to focus energy and support of his corps. If there is any question, support goes there. Subordinate commanders of all the various units in the corps (especially artillery, aviation, signal, engineers, and logistics) devise their own unit operation to assist the main effort.

At the same time, the corps commander might have another operation in progress that, while necessary, he will designate as a secondary attack or an economy of force. To this and other secondary operations will be allocated only minimum essential resources, so that maximum resources can be applied to the main effort. In this way, the commander can occupy the attention of enemy forces while allowing his main attack to succeed and freeing up some of his own forces for his main effort.

Sometime during the course of the main effort, the corps commander will adopt a basic form of maneuver to attack the enemy force. He will shift to this formation alignment when he determines that the enemy formations are identified well enough for effective plan making, and likely to remain in that posture long enough for the chosen corps maneuver to be successful. If this is not possible and the enemy is not precisely located or fixed, the corps puts itself into a form of the tactical offense called "movement to contact." This is a formation of units on the ground that permits the widest variety of maneuver options once the enemy force is more precisely fixed. It is like an offense in American football coming to the line of scrimmage and lining up in a basic formation from which it can shift rapidly once it determines the other side's defense. In the U.S. Army, this is called staying in a "balanced stance."

In a movement to contact, the lead element will normally be the corps armored cavalry regiment, and the regiment will be spread over the entire width of the corps sector. The regiment's mission is to cover the main corps movement while simultaneously finding and fixing the enemy force so the corps commander can maneuver the main punch of the corps in for the kill. Sometimes an artillery brigade (an additional forty-eight 155-mm howitzers and eighteen MLRS launchers) and an aviation battalion (twenty-four Apaches) will be added to the regiment's organic assets to accomplish its mission. The cavalry regiment so reinforced will have about 8,000 soldiers, 123 M1A1 tanks, 125 Bradleys, 72 155-mm howitzers, 27 MLRSs, and 32 Apache helicopters. It will project a lethal zone twenty to thirty kilometers to its front. On desert terrain, a regiment might cover a frontage of sixty to eighty kilometers and extend to the rear perhaps twenty-five kilometers. In Central Europe, its sector might be somewhat smaller. Meanwhile, the corps will be looking deeper in zone, partly with its own intelligence assets and partly with the assistance of theater reconnaissance assets. With the intel thus gained, the corps can attack key targets deep and thus influence the enemy's posture by shaping the upcoming battle for the divisions, which are its heavy punch. This intel also allows the corps to warn the cavalry regiment of enemy locations and dispositions. Theater air operations are vitally important to this early action. If air elements gain air supremacy, they will be able to attack freely targets at distances of up to 150 to 200 kilometers beyond the advancing corps while keeping enemy air and intelligence-gathering means away from the advancing corps.

Behind the advancing cavalry regiment, divisions normally follow by thirty minutes. In other words, they are at a distance from which they could take up the fight thirty minutes after the cavalry regiment has found and fixed the enemy. The divisions normally advance on a front about forty kilometers wide. In that posture they will usually have two of their three (ground) maneuver brigades side by side and one to the rear. Each of their lead maneuver brigades normally has 116 M1A1 tanks and about 40 Bradleys. Artillery battalions (twenty-four 155-mm howitzers) normally move with advancing brigades, and are available for immediate fire support. Supporting trucks and other logistics units follow behind the advancing combat units. Each advancing brigade brings its own support with it; this is replenished as required from division assets farther to the rear. An armored or mechanized division* so configured on desert terrain advances on a forty-kilometer front and extends to the rear about eighty to one hundred kilometers.

In the attack, there are normal additions to divisions. These include an artillery brigade of three battalions of artillery, two with twenty-four 155-mm howitzers and one with eighteen MLRS rocket launchers. There is also a

---

*Divisions normally differ only in the number of tank and Bradley battalions; an armored division might have six tank and four Bradley battalions, while a mechanized division will normally have five battalions of each.

MASH (mobile army surgical hospital). There are specifically tailored support groups from the corps with additional transportation assets for fuel and ammunition and other supplies. Depending on the mission, each division grows from its standard 18,000 soldiers to up to 24,000. (In Desert Storm the 24th Mechanized Division got so much additional fuel-hauling capability for its mission that strengths reached more than 24,000. VII Corps Divisions had from 20,000 to 22,000 soldiers.)

If divisions are part of the corps's main effort, they will receive other assets from corps to "weight" the main effort. In some cases corps attack aviation could be added to divisions. Additional artillery and more CAS (close air support) also can be added. And intelligence priorities can be shifted from corps units to assist main attack divisions. Meanwhile, other corps units are normally behind the divisions, but they can also be co-located with them, either operating independent of division control or else assigned temporarily to the divisions for specific missions. These corps units normally extend behind divisions by another 80 to 150 kilometers, and they can either be moving steadily or leapfrogging from position to position, depending on their mission. In total, the corps would extend from front to rear of its own formations 125 kilometers wide and up to 300 kilometers deep. Its reach into the enemy depth would extend another 150 to 300 kilometers.

As the corps advances, the corps support units will be accomplishing missions that keep the corps moving and ready to transition rapidly into the attack. For example, units of the engineer brigade will be ensuring mobility by building or maintaining roads and bridges, clearing obstacles, and even building airfields for C-130 aircraft or unmanned drones (which are used for intelligence gathering of enemy forces). Military intelligence brigade units will position themselves to listen to the enemy, jam his communications where appropriate, and fly drone or aviation unit missions deep to locate and target enemy capabilities. It will also use its specially trained infantry company by clandestinely inserting them deep into enemy territory to report directly on observed activity. The signal brigade will be operating a moving communication infrastructure that lets the corps communicate by voice and images on screens, as well as with paper orders and diagrams of future maneuvers. It will also establish continuing communications with the corps's higher headquarters, sometimes at great distances (in Desert Storm, higher headquarters was more than 500 kilometers away in Riyadh). The military police brigade will be securing roads used by the corps advance and by corps resupply going both ways (even in the desert it was necessary to have improved roads for resupply). Military police will additionally ensure disciplined use of those roads so that the right priority units can use them when required. And they will operate any prisoner-of-war compounds and move and process prisoners (a huge task in Desert Storm). The air defense units of the corps will alternately move and set up to provide continuous coverage over the corps as it advances.

The corps aviation brigade normally conducts attacks deep into the enemy rear with its two eighteen-Apache battalions. These attacks will be well forward of the cavalry regiment—normally at distances of up to 150 kilometers and normally at night. Meanwhile, the remainder of this brigade will be moving supplies with its heavy helicopters, providing command support with specially configured aircraft and providing troop lift where required.

Logistics support to a moving corps is provided by a combination of means. Some supporting units are placed directly with advancing units, providing area coverage (any unit in that area can go to that unit to get supplies). Meanwhile, logistics bases with fuel and ammunition are prepositioned at convenient locations, and unit supply vehicles from advancing units will go there for replenishment. The order of magnitude of supply is staggering: an advancing corps of five divisions will consume about 1.5 million gallons of fuel a day (an amount carried by about 600 trucks, each with 2,500- or some with 5,000-gallon capacity). In an attack, the corps will consume about 2,500 tons of ammunition a day (one truck carries 5 tons). In calculating the rate of movement and distances you expect for your corps advance, you have to figure in these numbers. Such calculations put a limit on advance. When the limit is reached, you either have to stop or else displace logistics bases forward. Without this displacement, advancing units travel so far from logistics bases that replenishment vehicles cannot make the turnaround from divisions to bases before units run out of supplies. This is especially the case with fuel.

While all of this movement and formation alignment is proceeding, the enemy is trying to do much the same thing you are doing. He is trying to gain intelligence on you that allows him to predict where you might be vulnerable; and he is seeking either to attack you or else to cause you to attack him where he is strong (which will dissipate your combat power and make you vulnerable to his counterattack). It is a deadly contest of hiding your intentions from the enemy and seeking to strike hard at the last moment, and keep striking, until you win.

Seeing a force like the one above bearing down on him, an enemy commander might choose to defend. If he began to set a defense with an extended security zone in front and supported by artillery, the attacking corps commander would want to discover this and to select his form of attack and act before the enemy commander can get set.

Both enemy and friendly forces are working on the same problem, and both are using the same time parameters and the same weather and terrain. Battle victory goes to the side that can more quickly solve those problems, and disseminate and act on the solutions, and that can keep doing that faster than the enemy until he quits or runs out of the wherewithal to continue.

Attack

When the commander determines (by a combination of means) the location and posture of the enemy force he is attacking, he arranges his units on the ground from their balanced formation alignment to his chosen attack formation (usually one of the forms of maneuver discussed above). If, for example, the cavalry regiment was leading, and it was followed by two divisions, with a third division in reserve, he would alter that alignment to a more potent combination. As soon as the cavalry regiment succeeds in finding and fixing the enemy force, he will quickly remove them from the lead and bring the full combat power of his divisions to bear. He does this with all units moving constantly toward the enemy.

If the cavalry regiment has surprised the enemy or has discovered an exploitable flank or gap in enemy forces, the corps commander might bring his reserve division forward. He might perhaps then concentrate two of his divisions on a narrow attacking front (maybe sixty kilometers) at the discovered or created vulnerability, while simultaneously distributing his third division on a broader economy-of-force front (maybe also sixty kilometers).

If an enemy facing the corps has a vulnerable flank, the corps commander might use his two lead divisions as a fixing force and maneuver his third division around to the flank and rear of the now-fixed enemy.

If there appears to be no assailable flank, the corps commander might concentrate combat power on a narrow front and force a penetration of enemy defenses, then pass follow-on corps maneuver elements through the breach rapidly into the enemy rear.

He will normally time his selected maneuver so his units have time to execute, but also late enough so that the enemy will not have time to react (he wants the enemy to stay fixed in the posture best suited for the attacking corps to be successful). In order to accomplish whatever maneuver he selects, the divisions will pass through the cavalry regiment (which is already engaged with the enemy). The 8,000 vehicles of each division will maneuver through parts of the cavalry regiment that are spread across the corps front. Sometimes this is done in daylight; sometimes in dark. It is never easy. Meanwhile the corps intensifies the deep fight with its own Apache aircraft, long-range tactical missiles, and support from theater air. These attacks are normally another eighty kilometers in front of the division attacks of fifty to seventy-five kilometers deep.

Divisions take up the fight from the cavalry regiment with their 300-plus tanks, 200-plus infantry fighting vehicles, 72 155-mm howitzers and 18 MLRS launchers (each with 12 rockets), and 24 Apache attack helicopters. They maneuver in their sectors, choosing their own form of maneuver (penetration, infiltration, envelopment, or frontal attack) for the mission. When the entire corps is brought on line, the seventy-five-kilometer-wide-by-thirty-kilometer-deep division sector of destruction is now extended in front by another seventy-five kilometers. This last zone of destruction will not be total, however, but will depend on available assets. Behind the main zone of attack, the supporting elements of the corps stretch some seventy-five to one hundred kilometers deep.

The corps will also normally have a reserve. The reserve can exploit an opportunity to maintain the momentum of the attack, or else it can be available to react to an enemy surprise. In a three- to five-division corps, the reserve might initially be a single division in the movement to contact, or it might be the cavalry regiment after the attacking divisions have passed through.

★ In short, the mounted corps will be the principal means of destruction of the enemy force. It not only is capable of attacking the enemy directly, but it also has the mobility to move deep in the enemy rear and do its damage there.

To create such a powerful force means putting together a complex organization with many moving parts. Such a force will usually be tailored for a specific theater of operations and a known enemy. It will usually have two to five armored or mechanized divisions. It will also have eight to ten non-division organizations, such as an armored cavalry regiment, an artillery command of two to four artillery brigades, an aviation brigade, an engineer brigade, a military intelligence brigade, a signal brigade, an air defense brigade, a personnel brigade, and a finance brigade. Its support command is normally bigger than any of the divisions.

To quote Franks: "Modern warfare is tough, uncompromising, and highly lethal. The enemy is found and engaged at ranges from a few meters to thousands of meters. Casualties are sudden. Because of that, commanders and soldiers at every level are also aware of the intense human dimension of war. The results are final and frozen in time for a lifetime. There are no real winners in war. Objectives are achieved, but always at a cost to your soldiers. That is why force protection is a vital ingredient of combat power. It is why at all levels the aim always is mission at least cost. Commanders and soldiers have to feel it all to really know what to do. But in feeling it all, they must not be paralyzed into inaction. They must decide, often in nanoseconds, make it stick, and go on. They must feel, but they also must act. They cannot give in to second-guessing themselves or to emotions. That is what makes combat leadership so demanding and why officers train so hard and constantly throughout a professional lifetime to make the few tough decisions they have to make in battle. It all comes down to that."

U.S. Army commanders, soldiers, and units regularly train to move and fight such a complex and powerful organization to achieve its full potential. Each officer and noncommissioned leader demonstrates competence at each succeeding level of command and responsibility before being entrusted with the next level. Moreover, NCOs and officers are afforded opportunities for education and training at each advancement progression to reinforce the level of competence. Normally it takes from twenty-eight to thirty years of experience, personal study, demonstrated competence, education, and training to develop a corps commander. A division commander normally has twenty-two to twenty-five years. Brigade commanders from twenty to twenty-two years. Battalion commanders and their Command Sergeant Majors seventeen to twenty years. Company first sergeants usually fifteen to eighteen years, platoon sergeants ten to fifteen years. In Desert Storm in 1991, most battalion commanders had entered the Army in the early 1970s. No other Army in the world has such depth in officer and noncommissioned officer leadership or goes to such lengths to train and educate that leadership.

Devastating combat actions executed by mounted units on the battlefield actions don't just happen. They are planned, synchronized, and executed by skilled professionals, always so that the combat power can be brought to bear to accomplish the mission at least cost to the soldiers.

7

MARCH TO THE SOUND OF THE GUNS

IT WOULD SOON BE TIME FOR FRED FRANKS TO PUT ALL THAT KNOWLedge into action—but in a way he never expected.

In the fall of 1989, the Warsaw Pact was collapsing, the Iron Curtain opened, and the Cold War seemed to be coming to an end. For over four decades, the U.S. Army in Europe, as part of NATO, had "fought" that war, not in actual battles, but in planning, training, and exercises. The mission in that war had been to deter and defend—to make the enemy unwilling to risk attack and, if they did attack, to throw them out. Now the mission had been successful.

But now what? What was the Army's mission in Europe—in the whole world, for that matter—now that it appeared to be no longer East versus West? The Army's leaders quickly began to move to answer such questions.

★ In August 1989, just as the Iron Curtain was beginning its final collapse, Lieutenant General Fred Franks took command of VII Corps—the "Jayhawks." With headquarters in Stuttgart, Germany, the Cold War VII Corps was 110,000 U.S., German, and Canadian soldiers (74,000 of them were U.S.). Its major units were the 1st Armored Division, 3rd Infantry Division, 12th German Panzer (i.e., Armor) Division, 2nd Armored Cavalry Regiment, 11th Aviation Brigade, VII Corps Artillery (three brigades), a Canadian brigade, the 4th CMBG (the 4th Canadian Mechanized Brigade Group, the Army Group reserve), logistics (Corps Support Command), and corps separate brigades of military police (14th MP Brigade), military intelligence (207th MI Brigade), signal (93rd Signal Brigade), engineers (7th Engineer Brigade), finance (7th Finance Group), and personnel (7th Personnel Group).

By the turn of the new year, it was evident that the end of the Soviet empire was likely to be permanent. That meant that Franks faced hard questions, not the least of them being how he was to deal with the drawdown of VII Corps units.

Now that the mission to defend against a Soviet-led invasion seemed over, the United States was sure to cut back in Europe. Two U.S. corps were then stationed in Germany, the V and the VII. In a matter of months, the two corps would be pared down to one, with units inactivating in each corp. Fred Franks would have the unhappy responsibility of presiding over the termination of many of his proud units.

That was several months down the road, however. In the near term, he had more pressing tasks. He had seen the flood of East Germans coming west in November. By early March 1990, he had pulled the 2nd ACR off their over-forty-year border mission. Formal mission changes would eventually be issued, but for Franks and VII Corps, change was needed now in training. He thought of new missions.

One thing was certain: they would be nothing like the terrain-oriented mission the corps had been used to. In a terrain-oriented mission, the lanes and routes the attackers can take are well known. You set up obstacles to slow him down while your own reserves are flown in. If you have to fall back, it is to already prepared positions. Your logistical support and command-and-control structure are clear and well worked out. Your command posts can remain in previously prepared positions where communications are dependable. After four decades of confrontation in Europe, defense against every conceivable attack had been minutely choreographed.

That would no longer be the case. In a rapidly changing world, the new mission for a powerful armored corps like VII would more likely involve finding and killing a similarly powerful opposing force at some distance from the corps's launch point. In other words, it would be a force-oriented mission, involving a long—100 kilometers or more—movement to contact, followed by a meeting engagement.

Thus the corps commander and the corps staff needed to know how to move the corps over those long distances. In contact, they needed to achieve coherence of formation—to keep units physically positioned relative to one another so that they could mutually support one another in a fight—and to rapidly focus their combat power—to arrange their tanks, infantry, artillery, and aviation in the right combination for maximum effect against the enemy. Formation alignments would have to be shifted rapidly . . . and units would have to be trained to know how to do that. Reactions and responses would have to be trained to a much greater quickness than in terrain-oriented operations. There would have to be far greater adaptability of mind and agility of units. Meanwhile, logistics would become stretched out. A lot of material would somehow have to find its way to the right units, all of them on the move: food, fuel, and ammo. And the entire corps—all of its many component units—would have to be orchestrated the way Franks and Brookshire had orchestrated the 2nd Squadron of the Blackhorse in Vietnam.

Training, training, and more training! More important, a different mind-set from the now-vanishing Cold War scenarios would have to be created. Agility and adaptability don't come easily.

In the fall of 1989, at the start of his command of VII Corps, Franks was already talking about fighting the corps as a corps, and not as a collection of individual units battling to defend a piece of NATO territory. Early in 1990, he published a "commander's intent" directive with a vision for an "agile" corps. He followed that in May with details. The corps, he said, must be prepared to "master rapid transition in tactical maneuvers, attack to defense, defense to attack, attack from the march. . . ." The tasks included "moving rapidly over great distances, fighting from the march, retaining the initiative in meeting engagements, conducting hasty attacks/defenses, sustaining combat power continuously. . . ."

Major exercises in 1990 put these ideas into practice. In January, General Butch Saint ordered that the annual REFORGER exercise engaging VII Corps against V Corps begin with tactical movement that brought them to contact and then a meeting engagement. Saint also had been talking about a "capable" corps, meaning one that clearly must be able to do more than its NATO mission. Later that winter, in a BCTP exercise with Major General Tom Rhame's 1st Infantry Division—the Big Red One—at Fort Riley, Kansas, Franks and VII Corps took the ideas even further.

Because of the old Cold War lineup of forces, VII Corps was the 1st Infantry's immediate headquarters (in the event of war in Europe, the division would have moved to positions in Germany under VII Corps as a REFORGER unit). Even so, VII Corps would not have normally supervised the BCTP, or any of the division's tactical training in the United States. However, Franks recognized that the BCTP exercise was another opportunity to train for the likely new corps mission, so with the okay of III Corps (their normal U.S. HQ) he brought a corps headquarters team to Fort Riley, plugged them into the Big Red One's command structure, and changed the training scenario from the old Cold War defensive mission to something completely different, again involving long unit movements climaxed by meeting engagements.

Adapting to these last-minute changes was no simple matter for Rhame and his commanders and staff, and it was a big risk, too. All those involved could fall flat on their faces in a big way. Specifically, they weren't used to working within the context of a corps offensive operation—that is, as one unit operating in concert with several others, all under the direction of the corps commander. At the same time, they were used to the Cold War scenarios, all set in Germany. This new scenario was not in their planning and training scheme, or their mission requirements, and it required some fast footwork on their part.

In fact, Generals Rhame and Franks did not even know each other. They were all starting completely cold.

As it turned out, it was a terrific exercise for everyone, and it told Franks a great deal about Tom Rhame and his commanders and staff—primarily that they could take rapid mission changes in stride and go on to execute the mission. Later on, this knowledge influenced Franks's mission assignment to Rhame's division not once but twice.

In May, then again later in the summer, Franks used a similar scenario for Major General Dutch Shoffner and the 3rd Infantry Division (their 3rd Brigade would deploy with 1st AD) BCTP exercises—that is, long movement to contact, followed by a meeting engagement, followed by an attack or defense, depending on the success of the meeting engagement. Major General Ron Griffith, on his own initiative, brought his entire 1st AD command element to the field during this exercise. He mirrored what 3rd Infantry was doing and in that manner was able to get an exercise for his division.

In June, VII Corps's 11th Aviation Brigade deployed Apaches to Israel for a live-fire training exercise in the Negev Desert. For Franks and his aviators, it was valuable training that they could not do in Europe, plus they were able to gain lessons on deployment of aircraft and units.

In September, Franks and his commanders and staff did a VII Corps seminar for one week as part of the preparation for their own BCTP WARFIGHTER exercise to take place in early March '91. That week was an intense series of discussions, tactical problem solving, and commander-to-commander interaction. In that seminar, Franks also used a scenario that required the corps to move a long distance and attack from the march. Elements of the corps also trained with a still-experimental JSTARS system (Joint Surveillance Target-Acquisition System), the first time that revolutionary technology had been used by an operational unit. JSTARS aircraft are modified Boeing 707s with the capability, through recently developed radar technology, of seeing unit moves on the ground over a wide radius, and showing these moves in real time over downlink facilities. JSTARS gives commanders the capability of knowing all the enemy's moves over the deep battlefield, a great advantage to have in the kind of force-oriented missions Fred Franks foresaw for U.S. Army corps in the future. Later, in Saudi Arabia, Franks recalled those capabilities and successfully lobbied for the use of JSTARS in theater. Though the system was still experimental, JSTARS was too useful to do without.

★ A leader has to know how his commanders will respond to situations they're likely to encounter in battle. Training exercises provide the most realistic opportunity to observe commanders in action. These exercises—

REFORGER, the BCTPs with the 1st Infantry Division, and the 3rd Infantry Division, VII Corps, BCTP seminar—also provided Fred Franks with the opportunity to see how he himself and his corps staff handled the new situations VII Corps would surely face if it was ever to fight another war.

It wasn't luck that VII Corps was ready, and *trained*, to fight Saddam Hussein's best in February of the following year.

✯ On 2 August 1990, the Iraqi army invaded and occupied Kuwait. Soon afterward, President Bush sent U.S. air, sea, and ground units to the Persian Gulf region to deter Iraqi aggression. An extension of Iraqi conquests a few kilometers down Saudi Arabia's east coast would put Saddam Hussein in charge of close to half of the world's known oil supplies. By mid-August the Army's 82nd Airborne Division and the 7th Marine Expeditionary Brigade were taking up positions in northeast Saudi Arabia, showing American resolve—if not a great deal of combat power. During the following weeks, more powerful ground units from the United States and other members of the Coalition that President Bush had created to stop the Iraqi threat arrived in Saudi Arabia. If Saddam Hussein was ever of a mind to continue his conquests toward the south, he now had second thoughts.

Meanwhile, in Stuttgart, General Franks was looking at ways his VII Corps might become useful to the Army in the present crisis. Whether or not VII Corps would eventually be deployed to southwest Asia was a national policy decision, but VII Corps was available, it was relatively close (Germany is about the same distance from Saudi Arabia as New York from California), for the time being it was not really needed for the defense of Europe, and it was a heavy, armored corps, much of which had recently trained for offensive, force-oriented missions—the kind of missions that would surely be necessary if the decision were made to forcibly uproot the Iraqis from Kuwait. So it was certainly possible that all or part of the corps would go to Saudi. More to the point, Franks knew that fellow soldiers were in a tough spot, the United States was deeply committed, and it was up to him to anticipate and look to the future where VII Corps was concerned. For Franks, the strategic situation resembled the days in 1945 when the European war ended, permitting forces to be shifted from that theater to the Pacific. The commanders had to find out first what was going on in that other theater of operations.

In consequence, he had the corps staff read themselves into the crisis—just in case. Corps G-2, Colonel Gene Klaus, and Corps G-3, Colonel Stan Cherrie, under the direction of the chief of staff, Brigadier General John Landry, set up a situation room at Kelly Barracks (an old Wehrmacht complex near Stuttgart that was the headquarters for VII Corps) in a vaulted-door, secure conference room facility in a basement. They set up maps, monitored the intelligence communications traffic they had obtained through their own parent headquarters in Heidelberg, posted the disposition of Iraqi forces, and of U.S. and other Coalition forces; they read up on the Iraqi army, and in general did their homework about the operation that by then was called Desert Shield. They were marching to the sound of the guns.

At the same time, Franks had planners looking into moving the corps from Germany to the Persian Gulf. Since he knew this would be a truly enormous undertaking, if they were called to do it, he wanted to know in advance what would be involved. As it happened, the most obvious route for the corps—to go through Italian ports—was not the best one. Heavy combat equipment could not pass through the tunnels in the Alps. Thus the fastest route, counterintuitively, looked to be through the northern ports of Germany.

He also had his planners look at an indirect approach to forcing the Iraqis out of Kuwait. "What if we moved VII Corps to eastern Turkey," he asked, "and then attacked toward Baghdad? Is that a workable alternative? Could we move our corps through the terrain and could we logistically support the operation?" After some corps planning work, it began to look like a workable option. As far as they could see, no Iraqi force was available to stop them. If Saddam saw an armored corps on the move to Baghdad, he might quickly decide his capital was worth more than Kuwait.

Franks informally discussed the Turkey option to his own higher commanders, General Crosbie ("Butch") Saint, the U.S. Army Europe commander, and General Jim McCarthy, USAF, deputy commander of U.S. forces in Europe, both bold thinkers, and they both liked the idea. But when they tried the concept out on still higher echelons, Franks's idea was squelched.

The American buildup in the Gulf was directed by General H. Norman Schwarzkopf, the commander in chief (CINC) of CENTCOM (Central Command), headquartered in Tampa, Florida. CENTCOM is one of six United States multiservice—joint—commands, its area of military responsibility covering most of southwest Asia and the Middle East, with the exception of Syria, Lebanon, and Israel, which are under EUCOM (European Command). Before the crisis in the Gulf, CENTCOM existed only as a planning body, which is to say that there were no actual troops under CENTCOM control. In case of need, troops from all the services would be given to CENTCOM (in Army terminology, they would be "chopped" to CENTCOM) from other geographical commands. CENTCOM would be the "supported" command, and other joint commands, such as EUCOM and FORSCOM, would be "supporting." CENTCOM trained with the various contingency units, who would normally be "chopped" to their command if need arose.

In August 1990, XVIII Airborne Corps from FORSCOM was chopped to CENTCOM and immediately began deploying to Saudi Arabia, along with air and naval forces. The XVIII Corps, commanded by Lieutenant General Gary Luck, was what the Army calls a contingency corps. It was specifically configured to deploy worldwide to meet a variety of circumstances, and to do so rapidly. It was made up of the 82nd Airborne Division, commanded by Major General James Johnson; the 101st Airborne Division, commanded by Major General J. H. Binford Peay; the 24th Infantry Division (Mechanized), commanded by Major General Barry McCaffrey (a heavy division); the 1st Cavalry Division, commanded by Brigadier General John Tilelli; and the 3rd Armored Cavalry Regiment, commanded by Colonel Doug Starr. Units of XVIII Corps began closing in theater in early August. The last to arrive, the 1st Cavalry Division, closed on 22 October.

Fred Franks was sure that if VII Corps or VII Corps units were to join XVIII Corps in the Gulf, they would know what to do. He was not certain who would be called, but knew his job was to have them ready if they were needed. If a whole corps was needed, they were the right team, he knew, to give the growing U.S. presence in Saudi Arabia real offensive punch on the ground. That decision would come in time, but there were false starts, false alarms, and zigzags along the way.

In August, after aviation elements from neighboring V Corps were alerted and then deployed, Franks asked and received General Saint's OK to alert his own aviation brigade for possible deployment of an attack aviation battalion. Though they worked hard to put the move together, the battalion did not deploy. Even so, Colonel Johnnie Hitt, the 11th Aviation Brigade commander, and his troops taught the rest of the corps a great deal about preparing for the move. As it turned out, this was an important planning drill for Franks and the corps staff. At about the same time, the first VII Corps troops to actually go to the Gulf were alerted and deployed—two NBC (Nuclear, Biological, Chemical) reconnaissance platoons, equipped with German-built FUCHS (FOX) vehicles.

Later in September, Franks had a meeting on force drawdown with General Saint at U.S. Army Europe Headquarters in Heidelberg, about forty-five minutes from Stuttgart by helicopter. It was clear by then that VII Corps HQ was soon going to be deactivated. "Look, sir," Franks suggested, "if another corps is needed, why don't you just send us to the Gulf? We're already halfway there. We're going to be out of a mission in Central Europe. The decision is, V Corps will be the residual European corps with headquarters in Frankfurt. Why don't you just send VII Corps? We know what to do. We've had our BCTPs. You know about the training we've been doing. Send us."

Saint was open to that idea and passed it on to higher command. But nothing immediately came of it, at least to Franks's knowledge.

By October, it was becoming increasingly obvious to the military leadership in Washington that the XVIII Corps was not going to provide them with an adequate offensive option against the Iraqis, if the President chose to exercise such an option. And so, in due course, Franks was alerted to send to the Gulf the 1st Armored Division, commanded by Major General Ron Griffith. But soon this deployment was put on hold.

Later in October, he received official instructions to begin planning to send the whole corps. But a few days after that, the message from higher up took another zigzag: "Stand down on your planning," he was told. "But don't throw anything away."

"WILCO," Franks and his team, good soldiers, replied, but the order was a painful jolt for all of them. They wanted to go; they expected to go; and they had all been working hard to prepare to go. And then . . . well, what did *this* new order mean?

And just a few days after that, on 2 November, there was still another zigzag: "No, revive that, but keep it very, very close hold"—meaning, under tight security, with very few people in the know.

A very small planning cell was reconstituted, including Franks's deputy, Brigadier General Gene Daniel; chief of staff, Brigadier General John Landry; Support Command commander (VII Corps logistics), Brigadier General Bob McFarlin; corps G-3, Colonel Stan Cherrie; G-3 plans chief, Lieutenant Colonel Tom Goedkoop; deputy G-4, Lieutenant Colonel Mike Stafford; G-4 planner, Lieutenant Colonel Bob Browne; and G-1 planner, Major Paul Liebeck. It was a smart, talented team.

★ The days after 2 November saw Franks shuttling back and forth to Heidelberg and General Saint. Under the cover of discussions on the planned drawdown of VII Corps, he and Saint worked on the troop list and all the other myriad choices needed for the deployment of VII Corps to the Gulf. It did not take them long to realize that the Cold War, NATO-oriented VII Corps would not work in that theater. The new mission demanded a new team. VII Corps would have to be reconstituted from a terrain-oriented, defensive corps to a maneuver, contingency corps, with fully modernized maneuver battalions, equipped with the latest M1A1 Abrams tanks and M2 Bradley armored fighting vehicles—not an easy transformation.

To make matters even more difficult, the corps would be moving to a location that was, for all practical purposes, empty . . . nowhere. VII Corps was now configured to fight in Central Europe, where they operated within a sophisticated infrastructure of communications, roads, railroads, supplies, and fuel. In Central Europe, the corps also normally availed itself of what is called host-nation support: that is, territorial units of the German army and some German civilian agencies were set up to supplement the corps's need for logistics, troops, equipment, and supplies. Saudi Arabia, at best, offered a much more austere operating environment. In Saudi, there was little to no infrastructure. When you're out in the middle of the desert, you have nothing . . . *nothing.* So you've got to bring your infrastructure with you.

They would have to deploy. It was never intended for a corps to plan and execute its own strategic deployment. Both USAREUR and EUCOM HQ sent planning cells to Kelly Barracks, and Lieutenant General John Shalikashvili, Saint's deputy, was to be a big help.

General Saint, who was himself the leading proponent of mobile armored warfare in the Army, wanted VII Corps to be successful and to give them what they needed, yet at the same time, he and his boss, General Jack Galvin, EUCOM commander, faced serious tensions between the needs of VII Corps in the Gulf and the needs of their own residual mission in Europe. VII Corps was already forward-deployed into a theater with an immediate and very serious mission; now it was to be deployed to still another theater. In such cases, conflicts between the two theaters' needs are inevitable. General Saint had to balance the residual Army mission capability of the forces remaining after VII Corps had deployed with the need to provide the corps with the necessary forces to accomplish their mission in CENTCOM in Saudi Arabia. It was not an easy choice for him, and it was not always easy for General Franks to accept what General Saint wanted him to take. At times the discussions between the two generals about the right mix of forces and amount of support grew heated.

Heated discussions between generals are not uncommon. To Fred Franks, this kind of candor is expected behavior. It goes with the job of general. Commanders who do not pound the table to make their case for accomplishing their mission are *not* doing their job. They should—and must—talk tough to each other. Generals do not tend to be delicate souls. Strong egos are part of their job description. They will stand up for what they believe in, normally in private meetings. A general who does not is almost surely a liability to his command.

Heated discussions require a particular kind of atmosphere in order to be productive, however. They demand openness on both sides. There has to be a true exchange, with each side asking questions and arguing his case, and then when all the arguments are exhausted, the senior commander has to make his decision. After that, it's "Yes, sir, WILCO," and you get to work and execute.

It's the senior commander's responsibility to create the work atmosphere that suits him, and that will be the most productive. It's called the command climate, and it's a function of a commander's command style. Coming out of cavalry, Fred Franks and Butch Saint were used to a command climate of fast-moving, open, often-animated discussions. Other commanders, either consciously or as a result of personality or the service culture they come out of, will favor something different. General Norman Schwarzkopf, for instance, was a passionate, charismatic leader with a famously thermonuclear temper and an equally famous propensity to verbally gut any subordinate who—in his perception—crossed him. All commanders like the visible and enthusiastic support of subordinates. Schwarzkopf went further. He didn't welcome contradiction, much less the kind of openness and candor that is often the way with other commanders. This difference would become important later.

★   This is the makeup of VII Corps that Generals Franks and Saint hammered out:

From their European VII Corps divisions, they would take only the 1st Armored. From Europe, they would additionally take the 2nd Cavalry Regiment, the Support Command, plus other corps regimental and brigade units, totaling about 42,000 of the original 110,000 soldiers—in the end, only 40 percent of the original European corps. The rest of VII Corps would come from other units in Europe and the continental United States. These would include units from the Army National Guard and U.S. Army Reserve, who would join the Support Command and the existing corps brigade units. VII Corps also would eventually include the British 1st Armored Division, but they had no idea of that in November. Some major specifics: The 3rd Armored Division, from V Corps, commanded by Major General Paul "Butch" Funk, would go in place of the 3rd Infantry Division (though a brigade from the 3rd Infantry Division did go). And the 1st Infantry Division would deploy with two brigades from Fort Riley, and add the 2nd Armored Division forward brigade from northern Germany, which would join them in Saudi Arabia. Three complete artillery brigades (one from V Corps in Germany, one from the Arkansas National Guard, and one from III Corps in the United States) were added to the 210th Brigade, one of three in NATO VII Corps, to form its corps artillery. The VII Corps support command in Germany—in that built-up modern infrastructure—numbered 7,500 U.S. soldiers. In Desert Storm—in the austere desert environment—they grew to over 26,000 soldiers, including a medical brigade of fifteen hospitals.

Each of the eight non-division brigades in the corps also grew. For example, two brigades of three battalions each were added to the 7th Engineer Brigade. And to increase air defense capabilities, a composite air defense task force of Patriot and HAWK units was added. Many of these additions, made by Franks's 1959 West Point classmate and FORSCOM commander, General Ed Burba, came from the Reserve component (National Guard and U.S. Army Reserve) in the States. From the Reserve component, 21,000 soldiers and their equipment were added (19,000 in units and another 2,000 as individual re-

VII Corps in Europe

Corps Headquarters   **76,000 Soldiers (US)**

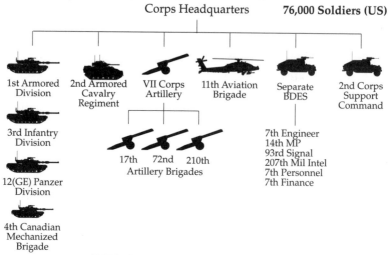

1st Armored Division
2nd Armored Cavalry Regiment
VII Corps Artillery
11th Aviation Brigade
Separate BDES
2nd Corps Support Command

3rd Infantry Division

17th   72nd   210th
Artillery Brigades

7th Engineer
14th MP
93rd Signal
207th Mil Intel
7th Personnel
7th Finance

12(GE) Panzer Division

4th Canadian Mechanized Brigade

VII Corps in Desert Storm

Corps Headquarters   **146,000 Soldiers**

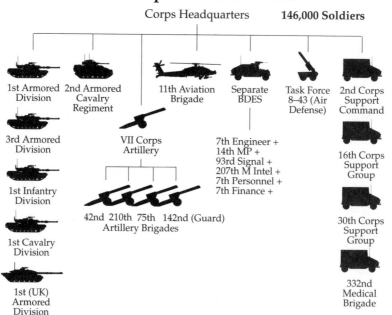

1st Armored Division
2nd Armored Cavalry Regiment
11th Aviation Brigade
Separate BDES
Task Force 8–43 (Air Defense)
2nd Corps Support Command

3rd Armored Division

VII Corps Artillery

7th Engineer +
14th MP +
93rd Signal +
207th M Intel +
7th Personnel +
7th Finance +

16th Corps Support Group

1st Infantry Division

42nd 210th 75th 142nd (Guard)
Artillery Brigades

1st Cavalry Division

30th Corps Support Group

1st (UK) Armored Division

332nd Medical Brigade

VII Corps changed dramatically from Europe to southwest Asia. In Europe the corps was geared to a terrain-oriented mission defending against a Soviet/Warsaw Pact threat. In Desert Storm, the mission was force-oriented, and the corps was tailored to find and kill a powerful opposing force in an attack that spread over long distance.

placements). In a little over ninety days, VII Corps grew by a total of 124,000 soldiers. And when the corps attacked the Republican Guards, it was a new corps team of 146,000 U.S. and British soldiers and close to 50,000 vehicles.

Once this essentially new corps team was in the desert, just to live and train, everything had to be created from what they brought with them—shelter, sanitation, waste disposal, mail system, water, and training ranges for weapons firing and maneuver practice. Beyond that, capabilities to attack over long distances had to be provided, such as additional trucks for fuel and ammunition, additional communication (capable of reaching longer distances), and additional support of all types, such as medical personnel and engineers (to build roads, airfields, and breach minefields).

Units and equipment had to be added to make up the difference. VII Corps had to become a corps much like XVIII Corps, capable of being deployed, then of fighting and supporting itself. That meant adding many units for a contingency role for which they had not prepared. Although XVIII Corps also had to add units for their mission, for them it proved less of an adjustment, for they were already trained and configured for that. VII Corps had been deployed, permanently stationed, and configured to fight in Central Europe. There had been no thought to making it a "contingency corps," capable of being picked up from Germany and deployed worldwide. In going through this experience, VII Corps was to be a microcosm of what the entire U.S. Army would be required to do over the next few years—that is, rapid tailoring to accomplish missions that were difficult to predict far in advance. Such rapid tailoring is now part of the U.S. Army's revised (1993) doctrine, and is now done with relative ease (as we have seen recently in Army deployments to Haiti and Bosnia).

So for VII Corps it was not a matter of picking up the existing Cold War VII Corps in Germany, moving it to Saudi Arabia, fighting the Iraqis, then boarding ships and planes and coming home. In a little less than 100 days, a new corps was built from a no-notice start; it was moved via ship and air to southwest Asia; units got used to operating together; and then they fought a major land campaign.

The VII Corps name was the same, but in the deserts of Saudi Arabia and Iraq, it was quite a different corps.

★ When VII Corps did deploy—and even at this late date it was not certain that they would—VII Corps would no longer be part of the NATO coalition in Germany, but of a new coalition, led by a new command team, General Schwarzkopf, CENTCOM, and Lieutenant General John Yeosock, Third Army, in a part of the world where they had absolutely no experience. They had a lot of work ahead of them, and not a lot of time to accomplish it.

On Thursday, 8 November, Franks was again in Heidelberg with General Saint. At that meeting, the final troop list was approved, and many other details were worked out.

Sometime during the meeting, Franks asked, "Sir, when do you think we might get the word to go?"

"Should be sometime later today, I think," Saint answered.

All right! Franks thought. Finally!

Later, back in Stuttgart, there was a phone call from Heidelberg. Major General John Heldstab, deputy chief of staff for operations, was on the line. "Fred, it's a go," Heldstab told him. "Watch CNN at 2000 tonight over Armed Forces Network."

"What about official notification, John?"

"As soon as we get something official, I'll get a message to your headquarters."

"Thanks, John. I've got some work to do."

They were going!

★ Just before 2000, Franks and all but three of his planning team assembled at the ops center. John Landry was on leave, and Bob Browne and Paul Liebeck were not available.

At 2000, President Bush came on the screen to announce that he was sending more troops to Saudi Arabia. He was followed by Secretary of Defense Dick Cheney and Chairman of the Joint Chiefs of Staff Colin Powell, who announced the units that would go: VII Corps from Germany and 1st Infantry Division from Fort Riley, Kansas.

As the President and the Secretary and the Chairman spoke, one thought flashed through every mind at the ops center: *That means us!*

The mood then was quiet, confident. There were a few "Hooahs" (an old Army rallying cry) and "Jayhawks" and "All riiights," a few fist pumps and excited grins. But this was a group of professionals. All of them had been working hard to prepare for this moment, and all of them knew they would soon be working even harder. The unspoken message in the air was "Okay, let's get the job done right."

It didn't take long for other thoughts to crowd into Fred Franks's consciousness, thoughts of the immediate challenges they all faced and of all they had to set in motion: teamwork, attitudes, training priorities, security.

Security is always a complex issue for commanders, and a particularly difficult one to get right. On the one hand, you have to be able to let staff and subordinate leaders know what they need to know to accomplish the mission. On the other hand, you want to keep your actions screened from the enemy.

All other things being equal, the more public a commander can be, the easier the move becomes.

The issue is not one the commander can himself decide. Ultimately, that is determined by civilian policy makers. Up to this particular evening, Franks and his staff had kept an extremely close hold on information relating to the move, but when the announcement over CNN specifically named the major units that would be going, Franks concluded that he and the rest of the corps leaders could now be much more public about who was going (though they could not be public about their strengths, their equipment, or their schedule of deployment). Having that option made the job much easier to coordinate within the corps itself, it helped inform families about what they needed to know most, and it allowed them to make the plans they needed to make. It additionally allowed the corps to coordinate more easily with the Germans and other NATO allies on the specifics of the movement.

Soon, Franks knew, he would have to go around to check the pulse of the soldiers and NCOs. How were they handling this? What about the families?

The family question was especially important for a corps based in Germany. Many American military families were living there—most married soldiers had their spouses and children with them—and in Germany, there was no external family and neighbor support on which the spouses and children could depend. That meant the families would either have to go home to the United States, which few wanted to do, or else depend on each other and on the entire military family in Germany.

Fred Franks knew he would have to begin working on family issues along with everything else.

"Let's go," he said to all the others, "we have work to do."

The TV set was in another part of the ops center, so Franks and his planners reassembled in the conference room. When they were there, he wanted to say a few words, to give the others a chance to collect their thoughts and capture the significance of the moment.

"Let all this settle in for a few minutes," he said. "This is part of history. You will remember this night for the rest of your lives, and well you should. It is something to tell your kids and grandkids about. There is a personal part for each of us as well. It affects our families. For some it is a first. Others will remember Vietnam. I know we have a lot to do, but I wanted to pause and reflect for a moment, because you will want to remember this night for a long time."

And then they got down to business.

Two hours later, they had a pretty good idea of the direction their next days would take. Their major challenge was to figure out the best use of their time.

Their major unknown was to answer the most important question: What would VII Corps's mission be? Franks had a pretty good idea that they would not be going down there to defend, but an attack can take many forms, and the corps had to be prepared to undertake any of them. Next, they needed to set an order of deployment quickly so that units could plan accordingly. It seemed best to lead the deployment with the 2nd Cavalry Regiment as the security force, which was one of the traditional roles of a cavalry regiment. But after that, the most immediate requirement was to get in as many engineer, transportation, and communication units as possible, so that they could build some basic infrastructure in the desert. Deploying combat units later would allow them to take advantage of the modern training facilities in Germany before they left. Franks had two other immediate tasks. First, he wanted to assemble the major unit commanders the next morning and issue guidance and listen to what they had to say. The second was to fly down to Saudi Arabia as soon as possible to make a leader's reconnaissance. The leader's recon took place from Sunday, 11 November, to Thursday the fifteenth.

At home, Denise had seen AFN, as had Margie in Bad Kissingen. This moment was hard for her—it was hard for both of them, as it was for all the families. She had seen him go away to war before, and she knew what that meant, and she knew what the separation meant for families.

"So now you know what those meetings and trips to Heidelberg have been about," he said after they'd had a chance to sit down and catch their breath in their family room.

"Now I know," she said. "Fred, I thought you were working to deactivate units in the corps."

"Look, Denise," he answered, "if it has to be done, VII Corps is trained and ready. We know how to do this. I know how to get it done at least cost to our troops.

"You and I have been through this before. We both know what to do. Now we have to help others. Who better to do this than you and me?" As he spoke, Franks thought again of Vietnam, the amputee ward, and the opportunities the Army had given him to come back.

As Fred spoke these words, he could see in her face two conflicting emotions. One, she wished she didn't have to hear them. And two, she was herself a veteran. In the crunch, she was a real rock. "OK," her face was telling him, "you and VII Corps have to go and do what you have to do. It's your job. Just as I'll have my own job here. We'll both do our best." She was an Army wife, and Army wives have their own kind of resolve, discipline, and duty.

The next day, she was rolling up her sleeves, getting involved with family support for the entire corps, and setting a positive example.

FRIDAY, 9 NOVEMBER 1990

Early Friday morning, Franks got two calls from Saudi Arabia. The first was from Major General William "Gus" Pagonis in Dhahran, and the second from Lieutenant General John Yeosock in Riyadh. Yeosock was commander of AR-CENT/Third Army, which had now been given the mission to command XVIII Corps and VII Corps under CENTCOM. Before VII Corps had been sent, ARCENT handled logistics and infrastructure for CENTCOM, and XVIII Corps reported to CENTCOM for operations. (This rapid transformation from an infrastructure command to also being a two-corps field command was to prove understandably difficult and take some time.) Gus Pagonis handled logistics for ARCENT, but also directly for the CINC—a job he accomplished so brilliantly that he was promoted to lieutenant general during the course of the Gulf crisis. Pagonis had a talent for making things happen, and for getting what needed to be got, no matter what it took to get it. Both Yeosock and Pagonis, it turned out, were primarily concerned with the immediate difficulties of bringing the enormous VII Corps into the already logistically strapped Gulf theater. The first problem was what to do with them and how to supply them. The mission against the Iraqis—whatever that turned out to be—would be dealt with later.

When Pagonis called, Franks had no idea who he was; they had never met. In fact, the name did not register; what Franks wrote down on his pad was "Bagonas." After all that was cleared up, Pagonis welcomed Franks and the corps to CENTCOM, and then got down to business.

"Right, Gus, thanks," Franks said in response to the welcoming words, and then asked, "And so what advice do you have?"

"That's what I called about," Pagonis said. "The theater is strapped for transportation, and for tents and cots for your troops. We were just getting up to speed in supporting XVIII Corps, and now we have your corps coming."

"How can we help?"

"First, you can front-load your deployment with as much support infrastructure as possible. I know you'll want to get your combat units in first. Don't do it."

As it happened, Franks was planning to send logistics in first, with most combat units to follow. That way the combat units could train as much as possible on the sophisticated training facilities in Germany. Pagonis's advice confirmed that plan.

"What about ports?"

"We'll bring you in through Dammam and Jubayl." Dammam and Jubayl were major ports on the Gulf, in northeastern Saudi Arabia. They had recently been upgraded and modernized with U.S. help and advice. As a result,

Dammam and Jubayl became world-class seaports. Without them the enormous Coalition deployment would still have been possible, but not in a workable time frame. "I can't emphasize enough," Pagonis went on, "that you need to bring as many HETs as you can from Germany. Otherwise we will have your troops stacked up in ports waiting for trucks. You also need to bring as much tentage and as many cots as you can find. We do not have any for you here. XVIII Corps bought all the Saudis had." HETs—Heavy Equipment Transporters—were used in Saudi Arabia mainly for transporting heavy tracked vehicles the 400 to 500 kilometers from the ports to the Tactical Assembly Areas—TAAs.

"Right, Gus," Franks replied in closing. "I've got it. Appreciate the advice. Look forward to joining the team and working with you."

It was a good phone call, Franks thought then, direct, candid, and to the point. In a few minutes he got the picture of what they were up against in this deployment. There were going to be shortages. It was going to be a lean theater, not at all like Germany, with its relatively luxurious logistical base. No use fighting it, he thought. That's the way it is. Deal with it.

Meanwhile, Gus Pagonis had been direct and forthright, true, but he'd had his own agenda as well. Pagonis was just getting his head above water with XVIII Corps. He was just about able to meet their requirements. And now VII Corps was coming down from Europe and the States, and he had very little left for them. He couldn't very well go to Gary Luck and ask him to give it back. Meanwhile, VII Corps was leaving a giant warehouse (in Pagonis's view) that was full of material that he could use in theater. And so, as soon as it was announced that VII Corps was going to the Gulf, the first thing he did was put leverage on Franks to bring some of that material down: cots, tents, fuel trucks, tank transporters, and much, much else. It was a normal request.

Pagonis took his needs to Franks. Other CENTCOM and ARCENT requests were going to Washington to the Department of the Army and the Joint Staff. EUCOM, with USAREUR as the land component, was one source of supply. Yet Saint proved in no way eager to raid all the warehouses of Europe and pull all of his stocks down to where he didn't have enough for his own mission. His mission remained large and CENTCOM had other sources of supply. At that point, CENTCOM was to be the supported command; it was the main U.S. operation in all the world, and General Powell had directed that they could have anything they asked for. What Butch Saint wanted was for Pagonis—and CENTCOM in general—to go to the Department of the Army and the Joint Staff and get them to support the theater. He wanted balance. He wanted Washington to look worldwide and task the Army all over the world to contribute to the Gulf forces, in ways that preserved mission accomplishment. He didn't want USAREUR to be forced to become CENTCOM's automatic supply source, simply because USAREUR was closer to the Gulf than everyone else. He wanted to supply VII Corps, but not the whole theater.

As it turned out, VII Corps got all the support they needed from Europe. Saint *did* want VII Corps to succeed, and in truth CENTCOM was unable to supply the corps with what it needed, so in the end Saint and Galvin opened up the caches of Central Europe not only to them, but to the theater. They got not only basic equipment (including, for instance, water trailers from what was once East Germany, now with German markings) but also consumables such as spare parts, ammo, medical supplies, and so on. VII Corps's deployment from Europe took almost double the number of ships than what was originally estimated.

The conversation with John Yeosock was more wide ranging than the earlier one with Gus Pagonis. Franks and Yeosock were friends and fellow cavalrymen.

"Fred, welcome to the team," Yeosock said as soon as they were connected on a secure line.

"John, thanks for calling. Proud to join the team. Bringing a lot of combat power with me. Think I can get an airplane and come down on a leader's recon on Sunday."

"That's perfect. We'll set up some briefings and get you around the area. Plan to stay through Wednesday, as the CINC wants a meeting in Dammam down through division commanders."

"Right, I'll do that," Franks said, then went on to summarize his conversation with General Pagonis.

"What Gus told you is accurate," Yeosock replied after he'd finished. "We were just about out of the hole with XVIII Corps, and now we are back to square one." And he went on to reinforce Pagonis's emphasis on logistics, especially trucks, tents, and cots, adding that they would also need units in early who could build an infrastructure—rough base camps, sanitation, communication, and the like. The desert was like nothing they were used to, he told him. You had to look hard in the States for anything that harsh and empty. Both men had served in the southwestern desert, at the 3rd CAV at Fort Bliss. But that was a tropical rain forest compared to the Saudi desert, Yeosock said.

He was exaggerating, but not much. One of the VII Corps troops remarked later that looking around the Saudi desert truly proved God rested on the seventh day.

"Going in first with logistics makes sense," Franks agreed, "and that is what we'll do. But I know the deployment order is your call"—as commander of Third Army, VII Corps's new next higher command. "What I have in mind is to send the 2nd ACR first for security. Then I'll send infrastructure. I'll have a recommended complete TPFDL for your approval when we come on our leader's recon."

The TPFDL—Time Phased Force Deployment List—lays out the order of deployment for each unit to go into a new theater. The commander in theater must approve this schedule before it can be set in motion. That happened early in Franks's visit to Saudi Arabia a few days later.

"Go with that plan," Yeosock said, "and we can look over your detailed list when you get down here."

They moved on to other matters.

"What about assembly areas?" Franks asked. "And any word on employment?"—mission.

"Right now, I see you to the west of XVIII Corps, with your 2nd ACR maintaining contact on the east with XVIII's 3rd ACR and on the west with the Arab Corps"—with the Arab part of the Coalition armed forces. "Then you can place your divisions behind the 2nd ACR."

Franks and some of his commanders would look over some of these Tactical Assembly Areas the following week during the leaders' recon.

"For employment, it is hard to read right now," Yeosock continued. "I suspect we'll get something from the CINC next week. It looks to me like you'll be the main attack and that you'll attack up the Wadi al Batin. You'll head north from Hafar al Batin with the corps deployed from that town east to Al Qaysumah."

Hafar al Batin is a Saudi town that lies near the junction of the Wadi and the major highway known as the Tapline Road, which runs north and west from the coast in a virtually straight line parallel to the Saudi-Iraq border. The town of Al Qaysumah lies on the Tapline Road about thirty kilometers from Hafar al Batin, and the entire area is approximately four hundred kilometers northwest of the ports on the Gulf coast. At the time, Fred Franks had only the vaguest notion of this geography, and the names he spelled out phonetically— and incorrectly. His ignorance was not destined to last for long.

"Thanks, John," he said, signing off. "That gives me enough to get the corps moving. See you Sunday night."

★ Small moments and not large occasions often wake us to the significance of enormous, earth-rattling changes. At nine A.M. that same morning a group of senior German military leaders and local civilian officials gathered with VII Corps leaders and families next to the VII Corps front gate there at Kelly Barracks. They were there to dedicate a memorial to the end of the Cold War. The twin highlights of the memorial were sections taken from the Berlin Wall and from the Iron Curtain. The piece from Berlin was donated to VII Corps by U.S. Berlin Command; the other piece was donated by the 2nd Armored Cavalry Regiment. There was a small stone patio, a bench, and a brass plaque. It was a modest affair, yet a small but visible reminder of the sacrifice and dedication it took to win America's "longest war."

The German guests did not know that VII Corps had been ordered to Saudi Arabia. The American attendees, of course, had watched AFN the night before. There was an unusual tension. As Franks looked out at the gathering and began to speak, he was struck by how the monument behind him was a visible sign of one familiar world now gone, and that VII Corps was now a visible sign of a different world whose outlines were not to be so sharp and clear as the one coming to an end. It was the end of one war in one theater under one set of strategic conditions well known to all, and the beginning of a deployment to another theater in another coalition for perhaps another war in a set of strategic conditions just beginning to emerge. There were consequences no one could predict with any probability or certainty. All the signs and symbolism were there. That reflection took all of about ten seconds to flash through Franks's brain as he realized he was neither poet nor philosopher at that moment, but a corps commander who had work to do and not much time for reflection.

A little later, at the reception, Franks announced to his German friends that the corps was going to the Gulf. At the same time he asked them, as friends, for their help.

He got it . . . more help from them and from the rest of the German people than he dreamed possible. The warmth and generosity of the Germans, from government and military officials down to families caring for families, gave splendid evidence of the friendship that had grown out of the long residence of the American army in Germany. Just as important, the Germans knew what to do and they got things done, efficiently and without complaint. ("We understand better than most what it means to send troops away," some of Franks's older German friends remarked.)

★ Later that morning, Franks assembled his new corps team in the command conference room, just upstairs from the secure conference room where they'd done most of their initial planning for the deployment: The 1st and 3rd Armored Division commanders, Ron Griffith and Butch Funk; the regimental commander of the 2nd ACR, Colonel Don Holder; the deputy corps commander, Gene Daniel; the chief of staff, John Landry; and the separate brigade commanders: the 14th MP commander, Rich Pomager; the 93rd Signal Brigade commander, Rich Walsh; the 207th MI Brigade commander, John Smith; the 11th Aviation Brigade commander, Johnnie Hitt; the 7th Engineer Brigade commander, Sam Raines; the 2nd COSCOM (Corps Support Command) commander, Bob McFarlin; the corps artillery commander, Creighton Abrams (son of the former Army Chief); the 7th Personnel Group commander, Jo Rusin; the 7th Finance Group commander, Russ Dowden; plus all of Fred Franks's staff, including the VII Corps base staff.

Fred Franks picks it up here:

There was electricity in the air. At the beginning of some meetings, you look around and can tell from body language and lack of energy in small talk that you need to do something dramatic to get everyone's attention. That was not the case today.

It was an impressive collection of talented and savvy commanders who were now ready to serve the same cause, only on a different continent against a different enemy. The only commander at that meeting from outside the regular corps lineup was Major General Butch Funk, CG 3rd Armored Division, normally assigned to V Corps. Following the two phone calls from Saudi, I had made myself some notes on three-by-five cards, as I did not want to leave anything out of this meeting. It was to be brief, but also important for all of us.

Attitude was important—mine and theirs. I needed to set the tone of command for this whole operation right from the start. I was pumped up. We had trained hard. We were confident. We were ready. I was sure of that. What I wanted was attention to thoughts we had previously adopted for VII Corps: focus on teamwork, discipline, agility, and skill in fundamentals. I wanted to reinforce the confidence, rapidly build this new team, set the attitude, and issue instructions for training priorities and rough order of deployment.

"Welcome. You all know where we're going unless you missed AFN last night. This will be a different kind of meeting than we originally had planned for this morning. Butch [MG Butch Funk], welcome to the VII Corps team. As I understand it, you will report here for operational matters, but stay plugged into V Corps for your deployment.

"I am proud that we are able to answer the call. Proud that the JAY-HAWKS are going. I told the CINC [General Saint] two months ago that if they needed another corps in Saudi, we were ready. We finished our mission in Europe and, besides, we are halfway there. Getting there will be a tough challenge, especially from a standing cold start. We can do it and will. We need to do what we know how to do. I want teamwork, since we will have a new lineup. We need discipline and reliance on the chain of command, since there will be a lot to do at the same time. There will be adjustments necessary, to be sure. Stay loose. This deployment will not go with the precision of laser brain surgery. Don't get frustrated because there

is not much you can do about it anyway. As deployment friction generates time, use that time for training, especially in fundamentals. Remember, skill in fundamentals wins in combat.

"In the absence of any mission orders, I want you to use your training time to concentrate on the following: chemical protection; weapons skills to be razor sharp, especially long-range gunnery; field craft, or living in the desert [later we would call it getting desert-smart and desert-tough]; and maneuver of large formations.

"One other thing. We will go do what we have to do and talk about it later. We are going to join our fellow soldiers who have been there now in a tough situation for three months. We are good, we know that. If we have to kick some ass, we know how to do that, too. But we do not need a lot of swagger bullshit about us coming into theater as saviors of the situation down there. Quiet professionalism is what I want. Inner toughness. My words to my cavalry friends fit here; that is, I want more gun smoke than horseshit."

We agreed on that.

Next was to arrange for a leaders' recon on Sunday to Saudi Arabia and look at our new area of operations, to talk to our fellow soldiers and leaders to get some lessons learned, and get some mission guidance from the CINC. One other benefit would be to remove some of the unknowns and stop some rumors, plus help commanders decide how much of what to take (not tanks or other major unit items, but things such as spare parts, training materiel, cots, tents, athletic equipment for whatever spare time the troops would have, etc.).

We then went over other things: preparation for the overseas move (all the coordination necessary to get soldiers processed—shots, wills, family-support plans for those single parents and dual military, etc.); the importance of physical training; making a thorough people check so that we would know if we had any deployability problems; and finally the alignment of how we spent our training time to practice skills required for our mission, whenever we got it.

Family support was a big issue since we were already a forward-deployed force with family members, and we would now deploy again, this time without family members. Our army had not done this on such a scale before, so we wanted to ensure we had well-thought-out military community family-support plans, that the Army would help our families take care of themselves. This was a particular point of pride with them, most of whom decided to stay at home in Germany rather than go back to the U.S.A.

Operations security was a question on everyone's mind. What could *we say and what couldn't we? Good question. Our rule was we could talk about what President Bush, Secretary of Defense Dick Cheney, and General Colin Powell had said on TV last night, but not much more. I did not want any mention of size of our units, or the sequence of our deployment (at this point that was also a mystery to my commanders, so no worry about that), or any speculation about what we would do when we got there.*

Finally, I told the commanders that we would lead with the 2nd ACR, followed by our signal, logistics, and engineer units, then the rest of the combat units. Details would follow when I got the OK on deployment order from CENTCOM.

It was a short meeting. I wanted to get things in motion rapidly. The corps needed to explode into immediate action. It is what we would have done if the Soviets had launched a surprise attack. For us it was something that we had lived with in Central Europe for forty years. For all those years, we had had unannounced readiness alerts every month, in which we would have to clear our barracks and motor pools, including ammo upload with all our vehicles, in less than two hours. We could handle this cold start. I was sure of it.

The other reason I was sure was that I was talking to winners. Leaders who had stayed the course, who had been part of a twenty-year rebuilding of the U.S. Army, who had just helped win the Cold War without a shot fired. I recognized this kind of an outfit.

I had been through this before. It would be the same in a lot of ways, but one thing was certain—this time the results would be different! I personally owed that to my fellow amputees from Valley Forge and to the soldiers now entrusted to my command.

Team Building

Since the VII Corps that had been stationed in Germany was only a portion of the VII Corps that went to Saudi Arabia, special efforts had to be put into creating the new VII Corps team.

For the commander, team building is not simply a matter of bringing the new units on board, showing them they are welcome, and incorporating their work styles into your own; team building is a matter first of assessing the following skills and then of acting on your assessment. You have to know (1) how well the new leaders communicate with you and with one another; and (2) how well they execute whatever it is they are supposed to be doing. You want the new people to fit in, yes, but fitting in is not the first goal. You want them to fit in in such a way that you can use them to achieve the goals you set for them within the mission.

Communication involves, first of all, knowing who you're dealing with. You find this out partly during the regular meetings with your subordinates and partly by visiting them on their own turf. The normal give-and-take of meetings will give you a sense of what's important to the various subordinates, how each looks at situations under discussion, and so on. In an organization as large as an Army corps, there will of course be particular practices and policies that have to be insisted upon. These have to be done in a certain way and no other, and that's the way it must be. They are not negotiable. Franks calls such items FARs—"flat-ass rules." Other policies and practices are up for discussion; there are several possible ways to accomplish them. From observing how subordinates deal with these and how they interact with one another and with you during meetings, you get a sense of who you're dealing with. You also watch to see how quickly the others understand what you have to tell them. Some people understand you almost immediately. Others need detailed explanations. Others are full of questions. Some need very precise language in order to understand you. Others "get it" on the fly. None of these communication styles is necessarily wrong, or bad, though quickness and precision in communication is obviously desirable in the Army.

In combat, you're rarely in the same room with your most important subordinates, and when you see them, you don't usually spend two hours with them. You're with them for maybe fifteen minutes to half an hour at a time, or perhaps forty-five minutes at the maximum; then you're off to somewhere else. In those fifteen or so minutes, the communication has to be exceptionally quick, accurate, and disciplined. With some subordinates, you can always get your business done fast, often in less than ten minutes. Others might take an hour to cover the same business. If a commander is not able to see all of his subordinates during a given swing around his command, he might choose to see face-to-face only those subordinates who are not as quick, precise, and disciplined as the others. The quick ones can perhaps be handled over the phone.

You have to know how subordinates communicate, and then you have to know how well they execute in leadership situations. You find that out by visiting their positions and talking to the troops and the small-unit leaders. In time you begin to get an idea of what your leaders are made of, how they issue orders, how they react in leadership situations; and you can determine from that what types of missions you're comfortable giving them in future combat situations. What you're looking for is a commander, and his subordinates, who can do whatever you ask them to do; who can execute it very thoroughly and quickly, and up to a standard of perfection that they themselves will be proud of; who are capable of handling two or three significant operations simultaneously; and who are very resilient in their ability to handle mission planning.

When you are building teams, and teams of teams, *that's* what you are trying to build. And to the credit of Fred Franks and his colleagues, that was the
kind of team he took to Saudi Arabia.

LEADERS' RECON
SAUDI ARABIA
11 NOVEMBER TO 15 NOVEMBER 1990

On Sunday, 11 November, Franks flew to Riyadh in an Air Force C-21—the
Air Force version of the Learjet. With him on the six-seater was the core group
he wanted instantly up to speed in the new theater. The rest of his leaders were
to arrive in Dammam two days later, on the thirteenth. On the Learjet with
Franks were Brigadier General Bob McFarlin, the commander of the 7th Support Command (in charge of VII Corps logistics); Colonel Stan Cherrie, the
G-3; Colonel Ed Simpson, the deputy chief of staff, whom Franks had appointed to be commander of the VII Corps port arrival unit; Colonel Rich
Walsh, commander of the 93rd Signal Brigade (communications in the austere desert environment was going to be a big challenge for the corps signal
brigade, so Franks wanted Rich Walsh to come down early to look around);
and Major Toby Martinez, Franks's aide. The journey took a full day, including a fuel stop in Cairo. They arrived in Riyadh after dark, and they were met
there by John Yeosock (to welcome Franks, Yeosock gave him his sand-colored
baseball cap to replace Franks's floppy issue hat). After a working meal with
Yeosock, the briefings started. The next four days were packed with meetings,
briefings, and field trips to check out ports and the Tactical Assembly Areas,
and to visit units and commanders already deployed in the desert.

For Franks and his leaders and staff, it was to be their first opportunity to
get a personal sense of this very strange, unfamiliar, and harsh place where they
were about to set up operations, of the people who lived there, and of the many
challenges he and VII Corps were about to face. They had a lot to do in a short
time; Franks's mind was working at top speed, taking in impressions from all
of his senses, concentrating on details of briefings, taking notes, asking questions, doing whatever he could to get a feel for the operational situation, the
training situation, the living situation for his troops. He was also aware that
they were making a first impression on the others in the theater. Many of the
units already there had been in theater for months, deterring further Iraqi aggression into Saudi Arabia. These soldiers had worked hard under exceedingly
uneasy conditions (if the Republican Guards had continued to the south in
August or September, Coalition airpower *just may* have stopped them, but the
Coalition forces then on the ground would have had a very hard time keeping the Iraqis out of the Saudi oil fields). And they were understandably proud

of their success. Franks wanted to make sure that his own people portrayed a professional force that was simply coming to do its part in a team that was already established. He didn't want any swagger or chest thumping.

And so Franks and the others went around—covering hundreds of kilometers. They saw the terrain, the ports, and the desert. They talked candidly to their fellow commanders and soldiers, and learned from them. And finally, General Schwarzkopf gave a mission briefing for all of his commanders, division and above. It was Schwarzkopf's most important briefing of the war, the first and only mission briefing they were to get from him.

It was held on Wednesday morning, 14 November, in Dammam, in a building the U.S. military leased from the Saudis for use as a dining facility. The security at the door that morning was unusually tight.

All the U.S. commanders from all the services were there, through the chain of command to division commander. From VII Corps were Franks, Funk, Griffith, and Rhame. XVIII Corps included Luck, Peay, Tilelli, McCaffrey, and Johnson. Third Army had Yeosock and BG Steve Arnold, Yeosock's G-3. The Army attendees were a group of combat-seasoned veterans, all of whom had been through Vietnam and the long climb back.

General Norman Schwarzkopf, a large, imposing man, with a lot of flair and spark, was a splendid public speaker—forceful, articulate, inspiring—and this was to be one of his more spectacular performances. It was a fire-breathing talk, and he expected everyone in the room to breathe fire after they'd heard it. He wanted them to embrace his concept for defeating Saddam Hussein with the same passionate intensity that he himself felt.

The CINC walked into the room after everyone was seated. During his remarks, he occasionally referred to an outline on Army standard "butcher paper" charts; off to his side was a fifteen-foot-wide map of Kuwait and Iraq.

Franks and those around him took notes. For Franks and the others from VII Corps—the new guys in town, who had had only a few hours to get a sense of the country and what they were about to face—it was a time to take in and internalize. (New guys should be seen, and not heard.) They weren't ready with anything like operational questions, and even if they had been, it was clear that Schwarzkopf was not looking for feedback that day. Thus, from the CINC's opening words, Franks was intent on mentally processing the concept the CINC was laying out. ("What do I have to do to make my part of it work?") He was excited ("Here is our mission! It's a great mission! It's exactly what I want us to do!"), but it was a sharply focused, interior kind of excitement.

The briefing followed logical military format: it was a statement of the mission, preceded by enemy and friendly capabilities, and some restraints the CINC wanted imposed on his commanders.

He started by talking about security. Since the best source of intelligence the Iraqis had was the Western press, and since it was certain that the press would hit all the commanders with questions whenever the chance presented itself, commanders *must not*, he emphasized fiercely, discuss operational matters with them. "I will deal brutally with anyone who compromises anything from operations," Franks quoted in his journal.

These were the CINC's strategic objectives: to throw Iraq out of Kuwait, restore the government of Kuwait, defend Saudi Arabia, and free the U.S. hostages then held by Iraq. To accomplish those objectives, he continued, they would have to go after the Iraqi center of gravity, which he identified as Saddam Hussein himself, their chemical and biological weapons capability, and the Republican Guards.

The Iraqis' strength was in their numbers (at this point twenty-six divisions) and in their chemical capability. Their weakness was in their over-centralized command and control, their supply lines (they fought during the day and resupplied at night), and their limited air.

U.S. strength lay in air (especially in projection of strategic airpower), in ground technology (especially in tanks and at night), and in leadership.

At that point, Schwarzkopf outlined U.S. battlefield goals: "The first thing that we're going to have to do is attack leadership, and go after his command and control. Number two, we've got to gain and maintain air superiority. Number three, we need to cut totally his supply lines. We also need to destroy his chemical, biological, and nuclear capability. And finally, we need to destroy—not surround—I want you to *destroy* the Republican Guards. When you're done with them, I don't want them to be an effective fighting force."

The campaign would have four phases:

• **PHASE I:** Strategic air campaign (six days) aimed at Iraqi command and control, gaining air superiority, and destruction of strategic logistics.
• **PHASE II:** Gain air superiority in the Kuwaiti theater.
• **PHASE III:** Conduct battlefield preparation; that is, conduct tactical air operations on Iraqi positions on the ground in the Kuwaiti theater of operations (about twelve days).
• **PHASE IV:** Ground attack.

By now you could feel the intensity in the room. There was total concentration. There were no questions.

At that point the CINC turned to the plan for the ground offensive.

He listed the forces available as principally four corps equivalents: the U.S. Marines, Arab Corps, VII and XVIII Corps. Though the strategic aim of the offensive was to drive the Iraqis out of Kuwait, the tactical aim of the offensive maneuver was to close the Iraqis—and especially the RGFC—in a box in and near Kuwait, to maneuver against them with the U.S. heavy punch, and then to destroy them. He talked about the adjustments that needed to be made as the enemy kept changing, and thought that it might not be until D-15 that battle plans would finally be decided.

The area of the maneuver was vast—larger than the state of Virginia. Part of the box's sides were natural, and part were, or would be, created by Coalition fighting forces. Looking at Kuwait: to the east was the natural barrier of the Gulf; to the north was the Euphrates, a potential barrier once air cut the bridges over it; to the south was Saudi Arabia, now closed to the Iraqis because of Desert Shield forces; and to the west was the desert vastness, the main corridor of attack. Schwarzkopf discussed the trafficability of the desert and directed the commanders to pay attention to that.

After noting that detailed intelligence of the Iraqi barrier system would be available by D-15, he emphasized, "Logistics is the long pole in the tent"— commanders *must* be prepared with logistics to support their operations—and directed them all to begin offensive training immediately. He added that he would reposition forces when the Iraqi recon capability was gone, and directed the Arab forces to liberate Kuwait City. And finally, he said, his worst-case scenario was that the attacking Coalition forces would be hung up in the Iraqi obstacle system and get hit by chemical attack. (Franks was to hear Schwarzkopf constantly stress the need to reduce casualties, a drive he shared with the CINC.)

He concluded, passionately, "Let me leave you with one thought, guys. In order for this to succeed—because the enemy is still going to outnumber us"— and because they had built what appeared to be a tough, extensive, potentially deadly barrier system along the border—"it is going to take . . . killer instinct on the part of all of our leaders out there. . . . We need commanders in the lead who absolutely, clearly understand that they *will get through*" the barrier system. "And that once they are through, will move. We will attack, attack. I will look for commanders who can attack. We cannot afford failure. We will not fail."

And that was it. It was a masterful presentation in content, in format, and in motivational language. No one there could possibly have a question about what he was supposed to do.

★   Many outside the Army erroneously imagine that when a commander like Fred Franks receives a plan—such as the one General Schwarzkopf outlined— all he has to do, more or less, is follow the numbers. People tend to think the whole thing is completely worked out, like a recipe in a cookbook, and all that's left for the subordinate commander is to say, "Yes, sir," and go execute it.

Not true.

General Schwarzkopf's campaign outline was indeed an excellent operations concept, but it did not provide—nor did it ever intend to provide—Fred Franks or Gary Luck or any of the other commanders more than a very general design for what they were supposed to do. The tactical details had to be worked out later. The outline defined the missions of each corps and its general scheme of maneuver; it gave each corps the sector it was to operate in (the corridors that Schwarzkopf talked about); and it laid out the phases of the campaign. But it was not at all specific in terms of the tactical operation.

So, in effect, the CINC was saying, "OK, VII Corps, your mission is to destroy the Republican Guards. And, XVIII Corps, your mission is to go up and interdict Highway 8. But how you do that, that's up to you." He even made a point of that during the briefing.

Consequently, as Franks was internalizing and processing the plan that morning, a host of questions was racing through his head: How extensive is the Iraqi barrier system in my sector? Will it go all the way across it? Will I have to breach the barrier before I can get my forces through? Or can I go around it, farther to the west? And how is the terrain out there? Can my heavy stuff pass over it? What options are available to the RGFC? What are my schemes of maneuver? How do I mass my corps for the RGFC destruction? How do I structure and orchestrate my corps for that attack? What are the battles and engagements I need to fight, sequentially and simultaneously, to get to and destroy the RGFC?

The CINC had nothing to say about that. That was Fred Franks's responsibility.

Some of them gave the obligatory expression of confidence and enthusiasm for the plan, but it was still little more than a concept or a notion. Fred Franks was already working the idea and analyzing the mission—keeping his own counsel until he had processed the task before him intellectually.

★ When the briefing was over, the CINC doubtless expected an outpouring of enthusiasm from his commanders, and he got it from some of them. But not from Fred Franks, which, for Franks, was certainly a mistake. For General Schwarzkopf, Franks's absence of outward display was interpreted as a lukewarm attitude toward the plan.

In fact, Franks was profoundly enthusiastic about the CINC's concept, and he was absolutely certain that when it came to a fight, his troops would win. Unfortunately, an excited outburst was the farthest thing from his mind just then. Instead, he was rapidly forming maneuver schemes in his head (hoping to give his commanders an early heads-up); he was thinking about Iraqi forces in front of the corps and about what the Republican Guards might do (since the VII Corps mission was force oriented), and he was thinking about force placement on the ground.

After General Schwarzkopf finished speaking, he invited the others up front to look more closely at the maps and the intelligence photos of the mine-fields and barrier systems, and the like. While Franks was up there, examining them, the CINC approached him and asked, "Hey, Fred, what do you think?"

And Franks answered, in a calm, confident, forceful, but professional voice, "We can do this. We'll make it happen."

For the CINC, that wasn't enough. It turned out to be a burr beneath Schwarzkopf's skin.

Later, in General Schwarzkopf's autobiography, *It Doesn't Take a Hero*, the general states that Franks was the one leader at the briefing who was not happy with the plan. In his words: "The only dissonant note was from Freddie Franks: 'The plan looks good, but I don't have enough force to accomplish my mission.' He argued that I should give him the 1st Cavalry Division, which I was holding in reserve. I said I would consider it when the time came."

This conversation did not take place on 14 November—though later, in a December briefing, Franks stated that as a planning assumption he presumed that the 1st CAV would be released to VII Corps, if they weren't required to save some situation elsewhere (also a Third Army assumption and a normal planning assumption, since VII Corps was the main attack).

The dissonance between Generals Schwarzkopf and Franks was to grow, with consequences that were unfortunate.

✯ Meanwhile, though Franks was certain that General Schwarzkopf's concept of attack was in fact the right one, with the right maneuver scheme, to achieve his goal of destroying the Republican Guard, nevertheless, he had a few questions about some of the tactical details that the CINC had left to be developed later. Franks actually thought he could help resolve these and be a team player. Since it would have been inappropriate and unprofessional to voice these concerns that day, he didn't, but later, at a more appropriate time, he went directly to John Yeosock and Steve Arnold, and even talked to the "Jedi Knights."

In his view, the CINC's campaign operational concept had three areas for further tactical discussion.

First: In the plan's original incarnation, XVIII Corps's attack corridor was many kilometers to the west of the VII Corps sector, which might limit the availability of XVIII Corps's combat power. Though XVIII Corps did not have the heavy combat power of VII Corps, it still had plenty. Yes, XVIII Corps should certainly push on up to Highway 8 and close that lane of escape for the Republican Guards, but if it was that far to the west, could it then move east fast enough to join its combat power to VII Corps's in a coordinated corps attack—if that was called for? If VII Corps attacked north-northeast, it would "pinch out" XVIII Corps. If XVIII Corps was just to sit on Highway 8 while the main battle was raging a couple of hundred kilometers east of them, all their combat power would be unavailable. (Later, the plan was altered, and the two corps were brought closer together).

Second: The concept made assumptions about the isolation of the RGFC. It assumed that if the RGFC attempted to escape the theater, then the Euphrates bridges would be destroyed by air, which would make the Euphrates an anvil against which the Third Army hammer could pound the Guards. That detail remained to be planned and then executed.

Finally: There was no discussion of a final air-ground theater maneuver to complete the action and achieve the strategic objectives. There needed to be discussion of the endgame—the tactical finish that would best realize the Coalition's aims. The idea was to come up with some vision of the final disposition of all relevant forces—both air and ground—that would make the most long-term strategic sense. Those discussions would follow.

For Fred Franks and his commanders and staff, however, the leaders' recon turned out to be a terrific three days. Gary Luck and XVIII Corps had given them lessons learned and welcomed them to the team. The few small discords (not in fact then apparent to him) in no way diminished that. It was an intense, packed, and immensely productive time. They had a clear mission, clear goals, and enough work to fill forty-eight-hour days for the next several months. They had to bring the newly retailored VII Corps to the Gulf and prepare the corps to fight our nation's toughest opponents since the Viet Cong and NVA.

When Franks flew back to Stuttgart, the little C-21 was so stuffed with papers and maps in the aisles and beneath the seats, there was scarcely room for passengers.

8

PREPARING FOR WAR

THE FIRST UNIT FROM THE 2ND ACR BEGAN LOADING TRAINS FOR German ports on 19 November 1990. The first troops from the 2nd Squadron, 2nd ACR, and support elements arrived in the Gulf on 5 and 6 December. This was a small wave foretelling the vast flood that was soon to follow.

Over the next two and a half months, VII Corps would be stretched and pulled in a hundred different directions. A commander's job is to focus his energies on the main objective while making sure that all the myriad activities that contribute to that objective's success are not ignored. For VII Corps, the main objective was to go to Saudi Arabia and, if needed, to attack and destroy the Republican Guards, and in order to achieve that objective, Franks fixed responsibility for the corps into four separate, but linked, areas. They would have to (1) deploy the corps while caring for families at home, (2) assemble the corps in Tactical Assembly Areas, (3) prepare for war, and (4) conduct combat operations.

Franks knew that he could not afford to take his eyes off any one of these activities, but his greatest focus had to be on the actual combat operations. In the other areas, he could accept some imperfection, and he trusted the commanders and noncommissioned officers to get the job done, but in preparing and conducting combat operations, the tolerance for failure to meet expectations had to be extremely low. Here was where he had to place his main personal effort, intervening in the other areas only when they needed him or when, in his own judgment, he needed to step in to break a logjam.

He threw himself into a series of meetings, war games, visits, and constant chattering over phones and tactical radios to get the job done on the combat side. In the meantime, to ensure family support, he established VII Corps Base in Germany. To handle the continued deployment of the corps after the corps headquarters had moved to Saudi Arabia, he left his deputy commander, Brigadier General Gene Daniel, and a headquarters element in Stuttgart to work with USAREUR and EUCOM. And to get the 152 ships and 927 aircraft of VII Corps debarked and then moved the 500 kilometers to the Tactical Assembly Areas in Saudi Arabia, he formed a special command called the Port Support Authority, or PSA, and to command it, picked his friend and 1959 West Point classmate, Brigadier General Bill Mullen, and his commanders and leaders from the 1st Infantry Division Forward.

It was time to begin.

GETTING MOVING

As a matter of priority in VII Corps, Franks had always stressed attention to fundamentals, agility, teamwork, and discipline. Though he would take those same priorities to the desert, there was now a new lineup of units and a new mission in a new set of conditions. The priorities would have to be adapted to these new conditions.

In mid-November, this is what he found when he looked at training specifics:

Third Armored Division had just completed their extensive semi-annual gunnery and maneuver training at Grafenwohr and Hohenfels, and they were currently engaged in a BCTP seminar, so the deployment order had come at a training peak for them. Good news. This was not the case with the 2nd ACR and the 1st Armored Division, however. They had not fired their major direct-fire tank and Bradley weapons systems in some time, and after they began deployment—which was very soon—their equipment would not even be available for training. Franks quickly reached out to the 3rd Infantry Division, which was already at Grafenwohr, but would not be deploying to the desert. In an act of great teamwork that proved to be of enormous training benefit to the corps, the soldiers and leaders of the 3rd Infantry Division formed a cadre and provided their own equipment so that 2nd ACR and 1st Armored Division soldiers could go through an intense period of training. Franks visited the 3rd ID often and never heard a grumble.

Initially, then, things seemed to be in good shape.

Yet after his return from the leaders' recon to Saudi Arabia, Franks began to notice that leaders at all levels were increasingly distracted by the myriad details of deployment. This was completely understandable, he felt, since deployment from a no-notice cold start was certainly not going to go with much precision. There was a lot of "friction." Some things just did not get done unless the commander got personally involved.

But some imperfection could be absorbed, because deployment was not the main effort. Training was. So in order to "get our heads out of CONEX*

---

*Large metal shipping containers

containers," as he put it, and into war-fighting thinking and training, he decided to convene a war council. They met at Schweinfurt, on 29 November, with 3rd Infantry Division* the host, and all the commanders present.

Franks did not want too many commanders' meetings, but it was useful to get them together from time to time, especially since some of them were new. His two consistent objectives at all of these meetings were to focus the commanders on what was important—for now, training, and later, operations—and to establish teamwork. He had a different group now and it was his job to unite them as one team. In a setting such as this, they could talk training and war fighting with one another, see how the rest thought, and Franks could both size them up and further encourage camaraderie.

The agenda that day was simple: the G-2 briefed them on the Iraqi order of battle and the latest from southwest Asia, then 1st Armored Division talked the commanders through a minefield-breaching operation; next everyone discussed how to assemble the corps—to deploy to Saudi Arabia and get everyone back together again in units—and the meeting closed with more "flat-ass rules" and training.

Some of the FARs were as follows: Because the corps must always fight in depth, they would discuss deep operations at every meeting. (As battle progressed, the tendency was to put one's attention on the battle in close contact and forget about depth—a situation Franks intended to avoid.) Next: though Franks would issue mission orders to encourage and indeed demand initiative, no one was a free agent. He stressed again the role of agility in the corps and the importance of commanders' intent. The intent must be understood two echelons in either direction, he told them. In other words, a battalion commander must know what the division commander intends and a brigade commander must know what a corps commander intends. He stressed that massed artillery fire was at least two or more battalions on the same target (reinforcing Franks's own belief in gaining a decisive edge over the enemy). And finally: "Get desert-smart and desert-tough," he said, "but don't overextend people and machines."

That meeting would set the command focus for VII Corps's training for their combat mission two and a half months later.

---

*Third Infantry also ran the convoy operations over German highways to ports in northern Germany and Holland and provided the cadre to load the ships at the port.

FROM A DISTANCE

There is an old saying that the toughest job in the military is to be a military spouse. VII Corps was about to prove that in spades.

Military families are accustomed to separations, but usually for predictable lengths of time, and there was nothing predictable about what was about to happen. Nor could they use Vietnam as a guideline. With Vietnam, soldiers had gone off to war for a certain amount of time, with certain hardships and casualties, but for the most part, after early unit deployments they had gone off individually, not as a unit, and here it was all different.

Now whole units were going, and family members knew one another, and knew other service members. They were a *unit* family, and so the impact of the departure—of friends and neighbors gone, of bustling *kasernes* suddenly emptied of soldiers—was profound and shocking.

Over the long years of the Cold War, military communities had sprung up in Germany, groupings of units and family members essentially into U.S. "towns," normally centered on garrison locations called *kasernes*, after the German word for barracks. In fact, they were mostly old German army locations, built prior to World War II, some dating as far back as World War I. Within these troop locations, which also included barracks for unmarried soldiers and motor parks for equipment, the U.S. Army had built family quarters (three-story, three-stairwell apartments and some individual dwellings), schools, shopping areas for PXs and commissaries, health clinics, athletic facilities, and other normal community facilities. In VII Corps alone, there were thirteen of these towns, which housed close to 100,000 U.S. VII Corps and other US-AREUR soldiers and close to 200,000 family members altogether.

Meanwhile, over the years, more and more Army service members had become married—60 to 75 percent by 1990—and because it had not been feasible for the Army to build more housing for them, many of them—up to half the families in some locations—lived in local German communities in housing leased from the Germans, some individually, others as blocks of units by the U.S. Army. Needless to say, such arrangements complicated living for those families, and at times, transportation, schools, medical care, and normal socialization with other American families proved difficult.

Such was the general situation when the announcement on 8 November hit VII Corps families with a thunderclap. The good news was that the announcement had named specific units and had gone out over the Armed Forces Network television station, so all the people connected with those units knew immediately. But not all the units had been named, so it was not until twenty-four to forty-eight hours later that everyone knew. And then the question was, what would the families do while the soldiers were off at war?

✯ Family support during periods of separations, and even during normal garrison operations, was not new to the Army. There had been support groups throughout the Army's history to assist families with the many challenges of living in faraway places—in the West after the Civil War, for instance. Such groups normally centered around units, and involved an informal grouping of spouses and a link to the unit's official chain of command. In the early 1980s, the Army even began a program called "command team seminars" to assist spouses, centering on a weeklong class at Fort Leavenworth while the military command spouse went to his or her pre-command course.

VII Corps deployment to Saudi Arabia built on the already existing informal, yet highly effective, family-support networks. And as for the families themselves, there was no complaining. The attitude was "We are part of the mission. Let's roll up our sleeves and get to work."

There also was official help. In General Butch Saint, for instance, they were fortunate to have a USAREUR commander who was both savvy in the ways of mobile armored warfare and acutely sensitive to family issues. He not only was intimately involved with units deploying throughout the command, but he realigned the military communities to see to it that VII Corps communities came under the direct support structure of his HQ, and he formed a family-support task force in the headquarters itself. He also set in motion plans to ensure the security of our families—understandably, there was a lot of anxiety about possible terrorist attacks—and he pledged the total support of the Army's assets for assistance. Wherever medical personnel and military police deployed with VII Corps units, he called in Reserve component units and individuals to come to Germany to replace them.

Meanwhile, on 6 December 1990, Franks published the detailed order to establish VII Corps Base, which would command those parts of the corps that would remain in Europe, an order that went into effect a week later, the day Franks deployed VII Corps HQ to Saudi Arabia. Though it was meant to accomplish a number of things simultaneously, it was aimed first and foremost at helping VII Corps families cope with the deployment and the war (if indeed there was to be a war, which was not yet certain).

To run the base, Franks and General Saint appointed Major General Roger Bean, current commander of the Pershing Brigade in Germany and an old friend of Franks, and as chief of staff Colonel Jerry Sinn, superb officer and the head of resource management. As an enlisted man in Vietnam, Sinn had been a tunnel rat, one of the soldiers who volunteered to go down into Viet Cong tunnels and look for the enemy, armed with only a pistol and flashlight.

As part of the order, Franks directed formation of a family-support directorate, whose sole responsibility was to help families in the corps. It was headed by Colonel Bob Julian, who had been running the corps's communications modernization program, now on hold because of Desert Shield.

Within each military community were formed what were called Family Assistance Centers—FACs—where the highest priority was to get information back and forth between families and forward-deployed spouses. Using faxes of newsletters, videotapes, phone calls, and messages, the FACs became nerve centers of information and comfort. At corps HQ at Kelly Barracks in Stuttgart, by converting an unused area with fresh paint and other internal construction, the spouses built a center where they could hold regular meetings and where teenagers of older military families could assume responsibilities and lend their considerable energies and talents. An e-mail system connected them to units in the Gulf. AT&T established a one-page "Desert Fax" program. Newsletters began all over VII Corps. Denise Franks started one of these, *Sandpaper-a-Desert Link*, which was published and distributed monthly. "This is a difficult time for all of us," she wrote in January 1991. "But I am inspired by all I see happening around me. . . . We all need help at one time or another. We aren't always able to repay the friends who helped us . . . but it is repayment in kind for us to offer help to someone else."

For all these efforts, the Army allowed use of transportation, copying machines, office space, and phones. For instance, Roger Bean let Denise use Fred's old commander's office for her own family-support work. She held her first of what turned out to be weekly meetings with a special task force on 13 November 1990, and also formed an informal advisory board with other senior commanders' spouses. Throughout the VII Corps area, similar arrangements sprang up, with Ron Griffith's wife, Hurdis; Butch Funk's wife, Danny; and others.

In an unprecedented act of friendship, the Germans poured out their support. Relations between the Americans and Germans had been genuinely warm and long-lasting, and now German army units provided security and transportation, and private German citizens contributed thousands of Deutschmarks for families, and sponsored Christmas functions.

Meanwhile, U.S. Army families in Germany began a yellow-ribbon campaign. The ribbons appeared everywhere to symbolize support for the deployed soldiers, and they stayed up until the soldiers came home. If there was a shortage of yellow ribbon, more was sent from the United States. Bolts arrived in Stuttgart. Every tree seemed to have one tied around it. Homes and office buildings and barracks became festooned with bright yellow ribbons.

Deployment reached and touched everyone. Some older families had more than one member deployed. In a spouse's absence, families bonded together to remember special occasions, such as anniversaries, births, graduations, and school events, and even to care for families where both spouses were deployed. The unofficial theme song in VII Corps Base was "From a Distance."

Security was tightened considerably, as threats from terrorism were real. Military police and local German police bonded together to provide a visible presence both on and off military *kasernes*. The presence of armed military police, complete with flak vests and Kevlar helmets, became a daily part of the military community landscape in Germany.

Schools also pitched in. Before Franks deployed, the head of the DODDS (Department of Defense Dependent School System) came to him and asked how the teachers could help. VII Corps immediately included DODDS in the information channels so that the teachers could explain what was going on to the students in school. The teachers also saw the children of the soldiers who were forward-deployed and at war every day, and were sensitive to their individual needs. They were quick to spot a student whose behavior might have changed, and to alert parents and offer counseling.

All of this activity was based on the simple yet profound idea that the Army takes care of its own. Following Desert Storm, the Army set about to capture valuable lessons learned, and published a TRADOC pamphlet in 1994 that would prove useful to future generations of families in similar circumstances, and would begin a formal program called Army Family Team Building. Many of the lessons were applied when U.S. Army forces deployed from Germany to Bosnia in 1995.

TIME IS A FOUR-LETTER WORD

The crush and variety of daily activities getting ready for war was almost mind-boggling. No one was exempt, from Franks commanding the corps to the Bradley or tank driver. It never let up. From the notification on 8 November to the week before the attack, when the last units from the 3rd AD arrived, it was the most intensive fourteen-week period of concurrent activities Fred Franks experienced in all his time in the Army. His REFORGER experiences were mild compared to this. His enemies quickly became accidents, troop sickness—and time: time to train, time to physically protect his troops.

The first thing he and his commanders noticed was the bare-bones nature of the theater. Everything became a struggle. Basic survival had to be created in the desert: shelters, sanitation, water, and food. Communications had to be set up, mail delivered, training ranges built, training started. And that was when they managed to get into the desert. It was hard enough just getting through the ports.

The VII Corps planners wanted to use the Saudi Arabian ports of

Dammam and Jubayl. Because Jubayl was over a 100 kilometers closer to their Tactical Assembly Areas, they wanted to bring the heavy forces through there, link up soldiers and equipment after two or three days, and move them quickly to the desert TAAs to begin training. They also had planned to combat-load* the ships, so that equipment could be speedily married up with units, and again moved to the desert.

None of these plans proved feasible. The airflow was smooth and uneventful, in fact, almost too efficient, because troops arrived on time, but ships did not. Some delays were caused by weather, some by ship breakdown. One crew jumped ship because they objected to arriving in a war zone.

In a perfect operation, the planners had estimated they would have a steady state of 8,000 to 10,000 troops in port at any one time, with a stay for each soldier of no longer than two or three days. They ended up with triple those numbers. Some troops waited in port for as long as three weeks for their equipment, which compounded the problems caused by the temporary living conditions in the port, fractured unit integrity, and seriously delayed plans for training in the desert. Though the command coped with these problems, they still had to face hundreds of unwanted daily issues. Stress on soldiers was high.

All of these problems continually proved the wisdom of placing Brigadier General Bill Mullen in command of corps Port Support Authority just after Christmas in 1990. The corps could not have gotten so ready to fight in such a short period of time with so many challenges to overcome if it had not been for the work of Mullen and his 1st ID Forward leaders and soldiers.

Their accomplishments were staggering. Between 5 December and 18 February, 50,500 vehicles were off-loaded and staged (checked and readied for heavy equipment transporter movement), 107,000 troops were billeted, supported, and secured, as well as thousands of other soldiers from other units. There were 900 convoys (the numbers of trucks in the convoys varied from twenty to fifty). More than 6,000 armored vehicles and other pieces of equipment were moved the 550 kilometers to desert assembly areas. Thirty-five hundred containers with spare parts and other critical items were sent forward. Eighty-six hundred vehicles were painted sand color. The maximum number of soldiers in port waiting for their equipment peaked at 35,981 on 9 January 1991 (many more than the eight to ten thousand soldiers they had planned for!). Maximum ship arrivals were eight in one day. On 12 January, nineteen ships were waiting to off-load. The last tanks and Bradleys arrived from Ger-

---

*Combat loading places a unit's weapons, equipment, ammo, and vehicles on board a ship in such a way that when these are unloaded at their destination, they'll be "ready to go." You can, for example, theoretically drive a combat-loaded unit off the ship and go fight it.

many from the 3rd Brigade, 3rd AD, on 6 February 1991. The last of VII Corps's units to arrive was the 142nd Artillery Brigade from the Arkansas National Guard on 17 February 1991. The types of ships varied: 11 U.S. Navy fast sea lift; 63 so-called roll-on roll-off ships; 74 World War II–type break bulk ships; and 4 lighter aboardship. Total ships: 152. The flow was not steady. In one week, 7 to 14 January, forty ships arrived.

Over Fred Franks's strong objections, ships were loaded for maximizing space and not for unit integrity. Analysis by the PSA indicated that equipment arrived on seven different ships over twenty-six days for nineteen different battalions. In some units, soldiers staged in one port while their equipment arrived in the other, over 100 kilometers away. One tank battalion in 3rd AD arrived on eight different ships over a twenty-three-day period. A corps signal battalion arrived on eleven different ships over sixteen days. A military intelligence battalion arrived on twelve different ships over thirty-five days.

Protecting the soldiers while in port from Scud attacks or terrorist action, ensuring good health in crowded conditions, and performing individual skill-training while waiting required both strong small-unit leader discipline and extraordinary overall leadership from Bill Mullen and his PSA. They not only got it done, they gave Franks and his commanders time to focus on training, planning, and eventually on conducting combat operations.

★ Meanwhile, to ensure the troops had the latest equipment, the Army decided to conduct a modernization program concurrent with the deployment. VII Corps would get the best tanks available. That meant swapping out some of the ones they'd brought for heavier-armor tanks, or bolting on heavier armor to ones they already had in the port (this was done by a group of civilians from Anniston Army depot in the U.S.A.). The 1st INF exchanged two tank battalions of 105-mm M1 tanks for 120-mm M1A1 tanks. In the 2nd ACR and in some 1st INF Division units, all the Bradleys were swapped for better-protected models. These were all command decisions linked to the battle being planned by the corps.

Additionally, VII Corps received a whole suite of mine-clearing equipment—plows, rollers, and a full vehicle-width rake. Hundreds of HMMWVs were added to replace older vehicles. Also new were the TACMS (ground-to-ground missiles) for their MLRS launchers and software to engage Scuds for their Patriots. Though corps units initially had no GPS receivers, they eventually received more than three thousand. Because there weren't enough GPS receivers to go around, some units had to use LORAN devices, or a combination of the two. LORAN and GPS are not compatible systems, which made for interesting navigation problems. The troops coped, but not without incident. There were two different tactical communications capabilities, the old and the new MSE (Mobile Subscriber Equipment—the Army's new tactical communication system that, among other things, establishes area communications just as a mobile phone does). They had to cobble these together to make both compatible. There were strategic comms, including a very few TAC-SAT* radios (essential, because of the great distances and the absence of reliable civilian comms). They also received the new reverse-osmosis water-purification equipment that allowed them to make their own water. And later they got the Pioneer UAV (*Unmanned Aerial Vehicle*) from the Navy, and employed it almost immediately.

Meanwhile, they had to deal with practical issues:

Troops had to get ammunition uploaded into vehicles and leaders had to make sure they had top-of-the-line wartime ammo. That meant distribution and uploading turrets and ammo trucks. Transportation was in short supply. The 1st INF had only forty-nine fuel trucks when they deployed from Fort Riley. At the end of the war, they had 114. It was an immense challenge for Gus Pagonis and the theater to find trucks to transport heavy tracked vehicles such as tanks and Bradleys from the ports to the desert. To augment the U.S. Army heavy equipment transporter trucks, he hired indigenous labor from Pakistan and other nations, with trucks, for the 800-plus-kilometer round trip to the desert. Compounding his challenge was the transportation required to haul new M1A1 tanks and Bradleys to the 1st CAV and 24th Division in order to swap for their old ones. And the limited truck supply had to haul U.S.A.F. ammo at the same time it was to haul the corps's late-arriving heavy tracked vehicles to the desert. When XVIII Corps began their truck move west after the start of the air campaign, the competition for truck assets intensified, causing a frustrated Ron Griffith at one point to order two Bradley battalions not to wait, but simply to drive the more-than-400-kilometer distance to their TAA on their own tracks.

Since the corps initially had no maps of the area, these had to be obtained and distributed by the tens of thousands, and in sets. (Military maps come in separate three-foot square sheets; for the VII Corps area, leaders needed about thirty separate sheets, which then had to be taped together to make one map.) It's a standing joke in the Army that you always go fight someplace where you can't pronounce the names of the towns and where you have no maps. For VII Corps, the joke wasn't all that funny.

Sanitation and waste disposal were also a serious issue—not only normal trash and garbage, but human waste. They burned it or buried it in deep pits. "Here's the most modern force our Army has ever fielded," Franks said at one

---

*Tactical Satellite Radio. When VII Corps deployed, they had none of these. They eventually got thirty-three for the whole corps. They could have used more.

point to Cal Waller, "using diesel to burn shit in fifty-five-gallon cut-off drums. It's no different from Vietnam." Black smoke plumes were everywhere.

Because they had very few cots, too many soldiers had to sleep on the sand. They worked at getting cots from every conceivable source in Europe and the United States.

Despite the efforts of everyone concerned, mail delivery was simply awful. Mail to and from Germany took up to a month. There was just too much volume for the system to handle, and of course transportation had higher priorities. Only after Franks ordered the formation of an ad hoc postal battalion, with a lieutenant colonel in charge, and gave them dedicated transportation, did the problem begin to get fixed. Of the spreading oil slick in the Persian Gulf, one frustrated soldier said, "Put a stamp on it and that way it will never get to Saudi Arabia."

On the positive side, water distribution worked well, which was aided considerably by the availability of cases of water in plastic liter bottles from the Saudi desalinization plant on the coast.

Meanwhile, the troops prepared for desert warfare:

They placed tape on the leading edges of the blades of almost 800 helicopters to save blade wear from the corrosive effects of sand. They installed particle separators on aircraft to prevent sand ingestion in turbine engines. To deal with the same problem in tank turbine engines, tankers got a fresh supply of "V" packs and spares to place in air-cleaning systems, and cleaned them at every opportunity. As a result, tanks ran at an availability rate of over 90 percent. They painted all of their almost 40,000 green Europe-based vehicles with desert tan chemical-resistant paint, one by one, taking precautions against the toxic paint spray by using tent enclosures and masks. Since the spare parts system could not be adapted fast enough, an ad hoc system sprang up, and vehicles got the spare parts they needed.

And finally, soldiers fitted chemical protective masks, using the tried and true method: You place banana oil around the mask before you put it on. If you smell the oil after it's on, you know you have a bad fit.

Soldiers made do with what they had. From the time they deployed from port to the desert until they redeployed in April and May of 1991, the troops lived in the desert with what they'd brought in. It was a help-yourself theater. The desert was hostile. Weather turned cold at night and it rained a lot. Fierce sandstorms blew up, reducing visibility to meters and getting sand into everything. Flies were everywhere. It was a hell of an adjustment for the troops, hardened as they were to living in the field in Europe.

Despite everyone's best efforts, nothing escaped "friction." It was everywhere.

Early on, Franks directed commanders to raise their tolerance for imperfection, to work on those things they could do something about, and when time was created by transportation delays, to use it for training. He did not want the command frustrated over things over which they had little control: "Keep your heads on the war fighting and preparing for war," he emphasized again and again. "Keep focused on the objective and do not take your eye off the ball." It wasn't easy, but the commanders and troops did it.

The whole Department of the Army operation in Washington was a masterpiece of organization by Army Chief General Carl Vuono, who held daily meetings to anticipate requirements. His vice chief, General Gordon Sullivan, quarterbacked the effort, and was constantly on the phone to Franks, Luck, Yeosock, and Pagonis, seeking ways to help. FORSCOM commander, General Ed Burba, not only deployed active component units, but put together combinations of active and Reserve component units to fit theater needs. It was exactly the kind of situation—the provisioning of a war-fighting theater—that the Goldwater-Nichols National Security Act of 1986 had anticipated. Franks and VII Corps became provisioned as a contingency corps almost overnight.

Not everything arrived on time. One minor frustration for both Sullivan and Franks, and a potential issue with the troops, was the fact that no one in the corps had yet received the desert battle dress uniforms, the sand-colored BDUs (called DCUs). XVIII Corps had them, as did the support troops in the port area, and troops in Riyadh. But not VII Corps. Rumors flew about the elusive uniforms: "They're at the port." "They're shipped." "One pallet arrived by air from Dover in Frankfurt. Meet the plane in Dammam." No DCUs. First it was frustrating. Then it was a joke. "To hell with the desert uniforms," one of the soldiers in 3rd Armored Division said finally. "Tell them we don't want them. We're the troops from Germany. We were trained to beat the best the Russians had. When the Iraqis see us, they'll know that and it will scare the crap out of them." Everyone in VII Corps felt the same way. They didn't get the sand-colored DCUs until almost April; and some of the troops only got issued a set on their way home after the war. Chemical overgarment protective suits covered them up anyway.

TRAINING

Everything in Saudi Arabia had to be started from nothing. That included training. There were no training facilities for VII Corps to use, and they *had* to train. Though the experience of XVIII Corps provided valuable lessons, they still had three months' lead. The enemy, as always, was time and the myriad concurrent activities that distracted commanders and soldiers from preparing for war. Nonetheless, leaders dived into training as an immediate priority.

Fred Franks had started out with a four-week plan for his units before he sent them into the attack: They would have a week to get individual units assembled, to find everything, and to get to Tactical Assembly Areas, and three weeks for training. He wanted a full three weeks of training in order to adapt European skills to the desert, and to get desert-smart and desert-tough. He also wanted time for mission rehearsals. This plan was not based on any scientific analysis, but on his best professional experience and judgment.

Though he did not think these plans were unrealistic, he realized he was not a free agent and might have to make some adjustments. Adjustments were OK, but not compromises that would cause his troops to be unprepared.

In the event, his three-week training goal proved hard to meet—he had to reduce the three weeks to two—and time kept pressing him harder and harder.

On 23 December, ten days after he arrived in-country, he made this comment in his journal: "How can we get ahead of time? Friction to overcome is enormous. . . . Maybe I need to change my style. Help yourself and do not worry. . . . Need some major muscle movement to make things happen. Not sure at this point we can make it and have three weeks' training. Settling in taking longer than I'd like. Thought seven days was OK, then three weeks to train. Unit integrity not good. Must get that fixed. We'll make another assessment end of this week."

During a meeting in Riyadh on 27 December, called by General Schwarzkopf and attended by Franks, Gus Pagonis, Gary Luck, and John Yeosock, the CINC announced that he thought they'd be at war in three weeks. After the meeting, Franks wrote in his journal, "What I must do is drive this corps to a new level of effort to get ready to go to war. We are not moving fast enough."

And on 2 January 1991, he wrote, "Time getting short. How to best prepare the corps. . . . Think we'll be OK if only I can give the troops two weeks." He'd had to adjust his earlier plan by then. "Must shoot. Must get some batting practice. Night moves. CSS on the move"—combat service support, or logistics—"Meet, plan, visit, assess, and make adjustments. Also have to get troops work at night."

★ The 1st Infantry Division Forward command team's running the growing port operations made a major contribution to the training effort. Since many soldiers were forced to remain in port for two to three weeks without their equipment, Franks asked Brigadier General Mullen to establish a training service for commanders and units in port. Mullen set up facilities where unit commanders could do individual preparation. Though these facilities were elementary, leaders immediately began exercises in firing individual weapons, chemical protection, driving in Saudi Arabia, and desert navigation.

Meanwhile, corps units needed gunnery ranges in the desert where they could refine weapons skills without endangering other units and whatever local populace might be in the area or passing through. An element in VII Corps headquarters was formed to assist unit commanders in acquiring the real estate, and unit commanders took it from there, building stationary targets from scrap lumber or whatever else they could get their hands on.

Franks gave directions to allow soldiers to fire service ammunition (actual wartime ammunition, something they had never done in Germany). He wanted soldiers—ground and air—to see the full capability of this ammunition, so that they would be familiar with it when the war started. This was both a risk and a trade-off, for wartime ammunition (especially Hellfire missiles) was in short supply. He took the risk.

In order to practice for the breaching operation, corps engineers (the 588th ENG Battalion from Fort Polk, Louisiana) built an exact replica of the Iraqi defensive system, complete with berms and antitank ditches. It was five kilometers long and even faced the same direction as the actual Iraqi system so as to replicate actual light data. It took two weeks to build at the rate of twenty-five meters an hour. Afterward, the 1st Infantry Division conducted full-up training rehearsals on this system, and the combat elements of the 1st UK Armored Division, with all of their nearly 4,500 vehicles, twice practiced their planned night passage of lines through the Big Red One.

The 1st UK was placed under tactical control of VII Corps in mid-December. The day before Christmas, Lieutenant General Sir Peter de Billiere came to see Franks at his trailer HQ in a parking lot in the port of Dammam. De Billiere was the senior British military officer in-country, and they had never met before, and it was crucial to talk about the conditions of employment of the British forces.

It was not the first time Franks would have foreign troops under his command. In Germany in NATO, he had commanded both Canadian and German forces, and he had also played in an exercise under the tactical control of the German II Corps, so he knew what it looked like from the other direction. Franks knew that building mutual trust was vital, and also that the mission assignment needed to be within that unit's capabilities and that he needed to be sensitive to different doctrinal processes for planning and for communicating orders. Logistics is always a challenge, because the official policy is that logistics is a national responsibility, meaning that every country is responsible for supplying its own troops—a totally unworkable policy from a tactical standpoint and one that needs changing. Finally, he was never satisfied that the staffs could work closely enough unless they were totally integrated. Armed with all those thoughts, he met de Billiere.

From his point of view, they hit it off right from the start. De Billiere was a no-nonsense soldier ungiven to posturing or reminders of the importance of his position. He wanted the best for his British troops and he wanted them to make a meaningful contribution to the success of the mission. It was purely a commander-to-commander meeting, also attended by Major General Rupert Smith, newly appointed to command the British division: just the three of them.

Their most important conclusions:

- The British would be employed as a division (in other words, Franks would not break up the division and place the parts under other American control);
- future U.S.-UK relationships depended on the success of their venture together;
- de Billiere agreed to make the switch as soon as Franks wanted (Franks said right away, because he wanted them to move out on planning);
- de Billiere was concerned about the impracticality of the policy that "logistics is a national responsibility"; Franks told him not to worry because it was his intent not to let that get in the way, including in the treatment of each other's casualties;
- de Billiere did not want to unplug from their national intel too soon, to which Franks was quick to agree, since he thought their products had to be better than what he was getting from his own national system (as it turned out, it was a valuable connection, even though U.S. intel got much better toward mid-January);
- they agreed to integrate their staffs rather than following the usual liaison cell practice (a new step at the tactical level, even though it was routinely done at strategic levels of command);
- Franks agreed to be sensitive to the British need for training and for forming the division, since it was happening on the fly, just as with VII Corps;
- they agreed on tight OPSEC, since they did not want anyone to know that the British were moving from the coast inland and joining VII Corps (to this day there are few official pictures or films of the U.S. VII Corps and the UK training and fighting together, due to rigid OPSEC discipline).

Their meeting lasted about forty-five minutes to an hour. They shook hands as soldier to soldier, in a mutual understanding that what they had agreed to verbally was the way it would be. No contracts, no treaties, no paper exchanged, just two soldiers trusting each other. Franks was proud of the corps's service with the British and of their mutual respect and trust. It all started that day.

After de Billiere left, Franks had a session with Rupert Smith and selected members of his staff, in order to get to know their capabilities and to give Smith some initial planning guidance.

Rupert Smith was bright, intense, focused, and very much at ease with himself, and Franks could see they would get along well. Although he had come from a Special Forces, light-infantry background, he was not intimidated in the least with commanding an armored division, and was also quite willing to listen and to give his subordinate commanders wide latitude in their methods for mission accomplishment. He wanted to get to work immediately. He took notes, asked questions, clarified guidance when Franks was not clear, and was candid in expressing his views but seemed quite willing and comfortable to take orders from an American. Franks was glad to have them on the team.

On 19 January, Franks visited them. At their assembly area along the east coast, the British had staked out a live-fire maneuver area where the down-range impact area for direct-fire systems was out over the water. There they could maneuver a brigade and conduct live fire with their tanks, artillery, aviation, as well as practice minefield clearing and berm breaching. During his visit, in the course of an attack exercise by 7 Brigade, commanded by then-Brigadier Patrick Cordingly, Franks rode a Challenger tank and fired a few rounds. They were training hard and aggressively. Franks liked what he saw and told Major General Rupert Smith so.

Smith had his hands full. The British were forming a division by assembling the most modern forces from all over their army. Only their 7 Brigade was a set unit. Smith was putting the others together as they flowed into theater. He had the same team-building and training challenge as Franks himself, and Franks understood. With that in mind, he determined to leave Smith and his division at this training area and close to their logistics base as long as possible. They could accomplish twice as much in the same period of time as they could when they picked up and moved to the west to join VII Corps's Tactical Assembly Area.

★   Meanwhile, units were crafting a variety of innovative training techniques. For example, they constantly practiced refuel on the move. They set up fuel trucks and long hoses, quick-disconnect nozzles, and the fastest pumps they could get and made an arrangement something quite like a service station crossed with an auto-racing pit stop. The tanks and other vehicles drove to the hose ends laid out on the desert floor at a spacing that could accommodate whatever size unit they wanted to refuel (within reason—usually determined by the terrain and the availability of refueling material). The drill was to anticipate when they needed fuel, preposition the fuel trucks at a spot, direct the tankers to it, get them there and through it as fast as possible, then get the unit back into its tactical organization . . . all the while maintaining some semblance of organizational integrity. It took lots of practice to get it right.

Units performed a lot of live fire, including what the Army calls calibrating, boresighting, and zeroing their major direct-fire weapons systems to make sure rounds hit where they aimed them—different procedures for each type of weapons system.

Major General Butch Funk at the 3rd AD had a particularly challenging training situation. Since his division equipment was the last to be shipped from Germany and it had been loaded in such a way that the tactical integrity of his units was lost, the assembling of his division was a major challenge. Yet in some ways he knew that 3rd AD was ahead of the game, since they had just completed their semi-annual gunnery and maneuver training in Germany. What they needed to do, he realized, was work on major unit moves and formation changes in the desert, maneuvers not possible to train in Germany, and so he turned the assembly of the division over to his junior officers and his noncommissioned officers, led by division command's Sergeant Major Joe T. Hill, took his commanders out into the desert to his Tactical Assembly Area, and used HMMWVs to move and navigate in the desert, spaced like the whole division. It was a masterful use of the entire chain of command to handle a variety of simultaneous activities.

Major General Ron Griffith had a different challenge. Though he, too, had to assemble his division amid fractured unit integrity, his division had had the bad luck of arriving when competition was highest for trucks to transport them the 400 kilometers to their desert assembly areas. On top of all that, Franks gave Griffith responsibility to be VII Corps reserve for an ARCENT mission to protect the ARCENT lines of communication (the road networks designated for unit and supply movements, in this case, the Tapline Road) from a preemptive Iraqi attack while XVIII Corps moved west. This was a real mission, requiring staff planning and orders—no small amount of work for a division-sized organization. Thus he had a real mission, plus he had to assemble and train the division all at the same time.

Griffith drilled his division hard and conducted as much live-fire training as he could fit in. He also worked his artillery, including MLRS, into his maneuver training. For their live firing, the 1st Armored used what was called Jayhawk range, a ten-by-fifty-kilometer piece of uninhabited desert the corps had arranged with the Saudis. A daily major exercise for all the units using this range was to make sure that no unsuspecting Bedouin and his herd wandered into the impact area—not to mention U.S. military vehicles or aircraft. There were no fences, no roads, no terrain features, and no electronic or phone communications with the Bedouins who shared the desert with VII Corps.

★ In the period before the battle, Fred Franks simultaneously devoted his most concentrated efforts—with the help of a great many smart, skilled people—to working out the corps's plan of attack. Before we get to that, though, we need to spend some time placing the story in its context. We need to look at the nature of military plans and maps, and then at the planning processes in the headquarters above his, in CENTCOM and Third Army, to show how his plans were formed out of those and how he helped influence them.

PLANS

Plans and orders are not the same. Plans are options. Orders make things happen. Units make many plans, but some never get executed.

The job of a unit's staff is to manufacture feasible options—and to continue manufacturing them. The commander needs as many options as possible. You try to be like the pool player, Franks likes to say, making a shot but also lining up the cue ball for the next shot.

Normally with plans, there are such words as "effective for planning on receipt, execution on order." This allows subordinate units to do their own planning and work out all the details. If events turn out anywhere close to the assumptions in your plan, then it is a matter of telling the organization to execute a specific OPLAN. That rarely happens without adjustment.

Sometimes you update the plan: when your mission or troops available to you have been modified, when your senior HQ modifies their own plan, when the enemy does something different or unexpected, when you get a better idea, or when you spot an enemy vulnerability to exploit. U.S. units make lots of plans, which on occasion causes concern with our allies. Their much smaller staffs are not capable of producing the prodigious numbers of contingency plans that Americans can generate.

Nonetheless, the more options, the better. Thinking through a situation and developing a wide range of options, then keeping your force in a physical posture where those options remain available to you, lets you outthink an enemy and then outfight him. It is a process that continues during a battle.

MAPS

Land forces use terrain. They fight on the ground. How they dispose their forces on that ground relative to the enemy and with what weapons are crucial to the successful outcome of a battle or a series of battles.

The U.S. Army still uses paper maps to picture that ground. As with service station maps, they have lines and use colors to represent various features, but they also include an overprinted grid system that allows soldiers and leaders to describe their locations from coordinates. They also include terrain contours that allow them to determine hills, valleys, etc. Newer technology will soon allow soldiers to see the terrain in three-dimensional virtual reality, and indeed fly over it, drive around on it, or walk through it. This technology will allow commanders to better apply their combat power on the ground relative to the enemy.

But for Desert Storm they had flat, one-dimensional paper maps.

Maps come in different scales to represent certain sizes of ground. In Desert Storm, VII Corps used three scales—1:250 000, 1:100 000, and 1:50 000. The smaller the scale, the more detail. In the desert, where the ground is relatively flat, scale does not really matter much—*except* that on large-scale maps it is much harder to indicate both enemy and friendly units and the speed of unit movements. That is to say, if you indicate an enemy brigade with a small map sticker (say an inch-by-half-inch rectangle) that sticker might cover an area on the map occupied by two brigades on the ground. It's not hard to imagine misperceptions and confusion resulting from that. Meanwhile, if you move an inch on a 1:250 000 map, you have in fact moved about ten miles on the ground. If you are attacking a determined enemy on tough ground, ten miles is a long way. But if you are looking at that map at a higher headquarters, or a larger-scale map, that inch might appear to you as no movement at all.

U.S. Army maps in a command post are normally mounted vertically on a piece of plywood and covered with acetate. The acetate allows you to mark up the map and change the markings. This procedure was begun in World War I and continues to this day. When the first U.S. tank crossed the Sava River into Bosnia in December 1995, the tank commander was standing in his hatch in the tank turret, looking at a map, and relating it to what he was seeing in front of him.

Skill in relating the map to the ground and in moving units in relation to one another to get the maximum combat power on the enemy (while the enemy is doing the same thing) is the art of war at the tactical level. When you are a small-unit commander, you can normally see all the ground your unit will operate on physically. The more senior you get, the more this skill becomes a function of your imagination, as you figure what combination should go where over terrain you cannot see and against an enemy with a mind of his own.

✮ Fred Franks spent a lot of time before the attack looking at maps, meditating on them, playing all the combinations over and over again in his mind, and then actually moving around on the ground. He wanted to inform his senses about what was possible on the ground, about how forces and various combinations of forces would fit, how much room they took, and how long it took them to move from one place to the other. He also did it with the Iraqis. Then he wanted to relate all that to a paper map. In that way he could begin to imagine the battle and the various combinations of possibilities.

He was helped in this by his experience in the deserts of Fort Bliss, Texas, with the 3rd Cavalry. Others in the corps had had similar experiences at Fort Bliss or at Fort Irwin. The desert was no stranger to them.

In early February, Franks asked his G-2, John Davidson, to put together a 1:100 000 map (the kind used most frequently in Germany at corps level) and put it flat on a table so as to better visualize the battle. It took an eight-by-ten-foot board to get the whole area on it. That flat map board became their primary planning and briefing tool in the last stages of attack preparation in the two weeks before the attack. It was around that map that Franks asked his commanders if they had enough room to carry out the missions he had given them. They all answered it would be tight, but they could do it.

By the time VII Corps attacked, that map, VII Corps forces, and the Iraqi forces were burned into Franks's mind. He had seen the fight ahead of time and could see the ground and his own forces on it. During the attack, his task was to relate what was actually happening on the field to the picture in his mind, and make adjustments. His big challenge was to keep his own forces continually arrayed in the desert in time, space, and distance in relation to one another for the first two days, so he could have all seven of his FRAG-PLAN options available to choose from when he saw the final RGFC disposition. That was why he spent so much time looking at the map. He was playing all the combinations over and over again in his mind. His subordinate commanders were doing the same in their sectors.

The end goal of all this thinking and meditation was to inform Franks's intuition. Commanders decide things because, they often say, "it feels right." What they mean is that all their years of training and education, that focused concentration, that intense desire to win at least cost to their troops, and their own intellectual capacity for synthesis tell them intuitively that their orders are the right thing to do in that given circumstance. Sometimes you cannot explain it.

THE CENTCOM PLAN

The VII Corps plan of attack was not an isolated grand concept entire of itself. Rather, in order to ensure harmony in the overall campaign, it was nested within the larger scope plans of Third Army, CENTCOM, and Coalition strategic objectives. CENTCOM planned the entire theater campaign—including the Coalition allies, land, sea, air, and Special Forces—to accomplish both national and Coalition objectives. Third Army planned the ground operation of VII and XVIII Corps in a way consistent with the overall CENT-COM plan. VII Corps planned its piece of the Third Army plan.

★ The concept that General Schwarzkopf briefed to Franks and the other commanders on 14 November grew out of another plan that had its origins in early October. At that time General Powell had instructed Schwarzkopf to devise an offensive option and then to send a team to Washington to brief it to the Joint Chiefs. The briefing was held on 13 October.

According to this plan, the heavy elements of XVIII Corps—the 24th MECH, the 1st CAV, and the 3rd ACR—and the Marines would attack just east of the Wadi al Batin in the general direction of Kuwait City. (Schwarzkopf and his planners had rejected a possible flanking move to the west of the Wadi, because logistics would be too difficult, and because the attack would be vulnerable to counterattack on its own flank by Iraqi armored divisions.) Schwarzkopf was not at all happy with this plan: he was by no means certain that it would get the mission accomplished, and there was a possibility of seriously unacceptable casualties (computer projections estimated 10,000, with perhaps 1,000 killed). Still, it was, in his view, the best course he had with the forces available.

In fact, the argument that Schwarzkopf made through his planners (he himself wasn't present at the briefing) was that the original plan's very inadequacies argued for more forces if there was to be a real offensive option. He had protested to General Powell about even sending a briefing to Washington because of his concerns. The problem at the time was that Schwarzkopf did not seem to know what to do with those forces if he got them.

The plan briefed on 13 October—even with Schwarzkopf's caveats—was not well received in Washington by the Joint Staff and the Secretary of Defense. It was less well received in the White House. Schwarzkopf's nervousness about the plan, his request for more forces, and the overall perception that he wasn't aggressive enough did not sit well there.

The briefing did not make Schwarzkopf look good, and that was a major sore point with the CINC. His sensitivity on that score continued even after the two-corps plan was developed.

Following the failed briefing, General Schwarzkopf directed General Yeosock to become involved in ground planning, and Yeosock turned to Brigadier General Steve Arnold, who had come from Korea just after Labor Day to become Third Army G-3. Arnold was called on to direct both Third Army planning and CENTCOM land operations planning, and he held these two responsibilities until final approval of the plan in early January. During that period, Arnold led the so-called Jedi Knights, the graduates of the U.S. Army's School for Advanced Military Studies, who were doing the planning work at CENTCOM and Third Army. (As it turned out, the planners of both VII and XVIII Corps also were SAMS graduates, which was a good thing for both communications and the overall planning effort.)

Meanwhile, General Powell had decided to go to Saudi Arabia to hear further plans discussions and, if necessary, to get personally involved in moving the planning forward. On 22 October, he attended a briefing on a two-corps option, but still was not satisfied. That evening in the guest quarters in Saudi Arabia, he sketched out for General Schwarzkopf on some hotel stationery a scheme of maneuver that would place the two U.S. corps west of the main Iraqi defenses in an enveloping maneuver.

Schwarzkopf agreed with this concept, which then became the basis for new guidance to Steve Arnold. Following Powell's return to Washington, Arnold and the planners sent copies of their early work on this new concept to the Joint Staff to demonstrate its feasibility. Once he himself was assured it would work, General Powell briefed the concept personally to the President on 30 October and secured approval (he already had Cheney's) for the introduction of VII Corps and an additional 250,000 troops into the theater.

The formal announcement was made on 8 November, the Friday after the fall elections.

The main question then at CENTCOM revolved around how far west the flanking maneuver should be. This had to be decided before Third Army could begin to do any definitive planning of its own. Likewise, the two corps would also have to wait for final decision from Third Army before taking their own plans very far. This was especially the case for VII Corps, the main effort, with their force-oriented mission.

Because he himself was under pressure from Washington to look at extremely wide flanking movements, General Schwarzkopf initially gave Steve Arnold guidance to look at sending some forces 500 miles to the west near the Jordanian border (where they could presumably attack Scud capabilities and perhaps cause the Iraqis other discomforts, such as threatening Baghdad); even after this option was discarded (it would have been a logistics nightmare), Schwarzkopf continued to press Arnold and the planners to consider options that placed forces far to the west of where they eventually ended up. This may have been craftiness on Schwarzkopf's part. Showing how insupportable they were may have been his way of getting "Washington ideas" off his back. Yet by the time of the 14 November briefing, XVIII Corps was still attacking far to the west of VII Corps.

Meanwhile, Arnold was convinced that an XVIII Corps attack to the west was not just logistically insupportable, from an operational sense it did not focus on the principal objective of liberating Kuwait and destroying the RGFC, and he continued to try to convince the CINC to agree with him on that. A number of options were considered, all focused on the question of how far west to put XVIII Corps.

As soon as Franks saw the plan on 14 November, he got involved with the planners and with John Yeosock in pressing for a two-corps mutually supporting attack against the RGFC. The concept of a wide attack by XVIII Corps was raised again at the briefing to Cheney and Powell on 20 December. Though Arnold's recommendation then was to drop it, there was no discussion either way about the option. In the end, it was logistics support that drove General Schwarzkopf finally to decide, on 8 January 1991, on a two-corps, side-by-side attack.

This decision freed Third Army to finalize its plans. From there the key decisions were about final force allocation to the two corps and about their mission assignments for the final attack on the RGFC.

Arnold and the planners, thinking conservatively, were convinced that in order to destroy the RGFC, Third Army needed more combat power than it then had. By mid-December they had succeeded in getting VII Corps an additional division, the 1st (UK) AD. (Since the British division was originally slated to join in the Marines' attack to the east of VII Corps, that ended up costing an armored brigade to replace them, which Franks persuaded Waller to ask Schwarzkopf to take from the 1st Cavalry Division rather than the 1st INF.) But in the view of Arnold and his planners, the 1st UK was still not going to be enough. In order to destroy all three heavy RGFC divisions, as well as their three infantry divisions and artillery, the planners thought the theater reserve division, the 1st CAV, should be released early to VII Corps—that is, to the main attack. The CINC, on the other hand, because he felt he might have to send it to help the Egyptians if their attack stalled, wanted to keep this division in theater reserve under his control, with no promises of release. Repeated discussions by planners with General Schwarzkopf on this issue made him very sensitive on that point. The release of the 1st CAV would consequently dog operational planning right up to and including the actual operation. And they were not in fact released from CENTCOM control until 0930 the morning of 26 February, or more than two days after the beginning of the ground war.

Picking the 1st CAV as theater ground reserve was a point for some discussion among planners. Normally, you choose as your reserve a unit that can influence the battle throughout the theater. In the choice of units for that role, the 101st Airborne (Air Assault) might have been a logical choice. With four AH-64 helicopter battalions, their long and lethal reach could influence the theater outcome. On the other hand, the 1st CAV was chosen because

CENTCOM wanted an armored unit available to reinforce the Egyptian attack if that became bogged down. Franks had spent time with the Egyptians and seen their plan. As far as he was concerned, they had what it took to accomplish their mission on the VII Corps flank.* If the theater had been willing to take a small risk on them, they could have given 1st CAV to VII Corps from the start, kept the 101st as theater or Third Army reserve, and effectively employed the 101st on the last two days to isolate the Kuwaiti theater of operations. Those are choices that are made early and are easy to second-guess later.

Meanwhile, planning efforts continued, and each corps worked on its own plans and kept both Third Army and CENTCOM aware of its work. There was no mystery to what each major HQ was doing. Commanders above the corps level also were well aware of planning work, and had the opportunity on several occasions to intervene if they did not like what they heard. Thus there should have been no surprise later on about the speed and tempo of the VII Corps attack. On 14 December, in preparation for a briefing of Secretary Cheney and General Powell, Franks and the other corps commanders briefed General Schwarzkopf on their plans so far. The CINC approved what he heard. In fact, it was now, in his words, "my plan." He had taken ownership of it.

On 20 December, during the briefing to Secretary Cheney and General Powell, Cheney made a somewhat mysterious comment to Franks, just after he had gone over his concept of attack. "Thanks," Cheney said, "I feel better now."

Franks didn't know then that Cheney was referring to the more than two months of discussions and planning in which he had participated. He had seen the early—and unsatisfactory—one-corps plan, the early two-corps planning, and had listened to General Powell sketch out a bolder two-corps plan to the President. Now he was seeing how the two-corps offensive concept would actually be put into action in the theater. And so for the first time, for him, all the pieces were really falling in place.

From 27 to 30 December in Riyadh, Lieutenant General Yeosock convened a MAPEX, which both Franks and Luck attended on the first day and the last. Yeosock had originally intended to use this as a war game of final Third Army plans, but couldn't, since the CENTCOM plan was not yet final. Instead, the

---

*Franks and the commander of Egyptian forces in the coalition, Major General Saleh Haleby, exchanged visits several times during the course of the preparations for war. They talked about command arrangements and exchanged plans. In fact, as it turned out, the Egyptian army knew the Iraqis very well, for they had seen them during the Iran-Iraq War. And during one of their visits Franks got from Haleby his appraisal of Iraqi forces. It turned out to be the most accurate assessment Franks would get of the Iraqis: He was right on target.

session became a discussion of resource allocation between VII and XVIII Corps, and of air support to the ground phase of the operation. Franks continued his discussions with John Yeosock over the necessity for a coordinated two-corps attack. Yeosock was sympathetic and, with Steve Arnold, went back to Schwarzkopf beginning on 4 January with a series of options.

On 8 January General Schwarzkopf made his final decision on Third Army positions for the attack. Instead of a wide west maneuver north by XVIII Corps, with a gap between corps, the two corps would attack abreast. It then became a matter of Third Army determining how to destroy the RGFC.

THE THIRD ARMY PLAN

Third Army planning intensified starting in mid-January.

The CINC directed Lieutenant General Yeosock to plan for offensive actions beginning anytime after the start of the air campaign on 17 January. Brigadier General Arnold and his planners, with the assistance of both corps, followed up on this. Taking into consideration the status of the two corps, the combat power available, and assumptions about possible RGFC choices,* they developed five different options for an attack.

Though timelines for the various attack options and forces available were developed, most of the planning energy was devoted to the one that assumed Third Army would attack only after all forces were ready and that the RGFC would defend in place. This timeline had both XVIII Corps and VII Corps in place by H+74 for a coordinated two-corps attack against the RGFC (H-hour—the start of the attack on G-Day). In actuality, since the heavy forces of both corps would not begin their attack until H+26, this meant these forces would hit the RGFC forty-eight hours from that point.

On 1 February 1991, a meeting to discuss final plans was held at King Khalid Military City, hosted by Lieutenant General Yeosock and attended by Franks and Luck and key members of their staffs.

Since, at that late date, a coherent Third Army two-corps order had not been published, Franks continued his strong argument to Yeosock at the end of the meeting (after General Luck had had to leave) for a two-corps coordinated attack against the RGFC if they stayed in place. He proposed that VII Corps would turn ninety degrees east and XVIII Corps would attack to their north. Both Yeosock and Arnold liked the concept. After that meeting, Third Army developed its plan for the Army to attack the RGFC and published the

---

*They thought the RGFC would attempt either to escape from the theater via Highway 8, to counterattack against attacking Third Army corps, or to defend the approaches to Basra. It was believed that the last was their most likely choice.

order on 18 February, during the time that Lieutenant General Cal Waller was temporarily in command.

The order's maneuver portion read, "ARCENT continues the attack with two corps attacking abreast to encircle enemy first-echelon forces in the JFNC zone and destroy the RGFC. On order, VII Corps conducts the Army main attack in the south to destroy the Tawalkana Mech and the Medina Armor; fixes then defeats the 17 AD and the 52 AD. On order, the XVIII Airborne Corps conducts the Army supporting attack in the north to penetrate and defeat the Nebuchadnezzar and the Al Faw Infantry Divisions and destroy the Hammurabi Armor Division."

XVIII Corps was not pleased with this order. In a message to the ARCENT commander, they listed three objections to it. First, they did not like being assigned the mission of attacking the RGFC infantry divisions, since that could cause unacceptable casualties. Second, they needed more maneuver room. Third, they did not feel they had the combat power to attack through the RGFC infantry and to destroy the Hammurabi.

At 2200 on 24 February—after the attack had begun—Third Army published a change to that order that allowed for the possibility that as the Third Army attack progressed, the Hammurabi Armored Division might either end up in the VII Corps zone of attack or in XVIII Corps's. It was not clear, in other words, whether the Hammurabi would stand and defend or move. If they stayed in one place, VII Corps was to be prepared to attack and destroy them, after destroying the Tawalkana and the Medina. Meanwhile, XVIII Corps would take on the RGFC light divisions and RGFC artillery, which were in their zone, and they also would take on the Hammurabi if that division moved into their zone. Third Army believed the RGFC had artillery positioned in XVIII Corps's sector that would fire south into VII Corps when VII Corps attacked the Medina. The order was for XVIII Corps to destroy that artillery.

These discussions and subsequent planning became the basis for the Third Army's two-corps plan. This was executed following the evening of 25 February, when Franks ordered VII Corps to execute FRAGPLAN 7 and when XVIII Corps subsequently redirected their attack toward Basra.

Even though Third Army had developed a coordinated two-corps attack, there was still no agreement on those concerns that had bothered Franks as far back as the 14 November briefing. No plans existed that laid out how the forces would be disposed (now probably in front of Basra) at the end of the war. Likewise, there was nothing like a CENTCOM air-ground plan to isolate and then finish the RGFC units in the Kuwait theater.

It was not that Yeosock and Third Army planners did not try to get this done. Rather, they intended to adapt to circumstances and put out a new "frag" order every twenty-four hours (which they did anyway) in order to adjust the two-corps attack. What caught them short was the timing of the end of the war.

Specifically, Lieutenant General Yeosock's intention was first to determine if the RGFC were staying in place. If so, then the two-corps attack plan would be executed. Then, based on the situation at that point, he planned to issue further orders to both corps for the final attack to complete the RGFC destruction in a coordinated air-ground action.

There had very definitely been thought within the Third Army about the war's end state, but the cease-fire preempted that final order.

THE VII CORPS PLAN

A military plan comes out of many minds working on a common problem, yet it is not a committee solution. The commander decides. How commanders decide, along with what they decide, largely determines the excellence of the final product and the confidence with which subordinates execute the plan.

The VII Corps plan had to be just that—the corps plan. Fred Franks knew from the start what he wanted to do and how he wanted to develop that plan: he had to come up with a simple scheme of maneuver that would accomplish his mission at least cost, and the way he did that had to reinforce the teamwork he was building in VII Corps. In other words, he not only had to come up with a workable scheme of maneuver, he also had to teach it, and do that in such a way that all of his leaders had internalized it, were of one mind with him, and were playing on the same team.

Someone asked Franks how much time in VII Corps he spent teaching. About 50 percent, he told them.

One might argue that in a military organization, where everyone follows orders, all you have to do is make a decision and then tell your subordinates "This is it, go do it." That is certainly true, and Franks did that a lot. But at the same time, a commander has the benefit of a great deal of experience in his subordinates and they also have large and complex organizations of their own, which they have to direct and move. For both reasons, they will have judgments worth listening to.

In other words, when you make military plans, you have to be aware of the human dimension. When things get tough, when opportunities and enemy actions require adjustments to the plan, and when you expect and indeed demand initiative from your subordinates, you want them to be on your wavelength and to really believe in what they are doing. Results are always better when your subordinates have been part of the plan. You form a team that way.

One of the ways Franks built his VII Corps team was to evolve the plan in such a way that all of his leaders took part in the plan building. From the start he had a good idea about what he wanted to do, but the process by which he arrived at it was a matter both of bringing the team along and convincing them that it was also their idea, and of consulting with his commanders, all savvy mounted warriors who provided valuable input. He also knew he was going to focus all VII Corps units' attack on a common corps objective, rather than assign individual objectives to individual units.

But in the end it had to be Fred Franks's plan. It had to come out of the will and mind of the commander, and not out of a patchwork of inputs from subordinates as an accommodation to all views.

In encouraging input from subordinates, he was not unlike many earlier commanders that he admired: Robert E. Lee, George S. Patton, Field Marshal Slim (the British victor over the Japanese in Burma in World War II). He did not consider it weakness or indecision. It was smart command style.

Though teaching the plan and listening to input are indispensable to the process, planning and decision making are primarily intellectual acts. They are problem solving, pure and simple—with the added dimension that the problem is two sided, and this is the tough, uncompromising arena of land war, in which the outcome is deadly and forever. In simple terms, the enemy shoots back and behaves in ways you sometimes do not want and haven't anticipated, while using the same time and the same terrain.

At the same time, the commander operates in a military and national hierarchy of ideas and policies. No military commander is a free agent—he can't do as he wants. He operates within a framework of orders and directives in a chain of command. In the United States, that means civilian control and orders issued either by the President as commander in chief or the Secretary of Defense. Those orders are translated into action at each subordinate headquarters. In Desert Storm, the orders came from President Bush and Secretary of Defense Dick Cheney via the Chairman of the Joint Chiefs of Staff, General Colin Powell, to General Schwarzkopf, the U.S. Unified Command commander for the region and the commander of Coalition forces in Saudi Arabia. That meant that General Schwarzkopf had to answer both to his chain of command and to the Coalition when he was putting together his strategic objectives and the military plans to achieve those objectives. It was not simply a matter of the United States devising a plan and then executing it. Though the United States by far had the preponderance of forces, it still had to involve the Coalition nations in the decision-making process. The United States needed their forces to accomplish the mission, wanted their ideas about the best way to do that, and wanted to conduct a campaign that would accomplish the mission in such a way that it would lay the groundwork for future cooperation in this very volatile region.

★ When the CINC finished his briefing on 14 November 1990, Franks was crystal clear about four things: He knew VII Corps was the main attack. He knew that if, through his fault, any details of this plan got into the media, he was history. He was convinced that XVIII Corps was way too far to the west for a mutually supporting two-corps attack. And he had heard nothing mentioned about how it would all end from a theater perspective.

Following the CINC's briefing, he did not give any guidance to his own planners for the better part of two weeks. There were two reasons for this: First, before he could do any detailed work, he needed from Third Army a basic mission statement and the units to be assigned to VII Corps. At that point, it was not at all clear what additional troops would come from outside the corps. As far as he knew, he would be attacking with three divisions (1st AD, 1st ID, and 3rd AD, three corps artillery brigades, the 2nd Cavalry Regiment, and the 11th Aviation Brigade). Second, because of operations security, he simply did not want to get involved in detailed planning while they were still in Germany. With all the media outlets and the intense speculation about what they were about to do, he felt it was best to wait until they were close to going before they did any detailed work. He issued his first guidance to his planners on 27 November.

His planners, meanwhile, had not been sitting on their hands. They had been busy in Riyadh. Heading his planning work was Lieutenant Colonel Tom Goedkoop. Goedkoop had been assigned to VII Corps after graduating from SAMS in the summer of 1989, and had arrived in VII Corps shortly before Franks. Goedkoop, a tanker, bright, focused, positive, and a hardworking officer, made several trips to Riyadh during November to better understand the planning climate there and to do what he could to help Third Army finish enough of its plan so that VII Corps could begin work.

Franks also had dispatched John Landry, VII Corps chief of staff, to Saudi with part of the staff for coordination meetings and, more specifically, to ask CENTCOM if VII Corps could move their Tactical Assembly Areas farther west (Yeosock had told him it would have to be cleared by the CINC). After a helicopter flight on 14 November over the area where the corps was supposed to locate, Franks was convinced they were too far east. To transfer from the planned TAA to the corps's attack positions would mean an extremely long desert move. The distance from the proposed TAA to King Khalid Military City was approximately 200 kilometers, and from there to the attack position—another 160 kilometers. Doing that would cost too much time, as well as too much wear and tear on the vehicles. Franks knew initial disposition of forces on the ground was vital, remembering Molke's dictum that "an error in initial disposition might not be corrected for an entire campaign."

Landry got permission from Cal Waller to locate west toward King Khalid Military City.

After Third Army came up on 24 November with a revised plan and mission statement, Franks met with his planners on 27 November and gave them guidance. He focused on three battles: the initial breach of the Iraqi defense, the defeat of the Iraqi tactical reserves, and mass to destroy the RGFC. He also wanted to find a way to keep the Iraqis from knowing where the VII Corps would hit.

At this point, intelligence indicated that the Iraqis had the capability to develop a complex obstacle system of mines, trenches, so-called fire trenches (trenches filled with oil they could ignite in the event of attack), and wire entanglements all across the corps's front. The big question, early on, was how far west the Iraqi barrier system would go.

Franks and his planners knew from the beginning that they did not want to get the corps tangled up in that system. He wanted a flank or to be able to create one. If there was a way in their sector to send heavy forces (at that point 1st AD, 3rd AD, and 2nd ACR) around it, and if the terrain would support heavy forces, and if they could logistically support heavy forces, then they would send as much of the enveloping attack out there as they could. (There were always reasons for making the breach—even if a way west opened up: to keep logistical lines short, for example, and to rapidly defeat the Iraqi tactical reserves.)

When they first looked at their sector, it appeared that the Iraqis would continue to build their barrier system all the way across it. If that happened, VII Corps would have to breach that line in order to achieve a penetration for the heavy forces to move toward the RGFC. After passing through the breach, the heavy forces would move north to a concentration area, and then they would attack to destroy the RGFC.

All of this was slow and deliberate, and Franks did not like it. During this analysis, he started asking about a flank. In fact, since at that time CENT-COM plans for XVIII Corps placed them far to the west of their eventual attack corridor, VII Corps could have gone even farther west than they eventually went, but their terrain analysis showed that traffic ability out there was not good for a large formation. Either it could not move rapidly north or the formation would have to spread out too much and be too far away to concentrate against the RGFC. Thus they assumed they had to punch a breach through the barrier and assemble the attack at a concentration point on the way to the RGFC. (As it happened, when the 3rd ACR traveled that terrain during the war they had a hard time getting through it, and had to move a lot slower than the 1st Armored to their east.)

VII Corps planners analyzed the breach in great detail. They figured its width and its depth, then how many vehicles could pass at what speed, then worked out specific time lines for each type unit in the corps.

Franks still didn't like it. None of his planners did. Not only would it take too much time to bring his forces through the breach, but once they were through, they would be strung out north to south when he wanted them aligned east to west and coiled to strike from south to north.

He again told his planners that he preferred to flank the Iraqi barrier so that he could achieve a more rapid concentration of forces for the attack on the RGFC. After some thought and examination of that option, he seized on the idea of an "audible." What he wanted to do was look over the Iraqi line of scrimmage, as it were, to determine how far west their defense was set. If they were in a defense for the play VII Corps had called—i.e., if the barrier extended across VII Corps's sector—then they would run the breach play. If, on the other hand, the Iraqis left an opening to the west, they would change their plan that put units in that opening and let them race to the RGFC and mass against them much faster.

They did this initial planning with only a few planners, all approved by Franks in their secure room in the basement of VII Corps HQ at Kelly Barracks in Stuttgart. His chief of staff and G-3 also were present.

In early December, he picked the Big Red One to make the breach. They'd had recent NTC experience in breaching, they were an infantry division, and Tom Rhame volunteered to do it.

On 6 December, Franks made a three-day return trip to Saudi Arabia with Corps staff Don Holder and 3rd AD chief Jerry Smith to personally greet the first arriving units from the 2nd ACR. He made this entry in his journal: "Saw 2/2 ACR. Troops look great. Spirited, cleaning weapons. Chain of command present. Landed in A.M. and right on their vehicles w/o sleep. Inspiring. Gave coins to soldiers cleaning weapons to remind them to continue." He discussed the plan with John Yeosock, as well as a myriad of other details of deployment, and briefed the breach option, stressing that he thought the VII Corps and XVIII Corps attacks should be mutually supporting. He discussed the need for deception and questioned how CENTCOM would conduct operations deep with air. Franks also met with Cal Waller, vital in any communication with General Schwarzkopf, but not with Schwarzkopf himself.

Franks made his final move to Saudi Arabia on 13 December.

In preparation for the briefing on 20 December for Secretary Cheney and General Powell, Franks briefed General Schwarzkopf on 14 December on his attack plan. His instructions from Schwarzkopf then were to brief the plan in sufficient detail (especially the breach) that when Secretary Cheney and General Powell left they would be convinced the plan was viable, and that it was set in concrete and difficult to change. Schwarzkopf wanted approval of what he was doing, and no more suggestions from Washington. Armed with that guidance, Franks and his planners prepared that type of briefing. The plan had six phases and the audible.

On 20 December, Franks principally briefed the breach-only plan, but explained that there was an audible plan available if the Iraqis gave him an opening farther west. As a point of interest, in the light of General Schwarzkopf's later dissatisfaction with the speed of the VII Corps attack, no one in Franks's superior chain of command commented about the laborious task of passing a three-division corps through a relatively narrow opening, assembling the corps, and then moving toward the enemy 150 kilometers away. Franks had misgivings about the plan, as indicated in his journal, even though he did not yet have an alternative.

"Believe operationally we might be violating principle of mass (if we send all our units thru breach one behind the other in column). In our scheme the principal worry is tight movement thru breach. Do not want a bridge too far (thinking of the WW II operation and piecemeal one-unit-at-a-time commitment on a narrow front)."

He is still pleased that he did not have to execute it.

In answer to a question from Dick Cheney about the mission Franks had for the British 1st AD, he replied that he anticipated giving them the mission to defeat the Iraqi VII Corps tactical reserve so that his heavy forces could move to destroy the RGFC without worrying about their rear, flank, and fuel.

A thornier issue had to do with the 1st CAV, the theater reserve (on which subject the CINC continued to be especially sensitive). As he went through his presentation, Franks explained that even though the 1st CAV was theater ground reserve, since it was a Third Army assumption and logical for the theater reserve to be assigned to the main attack (if it was not needed elsewhere), he was including plans for their use by VII Corps.

This assumption did not go down well with Schwarzkopf. Later, in fact, in his autobiography, he charged that Franks was not prepared to attack unless he had the 1st CAV.

The charge—with all its implications—is not true. In providing a place for the 1st CAV in his scheme of maneuver, Franks was doing what any commander would do and what Third Army had instructed him to do.

★ The last week in December was an intense period for Franks and his planners. There were many reasons for it: Franks wanted to settle on his intent, to nail down the plan, go over it with his commanders in a session (with a BCTP exercise) at King Khalid Military City in early January, and then lock it down and train and rehearse with specific tasks in mind. At the same time, he suspected that the air war was going to start soon. When it did, the Iraqis would be frozen in place. His suspicion was correct; the air war did start soon (on 17 January), and that did freeze the Iraqis in place—with the result that their picture of the Iraqis in mid-January turned out to be essentially the one they would have when they attacked.

Meanwhile, there were long sessions with Creighton Abrams, John Landry, Stan Cherrie, John Davidson, and the planners. There were still many questions about the breach and the audible, questions about logistics support (mainly fuel trucks), questions about when to move the British west to the corps TAA, questions about construction of an exact breach replica so that the 1st INF and the Brits could rehearse (this was done), questions about the feints and deceptions up into the Ruqi Pocket (so that the Iraqis would be deceived into believing the main attack would go up the Wadi al Batin), questions about air-ground rules in the theater that were totally different from NATO's, and questions about growing frustrations with lack of intelligence, especially imagery of Iraqi defensive positions. (At one point, Franks told Yeosock that tourists had better pictures of Iraq than he did. He'd be better off, he told him, sending his own C-12 to fly along the border with the door open and use a personal camera to get pictures. . . . He was exaggerating, but frustration was high.)

One serious disagreement between Franks and his planners was over whether or not there should be a pause by the corps before they hit the RGFC. Regardless of the final choice about the audible, they calculated that continuous movement and enemy action over the distances the corps would have to travel (over 150 kilometers) would require what doctrine calls an operational pause to refuel and rearm in an area they had called Objective Collins (after Lightning Joe Collins, the VII Corps commander in World War II).

Franks vetoed that suggestion. "No pauses," he ordered. He did not disagree with their calculations (friction was inevitable), with their recommendation for an area of concentration, or even with the possible need for adjustments to the rate of movement, in order to better focus the impact of the heavy forces, but he did not want to build a deliberate pause into the plan, especially one right in front of the main enemy location. A pause was bad motivationally: once you are two or three days into an attack and really rolling, it is better to keep rolling than to stop and then try to get tired troops moving again; and tactically: he did not want to give the Iraqis a chance to adjust their defense (it was Franks's belief that giving them time to set up a position defense was playing to their strength).

The planners then began to work out some other way.

As it turned out, Franks decided to adjust the corps's rate of advance during the first day and a half. Those adjustments allowed the corps to roll hard into the RGFC with the greatest possible momentum, with concentrated combat power, with fresh troops, and with a sustainable logistics posture. For these adjustments, Franks has since been sharply criticized by many analysts and chroniclers of the war in the Gulf, and most notably by General Schwarzkopf, their assumption being that several thousand M1A1s, Bradleys, and other heavy armored vehicles should have been able to charge across 150 kilometers or so of desert the same way horse cavalry in a John Ford movie charge down a valley. The issue goes back to knowing about what cavalry people call the "tempo of a mounted attack": You want not only to hit your enemy hard and fast with your heavy stuff, and hit them from an unexpected direction, but you want to hit them with a coherent formation so that your combat power is focused and can hit hard and keep hitting until the enemy quits. That meant that for Fred Franks the question was whether to stop in front of the main enemy objective or to "go slow now and go fast later," as the old German saying goes. He chose to do the latter.

★ On 28 December, Franks moved the VII Corps Main CP out of the port area of Dammam to the desert at a point about seventy-five kilometers east of King Khalid Military City.

On 2 January, he visited the soldiers who were by then erecting the exact replica of the Iraqi obstacle system. During the visit he determined that his people were building at the rate of twenty-five meters per hour.

That made for some interesting further thinking: Could the Iraqis, he asked himself, extend their defensive barrier west as fast as our engineers? And even if they could, how far west could they go at that rate?

The answer, it seemed to Franks, was that his soldiers were more skilled than the Iraqis. Based on his troops' timelines, he determined that in the time they had, the Iraqis wouldn't be able to extend their barrier system all the way across the VII Corps sector, especially if the air attacks began soon.

He called the "audible" during a plans and issues session in King Khalid Military City, 6 to 8 January, attended by all the major subordinate commanders of the corps plus their planners.

At that time, the two forces he had available for the enveloping maneuver were the 2nd ACR and the 1st AD. Third AD was then the VII Corps reserve; as such it was to be the force Franks wanted to put in the Ruqi Pocket to carry out the deception mission. According to the current configuration of the plan, 3rd AD would be feinting in the Ruqi Pocket before VII Corps attacked. When the real attack started, 3rd AD would back out of there and then either pass through the breach or follow 1st AD north through the gap in the west.

Franks was not pleased with this arrangement of units, because it probably meant that 3rd AD would take too long to disengage from Ruqi and catch up with 1st AD for the RGFC attack, and this would cause a piecemeal attack into the RGFC.

Even though he was to be CENTCOM reserve, John Tilelli attended the briefings. "Don't forget about us," he told Franks.

Franks didn't forget him.

During this meeting, Franks also talked to the new Third Army G-2, Brigadier General John Stewart. Stewart's area was intelligence, and in order to decide what formation to order VII Corps into for the attack on the RGFC, Franks had to know the RGFC's final disposition. He needed to make the decision about twenty-four hours before execution, Franks figured, and since it would take about forty-eight hours to get to the RGFC, he told Stewart he needed the final intelligence twenty-four hours after VII Corps attacked—no later. Stewart would deliver the information he needed on the afternoon of 25 February, right on time.

In the days following the meeting at King Khalid Military City, there were a number of what turned out to be false alerts that Iraqi forces were coming across the border.

On 11 January, there was a report that four Iraqi aircraft had penetrated Saudi airspace and had been driven back by F-16s. On 17 January, just after the air attack began, there was a report that fifty-five Iraqi tanks were engaging the Egyptians. At that time, VII Corps's 11th Aviation Brigade alerted their two Apache battalions, and the 2nd ACR sent a squadron out to intercept the force. When he got this intelligence, Franks was visiting Tom Rhame on a rifle-firing range. He dropped everything, immediately flew forward to 2nd ACR, and soon learned that no Iraqi tanks had crossed the border.

While none of these reports turned out to be accurate, they did serve to exercise the corps's rapid-response capability and communications. Franks was pleased with the ability of subordinate commanders to react quickly, to listen to the radio, to anticipate actions, and on their own initiative make things happen.

On 8 January, the 1st CAV and the 2nd Brigade, 101st Airborne Division, were attached to VII Corps for a mission to protect Tapline Road from a possible Iraqi preemptive attack south down the Wadi al Batin (Franks was also ordered to tie in with French forces west of King Khalid Military City in order to protect the western flank). The 2nd Brigade flew into position on 12 January. And on 13 January, because of reports of a probable Iraqi attack, Franks ordered the 1st CAV forward to a position just south of the road. It then occurred to him that now that he had the 1st CAV for this mission, it would be logical to move them forward to defensive positions just south of the Iraqi border and adjacent to the Egyptians east of VII Corps. Not long after that, he ordered John Tilelli north to this location . . . which was, as it happened, the Ruqi Pocket.

So why not use 1st CAV, Franks asked himself, instead of 3rd AD to conduct the feints and demonstrations up the pocket to deceive the Iraqis? If he could free the 3rd AD from that mission, he could move them out west to join the 1st AD and the 2nd ACR. It was a stroke of luck. Franks took advantage of it.

Once that was solved, he had another question: Was there enough room on the ground to place both armored divisions side by side? Or would he have to put them one behind the other? He had forty kilometers to work with in that sector, and uncertain terrain. Franks wanted the divisions side by side. He asked for analysis. The result: several opinions. Franks's staff favored putting the two divisions in column; they didn't think the terrain forward of the border would support two divisions side by side. He told his two commanders to take a look at the terrain. Butch Funk and Ron Griffith both favored two divisions abreast. It would be tight, they said, but they could do it.

To settle this question, Franks sent a ground reconnaissance party out to the area to look around, and on 24 January, he and Stan Cherrie went out to look at it from his Blackhawk. That same day, after his own look and when the recon report came back positive, Franks decided to put the two divisions side by side. Because 1st AD had farther to go, and more to do initially (they had to seize the Iraqi town of al-Busayyah early in their attack), Franks put 1st AD on a twenty-five-kilometer, two-brigade front, and 3rd AD on a fifteen-kilometer, one-brigade front. This would mean that 3rd AD would stretch to the rear over 100 kilometers, and that it would take time and considerable coordination for them to get in a combat posture of two brigades forward. But that was better than putting them behind the 1st AD.

Now Franks had the geometry of his forces that he wanted. He had an enveloping force to the west—2nd ACR, 1st AD, and 3rd AD. He had the 1st INF doing the breach, with the 1st UK following quickly through the breach to defeat the tactical reserves to the east. Logistics, particularly fuel, could also now be easily transported through the breach to the north, where it would be available to the enveloping force. Supporting artillery brigades could be initially passed through to join the enveloping armored divisions before their RGFC attack.

On 26 January, Franks made this note in his journal: "Planning session A.M. Trying to 'what-if' mobile Iraq forces. Think he will fight attrition battle from successive positions. Must shape battle with air, not extend myself logistically, and beat him to positions. East flank vulnerable. If Egyptian attack stalls, then flank thru UK is vulnerable. Must attrit 12th (Iraqi) Div (the one in reserve

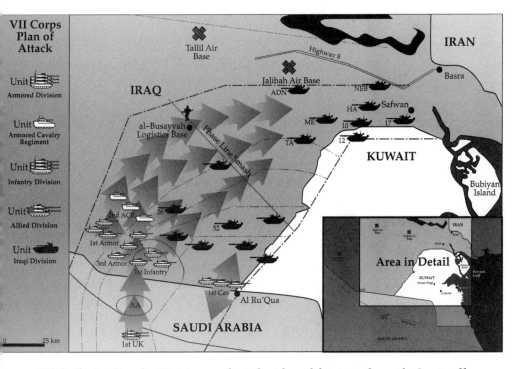

Tallil Air
Base

Highway 8

IRAN

Jalibah Air Base
ADN   NEB

Basra

IRAQ

HA   Safwan

al–Busayyah
Logistics Base

ME   10   17

Phase Line Smash

TA   12

KUWAIT

Bubiyan
Island

2nd ACR   26

52

1st Armor

Area in Detail

3rd Armor

1st Infantry

KUWAIT

1st Cav   Al Ru'Qua

AA

SAUDI ARABIA

1st UK

*While the 1st Cavalry Division conducted raids and feints to throw the Iraqis off
balance, the 1st Infantry Division would conduct a deliberate breaching operation
through the main Iraqi defensive positions. Further to the west, the 2nd Armored
Cavalry Regiment would lead the main armored punch of the 1st Armored and 3rd
Armored Divisions through the undefended border berms into Iraq.*

just behind the frontline Iraqi divisions) so UK can push east and hold while
I go north with 1st AD to threaten his flank. Keep 3rd AD in reserve in center able to go east to assist UK or commit north. Should not commit 3rd AD
until sure I'll get 1st CAV."

That day Franks also finalized VII Corps's plans for artillery raids across
the border and for feints. The purpose of these was to destroy Iraqi combat
capability, especially artillery in range of the breach, and to deceive the Iraqis
through the artillery fire and ground maneuver feints by the 1st CAV in the
Ruqi Pocket that VII Corps's attack was going north up the Wadi al Batin.

On 26 January, Franks also sent Tom Goedkoop, his planner, to assume
command of 4/66 Armor, an M1A1 tank battalion in the 1st AD, to replace
the unit's commander, who had been injured. Goedkoop went on to command
the battalion with distinction in combat. To replace him, Franks selected

Lieutenant Colonel Bob Schmitt, another SAMS graduate, who had been working at Third Army on their planning. Schmitt proved to be an excellent choice—well read in the situation, bright, motivated, and savvy.

On 13 January, the VII Corps attack order had been published to include Franks's intent. That basic order remained unchanged in its essentials from that point until the actual attack on 24 February—though modifications in it continued to be made as air attacks caused Iraqi dispositions to change and as they received better-focused intelligence.

Yet Franks knew there was a limit to how long such adjustments could be made. That limit, in his judgment, was to be about two weeks before the ground attack. "Now is not the time to tinker with the plan," he told Toby Martinez on 13 February, a few days before the attack. "The more senior you get, the less you must meddle—do not try and make 100 percent. We have a good plan, just let the people execute." He wanted subordinate commanders to have time to do their planning, to brief and discuss their options with their soldiers, and to be able to conduct rehearsals. That all takes time. If he continued to change the plan, they would never be able to do that. A good plan that is thoroughly understood will be better executed than a perfect plan that nobody has internalized and rehearsed.

To better see how all of this affected individuals units, let's take a quick look at how the 2nd ACR saw their own plan, which was published on 20 January. Their mission, it read, was to "attack through the western flank of enemy defenses and conduct offensive cover operations to develop the situation for VII Corps." In their concept of operations, it went on to say, the "regiment's task is to set the terms for action for the corps's main body and to serve as a base of fire and observation for the corps commander's maneuver. . . . If the enemy is moving, regiment meets and destroys advance guard battalions and develops the situation for the corps commander. If he is defending, regiment fixes the enemy from standoff range, finds his flanks, and assists in getting the divisions into the fight." Don Holder, the regiment's commander, and Franks discussed the regiment's maneuver many times both before and after their order was published. Since the regiment would be the key to finding and fixing the RGFC, Franks wanted Holder to be on the same mental wavelength with regard to possibilities for the coming battles. He was.

On 5 February, for instance, Franks visited a training exercise of the 3rd AD. Butch Funk had his commanders and key staff out in the desert in HMMWVs moving cross-country as though he had the whole division out there. At a break in their movement, he huddled all the commanders for a short AAR, and Franks spoke to them about the VII Corps plan and what he expected the Iraqis would do. The more the commanders knew, the better they'd be able to execute when the time came.

Late in January, Franks's planners began to develop the FRAGPLANs that would give the corps options off their basic maneuver and put them in the right attack formation to destroy the RGFC.

★ On 8 February, Franks flew to Riyadh for the final briefing with Cheney and Powell. The briefing was held the next day.

Franks had printed his most important conclusions on the bottom of his concluding briefing chart. These were:

VII Corps is ready to fight
Soldier will and attitude unbeatable
Support of body politic and public has been vital to date
Spare parts a big unresolved problem
Use of massed air with intelligence and ground maneuver is key to success

During the briefing, Franks went through the final iteration of the plan in detail, including a summary of combat actions up to that point, the RGFC's likely options, and a review of training time for each major unit.

Some questions came up, and then Cheney asked the biggest question of the war: "How will it all end?" It was a great question. Franks hesitated a moment, thinking Cheney should really hear the answer from General Schwarzkopf, from a theater perspective, instead of the perspective of one of five attacking corps commanders. But there was only silence. So Franks said, "Mr. Secretary, I cannot answer for anyone else, but I can give you my opinion from a VII Corps perspective. I believe the Iraqis will defend from positions about where they are now. We will get to a position about here"—he pointed to objective area Collins—"and then turn right ninety degrees, slamming into the RGFC with a three-division fist. We will continue to attack and finish around the area of the Kuwait-Iraq border here" where it intersects Highway 8. "XVIII Corps will attack to our north. We will be the anvil along the border area and they will be the hammer coming in from the north."

There was no discussion.

After the briefing, the CINC asked everyone to stay for a few minutes, and General Powell spoke in an informal setting. He told everyone thanks and related how Whitney Houston had sparked an emotional outburst of patriotism when she'd sung an inspired rendition of the national anthem at the recent Super Bowl. He said it was an indication of the lift the country had gotten from the operation so far, and said everybody should be proud of it. This operation was proof that the United States could do things well. He asked all the commanders to pass on to the soldiers how much they were supported at home. It really pumped Franks up. He was glad to hear it and pass it along.

General Schwarzkopf also spoke to the assembled commanders. He said he was "very well pleased" with what he had heard. "You should start on your countdown. February 21 to 24 is the window for attack."

Franks himself was really pleased with the outcome. He thought they were all of one mind on the attack, and on what the corps and Third Army would do if the RGFC stayed where they were. He also thought the ground and the air component saw eye to eye on what needed to be done, and that if the RGFC stayed where they were, the air would isolate them in the theater.

His only regret lay in one piece of coordination that didn't happen. While in Riyadh, Franks went to visit the Air Force to try to get better help in destroying artillery in range of the breach. He proposed to Major General John Corder, the deputy for Lieutenant General Chuck Horner, that the Air Force put up aircraft at the same time the corps flew their Pioneer UAV. When the UAV spotted an artillery target, Franks proposed, the corps could relay it to the circling aircraft, and the aircraft could roll in and take it out. Corder agreed to do it, but on 10 February Franks was informed that his decision had been disapproved and they would not do it after all. He never knew why.

Other than that, though, he was enthusiastic. The last time Franks had briefed them in December he had the 2nd ACR, two battalions of the 210th Artillery Brigade, and one AH-64 battalion in Saudi ready for war. Now he had a four-division corps ready to fight. It was a hell of an achievement by the commanders and soldiers of the VII Corps, with help from many outside the corps. Franks was proud of the VII Corps and proud to report to General Powell and Secretary Cheney that if called on, they were ready to fight.

★ During the period before the war, Franks never really stopped thinking about the upcoming battles—mentally preparing himself for what the corps was about to face. He was motivated to win at least cost, and he never concentrated so hard on anything in his life. It never left his conscious or subconscious thoughts. Total focus like that was a method of problem solving that had never failed him. An aspect of these meditations (as Napoleon called them) was to continue to sit in front of a map and concentrate on it—looking from that angle at the corps plan, at possible combinations, then thinking about something else, and then looking back again.

The corps was scheduled to move from its TAAs to its final attack positions starting on 16 February. During one of his map sessions before that move, Franks's concentration on unit dispositions paid off: he noticed that the corps units were now arrayed south to north in the same physical configuration as they would later—in the tactical maneuver toward the RGFC—attack south to north. That configuration meant that it would be possible to conduct a corps rehearsal of this difficult and complex maneuver as the corps traveled

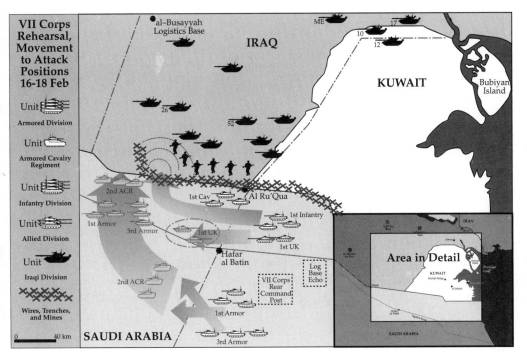

As a final "rehearsal," VII Corps conducted a corps-wide maneuver, in attack formation, as units moved to their final attack positions south of the Iraqi border. This provided invaluable training prior to execution under fire.

the 160 to 180 kilometers to its attack positions, an invaluable training opportunity. It was the only chance the corps had for such a rehearsal. Franks gave the order.

From 16 to 18 February, the rehearsal took place, and it was awesome, that massed wave of iron, itself over 100 kilometers wide, hurtling across the desert. Typically, they did an AAR after the move.

At the end of the move, on 18 February, Cal Waller became ARCENT and Third Army commander, as John Yeosock had been evacuated to Germany for emergency gallbladder surgery.

On 20 February, during a visit, Waller made it clear that from G-minus three to G-Day itself, it was imperative that the corps avoid getting into any fights that might force a strategic decision to go to war (this was during a time of intense, last-minute diplomatic maneuvering between the United States, the Soviets, and the Iraqis). At the same meeting, he also confirmed that there would be a coordinated attack by XVIII and VII Corps to the final objective, adding that VII Corps should not get in a hurry attacking the RGFC; he expected both corps might need the operational pause near Objective Collins. And he confirmed further that it would be twenty-four to thirty-six hours after the attack before there was a decision from CENTCOM on release of the 1st CAV Division.

Franks, of course, welcomed the decision on the mutually supporting attack, but he still did not want to pause in front of the RGFC.

At 2200 on 21 February, Waller called Franks to tell him G-Day would be 24 February. They would go on the twenty-fifth.

On 22 February, Franks had his final commanders' meeting. He told them to "fight tough and smart, close and deep, use arty and air, and cover each other," and gave a short pep talk about the importance of the mission and how well prepared the corps now was for combat.

Later that day, Franks visited a hospital and the 1st CAV soldiers wounded on 20 February. He told them thanks, and asked about their fellow soldiers and how soon they could go back to the division. Most of their wounds were from fragmentation or burns.

COMMAND OF GROUND FORCES

Meanwhile, an issue was still floating out there that needed to be resolved—the issue of overall command of ground forces. The designation of a land force commander, with a separate staff competent to direct land force operations in a joint theater environment, has been an issue in many U.S. joint operations back to World War II.

Normally in a theater of operations, there is a joint force commander, a CINC, who directs operations through what are called service component commanders of land, sea, and air. In the Gulf theater, there was no problem with sea and air component commanders. The Joint Forces air component commander was Lieutenant General Chuck Horner, and all air forces in the theater reported to him, including Navy air not needed for ship protection and Marine air not needed for close air support of marines. Likewise, all naval forces reported to Vice Admiral Stan Arthur.

On the ground, however, things were more complicated. On the ground were essentially five corps: two Arab corps and three U.S. corps. A lot of combat power. Yet initially no overall land forces commander had been designated.

Thus, for example, when Chuck Horner needed to coordinate air-ground actions, he had no land force counterpart with whom to coordinate, but went directly to the CINC.

In the end, General Schwarzkopf felt he had to assume the role of de facto land forces commander. This would still have been a viable choice if Schwarzkopf's staff had been able to direct land forces operations and be the theater staff. They were not. They had never practiced it, and were inclined not to get involved.

This is how the ground forces broke down: the USMC had a two-division corps-sized force, under Lieutenant General Boomer, reporting directly to the CINC; the two U.S. Army corps, with a total of nine divisions, reported to Lieutenant General Yeosock, who then reported to the CINC; and the Saudi composite—essentially two division corps—the Egyptian two-division corps, and the Syrian division each reported to the Royal Saudi Land Force's designated commander, Lieutenant General Khalid. In Riyadh, a staff coordination cell for all non-U.S. Coalition forces was created. It was called C3I (Coalition Communication Coordination Integration Center), and it was headed by U.S. Army Major General Paul Schwartz.

Thus, three land commanders reported directly to the CINC. But the CINC had no staff to direct land forces operations. During planning, this vacuum didn't have much consequence, but during operations, because there was no overall direction of land forces operations, it would matter a great deal. This continues to an be area of much discussion today.

OPERATIONS BEFORE G-DAY

Unlike forces in England preparing to attack German defenses on D-Day, who had no operational mission until they sailed to conduct their assault, VII Corps was an operational unit, part of CENTCOM's land forces, and had an operational mission, even as it deployed and planned the attack.

This meant that as soon as units were in-theater, they were assigned operational missions, which had to be planned for and trained for. They were not simply placed in some administrative area for sixty days to get themselves assembled and combat ready, at which point they could signal that they were ready to play. While they were assembling, training, planning, and dealing with the myriad other details of preparing for battle, VII Corps units had a number of tough things to do.

The 2nd ACR, the first unit in-theater, became operational on 21 December. At that time, the VII Corps mission was to provide a security force in the then-150-kilometer gap between XVIII Corps's western boundary (at this time XVIII Corps had a defensive mission from the coast to about 100 kilometers west) and the eastern boundary of the Joint Forces Command North (that is, the two Egyptian divisions and the Syrian division). The 2nd ACR had that job.

From that point on, VII Corps was directed to be prepared to fight with the forces they had in-theater. This directive required continuing adjustments in estimates, planning, training, modernization, debarkation and movement to TAAs, and in command, even as the corps planned for its attack toward the RGFC (if that proved necessary).

On 26 December, after a heads-up that Third Army might be called on to attack soon after the UN deadline passed on 15 January,* John Yeosock informed Franks that he wanted VII Corps's combat power (i.e., the forces they had then) available as of 15 January, 1 February, and 15 February. From that moment on, the corps planners had to be simultaneously available for war with what they had, while planning for war with the entire fully deployed corps.

On 27 December, at an informal meeting in his office in Riyadh, General Schwarzkopf informed Franks, Pagonis, Luck, and Yeosock that the President had called on Christmas Eve to tell him that they might be at war in three weeks. The CINC then instructed his commanders that he would try to hold off the ground attack until somewhere between 10 and 20 February, but that they should be ready to go earlier with what they had.

On 27 December, VII Corps was far from ready to go. They would be only slightly more ready to go in three weeks. Franks, in short, was not at all pleased to hear that they might be expected to attack then. All the same, he determined to drive the corps even faster to get ready.

He speculated in his journal on possible reasons behind the CINC's announcement: "[I] believe," he wrote, "some promises were made at the highest levels . . . that if we committed forces by early November they would be ready by 15 January. Then our gov't took that date and got the UN resolution passed. I'd like to meet the staff who came up with that projection. Here we are with 2nd ACR, one AH-64 battalion, and two artillery battalions. Have next to no CL IX"—spare parts. "Have no maps. Have no nav aids"—137 total. "Have lousy comms."

But an order is an order. So he kicked the corps into higher gear and planned accordingly. It was at this point that he adjusted his pre-combat training time from three weeks to two.

✦ Meanwhile, other missions came to them:

On 7 January, John Yeosock gave Franks the order to defend the Tapline Road against a possible Iraqi attack down the Wadi al Batin. To cut that would cut the major northern Saudi east-west supply corridor, as well as the avenue XVIII Corps would soon be using for their move west to their attack positions. For this mission, Franks planned to use the 1st CAV and the 2/101st

*The UN gave the Iraqis a 15 January deadline to get out of Kuwait, after which point the Coalition considered itself officially at war with Iraq. The deadline passed, and the air war began on 17 January.

to defend, while the aviation elements of the 1st AD would be his reserve. Air and the reinforced 1st CAV would be enough combat power to stop an Iraqi attack, he reasoned, and by using no more than those forces, he would be able to preserve his ground troops so as to protect their training and to allow them the time they needed to get out of the port area.

On 9 January, General Schwarzkopf met all of his commanders in Dammam. The air campaign would begin shortly, he told them, but—good news for Fred Franks—there was no longer pressure to start the ground campaign before 15 February. They were therefore to be ready to attack then. Meanwhile, the Iraqis were moving armor and artillery forward; it was likely that if they thought we were going to attack, they would conduct a preemptive attack. Thus, the CINC concluded, all should be in a heightened state of alert and prepared to defend themselves.

That same day, intelligence reported that the Iraqis were moving three divisions to the Wadi, either to attack or to blunt the U.S. attack.

The next day, Franks met with the French and tied their operations to his. He wanted them to defend the western approaches to Tapline Road and King Khalid Military City in case the Iraqis came wide through the opening in the west of their defensive line.

On 13 January, Franks and Martinez rode in their HMMWV with driver Staff Sergeant Dan St. Pierre cross-country in a driving rain to visit the 2/101st, now deployed into defensive positions west of Al Qaysumah. Once he personally saw their position, and met with Colonel Ted Purdom, the brigade commander, and after considering the recent intel about possible Iraqi preemptive strikes, he ordered John Tilelli to move the 1st CAV forward, and ordered reinforcement of the 2/101st with engineer support and artillery from corps. The 1st CAV moved within thirty minutes of the order, at about 1530, and closed just south of Tapline Road that evening. Later, on 23 January, Franks started the 1st CAV north of the Tapline Road. He wanted 1st CAV forward to the border to be in a better defensive position to protect the lines of communication and to begin artillery raids and feints for the deception plan.

★ On 17 January, the air war started.

The air campaign against Iraq, created and waged by the USAF, with no small tactical help from the U.S. Navy, the RAF, and elements of the French air force, was on many levels a brilliantly devised and magnificently executed operation. It brought the war devastatingly to the enemy's "head"—his centers of leadership, control centers, telecommunications centers, transportation centers, and centers of production for war and for weapons of mass destruction. Never before had these centers of gravity been so effectively and precisely neutralized.

Yes, the USAF claimed at the time more precision and more devastation than was actually achieved, but that does not diminish their actual achievement. Within hours of the start of the attack, one of the most sophisticated air defense systems in the world was rendered virtually harmless (above roughly 10,000 feet; below that, Iraqi SAMs and antiaircraft guns could hurt you). Within days, the Iraqi air force, armed with top-of-the-line Soviet and French aircraft, was chased out of the skies. These successes not only rendered the entire country naked to air attacks, they left the Iraqi army without any deep support or capability to maneuver, and allowed the U.S. Army to make its vast move to the west for the great "left hook" undetected. By 24 February, the air campaign had wrought considerable damage on the Iraqi army—not the 50 percent of Iraqi armor and artillery that the U.S.A.F. had set out to kill, but a lot. By G-Day, the Iraqi leadership's command-and-control capability over their army was seriously diminished, and the will to fight of Iraqi frontline troops, mostly in Kuwait, had been pounded and blasted into the sand.

The RGFC was another thing. At best, 25 percent of their armor and artillery had been knocked out of action. And their will to fight . . . ? When the battle came, they fought, and fought hard. To the benefit and credit of the U.S. Army, they were outclassed.

Back to VII Corps, when the air war started, it had been forty-one days since 6 December, when the first VII Corps troops had arrived, and twenty-six days since the 2nd ACR had become operational. More than half of VII Corps was still deploying, and there was not a combat-ready division available in VII Corps.

On 11 January , Franks had ordered the corps to begin conducting "stand to" at 0500 daily. He wanted to increase their combat-ready mentality and to get daily status reports.

On 19 January, in the first VII Corps combat action since World War II, a battery of the 75th Artillery Brigade, under the command of Captain Jeff Lieb, fired a TACMS missile in support of the USAF and destroyed an Iraqi SA-2 air defense site. Franks talked to the crew later that day. They called the TACMS "AT&T," or "reach out and touch someone."

The next day, another TACMS was sent against an Iraqi logistics site that supported their armored units just behind their frontline defending division. Franks reasoned that they would go nowhere without logistics and wanted the site destroyed to prevent a preemptive attack.

Intelligence reports intensified. There were reports on 21 January of terrorist infiltrators targeting command posts. VII Corps began tracking all civilian movement in their TAAs.

On 29 January, the Iraqis did attempt a preemptive strike in the east toward the Saudi town of Khafji. They were beaten back with high losses by a combination of air and U.S. Marine and Saudi land forces. Franks and his planners and commanders took lessons from the Marine report on that operation and applied them to their upcoming attack.

That same day, a Pioneer UAV (Unmanned Aerial Vehicle) platoon was attached to the corps's 207th MI Brigade. It began flying intelligence and target-acquisition missions two days later.

★ On 1 February, the 1st CAV began to assume operations up to the border, and from that day until VII Corps attacked on 24 February, the division fought what has become known as the battle of the Ruqi Pocket. Their mission was to conduct artillery raids and feints against Iraqi positions along the Wadi, to destroy Iraqi units and artillery in range of the breach, and to deceive the Iraqis that the Coalition main attack was coming north up the Wadi. As G-Day approached, the 1st CAV operation, by design, picked up intensity. Brigadier General Tilelli and his division kept constant pressure on the Iraqis by a combination of artillery raids, ground attacks up to brigade strength, and aviation attacks fifty to eighty kilometers deep.

Here are some of the notable events:

27 January—the 1st CAV captured five Iraqi deserters, the first of almost 1,800 captured during the next three weeks.

2 February—friendly fire. A U.S. HARM missile hit a 1st CAV radar site and wounded two soldiers.

5 February—the 1st CAV had its first exchange of fire across the border. Two days later, it destroyed an Iraqi border observation tower.

13 February—thirty-five EPWs (enemy prisoners of war, the new name for POWs) were collected. Later that day, sixty MLRS rockets were fired in two different strikes at targets determined by the 1st Brigade. The next day, the 1st Brigade began breaking holes in the twelve-foot-high border berm, and later that day 108 MLRS rockets were fired by the 42nd Artillery brigade under 1st CAV control. The following day, combat engineer vehicles used a variety of fire (165-mm demolition cannon, Copperhead laser-guided artillery, and TOWs fired by Bradleys) to destroy three Iraqi border observation towers.

15 February—in an operation named Redstorm/Bugle, the 1st CAV fired MLRS and cannon artillery, while the VII Corps 2/6 Apache battalion of eighteen AH-64s attacked approximately seventy-five kilometers deep into Iraqi positions.

17 February—using all of VII Corps's daily CAS (combat air support) allocations, the 1st CAV successfully destroyed numerous Iraqi artillery pieces, an MLR battery, a command post, and tanks in

front of the division's sector. The following day, 1/7 CAV and 2/8 CAV, both battalion task forces of tanks and Bradleys, conducted a mounted reconnaissance forward, capturing enemy ammunition and killing defending Iraqi infantry. As they withdrew, they came under Iraqi artillery fire, which was quickly silenced by twenty-four MLRS rockets and close air support.

19 February—the 1st UK MLRS unit, under 1st CAV control, fired 192 rockets against nineteen targets. That night, 2/8 CAV ambushed an Iraqi MTLB and destroyed it with a TOW missile. It also took out a pair of enemy infantry squads with artillery fire.

20 February—Operation Knight Strike was launched by Colonel Randy House's 2nd Brigade, in the largest tactical fight of the war so far for VII Corps. In a running battle with Iraqi dug-in units, 1/5 CAV, a Bradley battalion, came under heavy fire, and both a Bradley and a Vulcan air defense track took direct hits from five Iraqi tanks in revetments, followed by mortar and artillery fire. The CAV struck back with artillery and close air support, destroying the Iraqi tanks and twenty artillery pieces. During the fight, a second Bradley was hit, an M1A1 tank hit a mine, and three 1st CAV soldiers were killed (nine were wounded). One of those killed in action was PFC Ardon Cooper, who threw himself over his wounded buddies to protect them from incoming Iraqi artillery fire. For this, Cooper was awarded a posthumous Silver Star.*

Even though Operation Knight Strike was successful, it showed that the Iraqis were capable of heavy concentration of fire if an attacking unit got into their prearranged fire area. But it showed as well that Iraqi fire could be quickly silenced and that they had limited ability to shift their fires from their prearranged defensive positions. The lesson was to keep them from getting set in a defensive position. You had to hit them without pause with massed combat power from an unexpected direction.

21 February—703 MLRS rockets were fired by an MLRS unit of the 1st AD under 1st CAV control at known and suspected Iraqi targets as part of the plan for all units of the corps to get into combat operations.

Meanwhile, 1st CAV armor and infantry units kept up almost continual direct-fire attacks against Iraqi units in the Ruqi Pocket area;

---

*In July 1994, Franks directed that a building at TRADOC headquarters at Fort Monroe, Virginia, be dedicated in his memory. Present at the dedication were his family and his whole chain of command, from platoon leader to corps commander (by now John Tilelli was also a four-star general and Vice Chief of Staff of the Army.) It is the first building at that national historic landmark to be dedicated to an enlisted soldier. Ardon was a hero.

they continued to break holes in the twelve-foot-high border berm, and they continued their relentless raids against Iraqi defending units. First UK artillery joined this fight on 22 February, and along with 1st CAV artillery, they conducted a massive artillery raid. Later reports indicated that this raid deceived the Iraqis into believing the ground offensive had started in this area.

The actions by the 1st CAV Division in the Ruqi Pocket were hugely successful. They deterred any attack south by Iraqi units, destroyed significant numbers of Iraqi units and artillery (some in range of the 1st INF breach), captured prisoners, who were a valuable source of intelligence, deceived the Iraqi command about the size and direction of the VII Corps attack, provided valuable lessons about how the Iraqis could and could not fight, lessons other units in the corps would use, and allowed the aviation and artillery units of VII Corps to be skillfully employed in the artillery raids (code-named Redstorm). These raids inflicted damage on the Iraqis and gave the rest of the corps needed combat experience. It was a masterful and selfless performance by the 1st CAV that contributed in a major way to VII Corps's battle success.

✭   Earlier, during the first week in February, the corps began to position their logistics west to form Log Base Echo, which was to be the provisions center for the attack. To provide security for Echo, Franks moved an element of the 1st INF on the border in front of them, just west of the 1st CAV. Their orders from Franks were to show only reconnaissance units and aviation (he didn't want the Iraqis to know a force was west of the 1st CAV) so the 1st INF immediately began actions to guard the logistics site and cover the rest of the division move. VII Corps now had forces west from the Wadi approximately eighty kilometers.

On 14 February, a Scud missile hit Hafar al Batin, narrowly missing a 1st CAV shower point. That day Franks was twenty kilometers to the east at a COSCOM briefing and could hear the impact. There were no casualties.

More attacks were launched in front of the 1st INF on 16 February. Franks wanted to start to hit Iraqi artillery in range of the breach and to conduct some aggressive reconnaissance. He reasoned that by then the Iraqis would not be able to react very much anyway. And, besides, with the increased activity of the 1st CAV, they would not notice. But he kept the 2nd ACR and the two armored divisions hidden in the west until 23 February.

The next day was G-Day. Fred Franks continues from here.

9

COILED SPRING

I was up at 0400 after a good night's sleep, hoping my leaders and troops were as well rested. We would need our energy.

In a way, I was relaxed that morning—or at least relaxed in the sense that I knew we were ready and that we had the initiative. I did not think I would make any major decisions that day, one of those rare days in the last hundred when that was the case. Most of what we had spent those hundred or so days preparing was now ready to go. The main thing was we knew when we were going to attack: tomorrow, at about 0530, or BMNT. That seemed a sure thing.

This knowledge is a definite advantage for the attacker, one not available for the defense. You can get your unit both physically arranged and mentally ready. The defenders can only wait and wonder. After all those years conceding the initiative to the Warsaw Pact in our NATO mission, I liked this much better.

But truly relaxed? No.

I felt the stress—we all did, soldiers and leaders alike. All over the command, the pressure was constant. Some of it was physical, due to the extended austere living conditions, especially for the soldiers, and some was mental, because we were going to war and there were a lot of big unknowns. Those who had not been in combat probably wondered how they would handle it. Those who knew combat wondered what this war would bring. There was also a sense of isolation there in the desert. As a commander, you do your best to relieve some of the stress by the command climate you set, the way you treat people, the decisions you make, and the way you make them. But getting soldiers and units ready for war also means tough decisions, hard work, and being unyielding on the need to meet rigorous battlefield standards. As for myself, my own way of relieving stress wasn't to take days off, but to visit fellow leaders and soldiers, to try to do things for them: "To lead is also to serve." They always did more for me than I did for them. They never failed to inspire me

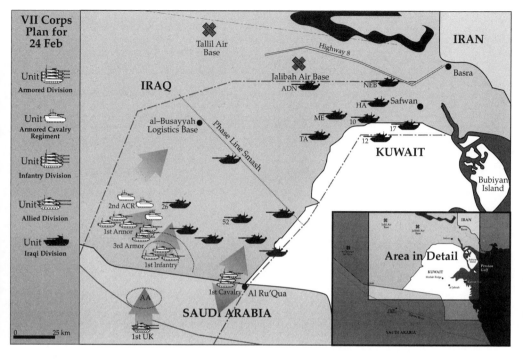

The plan for the first day of operation focused on the breach of the 1st Infantry Division. While the Big Red One conducted the deliberate breach, the 2nd ACR would continue to press on into Iraq as the 1st and 3rd Armored Divisions poured their combat vehicles through the holes prepared by engineers in the ten- to twelve-foot border berm. The 1st Cavalry Division would continue its deception operations near Al Ru'Qua, and the 1st (UK) Armored Division would begin moving forward on heavy equipment transporters to exploit the 1st Infantry's breach.

with their hard work, selfless attitude, sense of humor, and flat-out competence.

Like most mornings over the past hundred days, the transition from sleep to waking was not gradual. As soon as I woke up, my brain switched on full throttle. From the time we had gotten the mission, I had never stopped concentrating on the myriad issues confronting us, as well as on all the details that had to be dealt with in order to get ready for and execute combat operations. That focus consumed me that day and every day as we prepared for battle. I never concentrated as hard on anything in my life. It was seven days a week, every waking second; and it probably continued in my subconscious somehow when I slept. There were no days off; I just couldn't do that. General Hancock said right at Gettysburg: "Today, a corps commander's life is not important." I felt it was my duty to spend myself to the max for this mission and the troops for whom I was responsible. I lived it. I internalized the various parts of the corps so that I would know its behavior like my own. It was like a living part of me. We almost became as one. I was not alone in this. I had seen all my leaders and commanders do the same in their organizations.

So I was focused and intent on what we were about to do that morning, and especially on what we needed to do that day—to the point that I didn't notice much that was around me—yet I was also about as relaxed as a commander could be this close to a major attack. I was confident, but I knew that things rarely went exactly as planned, and I was acutely aware of my responsibilities.

My first focus that morning was on what we call a commander's running estimate—the continuing assessment in my own head of what was going on in the corps and of possible enemy actions. A commander does this constantly, looking at the situation and war-gaming possibilities, and his staff does the same, often separated in time and distance.

Here is how the corps looked to me that morning as I renewed our activities over the past few days.

The main issue for us that day was to move our enveloping force (2nd ACR, 1st AD, and 3rd AD) and our breach force (1st INF) far enough forward to make the start of our attack tomorrow release like a coiled spring. This would jump-start a momentum that would not let up until we destroyed the Republican Guards, in the sector Third Army had assigned us.

1ST INF DIVISION. Prior to this morning, elements of the 1st INF had moved forward once before. On 16 February, in order to get artillery close enough to reach Iraqi artillery in range of the breach, Tom Rhame had pushed his 1st INF, 3rd Brigade, commanded by Colonel Dave Weisman, forward to occupy the Iraqi security zone (an area in front of the Iraqi main defense that extended from the border about fifteen kilometers into Iraq). During this operation, the brigade had been in several sharp fights with Iraqi recon units and done well in their first combat. On the night of 17 February, we had had the first blue-on-blue (what some call fratricide, or so-called friendly fire) in the 1st Infantry Division, when a division Apache had fired on a 3rd Brigade Bradley and an M113, killing two of our soldiers and wounding six others. As a result, Tom Rhame, with my concurrence, had relieved the aviation battalion commander who had personally fired the fatal missile. The same day, an MLRS in the division artillery south of the border had fired by mistake into our attack positions. Though, as luck would have it, the rockets had fallen harmlessly into the sand, I was still concerned, because I wanted to build on early success. I had ordered Tom to pull the whole brigade back out of the Iraqi security zone that afternoon. That way, we reinforced our deception by signaling to the Iraqis that we were not coming at them from that direction.

CORPS ARTILLERY. During the period just before G-Day, Iraqi artillery was our main focus, especially those capable of firing chemical munitions. Because we didn't want to give away the location of our attack, we waited until about a week before the actual assault in which our artillery, attack helicopters, and close air support would hit the Iraqi artillery that was within range of the breach. We knew the Iraqis paid a lot of attention to artillery preparations, so if we'd been pounding the area out in front of the 1st Infantry Division for a couple of weeks, they probably would have reported to the RGFC: "Hey, they've got some sizable forces out here. Looks like they're coming farther west of the Wadi."

Later on G-Day, artillery would move into position before the 1st INF attack for two hours of preparatory fires into the breach area, in order to destroy the Iraqi artillery in range of the breach site. This prep fire had been planned by Brigadier General Creighton Abrams and Colonel Mike Dotson, the Big Red One Division artillery commander, and it would be shot by the 1st INF Division artillery, reinforced by three VII Corps artillery brigades, the 42nd, 75th, and 142nd, and the artillery of the 1st UK Division. After their firing mission, the 42nd and 75th Artillery Brigades would move through the newly opened breach and join the enveloping 1st and 3rd Armored Divisions, respectively, to reinforce the fires of their division artillery units in time for those division attacks on the RGFC.

ENVELOPING FORCE. Here our challenge was to find sufficient room to maneuver—1st AD, with their twenty-five kilometers of front on the Iraqi border, and 3rd AD, with their fifteen kilometers next to them.

I had given 1st Armored the extra room so that Ron Griffith could put two of his three ground-maneuver brigades side by side in a desert wedge (one brigade leading, followed by two brigades abreast). That way, he wouldn't be held up by time-consuming repositioning when we released the coiled spring. I wanted 1st Armored really fast off the mark—as though shot from a cannon toward Objective Purple, the Iraqi VII Corps logistics site at the Iraqi village of al-Busayyah, some 120 kilometers north of the border.

Given the enemy forces and the terrain he had to get through, I had estimated Ron would reach Purple about eight hours after H-Hour. Once he had seized that objective, we would have a major maneuver force north and west of the RGFC, one that was positioned to outflank any RGFC attack that might come west or southwest of their present locations to meet our enveloping force. (Iraqi forces habitually met a penetration attack head-on, and not from the flanks, as our doctrine advises.)

Because 1st AD had to be launched quickly, Butch Funk and his 3rd Armored Division had to start in a column of brigades that would initially extend almost 120 kilometers to the rear. Though 3rd AD was our corps reserve, they were not stationary. I wanted them moved forward across the border today, and I wanted them to get into a better offensive formation before they attacked tomorrow. Once he crossed the border and we got him more room, he could shift to whatever attack formation he thought necessary for the missions I had assigned him. It would take time, but I thought they would have time on G-Day and G+1 to get into another tactical formation before I committed them to any of the contingencies we had war-gamed.

While preparing for this maneuver, Butch also had to contend with another contingency, one that he handled with the kind of ease I'd come to expect from him: If CENTCOM committed the 1st Cavalry Division to JFC-North, then VII Corps was responsible for providing 1st CAV with a third maneuver brigade to replace the one 1st CAV had given earlier to the U.S. Marines. If that happened, I planned to order Butch to send one of his brigades to 1st CAV. Cal Waller had gotten my recommendation on this approved by Schwarzkopf, instead of CENTCOM's first choice, which had been 2nd AD (Forward) out of 1st INF.

The mission of our other enveloping force, the 2nd ACR, was to be out front and to provide offensive cover to cover the movement of the two armored divisions as they attacked toward Objective Collins about 150 kilometers from their line of departure. In order to get a better start on it, Don Holder had requested that his 2nd Cavalry Regiment move forty kilometers forward into Iraq to their Phase Line Busch* (2nd ACR had named all their phase lines after beers). This would not only put him about thirty minutes ahead of the two divisions, it would clear the area and allow the divisions to move up across the Iraqi border. (We wanted to lean as far forward as possible without tipping our hand.)

Yesterday, the regiment had moved forward about twenty kilometers beyond the border to their Phase Line Bud to clear the area south of the berm for the two follow-on divisions and to prepare for their move to Busch (they'd push their aviation forward of that). Though I had approved Don Holder's request for these moves, I had ordered him to show only aviation and artillery

---

*Phase lines are used to keep units abreast of one another when that is necessary, or to otherwise control a unit. It is easier to maneuver units if they have common reference points on which to orient—especially in the desert, where there are no landmarks.

to any Iraqis out there, in order not to tip our hand early. The regiment had fired their first round in combat at 1330 the day before in a ten-minute artillery preparation fire. By 1400, 2nd Squadron, preceded by the 4th, or Aviation, Squadron (nicknamed "Redcatcher" after our Cold War days), had all pushed across the border without incident. At 1628, however, two soldiers had been wounded when their vehicle had run over one of our own DPICM* munitions. The men were medevaced. At 1900, 3rd Squadron reported enemy dismounted infantry in their area, and the troops were assessed to be from the Iraqi 26th Division (thus confirming our intelligence that the 26th had a brigade in depth to refuse the west flank of the Iraqi VII Corps). Meanwhile, 4th Squadron reported that the twenty kilometers forward to Phase Line Busch were clear of enemy. By 2100, the regiment had reached Bud and had cut forty-three lanes in the double-border berm, both for their own passage and for assisting the two follow-on divisions, which would need to cut more.

The coiling of our coiled spring was to be on the Iraqi side of the border—just cleared out by the 2nd ACR. Both 1st AD and 3rd AD would have more room on the other side of the border, and they would also have gotten through all of the friction of passing through the lanes in the berm and reassembling.

Making it through the border berms turned out to be slow going for some of our units. The holes we had cut in the berms acted like "filters," and it took time to go through one by one, and then to get into some sort of tactical grouping. In one battalion, units got so disoriented in the dark and mixed with vehicles from other units that the commander pulled them south of the berm to reenter Iraq the next day.

207TH MI BRIGADE. Our newly acquired Pioneer UAVs (the first UAVs used in combat by the U.S. Army) were an immediate help in targeting Iraqi artillery. By G-Day, through bomb damage assessment provided by Pioneer flights, we had detected the destruction of sixty-five Iraqi artillery pieces and FROG (Free Rockets Over Ground). The Pioneers had also flown a mission in support of General Saleh Haleby's Egyptian Corps on our east flank.

I had previously cleared all of our forward movements across the Iraqi border with John Yeosock. The main attack on G-Day was in the east—the Marines and the Arab forces of JFC-East, together with a very well planned and, as it turned out, well-executed Navy and Marine amphibious deception maneuver toward the Kuwaiti coast. Since the aim of that attack was to freeze the RGFC in place and to draw their attention to Kuwait, and since General Schwarzkopf rightfully wanted a synchronized first- and second-day ground

---

*Dual-Purpose Improved Conventional Munitions—small hand grenade–sized bomblets packed into an artillery shell and dispensed when the shell bursts in the air; about 5 percent were duds.

attack scheme, John had directed both us and XVIII Corps to clear any such forward movement with him. If the eastern attack was successful in its aim, the Third Army heavy forces attack on the second day could better achieve positional advantage to destroy the RGFC.

★ That was my running estimate that morning of G-Day, and everything looked in place. After a paper cup of coffee brought over by Staff Sergeant Dave St. Pierre, my driver, I strapped on my leg, pulled the leg of my tanker's Nomex suit over it, strapped on my shoulder holster containing my 9-mm Beretta, and put on my Kevlar helmet. Today we'd get into our coiled spring. Tomorrow we'd attack.

I walked the thirty feet through the sand in the early-morning cold and quiet darkness to get a quick breakfast before the morning update. John Landry and a few other members of the corps staff were in the small van where we took meals and sometimes had short meetings. As we ate a hot breakfast of B rations and coffee, we talked informally. At this point, most of the corps were eating two hot meals a day, breakfast and supper, with Meals Ready to Eat (MRE) during the day. That was about to change. Until the war was over, we all ate a steady diet of MREs.

We talked about our activities for the day. Nothing unexpected had happened during the night. I would get a complete staff update shortly.

0600 VII CORPS MAIN COMMAND POST

After breakfast, I walked the short distance to our newly arranged CP, two Army general-purpose tents hooked together and pitched over sand, where I would get a quick morning update before moving on to the TAC CP.

I took a fast look around. The CP was a working area, and work continued even as we had our meeting. The atmosphere was informal. We had been at this for three months now, and during that time I'd lived there, often just wandering around and chatting with people, so by this morning, I knew nearly all personnel by their first names, and the feeling was relaxed. We were like a family in many ways, and the meeting was much more like a family gathering than the stereotypical image of some Prussian war council—the supreme field marshal marching in and arranging himself grandly in the highest-backed of a line of high-back chairs. Our chairs, in fact, were mainly gray metal fold-up things, with a lot of dents and chipped paint from constant use. Since there weren't many of them, people dragged up their own or stood.

The various corps staff seated themselves. Standing behind them were most of the rest of the tent's staff, who'd left their stations so that they could be present for the update on this first day. Also standing were the liaison officers from the various corps units, there to report any orders back to their commanders. By this time, everyone knew what to expect when I had a briefing. On this day, as usual, I was serious, but I also wanted to project the confidence I genuinely felt . . . and wanted everyone there to feel. I looked at the faces around me. What a talented team, I thought, their skills developed through years of schools and training exercises. It had taken our Army almost twenty years to get here.

I sat in the middle chair, about ten feet in front of a 1:250 000-scale situation map with the latest enemy and friendly situation posted. To my right was my deputy, Brigadier General Gene Daniel, and to my left was Brigadier General John Landry, chief of staff. The tent was quiet in anticipation, except for the occasional radio and phone calls coming in on this first day.

Normally, I liked to start with the G-2 for a picture of the enemy.

So far, based on what I'd seen, we had the Iraqis where we wanted them, and we had the right moves for that day and the next. But I was searching now for any indicators that would cause me to make last-minute adjustments, as I looked ahead to the next day and the day after that. Tactics is always a series of adjustments, as you attempt to get an edge on the enemy and keep that edge.

I still anticipated that my next big decision would come in about twenty-four hours, when I ordered the corps into a maneuver to attack and destroy the RGFC. I anticipated selecting one of the seven FRAGPLANs we had proposed—I still preferred FRAGPLAN 7, which turned VII Corps ninety degrees east, formed a three-division armored fist, then attacked into the flank and rear of the RGFC if they remained fixed or defended where they were. Over the next twenty-four to forty-eight hours, I needed to maneuver the corps so that when we executed that FRAGPLAN, we would be in a continuous rolling attack and wouldn't have to stop and form the fist. The only two missing pieces from FRAGPLAN 7 were the Iraqi RGFC dispositions and the third division for my fist. If CENTCOM didn't release the 1st CAV—or if they didn't do it in time—I'd have to come up with another division from somewhere.

Why three divisions? For two reasons: First, if the RGFC and the 10th and 12th Iraqi Armored Divisions stayed fixed, we would be attacking into five heavy divisions (with our three), with XVIII Corps to our north attacking three RGFC infantry divisions. Even if CENTAF had succeeded in reducing the Iraqi divisions by 50 percent, that would still leave a 1:1 fight (again with our three). We could defeat the Iraqis with two divisions instead of three, but at a risk of sustaining many more casualties. The second reason I wanted the three divisions was so that we could sustain our combat power for at least two or more days. I did not want our attack to run out of combat power after twenty-four hours. Our mission was to destroy the RGFC in our sector, not just defeat them.

As for the question of which would be the third division, I had always kept open the possibility of using the 1st INF somehow in the RGFC attack after they completed the opening-up of the breach. The issue there had to be how well they came through their breach attack. If they got hurt badly in the breach, then I would leave them there. If, on the other hand, they came through all right, then I wanted to use them. In fact, I hoped to use them— possibly as reserve—even if the 1st CAV had been committed to us earlier than they in fact were.

"OK, John, what have you got?" I asked Colonel John Davidson, the G-2.

After John gave us a complete enemy lay-down, he concluded, "Sir, the Iraqis have not moved and show no reaction in our sector so far to Coalition attacks or to our early movements. Iraqi VII Corps remains fixed in front of us. RGFC still has capability to relocate. Looks as though they are remaining in place and will stay that way. Estimate main force Iraqi units at between 50 and 75 percent strength. Morale continues to be low in Iraqi VII Corps. RGFC will fight."

Let me expand on this a little: First, it looked as though our 1st CAV deception into the Ruqi Pocket was working. The Iraqis weren't aware that the main attack would come from west of there. Good. Next, we had predicted that a brigade of the armored division in reserve (the 52nd) could reinforce Iraqi units defending against our breach, and that prediction still held. I had instructed fire support and G-2 to hammer it relentlessly. The Iraqis had five frontline infantry divisions in our sector. Their tactical reserve was the 52nd, positioned in the Wadi al Batin and stretching westward behind the frontline divisions. One brigade of the 52nd was positioned close to the place where the British would turn east as they left the breach. If that brigade was left alone, they could hold up the British and clog the whole breach. That is why I had ordered our fire support people to make it "go away."

We also estimated that deeper in their strategic theater forces, the Tawalkana, Medina, and 17th Armored Divisions could reposition west to the vicinity of our Objective Collins. Collins was a corps "way point"—or the place where I had estimated I would commit the corps to one of the FRAGPLANs. It was a large circle on the map to indicate a corps concentration point, about 150 kilometers from the line of departure, and it had significance only as a point of orientation. There was no attack to "seize" Collins, for example. Rather, in the absence of towns or crossroads or some other orienting feature, we had to create "features" of our own. Collins was one of these.

And lastly, we continued to think that they would attempt to defend in depth in successive positions from the border over to Basra and use chemical weapons against us, either at the border or as we attacked the RGFC.

John was followed by the staff weather officer, Air Force Major Jerry Thornberg, who gave a not-too-encouraging picture of the February desert weather: High winds would develop later, with blowing sands limiting visibility, plus low clouds and chance of rain. Temperatures were to climb into the low fifties during the day and go down to close to freezing that night. He predicted more of the same all week.* I knew that would probably complicate movement and resupply, and might interfere with aviation. But I also knew there wasn't much you could do about the weather except work around or through it.

Since my G-3, Colonel Stan Cherrie, was at this point already about fifty kilometers northwest at the TAC CP, Colonel Mike Hawk gave the G-3 portion of the briefing. I would join Stan shortly and get from him a complete report on what the friendly units were doing. Mike reported that to this point the movements of our forces were proceeding without enemy contact and without problems.

He added that reports of progress outside the corps early in the morning of 24 February were sketchy at best. As 2nd ACR had moved forward, they had maintained contact with 3rd ACR on our VII Corps western boundary (they were XVIII Corps's easternmost unit). And since we had a liaison officer directly linked to XVIII Corps in our main CP, we had reports of early success by the 82nd, 101st, and French 6th Division operation in the west of XVIII Corps.

Meanwhile, effective midnight, 1st CAV had been placed back under control of CENTCOM as theater reserve. We continued to stay in communication with them, however, as I anticipated their coming back to us at some point. They were also still operating in our sector, and we were providing their logistics support.

As for Marine actions or the Arab forces (JFC-E) on the east coast, we had no reports.

Fire support came next: Colonel Ray Smith** reported that we would get a total of 350 sorties of air that day, 100 of them close air support.

"What about targets beyond the FSCL?" I asked. The FSCL was a line usually drawn about thirty to forty kilometers forward of the line of enemy contact; beyond it, the air could attack targets of their choosing.

"Sir, the correlation between what we asked to get hit and what got hit is still poor, less than 50 percent."

The FSCL issue continued to be a point of great disagreement between me and CENTAF and had plagued our operations from the start (Gary Luck and Third Army were having the same problems). My ability to influence air

---

*As it turned out, this period set a ten-year record for rainfall.
**Ray died of a heart attack in 1993; he was a superb officer who knew more about corps deep operations than anyone I knew. He was also a meticulous planner and relentless in seeing orders executed to completion.

interdiction attacks against ground targets beyond the FSCL was poor. CENTAF kept rejecting our targets and hitting their own. Though I had made my feelings on this well known to both Yeosock and Waller, I was not confident the situation with air would change. It did not.

By now, the staff knew all this was a raw issue with me. I had no arguments with how many air sorties CENTAF flew in and beyond our sector. That was the CINC's decision. But I wanted to synchronize the sorties in our sector with my own assets in a well-orchestrated scheme of attack. I had the mission here, not the Air Force! So when the subject of targets beyond the FSCL came up, my reaction was likely to be heated and sharp. I thought I knew a hell of a lot better what targets should get hit in our sector than CENTAF in Riyadh, especially after the attack began and the situation started to change rapidly.

In his brief, our chemical officer, Colonel Bob Thornton, reported that the orders were understood in the corps that forward of the line of departure (the Iraq-Saudi border), troops would be in MOPP 1 and would take the nerve gas (PB) pills. He continued to maintain that the Iraqis had the capability to use chemical and bio against us, and I believed him. I expected the Iraqis to use chemical weapons, and I never rested easy about it.

G-4, Colonel Bill Rutherford, reviewed the status of major pieces of equipment. Availability was in the high 90 percentile, better than we'd ever had in Germany, and a testament to the hard work put in by soldiers and sergeants. It also showed pride: no one wanted to be left behind with a broken vehicle. Our biggest challenge, we all knew, would be fuel. Though consumption would be enormous—the divisions would burn up to 800,000 gallons a day—the problem would be distribution, not supply. I did not want to be the armored commander who ran out of fuel on top of the world's greatest supply of oil. Logisticians can work only so much magic, however, and I was very aware that my tactical decisions would be influenced by logistics.

Over the past few days, I had ordered a number of operations to prepare for our attack on G+1, but because of the diplomatic maneuvering and the constant possibility of last-minute changes, I had been in the habit of confirming those orders each day. That day, I *knew* I needed to confirm that: 2nd ACR was to continue to execute a movement to contact twenty kilometers to Phase Line Grape (their Busch), 3rd AD was to conduct a planned deep attack that night against artillery in range of the breach with their Apaches, and 11th AVN BDE was to execute CONPLAN Boot, an attack the following night against Iraqi VII Corps tactical reserves, their 52nd Armored Division (this would complement both the 1st INF breach on G+1 and the subsequent attack east by the British).

It was a quick staff update, perhaps twenty minutes in all, and when it was over, I made a brief recap. This was an important day, I said, the last day for us to get ready for our attack. The diplomatic maneuvering was over, I told them. Now it was up to us. I thanked them for all their hard work, and said, "JAYHAWK."

It was a great team. As I had said many times, I was confident we would do what we had to do, and save the talk for later. I was proud to be with them, as well as with the larger team, the 146,000 (counting 1st CAV) American and British soldiers who were the JAYHAWK VII Corps.

After a brief huddle with John Landry and Gene Daniel to go over that day's key operations and review my expectations of the next two days, I departed for the twenty-minute Blackhawk trip to our TAC CP.

VII Corps Command Posts

Though we had spent considerable effort to think our way through command post arrangements and to keep each other informed during the anticipated fast-moving operation, these arrangements, we knew, were fragile. Even so, I was confident they would work. While there was still time, though, I took one final look at them:

Of our three command posts, the rear CP would stay at Al Qaysumah, a town with an airfield about thirty kilometers east of Hafar al Batin on the Tapline Road; the main would stay right where they were, about forty kilometers south of the border; and the TAC CP and the two "jump TAC" CPS would move and stay physically close to the battle.

The TAC CP would initially remain close to the middle of the 3rd Armored formation. It would move late on G+1, after the success of the breach was assured and I shifted the main effort of the corps to the enveloping force.

One "jump TAC" would stay well ahead with the 3rd Armored, so they could communicate with 2nd ACR, 1st AD, and 3rd AD. The other "jump TAC" would be at the breach site, where Brigadier General Gene Daniel was to command passage through the breach of the appropriate corps units—the British, our two artillery brigades moving to join their divisions, the 400-plus vehicles that would make up Log Base Nelligen, the 1st CAV (as I hoped), as well as other corps units needed north in the attack. We also needed two-way traffic in the breach to evacuate prisoners and for resupply.

My personal plan was to stay closest to the corps main effort. That meant I would spend that night at the main CP (its location was closer to the breach than the TAC's), then shift to the TAC on G+1. I planned to use the main TAC and the two smaller jump TACs as my operating bases and command the corps from the front. To ensure a positive link to my nerve center at the main CP, we had arranged for my executive officer, Lieutenant Colonel Russ Mulholland, to make two courier runs to the main TAC daily, at 0900 and at

1700 (John Landry had directed the staff to have information current as of 0830 and 1630). In this way, I could be forward to command face-to-face, get my "fingerspitzengefuhl" of the battles, and obtain the latest information from the corps main, which had much better long-haul comms.

We also planned to use aerial retrans capability—a helicopter relay of line-of-sight comms, like a manned low-orbiting satellite, to essentially double our comm range. This worked reasonably well, except when weather kept the helos on the ground (quite often, it turned out).*

STRATEGIC CONTEXT AND TACTICAL COMMANDER

During the flight to the TAC CP, I shifted my thoughts to our part in a larger theater campaign plan. We were not operating alone, and I could never let myself lose sight of that.

Nobody in an operation this vast and important was a free agent. We all operated within the context of a mission and objectives, and the discipline to stay within those. That applied to me as well as to Generals John Yeosock, Norman Schwarzkopf, and Colin Powell, Secretary of Defense Cheney, and even to President Bush. I always had the opinion to go to my commander and try to get something changed if I thought it was getting in the way, but in re-ality, as a senior commander, you have to pick your spots, and you don't do it often. Otherwise, you're either a whiner or a disruption to the operation. So, as in any operation, there were some constraints (must-dos) and restraints (do-nots).

They were not unreasonable, and I agreed with them.

The major constraint on us was to reinforce the theater deception scheme. That meant we had to stay hidden from the Iraqis out west until we attacked and reinforce the 1st CAV deception.

As for our major restraint, this had been set out to us in an order that my chief of staff, John Landry, had gotten from Third Army on 22 February. We were directed not to conduct any "irreversible" actions—that is, actions that would throw off the theater attack timetable. During a call to Cal Waller (when he was Third Army commander in Yeosock's absence), I told him I as-sumed that meant we were not to conduct any operations that might affect the diplomatic maneuvering then going on. Cal agreed but left further inter-

---

*Such is the nature of investment decisions for strategic and tactical communications. Strategic comms work well and get big dollars for development, while the closer you get to where rounds impact, the less money and the more primitive the comms. So you improvise and do other things. Except for 3rd AD, we had tactical line-of-sight communications that dated back to the early 1960s and had been used in Vietnam.

pretation up to me. My choice then was to interpret the restraints as very tight. This was my interpretation and no one else's.*

This order had been a formal follow-through on Cal Waller's informal instructions during his 20 February visit that we should not conduct any battles that could provoke a strategic decision (that would get ground forces so involved it would set off a clamor for the beginning of the entire ground war in the United States). At that point, a couple of days before the attack, there was still a possibility that the ground war would be called off.

Why is all that important? Because this restraint and my own interpretation tied our hands for cross-border operations with Apaches (although we had in fact conducted one with our 11th Aviation Brigade earlier in February). Both the 1st Armored and the 3rd Armored Divisions, for example, had well-thought-out plans to send their Apaches into Iraq. Though I had gotten excellent briefings from both division commanders on both operations and had no hesitation about executing the plans, the restraint put any such plans on hold.

The 3rd AD wanted to go after artillery that was about fifty kilometers from the border in their assigned zone. Because this artillery was also in range of the 1st INF breach, the attack would help out the Big Red One as well. We were having difficulty getting TAC air to go after the artillery, and we couldn't reach it with our own artillery, so I had talked to Butch Funk about using our Apaches. Soon after that, Colonel Mike Burk, the aviation brigade commander, put together a plan to go after the artillery, and I told Butch to execute. But then I got the instructions from Third Army to restrain, and the attack had to be put off. (On G-Day, I authorized Butch to conduct the attack that night.)

Meanwhile, Ron Griffith wanted to conduct an armed reconnaissance with Apaches in front of the 1st Armored Division out to a depth of some sixty or seventy kilometers to confirm, as we thought, that parts of a brigade of the 26th Division were out there trying to refuse the Iraqi west flank. He also wanted a better assessment of the difficult terrain through which the division would have to travel for fifty kilometers just north of the border. The confirmation of that intelligence on the enemy and terrain would allow Griffith to fix and bypass the Iraqi force (and the Apaches could take out some Iraqis on their own as well), and also speed Ron's advance toward al-Busayyah. I had to

*Cal Waller died of a heart attack in 1995. He was an invaluable line of communication with General Schwarzkopf, and in January had the courage to say that we weren't then ready to attack (even though several people wished that was somehow so); he was for a time Third Army commander, a job he handled with professionalism and skill; and he was a friend.

disapprove Ron's plan for the same reason. (As with Butch, I gave the OK to Ron to execute on G-Day after the restraints came off.)

Though the reasoning behind this Third Army restraint made complete sense to me, it is still an illustration of the fits and starts that last-minute diplomatic maneuvering cause in military operations. As uncomfortable as this may be for commanders, we all better get used to it. More recent diplomatic maneuvering at the last minute forestalled our airborne assault in Haiti.

If I had known that our attack was going to be moved up from G+1 to G-Day, my decisions on the twenty-third would have been much different, and I would have put the corps into a much more aggressive posture on the twenty-fourth. In particular, I would have hit the Iraqis hard with our own aviation for a few days before our ground units attacked. You can turn some operations off and on in a short period of time; but not most of them.

0850 VII Corps TAC CP

After we landed at the TAC CP, I went immediately inside the tent extensions behind the M577s. The weather was still good for flying, but the wind was picking up. The temperature was in the low forties.

Inside the TAC there was a roughly twenty-by-fifteen-foot "floor" of sand with three M577s on one end and two on the other. Four vertical poles and long horizontal tube steel poles held the canvas up to a height of about seven feet. Behind each M577 was a small work area for that section, usually consisting of a green, wooden two-by-three-foot collapsible field desk with field telephones. There was the ever-present, never-shut-down coffeepot working away nearby as well as the steady hum of the generators. At the rear of the G-3 M577 were two desks, one for me with my own phones and one for the G-3. In front of those desks was a situation map, 1:250 000 scale, over which you could put separate sheets of heavy acetate, each annotated with information, such as enemy, engineers, fire support, air defense, etc. Enemy and friendly locations were posted using one-by-two-inch pieces of acetate with adhesive on the back (cut out and posted by hand). Since they were not to scale, you had to interpolate. An enemy brigade unit sticker might cover twice the area they actually occupied on the ground. Same for our own units. Worse, the glue tended to dry out, so on occasion the stickers fell from the map. When you picked them up, you hoped you put them back where they belonged. Reports came in via radio, fax, telephone, or teletype, then the info got posted on the maps by our NCOs. It was far from high-tech, and a reminder that even today, war on the ground and at the front was done by hand.

The team in there was hard at work. We had been at it for two months, and were a smooth-running operation. I was pleased with what we had done and confident we were up to the task of commanding what was potentially a five-division multi-national corps of 1,584 tanks and a total of close to 50,000 vehicles on the move.

After I walked in and said good morning to the troops, I sat down on the gray metal folding chair behind my field desk and turned my attention to Stan Cherrie's update. Though I had already gotten most of what I needed at the main CP, information on our own units' operations was usually more current at the TAC—they were closer to the units than the main CP and had direct line-of-sight communications—so that is what I focused on. I paid attention to our own early movements, because I wanted them to go right and to build an early momentum of success. I did not anticipate any problems, but you can never discount chance. In other words, though I was still confident, I was also still wary.

1ST INF DIVISION. In order to make room for our artillery far enough forward to range the Iraqi artillery, at 0538, the division attacked into the Iraqi 26th Division security zone, with 1st and 2nd Brigades on line, and one in reserve. By 0930, they had reached Phase Line Kansas without enemy contact, and were set to begin the breach the next day.

2ND ACR. The regiment had moved out toward Busch at 0630, with 4th Squadron (Aviation) in front and the 2nd and 3rd Squadrons following side by side on the ground. At this point, Don Holder had three squadrons forward (one air and two ground) and one (the 1st) back (on the ground). By 0708, the 4th Squadron had engaged six unidentified enemy vehicles with MLRS, and was reporting empty fighting positions. At 0812, P Troop (Aviation) had engaged six enemy infantry about twenty kilometers into Iraq. At 0910, the regiment received enemy artillery fire and quickly silenced it with counter-battery fire. By 1117, the entire regiment was across the border berm, clearing the way for follow-on divisions.

1ST AD AND 3RD AD. Both divisions had been moving forward into the area now vacated by the 2nd ACR and were preparing for the next day's attack by cutting additional holes in the double ten- or twelve-foot-high hard sand border berm. First AD had two brigades forward and one back, and their roughly 8,000 vehicles stretched about eighty kilometers to the rear. Third AD was in a column of brigades, and their own 8,000 vehicles stretched over 100 kilometers to the rear.

BRITISH. The British were beginning to load their heavy armored vehicles on Heavy Equipment Transporters. Today they would move those HETS the seventy or eighty kilometers from their position, called "Ray,"* forward to a location just behind the border. From here they would be ready to move through the cleared breach just after dark on G+1. Rupert Smith wanted to do this in order to conserve wear and tear on his vehicles and to save them for the fight. (The British were genuinely concerned about breakdowns of the Challenger tank. As it turned out, Challenger performed much better than expected.)

LOGISTICS. Our logisticians were assembling the over 400 fuel vehicles and other support required to establish the corps's Log Base Nelligen. Those vehicles and soldiers were to go from Log Base Echo 100 kilometers forward through the 1st INF Division breach and into the open desert just to its north to set up a 1.2 million–gallon fuel-storage capability on the ground. There they would refuel the attacking enveloping force after that force had used the fuel in their own vehicles and the reserves carried on their own assigned trucks. South of the breach would be another fuel site (called Buckeye) with a similar capacity, also requiring 400-plus fuel vehicles, which would fuel the breach operation and be available for the British should they need it.

ENGINEERS. Our engineers were up front with each of the attacking units where they would break holes in the border berm with bulldozers or Armored Combat Engineer (ACE) vehicles. They also would fire mine-clearing line charges (MICLIC) into the Iraqi minefields to clear lanes for follow-on tanks equipped with mine plows and rollers.

Colonel Sam Raines, CO of the 7th Engineer Brigade, captured in his journal a lot of what we were all thinking: "Looking in the faces of my soldiers, I see some fear; but overwhelmingly I see determination and seriousness. These are the same faces that were in landing craft off Omaha Beach, 6 June 1944, on Iwo Jima, at Pork Chop Hill, the base of Hamburger Hill, or in a C-141 aircraft just prior to the airborne drop on Grenada. It is a serious, anxious look, no horseplay, just pure professional dedication to the task at hand. In every heart there are prayers. . . . All of us are now wearing cumbersome chemical protection suits and rubber boots over our regular uniforms. They are uncomfortable, very hot; and the charcoal filter lining turns hands, face, and neck sooty black. . . . We live in the miserable chemical suits for several days."

---

*Lieutenant Colonel Tom Goedkoop and my corps planners had on their own initiative named all the assembly areas and attack positions of the VII Corps after World War II Medal of Honor winners: Garcia, Butts, Henry, Thompson, Roosevelt, Keyes, and Ray.

207TH MI BRIGADE. To ensure we had continuous coverage as we attacked north, then east, Colonel John Smith, CO 207th, had formed Task Force Sand Hawk to move his UAV platoon closer to the Iraqi border. The next day they displaced forward into the 1st CAV sector to operate off a 188-by-60-foot aluminum runway built by the 527th Engineer battalion. There they flew a total of fifteen missions, totaling just under sixty-one hours (ten further missions were canceled because of bad weather, and one aircraft crashed and was destroyed). Their contribution was important, for they located for attack Iraqi artillery battalions, FROG batteries, infantry trench lines, and other targets. And the UAV platoon also would capture 303 prisoners. Because I had concerns that the platoon needed some firepower (there was nothing between them and the Iraqis), I had ordered them to be provided with a platoon of tanks (3rd Platoon, Company B, 3rd Battalion, 77th Armor, from the 8th Infantry Division).* Our soldiers and leaders did all this after getting them in theater just three weeks earlier, with no prior experience with UAVs. It was remarkable, and a great tribute to our soldiers and leaders.

⋆ After Stan's update, I was satisfied that we were doing what we had planned and that, as I read the Iraqis, no adjustments were necessary so far. I planned to stay at the TAC a little while longer, then go visit commanders, starting with Don Holder in Iraq and working my way around. I wanted to confirm what I had just heard, see it with my own eyes, and get the face-to-face judgments of my commanders.

Meanwhile a lot was going on in the theater outside of VII Corps, but I knew very little about it at the time. Tom Clancy now brings us up to date on some of these events.

ATTACK

On G-Day, at 0400, on a front running from the Gulf to about 400 kilometers deep into the desert, a force of 620,000 soldiers, Marines, and airmen from close to forty different nations took part in launching the most massive attack since World War II against an Iraqi force of approximately 540,000 men.

• In the Gulf near Kuwait, a Marine amphibious group thrust toward the coast, threatening the seaborne invasion for which the Iraqis had prepared mightily . . . and that never came.

---

*On a visit to Fort Huachuca on 19 December 1991, I was surprised to receive a UAV propeller blade from one of the task force members with the inscription "Thanks for the TANKS, Sir."

• The Saudi-led Arab JFC-East force attacked up the coastal highway toward Kuwait City.

• Just to their west, in the Kuwaiti boot heel, Lieutenant General Walt Boomer's two divisions, the 1st and 2nd Marines, started their breaching operations into the Iraqi minefields and other static defenses a few kilometers inside Kuwait. The 1st CAV's "Tiger" Brigade (as part of the 2nd Marine Division, on the west flank of the Marine attack) followed close behind, to give the Marines additional heavy M1A1 punch. (The Marines also had a battalion of M1A1s.)

• To their west, the Egyptian-led JFC-North continued to prepare to launch their 25 February attack into the Iraqi security zone.

• To their west, in VII Corps, the 1st CAV, now under CENTCOM command, continued their deception into the Ruqi Pocket.

• To their west, 1st INF attacked into the Iraqi security zone, to take out reconnaissance and observation posts, and the 2nd ACR moved twenty kilometers into Iraq to their west.

• And, finally, to their west, XVIII Corps launched their attack toward the Euphrates with their light infantry and air assault elements.

There were three initial phases to Gary Luck's attack plan to cut off the RGFC escape routes and supply corridors along Highway 8:

First, elements of Major General Peay's 101st Airborne Division were to airlift to an objective about 150 kilometers from their launch point and set up there what was known as FOB (Forward Operating Base) Cobra, which would be their logistics and operational anchor for their second phase.

Second, the next day, another helicopter assault by the 101st would establish an airhead near the Euphrates.

Third, Major General Barry McCaffrey's 24th MECH and 3rd ACR would drive east of the 101st, toward Highway 8.

Meanwhile, on the western flank of XVIII Corps, the French division, beefed up by the 2nd Brigade of the 82nd Airborne and the American 18th Field Artillery Brigade, attacked toward Objective Rochambeau, fifty kilometers into Iraq. When that was taken, they were to move on toward Objective White, the town of as-Salman, and the airfield north of town.

To say that all of these attacks went well is an understatement. The Iraqi frontline defenses crumbled. The fearsome Iraqi defensive barriers proved to be far less fearsome than everyone believed, or dared to hope for (though they still weren't easy, and there were casualties and deaths). Some Iraqi troops and entire Iraqi units surrendered without a fight, while others fought back. Predictions of U.S. casualties into the tens of thousands never happened. No chemical or biological attacks were detected. Such a result had been far from a sure thing only hours before.

By 1800 on the twenty-fourth, the two Marine divisions had advanced through the two Iraqi defensive belts. The 1st Marine Division had gone about forty kilometers, and the 2nd, on the west, had gone twenty kilometers. As the official Marine Corps history states: "During the night of 24–25 February, both divisions assumed defensive postures. . . .

"In the early afternoon, Lieutenant General Walter Boomer received a call from General Schwarzkopf concerning the allied main attack with VII Corps and the Joint Forces Command–North immediately to MARCENT's left"—i.e., to the left of the Marine divisions. "The Marines' speedy progress caused Schwarzkopf to worry aloud about possible exposure of I MEF's left flank once they became abreast of Manaquish, where the border turned due west. . . . General Boomer recommended that the main attack begin as soon as possible. Shortly after this conversation, General Schwarzkopf ordered the main attack to commence. Although ARCENT's VII Corps crossed its line of departure at 1500, the Joint Forces Command–North attack on MARCENT's left was delayed until after 1800. It stopped just inside their breach for the night."

Thus, the wheels were set in motion for an early attack by VII Corps— much, as it turned out, to Fred Franks's surprise.

EARLY ATTACK
SUNDAY 24 FEBRUARY
VII CORPS TAC CP

At 0930, John Yeosock called.

"Fred, John, CINC wants to know if you can attack early."

"Say again." I was not sure I heard this right.

"The Marines have been having success, and the CINC does not want to wait until tomorrow to attack. He wants to know if we can go early, today."

I was genuinely surprised—shocked maybe was more accurate. We had considered every other possibility except this. In a flash, my brain went from the reflective, intensely focused, get-ready pace of a moment before to "warp-speed" active. Before I replied to John, dozens of thoughts flashed through my head, along with dozens more about what I would have to do to make it all happen.

What is the CINC really asking? was the first mental question. I quickly concluded that it wasn't actually "*Can* you attack early?" but "How *soon* can you attack?" I quickly ruled out telling John we could not do it, because I had no doubt that we could.

Other questions shot through my head.

What about unit positions in relation to one another? Would they have to move? What about artillery preparations, logistics (especially fuel), the British move forward, and the orders already disseminated and rehearsed? And how would an early attack affect day and night operations, and operations forty-eight hours from now?

I told myself, Whatever you do, keep it simple. I knew that success early on in an attack builds its own momentum. I had seen that many times before. So, given this go-early situation, I did not need to put additional barriers in front of the corps by making some sudden change of plan. If we could simply back everything up to today that we had planned to do tomorrow at BMNT, then that would be the best way to do it.

All this raced through my brain in nanoseconds. OK, I decided, keep it simple and continue with what we've already set in motion, but with some major time and tactical adjustments. Now I had to see whether that was possible.

"Yes, we can do it," I told John, after a pause of no more than a second or two. "Tell the CINC yes, but I still want to talk to my commanders."

"XVIII Corps said they could go on two hours' notice," Yeosock answered. "How does that sound to you? Based on how soon the Egyptians can get ready, it looks like 1500 at the earliest. Take that as a warning order, with a confirmation at 1300, for a 1500 attack."

"Sounds OK to me, but I still want to talk to my commanders."

★　That call, and the cease-fire decision four days later, turned out to be the biggest surprises of the war for VII Corps. We had been over the plan with Third Army and with CENTCOM so many times that I thought we had considered every possibility. And now came one that we had never considered; it was *that* unexpected.

Why did the CINC want us to go early? What had brought on this very large, very sudden change? Except for John's remark that the Marines were doing well in the east, I was without a clue. The best understanding I could come to in the first moments after John's call was this: Since the Marines were going faster than expected, the fixing operation to our east was now going to take much less than a full day; this would allow us to attack today instead of tomorrow. Thus, as I understood it, the call from John Yeosock was primarily a matter of moving up the attack timetable fifteen hours.*

If that was the case (and I had no indication from John of anything else; he hadn't mentioned any change of missions or different methods of attack), I figured that the CINC was making no other changes in the plan. Nothing in my own intelligence indicated that the Iraqis in our sector were doing anything different from what we expected. There was no release of the 1st CAV Division from theater reserve, which would have signaled that all was well in the east, and that the Iraqi situation was so well known that early commitment of the reserve was a good choice. There was no "go as soon as you are ready." There was only "go early," but in coordination with XVIII Corps and the Egyptian Corps, just as the original plan said.

On the other hand, if the Iraqis were totally crumbling and we were now involved in a rout of the Iraqis and were in (technically) a pursuit, then there would be no need for flank protection or any coordinated attack. We could all go as soon as ready and get immediately in pursuit of a broken enemy.

If the enemy situation is completely known, then you have no reason to keep a reserve for contingencies. In other words, reserves are insurance policies against unexpected enemy actions or to exploit enemy vulnerabilities by piling on at a decisive location. Thus keeping a reserve signaled—at least to me—that the CINC still needed an insurance policy.

★ Turning my attention back to immediate practical matters, I knew we would have to make adjustments. According to the old saying, when you meet the enemy, the first casualty is your plan. Well, we went that one better. We had not yet met the enemy, and the plan was already a casualty.

As my first order of business, I wanted to do three things: to talk to my commanders to get their assessments, to determine what adjustments needed to be made to move our attack up by fifteen hours, and to determine if we needed to make any tactical adjustments from our planned maneuvers following this early attack. We were going to do it. That wasn't an issue. It was a matter of when and how.

---

*After the war, I learned from the USMC history that a decision to go early really did not happen until early afternoon—despite the flurry of phone calls in the morning. The 0930 phone call from John Yeosock was therefore a "what if" . . . a trial balloon. In other words, contrary to some postwar analyses and commentaries, the decision to attack early was not predicated on some kind of perception of a rout of the Iraqis or that the Iraqis were getting away. The motive for the early attack was protection of the Marines' left flank. That makes sense.

The major factor for me was that each piece of the corps had to fit together to make a coherent whole. Coherence was necessary because of the confined space in which we were working and because we had a single corps objective: to destroy the RGFC in our sector. That meant coordinating the movement and positioning of *all* corps units toward that single, common objective, and staying balanced, so that several options were available when we attacked the RGFC. I wanted to go early in a way that preserved that balance. That was the key challenge on which I focused.

It would have been different if each of the VII Corps units had had its own individual objectives. If I could have lined up my units along the border, given them a zone or lane in which to operate, and then turned them loose to head north in their own lanes to their own individual objectives at their own speed, it would have been much easier. We were not in that situation.

Meanwhile, a question kept flashing in the back of my mind: What do we do in daylight and what in darkness? I knew that I'd have to adjust the day-night scheme we had worked out and rehearsed in training, but now that we were going early, would I be calling on units to perform operations at night that would get us either bogged down or else so tangled up that the RGFC focus could be jeopardized?

I had wanted the breach done, minefields cleared, and passage lanes marked in daylight. Then I wanted to pass through the follow-on forces under cover of darkness and move the enveloping force close to the RGFC at night. That way, I had reasoned, they wouldn't know what was coming at them either from the breach or from the envelopment, and the RGFC would have only the minimum time to react to our attack. Such a sequence also would make it more difficult for the Iraqis to target us and to employ chemical weapons, even if they were able to move artillery to replace what our two-hour prep had taken out.

Breaching a complex obstacle covered by enemy fire is the toughest attack mission a unit can get. By doing it in daylight, there would be much greater exposure to Iraqi direct-fire weapons than at night, but we would more than make up for it by greater speed, greater avoidance of blue-on-blue, and our greater ability to mark lanes for follow-on units to pass through. We also would have a better setup for the RGFC attack. I had discussed all this with Tom Rhame and his commanders over and over again, and they all had agreed. Daylight it would be. That meant a start at BMNT tomorrow.

Now that timing was out the window.

At that point, I intuitively felt that we were going to run out of daylight for our breach attack, even given our early success in moving through the Iraqi security zone. And I sensed that time was suddenly slipping through our fingers. We needed as much daylight as we could get.

If we could handle the early attack simply by moving up our attack time—and keeping all the other pieces of the operation about the same—then the sooner we attacked, the better. If we could move it up fifteen hours, we could move it up more. We were losing valuable time. You just sensed that.

Since I was coming to the conclusion that earlier was better, and that going earlier might even reduce some of the tactical risks, I knew I needed to talk to Tom Rhame and confirm it with him. As for my enveloping force, they could continue doing what they had already begun.

Stan Cherrie had heard my end of the conversation. So had Creighton Abrams.

"Stan," I said, "get a warning order out that we are going to attack early. Talk to the commanders and get their input. Get Butch Funk and Don Holder in here." Since the 2nd ACR would be pacing the corps advance, I wanted to talk to my covering force commander. Meanwhile, I'd had some ideas about a possible contingency operation on the east flank, so I wanted to talk to my reserve division commander about that. This contingency operation carried some risks with it. The issue, as I saw it, was that by going early, the enveloping force would be way out ahead toward the RGFC by the time the 1st INF could complete the breach and the British could pass through and move on to defeat the Iraqi tactical reserves to the east. That meant that my east flank would be exposed during that gap. What I was thinking of doing was committing Butch Funk in a shallower attack to the east than we had originally planned. If I did that, and used the 2nd ACR in between the two armored divisions, we could possibly protect our east flank and get to the RGFC faster, though at the cost of reducing our combat power. With that in mind, I wanted to brainstorm a quick maneuver adjustment with Butch and Don.

I then called Tom Rhame. No problem, he told me. They could go early around noon. Ron Griffith told me the same.

As I made these calls, Creighton Abrams was working on the adjustments he would have to make to the two-hour artillery prep fires planned before the breach. Two hours was impossible now; we could not get all the ammo into position in time. How much prep was enough? How much would kill the Iraqi artillery in range of the breach and their chemical delivery means? If two hours was the minimum necessary, and we did less today, were we risking chemical strikes?

Meanwhile, I needed someone to call the British. Since they had a liaison element with us at the TAC CP, they knew what I knew at that point. But I needed to find out if Rupert Smith could adjust his movement from Area Ray forward fast enough to be ready to pass through the breach once the 1st INF opened it up and cleared out of the way.

I also needed a quick logistics estimate. Would log elements (more than 400 vehicles) be ready to go forward to establish Buckeye (then about 400 more vehicles), then through the breach and establish Nelligen to provide fuel for the enveloping units?

And finally, I needed to make an adjustment to CONPLAN Boot—the 11th Aviation Brigade attack planned for tomorrow night on the eastern flank. I wanted them to hit the Iraqi reserves there and speed the British exit from the breach. Could they go tonight?

Don Holder and Butch Funk arrived at about 1015. We huddled outside the TAC enclosure because Stan and the troops in there were burning up the comms lines getting all the orders out and getting input on what I had asked for.

I used butcher paper to sketch out my ideas for Butch and Don.

What I had in mind was to commit to FRAGPLAN 7 right away. Third AD would initially make a shallower attack that would drive almost directly east while keeping clear of the northern forward limits of the breach. This maneuver would very quickly place a major force just east and north of the planned British attack. Meanwhile, the 2nd ACR would attack in the center between the two armored divisions. They would then give up their cover mission and become an attacking force—actually, part of a smaller fist. If I could not come up with the third division for my fist, then they would continue the attack in the center—a risk. If I did find another division, I would eventually relieve them, and the added division would pass through them. And in fact, in the back of my mind, was the growing likelihood that the 1st INF would come out of the breach in a posture that would allow me to use them again against the RGFC.

There were other risks. The plan would require rapid adjustment by two major maneuver units, 3rd AD and 2nd ACR, which would take time to disseminate. It would also commit us early to FRAGPLAN 7. If two days from now the RGFC did something different from what we expected, we were out of options.

Still, I wanted to explore maneuvers quickly that could adjust our attack for the better without totally unraveling the corps. Such adjustments open new risks, and I was aware of that, but I also was aware that such risks were not so unusual. When you change your attack scheme, you have to look for possible adjustments. That's the nature of tactics.

After I finished laying out my concept, Don told me he could do it—but he didn't think it was a good idea. His operation was going well, he was building a successful momentum that he did not want to interrupt, and he thought our original maneuver gave us more combat power against the RGFC to accomplish our mission.

Butch also told me he could do it. It was a matter of adjusting his graphical control measures (drawing new lines, or boundaries, for the units) and of attacking shallower but he, too, was concerned about our combat power against the RGFC.

I listened to them, and I remembered my focus: Keep it simple. Don and Butch verified what I already knew: I could be introducing additional friction if I went forward with my change. I decided to stick with the plan we had made, after all, and to make only the adjustments, such as artillery preparation, movement of the British forward, and positioning of logistics, necessary to compress the time by fifteen hours. All these would introduce friction of their own. I did not need to add to it unless the tactical advantages far outweighed that disadvantage, and they didn't.

So I told both commanders to continue as planned, with one adjustment: I ordered Butch Funk to cover that eastern flank until the British got out there. That way I had the flank secured and could still remain focused on our objective: the destruction of the RGFC, in our sector.

The meeting lasted twenty minutes.

I went back inside to talk briefly to Stan and to tell him of my decision. It was my final decision that day concerning the scheme of maneuver. I'd figured I had a small window in which to adjust tactics, and had now used that window to consider the adjustment I had just rejected. Window closed. Decision made. I call this moment, and moments like it, the "good-idea cutoff time"—the point at which a large organization just cannot make any further major changes. One element in the art of command is to know when you've reached that point. I knew we had just passed it.

When I walked up to him, Stan was busy with all the tasks that needed to be done and coordinating it all with John Landry at the main CP. In fact, things were breaking so fast that I had not told Stan that I was even thinking of making the adjustments I had discussed with Butch and Don, so it was important to tell him that I had decided to stick with what we had planned to do tomorrow, but that the time schedule had to be compressed so we could do it all today.

Before I left, Stan further heightened my concern that time was escaping us. "You know, boss," he remarked, "we might run out of daylight."

Night operations, even with night-vision equipment, are not the same as those during the day. They are more difficult. They take more time. There is more friction. You try to keep the tactics simple. You try to give troops time to plan and rehearse what they will be doing at night. I sensed all that—and kept on moving.

1st Infantry Division

At 1115, I flew twenty minutes out to the 1st INF Division. The weather was still good, although by now clouds covered the sky and the wind was picking up. Beneath us was vehicle movement as far as the eye could see. Although the units did not yet know that they would be attacking early, they were repositioning for the attack that they thought would be under way tomorrow.

When I arrived at the 1st INF TAC CP, I was met by Brigadier General Bill Carter, the assistant division commander. Tom Rhame was supposed to be there, too, but he was at the 1st INF main CP—a screwup of comms already. No matter. Bill could answer my questions about an early attack into the breach at 1500.

He outlined the status of the artillery positioning (at this point still aligned for the prep to fire the next day), the ammunition for the prep, the possibility of seizing Phase Line Colorado (the line where they would complete the breach) by nightfall if the division attacked at 1500, enemy activity and disposition, and the status of the lanes opened for the passage of the British (they had already begun marking these). The bottom line, Carter said, was that Tom Rhame felt they could go at 1500 with no problem or undue risk, but unless they went earlier than 1500, they would probably not finish by dark. They could go earlier if ordered. In fact, Rhame preferred that.

At the 1st INF TAC, I again ran into Brigadier General Creighton Abrams. (Creighton had a great knack for showing up at precisely the right time. Uncanny the way some people can do that.) Creighton told me there'd be no problem shooting the prep, but we'd have ammo available for only a thirty-minute attack.

I said, "OK, thirty minutes it is."

I knew the risk. Certainly, the Iraqi artillery in range of the breach, and able to fire chemical munitions, might not be silenced by a shorter thirty-minute prep—if we had thought two hours necessary before, then why was something less all right now? I also remembered the Iraqi artillery fire against the 1st CAV Division on 20 February in the action that had resulted in three soldiers KIA and six wounded. However, a few things had changed. What I'd seen so far today was how ineffective Iraqi artillery fire had been at the 1st INF in its move forward into the Iraqi security zone and at the 2nd ACR movement forward. I'd also seen our own artillery and witnessed its counterfire capability to rapidly silence Iraqi mortar and artillery fire. In addition, our attacks the past week had caused Iraqi artillery to take a severe beating. It was a risk—but it was acceptable.

That settled it. We could do it. We could go early. Though there were tactical risks, they were acceptable. In fact, the bigger risk now was in waiting. If we could go at 1500, we could go now. Since John Yeosock's call, I'd been feeling we were wasting daylight. If we went right away, it would be no more risky than later—it might even be less so. Maybe we would complete the breach that day and pass the British the same night instead of the following night. That way we could save a whole day. I could see no advantage to VII Corps in waiting. I was seized with the urgency to get this thing going *now!*

"The wasted minute," Napoleon called it. In battle you cannot get it back. There are times when you just feel that time is getting away from you or that you are wasting time that would be a combat asset if you had it. This was one of those times, and so I was getting impatient.

Tom Rhame was feeling a similar impatience, I think. When I talked to Tom on the radio and ordered him to attack at 1500, he made it clear what Bill had already told me, that he wanted to go earlier, if he could.

"I'll see about that," I told him, "but for now plan on 1500."

If I wanted to go early, the first thing I had to do was put in a call to John Yeosock to get his permission. But when I walked over to my jump TAC nearby, the comms weren't working! I could not get through.

"Damn! Just when I need them, the comms are not there."

I was frustrated, but there wasn't much I could do except get in the helo and go back to the TAC and the comms there.

ATTACK
VII CORPS TAC CP

I got back to the TAC at about 1250.

Stan told me 3rd AD had said they were ready to attack right away—they were already moving. That was good. That gave me more proof that we might as well just keep this thing rolling.

I immediately called John Yeosock. I told him we were ready to attack by 1500, but we were also ready to attack now. It would be just as easy to go now. If there was urgency in Riyadh for us to attack early, I reasoned, then keeping tight coordination between the attacking corps was no longer necessary. We were ready now. We had five hours of daylight left. Based on what I'd seen myself and on what had already been reported by 2nd ACR, I thought we might get through the breach today if we got started now. And if we did that, we could put ourselves back to our original day/night scheme, only twenty-four hours earlier. We did not have a long discussion, but I was clear that we could go immediately if required.

But John said no. The CINC wanted to keep our attack coordinated with the Egyptians on our east, and they could not be ready before 1500. When I protested again that we were losing valuable daylight, no was still the answer.

At this point I was getting mixed signals. Go early, but not too early. Go early, but the coordinated attack—XVIII Corps, VII Corps, Egyptian Corps—still ruled. From all I gathered from the call to John, there was no unusual sense of urgency other than that, for some reason or other, the CINC wanted us to go a bit early. He still wanted us in a coordinated deliberate attack, and all the other pieces of the mission remained unchanged.

I turned to Stan. "Get the order out," I told him. "We attack according to the same plan, but at 1500 today. Artillery prep starts at 1430 for thirty minutes. I want to cheat with the 2nd ACR and start them at 1430."

"WILCO."

The order went out.

ACTIONS

Then the weather turned bad. While VII Corps units attacked, there were high winds and rain, which severely reduced visibility in some places to less than 100 meters. Though all this probably helped conceal our attack, and so worked to our benefit, the effect for me personally was to trap me for most of the afternoon at the TAC, where I listened to the radio transmissions of the battle reports. Here is what was happening.

1st INF Division

At 1430, an almost 6,000-round prep was fired for thirty minutes. This was fired by the division artillery of the 1st INF, the 42nd Artillery Brigade, 75th Artillery Brigade, 142nd Artillery Brigade, and the Regimental Artillery of the British: a total of over 260 cannons and 60 MLRS; 414 MLRS rockets were fired, and cannon accounted for the rest. It was an awesome display of firepower, and of coordination and soldier-NCO skill in getting it together in such compressed time. From a standing no-notice start at 0930, they had put it all together in five hours. Creighton Abrams, Colonels Mike Dotson, Morrie Boyd, Gunner Laws, 142nd commander Colonel Charles Linch, and Brigadier (UK) Ian Drurie were masterful in their teamwork and leadership.

Following the prep fires, the 1st INF attacked, with Colonel Bert Maggart's 1st Brigade on the left and Colonel Tony Moreno's 2nd Brigade on the right. Colonel Dave Weisman's 3rd Brigade was in reserve, to be committed when the division expanded the breach head to three-brigade width beyond Phase Line Colorado to New Jersey, at a distance of about forty kilometers.

The Iraqi defense was laid out like this: First there were wire obstacles, then mines (the wires and mines extended back about five or ten kilometers). Then came bunkers and trenches, extending another ten kilometers. This far west, there were no fire trenches, though they did have them in front of the 1st CAV and perhaps thirty kilometers west of the Wadi al Batin.

Tension was high as the two brigades attacked. Their mission was to clear the breach zone of not only direct fire that could be placed on the units following them, but also of Iraqi artillery observers who could send indirect fire from Iraqi artillery units. (I didn't want *anything* left—not artillery, not forward observers, not tanks, not RPGs, not even rifles or machine guns that could cause problems to, say, our 5,000-gallon fuel trucks.) They were also to clear and mark twenty-four lanes through the obstacle system, each wide enough—about four meters—for a tracked vehicle. The Iraqis were in bunkers and trenches behind the minefields and barbed-wire obstacle system. Some of their artillery was still operable, plus heavier weapons such as tanks thickened their defense.

The breach was to be made slowly, steadily, and deliberately. The 1st INF lead tanks were equipped with mine plows that had been fitted in front of each track to plow up mines and push them to the side. Behind the plows came tanks equipped with heavy rollers in front of each track to set off any mines missed by the plows. To be sure lanes were cleared, a tank with a full track-width blade followed the rollers to scrape the entire width of the lane. This ensured positive clearance for the many fuel trucks that would soon use the lanes.

Crews in the lead mine-plow tanks were the tip of the attacking VII Corps spear. In those vehicles tensions were way up. They were out front and ready.

While mine-clearing tanks did their work, the rest of 1st Brigade and 2nd Brigade kept up relentless suppressive fires on Iraqi positions, forcing the defending Iraqis either to die in their bunkers or to surrender. And 1st INF artillery continued to fire on Iraqi positions just in front of advancing tanks and Bradleys, as well as deeper, to silence the remaining Iraqi artillery. Apache helicopters joined the fight by firing deep over the top of the attacking brigades to destroy Iraqi tanks. It was a masterful coordinated combined-arms fight by those lead brigades and the division to get all the combat power of the division into operation.

The Iraqis never had a chance. The Iraqi 26th Division had been defending with two brigades forward, the 110th and 434th, each on a fifteen-kilometer front. They were surprised and stunned by the speed and violence of the 1st INF attack, and rapidly cracked. Though there was return fire, mostly small arms and some heavier weapons that were quickly silenced, the Iraqis could not effectively coordinate their defense; pre G-Day artillery raids had knocked out much of their telephone wire and they feared getting on radios, in the belief that U.S. forces would use the transmissions as a source to target. Their third brigade was to the north, refusing the western flank, and could not assist.

The Iraqi trenches were anywhere from two to six feet deep, and the bunkers had two feet or more of sandbag cover overhead. The Iraqis would come out of the deeper bunkers to man the trenches, and interspersed among their positions were heavier vehicles such as tanks and BMPs. Mortars and artillery fired sporadically. One of the units to receive mortar fire was Company C, 2nd Battalion, 34th Armor, and it quickly became involved in a typical situation. U.S. engineers and mortars fired smoke in an attempt to blind the Iraqi defense, and some of the smoke blew back on the attacking units, making progress difficult, although more of the smoke fell in front of the Iraqis and was helpful. Meanwhile, the mine plows tried to keep at a speed of five mph or less, and on line to clear the mines evenly in the twenty-four lanes, while other units fired over them to suppress Iraqi defenders.

Rather than send our own troops into the bunker systems when we got there, we had decided to put tanks with bulldozer blades on each side of the fortifications and run them alongside the trenches, burying whatever was in there under a wall of sand. The Iraqis were given the opportunity to surrender, and some of them did; others were buried. It was their choice. It made no sense for our troops to get tangled in the Iraqi trenches and bunkers.

The battle was sharp and violent, with a high sustained tempo of fire and movement from our side. This was just as Tom Rhame and the Big Red One wanted it to be.

Once on the Iraqi side, the fighting was sporadic. Faced with this overwhelming force, many Iraqis surrendered, yet some fought back the best they could. They returned fire. Some of them died in their bunkers. But it was no use.

At about 1630, the weather cleared enough to permit flight, and I went forward to see Tom Rhame at his TAC CP, which was still in Saudi Arabia at that point. When I met him, Tom was ecstatic over the success of his division and the courage of his troops. I told Tom I was proud of them and what they had done so far. I was also relieved that we had seen no chemical attacks. We were all so highly sensitized to the possibility that I listened for any indications, and I almost could not believe that the Iraqis had not used them yet.

After I left Tom, I flew into Iraq to link up with Colonel Don Holder and the 2nd ACR Command Group. By now it was about 1715. We flew over attacking 1st INF units, stretching back as far as I could see. Some were moving forward through newly cleared lanes; others were waiting to pass through. When we reached the border, we headed northwest over the 3rd AD, which was now crossing the border and making its way through the berm (we could also see part of the 1st AD). The vehicle movement visible to me was slow,

With the Blackhorse on the German-Czech border, early 1960s

Major Franks in Vietnam, halfway between Loc Ninh and Bu Dop, Christmas Day, 1969. A familiar pose— on the radio.

Snoul, Cambodia, 5 May 1970. Franks is carried off the battlefield after a grenade shatters his left leg and foot. In the foreground is Colonel Donn Starry, regimental commander. (Photo by James P. Sterba.)

Fort Bliss, 1975–76. Back on active duty, with a prosthetic leg.

Fulda, Germany: the 11th Armored Cavalry Regiment's first M1 tank—Franks cuts the ribbon. With him is Captain Greg Bozek, Troop A commander.

Saudi Arabia, 16 January 1991. Lieutenant General Franks discusses his intent for the first phase of the war at a corps war council.

The VII Corps TAC command post being set up in Saudi Arabia, 23 February, "the day before"

Talking with soldiers of the 4th Squadron, 7th Cavalry, 3rd Armored Division, the day before the attack

G-Day, 24 February. Meeting with Major General Rhame, commander 1st Infantry Division, to discuss the breaching operation and follow-on missions.

A Multiple-Launch Rocket System (MLRS) firing

The 3rd Armored Division moving toward Iraq

An M2A2 Bradley

A destroyed Iraqi tank

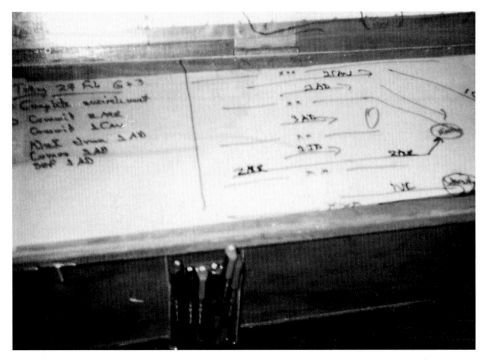

Notes and sketch of the corps encirclement Franks drew on the UH-60 map board first thing the morning of 27 February

Commanders meeting at corps TAC the day of the cease-fire, 28 February. Left to right: Brigadier General Tilelli, commander 1st Cavalry; Major General Funk, commander 3rd Armored Division; Major General Rhame, commander 1st Infantry Division; Major General Griffith, commander 1st Armored Division; and Franks. Major General Smith, commander 1st UK Armored Division, is behind Tilelli.

Franks presenting Army Chief of Staff Carl Vuono with a captured Iraqi helmet autographed by the commanders

America welcomes back the soldiers of Desert Storm, 8 June 1991. Arrayed behind Franks, left to right, are his VII Corps staff, Colonels Art Hotop, Bill Rutherford, Stan Cherrie, John Davidson, and Johnnie Rusin.

After the parade, Franks and his wife, Denise, visit the Vietnam Veterans Memorial.

Franks with his family, 1996: Denise on the right; Margie on the left; Margie's three children, Jake (left), Mickey, and Denise (in arms); and her husband, Lieutenant Colonel Gregory Bozek

Franks gets his fourth star from Army Chief Gordon Sullivan and Denise.

and many vehicles were stopped—but that was not that unusual in a large unit movement and attack. After we passed over the 3rd AD, we flew over nothing but empty desert until we reached the 2nd ACR.

From 1015, when I'd last talked to Don, the regiment had seen some action against the deep brigade of the Iraqi 26th Division, about twenty kilometers from the line of departure. The Iraqi division commander had had to fight the Big Red One and the 2nd ACR simultaneously from two directions, with few workable communications. The 2nd ACR was continuing to attack while I visited with Don.

The 2nd ACR had captured some officers, he reported, engaged enemy armored vehicles with their aviation and close air support, and their helos had taken some fire. From 1430 until later that evening (a report I got after returning to the TAC), Troop L on the regiment's eastern flank had fought nine engagements over a space of twenty kilometers against T-55s, BMPs, infantry, and bunkers. They had destroyed one T-55, a BMP, and a PT 76 (a Soviet-built light amphibious tank), and taken approximately 300 prisoners. They had also refueled twice and gotten some fifteen ammo tractors stuck in the soft sand.

I gave Don the status of the 1st AD and 3rd AD behind him since I had just flown over them. I figured it would take them most of the night to close in behind the regiment, even unopposed. Don and I talked about the wisdom of his continuing the attack that night. Though I wanted to continue, I was aware of the growing gap between the now-fast-advancing regiment and the rest of the divisions. It was now at least twenty kilometers, and the gap was about to grow, since the regiment was now in full deployment and moving, while the divisions were in the process of squeezing themselves through the berm and getting into their formations.

Based on the rapid movement of the regiment, and their success this day, Don's recommendation was to continue aviation and artillery throughout the night but to stop forward ground movement. In that way, the divisions could close up behind the regiment and remain concentrated for our closure on Phase Line Smash, another fifty to seventy-five kilometers ahead, the next day.

Phase Line Smash, about 150 kilometers from our starting point on the Saudi-Iraqi border, was the last reference line we had drawn before we anticipated significant combat with the RGFC. It was a control measure for me to get the corps into whatever attack configuration I decided on to attack the Guards. Smash was named deliberately, because that is where we anticipated "smashing" into the RGFC. It was like a line of departure for our attack, and by the time we reached it, I wanted us to be rolling through it without stopping. Because I had Smash there, I was able to meter the movement of units so that they would reach Smash at about the same time for a concentrated attack.

What Don said made sense, and I told him I'd let him know later, but for now I wanted him to slow his rate and continue aviation and artillery attacks well forward to keep the Iraqis off balance. What I wanted to do in the meantime was check the progress of the 1st INF to see if they were getting any artillery fire from the Iraqis and if they might be vulnerable by not continuing to move.

Meanwhile, all the Iraqis had seen so far was a cavalry regiment and two brigades of the 1st INF. That meant that the RGFC still did not know what was bearing down on them. The less the Iraqis knew about the size of the force descending on them, the less would be their sense of urgency to organize a fortified defensive line. I wanted to stay hidden from them for as long as possible. If I continued moving the 2nd ACR forward, and in so doing tipped off a larger force to their presence, and if I could not then bring my own larger force into a coordinated attack before the Iraqis got big units in the way, it would make for some tougher going.

In addition, on 19 February, I had told Don Holder that if he was successful on Smash and found a soft spot in the Iraqi defenses, he should not be surprised if I blitzed him directly to Objective Denver on Highway 8. In my mind that possibility still remained for the following day. I wanted the regiment fresh for it.

I left and was back at the TAC just at dark.

When I got there, I got a quick, informal update of our situation:

The 1st INF Division had reached Phase Line Colorado, which meant they were halfway through the breach mission, or about twenty kilometers deep. At this point, Tom had two brigades abreast, with the rest of the division strung behind, all the way back into Saudi. To make room for the British, we had planned to expand the breach head another twenty kilometers north, to Phase Line New Jersey, and also expand it west and east. That would allow the 1st INF to move all its vehicles through the lanes and into this expanded area. To get that much area required three brigades on line, which meant Tom had to bring the 3rd Brigade through the cleared but not yet marked lanes, then attack forward with the two lead brigades northeast and northwest so that they could open up the middle for the 3rd Brigade. That was no easy maneuver, especially in contact with the enemy, and especially at night, but it was necessary, both to ensure that the area was totally secured and free of any artillery in range of the breach, and to finish passing the Big Red One through the breach and make room for the 1st UK.

I was pleased with the operation so far. But I also knew the risk of moving a brigade in between two others and attacking forward twenty kilometers at night from Colorado to New Jersey without any preparation or warning. And so I was beginning to question the wisdom of continuing the attack at night. . . . Once again, the wasted minute. We could have gone earlier than 1500. I would not have been in this situation if we had. But that was past. I had to deal with *now.*

Meanwhile, 1st INF aviation ranged far beyond Colorado into Iraqi depths, and 1st INF artillery fires also were striking deep. By 1800, the 1st INF had reported more than 1,000 prisoners, a rough count, as no one was particularly worried about statistics at this point. The division so far reported no losses of its own.

Things had gone far better than we had expected. Better still, the Iraqis had still not used chemical or bio.

I got an equally encouraging report from 1st AD. Ron Griffith reported that their cavalry squadron had crossed the Iraqi border at 1434, following the 2nd ACR. By 1500, sixteen D-7 combat engineer bulldozers had cut 250 eight-meter-wide lanes through the border berm (they had been working for ten hours). The division was passing through. At this point, Ron had the division in a wedge formation, with one brigade at the tip and two following on each side. By 1800, the lead elements of their brigades had moved about fifteen kilometers into Iraq, and they were continuing to move. Their cavalry squadron had actually moved sixty kilometers into Iraq that day.

Third AD movements also were continuing. Butch Funk (still corps reserve at this point) moved his column of brigades behind 2nd ACR. As his elements streamed north into Iraq, Butch had his division band at the border berm playing cavalry music. So far, the division had reported some minor enemy contact and had taken some prisoners bypassed by 2nd ACR.

When I called John Yeosock at 1810, I reported all this, and I also advised him we would more than likely suspend offensive operations for the night, but would continue other combat operations, such as aviation and artillery, as well as finish the passage of the remainder of the two armored divisions across the berm and into Iraq. We would then resume offensive operations at first light. He concurred without discussion. John usually said that tactical decisions were up to me, since I was closer to the action, and then he supported them. My report was quick, with little deliberation: a routine affair, and then I went on to other duties.

I called Don Holder and confirmed that I wanted him to cease offensive movement, but to continue artillery fires and aviation attacks forward.

A few minutes later, Ron Griffith, who had monitored the order to the 2nd ACR to cease forward movement, called me at the TAC to ask if the order also applied to him. I told him yes.

I did not actually think that decision through as well as I had Don's. As it happened, I could just as easily have ordered Ron to continue . . . even though elements of 2nd ACR were in front of him, and he could not have gone far.

To allow 1st AD to continue to move toward al-Busayyah and Objective Purple, I would have had to order Don Holder to uncover in front of 1st AD tonight (since 2nd ACR had moved their elements forward all that day, by about 2000 many of their ground elements were actually out from in front of 1st AD; 2nd ACR aviation, however, was still operating there). Yet since I figured it would take most of the night to get all that done and would possibly cause some fratricide, I told Ron to stop. I really did not think we would net any advance time by uncovering and advancing that night, and I also knew that Ron would continue to move his division forward through the border berm well into the night, refuel, get orders out, and continue the attack at first light. Besides, our intelligence indicated little reaction from the RGFC.

We had one disappointment that day. The 11th Aviation Brigade reported that they could not execute CONPLAN Boot that night. When we had gotten the word to go early, we had caught them moving both FAARPs (Forward Arm And Refuel Points, temporary fuel and ammo sites meant to be set up and broken down quickly) and aircraft forward, in anticipation of attacking the following night. There was no way they could go tonight. Too bad. The weather was still good, and that attack really would have helped on the east.

Our casualties so far were one soldier KIA and one WIA in the 1st INF, three soldiers WIA in 1st AD, and two soldiers WIA in the 2nd ACR from the DPICM incident earlier, when they had run over our own munitions. These were our first, but regretfully not the last, casualties from our own unexploded ammunition on the battlefield as we advanced.

Meanwhile, I had forecast we would be at Phase Line Smash the next day. At that point we would know whether we had been successful in surprising and fixing the Republican Guards. Late in the day, I would make the decision about which FRAGPLAN to use to destroy the RGFC. As for now, I was continuing to maneuver the corps to keep all my options available until the following afternoon. All of this was clear to my commanders. It also was in the heads of my two key maneuver operators at my command nodes, Stan Cherrie at the TAC and John Landry at the main CP. In short, I was pleased at our progress to this point and felt good about the coherence of our formations and our logistics, even though we had had to advance our attack by fifteen hours.

One last piece of maneuver remained. Did I order Tom Rhame to continue to attack to New Jersey? I got both Tom and Rupert Smith on the TACSAT radio from the TAC:

Enemy contact was light, Tom told me, and they had taken many prisoners. I asked him about continuing.

"I recommend we wait until daylight," he answered, "to avoid the night passage forward of 3rd Brigade, 2nd Armored Division." Tom had gotten his 3rd Brigade from northern Germany in USAREUR. "We can have New Jer-

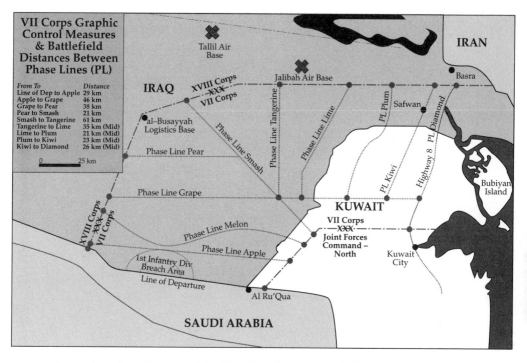

The major phase lines used by Fred Franks to control the movement of forces within VII Corps. To further coordinate their actions, subordinate units supplemented these measures with graphics of their own (2nd ACR named all its phase lines after beers, for instance, and 1st INF after states). The legend indicates the average distance between the phase lines, which was dependent on the location of the force.

sey secured and be set to support a passage of the 1st (UK) AD by noon on the twenty-fifth."

When I talked with Rupert Smith shortly afterward, he concurred. He could use more time—and daylight. All day he had been aggressively moving his division forward. Considering his unplanned early move forward with his almost 5,000 vehicles, he preferred a late-morning passage. When they had moved forward, they'd been arranged in column—i.e., they were pretty strung out. Then they'd had to regroup for the twenty-four-lane passage through the breach, and coordinate that passage, and then later they'd had to link up and get fires coordinated with the U.S. 142nd Artillery Brigade of about 600 vehicles from the Arkansas National Guard, with their two eight-inch battalions and an MLRS battalion. Following their participation in the breach prep fires,

I had ordered the brigade to be in direct support of the British. It had turned out to be a great combat arrangement (even though it had sparked some laughs when the British troops and our troops from Arkansas and Oklahoma talked on the radio).

After I thought for a moment about what Rupert and Tom had told me, I ordered Tom to continue his attack at first light. He would then pass the British through at noon tomorrow.

I knew this was a gamble, but it was the best choice I had then, given the alternatives. Here is how I weighed them quickly in my head.

On the one hand, it was a gamble not to continue. If the Iraqis fired chemical or biological agents into the breach that night, then we would not be able to recover from it. In addition, if the Iraqis had already discovered the strength of the wide enveloping attack, it would give them twenty-four to thirty-six hours to set their defenses more skillfully, and to make our coming attacks more costly.

By continuing, we might keep them from firing those chemical or biological weapons, and we would get to the RGFC twelve hours sooner. But continuing was also a gamble.

By continuing, we could get ourselves physically tangled up expanding the breach at night—by trying to fit a brigade in between two others while marking cleared lanes and moving the rest of the Big Red One forward. While we were untangling them, our enveloping force would be so far ahead, they would hit the RGFC while we were still getting the British through the breach. Even if the two armored divisions were successful in staying close behind the 2nd ACR, the rear of the enveloping forces would still be vulnerable to Iraqi attack from the east. In addition, the situation would prevent needed fuel from coming through the breach, and cause the enveloping attack to grind to a halt at the beginning of their RGFC attack. It also would deny our two armored divisions fire support from the two artillery brigades, which would be stuck behind the breach and thus be unable to join them for the RGFC attack.

It also was possible that the two divisions would *not* be able to close quickly behind the rapidly advancing 2nd ACR. In that case, the regiment would likely find itself way out ahead of those two follow-on divisions, and it would hit the RGFC, alert them, and give them time to react before I could mass the corps.

All in all, I thought the gamble was far greater if we continued that night than if we continued the next day. I would gamble that we had silenced all the Iraqi artillery and that, even if they noticed, the RGFC would probably underestimate the size of our force and that our three-division fist would overcome any time advantage on the RGFC side and smash them anyway. It was more important to preserve the three-division fist.

One other consideration operated as I made this decision. In the back of my mind, the idea was forming that if I did not get the 1st CAV in time, the third division of my three-division fist would be Rhame's Big Red One.

I recalled something Tom Rhame had said to me before the attack: "Boss, don't leave us behind in the breach." It was beginning to look as though Tom would get his wish.

Though the Big Red One had always seemed a possibility for that mission, I couldn't make that choice until I knew how much the breach mission had taken out of them. If they'd taken heavy casualties, for instance (some estimates had them losing up to a brigade total in the breach), it would have been impossible to use them for my third division.

As it happened, the 1st ID's casualties turned out to be unexpectedly low. Though I never expected casualties as high as some of the estimates, I still anticipated more than Tom actually reported—which was the best news I got all day. Now that it was clear that the division was in relatively good shape, I wanted to preserve them for use against the RGFC. Continuing that night might remove that option.

I consulted my commanders, but it was my decision alone. It was the right one.

★ At about 2000, the G-2 reported that all the Iraqi heavy units had remained in place. This included the three RGFC heavy divisions, the 12th AD, the 46th MECH (actually the 10th AD), the 52nd AD, and the 17th AD. There was, however, a report that a brigade of the Hammurabi was moving out for training. Based on tendencies we had studied from the Iran-Iraq War, such a move was usually a precursor to some offensive maneuver: they would set out from their locations, do some training—what we called rehearsals—and then attack. That got my attention.

Why? Because it was an indicator that the Iraqis might not be going to defend in place after all, but would try some kind of maneuver against us, a capability they still had. In that case, I would have chosen some other maneuver besides FRAGPLAN 7.

What did all this add up to? There was no indication at this point of an RGFC retreat. Of the three options we had originally given the RGFC, we were down to two. Every indication was that they were going to stay and fight from where they were or maneuver against us. It heightened my sense that I needed to keep the corps balanced to preserve my options for the attack tomorrow.

Shortly after the G-2 update, Stan reported that at this point our line of advance put the 2nd ACR on Phase Line Grape; both 1st AD and 3rd AD were on Melon; 1st INF was on Apple (their Colorado), with twenty-four lanes completed; and 1st CAV was conducting another feint into Iraq. Total prisoners reported were 1,000 in 1st INF, over 300 in 2nd ACR, over 100 in 3rd AD, and

50 in 1st CAV. (Throughout the course of the war, prisoner totals were very inaccurate. Rather than tie down combat formations to process prisoners, units would disarm the Iraqis, give them food and water, keep the officers, and point the rest south. Some estimates placed our prisoner totals at almost double the official figures.)

★ From the first moment of my involvement in Desert Shield, and all during Desert Storm, I had been in frequent communication with John Yeosock. John and I had agreed that I would call him as often as possible during the ground war to keep him informed. It was especially important for me to try to talk to him around 1800 so that he would have the latest when he went to General Schwarzkopf's regular 1900 evening briefings.

I called John Yeosock that evening to report what I was doing and why— a simple conversation between two cavalrymen who understood what it took to maneuver VII Corps. I told John that in my judgment the immediate situation and complexity of what we had to do at night was not worth the risk of continuing the attack. Just as he had done a few hours before, he told me he agreed with what I was doing and trusted my judgment.

We kept our higher headquarters informed in other ways, as well. As a matter of routine, and of Third Army rule, just as we had done throughout Desert Shield, at midnight, every twenty-four hours during the war my main CP sent a written "Commander's SITREP (Combat)" to Third Army. It was the official report of what had gone on in VII Corps for the previous twenty-four hours and a forecast of what we would be doing for the next twenty-four. An info copy also went to CENTCOM. As it happened, this was not well timed, as the CINC got his daily briefing at 1900 and an update the first thing in the morning.

Before the attack, I had been in the habit of writing the commander's evaluation portion of the SITREP—or at least going over it. (These were often brutally candid: I complained about poor intel and about logistics shortages— lack of spare parts, medical supplies, and transportation. This at times got the CENTCOM staff in hot water, thus not making me a popular guy with some of them.) But during the war I stopped this practice, relying on John Landry and Stan to listen to me and to capture the essence of what was going on in the corps. Besides, I was talking directly to John Yeosock so much that he was getting commanders' evaluations directly from me. Though I wasn't aware of this at the time, after the war I found out that John Yeosock had had his staff pay close attention to these reports, and had often had them follow up on the key items that he would need for the CINC's regular 1900 briefings. But I have no idea of the effect of all this at CENTCOM.

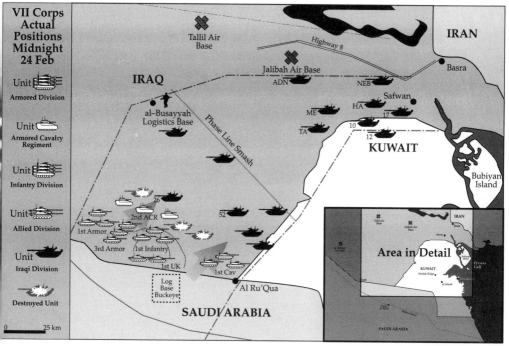

By the close of the first day, the 1st Infantry Division breach was completed to twenty kilometers, and the 1st (UK) Armored was flowing toward the passage points to continue to push the attack. The 2nd ACR had advanced well forward toward Phase Line Smash, and the 1st and 3rd Armored Divisions were continuing to maneuver into attack formation and getting their vehicles through the berm choke points. First AD had combat actions on the west of the corps sector.

All commanders make a choice about what to pay attention to and what to ignore. There was no lack of information at Third Army about what was happening in VII Corps. They got it by way of direct calls from me to Yeosock; direct calls from the Third Army liaison, Colonel Dick Rock, to Third Army HQ; direct calls from Stan Cherrie, John Landry, Colonel Mike Hawk, and others to Brigadier General Steve Arnold and others in Riyadh and Third Army TAC CP in King Khalid Military City; periodic situation reports from staff officers to Third Army; and finally, from the written summary submitted as of midnight each day. (As a practical matter, this report was prepared much earlier than that, so by the time it went in, much of the friendly information was less than current, especially as the action picked up tempo. That meant that the information reported at the CINC's morning briefing could be as much as twelve hours old if the CENTCOM staff did not update their reports.)

2300 VII Corps TAC CP Saudi Arabia

That evening, I continued to monitor reports of corps activity coming into the CP over the radio. Per my orders to Don and his assessment of his situation, 2nd ACR kept up attacks and combat activities all night. In other words, they did not stop at sundown, get out their sleeping bags, and get eight or ten hours of sleep. They continued movement to adjust unit formations, get better force protection, and also put out reconnaissance. They also fired artillery and pushed aviation forward, and some units even advanced forward if the local commander thought it would improve his posture for his operations the next day. Many of the leaders and the troops were up all night. Few would get more than three or four hours of sleep . . . and that was "combat" sleep, without tents or cots.

They also had some combat actions. Later that night, at 0200, in order to keep the Iraqis off balance, and to keep them from being set when the regiment attacked at first light, they were planning to attack the eastern half of their Objective Merrill, about sixty kilometers into Iraq, with the AH-64 battalion from 1st AD that I had placed under Don's operational control.

Meanwhile, they reported their lead aircraft scouts were at Phase Line Smash—or at the 78 Easting* longitude line—where it was vital to me to have immediate intelligence because of the proximity of the RGFC. At 2200, they reported their 2nd Squadron had taken 385 prisoners. At 2359, an Iraqi infantry battalion surrendered to their 2nd Squadron in Objective Merrill, and soon after that, they reported that they were inundated with prisoners all across their area. Later, after I went to get some rest at 0324, the aviation battalion reported destroying a building with antennas, numerous bunkers, a BMP, and six trucks; one AH-64 was hit by ground fire.

The rest of the corps was not idle that night. Other combat activities were going on:

• In 1st AD, the lead unit, 1-1 Cavalry, had pushed sixty kilometers into Iraq, well forward of the rest of the division. Elsewhere in the division, three soldiers were wounded when a vehicle struck a mine just over the border. Meanwhile, refueling operations and movement forward of the division into

---

*Easting lines—north/south grid lines—were another means of orientation. As you moved from west to east, the numbers grew higher. Thus 60 Easting was farther west than 70 Easting.

their division wedge would continue until after 0200 on the twenty-fifth. The division had taken prisoners, but by now the count was not accurate.

• Third AD also continued moving units forward over the border and re-fueling operations well into the night. Their lead unit, 4-7 Cavalry, had reported engaging twenty-nine tanks with close air support and later capturing more prisoners. Other prisoners, bypassed by 2nd ACR, also were captured by division units.

• As 1st INF continued to mark lanes, their aviation forward also conducted a screen of their ground elements so as to preempt any Iraqi artillery from firing on forces refueling for tomorrow's operation.

• The British reported closing into an area just south of the breach ready to begin passage of lines.

• Finally, I learned we had used forty-four close-air-support strikes today.

At midnight the commanders' SITREP went in from our main CP. In it no casualties were reported (in fact, we had seven—two in 2nd ACR, two in 1st INF, and three in 1st AD). The report described major units of the corps as involved in security and reconnaissance operations that night and positioned to continue the attack on 25 February.

As for the Iraqis, we assessed that in their VII Corps there was little chemical capability. They could continue local counterattacks, but use of mobile reserves was limited to local repositioning. The report went on to say: "Indications of minefields and defensive positions in Tawalkana Division sector indicate intent to defend in place. Alpha Brigade, Hammurabi Division, has moved out of revetments and appears to be conducting local maneuver training. . . ."

This report—like most of those from our main CP throughout the war—was right on the mark with respect to possible enemy courses of action and our own future plans. Although they were mostly out of direct radio contact, the troops there tracked the battle as well as they could. Because they were out of direct radio contact, there were some exceptions to the overall accuracy of these reports: Normally, reports of our own actions tended to understate what was going on—as, for instance, the destruction of Iraqi units and the numbers of Iraqi prisoners and KIA. Reports of our own casualties also lagged considerably.

In sum, I was pleased with the corps that day. Our agility in adjusting to the fifteen-hour advance in attack had been superb. Second ACR and lead elements of 1st AD were now sixty kilometers deep into Iraq and continuing actions. First INF had completed twenty-four lanes. Through these the 2,500 tracked vehicles and 5,000 wheeled vehicles of the British would move, followed by the 400 logistics vehicles (and the fuel that would allow the enveloping divisions to attack the RGFC without stopping) and the over 1,000 vehicles of the two-corps artillery brigades that would join the enveloping divisions. We were in the posture I wanted.

★ Later that night, I learned from Major Bernie Dunn, our Arabic-speaking liaison officer with the Egyptians, that the JFC-N attack on our east had not yet gone forward of the border. This information further reinforced my urgency to get the British out to the east before I got my enveloping forces logistics elements too far forward and vulnerable to an Iraqi move from that direction.

My decision not to continue with most of our offensive operations that night was a gamble. I knew that, yet I was convinced the risk was worth taking. To gain a massed three-division fist against the RGFC more than offset any advantage they might gain from a warning of our attack that gave them time to prepare. Meanwhile, they showed few signs of reacting, and Iraqi artillery fire was by now almost nonexistent—or quickly silenced by counterfire.

★ Still later that night, I gave some more thought to the go-early order and to whether, because of that, the intent of my higher HQ had changed.

My conclusion: Everything I'd learned today from higher headquarters told me we were operating only with the intent of moving the attack up fifteen hours, nothing more.

John Landry was to tell me the next day that he was surprised by my decision because I had been so adamant about "no pauses" and would not even let the word be used.

He was right, I didn't want pauses. What I meant was I didn't want them in front of our main objective, the RGFC (as Burnside had paused before Fredericksburg in December 1862, during the Civil War, when he'd waited for bridging for two weeks while Lee built his defenses). I would not permit planned pauses because they might not be needed and would break the natural momentum of an attack once it got rolling. On the other hand, I was prepared to accept *battle-event–caused* pauses in order to keep the corps balanced and thus use them to adjust tempo to gain mass and continued momentum with our troops reasonably fresh and the corps supplied when we hit the RGFC.

I did not agonize that night over my decision not to continue, much less second-guess myself. I was looking ahead to our objective. As we approached the RGFC, I thought about the moves and countermoves available to us and to them. I wanted them fixed and out of options while we still had some left. As I had been doing all along whenever I could, I stared at the map, making it come alive in my head. We are here, they are there. What do I want it to look like when we are successful? How do I get us from this state to that state at least cost?

I war-gamed in my head, involved some others, thought out loud with Stan. That not only helped me think my way through the next few days, it also got Stan inside my head, where he needed to be.

The bottom line that night was that I thought the RGFC would stay in a posture that would make FRAGPLAN 7 the best scheme of attack. I needed one more look to confirm it the next day. The timing depended on our being able to go from our current formation alignment to our attack alignment in less time than the Iraqis could react. I also could not wait too long or the corps would not be able to execute. My key "reads" the next day would be our posture and the Iraqis'. Then I would decide.

★ Commanders of large campaigns and of large land forces don't think in chronological terms. They think in terms of the mission against a particular enemy, the organization of their forces on the ground, the time it takes to get their forces in a posture to accomplish their mission on that terrain and at the least cost to their own side. Sometimes they will think in terms of hours to accomplish all this, sometimes in terms of days. Sometimes the mission will take hours, sometimes it will take days.

Thus, when we examine what happened in a campaign such as Desert Storm on Day 1 (24 February), on Day 2, Day 3, and Day 4, rather than at the actual phases of the battle as they developed (and which didn't follow the rhythms of day and night), we miss the context within which a senior tactical commander views the battle and uses time.

In other words, during Desert Storm, I did not think in terms of discrete days. On the first day, on the twenty-fourth, when we were ordered to attack early, I was thinking in the present: we had lots to do to pull that off. But I also was thinking two days in advance. I knew that decisions I would make that first day would influence the posture the corps could get into on the third day, the twenty-sixth.

The third day was the key day, for in my judgment, that was when we would attack the Republican Guards. I would make the decision about how to attack them on the second day, and the first day's decisions would determine the range of alternatives available to me then. So in Desert Storm (other situations would have required different kinds of thinking), I thought in continuous periods of 12, 24, 48, and 72 hours, regardless of days. I also was aware that in large tactical organizations in large land battles, you cannot make many decisions over short time spans that cause major maneuvers. That is why you forecast key decision points and make decisions that stick. For that reason, my intent was to issue orders to my subordinate commanders that would last at least twelve hours before I had to change those instructions. In the event that I had to issue instructions that would cause a major rearrangement of the corps within our overall basic plan, I needed to give them as much as twenty-four hours. A total plans change, done from a cold start without warning— such as, for instance, an attack to Baghdad—might have taken as much as seventy-two hours from receipt to execution.

★ About midnight, I told Toby to wake me for anything significant, then left the enclosed area and went to get some rest. Stan and most of the TAC team were still at it when I left.

At 0500 on the twenty-fifth, I was awake and back at it. A quick paper cup of coffee, a few moments to strap on my leg and the other boot, shoulder holster, and Kevlar, then a short walk over to the TAC CP. The charcoal-lined chemical protective overgarment we all wore felt good in the early-morning cold. Stan Cherrie and the TAC team were already in there, and radios were already alive with reports.

10

TURN EAST

**0600 VII Corps TAC CP Saudi Arabia
25 February 1991**

During the very brief—less than twenty-minute—morning update, I was interested in answers to the following questions: What was our situation? The enemy's situation? Where were we vulnerable? Where was the enemy vulnerable? What was happening on the flanks? Had higher HQ issued any changes? Did we need to make any adjustments to exploit an enemy vulnerability or to protect one of our own? Did anyone have any recommendations? Wherever I went, I looked for answers, for these formed the basis of my continuing running estimate.

I hadn't been away from the map long; things hadn't changed a lot.

G-2 went quickly over the enemy situation, then Stan reviewed the battle activities since midnight. Our units reported more prisoners. There were reports from 2nd ACR, as it approached Phase Line Smash, of battalion-sized units and heavy Iraqi equipment, such as tanks, which were early indicators that we could expect increased enemy actions the closer we got to the RGFC. As for the actual RGFC divisions, they did not appear to be going anywhere. They were still in position, attempting to set a defense. The earlier report that a brigade of the Hammurabi was moving out indicated that they might even be trying some kind of maneuver or repositioning north or west. As we had expected, they were not retreating. At this point, I did not know how much they knew about us. By now they were probably aware of a force out to the west, but I did not think they realized our size and capabilities. The early indicators showed some attempt at reorientation, but at this point it seemed to me they still believed the main attack was coming north up the Wadi.

I had no information otherwise from my own VII Corps sources or from Third Army. Because the Iraqi defense was hasty and not well coordinated, they were vulnerable to a massed fist attack. Good.

We had not gotten any change in orders from Third Army.

While I received this short briefing, the radios in the TAC continued to come alive with short-burst transmissions, as corps units reported moves, locations, and enemy contacts, and gave situation reports. Each staff section was busy on the phone getting longer messages or reports, and our NCOs were back and forth in both G-2 and G-3, posting the latest friendly and enemy situations on the map. Troops were already beginning to break the TAC down, getting ready to move as soon as I left. The breakdown of the TAC normally took less than an hour if you had had a lot of practice, and by now these soldiers had had a lot of practice.

Throughout all this, I was both thinking and listening—redoing my mental map of enemy and friendly units based on the briefing, looking forward to key decisions I needed to make that day in order to set corps action in motion to accomplish objectives the next day. First, I did not want to give the Iraqis any more time to set a defense. Second, this was the day to commit to our attack formation. FRAGPLAN 7* still looked like the best choice, though questions remained about 1st CAV, which was still being held by General Schwarzkopf in CENTCOM reserve.

I was also thinking of where I needed to go that morning to get information (or to confirm what I already had), to get a feel for the battles and their tempo, and reinforce what I wanted done face-to-face with the commanders.

Right now, I was getting maybe 20 percent of my input from my staff at the CP; 40 to 50 percent from what I was seeing and hearing myself, and from my commanders as I met them; and the rest came from my own professional knowledge, training, education, and combat experience.

As we saw in an earlier chapter (but it bears repeating now), most often you decide to decide. You ask yourself the question: Do I need to intervene and make an adjustment, or do I let the battle continue as it is? Most often a senior commander does not need to decide; he can leave things to subordinates rather than tinker at the margin. Senior tactical commanders really get to make only a few key decisions. It is better for them to focus their energies there, and trust their subordinates, who are in a better position to make their own decisions. Knowing the difference is the art of command. So is determining the tempo of the attack to keep your enemy off balance, and knowing when to be bold—when to take risks and gamble—and when not to.

I would take all those elements into consideration that day as I selected the attack formation to destroy the RGFC. I would also have to find a third division for the attack . . . or else do without and use the 2nd ACR. Earlier, I had told Don Holder to be prepared to go all the way to Objective Denver if

---

*FRAGPLAN 7 had originally been the proposal of my chief of plans, Lieutenant Colonel Bob Schmitt, and British staff planner Major Nick Seymour, a fact that accounted for some British names for objectives, such as Norfolk and Minden.

the opportunity presented itself. (Denver was on Highway 8, just south of the Iraq-Kuwait border.) By looking at our unit locations on the map and the enemy situation, and by doing some quick mental time/distance calculations, I could sense the time for that decision getting close.

That meant I had to get on the move, and I needed to talk to my commanders face-to-face.

But I was going nowhere right now. High winds and blowing sand, which reduced visibility to a few hundred meters, had grounded us. I was now a prisoner of the CP and tied to the comms.

★ Meanwhile, I got reports from our flanks.

Word from our eastern flank was that the Egyptian attack was slow in getting under way. Earlier, that might have bothered me, but not now, because so far the Iraqis had been unable to react. More important, I would have the British out there shortly.

That was important, because until the British could attack out of the breach to the east, Iraqi forces now opposite the Egyptians could be ordered to back out in order to thicken the RGFC defense, or even retreat across our sector along the blacktop road that ran roughly northwest on our Phase Line Smash to al-Busayyah. If they did either, they would threaten the steady stream of fuel tankers moving north from Nelligen to the 1st and 3rd ADs. If any of those Iraqi units—even by accident—ran into one of our convoys on the way to refuel the enveloping units, it would be a disaster from which we could not recover. Leaving logistics that vulnerable was a gamble I was not prepared to take.

On our western flank, 1st AD 1/1 Cavalry was maintaining physical contact with XVIII Corps. Internal flank contacts were also good. In the desert, where there were no navigation features to act as guide points, we had to pay close attention to flank contacts. For navigation, units only had GPS, and at those times of the day when there were no satellites, most of them had to use old-fashioned dead reckoning. As a result, the risk of units running into, or else crossing in front of, one another was high throughout the war. When you have tank cannons that fire projectiles that are lethal past 3,000 meters at a mile a second, and when there are no natural terrain features to stop those projectiles, commanders at all levels pay close attention to flank contact.

At that point, I used the delay to talk to John Yeosock. Because John's liaison in my TAC CP, Colonel Dick Rock, had been keeping Third Army well informed of our locations and actions, John had a pretty good picture of our situation (Dick Rock was excellent at giving this information as he knew it; his challenge was that he often was not completely up-to-date, either because the TAC was moving or because he was not with me and could not hear my discussions with commanders). I explained to John what I anticipated doing today, and he agreed with it.

It was after that, though, that John dropped some surprising news on me: the CINC was concerned that we were not moving fast enough. For a moment, that hit me hard. It takes a lot of wind out of your sails when your theater commander seems disappointed in your progress. As a subordinate, you do not want to get on the bad side of your boss, so it was a blow when I learned that my boss's boss was not happy about our progress.

My first thought was defensive: We had done well even to have gotten to where we were this morning, given the fifteen-hour advance start, I said to John; you know what we have been doing and why. And he agreed: he was pleased with our progress and convinced that, as the commander on the ground, I had the best feel of what to do. And, in fact, he gave me no new orders, nor was there any change of mission.

When John told me that in fact he thought we were doing fine, I decided not to give the CINC's concerns much more thought (at the time). It looks like they don't have a good picture of the corps situation in Riyadh, I told myself, and when they do, this will blow over. It had just been a quick, passing comment. I chalked the whole thing up to the usual emotion of battle.

Certainly, nothing John had told me led me to change my mind about what I needed to do, and in fact, in the press of commanding and maneuvering the corps, I soon forgot all about it (and the episode did not get noted in either my own journal or in Toby Martinez's log). Changes of orders I understood; I would have executed them. But concerns were not orders. There were concerns all over the place. If commanders want to do something about them, they give orders to their subordinates, but neither the CINC nor John Yeosock had told me to do anything different.

After the war, I was to find out that John had been shielding me from an extraordinary emotional outburst from General Schwarzkopf during his morning update. He had—I have gathered from later reports—hit the ceiling. He had expected a VII Corps cavalry charge to the Republican Guards, and when he didn't get it, he blew up into one of his well-publicized rages. Since John Yeosock had much more experience with large armored maneuvers than Schwarzkopf, he knew that the CINC's expectations were illusory. And so he did what many commanders do—he absorbed the blow and shielded his subordinates. He toned down the CINC's blowup to "concerns" when we talked that morning. Yeosock did that a lot both before and during the war for both VII and XVIII Corps.

It is also important to note that Third Army HQ in Riyadh was three miles away from the CINC's underground war room. Most communications between Yeosock and Schwarzkopf were by phone.

Later commentators—including General Schwarzkopf—have claimed that from virtually the first moments of the G-Day attack, the U.S. Army should have been in "pursuit mode" rather than in what we call "movement to contact." More bluntly: they have accused VII Corps of failing to go into pursuit when we should have. However, you go into pursuit when your enemy is in retreat or fleeing. Though that's what Iraqi units elsewhere were doing, that was not the case with the RGFC. They were setting up a defense. Even if the CINC had told us to go into pursuit (which he did not do), it would have been a mistake. His concern should have been to isolate and cut off the RGFC, mostly by air, so that VII Corps and XVIII Corps could destroy them. Instead, he flew into a rage about how fast we were going, based on blue lines on a map in Riyadh that probably were not even accurately posted.

0725 VII Corps TAC CP

Because we were co-located with 3rd AD (which was still corps reserve at that point), Butch Funk took the opportunity to come see me.

At that time, Butch, real pro that he is, was doing what any good reserve commander would do. He was trying to anticipate the possible commitment of his unit so he could make plans—and maybe even rehearse them. When he came into the CP at 0725, I had two things on my mind: I wanted to keep him moving toward the RGFC, but I also wanted him to continue protecting our right flank from stray Iraqi units or vehicles until the British got out there in force. Butch "rogered" that, then gave me a quick update: he was maneuvering his division from a column of brigades to two brigades up and one back. I acknowledged it, and told him my intent was to position my TAC CP with, or close, to his own, in the center sector.

It was a good, relaxed moment for both of us, and we were able to enjoy a paper cup of black coffee together from our coffeepot in the CP. The operation was going well. Because he and I saw eye to eye on the maneuver, we did not require a whole lot of communication. I was fortunate in all of my commanders—it worked that way with all of them.

After my talk with Butch, I had a few minutes to myself (for the time being, the weather made it impossible to go anywhere). It was a welcome respite, and it gave me the opportunity to go over again what it is we were doing and why. Before I went out to visit commanders, I wanted to take a hard look at our primary mission and our tactics. I wanted to be as certain as I possibly could that what we were about to do would destroy the RGFC, and I wanted to review for myself that my intent and orders to the corps were still the right ones. These thoughts had been on my mind constantly, and they remained on my mind until the battles with the Iraqis ended. I looked at them from every possible angle, again and again:

I had planned a rolling attack through Objective Collins into the flank and rear of the RGFC. We were not in pursuit of a retreating enemy, but preparing to attack a hastily defending enemy armored force.

I had not considered any maneuver except to aim VII Corps directly at that force. That was our mission: to destroy the RGFC, not surround them. The only way to do that, in my judgment, was to hit them in such a way that they could not contend with us, and to keep hammering them until they quit or we had destroyed them. I remembered again what George Patton III had said in Vietnam, in the Blackhorse: "Find the bastards, then pile on." After we had found them and fixed them, I wanted to maneuver VII Corps into a position from which we could not only attack them, but pile on.

In all of our briefings, it had been made clear that if the RGFC defended from where they were, the theater plan was for CENTAF—the Air Force—to isolate them. In Colin Powell's words, they were the ones who would "cut them off." We were the force that would "kill them."

After I thought about the mission, I thought again about the time it would take. From the first, I had thought the campaign would last eight days: two days to get to the RGFC, four days to destroy them, and two days to consolidate what we had done. Those first two days were not only a function of the Iraqi army, but of time/distance, the coherence of our formations, and the freshness of our troops for the anticipated fight. From our line of departure to Collins, our way point just past Phase Line Smash, it was about 150 kilometers. If I decided on FRAGPLAN 7, I wanted a three-division moving fist of reasonably fresh troops at Collins, with enough fuel to sustain the attack until the RGFC was destroyed.

Third Army had its own campaign timing figured out and it was well known to CENTCOM and to us. Third Army's planning had us taking seventy-four hours after H-Hour (i.e., BMNT on 24 February) to reach the RGFC. Our timing was in harmony with theirs.

And then there was the issue of "operational pauses." I wanted to go over that again as well.

As we saw earlier, my staff had estimated that if the corps moved continually to Objective Collins, we would need to make a preplanned halt so that our units could replenish themselves before they resumed the attack, and they were correct. The physical endurance limitations of soldiers and the need to fuel our vehicles meant that we could not move constantly for forty-eight hours, and then shift right into a major attack that might go on for up to four days.

While Cal Waller was acting Third Army commander, I had briefed him in a four- to six-hour "rock drill" at the VII Corps CP. All my senior commanders had been present, and they had moved their own markers around on the flat 1:100 000 map board. During the drill, Waller had suggested needing a twenty-four-hour operational pause at Collins as we shifted from a north-south to an east-west attack. But I did not want to stop at Collins, directly in front of the RGFC—I wanted a rolling attack right into them: "no pauses." Therefore, I adjusted the tempo during the first two days to meet that goal.

To get in the right attack formation without stopping meant a number of adjustments as we approached Smash. It also meant finding a third division for the fist. Today I would pick the third division or decide to use the 2nd ACR. As for the tempo adjustments, I had already begun making them the night before, and others would be made by my subordinate commanders as they maneuvered their units. For example, Don Holder was maneuvering the 2nd ACR at a tempo that would keep him about thirty minutes ahead of the divisions, and Butch Funk and Ron Griffith would do the same. Rupert Smith would move his division rapidly through the breach, then attack aggressively to the east. If I thought they needed to change their tempo to keep the corps physically balanced for our attack, I would tell them.

When Butch left the TAC, the weather had cleared enough for me to fly forward. By now I was getting antsy about remaining too long at the CP. I hated to listen to the battle in the CP. I did not belong there. The inputs I needed to make decisions were not all there. They were forward.

RENDEZVOUS WITH MAJOR GENERAL GRIFFITH
SOMEWHERE IN IRAQ ABOUT 0830

Though the wind had slowed down enough to fly, the sky was overcast and the temperature was fifty degrees.

First, I went forward to meet Ron Griffith.

I spent the twenty minutes of flight time staring at the map. It was coming together. The time and distance factors, as well as the position of VII Corps's units resulting from last night, gave me the mental picture I needed. If the RGFC stayed fixed, we were in an excellent position to turn ninety degrees east with our main attack—FRAGPLAN 7.

With the intelligence indicating that the RGFC was staying in position—or perhaps beginning a movement that might denote an offensive maneuver—I felt it more important than ever for Ron to move 1st AD fast to Objective

Purple, and achieve a positional advantage on the northwest flank of the RGFC in case they came toward us. With that done, I wanted him to be in the northern part of Objective Collins by midmorning the next day. By this time, I felt sure enough of the RGFC indicators that I could now give that order to Ron. Even though I could still maneuver 1st AD in a different direction if intelligence on the RGFC changed during the day, this order would essentially start us into the ninety-degree turn east. However, since the conditions for the FRAGPLAN 7 decision were still not completely certain, for the rest of the day I looked for information that either would confirm my hypothesis or cause me to decide to do something else.

Either way, I knew I would make the go/no-go decision later in the day.

Ron and I met somewhere in the east of his sector, about fifty kilometers into Iraq. It was flat, empty desert, with no vegetation. Some of his units were visible moving forward.

Ron had landed his helo and was in radio contact with the division. His aviators had rigged up a portable generator so that they could set up quickly to power the radios. With him in his helo were his G-2, Lieutenant Colonel Keith Alexander; his G-3, Lieutenant Colonel Tommie Straus; and his aide. It was a good setup that allowed Ron both to move around the division and be present up front. While he was moving around, his ADC, Brigadier General Jay Hendrix, stayed on the ground at his TAC CP, while his chief of staff, Colonel Darryl Charlton, ran his main CP. Brigadier General Jarrett Robertson, ADC for support, moved around the division sector, making sure he and the DISCOM* commander, Colonel Verne Metzger, were on top of the division's considerable logistics challenges.

I did not care how the commanders arranged things as long as they were personally up front and knew what was going on and I could find them. I always tried to go to them rather than have them come back to me.

Ron was clearly on top of the situation and feeling good about his operation—I could see it on his face and hear it in his tone of voice. That was the way I liked to find my commanders, and it was also the way I felt about the entire corps just then. Up to now, they'd been facing parts of a brigade (and other units in the area, Ron estimated) of the Iraqi 26th Division in depth, but they'd had no problem defeating them (they had many prisoners).

In fact, he reported, their main problem so far wasn't the Iraqi army, but the Iraqi terrain in the forward parts of their sector (that is, for the first fifty kilometers or so after their line of departure). They had encountered boulder fields, *sabquas* (soft sand), and blowing sand on the previous day, which had

---

Division Support Command, of four battalions, responsible for the resupply of the division.

made it difficult to maintain unit integrity and had caused them to consume more fuel than they had anticipated. Fuel vehicles had gotten stuck in the sand, and some rocky terrain had proved more difficult to get through in coherent formations than we had thought. (My staff had predicted—quite accurately—that the going would be tough early on in 1st AD sector. I had largely ignored this estimate!) As it happened, CENTCOM/ARCENT had earlier read this terrain as impassable for armored formations. The Iraqis had read it the same way. Thus, not only did the Iraqis not occupy it, they thought it would help their defense refuse the left flank.

Once through this area, the 1st AD tempo picked up dramatically. Its navigation challenges were exacerbated by the lack of GPS—the division mainly had LORAN* navigation devices. It sometimes took as long as two or three minutes to get accurate readings from LORAN towers (the Iraqis left these towers standing the whole war!). Because of the two- or three-minute lag time of readings, units wandered around some, and made some "S" maneuvers through the already difficult terrain. It was even more difficult for logistics to keep up. In other words, up to now, navigation, refueling needs, and changing division formations had regulated the 1st AD's tempo more than any Iraqi action.

Meanwhile, in order to maintain the momentum of his attack, Ron was about to shift the division formation out of its wedge. What he wanted to do was destroy the brigade of the 26th Division that had been out there refusing the flank while he bypassed with the other two brigades and moved rapidly to al-Busayyah. His third brigade got the mission of destroying the Iraqi brigade.

Finally, all along, he had kept his cavalry squadron well out in front of the division, much the same as I had the 2nd ACR out in front of the corps. He continued to do that now.

"Ron," I said, when he had completed his update, "I want you on Purple before it gets dark today. I'll get 2nd ACR out from in front of you."

"Roger, I understand and do not think that will be a problem," Ron answered.

I recalled then my own original estimate of eight hours from LD (line of departure—in this case, the border) to Purple. After I learned about the navigation problems the division had been facing, as well as the enemy action they'd run into along the way, I realized that my estimate had been overly optimistic.

---

*LORAN is a commercially available system used mainly by the oil people in Iraq. It depends on signals sent from towers and uses triangulation to get accurate readings. There are, however, delays in getting signals back from towers.

Still, they had done very well, considering the problems they'd faced. On the twenty-fourth, 1st AD had moved all day. They'd started before 0500, after 2nd ACR had vacated the terrain in front of them, and they'd continued until well after 2100 (the process of collecting and refueling vehicles, plus local security and reconnaissance operations, went on all night). Then the troops were back into it at first light that day. The leaders got even less rest. Now they were about halfway to Purple—maybe seventy kilometers. So when I left Ron, I had every reason to believe they could be there and seize al-Busayyah by dark.

"I also want you to have 1st AD in the northern area of Collins by midmorning tomorrow," I went on to tell him. "It looks as though the RGFC will remain fixed. If that is the case, then our FRAGPLAN 7 will work. You are the northern part of that attack."

Ron gave me a WILCO and said they could do both. They would seize Purple and be in the northern part of Collins by midmorning the next day.

✶ As he and I were meeting, Ron's division cavalry squadron was beginning a series of actions that went on for the rest of the day. At this point, they were about 20 kilometers in front of the division, close to 80 to 90 kilometers from the border, and about 50 to 60 kilometers from al-Busayyah, and they were already in a fight. During this early action, they destroyed a BMP and captured more than 200 prisoners, then, passing the action over to the newly arriving 1st Brigade, they had pressed on. Soon their Bradleys and Cobras had destroyed several more armored vehicles, including two T-55 tanks, and they had captured additional prisoners, bringing their total to more than 500 in a little less than three hours. More action followed. It kept up until they reached the outskirts of al-Busayyah just before dark.

Al-Busayyah, or Objective Purple, was a key in our planning. It was the major Iraqi VII Corps logistics base—thousands of tons of equipment and ammo there—and an airfield was nearby. After 1st AD took it, Third Army planned to use this area as a logistics base for XVIII Corps and to push supplies up to XVIII Corps through the 1st AD zone in order to avoid the circuitous and much longer route to the west. Getting it also secured XVIII Corps's flank.

In order to protect the follow-on logistics units of both XVIII Corps and 1st AD, I told Ron Griffith to clear the zone of all Iraqi combat units, which he did. Al-Busayyah was a significant battle. Ron attacked it with his 2nd Brigade (Colonel Monty Meigs, commander) and bypassed with the rest of the division so that they would arrive in Collins to the east by midmorning of the twenty-sixth, as I had ordered. Later, Ron told Meigs to leave a task force behind to clear al-Busayyah, and Meigs left Lieutenant Colonel Mike McGee and his Task Force 6/6 Infantry to accomplish that mission, which they did by killing the defending commando battalion after they refused to surrender.

I had given a lot of thought to assigning this mission and this sector to 1st AD. Assigning particular missions to particular units is one of the ways senior commanders influence the outcome of battles and engagements. Who do you put where in the formation and what objectives do you assign? Who is on the outside? Who is in the center? Who can move the fastest? Who needs detailed instructions and who does not? Who exercises initiative and who needs continuing instructions? You also consider the combat power available, the equipment and troops, and the state of training. A big factor is the condition of the troops. Are they tired? Have they been in the lead and in constant combat for some time? What success have they had recently? And have they taken losses? It is no small decision. All units are not the same.

The choice had been between the 1st AD and the 3rd AD. Whichever one it was, the division had to be able to move fast to Purple and to stay in contact on our west with XVIII Corps (to preclude cross-border fratricide and to prevent the escape of Iraqi units). Then, from Purple, I needed them to be able to rapidly turn ninety degrees east into the northern part of the RGFC, if that is what I decided, or else to accomplish such other maneuvers as the situation might demand. Of all my units, they would have the longest move (and maybe an open flank if we turned east, and XVIII Corps did not move east with us). Either division could do these missions, but of the two, I had commanded 1st AD; I knew them; they were a VII Corps division and used to our FARs; and, most importantly, they had been in Saudi longer than 3rd AD. So I picked 1st AD.

That meant I would put 3rd AD in the middle, and because they were getting into theater last, I would initially keep them as corps reserve and give them a wider number of contingencies to plan.

After I left Ron Griffith, I flew about forty kilometers to the jump TAC, manned by Lieutenant Colonel Dave McKiernan and Major Ron McConnell, which was now forward with the lead elements of the 3rd AD, or almost due east of the place where Ron Griffith and I had met. By this time, Stan Cherrie had the main TAC breaking down in Saudi Arabia south of the border and was starting to relocate toward the 3rd AD. Meanwhile, the jump TAC was with the lead elements of the 3rd AD. When I reached the jump TAC, they had no word on the release of 1st CAV, no change of mission from Third Army, and no change in intel from what I had gotten a few hours earlier.

At this point, I made a decision: 1st INF would be the third division in our fist. Now I needed to get them free of the breach and forward behind the 2nd ACR.

My aircraft and two M577s were by then at the jump TAC with its line-of-sight comms, but I anticipated that my main TAC, with its better comms, would be well into Iraq and set up by the time I finished moving around the corps that day and was ready to make the decision on FRAGPLAN 7. That did not happen.

1100 1st Infantry Division Breach

After the quick stop at the VII Corps jump TAC, Chief Warrant Officer 4 Mark Greenwald, my command pilot, an SOF veteran* and a ten-year Blackhawk pilot, flew us at about fifty feet over the forty to fifty kilometers to link up with Tom Rhame and Rupert Smith.

With me in the helo were Toby Martinez, my aide; Lieutenant Colonel Pete Kindsvatter, the VII Corps historian and an old 3rd ACR mate; Sergeant Park, who was in charge of the TACSAT radio; and Sergeant John McInerney, who was there for local security, if we needed it. Toby also helped navigate, listened to the corps TACSAT radio net with Sergeant Park when we were on the ground, and sat in on my talks to the commanders, so he could feed the result back to Stan at the TAC.

In the back was a map stand that Toby had gotten two engineer NCOs to build out of scrap lumber with hand tools. They'd painted it a dark red, the only paint they could find. It was close to the width of the helo, about four feet high, and had an acetate cover, under which we slid the 1:250 000 map on which Toby kept the current enemy and friendly situation posted. On the map stand was a small shelf, also covered with acetate, where I could make notes. And there was a crude drawer where we kept all kinds of "stuff," such as granola bars and MREs. It worked, but again it was far from high-tech.

At this point, the main communication available to me in my helicopter was my FM line-of-sight radio (which had about twenty or thirty kilometers' range at the altitude at which we were flying), but Sergeant Park also carried a portable TACSAT radio, which he set up when we were on the ground; the antenna went up like an umbrella. He and Toby would eavesdrop** on the VII Corps SATCOM command radio net and make notes on a card for me. We had only one TACSAT in the corps that could be used while flying. Park did a magnificent job keeping the radio working and setting it up in the rain and wind; I decorated him after the war.

When the common folks wanted to put the single air-carried TACSAT on

---

*Special Operating Forces—Mark had flown with Task Force 160, an elite Special Forces unit.
**"Eavesdropping" is important, and should be constant during a battle. You "eavesdrop" by listening to a radio net for significant information passing between two other stations on the net; another technique is to turn to a subordinate radio frequency and listen to what is going on. That way you can get a feel for their situation without calling them.

my Blackhawk, I told them no, put it in the 11th Aviation Brigade. They needed the comms on the move for their deep strikes. I could wait until I got where I was going and use the portable, hand-carried TACSAT.

As we flew in, I could see evidence of success all around. Specifically, the 1st INF had pushed their third brigade forward in between their 1st and 2nd Brigades as they expanded left, right, and forward. The three brigades were now abreast of one another on a semicircular line that marked their expanded breach-head line, which they had named New Jersey, forty kilometers into Iraq. By doing this, they had cleared the breach so that the British could flow through it and attack to the east.

Moving a brigade in between two others that are simultaneously moving out of the way, moving forward, and fighting is a great feat of coordination. The 1st INF had done it in less than four hours without incident.

They'd also had additional combat: in expanding the breach head east and north, their 2nd Brigade had attacked into and destroyed the 807th Brigade of the neighboring 48th Iraqi Division.* In expanding west and north, their 1st Brigade had added to the destruction of the 26th Iraqi Division's 806th Brigade (the 3rd AD, 2nd ACR, and 1st AD also had run over elements of this Iraqi brigade). And I could see overrun Iraqi positions and destroyed Iraqi equipment.

I also could see a steady movement of 1st INF vehicles forward into the newly expanded breach-head area to make room for the British passage. Their biggest challenge, I knew, was handling the thousands of prisoners. Our combat units were just not able to spare the combat power to escort prisoners to the rear. Many times, all over our corps sector, prisoners were disarmed, given food and water, and sent south to the rear on their own. The 1st INF had started that practice here.

As we landed, I could not hear any firing.

Tom Rhame came out to greet me, cigar in hand, obviously animated. Rupert Smith was there as well, clearly ready and eager to get his division into the fight. Tom had a hastily set-up CP arrangement with two expando vans (one each for the G-2 and G-3) and a few other vehicles. His TAC CP was farther forward, closer to New Jersey. We went inside Tom's G-3 van and sat down.

"Boss, this operation is going great," Tom began. "We've pushed out to New Jersey, and Rupert is beginning his passage."

By this time, he went on to report, they had destroyed all of the Iraqi 26th

---

*In case you need your memories refreshed, here is the layout of the Iraqi frontline divisions: West to east were the 26th, 48th, 31st, 25th, and 27th Divisions, with the 52nd mostly positioned in reserve behind the easternmost divisions. One of their brigades was farther west, however, behind the 48th.

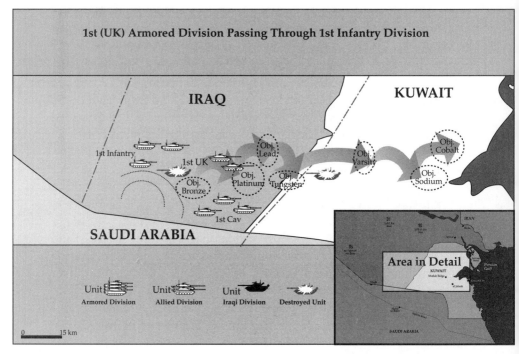

With the breach successful, the 1st (UK) Armored conducted its passage of lines with the Big Red One, and then attacked to secure the east flank of VII Corps. These attacks would take it into Kuwait.

Division, which had been facing them, a brigade from the adjacent 48th Iraqi Division, all artillery in range of the breach, and other unidentified units in the area; and they had marked the twenty-four passage lanes through the breach. They were now clear of the breach lanes and well forward to New Jersey. Tom was really pumped . . . and I think a bit relieved that the breach had gone so well and at such a small cost. He was proud of his troops, and rightfully so. They had trained hard for this mission and had done it superbly.

I was glad to get his report and see it for myself. Because of what we had done so far, now further confirmed by Tom's report, I felt we were building a momentum of success that would fuse with our physical force just as we were hitting the RGFC. Such momentum lifts the whole unit—from platoon to corps. It is contagious. Here, and earlier with Ron Griffith, I was seeing exactly what I had anticipated, and that pleased me a lot.

As he finished, he added, with the same enthusiasm with which he had made his report, "Don't leave us behind, Boss." What a great team we had.

"No chance of that," I said, then told him what I'd come to tell him, that the Big Red One was to become the third division in our fist. "I want you to leave a task force"—a battalion—"in the breach for security, and after 1st UK passes, move your division forward here." Pointing to the map, I gave Tom a location I had picked just south and west of the place where 2nd ACR would be by that time. "Be prepared to make a forward passage through 2nd ACR sometime late tomorrow afternoon to attack the RGFC."

"WILCO." Tom was not one to waste words.

Meanwhile, the British had been moving forward most of the day before and into the night to an area just south of the border berm. Although they had originally planned to come forward on HETs (in order to save wear and tear on their vehicles), they'd realized they didn't have time to load onto the HETs, move forward, off-load, then reassemble the division, and so they had rapidly changed their plans and moved the sixty to seventy kilometers forward on their own power.

They had done a splendid job of adapting rapidly to changed circumstances: they had had to change their plans, get the orders out, move in formation, and get the leaders into huddles to talk about adjusted times for their attack. They'd also needed to talk about the usual "machinery" of passage, such as recognition signals, exchange of routes, fire plans, logistics, co-location of CPs, and face-to-face coordination. There had been many things to get done simultaneously and they'd done them.

Although they'd gotten themselves assembled and ready to move through the breach quickly, however, the quick change in plans had strung the division out a good bit more than they would have liked. In spite of these difficulties, though, they were ready to pass their 7th Brigade through the breach as soon as the 1st INF expanded it forward and cleared their units from the lanes the British needed. As Tom, Rupert, and I met, they had already begun forward movement. I now wanted to explain to Rupert his part in what I had just ordered Tom to do.

Major General Rupert Smith was a fast-thinking, decisive commander, who had his 1st UK Armored Division ready for action. Although he had not had a lot of time in mounted units, he had a nose for the fight and permitted his subordinate units maximum freedom of action at small-unit level to accomplish their mission. I had watched him prepare his commanders in war games. He always sketched out what he wanted done, drew in some basic control measures, then left his brigadiers, Patrick Cordingly in 7th Brigade and Christopher Hammerback in 4th Brigade, to execute. At the moment, they had a series of objectives: to move out of the breach to the east, which would put them into the rear of the Iraqi frontline divisions and into the front and flank of the Iraqi 52nd Division. During the next few days, they performed those maneuvers skillfully, and they were in a series of stiff fights day and night.

I was proud and happy to have the British with us. They were fast off the mark, aggressive, and pressed the attack. I liked them. They were family.

"Rupert," I said, turning to him, "what I've just told Tom means your division must move through here as quickly as possible and clear out so that Tom can move forward."

As soon as he understood my intention, Rupert told me that he saw no problems, and that he and Tom would stay in communications and make it happen. They then estimated that it would take the Brits about twelve hours to make the passage through the breach—four hours longer than earlier staff estimates. But the estimates had not taken into account the number of vehicles now in the division. With the additional 142nd Artillery Brigade, U.S. Army National Guard from Arkansas, these now numbered about 7,500. Since the British had actual experience of two full-up rehearsals in our recent training, I figured Tom's and Rupert's estimate was accurate.

★ After I left Rupert and Tom, I huddled for a few minutes at my other jump TAC, which was at the breach.

While I was there, I got a flash report from the 2nd ACR: at 1240, they reported that they'd found the security area of the Tawalkana Division, and identified the unit as the 50th Brigade of the 12th AD.

The security area is a zone of about fifteen to twenty kilometers (sometimes less) in front of a main defense, and is intended to deceive the attacker as to the location of the main defense and to break up the momentum of the attacking force by causing them to fight, deploy, and thus expose their intentions early.

Finding the RGFC security area was a big deal for me, for it indicated that our main attack was beginning. Once that zone had been found, I wanted the CAV to attack through it and into the main defense, while I simultaneously maneuvered the corps into a fist and kept them concealed from the RGFC as long as we could.

Other reports from the 2nd ACR indicated that their Troop I had destroyed twelve Iraqi personnel carriers, and soon after, 2nd ACR reported another contact and combat with an Iraqi mechanized battalion reinforced by tanks. All this was happening around our Phase Line Smash.

My orders to 2nd ACR were to press on to develop the situation, but not to become decisively engaged. I wanted the regiment to collapse that security zone and find where the main defense was. I did not want them stuck in a situation they could not handle while I was maneuvering the heavy fist of the corps against the Iraqis' main defense area.

But as of now, the timing seemed about right to me. The 2nd ACR had the combat power to continue east through the Iraqi security zone, while I turned the rest of the corps ninety degrees to take up the fight they were now beginning to develop for us.

By now it was getting close to 1400, time to go forward and get a firsthand, face-to-face assessment from Don Holder.

We lifted off from near the 1st INF CP and flew the seventy or eighty kilometers forward to link up with Don Holder. This flight gave me a chance to look over the 1st INF's accomplishments, then to fly over the 3rd AD and the empty stretch between the 3rd AD and the 2nd ACR.

What I saw were signs of Iraqi defenses, now destroyed. Some destroyed Iraqi equipment was also visible. Bunkers and trenches were everywhere, either abandoned or destroyed by 1st INF vehicles running over them. Though I had seen no prisoners while I was on the ground, Tom had told me there were so many they had almost overwhelmed their capacity to move them to the rear. (This information gave me some concern, for the breach lanes needed to be running south to north. We didn't need EPWs moving south and clogging lanes.)

Moving south to north, meanwhile, was a steady stream of equipment: the British. The whole scene was just as Tom and Rupert had described it.

We doubled back and flew over the incredibly massive 3rd AD formation that was moving forward—vehicles as far as I could see, about 10,000 of them, counting corps support units. And this was only one of the four divisions! By this time, they were stretched from south of the border forward by sixty to eighty kilometers. Though I wasn't aware of it at the time, the 3rd AD was having some combat actions of its own as we passed over, and taking prisoners. The area they covered was simply too big for me to see everything they were doing in a quick overflight.

After we passed their lead units, flying very low and fast, there was nothing but sand until we reached the 2nd ACR. It was a strange feeling, flying over this now mostly empty "no-man's-land" through which the 2nd ACR had attacked earlier. Though there were bypassed Iraqi units in this area, plus who knew what else, I was too focused on the 2nd ACR to pay too much attention to what lay beneath us.

1550 2ND ACR MAIN CP

Right now I needed to look at the current situation in front of the 2nd ACR before confirming the attack formation for the corps. I also needed to decide whether to push the 2nd ACR straight to Objective Denver or to pass the 1st INF through and put 2nd ACR in corps reserve. We landed at the regimental TAC CP, where there were three M577s and a scattering of other vehicles under some canvas extensions. Inside the CP, I immediately sensed that the regiment was engaged with the Iraqis. Radios were alive with almost constant battle reports. Maps were being posted and adjusted with new information. Small huddles were taking place as officers exchanged battle information.

I could tell from Don Holder's voice and his eyes that he was in a fight. I also sensed he had it firmly under control and needed no additional help from corps assets at this point. He quickly confirmed the earlier report that the regiment had found the RGFC security zone. His third squadron, he added, had been engaging tanks, APCs, and MTLBs around the regiment's Objective May, close to Phase Line Smash.

Here is the essence of the rest of Don's update:

At 1245, Troop P (aviation) reported numerous enemy contacts just west of Phase Line Smash, and aviation was continuing to push east across Smash. Troops I and K (of 3rd Squadron, on the south of the regiment's northeast advance) engaged an Iraqi mechanized infantry battalion reinforced with tanks about five kilometers west of that sighting and destroyed thirteen BTR60s (wheeled infantry carriers), four T-55s, one BMP, and captured a lieutenant colonel.

At about 1321, Troop L (of 3rd Squadron) crossed Phase Line Smash.

At 1343, 4/2 (aviation squadron) reported Iraqi armor almost twenty kilometers east of Phase Line Smash but out of 4/2's range. At 1400, Troop G (of 2nd Squadron, on the north of the regiment's advance) reported that they had attacked and destroyed an Iraqi infantry company of MTLBs. This meant that Don had not only both his leading squadrons engaged with Iraqi defending units, but reports that his aviation, out front by twenty kilometers, had spotted additional Iraqi tanks. When close air support was available, the regiment was employing it. That day it would use twenty-four close-air-support strikes against the targets being located by the ground and aviation units. Don also had the 210th Artillery Brigade from VII Corps artillery, and a battalion of Apaches out of 1st AD that I had put under his operational control. He was using them all now, except for the Apaches. Those he was saving for that night, because their night-fighting capabilities were much better than those of the Cobras in his aviation squadron. These he used during the day.

At this point, we were at the 29 grid line (29 Easting) and these fights were going on at the 41 grid line (41 Easting), twelve kilometers away.

The desert was featureless, just it had been at the spots where I had met Tom Rhame and Ron Griffith. There were small twenty- to fifty-foot rises and drops to which the small-unit commanders had to pay attention, but almost no vegetation. Despite the intermittent rain, where armored vehicles passed, sandy dust still got churned up quickly. Though the weather now was mostly calm, the cloud cover indicated that the weather would soon turn bad.

Don's conclusion was exactly the same as mine: he had found the RGFC—the Tawalkana—defending and moving units into position, with a hastily formed security force of other units to its west. From all these battle events, the regiment's intelligence assessment and Don's judgment was that the Tawalkana Division was along the 65 Easting (about twenty kilometers east of our Phase Line Smash), covering the Iraqi army's withdrawal from Kuwait, and with a security zone that extended eight kilometers west.

That got my attention . . . though I was far more fixed on the location of the Tawalkana and the rest of the RGFC than I was on the possibility of the Iraqis leaving Kuwait. True or not (it turned out to be correct), I had no way to confirm Don's judgment at that point. Instead, I focused on our mission. If the Tawalkana was along the 65 Easting, then that was where we would fight them. It also meant they were fixed or had fixed themselves—either way was fine with me—and that the Medina and Hammurabi Divisions, as well as other armored units, also would be in the vicinity and part of this forming defense.

That battlefield report and Don's judgment confirmed the conditions for FRAGPLAN 7.

Here is how I was thinking: We had the Tawalkana fixed. Other armored and mechanized units in the same vicinity would probably join the defense, as would the two other RGFC heavy divisions. At this point I did not know how much they knew about our enveloping attack. When the regiment hit them, however, they had to realize that they were now facing some forces west of the Wadi. If they were expecting us up the Wadi, they now had to adjust rapidly. They were not good at that (though they could rapidly reposition). After their adjustments, their defenses would not be well coordinated, their obstacles and artillery would not be tied in . . . unless we gave them time to get set. I was not going to give them that time. The regiment had done what I asked. The Iraqis were fixed. It was time to swing into our attack formation.

★ One other question remained: If I passed the 1st INF through the 2nd ACR, then where and when should I do it?

In Don's judgment, the regiment did not have the combat power to attack through the Tawalkana and other forming Iraqi units to Objective Denver, and I agreed. That settled the if. As to the rest, it was a matter of a quick time/distance mental calculation. There was no time for detailed staff work. This was an in-your-head commander-to-commander mounted maneuver (and again, the reason why a mounted commander must be up front in the ck with his finger on the pulse). The 1st INF was in the breach securing it, while the British passed through them and attacked to the east. Rupert and Tom had estimated it would take the British twelve hours. If they were correct, the 1st INF could begin moving forward sometime after midnight on the night of the twenty-fifth to the twenty-sixth. Given the almost 100 kilometers separating the 2nd ACR and the 1st INF, and given my imperative that the 2nd ACR keep the pressure on the Tawalkana (so that they would not have time to set their defense), I had much to consider. My first thinking was for the passage to happen late the next afternoon, but that was beginning to look doubtful. If they could not make it by then, I had another decision: should I continue to push the 2nd ACR and pass the 1st INF early in the morning of the twenty-seventh, or pass them forward tomorrow night? That decision was coming, but I didn't have to make it now.

I had a quick huddle with Don and his executive officer, Lieutenant Colonel Steve Robinette. Don was a superb commander, with a great feel for covering force operations and the tempo of the covering force in relation to the main body. A year before, during REFORGER 90, when he had been in a covering force mission in front of VII Corps, he had developed a situation that exposed an enemy vulnerability (an opening for a preemptive attack), but the main body (or follow-on force) had been too far behind them to exploit the vulnerability. Neither of us wanted that to happen again. I had known Steve Robinette in the Center for Army Tactics at the Command and General Staff College at Fort Leavenworth, and I had seen him in action at Hohenfels and in REFORGER in Germany. He was a superb tactician, who could picture the tactical situation in his head and accurately assess friendly abilities as well as any officer I knew. I trusted both their judgments completely. Tactically, we were in one another's heads.

What Don had in mind just then—based on my mission to him not to get decisively engaged, and on the expectation that the 1st INF was closer than they actually were—was that the regiment should go over to the defense very soon and let the 1st INF pass through the next day. (More accurately, he wanted to get into a stationary position that would allow the follow-on division to pass through the regiment with the fewest potential complications.) He was unaware that the British were just now only partway through their passage, or that the time/distance to get the 1st INF forward was greater than he thought.

After I clarified the actual time/distance for 1st INF, I pointed out that I was not yet ready for him to go on the defense. "What I want you to do," I said, "is continue to maintain contact with the enemy. Keep pressure on the Tawalkana. Fix the RGFC. Locate flanks. And then be prepared to pass 1st INF to the east."

Don understood.

It was not an easy mission. He'd have to revise his formation alignment, then go into the teeth of the stiffening Iraqi defense in order to both fix and find the flanks of more than a division, and figure out the tempo to do all of that. And he'd have to do it all without getting so tangled up that I'd have to rescue him by committing combat units at a time and place dictated by the enemy and not by our own initiative . . . with the end result that I wouldn't be able to pass the 1st INF through. I trusted Don and the 2nd ACR to get the job done. And I knew I'd go back to see how they were doing it.

What I had just done with 2nd ACR was to reinforce the offensive cover mission. So far, 2nd ACR's mission had been to protect the movement of the main body from enemy action, and Don and the regiment had been adjusting their tempo to stay about thirty minutes in front of the main body. Now that was about to change.

I had now ordered Don on a reconnaissance mission—part of an offensive cover—which meant that he now had to orient himself more directly on the enemy in front of him than on the corps behind him. It also meant that the movement tempo could change, that is, he was no longer restricted to keeping about thirty minutes ahead of the lead elements of the rest of the corps. Don and the 2nd ACR were now focused on the enemy, while at the same time estimating a place where they could pass the 1st INF through. I would rely on Don's tactical judgment to decide the tactics and to adjust the tempo for this mission.

Estimating where to make the forward passage of two moving units is more art than science. You could attempt a passage of one unit through another while both are moving in the same direction, like a relay team in track, but in my experience that does not work. You must designate some battle handover point, a clear separation of the responsibilities for where the passing unit is to take up the fight.

In our NATO missions, all our passages of lines had been in the defense, called a rearward passage of lines, where a defending unit on the move backward had passed the fight to a stationary unit in a defensive position. We had done it many times when I had commanded the Blackhorse in the Fulda Gap from 1982 to 1984.

Those were easy compared to the maneuver facing us soon. For one thing, we were attacking. In the attack, I wanted the maximum out of the 2nd ACR, that is, I wanted them to find, fix, and locate the enemy flanks, and also to push as far east as they could go before passing the 1st INF. Sooner or later, however, the 1st INF would be ready to pass, and the 2nd ACR must stop, either of their own accord or because of enemy actions. As they tried to fix that point (judging both enemy resistance and the availability of the 1st INF to pass), the 2nd ACR would almost surely have to go through some fits and starts, and there would also almost surely be some frustrations among junior leaders in the regiment who wanted to press east. I liked that aggressive attitude, but it was better for the larger 1st INF to keep moving steadily while the 2nd ACR did the fits and starts; a cavalry regiment is much more agile and able to handle the interruptions than an 8,000-vehicle, three-maneuver-brigade division.

All this was in my mind as Don, Steve, and I worked things out.

Based on his estimate that the Tawalkana security zone started at 65 Easting and extended about eight kilometers west, Don figured that from where they were, the 2nd ACR should attack to about 60 Easting in order to collapse the security zone. By that time, the 1st INF would be ready to pass through. However, if the RGFC turned out to be farther east than that, or if the 1st INF turned out to be farther behind than we expected, or if the 2nd ACR was able to go farther east than the 60 grid line, then they would continue to attack east.

I thought about that for a second—and about a larger issue that I had to keep forcing into my thinking. Just then I was intensely focused on the present. As tempting as that might be, I knew I had larger responsibilities. I could concentrate on the present only to the extent that its outcome affected future operations. It was not easy—I had commanded a cavalry regiment and there I was in the middle of combat with one—but I had to let that pass and force myself to look to the future—and especially at the decision on FRAGPLAN 7. It was up to Don to fight the regiment in the present.

After a quick look at FRAGPLAN 7 on the map, I looked ahead at both 3rd AD and 1st INF in relation to the 2nd ACR. We needed to pass both divisions through the 2nd ACR to take up the fight against the Tawalkana and the developing RGFC defense, but the two divisions were in different circumstances.

The 3rd AD was immediately available to execute, and was to the west-southwest of the 2nd ACR by about thirty minutes to an hour—just about right. It'd been a hell of a feat for them to get there only twenty-four hours after we had launched—they'd had to start fifteen hours early, and in a column of brigades; they'd had few cuts in the border berm to use, and so the tactical integrity of their formations had been fractured, forcing the units to go through single file, and then reassemble on the far side into two brigades forward and one back. The 3rd AD had taken hundreds of prisoners, some bypassed by the 2nd ACR, and they'd had some combat: Iraqis retreating away from the 1st INF attack had run into the 3rd AD's eastern flank. Because we were concerned about fratricide on that flank, I had placed a five-kilometer buffer zone in between the two divisions. Some Iraqi units in that zone had been attacked by both divisions. In other words, it had not been an idle or combat-free twenty-four hours for the 3rd AD.

On the other hand, the 1st INF was in the breach about sixty to eighty kilometers away from the 2nd ACR, and fixed in place until the British could pass through. By the time the British finished passage, the 1st INF would be a good eight or ten hours behind the 2nd ACR. The next day I would need to make the tactical judgment about how to keep the 2nd ACR attacking east while moving the whole 1st INF forward to catch them, pass through, and take up the attack.

It was all coming together. I knew what I wanted to do. I would use FRAG-PLAN 7—but with the 1st INF in place of the 1st CAV, who were still held in CENTCOM reserve. This would cause major adjustments to be made in the 1st INF and adjustments in graphics overlay at corps. To do both on the move would require many orders to be oral rather than written, and maps would have to be hastily marked. But it all could be done.

With the decision came an assumption: Since the Tawalkana was fixed, the other two RGFC heavy divisions would also doubtless fight in that defense. So far, I had the Tawalkana intelligence I needed from the 2nd ACR. I would soon confirm my assumption about the other two RGFC heavy divisions from the intelligence update from my G-2, and from Third Army. Earlier, I had figured with the Third Army G-2, Brigadier General John Stewart, that this was about the point in the fight when we would have to make a prediction about the disposition of the RGFC. I was confident they would have that intelligence for me when I rendezvoused a little later at the TAC with John Davidson, VII Corps G-2.

Meanwhile, the orders that set the plan in motion were clear. I had ordered Tom to move forward. I had ordered Don to continue to attack. I had ordered Ron Griffith to be in the northern area of Collins by midmorning the next day. Now it was time to get an update from my staff and see if Third Army had any orders for us before I gave FRAGPLAN 7 orders to the corps.

★ I left Don and the advancing 2nd ACR and flew about forty kilometers to the southwest to a spot in the desert where my jump TAC was co-located with the 3rd AD TAC CP. The sky was dark and the wind was picking up; it looked like rain.

Earlier, I had asked my chief, John Landry, to bring a small staff group forward so I could review the situation, compare what they had with what I had seen and gotten from the commanders, and confirm the deep attack by our 11th Aviation Brigade that night.

1630 SOMEWHERE IN IRAQ

After a few radio calls back and forth, and some flying that was in less than a straight line, we found the jump TAC, JAYHAWK Forward, located with the 3rd AD TAC CP. Waiting for me were John Landry, John Davidson (G-2), Colonel Johnnie Hitt (11th Aviation Brigade commander), Colonel Ray Smith (corps deputy fire-support coordinator), Colonel Bill Rutherford (G-4), and Stan Cherrie. Much to my disappointment, the TAC CP were stuck somewhere in the sea of vehicles behind us that stretched all the way back to the Saudi border. Considering the 8,000 vehicles of the 3rd AD, plus those of the 42nd Artillery Brigade that had linked up with them, plus the corps support groups that were moving supplies behind the 3rd AD, it should not have surprised me. But it put me in a slow burn that I had only two M577s and one PCM line* with which to command an entire attacking armored corps.

In the fast-fading daylight, we huddled around a HMMWV hood, with a map spread over the top. The jump TAC was still setting up.

"The RGFC situation is about what we reported to you this morning," John Davidson began. "It looks as though they are forming a defense along here." He pointed to a location that was close to an estimate that the 2nd ACR S-2, Major Dan Cambell, had given to me earlier. "We talked to Third Army. Brigadier General Stewart knew you wanted to make a decision about now and that you needed his best estimate on the RGFC. The way it looks, he told me, the RGFC will defend from where they are now."

That was the final intelligence piece I needed, which confirmed everything I'd learned at the 2nd ACR.

Bill Rutherford, G-4, reported that our logistics situation was green for now, but that fuel would continue to be a close call. Log Base Nelligen, north at the breach, would be operational by sometime tomorrow and available to provide fuel to trucks returning empty from the divisions. He also reported an emergency resupply of ammo to 2nd ACR by CH-47,** because some of the CAV ammo vehicles had gotten stuck in soft sand. In major end items, that is, major pieces of equipment such as tanks, Bradleys, and the like, we were in excellent shape. Over 90 percent of them were available, as combat and maintenance losses had been few.

"That does it," I said, voicing the decision I had already made. "We execute FRAGPLAN 7. Get the orders out. I want 1st INF to pass through the 2nd ACR and continue the attack tomorrow afternoon. I want 3rd AD to pass

---

Long-haul comms to Riyadh and the VII Corps main CP.
**We had a company of these large cargo helicopters in our aviation brigade that were used for emergency resupply.*

through and around to the north of the 2nd ACR and attack east. I already told Ron Griffith I want him in the northern part of Collins by midmorning tomorrow to attack east from there."

VII Corps would now turn ninety degrees east and activate the new Third Army northern boundary between us and XVIII Corps, which would open an attack lane for them and make possible the mutually supporting corps attacks I thought we needed. It also meant that the RGFC was now in two sectors, ours and XVIII Corps's—or rather, in a Third Army sector, as drawn in the contingency plan of 18 February and amended just the day before, on the twenty-fourth.

I knew I needed to call John Yeosock right away to tell him what we were doing. It would confirm what I had told him that morning.

Earlier, there had been some differences over how and when to commit to this Third Army contingency plan. As we have already seen, while Cal Waller was Third Army commander, he had committed to it ahead of time—in fact, he had thought we might even have to pause to make sure we had a coordinated VII and XVIII Corps attack against the RGFC. When John Yeosock had returned, however, he was not ready to commit. Instead, he had published the plan, to be executed "on order." I knew, however, that it was his intent to order its execution if the RGFC stayed fixed, and so when I became convinced that the RGFC was indeed fixed, I thought I had the green light from Third Army to make this decision. And I did it.

Getting hold of him did not prove to be easy.

G+1 . . . The Rest of the Theater

Meanwhile, many other things were going on in the theater of operations. On Monday morning, 25 February, this was the state of affairs in the Iraqi-occupied emirate that the Iraqis called Al Burqan Province and everyone else called Kuwait.

The Marines were in possession of the better part of the Kuwaiti bootheel, twenty to forty kilometers into the Iraqi defense. In the process of taking it, they had mauled three Iraqi divisions and captured 8,000 Iraqi prisoners. JFC-North, to their west, with only enough breaching equipment to open eleven lanes, had not by then made much of a dent in Iraqi lines. Even so, though they were deliberate, the Egyptians were getting the job done. And on the coast, the forces of JFC-East had advanced steadily, though not especially speedily, toward Kuwait City.

The Iraqis in Kuwait were in a wretched condition, and that was just fine, as far as the Marines and the Arabs fighting them were concerned.

At least five frontline Iraqi divisions were, for all practical purposes, no longer in existence, and several other divisions, including some heavies, were so severely battered they were close to ineffective. A number of other divisions and special forces brigades remained facing the coast, still waiting for the Marine amphibious assault that was never to come. These units were effectively tricked out of the war. In the end, the Iraqis in Kuwait proved more efficient at destruction and looting than at organizing a defense and fighting a determined, well-trained foe. Most notably, the Iraqis had sabotaged refineries and more than 150 oil wells. Black, greasy plumes of smoke darkened the skies over Kuwait.

Meanwhile, in Iraq, several hundred kilometers to the west, the 101st Airborne was preparing to be airlifted out to Highway 8 and the Euphrates valley, while the 3rd ACR and the 24th MECH were moving north, without opposition, on VII Corps's western flank.

The rest of G+1 was not to go so smoothly.

Early that morning, in Kuwait, T-55s from the 3rd and 8th Armored Brigades of Iraqi Major General Salah Abdoul Mahmoud's Iraqi III Corps (Mahmoud had been the Iraqi commander at the Battle of Khafji) attacked the eastern flank of the 1st Marine Division out of the oil smoke–grimed fog covering the Burqan oil field. The Iraqi counterattack that everyone had expected had finally come, and from an unexpected direction. Iraqis traditionally took attacks head-on. This time they tried a surprise out of the oil field on the Marines' flank. It was a sharp battle—perhaps the largest tank engagement in Marine history. It was also, for all practical purposes, a rout. The poorly trained Iraqis were no match for the Marines, with their M-60 tanks, their LAVs (APCs), their Cobra attack helicopters, and their Harrier fighter-bombers—not to mention TOWs and other missiles. The Iraqis did not have effective artillery, their tankers couldn't shoot straight, and their attack was piecemeal and uncoordinated. If they had hit the Marines in a coordinated fist (the kind of fist Fred Franks was aiming at their Republican Guards), it could have been a very nasty morning for the Marines.

As it happened, the Iraqi defeat was not a total loss for them. It bought time. The battle put an end to the Marine advance for the rest of the day, and this gave major elements of the Iraqi army time to pull out of Kuwait City.

To the west, the French 6th Light Division and the 82nd Airborne were advancing to as-Salman to secure the Coalition's left flank. Meanwhile, that afternoon, a thousand paratroopers from the 101st Airborne's 3rd Brigade were lifted by Blackhawks north to a spot in the Euphrates val-

*ley near the town of Al Khidr, between the larger towns of as-Samawah
and an-Nasiriyah. They carried with them their M-16s, their machine
guns, a few TOW missiles, and their mortars. Their artillery and most of
their TOWs, with most of their launchers mounted on Humvees, came in
nearby on big Chinook helicopters. Because the Chinooks didn't have
range enough to reach the 3rd Brigade landing zone, they landed about
forty kilometers south of Highway 8. From there the Humvees and cannon would travel overland to rendezvous with the paratroopers.*

*Both landing zones, it turned out, were a sea of mud, which made it
hard—and miserable—for everybody, but especially for the artillery. It
took the entire night and most of the next morning to plow through the
axle-deep slop and reach the other men.*

*Meanwhile, because the weather was so grim, Colonel Robert Clark,
the brigade commander, decided to hold off on reinforcing the 1,000 who
had already landed. That left a lightly armed force of paratroopers to spend
the very cold, wet night between G+1 and G+2 setting up ambush positions to close off Highway 8, and waiting nervously for Iraqi armor to
counterattack. The Iraqi armor, blessedly, never showed up. The worst the
Americans had to face, as it happened, were fifteen Iraqi infantrymen,
whom they drove off with mortars. Later they stopped a convoy, whose
trucks turned out to be carrying onions (which they gave to hungry local
villagers the next day).*

*Though the 101st's hold on Highway 8 was just then tenuous (they
were soon reinforced), it proved real, lasting, and effective. For the rest of
the war, if the Iraqis wanted to drive from Basra to Baghdad, they didn't
do it on Highway 8.*

11

ATTACK EAST

At 1800 I got a call from Ron Griffith. He was in a situation that would delay his attack into al-Busayyah.

First AD was just outside Purple, he told me, and his G-2 had estimated that an Iraqi commando battalion, tank company, and some other infantry were in al-Busayyah, all positioned to protect the VII Iraqi Corps logistics base. The area around al-Busayyah was laced with four- to six-foot-deep wadis, and the Iraqi tanks were dispersed and dug into the terrain, as was the infantry. The commando battalion was in the town itself, thirty to thirty-five buildings of stone and thick adobe. Because he preferred not to get into a night fight that would set his mounted units against dismounted enemy troops, he wanted to request my OK to hold his mounted ground attack until first light the next day (though he would continue to attack by artillery and Apaches all night).

I figured the tactics were up to Ron, but the corps tempo was my business. My main corps focus for Ron was that he have 1st AD in Collins the next morning at 0900. On the other hand, since the RGFC and associated units were moving into a defensive set and were not a threat to maneuver against us, the sense of urgency to hit Purple by the end of the day and to position 1st AD on the northwest flank of the RGFC was no longer that great.

So Ron had it right. It made no sense to risk the casualties and possible fratricide that could result from a mounted attack at night into a dismounted defense in a village. (To do a night attack correctly, he would have had to go very slowly and deliberately, which would have ended up compromising our much greater firepower. If he had tried to go faster, he would have risked bypassing Iraqi infantry and getting involved in a 360-degree fight in a village.) It was better to secure the town in the morning, in daylight, when all the advantages would be with his troops. That should still give him plenty of time to turn ninety degrees right and be where I wanted him by 0900.

"Permission granted," I said, "as long as you are in the northern part of Collins by 0900, attacking east beside 3rd AD."

"Roger. We can do both."

Meanwhile, we were getting reports that the British had had enemy contact right after noon, soon after their lead units had exited the breach-head line attacking east. Between then and now, they had been overrunning HQs and capturing prisoners, and they were continuing to fight on into darkness (it got totally dark at about 1845 each day, which was around fifty minutes after sunset). The entire division was still not clear of the breach.

This was not good news, as it would delay the 1st INF move north to pass through the 2nd ACR.

Meanwhile, I heard from John Landry that we had no additional orders from Third Army, but he had learned from Steve Arnold that there was still concern about the VII Corps pace of attack. That really got my attention. I blew up over the phone to John.

"What the hell is wrong with them in Riyadh? Do they know what the hell is going on out here? I've talked to John Yeosock constantly to let him know what's happening. Here we are maneuvering the corps to get in position for the knockout of the RGFC, and they are concerned about progress? God damn it."

I had a lot on my mind from a long day of complex maneuvering and advance planning, and now this. No new orders. Only "concerns." Give me a break. If you want me to do something different, just tell me. I'm a soldier; I will execute. But "concerns"? Thoughts from J. F. C. Fuller's book *Generalship: Its Disease and Cures* and images of "chateau generals" during World War I danced in my head, but I said nothing of that. It was just normal commander frustration with higher HQ, I told myself. I let the moment pass. I thought the "concerns" in Riyadh also would pass when they had a clearer picture. But I also thought that I had better find out what the problem was.

As a commander, I was not prone to wide mood swings or loud outbursts. Some are, and use it as an effective command style. Not me. Competitive, yes. Hate to lose, yes. Iron will and fierce determination. Yes. But not a screamer. You work hard at keeping a cool head and maintaining the right balance of patience and impatience, at staying under control, able to think clearly when chaos threatens. If you constantly blow up at the least setbacks, your subordinates have a hard time understanding you, and soon get numb to the emotional outbursts, plus it clouds your thinking.

I also felt intense loyalty to my unit, like you do in a tight family. When something threatened my family—as these Riyadh "concerns" did—I got very combative. My first reaction was anger, but then I quickly cooled down and blamed it all on misunderstandings. I figured an explanation would clear it up. If that did not do it, then I would get some new orders to replace my current orders and intent from Third Army and CENTCOM.

"I'll call John Yeosock later and talk to him about it. Let's get the rest of this done," I said.

The other issue was our deep attack. I had wanted to attack deep with the 11th Aviation Brigade the previous night, but because of the time change of the corps attack, we hadn't been able to execute. Tonight I wanted them to go deep in front of 2nd ACR to help isolate the Iraqis in the battle space—to keep the units in the rear from reinforcing the units forward—and to destroy Iraqi units that were deep while 2nd ACR was doing the same thing close. That way, 2nd ACR would be better able to continue its advance until I got the 1st INF forward to take up the fight. The 11th Brigade was ready, and I had already ordered them to execute.

Then, at around 1800, the weather turned bad. Of all the four days of our battle, this night brought the most violent rainstorms: thunder, lightning, torrential rain, fast-forming ponds, and running water. Because of the bad weather, John Landry and John Davidson were unable to fly back to the main CP, so they spent the night at the jump TAC.

For most of the evening, we kept current inside the two M577 extensions behind the tracks. The maps were up, showing friendly and enemy situations. We were located with 3rd AD, of course, and had radio contact with 1st AD and 2nd ACR, but not with 1st INF or the British. Our communications were terrible. At that point, I did not have a single dependable long-haul comm line with which to talk to Third Army or my main CP.

The weather and commo situation, on top of the "concerns" from Riyadh, had me totally pissed off. To complicate matters, the main TAC was moving to catch up, but by now there was no hope that they would make it to our location before morning. So that night I was as frustrated as I had ever been as a commander. Worse, I could not do much about it.

It was not a good situation. There I was, commanding a four-division corps, and I was located in two M577s with twenty-four-foot canvas extensions, I had line-of-sight radios good for only about twenty kilometers, and one intermittent PCM line, and water was running through the sand in small rivers underneath the sides of the canvas extensions and right through the inside of our jump TAC. There were some dry islands, but mostly we stood in ankle-deep running water. The extensions on the M577s had been taken from the theater reserve in Germany, so they were old and they leaked. On occasion, water ran down our situation map, carrying with it to the wet ground some of the map stickers showing friendly and enemy situations and streaking the markings on the map. And in the middle of all that, Riyadh was expressing concerns.

✭ We talked through FRAGPLAN 7 again that evening, and I got as much of an update as possible on friendly actions. Since I had just visited most of the units, there was not much new to report, and in any case the weather had slowed actions down. Aviation was completely grounded. When it storms in the flat desert, it storms. The troops must be having a miserable night, I thought.

At about 2100, I tried to call John Yeosock, but no luck. I could not get through on our comms. We continued to try on into the night. I decided to go over to Butch Funk's TAC, so I could get an update, order FRAGPLAN 7, and use Butch's comms—he had the more advanced MSE (Mobile Subscriber Equipment).

It was about a hundred meters' walk in the wind and driving rain and pitch blackness. We stumbled around and finally found the entrance.

Their TAC was complete. Four M577s were parked parallel, with canvas extensions out the back, making a work area of about thirty by thirty feet, all lit by power from their ever-running portable generators. Butch was inside an M577, busy with updates and planning of his own.

"Butch," I said, "give me a SITREP on your situation, and see if your folks can get through to Third Army in Riyadh."

"Roger," he answered, then gave me a complete rundown.

So far, 3rd AD had moved forward aggressively about eighty-five kilometers. At noon, they had gone into a division wedge, a formation of one brigade forward and two back side by side. To go from a column of brigades to a division wedge takes time and coordination; and since they were on the move, the maneuver had taken them the better part of four hours to complete. They were still moving.

During the day, they'd had some enemy actions, primarily from elements from the Iraqi 26th Infantry Division that had been bypassed by the 2nd ACR. The 4/7 Cavalry Squadron, whose mission was to guard the corps's east flank, had captured almost 200 prisoners. Other units in the division also reported prisoners and occasional incoming artillery. The total prisoner count was between 500 and 1,000.

The division was approximately thirty-five kilometers from Objective Collins, and not long ago his lead brigade had closed within about twelve kilometers of the rear of the 2nd ACR. They were right where I wanted them, reasonably well rested, and in an excellent logistics situation. I would now commit them to attack into the heart of the RGFC and associated units just to the east.

"Butch, I've ordered FRAGPLAN 7. Use those graphical control measures, except 1st INF will attack in place of 1st CAV. I want you to turn east, pass through and around the 2nd ACR at first light, and attack the RGFC as the middle division between 1st AD in the north and 1st INF in the south. You and 1st AD will be roughly on line, as Ron should be in the northern area of Collins by 0900 at the latest. First INF will probably not pass through 2nd ACR until late afternoon, so maintain contact with 2nd ACR to your south. Press the attack against the RGFC. No pauses."

"WILCO," Butch replied. He knew what he had to do. I did not need to give him any more orders than that.

After I finished my business with Butch, he went on to take care of other matters, and I tried once more to get John Yeosock.

Because Third Army was not hooked up directly to 3rd AD's MSE radio grid, the comms had to be rerouted through an improvised series of communication gateways in order to reach Third Army in Riyadh, which by now was almost 600 kilometers away. No easy task. It was close to 2300 before I got to talk to John Yeosock. I was inside one of the 3rd AD M577s, sitting on the floor of the track, straining to hear John over the noise inside the TAC.

"John," I said, "I ordered the corps to turn right, according to our FRAG-PLAN 7. That activates the boundary between us and XVIII Corps to run east-west, and opens the attack corridor for XVIII Corps in the north for a two-corps attack. I am using 1st INF as my third division in the VII Corps fist. I assume all this is OK with you."

"Good," John replied. "Continue to attack. You are doing exactly as I want done."

That confirmed for me that we were doing precisely what we had discussed and war-gamed, and what Third Army had published in its order of 24 February.

"John," I went on, "my chief mentioned there might be some continuing dissatisfaction with corps movement."

"Not from me, but the CINC blew up this morning. He thought you should be moving faster."

"Don't you know what the hell is going on?" I shot back, frustrated that they did not seem to have a grasp that we had maneuvered the corps to deliver a deathblow to the RGFC. "We are turning the corps ninety degrees east into the RGFC and will hit them with a three-division fist tomorrow. I thought we were doing great, considering the number of units and vehicles we've got crammed into this small maneuver space."

"I'm aware of all that," John replied, "and I understand everything you're trying to do. You have the best feel for the situation, Fred. I'm pleased with what VII Corps is doing."

"Would it do any good for me to talk directly to General Schwarzkopf and explain what we are doing?" I asked, not yet satisfied that the "concerns" issue had been laid to rest.

"Settle down, Fred. It's OK now. The CINC is satisfied with what is happening. He doesn't want the pace any faster now. He's concerned with fratricide if the pace gets too fast. So his intent is for deliberate operations with low casualties. Right now, the CINC wants us to fight smart, deliberately, with small casualties, develop the situation, and fix by fires."

"That's good to hear," I said. So the flap in Riyadh really was no big deal, just the normal give-and-take of command in war. You do not record every mood swing or discussion with subordinates. But I did think that if I talked to Schwarzkopf, I could give him some direct info from the battlefield. I knew that I would have appreciated a call from the actual battlefield if I were in his place.

"Do you still think I should talk to the CINC . . . ?"

"Good idea. Go ahead and talk to him, probably tomorrow," John said.

That made sense—it was past midnight by this time, and from what John just told me, I could tell that the storm in Riyadh had passed. But I still had no idea what it all meant.

I do not think I shared any of this with Butch. It was my business to deal with higher HQ, absorb any problems, and shield the corps from them, just as John Yeosock was doing for me.

TACTICAL MANEUVERS

All that night, out in the rainy, windy desert ahead of us and for dozens of kilometers on either side, commanders of smaller units were performing the same kind of tasks we were—the difficult, highly skilled, and intensely focused work of organizing their forces and maneuvering their teams in such a way that their piece of the corps fist would hit the enemy with maximum impact.

How do you do that? How do you maneuver for maximum combat power concentration at the right place at the right time? By watching combat alignments and movement friction, and by a lot of advance practice.

You have to keep your own individual unit in the right formation, while keeping those units who are supporting you, or who are part of the same attack, in the right position relative to your unit. You need the appropriate combination of tanks, infantry, artillery, and maybe engineers to be where they're supposed to be. You need the intelligence units positioned so that they can give you the latest information. You need your formation fueled and supplied with ammo and other classes of supplies, so that they don't run out during the fight. You also want to finish the current fight in the right position and combination of units to flow right into the next one.

In the desert, taking care of all of these requirements means constant formation adjustment. For example, if you want to take a unit out of the lead and put in a fresh formation, that means you have to pass one unit through another. For armored brigades, this involves 2,000 vehicles passing through another 2,000, which requires careful coordination just to keep the units from running into one another. If a battle is going on, then the passed unit also has to render tactical assistance to the passing one in order to shift the battle to them.

While you are arranging and maneuvering, you can never lose sight of physical friction. Armored formations have to refuel and rearm, which takes time. They have to repair vehicles with maintenance problems and perform preventive maintenance—clean air filters, check oil levels, adjust track tension, and the like. If you can, you combine maintenance with fuel-rearm halts.

Meanwhile, different vehicles move at different speeds. Tanks go much faster than artillery vehicles, so in an attack you have to make sure that one doesn't outrun the other. Fuel trucks also are slower than tanks and Bradleys cross-country, and since they often can't go where the others can go, you have to bring the tanks and Bradleys to them.

Movement at night is much slower than in the day. You have to work extra hard to maintain unit integrity and to keep vehicles from wandering off course, and when combat is imminent, the pace is even slower. You want to be certain you know where all your vehicles are located before you engage the enemy. Because only a few selected commanders' vehicles in each formation had GPS or LORAN, everyone else had to use those vehicles as a guide, employing either night-vision devices or light signals—a tough task. The high winds and rain complicated these maneuvers . . . which became especially difficult if the enemy had been bypassed and there was action both to the front and rear.

Soldier fatigue also affects speed. If you're standing in turrets or lying in drivers' compartments for a long time, you get tired and lose concentration. You must give them breaks from time to time.

To do everything you need to do rapidly takes much practice. Because of the limited maneuver possibilities in Germany, VII Corps hadn't had much major unit maneuver practice there, and there hadn't been any opportunity at all to practice desert formations such as the wedge or the box until we actually deployed in Saudi Arabia (some of the formations hadn't even been invented yet). That was why I had so forcefully stressed large-unit training skills in our first meeting on 9 November. As it was, the training time had been limited, and our only full-scale rehearsal was the 180-kilometer move from our TAA to our attack positions in mid-February. If we had gone to war right off the ships and without GPS, our maneuvers on the night of the twenty-fifth and all through the rest of our attack would have been more difficult. That we got it all done in a small attack zone during the eighty-nine hours of the war was a great tribute to the leaders, the soldiers, and to mission-focused training.

As Ron Griffith put it after the war: "The thing that we didn't have a sense for, because we had never maneuvered on that scale before, is how to array your battle formations. How long does it take, for example, if you decide to provide a base of fire with one brigade and to envelop twenty-five or thirty kilometers into the rear with another brigade? Sometimes our assessment of how long it would take to conduct a particular maneuver would be off by as much as 300 percent. . . . Well, it might take five hours to do that or it might take an hour and fifteen minutes. And so we practiced."

These were our basic maneuver formations:

DIVISIONS had four formations: a column of brigades; a "desert" wedge; two brigades forward and one in reserve; and three brigades abreast. From those basic maneuver sets, division commanders could set a base of fire and maneuver to attack.

The division commanders also experimented with aviation. They started out by using their AH-64s' fire to support the attacking ground units, but when they discovered that in-close did not work due to sand clutter (the normal swirl of sand dust kicked up by maneuvering tracked vehicles obscures vehicles from the air and makes laser designation of targets difficult), they quickly adapted by sending the Apaches deeper in front.

On the other hand, since in many cases the Iraqi artillery outranged ours, the commanders pulled their cannon and rocket (MLRS) artillery in close to the lead maneuver units so that they could range Iraqi artillery in counterfire. This even meant pushing the MLRS well forward, which was a violation of doctrine, but it fit the battle conditions.

BRIGADES also had their own attack formations, which resembled division formations: a star, with two battalions forward and two back, plus artillery behind; a wedge, with one battalion forward and two abreast and behind, plus artillery right behind the lead task force; a column of battalions (one behind the other); two brigades up abreast and one back; and the brigade on line with three or four battalion task forces abreast. These basic formations gave the brigade commanders the versatility and options they needed. They used them all.

BATTALIONS. Normally there were no "pure" battalions of "only" tanks or Bradleys. In order to get the versatility and combined-arms effects of tanks and infantry, the U.S. Army combined them into task forces, which used the battalion command structure, but involved exchanging companies between battalions. In other words, a tank battalion of four companies would send one of its companies to a Bradley battalion in exchange for a Bradley company, thus making both battalions into task forces. They used the same maneuver formations as the brigades, except that the companies replaced the battalions in the formation alignments: a box—two companies up and two back; a diamond—one company forward, two behind, and one trailing; or all companies on line abreast.

Refueling on the move (ROM) was another thing that units worked hard to perfect, and our soldiers' skill in execution would have made a pit crew at the Indy 500 proud. By G-Day, ROM was a well-choreographed drill, practiced many times in training in the desert: Fuel trucks were brought forward and set up at spots in the desert, then unit vehicles lined up at these "pit" stops and took on fuel on either side of the truck. Simultaneously, tank crews, before or after refueling, removed air filters (twenty- to thirty-pound metal boxes) from tanks, blew compressed air through them to clean out sand, and performed other maintenance while also checking the tank's main gun boresight (to ensure that the cannon and sights were both on the same spot).

VII Corps Jump TAC CP

At around 0100, I went back to the two M577s to see if there had been any change while I was gone. The rain and high winds continued, and the soldiers were wet and cold. The official weather data said we were to have 81 percent illumination, but with cloud cover and rain, I could barely see Toby a few feet away as we stumbled around in the rain getting back to the TAC. I could picture the commanders and soldiers trying to keep the units together while continuing to move and refuel in this weather.

Though the bad weather had caused cancellation of our deep aviation attack, other actions continued.

Since 1500 the day before, 1st AD had attacked the almost 140 kilometers to al-Busayyah and destroyed the better part of a reinforced Iraqi brigade and other Iraqi units in their zone. They had reported destroying 2 tanks, 25 armored personnel carriers, 9 artillery pieces, 48 trucks, 14 air defense pieces, and capturing over 300 prisoners (the accounts of prisoners continued to vary widely). Before the violent rainstorms, their aviation brigade Apaches had struck hard at Iraqi positions in al-Busayyah, and the division was continuing to pound Iraqi targets in the town with cannon and MLRS artillery. Ron had them exactly where I wanted them. The division was in an excellent logistics posture, and the troops were reasonably fresh, although there would not be much rest with the weather that night.

Second ACR had also been active in combat. Though Don Holder had had to cancel a planned Apache attack into the Tawalkana, he had managed to launch a successful MLRS raid that night as a follow-through on my order to keep the pressure on the RGFC. He'd sent Company M of 3rd Squadron to escort the nine-launcher MLRS battery C/4-27 FA.

The unit commanders remembered the action like this: C Battery:

"Guarded by the tank company from 3/2 ACR, C Battery moved outside the regimental defenses to fire the missions. The first two, at 2230 and 0100, were executed unimpeded. The third, at 0430 on the twenty-sixth, was interrupted as the launchers moved behind the tank company through the regimental defenses. An MTLB unit of estimated company size was moving up the MSR to investigate the rocket fires. The MTLBs ran into the tank company and a short, violent fight ensued. The launchers quickly returned to the regimental sector while the 3rd Squadron tanks destroyed the MTLBs."

The account by Company M reads, "At 0135 the first platoon reported five possible enemy vehicles. . . . The vehicles had been positively identified as two T-55s, MTLB-PC, jeep, and a truck by several gunners in the company and reported their ranges varying from 3,000 to 3,500 meters and moving out of the effective direct-fire range. The gunners' fingers were getting itchy as the commander gave permission for the first platoon elements who could observe the enemy vehicles to engage. The weather was still zero from cloud cover. The first rounds from the M1A1 120-mm main guns rang out and declared target hits. Brilliant sparks flew from targets as M829A1 sabot rounds found their mark. The engagement lasted all of ten minutes, as twenty-three sabot rounds traveled downrange, destroying the enemy vehicles at ranges from 3,000 to 4,100 meters. . . . The enemy had been completely surprised and seemed confused as vehicles moved in every direction. It had been a simple ambush that had taken place, and was so effective and ran so smoothly that the men of Mad-Dog developed unimaginable confidence and were actually ecstatic that the mission went so well in such miserable weather. At 0530, Company M conducted stand-to and at 0615 moved out due east. . . . All of the men were silent as we made our way through the area. Vehicles were still burning and bodies were strewn about the sand. We found two survivors in the area and brought the medics forward to treat them. We felt no regrets. We had done our job and done it well. We were alert that night and were alive to see the next day."

★ Meanwhile, I knew that the British were having some actions as well, but I didn't know the nature of them. My British liaison team was with the main

TAC, caught in the middle of the 3rd AD mass of vehicles. Rupert's passage had begun around noon, and given the usual friction of lanes closed or wrong-way traffic, I figured that both his 7 Brigade and 4 Brigade were through the breach by now and well into the attack. Rupert had planned a generally due-east attack on two axes out of the breach, one in the north for 7 Brigade and one on the south for 4 Brigade.

I found out later that 7 Brigade had passed at about midday, immediately run into enemy contact, and had destroyed tanks and other armored vehicles. They had been joined just after dark by 4 Brigade attacking south of them on a due-east axis.

All this was happening as we listened to the rain crash on the canvas extensions and watched the water run through the sand all around our feet.

For a time, I stared at the map in silence, focusing on what we had to do the next day and the decisions I needed to make then, and trying to think ahead to the day after that. So far I was really pleased with our tactical situation: the hastily defending enemy versus our available combat power, our ability to focus it on the enemy, and the general condition of our troops. Based on the developing clearer picture of the Iraqis, we were in the right place at the right time in the right combination; and I knew I had picked the right time and place for our RGFC battles. We had the Iraqis where we wanted them.

The rain showed no signs of letting up. Shortly after 0100, I decided to get some rest.

Because John Landry had not been able to make the trip back to the main CP, he and I shared a small tent with two canvas GI cots and no lights that Toby had gotten from 3rd AD. It was better shelter than most of the soldiers of VII Corps had that night. At least we were dry. I slept on the cot minus only my shoulder holster, which I set down in my Kevlar, within easy reach.

0400 VII Corps Jump TAC Eighty Kilometers into Iraq

It was a short night. Toby shook me awake at about 0400 with some black coffee he had scrounged up from somewhere. I used a portable electric razor to shave quickly, then strapped on my shoulder holster and Kevlar and went the fifty feet to the jump TAC. John Landry joined me, and we got a tactical update before John went back to the corps main CP. It had stopped raining, but it was still dark. I could not hear any weapons firing, but I could hear sounds of tracked and wheeled vehicles moving. Third AD would be rolling into the attack.

My sleep had probably been longer and more comfortable than what most of the soldiers in VII Corps had gotten. Since we were right out there in the middle of the corps, I had a good idea of how most of the soldiers and lead-

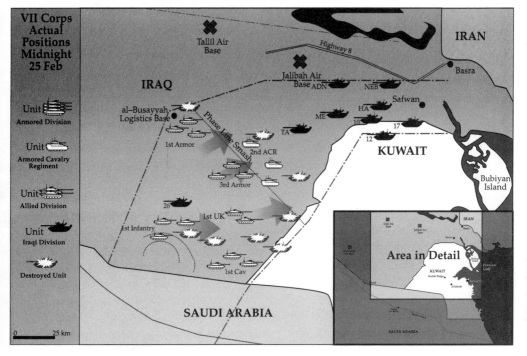

IRAN

Tallil Air Base

Highway 8

Basra

Jalibah Air Base   ADN   NEB

IRAQ

Safwan

al-Busayyah Logistics Base

ME   HA

1st Armor   TA   10   17

Phase Line Smash   2nd ACR   12

KUWAIT

3rd Armor

Bubiyan Island

26

1st UK

1st Infantry

Area in Detail

1st Cav

KUWAIT

SAUDI ARABIA

By midnight on 25 February, 1st UK Armored was through the 1st Infantry Division, and both were directing their actions east. Second ACR had uncovered from the front of the 1st Armored Division, and the regiment was now searching for the lead elements of the Republican Guards. The 1st Armored Division began pounding the al-Busayyah logistics base, which contained armored vehicles and special forces units, as well as resupplies for the Iraqi army.

---

ers had spent the night. Many were in combat. Others were refueling and doing maintenance. Commanders were collecting units, planning for their next move, and looking to execute their part of FRAGPLAN 7.

I wondered what picture they had in Riyadh of what we were doing.

The comms were still not good, but the troops were working as best they could to fix them. The long-haul comms continued to be intermittent, so I could not talk reliably either to the main CP or to Third Army, but we could get through; nor did I have consistent communications with the British or 1st INF.

In one respect, the fragile comms were a consequence of a deliberate choice I had made. I had wanted to be up front so that I could talk face-to-face with my commanders, feel the tempo of the fight and of our own move-

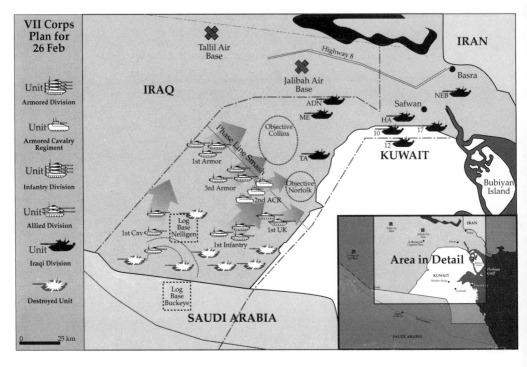

The plan for 26 February was to continue to press the attack toward the east. The 1st Cavalry Division was "chopped" from CENTCOM reserve to VII Corps, and was immediately moved through the recently deserted 1st Infantry Division breach sites toward the left corps boundary. While the corps logisticians continued to develop the log bases that would provide the much-needed fuel and bullets to combat vehicles proceeding into the attack, all combat units would continue toward establishing the formation that would provide the "fist" for hitting the Republican Guards.

ment, and monitor the condition of my soldiers. I had known the comms would be fragile from time to time, but had decided it was a risk I was prepared to take rather than be where my comms were good but I was out of personal touch with commanders and soldiers and the rapidly changing situation. What I lost in comms, I gained in "fingerspitzengefuhl."

However, one effect of the situation was that the official hard copy of the FRAGPLAN 7 execution did not reach all units until well past midnight. Third AD plans officer, Major John Rosenberger, wrote the 3rd AD attack order out longhand, three pages, double-spaced, and faxed it to subordinate units. Others made similar arrangements. Tom Rhame did much of his orally as his units began to move forward. It was no problem. From our meetings, I knew they knew what to do.

Today we would hit the Tawalkana and subordinate units hard. In fact, we had hit the security zone of the developing defense the day before at around noon; and 2nd ACR had continued to intercept units moving to get into the forming defense. With that in mind, I'd figured the 2nd ACR would be well into the fight by midmorning, which is why I had wanted Griffith and Funk on line to their north by that time. So that, later this morning, we would be in our fist, with 1st AD in the north, 3rd AD in the center, and 2nd ACR in the south. Later, the 1st INF (replacing the CENTCOM-held 1st CAV) would pass through the regiment and give us our three-division fist. By that time, in addition to the RGFC Tawalkana and other armored divisions in the area, we also would be fighting the RGFC Medina. We would do all that today, while maintaining the momentum of the attack through the following day to destroy the rest of the RGFC units in our sector.

Even though I was aware that the comms limited our information, I asked for a quick update on the battle activities of VII Corps units. I wanted to hear what they had, then go look for myself.

I was interested in the same questions discussed the morning before.

First I wanted to hear about the enemy, and I had a number of sharp questions for the assistant G-2, Captain Bill Eisel, about what the RGFC* was doing.

It was ever more clear that the RGFC theater command had a *defensive* plan and were executing it. They were not as skillful at the tactical level as our troops, but they had a plan! By now I figured they knew we were here. What they still did not know was the size of our force, the power of our rolling armor attack, or the direction from which we would hit them. They would find out the answers to those questions shortly. They were about to get hit by the largest combined-armored corps in the history of the U.S. Army ever to engage in an attack.

So, as battered as they might be from Coalition air attacks, the RGFC HQ was trying to set a defense in depth that would allow its forces to get out of Kuwait (as Don Holder had suggested yesterday) and would set a series of defensive belts in front of Basra, their only port. We knew from studying the Iraq-Iran War that the Iraqis had put up a tough defense of Basra.

The RGFC tactic was to throw armor/mechanized infantry in our way. As they could perform only limited maneuvers, it was mainly a brute-force defense thickened by all the units in the area (as confirmed by the Third Army

*I should make clear that the term RGFC connotes their command HQ, not individual units; the RGFC HQ controlled all the operational reserves, including non–Republican Guards subordinate units.

intel feed and our own intel sources). That is why we ran into so many different units during the battles over the next two days. The 1st AD and the 3rd AD fought elements of the 12th, 17th, 52nd, and 10th Armored. In addition, the 1st AD fought the northern brigade of the Tawalkana, the Medina, and a brigade of the Adnan.

As what the Iraqis were doing became ever clearer, it also became clearer to me that our tactics and maneuvers had been exactly right. We had them where we wanted them. They had fixed themselves. The timing was perfect, and, further, the time we had taken to keep concentrated had not hurt us at all, for at that moment on the twenty-sixth, we were still catching the Iraqis trying to form a defense. In other words, our forecast had turned out right for both our own force and the enemy, and we had our force in the right place at the right time. It does not get much better than that in maneuver warfare!

Meanwhile, as we turned ninety degrees east, I also wanted to keep track of the progress of XVIII Corps. If their attack east did not move at the pace of ours, Ron Griffith and the 1st AD would have an open flank. Open flanks in the desert are no big deal, unless the enemy can do something about it. At that point, the RGFC still had its three Guards infantry divisions to the north of our attack zone (that is, in the XVIII Corps zone). As for the third heavy Republican Guards division, the Hammurabi, I was not sure where they were just then or how the RGFC would play them in the defense. (I learned later that they were in fact still east of the Tawalkana and Medina, standing between these divisions and Basra, and also moving north to reinforce the Nebuchadnezzar, which was an RGFC infantry division.) But it was at least clear that we had the Tawalkana and Medina in our zone now, along with three or four associated divisions of 50 percent strength or better. With the new Third Army boundaries, significant elements of the RGFC were now in the zone of attack of XVIII Corps, not just of VII Corps.

★ Our own situation was still good.

The British 1st Armored Division had completed its passage of lines through the 1st INF at about 0300. My division commanders had estimated it would take twelve hours, but it had actually taken them fifteen.

It was then that I learned that the British had been in contact with the Iraqis almost from the time 7 Brigade had exited the breach the afternoon before. Rupert had then had 7 Brigade attack in the north of the British sector, since that sector contained the Iraqi forces that could threaten the rear of our envelopment force. Four Brigade soon followed and attacked in the southern half of the British sector. The lead units of 4 Brigade had had combat actions the previous night, even as the rear of the brigade and division support units were clearing the breach. Both brigades were continuing to attack elements of what was left of the Iraqi VII Corps frontline infantry divisions (the 48th, 25th, 31st, and 27th) and the deeper-positioned tactical reserve, the Iraqi 52nd Division.

Later I would know the details. According to Brigadier Patrick Cordingly of 7 Brigade, that afternoon at 1500, after passing through the breach, "It was cold; it was wet and it was overcast and we were wearing NBC suits and quite expecting the enemy to use chemical weapons against us. . . . During the ground war, the brigade was involved in six formal . . . attacks in the first thirty-six hours. . . . We destroyed some 150 tanks and armored vehicles and took over 3,000 prisoners (in an attack that covered over 300 kilometers)." He relates the first of those attacks (actually the first tank and armored infantry attack in British army history) early on the evening of 25 February by the Scots Dragoon Guards on an Iraqi communication and logistics site: "As night fell, the columns of tanks closed up. Only the red turret lights betrayed the presence of the mass of moving armor. Suddenly, reports of the enemy came in from D Squadron (Challenger tank company) on the right. It wasn't a preplanned attack, but we knew that there was a defended divisional headquarters in the area. As we advanced into the mine belt, the tanks began to pick up the objective with their thermal sights. . . . It was a particularly unpleasant night; it was raining quite heavily, and visibility was down to about fifteen meters before you could see anything the size of a Warrior. It was absolutely black. Thirty seconds before we went in, the tanks opened up, and when the vehicles they hit started burning, the infantry had a reference point to aim for. . . . And when the infantry debussed and stepped into the blackness, it was a step into the unknown for them. . . . Bullets, both friendly and enemy, seemed to be flying everywhere. Private Evans's life was saved when an AK-47 bullet lodged in a rifle magazine in his breast pocket. . . . We also had another tank and one of the Milans grouped together, putting down fire support as that platoon ran in. As soon as another position was identified, fire was put down. . . . Some of the assaults were very tight and it was undoubtedly a concerning time . . . although we had taken five casualties, we all knew that whatever else happened, we had done it, and despite atrocious conditions, it had worked."

Here is another battle account by Major Simon Knapper, commander of A Company, Staffordshire Regiment—an armored infantry battalion comprising two Warrior and two Challenger tank companies commanded by Lieutenant Colonel Charles Rogers, 7 Brigade. The time was approximately 2100 25 February. "It wasn't a preplanned attack. We knew that there was a communications site in that area and we knew our battle group had been tasked to clear it. . . . The whole area was quite clearly still occupied, and therefore we went into a quick attack on it. . . . Thirty seconds before H-Hour, the tanks opened fire, destroying the vehicles and generator. . . . The tanks led us to exactly the right places, and in the last 300 meters, the Warriors broke forward of the protective screen of tanks and opened up with their chain guns. We debussed the men on site. . . . All the time there was this incredible noise of firing; cannon fire and small arms and tracer bouncing everywhere." As part of 7 Brigade, this battalion had crossed Phase Line New Jersey out of the 1st INF Division breach at 1525 on 25 February, and attacked east. The attack described by Major Knapper was conducted in a driving rainstorm, lasted about an hour and a half, and resulted in one British soldier wounded. They captured about fifty Iraqis, and the battalion destroyed the CP complex. Other units of the 1st UK had been in similar engagements. "I am very proud of what the company achieved that night," Major Knapper ends his account. "It was the first armored infantry attack of the war, and it worked."

1ST INF had left a task force in the breach and were just now beginning to move forward to get into position to pass through 2nd ACR. As I heard this, it went through my mind that 2nd ACR would be moving east and attacking Iraqi units as 1st INF caught up to them, also moving east. That posed a difficult time/distance problem.

The key question was: Where should we make the passage and when? I needed to make that decision today. In the back of my mind, I wanted the passage to be event-driven and not time-driven—that is, I wanted the 2nd ACR to get as far into the Tawalkana as their combat power permitted, and then I'd pass the 1st INF to take up the attack. I did not want to set a definite time for the passage to happen. To do that might prematurely stop the 2nd ACR or cause them to wait while the 1st INF made its way forward, thus giving the Tawalkana more time to thicken the defense with more units, mines, and artillery. At this point, I still believed that 2nd ACR would get about as far as they could into the Tawalkana defense by late afternoon—still in daylight. By that time, 1st INF should be ready to make the forward passage and take up the fight.

What I did not know then, and did not learn until after the war, was that the zone for the 1st INF to move forward, between the 1st UK attacking east and the 3rd AD moving northeast, had been drawn so narrow that Tom Rhame was forced to move in a column of brigades, thus slowing his movement and forcing him to shift formation later—a time-consuming task. Our staff had to rush the drawing of a sector after I had made the change to FRAGPLAN 7 that replaced 1st CAV with 1st INF. The weather also affected their movement rate. It continued to be lousy, with sandstorms.

1ST AD had pounded Objective Purple for the rest of the night and were about to attack to seize it. During the night, they had fired a total of 340 MLRS rockets and 1,920 155-mm DPICM* artillery rounds into targets on and around Purple. Ron liked to pound the Iraqis with artillery, and so did I.

Between 1500 on the twenty-fourth until midnight on the twenty-fifth, the division had crossed the berm, moved the fifty or so kilometers through the boulder- and wadi-laced terrain, then taken over the sector from the 2nd ACR, fought a brigade-sized fight, and moved the 8,000-vehicle division nearly 140 kilometers to al-Busayyah. They had been moving during the twenty-fifth in a division wedge, with 1/1 Cavalry Squadron as a covering force. The 1st Brigade was the lead of the division main body, followed by the 2nd Brigade on the west and the 3rd Brigade on the east. Artillery was in the middle of each brigade formation.

When Ron had encountered elements of a brigade of the Iraqi 26th Division, he had left the 3rd Brigade to finish that fight and pushed the rest of the division forward to just outside al-Busayyah. That meant shifting to a formation of two brigades on line, the 2nd on the left and the 1st on the right. The 3rd Brigade, commanded by Colonel Dan Zanini, closed behind the 1st Brigade later that night, after finishing their fight. At 0500 the morning of the twenty-sixth, after refueling, 3rd Brigade bypassed Purple to the east, wheeled ninety degrees to an easterly attack orientation, and set the 1st AD baseline along Phase Line Smash. Later that morning, 1st and 2nd Brigades would join them giving the division the 1/1 CAV out front, followed by the 2nd, 1st, and 3rd Brigades from north to south. It was a hell of a maneuver, fighting and moving without stopping over thirty kilometers of territory. The division reported that on the twenty-fifth they had destroyed 27 armored vehicles, 9 artillery pieces, 48 trucks, 14 air defense systems, and had counted 314 prisoners, although the total was probably double. The 3rd Brigade of the Iraqi 26th Division had ceased to exist; they had overrun it.

Today they would move farther, after the right turn, and would attack into the northern part of the defense that the Tawalkana was trying to set. After the turn, they would have an open flank to the north, if XVIII Corps did not rapidly refuel and turn east as well.

Meanwhile, the 75th Artillery Brigade was not yet back with them from their breach mission. That was troublesome to me, as the 42nd had already linked up with the 3rd AD. I'd have to keep that on my mind and make sure it happened.

Ron and 1st AD would have their hands full today.

Here is how TF 2/70, 1st AD, commanded by Lieutenant Colonel Steve Whitcomb, which consisted of three M1A1 companies and a Bradley com-

---

*Each of these rounds has eighty small bomblets that are released when the shell bursts in the air.

pany, spent the night on the outskirts of al-Busayyah: "TF 2-70 arrived at PL South Carolina [about 120 kilometers into Iraq] after 2130 and began its move into position. I wanted to get ourselves set to kick off the attack so that we would not have to reposition the next morning. The wind howled at fifty-plus knots, the cloud cover was low, and we had driving rain. Vehicles were refueled and limited maintenance pulled. The task force was settled in by 0030. The brigade's direct-support artillery battalion, 2-1 Field Artillery, Iron Deuce, commanded by Lieutenant Colonel Jim Unterseher, fired harassing and interdiction fires all night on al-Busayyah. Multiple-Launched Rocket Systems pounded the town in preparation for the morning attack. The task force S-3 coordinated with the brigade S-3, and at 0100 returned with the attack order. The task force plan was prepared and approved by 0230. We issued a frag order and briefed the plan at 0500."

This task force attacked that morning, 26 February, at BMNT (about 0540) as one of four task forces subordinate to 2nd Brigade and as part of a two-brigade attack (the first brigade had three task forces) on al-Busayyah. When they finished the almost four-hour attack, this task force had destroyed seven tanks, two BRDMs (wheeled infantry carriers), one BMP, and twenty-five trucks, and captured sixteen enemy soldiers. They had no casualties (their medics treated Iraqi wounded later that morning). They then turned right ninety degrees with the rest of 1st AD and pressed on toward the RGFC.

3RD AD was poised to pass around the 2nd ACR to the north and slam due east into the Tawalkana. They had been in a division wedge and had reported taking more than 200 prisoners the night before (in fact, I knew from my meetings with Butch Funk that the totals were much higher than that). Because they had been corps reserve, they had had little enemy contact the first day and a half, and so they would be the most rested of our divisions. When I had given Butch the FRAGPLAN 7 execute order the night before, that had meant, among other things, that they were no longer our reserve, and I was sending them into the heart of the setting Iraqi defense. They were going to be the first division to hit the Tawalkana—which was the right spot in the attack for my freshest division, especially since their nickname was the "Spearhead" Division (Butch Funk had even found the original "Spearhead" emblem from World War II and had it stenciled on the 3rd AD vehicles. In the coming attacks, they would live up to their World War II reputation and then some).

The night before, after a cross-desert journey of 100 kilometers, the 42nd Artillery Brigade, commanded by Colonel Morrie Boyd, had linked up with the 3rd AD with his approximately 600 track and wheeled vehicles. The feat did not surprise me, as I had seen Morrie Boyd in action in a few other leadership situations and knew he could make that happen.

Here is how TF 4/67, 3rd AD, which consisted of three M1A1 companies and a Bradley company, and was commanded by Lieutenant Colonel Tim Reischl, spent the night: "At dark the task force continued to move, now into rain, blowing sand, and cloud cover that reduced visibility to less than fifty meters. The move was complicated by loss of satellite and LORAN coverage from 1800 to 1900 hours; the GPS and LORAN position-locating devices were useless. The task force tightened up the formation and used compasses and a lone inertial navigation device in a Fuchs chemical recon vehicle as guides and continued to move in sector. A halt was called at 2030 hours, and the next few hours were spent collecting vehicles, refueling, and repairing weather damage to the equipment. . . . On 25 February the task force had advanced another eighty-five kilometers. . . . Fifty percent alert for security and four hours of sleep nightly for all personnel was the norm during the move through the desert. The advance was resumed at first light on 26 February, amid reports of enemy movement and contact forward of the brigade."

The nights referred to were 24 and 25 February. This task force was part of the 3rd Brigade, at that time in reserve in the 3rd AD, directly behind the two leading brigades, 1st and 2nd. Third Brigade was part of the 3rd AD attacks the nights of 26 and 27 February.

2ND ACR had spent the remainder of the night in an active horseshoe defense astride an Iraqi main supply route that the regiment called Blacktop. It was actually the IPSA Pipeline Road along Phase Line Smash. They were there in position to stop Iraqi units from using that route out of Kuwait, either to join the Tawalkana's defense against our attack or to escape the theater.

Though I was a little surprised to see that the 2nd ACR had not moved forward during the night to "maintain pressure," I had left the tactics up to Don Holder. Don had used the time for local actions to block the Iraqis and to get orders out appropriate to the change in mission I had given him. Given the terrible weather that had canceled the aviation strikes, and the change in mission, I supported his choice.

Even if they weren't pressing ahead, they weren't sitting on their hands, either. In addition to the action of Company M and the MLRS, they had also had other enemy actions, from an engagement against Iraqi dismounted infantry to heavier action by 2nd Squadron, which had destroyed nine MTLBs and a T-55. Until 0300, most of the action seemed to be in the north of their sector, which is where we were about to attack with the 3rd AD. At a little after 0500 this morning, they reported that 3rd Squadron had turned back an Iraqi recon company attack, destroying twelve vehicles and taking sixty-five prisoners. It had not been an uneventful night for the 2nd ACR.

Today, they were moving out to gain and maintain contact, to pass 3rd AD to their north, and to be prepared at some point to pass the 1st INF through.

★ The reports to Riyadh, meanwhile, lagged well behind many of these actions, and once or twice they were downright wrong. For instance, the official VII Corps situational report that went to Riyadh as of midnight 25 February (almost two hours after these engagements and actions) said, "Units are in hasty defensive positions preparing to attack BMNT 27 Feb"—!!?? And of the British, it said, "The passage of lines through 1ID went extremely smoothly and according to plan. . . . By 1800C [local time] 7th ARMD had cleared the breach. Fourth ARMD began moving at 1325C from staging area and should complete passage NLT [not later than] 260300C" (that is, at 0300 on the twenty-sixth). Because I was out of communications with the corps main CP, the main was out of line-of-sight communications with the units, and many CPs were on the move, I should not have been surprised at this information error.

Friendly information was always behind in the attack. The faster the tempo of the attack, the more behind it was.

There was no mention of the fact that the British had been in contact with the enemy and were fighting, nor of 2nd ACR's activities, nor of the 1st AD attacks by fire on al-Busayyah. It was not surprising, since the VII Corps main relied on reports from subordinate units, and just as the main usually cut off its information at a definite time, subordinate units usually cut off their information at a somewhat earlier time. If they had to get a report to the VII Corps main CP by 2300 (to give the main an hour to prepare for its midnight transmission to Third Army), they would probably cut their own information off at 2200 or earlier. So by the time the consolidated VII Corps report went to Riyadh at 2400, the information from the division CPs was already at least three hours old.

Throw in the weather and interrupted communications from the jump TAC to the main CP, and matters get worse. Worse still, the Third Army liaison officer, Colonel Rock, was stuck with the corps TAC CP in the middle of the 3rd AD sea of vehicles.

In the absence of any kind of automatic electronic update of the maps at each echelon, this is the way it got done. So by the time the CINC got his morning update at around 0700 or so, the information on VII Corps units was almost twelve hours old.

Ironically, the enemy information was more current, while Third Army (and CENTCOM) received information on VII Corps primarily from the fragmented voice reports sent by our CPs through the fragile communications 600 kilometers away. If the staff in Riyadh was relying solely on those reports to post their maps and brief the CINC, then the information gap was beginning to widen considerably.

Mind you, this was not unexpected. All experienced tactical field commanders know and deal with this phenomenon. Even at the edge of the so-called information age, such a lag is simply characteristic of fast-tempo operations and long-distance reporting.

It is only when senior commanders at higher HQ act on old information without validating it that they can get their decisions wrong. Most of them correct the possible misinformation by finding out for themselves—by visiting subordinate commanders or, at a minimum, calling the subordinate unit to verify facts and discuss the situation. I was later to learn that John Yeosock constantly attempted to ensure that the CINC's briefers had current information.

During the four days of the ground war, I never saw the reports that went to Riyadh. I trusted my chief of staff and the troops at the main CP to get it right and to do the best they could with the information they had. As it turned out, their reports were particularly sharp on the enemy situation and on our future plans, but the friendly situation was just as I've described. It is a fact of land warfare that you cannot have perfect knowledge of everything going on, so if you want to act, or think you need to act, then the higher you are, the more imperative it becomes to validate the information if your actions will affect the tactical battle.

The main problem that came out of all this was Riyadh's sense of our movement rate. On the one hand, there seemed to be a perception down there that all the Iraqi forces had been defeated virtually from the get-go (including the RGFC) and that all that was left was to pursue the defeated enemy and mop up (that nothing much was left for the Army and Marines to do but garrison the ruins).

Well, the RGFC was still very much a fighting force, though greatly weakened. And we were not taking our own sweet time in getting ourselves to them—especially considering the lousy weather and the maneuver skills needed to put together a three-division fist. This wasn't some kind of a free-for-all charge, with tanks instead of horses and raised sabers. It was a focused maneuver involving several thousand fighting vehicles to concentrate combat power in a rolling attack against an enemy defending with tanks, BMPs, and artillery.

By this time, I was getting sensitive to movement rates, but unless I got specific orders to the contrary from either Yeosock or Schwarzkopf, I was determined to do what I thought looked right to accomplish my mission at least cost to our troops. Suggestions and innuendoes were not what I needed. Commanders with units in combat and taking casualties get very focused. They are not sensitive to casual comments or sideline suggestions, and it is not a time for subtle mind-reading or communication games. You use very direct language and remove as much ambiguity as possible. *"Here's what I want you to do. I want you here by such and such a time. Do you understand?"* In my own experience, the more tired commanders get, and the more engaged they are in battles, with successes and setbacks and casualties, the more you have to use precise language, commander to commander. So give me a change in orders, I thought, or stay out of the way. Don't second-guess us at 600 kilometers from the fight.

★ My other focus was air. So far, we had had plenty of close air support . . . as much as we wanted, and we got as much as we wanted for the rest of the war. When CAS was able to fly during the previous two days, we had used 98 CAS sorties—38 by 2nd ACR, 44 by 1st INF, and 16 by 1st UK.

We did have two problems with CAS, however: First, the aircraft normally flew at 10,000 feet (for good reason; twice they came below that in the 1st AD sector and they had two aircraft shot down). Because they had to fly so high, though, the low weather ceilings became a problem. Second, because of the sand stirred up in the battles, the irregular nature of what even loosely could be called front lines, and the need to prevent fratricide, when CAS attacked targets in the immediate battle, everything else we were doing had to stop. Since ground commanders, for obvious reasons, found that situation unsatisfactory, they soon pushed CAS and their own organic Army aviation well forward of their ground elements, thereby creating a lethal zone in front of our maneuver units about twenty to forty kilometers deep.

Aside from these relatively minor issues, though, the close air support was there for us. It not only destroyed enemy targets and produced a shock effect on the enemy (who would not have been able to see them at 10,000 feet even if there had been no clouds), it also gave a lift to our troops when they saw their comrades in blue working with them as a team. Before the ground attack on the twenty-fourth, the Iraqis particularly feared the A-10; it never seemed to go away, they told us after the war. "I know you are not into it yet," an A-10 pilot told me before the ground war, "but when you are, we'll be there for you." It was the same kind of air-ground team loyalty I had seen in Vietnam. It's powerful.

That day, we were scheduled to get 146 CAS sorties and 86 AI sorties flown in support of the corps. I decided to allocate the CAS to the three attacking U.S. units—40 percent to 1st AD, and 30 percent each to 3rd AD and 2nd ACR. Since 1st UK also needed CAS, we allocated some for them as well and made appropriate adjustments.

Even though close air support was never a problem, coordination with

CENTAF of the deep attack *beyond* CAS did continue to bother me. Now that we were in our attack maneuver to destroy the RGFC, I wanted to use air to help me isolate the battlefield, to build a wall of fire that would keep the RGFC from organizing a withdrawal. As we turned east, I wanted a death zone in front of the VII Corps that extended from the forward tanks in our sector all the way to the Persian Gulf, and I wanted to synchronize the sorties with our own attacks.

But CENTAF still controlled the sorties beyond the FSCL, and as a consequence, I had very little influence on the choice of targets in my sector, and the same was true for Gary Luck and John Yeosock. Since the theater commander made the rules, I had to assume the theater commander would take care of isolating the RGFC.*

These differences never did get resolved. The result was that I largely ignored the area that CENTAF said they would handle. Even without CAS, there were still the better part of more than 1,000 sorties a day, and CENTAF could do whatever they wanted to with them. So, after the war, when in some accounts the escape of the RGFC was laid at my feet, I had to wonder what CENTAF and the theater commander had been doing with all those sorties and with the other assets at their disposal to isolate the battlefield.

Meanwhile, since the most likely escape routes for Iraqi forces to get out of Kuwaiti theater of operations—north from Basra and north over the crossings of the Euphrates—were now in XVIII Corps's, Third Army's, and CENT-COM's area and out of mine, the focus of my attention had turned due east, toward the Gulf and the RGFC and the other forces forming a defense in depth.

Of course, now that XVIII Corps had the sector to our north, I was very curious about what they would do deep up there, and how that might affect the RGFC units in our sector. I had no information about that, however. At this point in the battle, I was forward about 100 kilometers into Iraq, John Yeosock was 600 kilometers away in Riyadh, and Gary Luck was about 300 kilometers away in XVIII Corps's sector.

So, now that the RGFC was clearly in the Third Army zone (and not solely in the VII Corps zone), how was Third Army going to use the two corps and the deep air to destroy them? And what would CENTCOM do to influence the outcome?

My assumption was that XVIII Corps units would swing east with us that day, and that together we would attack to destroy the RGFC divisions and their

---

*On the afternoon of 27 February, General Schwarzkopf personally moved the FSCL into the Gulf in our sector and north of the Euphrates in XVIII Corps sector. When he did that, he eliminated air's ability to interdict escaping Iraqi units.

subordinate units. I also assumed that the theater commander would isolate the battlefield with air. But these were only assumptions, and besides, at this point I had my hands full commanding VII Corps, without trying to do John Yeosock's or the CINC's job as well.

★ I turned my attention to our combat strength.

To this point in the fight, I was aware of two soldiers KIA and twenty-three soldiers WIA,* and fifty-six soldiers classified as DNBI (disease non-battle injury). Today I knew there would be more. The pace of battle was about to pick up sharply as 2nd ACR and the divisions slammed into the Republican Guard and other units. Today we would see some heavy fighting both close and deep; it would go on into the night and continue tomorrow. We had the corps ready to fight those battles and to accomplish the mission at least cost. But there would be a cost. There always is.

We'd already had some fratricide from our own munitions—duds** from MLRS and Air Force cluster bomblets. It was another difference between attacking and defending. When you are in the defense, it's rare that you would move through an area you have just plastered with air and artillery, so unexploded munitions are usually not a problem. For attackers, it's a different story. Unexploded munitions form de facto antipersonnel minefields through which you must pass, and in fact, the situation in Desert Storm was much worse than most of us had expected. We were surprised at the density of our own stuff on the battlefield. It was a real enemy.

In Vietnam, if we had been about to attack through an area, we would not have put in air strikes with cluster bombs; we didn't want the duds to wound our troops. There, though, our artillery did not have DPICM bomblets, nor did we need the volume of artillery fire that we needed here, and here, as well, we had no control over the types of munitions used by the air. However, we did have control over our own artillery, and despite the risk to our own troops, mission requirements saw us fire lots of DPICM and MLRS bomblets.

Turning to logistics: Our posture there was good. The availability rate for the major end items—that is, tanks, Bradleys, British equipment, and the like—continued to be well into the 90 percentile range, and supplies—including fuel and ammo—also were doing well.

By this time Log Base Nelligen was beginning to be established about sixty

---

*Casualty reporting considerably lags combat action and did in Desert Storm.
**The technical term is unexploded munitions. But they were duds because they did not go off as they were designed to. Even the slightest movement may be enough to set unexploded munitions off. Thus, the saying "Duds can kill."

kilometers inside Iraq. By this afternoon, it would have more than 1.25 million gallons of fuel, ready for issue to our attacking force. Prior to Nelligen, COSCOM (Corps Support Command) had established PTP* Buckeye, just south of the breach, with more than 1.2 million gallons of diesel, to refill the fuel vehicles of the 1st INF, 1st UK, and 2nd ACR (in Desert Storm, our divisions used up to 800,000 gallons or more daily). Both Buckeye and Nelligen were operated in part by troops from the U.S. Army Reserve called up for Desert Storm, and both had been set up on the initiative of Brigadier General Bob McFarlin and his COSCOM commanders as a result of my "no pauses" intent. They proved to be lifesavers in maintaining tempo—and the troops driving the fuel vehicles through the trackless desert in long convoys past sometimes bypassed Iraqi units were real heroes.

As the battle continued, I remained much more sensitive to fuel than to other classes of supply, including ammunition; none of the others ever seemed to be a problem. But as we turned east and got farther away from Log Base Nelligen, we knew that this would be a critical day for fuel.

My orders that morning were simple:

1. Continue to execute FRAGPLAN 7, with 1st INF in place of 1st CAV.
2. Focus the deep air beyond the FSCL that we could influence on the Iraqi 12th AD and Tawalkana Division.
3. Get the corps 11th Aviation Brigade into the fight that night to execute their CONPLAN Saddle about eighty kilometers deep, near what we had named Objective Minden. (Saddle was their contingency plan to support execution of FRAGPLAN 7, while Minden was an area in front of the 1st INF direction of attack where we anticipated the Iraqis would set another line of defense.)

At about 0700, Butch Funk came into the TAC for a chat. I was always glad to see Butch. He rested easy in the saddle and was always upbeat and forward-looking. (Butch was from Montana, and had a Ph.D.; in Vietnam he'd been an aviator, and had later commanded at all levels of armor; he'd also commanded the NTC, and been the III Corps chief of staff.)

His news for me was good. He was moving out with two brigades forward and one in reserve, he said, which were fully coordinated with the 2nd ACR,

---

*Petroleum Transfer Point. There fuel was transferred from larger, less mobile trucks to smaller, more mobile fuelers, which could travel with relative ease through the terrain and keep up with advancing units. Fuel was also placed in huge bladders on the ground as temporary storage, and could refuel returning division fuelers that way.

and would pass around to the north of Don Holder's northern squadron, rather than making a passage of lines. I liked that. It was a fine piece of initiative on the part of both units, and would mean a much swifter attack into the Tawalkana.

Next he had a request for more room to maneuver his division, which, unfortunately, was something that I didn't have to give him. I could do that only if I attacked with two divisions, instead of three, and kept both the 2nd ACR and the 1st INF in reserve, and I did not want to do that. Two divisions might have served for twenty-four hours, but I figured we needed to sustain our attack for at least forty-eight, and maybe longer.

"I can't give you any more room, Butch," I told him. "I need you to pass around the 2nd ACR and take up the fight with the RGFC. Press the fight. We're going to crank up the tempo."

Though he understood, he had to be disappointed that his division was in such a straitjacket. Nonetheless, he said "WILCO," and left to execute.

★ After Butch left, I gave some additional thought to our corps's restricted maneuver space. In order to get the focused combat power we needed and to sustain it at a peak, I had given the divisions a front about thirty to forty kilometers wide. They didn't have much room to maneuver laterally, but lots of depth. Though our VII Corps sector was about as wide as my covering force sector in front of V Corps had been in the Fulda Gap in Germany from 1982 to 1984, our VII Corps sector now had four divisions and an ACR with about 130,000 troops, while the Blackhorse had only had about 10,000 troops. In the relatively flat desert, it was a risk to focus that many troops and that many vehicles, with that kind of combat power, on one corps objective. We all knew that a wrong orientation of a gun tube—or of a unit with many tank gun tubes—meant rounds crossing boundaries, and fratricide. After they're fired, tank rounds cannot be recalled. Minimizing the risk, while maintaining the tempo of the attack, meant keeping my finger tightly on the pulse of the maneuvers. It also meant that in the overall corps rolling attack, some units would be stopped while others were moving. We would have to rely on the boundaries on our maps, GPS, and LORAN to keep our units from running into one another.

Where we did have additional room was in depth. That is why the problems of coordinating our deep attacks with CENTAF were so frustrating. Given control of all the air attacks in our sector from Smash to the Gulf, we could have created a 150-kilometer-deep death zone.

★ At 0800, I called John Yeosock to give him a report on the progress of our maneuver, and to tell him that I expected the corps to be in contact with the

Tawalkana that morning and that I would pass the 1st INF through the 2nd ACR to continue the attack later that day.

After I'd delivered the basic facts, I continued to voice my frustration at the apparent lack of a common picture of the battlefield between Riyadh and the field.

He himself understood what we were trying to do, John explained. As far as he was concerned, we were right where he expected us to be, and in the right posture. However, the CINC had gotten heated up again that morning about the pace of our attack.

When I heard that, my frustration leapt into high gear. I was genuinely frustrated about the command mood swings in Riyadh, and I once again wondered what the hell they knew about what was happening. And the question again entered my mind: What were they doing there about isolating the battlefield? But I did not talk to John about that.

Then, to top it off, John wanted me to order the British to attack south, in order to clear the Wadi al Batin area from the Saudi border north into Kuwait.

I didn't like that idea at all, and I said so strongly. We had come out west so that we could avoid all the mines and obstacles the Iraqis had put up the Wadi. Why in the hell would we go in there now? When John insisted, I asked if I could give the order but not execute it, and then look again later that night, and he okayed that. (After the war I discovered that he was thinking that a British attack south would open a lane for 1st CAV to attack north past the British. That way 1st CAV could still get into the fight in time. It would also ease the logistics flow north in case the war went on around Basra for some time. It was a logical thought.)

Once we had worked our way through that issue, I asked if and when the 1st CAV would be released. Sometime today, John answered. And to us.

John's attitude had undergone a distinct change from the time of my late call to him the night before to today: The night before, we were doing OK. The CINC's intent was for us to conduct a deliberate attack to minimize casualties. Now there was abruptly a greater urgency, a change I was not to understand until long after the war.

In a student monograph at the U.S. Army's War College at Carlisle Barracks, Pennsylvania, Colonel Mike Kendall unraveled some of the knots that had long puzzled me. During the war, Mike had been John's exec, and he kept excellent notes of John's discussions with General Schwarzkopf. The monograph bases its conclusions on these notes.

On 25 February, Kendall writes (as we have already seen): Yeosock "concluded that the CINC was satisfied with the operational pace" of VII Corps, and even "expressed concern with possible fratricide if the pace increased; the

CINC stated that the intent was for deliberate operations with low casualties. In Yeosock's words, the CINC's intent was, 'fighting smart, deliberately, with small casualties, developing the situation, and fixing by fires.' " Yeosock "concluded that the CINC expects 26 February to be a slow day because of weather," and Yeosock "passed this information to the corps commanders during late-night discussions." It was this attitude and guidance that Yeosock had passed to me during the night of the twenty-fifth. But at "0215 hours on 26 February, the CINC was awakened by Brigadier General Neal, his night operations officer, with a report that the Iraqis had ordered their units out of Kuwait City. The CINC talked to CJCS [General Powell] and expressed concern that a cease-fire could occur within two days, resulting in the escape of the RGFC."

In "private conversations with me during the morning," Kendall continues, "General Yeosock discussed the atmosphere of the moment. He understood the CJCS's call to the CINC had caused the intent to change . . ." from, in Yeosock's (unforgettable) words, " 'slow and deliberate to magic units forward.' " This "reflected a CENTCOM lack of appreciation, in Yeosock's view, for the time/distance factors associated with the movement of a heavy corps against enemy forces whose intent was still ambiguous."

In other words, John Yeosock was aware that the CINC's perception had changed after his discussions with Powell. Because the Iraqis seemed to be abandoning Kuwait, which could result in an early cease-fire, Generals Schwarzkopf and Powell now believed that the Army—i.e., VII Corps—would have to speed up the attack against the RGFC, if there was any hope of destroying them.

However, I do not think Schwarzkopf recognized that it was Third Army, not VII Corps alone, attacking the RGFC. CENTCOM had the means and, it seemed to me, the responsibility to seal off the theater and bring land, sea, and air forces together to end it right. That was the time to set it in motion.

And yet, because Yeosock was aware that there was no way to make the corps go faster, and because he was aware that we had a defending enemy in front of us and XVIII Corps with a defense plan, he simply told me to keep pressing the attack.

And that is in fact the only intent I got from John that morning. There was nothing about the CINC's or Colin Powell's concerns. "Press the attack," John told me.*

---

*I should say here that I knew nothing about Colin Powell's wartime conversations with General Schwarzkopf until long after the war. Likewise, I knew nothing about General Schwarzkopf's criticisms of me until February 1992 (the criticisms were later spelled out in his book).

It was like telling me to do something we were already doing. We were already committed east. We were already attacking. I soon forgot the discussion.

We had maneuvered the corps into a posture that would allow us to sustain the intensity of our attack for two to three days, as necessary. That was what we were out here to do . . . or at least, so I thought. CENTCOM could orchestrate the air deep to isolate the RGFC with the Third Army attack on 26 to 28 February. It would also help if Third Army could rapidly turn XVIII Corps east to attack to our north, so there would be a two-corps coordinated attack.

★ Before he left for the main TAC, I said to John Landry, "John, make sure Third Army knows what the hell we are doing out here. Call them yourself. I talk to Yeosock all the time and tell him, but I'm not sure what picture they have."

He assured me he would. John was as good a tactician as I knew and had a great feel for what was going on. If anyone could get our ratings up in Riyadh, he could. And he did make sure that reports of our unit combat actions during the rest of the war were as accurate as they knew them at the Main CP.

WEATHER AND AIR

On 26 February, the rotten weather of the night before did not let up. Most of the day, we had intermittent heavy rain, blowing sand, and low cloud cover—with lucky breaks when we could fly helos and CAS. The weather was local and spotty. Some places would be relatively clear and others would have rain and blowing sand. This was our worst weather day.

It was a real tribute to both Army aviators and USAF CAS pilots that they were able to give us so many air attacks. By unit, 2nd ACR had 48, 1st AD 32, 3rd AD 26, and 1st UK 22, for a total of 128. And more were available if we'd wanted them. CENTAF had originated a system they called "push CAS," whereby they would push sorties of CAS into our area without request. We could then employ them or send them to someone else.

It worked well—just as CAS had worked well for us in the Blackhorse in Vietnam. CAS pilots went way beyond their duty in order to give us their best. Pilots even ignored the 10,000-foot altitude limit, which put them at considerable risk. Our own Apaches were no less selfless—flying day and night in weather that would have grounded us in Germany in peacetime, and with little regard to rest.

0730 En Route to 1st AD

"JAYHAWK 6, this is JAYHAWK 3 OSCAR." I was in my Blackhawk, and this was my TAC FWD calling.

"This is JAYHAWK 6."

"Dragoon reports contact with RGFC, Tawalkana Division." Dragoon was the 2nd ACR.

"Roger, location?"

"PT 528933." That was about the 50 Easting, or right on Phase Line Smash.

"Have them continue to attack."

"WILCO."

I found out later that, at 0713, 3rd Squadron had killed a T-72 at 52 Easting. The regiment read this as first contact with the Tawalkana. Then, at 0754, a T-72 company was sighted at grid line 5299. And the regimental log records, "At 0847 T'kana Div screen at 52 Easting. 2/2 reports all units in contact. 3d sqdn had incoming arty fire. At 0915 3d sqdn reported visibility dropped to less than 1,000 meters. At 0918 3 AD passing to north of 2nd ACR."

That was a big report. It confirmed what I had been expecting. We had them fixed.

What surprised me a bit was the location given; it was about ten kilometers farther west than I had thought. No matter. We were in the RGFC security zone, maybe deeper, and the regiment was doing exactly what a cavalry regiment in front of an attacking corps should be doing in an offensive covering force mission.

Now to keep them attacking while bringing the corps fist together to smash the RGFC. We had been maneuvering the corps for the past day and a half to put ourselves in this position. Now we had them fixed and were going to attack and hit them hard and keep hitting them until they were finished.

0800 1st AD Field Location

As I approached 1st AD, I was thinking that I needed to make clear what I wanted done today and my continued intentions. In light of this 2nd ACR report confirming the location of the Tawalkana, I wanted to be sure that the 1st AD and all my commanders understood my intent: no pauses in front of the RGFC. It was still possible there might be misunderstandings on that score, despite my repeated and forceful orders. I wanted nothing but hard forward momentum into the enemy. It also occurred to me that once 1st AD got to al-Busayyah, they might conclude they'd have time to stop, read the RGFC, get an attack order out, and even change map sheets, while the rest of the corps closed on Phase Line Smash.

So I needed to be crystal clear to Ron.

The battle tempo of VII Corps was my responsibility alone. It made no difference if there were misunderstandings or internal stops because of tactics selected by subordinate commanders—I alone would be accountable, and that was the way it should be. So if I did not like what a unit was doing, then it was my job to tell the commander to do something else, or else to go see him, get an explanation, and then decide.

As Ron Griffith and I met, the fight for al-Busayyah was well under way. Ron was attempting to finish that fight and press forward to Collins, where I had ordered him to be later this morning.

First AD had attacked al-Busayyah with two brigades abreast. On the left was the 2nd Brigade, commanded by Colonel Monty Meigs, with four battalion task forces (three tank and one Bradley). On the right was the 1st Brigade, commanded by Colonel Jim Riley, with three battalion task forces (two Bradley and one tank). Riley's brigade passed to the east of Purple in the early morning and turned ninety degrees east, continuing to attack in the center of the 1st AD and north of 3rd Brigade. Most of the fighting inside al-Busayyah was done by Lieutenant Colonel Mike McGee's 6/6 INF, supported by a combat engineer vehicle that turned many of the buildings to rubble, and killed or buried the commando defenders who refused to surrender. Most of the action fell to the 2nd Brigade.

I greeted Ron with the news of the RGFC contact to his south.

The attack on Purple was going well, he reported. He would finish it with one brigade, and would be in the northern part of Collins with the other two brigades to continue the attack by late morning. That was a little later than I had wanted, but all right, since he'd have two brigades to continue the attack (the second brigade would rejoin the others after Purple was secured). It was not an easy maneuver, but Ron and the 1st AD would do it and form the northern part of our fist.

"Ron," I said, giving him essentially the same order I had given to Butch Funk earlier, "I want you to press the fight all day. Do not stop. Continue the attack all day and into tonight."

Ron was a strong commander and knew what he had to do. He would make it happen.

I returned to the TAC FWD, about thirty kilometers away.

1000 TAC FWD

By now the 3rd AD had moved out to execute its maneuver east around the 2nd ACR and attack the Tawalkana, and so the TAC FWD stood by itself—two lone M577s with their twenty-foot canvas extensions still out the back. A few HMMWVs were scattered nearby, as were several commo trucks for the long-haul comms hookup. The troops were tired. Many had been up all night trying to make the comms work, while at the same time performing the Herculean task of keeping track of both a rapidly developing enemy situation and VII Corps units, all of which were on the move or in combat. I don't know how they did it.

Our main TAC, with all the comms and G-3, still had not arrived, so the comms situation was not good. Good or not, there was not much I could do about it. We did have line-of-sight FM and two TACSAT radios, and a long-haul comm line into the main CP gave us a connection to Riyadh. As for my main TAC, I knew they could feel the situation wherever they were, and were making every effort to get forward out of the tangle of vehicles and get the TAC set to control the RGFC battles.

Even without the comms, I was confident that all the commanders knew my intent and would make it happen. We had been over this situation in war games and were in one another's heads. I trusted them.

At 1000, Tom Rhame showed up. I had told him to come forward and meet me at the TAC. I went over the friendly and enemy situations as I knew them at that point, then told him I wanted him in the fight as soon as possible, and I especially wanted to know when he would be ready to take the fight from the 2nd ACR. I figured that in another four hours or so, the regiment would be at the main positions of the Tawalkana. Based on what Don Holder and I had discussed the day before, I did not think that they would be able to go much farther.

After I took him through these points, Tom gave me a quick SITREP on his progress.

"Boss," he said, "we began movement at 0430, as soon as the British cleared, and we are now moving forward in the worst sandstorm I've ever seen. I had a hell of a time even finding you. Only GPS got me here. Worse, the sector to move in was so narrow that I had to put the division in a column of brigades. We'll be set on Phase Line Hartz before dark." Phase Line Hartz was about twenty kilometers west of Phase Line Smash.

That was much slower than I had expected, but it was real. I knew Tom wasn't making excuses. If he could have gone faster, he would have. To act on what you have, not on what you wish you had, is another acquired skill for commanders. Friction is everywhere. You have to deal with it. You can't wish it away.

"Roger," I replied. "Here's what I want you to do. Continue to move forward to Hartz as fast as you can. Then, from there, close on the rear of the 2nd ACR. Pass through the 2nd ACR, and continue the attack to seize Objective Norfolk. You are the southern division of our corps fist." In other words, I wanted him to attack through the Tawalkana and deep into the Iraqi stiffening defenses. Norfolk was on the other side of the Tawalkana.

"WILCO."

Tom left to make it happen. My orders had to be translated into division orders, and graphics had to be hand-drawn on paper maps (since the original FRAGPLAN 7 had 1st CAV listed on the overlays). And all this had to be done on the move.

★ Meanwhile, I stayed at the TAC FWD. Though the comms there were marginal, I wanted to be near them—our own situation was fluid at the moment and I felt that was the best place to be. I also had the comfort of knowing that in the space of the last three hours, I had talked face-to-face with all of my division commanders, except Rupert Smith, and was confident that they would do what I expected them to do. The weather continued to be bad, with blowing sandstorms that limited visibility to 500 meters, or in some places less.

A call came in from my main CP that an Air Force A-10 (a close-air-support aircraft) had fired on two British Warriors, killing nine British soldiers and wounding ten. Blue on blue—our worst nightmare. Because I was out of comms with Rupert Smith at that point, I thought about flying down to talk it over with him. But then I realized there was really nothing I could do.

Could the British absorb that terrible loss and continue to drive on? I asked myself. I knew Rupert and his troops by now. I knew they would continue despite the shock that temporarily stuns a unit when such a tragedy occurs. It is one of those moments in battle when commanders and soldiers have to reach inside for the steel they know is there, and then go on. It would not be easy for them. It never is. Battle results are final and last forever. They are frozen in time. Dealing with such moments is the reason why you spend a lifetime training, learning, gaining experience. But you never get used to it. Never.

★ Later I got a call from my main CP: at 0930, the 1st CAV had been released from CENTCOM reserve to VII Corps. This was H + 53.5 hours. A few days earlier, Cal Waller had estimated it would take twenty-four to thirty-six hours after H-Hour to get them released. John Yeosock wasn't so optimistic, but he did expect the 1st CAV release sometime that day.

After the war, I learned that the tactical judgments at CENTCOM in Riyadh held that, soon after 0400 on Sunday, 24 February, we were in a state of pursuit. That meant that they were convinced the enemy was defeated and on the run, and that our job was to race after them and catch them. If such was the case, I wonder why it took more than two days to release the theater reserve so that they could take part in the pursuit.

Because of John Yeosock's forecast the night before, I had been anticipating the 1st CAV release. I figured I would tell John Tilelli to back his division out of the Ruqi Pocket (he had two maneuver brigades at that point) and to go west to the breach, then move through it to Lee, a position we had designated eighty kilometers north of the breach and just west of where the 1st INF would pass through the 2nd ACR. Though it would be a move of about 150 kilometers, I estimated that John could be at Lee early the next day if he moved all night. The 1st CAV was well practiced at long unit moves—the best in the theater.

Just as Tom Rhame had done, John Tilelli used his initiative and called me right away—though how he got through to me with the fragile comms was a mystery. It also was a tribute to our signal troops, who were busting their butts trying to keep us in touch with the rest of the corps.

"JAYHAWK 6, PEGASUS 6." PEGASUS 6 was John's call sign. "We've been chopped to VII Corps."

"Roger," I answered, "welcome back to the team." Then I moved quickly to what I had in mind. "I want you to move your division as fast as you can to Area Lee. We are executing FRAGPLAN 7, and have just hit the RGFC. First INF will pass through 2nd ACR later today and attack east. Depending on how our attack goes today and tonight, I will commit you either around to the south of the 1st INF or around to the north of the 1st AD. Too soon to call."

"WILCO. We're on the move."

Even though he had still been under the command of CENTCOM, John had been thinking ahead and monitoring our situation. On their own initiative, he and his commanders had prepared for the two release possibilities: that they would either reinforce the Egyptians or go to us. John had had tentative plans and was ready to execute them, whichever way CENTCOM turned. And so they were soon on the move.

DEVELOPMENTS IN-SECTOR THAT MORNING

True to his earlier assurances, by late morning Ron Griffith had the 1st AD in the northern part of Collins and was attacking east. They had secured Purple and were on line with the 3rd AD to their south. The only disturbing note was that by now units of XVIII Corps were thirty to fifty kilometers behind the 1st AD, leaving Ron an open flank. To Ron's north in that sector were RGFC army-level artillery and three RGFC infantry divisions, reinforced with some armor. In other words, the open flank gave Ron other tactical situations to deal with until the XVIII Corps attack closed the gap. In my own mind, I began to question the feasibility of executing the Third Army two-corps attack plan.

Meanwhile, Butch Funk had maneuvered the 3rd AD into two brigades forward (the 2nd on the left and the 1st on the right), with his 3rd Brigade in reserve. By a little after 0900, he was passing north of the 2nd ACR. Once that was done, Butch turned the 3rd AD sixty degrees east into his FRAGPLAN 7 attack zone, no easy maneuver on the move, and he would soon be in contact with the middle of the Tawalkana's hastily drawn defense.

We now had a giant left hook forming, with 1st AD coming around on the outside, 3rd AD in the center, and 1st INF coming up on the right to take over from 2nd ACR, which was already moving east to initiate the attack. We had formed on the move the most powerful attacking armor force in the history of the U.S. Army, and maybe ever; the tank battle that followed was as big or bigger as any in history. We would hit the forming RGFC defense from south to north with a force the likes of which they had never imagined.

I was later to learn that on his own initiative, Don Holder had linked the 2nd ACR TAC with the 3rd AD TAC, and smoothly coordinated the passage of 3rd AD to 2nd ACR's north. (He also was in contact with the British, on his south, who were pressing their attack aggressively to the east.) Simultaneously he had brought his regiment on line, with three squadrons abreast to get maximum combat power forward. By now his sector was the same as a division's, about thirty kilometers wide. I also later learned that, in order to prevent fratricide, Zanini's 3rd Brigade of 1st AD and Colonel Bob Higgins's 2nd Brigade of 3rd AD had established physical contact and put units together throughout the attack.

All in all, it was an impressive display of teamwork. Much maneuvering of major forces and vehicles in a confined space in a short time. Much initiative at small-unit level. Everyone doing the little things to reduce the friction without being told. A combat team. I was proud of them.

2ND ACR LATE MORNING

Around noon, I flew over to 2nd ACR to see how much farther to push them into the RGFC and to learn if they had found the RGFC's southern flank. I was still thinking of passing 1st INF forward during the daylight, a much easier move than a night passage, and less risky for fratricide. But I also did not want to break the momentum of the attack and give the RGFC any more time to set their defense.

Command judgment time. After 1st INF's all-day move, should I then push them in a night forward passage of lines into the attack? Or should I continue the attack with the 2nd ACR and pass the 1st INF the next day early in the daylight?

In the back of my mind, I also was trying to figure what our next move should be, because if I wanted to continue the momentum, I needed to set it in motion soon. I needed to sustain the regimental attack until the last possible moment, and maybe even reinforce them temporarily. Perhaps another AH-64 battalion from corps? Hard to manage. I had the 11th Aviation Brigade focusing on a deep attack that night. Using them for this purpose would screw that up.

At 1130, while I had still been at the TAC FWD, I had gotten the following SITREP over the radio from Dragoon:

"Regiment along 52 Easting, encountering covering force of Tawalkana Division. Attached infantry and armor. Destroyed tank company by air. Contact with dug-in tanks. Possible cuts in flanks north-south." They knew they had located the southern flank of the Tawalkana when they stopped seeing T-72s and started seeing older equipment.

I asked them then if they needed more AH-64s.

"Request a battalion." The CAV never turned down combat power.

They were already employing a battalion of Apaches from the 1st AD. If they needed another to continue, they might soon be at the end of their attack. I had to go talk to Don.

At 1250, I arrived at the Dragoon TAC and got a quick SITREP from Don Holder and Steve Robinette.

The Iraqis were in defensive positions. There were numerous reports of dug-in tanks, battalion defensive positions, some artillery fire. You could feel the defense beginning to stiffen. They might not be as skillful as they could have been, because we had not given them time to set a defense, but they were not running away, not here, and not in 1st AD or 3rd AD sectors. This was a different enemy from the one we'd encountered in their frontline infantry divisions. Those divisions had put up some fight, but they'd soon cracked when hit by our firepower. These units fought back; they were not surrendering at the rate we had seen earlier.

Now to the question of where to make the passage with the 1st INF.

Tom Rhame had said he would be at Hartz, ready to pass at dark. Hartz was at about 40 Easting (named after the north-south 40 grid line that ran through the battle area), or a little more than ten kilometers west of 52 Easting, where the 2nd ACR now was engaged. Don, Steve, and I estimated that the 2nd ACR could go another ten kilometers before they would be ready for the 1st INF to begin passage, which would make passage at about 60 Easting. That meant the 1st INF would roll into an area about twenty kilometers to the rear, take care of coordination, then move forward and make the passage.

It was a judgment call. Don was reaching out to around 80 Easting with air, and he had a good feel for what was in front of him, and I could see in their faces that they still had a lot of fight left in them. But I had to decide where I thought the regiment would run out of combat power. Sixty Easting was my best judgment at the time. Don agreed.

After I left, I went back to the corps TAC for some quick discussions with Brigadier General Mike Hall about our continuing frustrations with air/ground coordination. Mike promised to see what he could do to help. And just then—finally—the main TAC arrived.

1325 VII Corps TAC FWD

Stan and I immediately huddled so that I could fill him in on the situation and on the orders I had given to the commanders, and then we talked over the best way to deal with placing the main TAC. Because the battle was rapidly moving east, we decided not to set up the TAC here, but instead to move forward to a location closer to where we anticipated the battles would be that night.

Meanwhile, 1st INF's arrival estimates had been pushed back even further, but the 2nd ACR was still doing well; continuing the attack was no problem.

At 1509, according to the 2nd ACR battle log, I called Ron Griffith and ordered him to "move east, gain contact," a reinforcement of the early-morning orders I had given him and a signal to anyone monitoring the command net of my intent for an increased tempo.

At 1513, I got Don on the radio and amended my previous order to him to stop at the 60 Easting. "Recon forward. Gain contact," I told him. I now judged that 60 Easting was too soon, that they'd have to wait too long there for the 1st INF Division. . . . Remember, this was art, not science. You can always change your mind as the situation changes, and especially if you have a unit with the agility and the aggressive young leaders of the 2nd ACR.

With that, it was time to return to the 2nd ACR—who by then had engaged in a major battle with the Tawalkana.

1600 2nd ACR

Though by then the weather was marginal for flying, the high winds and sand-storms, having picked up, I got back to the 2nd ACR after a quick twenty-minute helo flight. I was glad that we had been able to make it back. There was an air of electricity in their TAC. Radios were alive and the noise level was high.

The 2nd ACR TAC was feeling great.

Meanwhile, what was to be called the Battle of 73 Easting was just getting under way. Here is what led up to that battle.

Almost immediately after first light that morning, as 2nd ACR had been nearing the vicinity of 50 Easting, they'd had enemy contact, and the contact had continued all morning. But as they had continued to push their attack east, they'd come into contact with, and destroyed, increasingly stiff defenses until they'd reached 60 Easting. At that point, they found themselves in between the now-destroyed security zone and the main defense of the Tawalkana, which appeared to be set somewhere east of them.

At 1400, regimental S-2 had picked up a report of eighty enemy vehicles moving north along 64 Easting. That gave them some warning that a major enemy force was close, though the precise nature of the enemy force was not clear. And in fact, after I amended my order and they resumed their attack east of 60 Easting, they ran head-on into the main defense of the Tawalkana, which began around 69 Easting. Tanks and BMPs faced them directly.

Because they had had no advance warning, other than the 1400 intelligence report, the 3rd and 2nd Squadrons found themselves in a meeting engagement. Though we knew the approximate locations of major enemy units, the troops on the ground who had to engage in close combat were essentially blind until they actually ran into the enemy. This was not a surprising situation. It happens more than we'd like it to.

Three things helped the 2nd ACR troopers: the boldness of their small-unit leaders, the training of their soldiers, and the weather. They attacked in a sandstorm. The Iraqis never saw what hit them until it was too late.

The Iraqis were in what is called a reverse-slope defense, a tactic they had used successfully against Iran. Taking advantage of the normal 50- to 100-foot undulations in the rolling desert, they had positioned part of a unit on the leading edge of a rise in the desert floor, while the remainder of the unit was concealed on the other side of the rise, or on the reverse slope. Their intent was to lure unsuspecting attackers into believing that they had to contend with only the small unit on the forward slope, but when attackers came over the rise, they would be hit by volley fire from the rest of the Iraqi defenders on the other side. It had been a good tactic against the Iranians. It did not work against our troops.

Though there were few bunkers, as this had been a hastily drawn-up defense, most of their tanks and BMPs were in horseshoe-shaped sand revetments—sand pushed up to about turret level on three sides of the vehicle, with the rear left open, so that the vehicle could back out. Some of the revetments had been dug out, some not. The revetments helped to hide vehicles, but they did nothing to stop the long-rod penetrator of the M1A1 120-mm cannon from destroying the Iraqi tanks. (After the engagement we found many "notches" in the berms indicating where the penetrators had gone through to find their mark.) In other places, when they had time, the Iraqis would erect screens in front of their tanks to deflect HEAT projectiles. But they did not have time for that here. Likewise, though their artillery was in position behind the defense, they also did not have time to get very well coordinated. Behind the defenses by about fifteen kilometers were logistics vehicles.

In addition to the reverse-slope defense, the Iraqis had some other devices. In some places (though not much in this engagement), they placed fifty-five-gallon drums out in front that could be heated at night and used as target reference points for their infrared night-sight equipment. They sometimes also (but not in this engagement) put out burning rubber tires to decoy laser-guided bombs or heat-seeking target designators away from their real targets.

In other words, the Iraqis were doing the best they could. They were not totally immobile, either. At 73 Easting and elsewhere they tried to reposition to meet the attack better, or even to counterattack. Thus, 73 Easting was a running three- to four-hour fight.

On this day, the weather was particularly bad, with visibility in the hundreds of meters, if that. The Iraqis never thought anyone would attack them in that kind of weather.

Captain H. R. McMaster, Troop E commander, offers this account: "I was issuing final instructions to the troop when my tank crested another, almost imperceptible rise. As we came over the top, my gunner, Staff Sergeant Koch, yelled, 'Tanks direct front.' I then saw more of the enemy position that Magee and Lawrence had spotted. In an instant, I counted eight tanks in dug-in positions . . . on the back slope of the ridge . . . so that they could surprise us as we came over the rise and equalize their weapons' capability with ours. We, however, had surprised them. . . . They were close. Koch hit the button on the laser range finder and the display showed 1,420 meters. I yelled, 'Fire, fire sabot.' The enemy tank's turret separated from its hull in a hail of sparks. . . . All the troop's tanks were now in the fight. Eight more T-72s erupted into flames. Enemy tanks and BMPs . . . erupted in innumerable fireballs. The troop was cutting a five-kilometer-wide swath of destruction through the enemy's defense. . . . In twenty-three minutes, Eagle Troop had reduced the enemy position to a spectacular array of burning vehicles."

After he looked at the battle area the next morning, H. R. wrote, "Our Bradleys and tanks destroyed over thirty enemy tanks, approximately twenty personnel carriers and other armored vehicles, and about thirty trucks. The artillery strike had destroyed another thirty-five enemy trucks, large stocks of fuel, ammunition, and other supplies, and several armored vehicles. We were faced with the gruesome sight of a battlefield covered with enemy dead. One of the enemy prisoners claimed to have commanded a Republican Guards mechanized infantry battalion of over nine hundred men, reinforced with thirty-six tanks. He said that forty of the prisoners were all who remained alive. Eagle Troop had taken no casualties."

Captain Joe Sartiano, Troop G commander, gives this report: "The ensuing move due east was based upon north-south grid lines. Ghost and Eagle moved abreast of each other. Eagle had contact at about the 70 Easting, and Ghost continued to move forward. Ghost encountered enemy vehicles dug in at the 73 Easting. After destroying the mass to our front, more enemy vehicles came into our zone, and the troop engaged them with assets available. The scout platoons went 'black' [ran out of ammo] on TOWs at 1800 hrs; each tank fired an average of fourteen rounds (14×9 tanks in troop = 126 tank rounds, each deadly accurate), the mortar section (two SP 4.2-inch mortars) fired 256. Early in the evening, due to the ammunition expenditure, Hawk Company (squadron's tank company) was to relieve Ghost Troop. . . . Battle damage was unknown at the time due to the limited visibility during the day. The troop lost one soldier, Sergeant Nels A. Moller, when an enemy tank hit his Bradley with a main gun round. . . . The troop closed in on its TAA at 0100 and stayed there until 1500. During this time, the troop held a memorial service there for Sergeant Moller."

And Captain Dan Miller, Troop I commander, gives this report: "Enemy tank turrets were hurled skyward as 120-mm sabot rounds ripped through T-55s and T-72s. The fireballs that followed hurled debris 100 feet into the air. Secondary explosions destroyed the vehicles beyond recognition. . . . The annihilation of this Iraqi armor battalion continued when the troop found itself surrounded by burning hulls and exploding ammo bunkers. . . . The report of advancing T-72s from the east told us the battle wasn't over. Seven T-72s had managed to crawl out of their reveted positions and attempt a counterattack. The enemy was advancing at about 2,500 meters to our front. The flash from their gun tubes confirmed they had a fix on us. The scouts were in no position to continue the advance on T-72s. The T-72s' 125-mm main guns splashed short and kicked up a wall of dirt. In seconds they would have us in range and a Bradley was not built for such a hit. Again, the tanks quickly bounced forward. At 2,100 meters, the inferior T-72 didn't stand a chance against the Abrams M1A1. The depleted uranium long-rod penetrators from the sabot round passed through the T-72s like a hot knife through butter. The TOW missiles also had no problem with the range on penetration, and the counterattack was squelched like a match in a cup of water. . . .

We lost one vehicle in the armor battle [I-14] but thankfully the crew . . . all survived. Three of the crew members returned the following day, and the other two were medevaced for burns."

I learned later the extent of the damage the 2nd ACR had inflicted on the Tawalkana. The Battle of 73 Easting, which went on the rest of the afternoon and on and off into the evening until about 2300, proved to be a watershed event for our VII Corps attack and, in the longer run, for the U.S. Army.

For the Army, it was a vindication in microcosm of all our emphasis on tough performance-oriented training; of our investments in combat maneuver centers at NTC and Hohenfels; our quality soldiers, NCOs, and leaders; our leader development; and our great leading-edge equipment. It had taken the U.S. Army almost twenty years to get to the results of 73 Easting. When Troop G commander, Captain Joe Sartiano, was later asked how his troop had been able to do so well their first time in combat, he answered that this hadn't been their first time; he and others in his troop had been in combat before—at the National Training Center.

Here was the ultimate battlefield payoff of performance-oriented training under realistic combat conditions against a world-class opposing force at the National Training Center and at other combat maneuver centers. Later, other actions by units in 1st INF, 1st AD, and 3rd AD would lead many to the same conclusions. "After the OPFOR," a soldier in 1st AD said, "the Medina ain't nothin'."

For VII Corps, the battle was critical because the 2nd ACR not only succeeded in collapsing the security zone of the developing Iraqi defense, but delivered a resounding defeat to the Tawalkana first echelon and kept the Iraqis off balance until we got the 1st INF into the fight. Moreover, as I noted earlier, the 2nd ACR had found a seam between the RGFC defense and its subordinate units. Though there was no physical break in the defense, the identification of a seam or boundary is important. Where two different units have to tie together is a vulnerable area in any defense, and one you always try to attack. This was especially the case where two units had been thrown together as quickly as the Iraqis had done.

While I was at the 2nd ACR TAC, I talked mainly to Lieutenant Colonel Steve Robinette. What I wanted most was to get a picture of the battles, of what they had learned about the Iraqis, of the passage forward of the 1st INF, and how to exploit that seam. My first instincts were to use the 2nd ACR by sending them toward Objective Denver. The 1st CAV was another possibility, since by that time they would be ready in Lee.

My most important thought just then, however, was that the 2nd ACR had found the security zone and collapsed it, and then had severely punished the first-echelon defense of the now formerly elite RGFC.

Some quick considerations led to a decision to pass the 1st INF somewhere between 65 and 75 Easting. I now left the specific location of that to the commanders of the 2nd ACR and the 1st INF to work out. I still wanted the passage to occur in daylight, but at this point that no longer looked possible. (It actually started at around 2200 that night, soon after the Battle of 73 Easting was winding down.)

At 1600, I left the 2nd ACR and flew over to the 3rd AD TAC CP, by now forward in their new zone.

1650 3RD AD TAC CP

At the 3rd AD TAC, I met briefly with both Butch Funk and Ron Griffith. Ron was there to personally coordinate boundaries and flank contact between the divisions. The normal rule of thumb in units is that contact responsibility is from left to right. Since Ron was on the left, he had come to 3rd AD.

Both commanders were concerned about boundary coordination and had gone to great lengths to see to it they were tied in on the flanks. Because they were about to enter a night attack posture, we all were increasingly concerned about fratricide.

Meanwhile, both divisions had done a superb job of making the sharp ninety-degree turn in the trackless desert with no landmarks and only GPS and LORAN to guide them. Complicating navigation was the fact that 1st AD used mainly LORAN while 3rd AD used mainly GPS.

At that point, Butch Funk was right at the beginning of what they would call the Battle of Phase Line Bullet.

Butch told me he had two brigades on line, Colonel Bob Higgins's 2nd in the north and the 1st of Colonel Bill Nash (of recent Bosnia command) in the south. Both brigades had units in contact. At around 69 Easting, their 2nd Brigade reported sixty to seventy T-72s in revetments and began a fight. At 1610, farther south, their CAV squadron (4/7 CAV) and 4-18 INF (1st Brigade) were in a battle from 69 to 73 Easting with T-62s and infantry in bunkers. At 1645, both brigades passed through Phase Line Tangerine. From there and on into the night, they had a series of running tank fights with Iraqi defending units in reverse-slope defenses with T-72s. It confirmed what I already knew. Along 70 to 80 Easting, we had hit a hastily defending RGFC division plus reinforcements. They were fighting back—just as they had fought back against 2nd ACR.

So Butch had a lot to tell me.

Ron Griffith also had a lot to report.

By now, after his ninety-degree turn, he had three brigades on line, with his aviation out front. He was anxious, though, to get his Apache battalion back from the 2nd ACR for his coming fights.

He'd get them back, I told him, after the passage of the 1st INF through the 2nd ACR.

There were several other things on his mind: First, he had left an infantry battalion in al-Busayyah to finish the action there (6/6 INF under command of Lieutenant Colonel Mike McGee). Second, because XVIII Corps units were a good sixty kilometers or so behind him, he now had the open flank. And finally, he told me about a possible fratricide between one of his engineer units and an element of the 3rd ACR that had crossed the boundary into our sector.

All combat elements of 1st AD were by then forty to sixty kilometers east of al-Busayyah. On a number of occasions, the 3rd ACR had been told over the radio by both Griffith and Brigadier General Jay Hendrix, his assistant division commander, that only friendly logistical/support elements were on or near the airfield near al-Busayyah. (At that time, they were highly concerned about seizing this airfield, because it was planned as the center of a log base to be established if combat actions were extended.) The blue-on-blue event resulted in the deaths of two soldiers, while two others were wounded.

That shook me up.

Apparently, Hendrix, with corps approval, had denied the 3rd ACR permission to cross the VII Corps/1st AD boundary. This refusal had been needless, since the battle for al-Busayyah had long been over, and 1st AD was well forward. But it had happened. Ron and I both exploded . . . and then we had to go on the move again.

1700 VII Corps Main TAC

I flew the short distance to the TAC, which was now set up at our new location.

I still had to make the decision on the Big Red One. Should I pass them forward at night or wait until morning? Clearly, the 2nd ACR had not only collapsed the RGFC security zone, they were now attacking main RGFC defenses and had found a seam between the RGFC and another unit. If we were going to sustain the attack momentum the regiment had started, I needed the 1st INF's 348 M1A1s fresh into the fight to replace the 2nd ACR's 123 tanks, which had been fighting most of the day.

But a hastily coordinated night forward passage of lines leading right off the march into a night attack was a tough and highly risky operation. Though we had trained some forward passage in simulations during our BCTP scenarios with the 1st INF in March 1990, I knew that wasn't going to help us a great deal. I also had a certain amount of experience with passages of lines and reliefs in place as a squadron commander in the 3rd ACR, then as commander of the 11th ACR and of the 1st AD. Yet all that had been a rearward passage in the defense.

I weighed the pluses and minuses once again. The risk to our troops was that units could get misoriented in the dark and there could be fratricide. But waiting until morning also was a risk. The RGFC was right in front of us, and it was moving units into the defense. At the same time, continuing the attack with the 2nd ACR posed no less a fratricide risk as making the passage at night—and they had only one-third the combat power of the Big Red One. That meant that the 2nd ACR might run out of combat power in the middle of the RGFC defense. Worse, the Iraqis might be able to set a stronger defense with mines and better-coordinated artillery fires.

I weighed these considerations quickly, then made my decision. I needed the 1st INF combat power attacking the now-stunned defense before they could recover. The Big Red One had the combat power I needed to keep attacking and maybe break through to Highway 8. It was a risk, not a gamble. But it was a risk.

At 1700 hours, I called Tom Rhame and ordered him to pass through the 2nd ACR and attack to seize Norfolk. It was a heavy decision for me: I knew what I was asking the soldiers and leaders to do. Though I did not second-guess myself, I thought about it all night long as I listened to reports of our battles on the radio in the TAC close by.

G + 2 . . . THE REST OF THE THEATER

For the first twenty-four hours after their launch on G-Day, XVIII Corps's powerful 24th MECH had relatively easy going, with virtually no enemy opposition, over hard desert highlands as they thrust north toward Highway 8 and the Euphrates. They had a very long way to go, however. It was roughly 300 kilometers from their line of departure to Highway 8. But then, about sixty kilometers south of the highway, as the terrain sloped down toward the river, the going got considerably rougher. After rains, much of the area turns into nearly impenetrable quagmires. There were rains aplenty.

And so it took the division the better part of the night of 25 February until midday of the twenty-sixth to negotiate "the great dismal bog," as they called it, and begin the final attacks to put an armored cork on the Euphrates River valley.

The division had a number of objectives on or near Highway 8. South and east of the town of an-Nasiriyah were two airfields: Tallil, near the town, and Jalibah, not quite halfway (about seventy-five kilometers) between an-Nasiriyah and Basra. After they got through the bog, the 24th MECH took aim at the two airfields and at the highway itself. Soon the Iraqis were checked and the highway was secure. (Iraqi command to the east seemed unaware of this fact, for later that evening, a convoy of several dozen trucks and tanks on HETs were motoring up the highway—a brigade of the Hammurabi Division, it later turned out, trying to escape to Baghdad. First Brigade soon let the convoy know that the XVIII Corps had slammed the most direct route from Basra to Baghdad in their face.)

By early evening of the twenty-sixth, 2nd Brigade was in position to attack Jalibah, and by early morning of the following day, 197th Brigade had fought another 300 Republican Guard commandos in the vicinity of Tallil Airfield and secured a position southeast of the field. The 24th Division spent the morning of the twenty-seventh attacking the airfield.

Meanwhile, Lieutenant General Gary Luck had been briefed on CONPLAN Ridgeway (Contingency Plan Ridgeway), XVIII Corps's accommodation to the developments to the east. He ordered XVIII Corps to attack east into the Republican Guards. The 24th MECH and the 3rd ACR (under the 24th's operational control) would be the main effort, attacking east along Highway 8 late on the twenty-seventh, while the 101st Airborne would attack into an objective (Thomas) ten kilometers north of Basra with Apache and Cobra helicopters.

XVIII Corps was now prepared to synchronize its operations with VII Corps. But they had to hurry. By late on the twenty-sixth, while XVIII Corps was completing its airfield attacks and mission to interdict Highway 8, VII Corps was at least fifty kilometers farther east than Gary Luck's easternmost unit, and the gap between the two corps was growing.

Over in Kuwait, on the night of 25–26 February, there began an episode that would later turn out to be a major reason why the war ended early.

Late on the evening of the twenty-fifth, the Kuwaiti resistance let the Saudis know that the Iraqi army in Kuwait City appeared to be forming convoys out of military and civilian vehicles. It looked, in other words, as though the Iraqis might be starting to move out. The Saudis communicated this news to CENTCOM, and it was confirmed by a J-STARS aircraft tracking ground movements out of Kuwait City. Something approaching 200 vehicles was tracked moving on the freeway connecting Kuwait City and Basra near the town of al-Jahra, at the western end of the Bay of Kuwait.

Soon CENTAF *had Navy and USAF F-15s attacking these vehicles (only a very few of which were tanks or BMPs) along the highway, on what is known as the Mutlaa Ridge. And during the early-morning hours of 26 February, Air Force and Navy aircraft flew hundreds of sorties against what indeed proved to be the fleeing Iraqi army. The attacks were so successful, the Western media dubbed the highway near al-Jahra "the Highway of Death." Close to 1,500 smashed and burned-out hulks clogged the road to Basra (though loss of life, it became apparent later, was not nearly so great as the press at first reported).*

An article appeared in the 26 February Washington Post, *entitled " 'Like Fish in a Barrel,' U.S. Pilots Say." Another appeared the same day, describing Coalition air attacks as "a combat frenzy." Such views half a world from the action were about to set in motion decisions that would determine whether or not Norman Schwarzkopf's imperative—"Destroy the Republican Guards!"—would in fact be achieved.*

By the afternoon of the twenty-sixth, the 2nd Marine Division, spearheaded by the Army's Tiger Brigade, had captured Mutlaa Ridge and cut off the highway to Basra, while the 1st Marine Division had sealed off the Kuwait International Airport. JFC-E continued north along the coastal highway. Kuwait City was now encircled.

12

NIGHT COMBAT

VII Corps TAC CP Iraq

Activity level was high in the TAC. With enormous effort, they had traveled 150 kilometers to a position just west and north of the 2nd ACR's 73 Easting battle, set up the five M577s, and reestablished the communication channels. By now, the sandstorms, limited visibility, and rain of the late afternoon had passed us by, the wind was relatively calm, and temperatures were in the high forties. We had been in a fight with the RGFC since noon the day before.

I could see the troops were tired. Some were unshaven, and their chemical suits were soiled from three days of continuous wear. Yet everyone was working hard with focus and quiet professionalism. No one was hollering, and everyone had kept his sense of humor, although that was being seriously challenged.

Maps had been put up on the boards, situations quickly posted, field desks set up. Somebody somehow managed to make coffee—using paper towels for filters; real filters had run out long ago.

With the canvas extensions pulled out behind the backed-up M577s, our open work space (minus the vertical extension supports) was roughly twenty by thirty feet, all over uneven sand. The constant moving back and forth of the almost thirty people inside created a constant brown sandy haze under the artificial light.

A total of about 150 troops were at the TAC, and about fifty vehicles, counting our command group tanks and M113s. Located as we were in the middle of the 3rd AD sector, we could see the tracers from the rounds fired against the Iraqi defenses, and could hear the sounds of the battle, the low rumble of outgoing artillery, the boom of tank cannons, and the three-round thuds of 25-mm Bradley chain guns.

The radio crackled with continuous transmissions: "Enemy tanks at . . . Passage of lines beginning . . . T-72s at . . ." One after the other they came in . . . almost too fast to record manually. Each of the five M577s had two or more radios, so the noise was multiplied. Our battle staff NCOs were manning the radios and posting maps and staff officers were on the phone to VII

Corps main CP—now more than 200 kilometers away—so that the main could keep its situation maps current for reports to Riyadh. Main also was giving us the latest intelligence from Third Army. I would want to hear that soon.

A few moments after I returned, I asked Stan to assemble the TAC crew so that I could brief them about what had gone on that day and outline what I had in mind for the next VII Corps maneuver.

"For the next twenty-four to thirty-six hours," I told them, "we are going to drive the corps hard, day and night, to overcome all resistance and to prevent the enemy from withdrawing. We will synchronize our fight, as we always have, but we will crank up the heat. The way home is through the RGFC."

I went on to thank them for their efforts so far, but, I added, we needed to run right through the finish line.

Since we were all getting tired—the TAC crew especially, after they'd moved all night and most of the day—I thought I needed to give us all some motivation, but I also wanted to outline some guidance for a plan of maneuver for the next day. I explained that we had the opportunity to engage in a double envelopment of the Iraqi forces to our front. We could close around them from the south and from the north, and trap the remaining Iraqi forces in our sector. From what we could see of the movement of XVIII Corps units, it did not appear that they would catch up to 1st AD for at least another twenty-four to forty-eight hours, as they had a long way to go after getting north to Highway 8 and then turning east. It was not an easy maneuver for them and one with significant logistics challenges, especially concerning fuel. So we'd better do what we could ourselves, in the time we had, to destroy the remaining Iraqi forces in our sector.

CONVERSATION WITH THE CINC

At around 1830, I called CENTCOM HQ and asked for General Schwarzkopf, but he was not in. They told me he would call back, and we finally connected sometime before 2000.

Since I have no exact notes on this call, I won't try to quote our exact words, but this was the gist:

I'd wondered if he would raise the issue of the speed of our advance, but he didn't, which pleased me. It seemed to indicate that the issue was closed. Otherwise my report was the same kind of SITREP that I normally gave to John Yeosock, though I hoped I could also communicate to him an awareness of the magnificent job our troops were doing under tough battlefield conditions. I just sensed he did not have an appreciation of all they were doing.

During our conversation, the TAC kept working hard. Radios continued to crackle, and people went about their business as I pressed the phone close to my ear so that I could hear. It was a straightforward, commander-to-commander discussion, and throughout he gave every indication that he understood what I was saying. I wanted to lay out what we were doing, and intended to do, and see if he had any further guidance for us, but I also wanted to let the CINC know that, in my judgment, the maneuver John Yeosock wanted to make with the British—to attack them south into the Wadi—was not a good idea. (I wanted General Schwarzkopf to be aware of this issue, because I wanted to use the British as the southern arm of the envelopment instead, and because we needed the CINC's help to get an Army boundary changed. Otherwise I would have simply argued the whole thing out with John Yeosock.)

I began by reporting that we had turned the corps ninety degrees east and were attacking the RGFC, that 1st INF would pass through 2nd ACR that night and form the three-division fist of the corps to destroy the RGFC, that I had Apaches going deep that night, and that we were pressing the fight hard. He seemed to take it all in.

Because I assumed he already had a good picture of our activities, I did not give him details of the fighting, or of the battle damage to the Iraqis. As I discovered after the war, though, his HQ was twelve to twenty-four hours behind in tracking the fight. If I had known that then, I would have filled him in more completely. As it turned out, what the CINC apparently thought we were doing and what we were actually doing were worlds apart.

After I had taken him through our basic situation, I told him about our orders from Third Army to attack south with the British, and told him that instead we should continue east and maybe north with the British, and he agreed. He thought going south was a bad idea as well.

Once again, I thought we understood each other. Again, I discovered after the war that I was wrong. In his autobiography, General Schwarzkopf reports that he heard me say that I was worried about some bypassed Iraqi units that might hit us in the flank and that, in his words, I "wanted them destroyed" before his forces turned to the Republican Guards, and therefore was about to order an attack toward the *south.*

" 'Fred,' I interrupted, 'for chrissakes, don't turn south! Turn *east.* Go after 'em!' "

A few lines later, he chalked it up to understandable pre-battle jitters but what he seemed to be saying was that I intended to have the whole corps attack south before I got around to hitting the Republican Guards. Such a thought couldn't have been further from my mind. I didn't even want to attack south with the *British,* much less the whole corps. How he got that impression is almost unimaginable to me. I was stunned. Here we were in a fist;

we had been attacking relentlessly into the Tawalkana most of the day; we were also less than two hours from an Apache battalion attack about 100 kilometers east of those battles; and all of it heading due east! How could he think I was about to turn south? (That would have meant, for example, turning 1st AD and 3rd AD ninety degrees, which would have put them on the axis on which they had just attacked north for 150 kilometers! Plus, we were about to pass the 1st INF through the 2nd ACR at night!)

Lastly, I told him about our commitment of the 1st CAV in the north and our double-envelopment scheme of maneuver.

After he had listened to it all, he answered, "OK, Fred, good work, and keep it up," or words to that effect. He went on to add some compliments to the corps, yet he also left me with the clear intent that we should continue to press the attack hard . . . as we were in fact doing. Then he added some intelligence that was new to me: the Hammurabi Division were being loaded onto HETs and were trying to escape the theater. We had thought the Hammurabi would be defending in the vicinity of the Medina, or even up north in XVIII Corps sector. Now that they appeared to be trying to get out, my sense of urgency increased. However, since we were then close to 100 kilometers from the Hammurabi, they were split between us and XVIII Corps, and our troops were fully committed at this point, there wasn't much else we could do.

Finally, he thanked me for the update, added a "good luck," and that was it. I got no change in orders from General Schwarzkopf.

It was our only talk during those four days, and afterward, I could not help but conclude that he was satisfied with what we were doing. He also left me with the feeling that we had maybe another forty-eight hours to finish this war. It was nothing he said specifically, yet I put together the new intelligence about the Hammurabi with what we were doing to the Tawalkana, and that told me intuitively that time was running out. I still thought we had enough time to destroy the RGFC in our sector.

I felt I had had a clear meeting of minds with Schwarzkopf, and I chalked up the earlier reports of his displeasure to the usual ups and downs all commanders go through in a fight. We had maneuvered a large complex formation into a physical posture that in my judgment was perfect for the enemy and the mission. I had just finished pumping up the TAC and telling them we would drive this to completion. If ever I felt I had my unit in a position to have a decisive edge over an enemy, this was it.

I called John Yeosock to report the conversation, and my impressions, and also told him that I had raised the issue of the British attacking south, and that the CINC had agreed that it was not a good idea. John then released me from it (in all fairness to John, the mission south had not been a stupid or ill-considered idea: in addition to the possibility of getting the 1st CAV into the fight earlier, he had also been thinking that, by clearing the area, he could more quickly establish a log base in Kuwait that would give us a much faster turn-around time for fuel, in case we and XVIII Corps continued fighting in and around northern Kuwait and near Basra).

ENEMY FORCES

During the day, our main CP had been developing a clear picture of the Iraqis' activities, and after my phone calls, our G-2 folks gave Stan and me a quick intelligence update. This is what they reported at 2030:

"Tawalkana Mech Division and one brigade of the 52nd Armored Division will continue to defend along Phase Line Tangerine until approximately 262100C"—that is, at 2100 on 26 February ("C" stands for local time)—"at which time, Tawalkana Division has been ordered to withdraw to a subsequent defensive position. This subsequent defensive position will probably be reinforced by the remainder of the 52nd Armored Division and possibly the 17th AD. On 26 Feb, elements of the Medina Division moved out of revetments to orient forces to the SW. Similarly, up to 9 bns of the Hammurabi Division moved to the NE about 10–20 kilometers in positions to defend the Rumaila oil fields." The oil fields were about thirty kilometers west and southwest of Basra, running north to south about ten kilometers; they were about half in our sector and half in XVIII Corps's. We thought they might be impassable for heavy tracked vehicles (it turned out we were wrong). "Other Iraqi forces in Kuwait will continue to withdraw to the north toward the Iraqi border. The Iraqi goal will be to delay VII Corps and MARCENT* along successive defensive lines, while withdrawing the bulk of his armored and mechanized units into Iraq. Iraqi forces, particularly RGFC units, will remain capable of maintaining a defense in depth and conducting up to brigade-sized counterattacks. He will become increasingly vulnerable to Coalition air strikes as he withdraws from prepared defensive positions, as well as to rapid and coordinated fires and maneuvers."

This statement was later included in the report that went to Third Army from our VII Corps main CP. What it meant to me was that the Iraqi strategic reserves were attempting to form a series of defensive lines between us and Highway 8, so that they could continue to move their forces out of Kuwait, that the RGFC was the HQ directing this defense, and that the Tawalkana and Medina RGFC divisions were still immediately in front of VII Corps.

The Tawalkana had their three brigades on line from north to south ap-

---

*We thought MARCENT was then attacking north, roughly on Highway 8. In fact, they had actually reached the end of their attack.

proximately along the 70 north/south grid line. These three brigades were the 29th MECH, the 9th Armored, and the 18th MECH. South of the 18th MECH was the 37th Armored Brigade of the Iraqi 12th Armored Division. Earlier in the night of 24–25 February, the RGFC had deployed the 50th Armored Brigade, with close to ninety tanks, in a security zone in front of this defensive line. That force had been decisively defeated by the 2nd ACR the day before, 25 February. Behind the Tawalkana defense were brigades of both the 10th and 12th Iraqi Armored Divisions. The Medina, meanwhile, was moving two armored brigades west, the 14th and the 2nd, to defend a theater logistics site just to the east of the 70 north/south grid line. They were being joined by two unidentified armored brigades moving up from the south. At this time, the Iraqis still had the ability to reposition brigade-sized forces and were doing so. The Adnan Division also appeared to be sending a brigade south to help the Tawalkana and Medina Divisions defend.

For some time, it had not been clear to me either how much of the Hammurabi was in VII Corps's sector or how much they would become involved in this forming defense, and that was still the case. Our VII Corps estimate was that they were moving out of positions to defend the Rumaila oil fields and would move forward to defend if the Medina could not hold our attack. The 17th Armored also was part of the defense. (Earlier, in chapter 1, we mentioned that some Iraqi units had been wrongly identified. That was true in this area. Thus, the 52nd Division was actually the 12th Armored.)

Clearly the RGFC were attempting to defend, and were positioning forces to do so. Though I did not know their precise strength at this time, I believed it was closer to 75 percent than 50 percent. Not only were they repositioning units, they were also attempting fairly crafty defensive tactics, such as the reverse-slope defense mentioned earlier.

I put the intel update together with the information my commanders had given me during my battlefield visits earlier that day, and they matched. From there my commander's running estimate led me to these conclusions:

I knew we had the Iraqi forces fixed. We had also surprised them with the speed and direction of our attack, and they were now scrambling to reorient and to thicken the defense. I needed to continue to press the corps attack so that the Iraqis could not get any more set than they already were. We had opened up a window of vulnerability in the Iraqi defense, and we needed to complete our mission before that window closed.

As for us, it was clear to me again that we had the right forces in the right combination at the right place at the right time. The decision to mass into a three-division fist, the changes in tempo, the rolling attack—all were proving correct.

By turning east into the forming RGFC defense, we also had opened an attack lane to our north for XVIII Corps. We had not pinched them out and tried to do it all ourselves—their combat power would also be in the fight. It would make the complete destruction of the RGFC a Third Army, not just a VII Corps, fight, and it would also facilitate the ground/air coordination needed to finish it off, since both commands were in Riyadh. Because CENT-COM, Third Army, and CENTAF were co-located in Riyadh, all the command elements needed to isolate and destroy Iraqi forces in the Kuwaiti theater were in one place.

In the air, CENTAF had all the aircraft necessary to seal off the escape routes. On the ground, Gary Luck and I had the combat power to completely destroy all Iraqi forces in the Third Army zone. It was all coming together, just as we had discussed in our war games. Now we just had to complete the execution.

It would not be easy. For the soldiers and small-unit commanders conducting the attacks, it would turn out to be a night we would all remember.

PERSONNEL AND LOGISTICS

Once I had looked over the enemy and friendly situations, I asked for a quick report on our logistics status. Because I did not have a staff section to track logistics at the TAC CP, I was not current on our situation, and did not have a good feel for our fuel posture.

I did know I had a talented group of logisticians who could do the fuel arithmetic as well as I could. An M1A1 tank uses about fifty gallons an hour. You refuel about every eight hours or less, or at every opportunity. The tank's turbine engine burns as much idling as it does rolling at forty miles per hour. Divisions consume about 600,000 to 800,000 gallons of fuel a day. We were rapidly moving away from our supply points, so the turnaround time for returning trucks was stretching out to as long as twenty-four hours, or over 200 kilometers. But with Nelligen now established, I thought that we were still all right.

Though fuel availability in the battle area was becoming increasingly short, the percentage availability of our major combat systems was still in the high eighties to low nineties—even after the 150-kilometer move and some combat.

The equipment losses did not bother me—the soldier losses did. Our casualties for the first two days were fourteen KIA and forty-six WIA. That was not just a number to me. These were individual soldiers who had come here to do their duty. I did not agonize over these last reports, but I paused a minute and thought about those soldiers and what we needed to do over the next hours and days to continue to get our mission done at least cost. You feel it all, and then you decide and go on.

DOUBLE ENVELOPMENT

Earlier that afternoon, even while paying attention to the current battles, I had been intermittently thinking about the next move. How would we end it?

What I knew about the Iraqis that afternoon was this: The RGFC were defending and getting units into position in a hurry. We had clearly attacked into the Tawalkana in a defensive alignment from south to north. They had also attempted to put a security force of tanks and BMPs another ten to fifteen kilometers west of their main line of defense. Artillery was present, as well as mortars, but the Iraqis did not have time to coordinate their artillery fires very well with the defense, or to set any barriers in place, such as mines or antitank ditches. To the south of those three defending Tawalkana brigades was a brigade of the 12th Armored Division. The remainder of the 12th and the 10th Armored Divisions seemed to be in depth behind the Tawalkana. To the north of the Tawalkana and just slightly to the east, the Medina appeared to be relocating west from their earlier positions to tie in with the Tawalkana to their south. Augmenting the Medina defense was a brigade of the Adnan Division, which had come south to tie in with the northern brigade. Behind the Medina was the Hammurabi, whose intentions at that point I could only guess. They could stay and help the Tawalkana and Medina fight or leave. As far as I could determine, those were their only two options. I also did not know how much of the Hammurabi was still in the VII Corps sector.

Our own situation was clear to me. We would soon have three U.S. divisions on line attacking east. The 2nd ACR had found the southern seam between the RGFC and other units (it was between the southern brigade of the Tawalkana and the 37th Brigade of the 12th Armored Division). The XVIII Corps was about a day behind us now in the north after 1st AD had turned east. I figured we had two complete RGFC divisions in our sector (Tawalkana and Medina), one brigade of the Adnan, and probably one or two brigades of the Hammurabi, plus other divisions by now subordinated to the RGFC. Two complete RGFC infantry divisions were in the XVIII Corps sector now, as well as one or two brigades of the Hammurabi, plus an unknown amount of artillery.

The Iraqis had only two options: to fight us or attempt to escape. Our options were greater, but the two key factors were these: we had to choose how to cut off the RGFC in our sector, and we had to choose how to destroy them.

Destroying them meant keeping up the relentless series of attacks, and I felt confident we had the combat power for that. Choosing how to cut them off was going to be tougher.

Our sector now ran due east toward the Kuwaiti border and extended to the Gulf. The northern line ran directly east to west, from al-Busayyah to the coast, passing just north of Safwan. It did not include Basra, or the crossings over the Euphrates north of the east-west portion of Highway 8. The southern line ran from the Kuwait/Iraq border to about fifteen kilometers north of Kuwait City across the north-south portion of Highway 8 and to the Gulf.

I considered the tactical means available. I did not think we could cut off the RGFC with attack helicopters alone, and my success in getting fixed-wing air to hit our targets deep had been poor. So I figured we'd have to use maneuver forces. How to do that? To the south of our sector, the British were rapidly closing on their Objective Waterloo. Once they reached that, they would run out of maneuver space east of the Wadi al Batin (since the area east of the Wadi was in the Egyptian sector). However, 1st CAV would be in area Lee behind the 1st INF attack by early the next morning.

That afternoon the answer jumped off the map. We had the maneuver forces for a double envelopment. This is a complex maneuver involving a direct attack at the enemy's strength, to keep the enemy fixed, while other forces go around as "enveloping arms" on each side and link up behind the enemy's main formation. The result is an entrapped enemy force. It is a rare maneuver, because conditions for its execution don't happen that often, but here it was clearly within our grasp. Trapping a significant part of RGFC forces in a vise would be a perfect way to end our mission.

This maneuver also dealt with questions that had occurred to me by then about whether XVIII Corps would have time to execute the Third Army–directed maneuver to attack to our north and pin the Iraqi forces against us. If XVIII Corps could attack across the north while we came up from the south and applied pressure in the center, that would be the best use of available Third Army forces—but if time ran out before XVIII Corps could attack into the RGFC, at least with the double envelopment we would have destroyed or captured all the Iraqi forces in our sector.

Because I had been more certain earlier that there would be a Third Army envelopment, using XVIII Corps as the northern arm of the enveloping force, my instinct then had been to send the 1st CAV around the south of the 1st INF, then north to Objective Denver, while continuing to send the British due east to interdict Highway 8, north of Kuwait City. (Also, since the British had been so successful that they had run out of maneuver space, I needed to get a boundary adjustment from Third Army to give them room.) Late in the morning, I called Third Army and hastily sketched that scheme to John

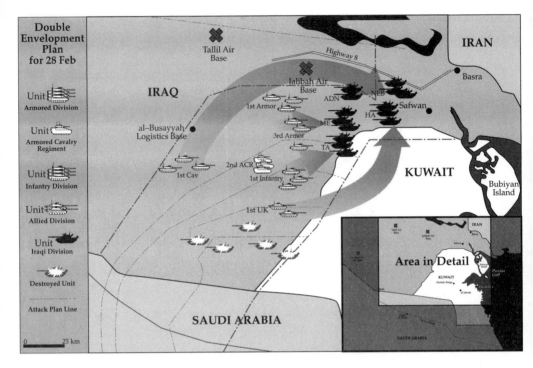

On 26 February, while current battles raged, General Franks was also thinking about how to shape the battles he wanted VII Corps to fight twenty-four to forty-eight hours in the future. With confirmed locations and intentions of RGFC units, he began shaping the plan for a double envelopment, initially intending to use the 1st (UK) Armor as the southern pincer and the recently released and on-the-move 1st CAV as the northern pincer.

Yeosock's XO, Lieutenant Colonel Mike Kendall, who passed it on to John.

In the early afternoon, when I talked to John Yeosock about my intention for 1st CAV, he told me he did not like the idea of sending them around 1st INF toward Denver, since, from what he could see, the bulk of the RGFC was farther north, and that was our objective. Since at that time I had figured XVIII Corps would be attacking in the north, I continued to argue for my own proposal. I figured that we had enough combat power up there and that I could get the 1st CAV around the south faster to close the door on the RGFC.

For a time, each of us argued the merits of each point of view in a good commander-to-commander discussion. Then, after we had both expressed our views, John still wanted me to weight the attack to the north, so I had said, "OK, I'll send them around the north of the 1st AD." John had a better picture of what XVIII Corps was doing and of whether they could close the gap in the north, and he probably had a better feel from the CINC about war termination, although at that time neither of us discussed it.

(What would John and I have decided if we had known on the afternoon of the twenty-sixth that it would end at 0800 on the twenty-eighth? Knowing now what I did not know then, I probably should have gone with my instincts and sent the 1st CAV attacking east from Lee, then north, early on the morning of the twenty-seventh, rather than sending them north, to the rear of 1st AD. However, since neither John nor I did know then, going north was then the right decision, especially in light of the growing gap between us and XVIII Corps.)

Once it was clear that 1st CAV would be the northern arm of our envelopment, I picked a new area for the 1st CAV north of Lee by about another eighty to one hundred kilometers, called it Horse, and ordered Tilelli to move his division there to be committed east and north of 1st AD. Though Horse was then occupied by 1st AD, we anticipated that by the time the 1st CAV got there, the 1st AD attack would have moved east and it would be vacant.

After I'd determined that move, my attention turned to the southern arm of the envelopment. My choice for that was the British, and later that day, before I talked with the CINC and Yeosock, I gave that planning contingency to Rupert Smith (at the same time, I told him he did not have to execute the mission south back down the Wadi). The series of planning contingencies we were giving the small British tactical staff severely strapped their capabilities—even as they were busy directing the battles toward Waterloo. In fact, I'm sure they thought their corps commander had them planning too much. And they were right; I did ask a lot of them.

So the double envelopment was going to be our next major maneuver. Most of the orders would be oral, and there would be some hastily drawn boundaries (the Germans call all of this *auftragstaktik*, or mission-type orders—that is, orders that veteran units can handle and that our doctrine tells us to use). These would be all we would need. By now we were a veteran corps.

PLANNING AND FIGHTING

I turned my attention back to fighting VII Corps and to the next day.

We had to do three things almost simultaneously at the TAC: to press the current developing attack; set the next move in motion; and keep Riyadh informed. After the short meeting with the TAC staff and my phone call with the CINC, I huddled with G-3 Stan Cherrie for further details.

At the 9 February briefing in Riyadh, Defense Secretary Dick Cheney had asked, "How will it all end?" Now—at least in our sector of attack—I could see an emerging opportunity to answer the Secretary's question. We now had a final plan to close off the RGFC and destroy them.

Here is what we figured at that point: The 1st CAV, our northern envelopment arm, would attack east and just to the north of the 1st AD toward Objective Raleigh, which was where we thought the Hammurabi Division was located. The British, our southern envelopment arm, would attack northeast from their current location near their Objective Waterloo to Objective Denver. The two arms would link up behind the surrounded Iraqi forces near or just to the north of the town of Safwan, which was itself just north of the Iraq-Kuwait border on Highway 8. In between these two divisions would be the pressure force—the 1st AD, 3rd AD, and 1st INF. They would all attack due east toward Objective Denver. Finally, I would have the 2nd ACR in reserve, possibly to attack south of the 1st INF and toward Denver, inside the British. Though the concept seemed to make sense on the surface, I knew the real challenge would be getting the 1st CAV fitted in north of the 1st AD.

At around 2000, Stan Cherrie communicated our concept to the main CP for some further planning, while we set about to examine quickly its overall feasibility. Though Third Army was already well aware of what we had planned by that time, John Landry sent the double-envelopment scheme of maneuver to Third Army as part of the midnight VII Corps official situation report. Thus the CENTCOM staff had that report to include in General Schwarzkopf's 27 February morning update, but whether the update included mention of the double envelopment—or if in fact he ever learned of it—I do not know.

At a little past midnight, the Third Army liaison, Colonel Dick Rock, reported to Third Army that we were planning a double envelopment. And at his 0615 report on 27 February, he added details on the identification of units and location of objectives.

REPORTS

By 2100 the main attack was well under way.

When the 2nd ACR attacked through the RGFC security zone into a brigade of the Tawalkana, the orientation of the Iraqi units was either west toward us, or else south and southeast, as though they still expected the attack to come north up Wadi al Batin. North of the 2nd ACR, the 3rd AD had also begun to hit more and more Iraqi units, and by late afternoon had hit what appeared to be another brigade of the Tawalkana. To their north, lead elements of the 1st AD had also hit Iraqi armored and mechanized units. Although we were still getting prisoners, most Iraqi units were in defensive positions and fighting back. So far it appeared that both the direction and power of our attack had them surprised. We had the Tawalkana Division fixed, and possibly the Medina, as well as elements of other Iraqi divisions that had been incorporated into their building defense. I wanted to keep it that way by continuing the attack all night and all the next day . . . and for as long as necessary to accomplish our mission. And I wanted to press the attack both close and deep in order to keep the Iraqis from getting set, and permitting them to better coordinate their artillery fires or to emplace minefields.

While all this was happening, the British had been highly successful. While protecting our advancing corps right flank, they had defeated the 52nd Iraqi Division and overrun the HQ of most of the defending Iraqi frontline infantry divisions.

Thus, by late afternoon of 26 February, we had three divisions and a cavalry regiment in direct contact with the enemy. North to south: 1st AD, 3rd AD, 2nd ACR, and 1 UK. The 1st INF Division had been moving since 0430, and would pass forward through the 2nd ACR later that evening to give us four divisions on line in a night attack.

By this time, with so many units engaged in combat, there were more events to report in the battle than time to report them. The best we could do for our higher HQ was to summarize our plans and the enemy actions. It was just not possible to attempt the sort of specific detailed reporting of the battle at the corps level that one would normally get at a lower echelon, such as a battalion or a brigade.

The reporting did have to get done, though, and there we were, beset with problems, none of them having to do with talent or motivation.

The biggest problem, ironically, was our success on the battlefield. At every level, commanders and soldiers were more focused on fighting their units than on reporting, and so the latter suffered. That's normal in heavy fighting, of course—it was the same in Vietnam—and in fact, the heavier the fight and the faster the pace, the greater the lag time, but still it was a problem.

Another one was the constant movement of the command posts. Reports are assembled in the CPs and passed on, and maps kept current—yet everyone's command posts kept moving. They'd be set up for a short time, then they'd be gone again.

To control the 1st AD movement and early contacts, Ron Griffith had set up what was essentially a rolling TAC CP—a group of vehicles directly behind the attacking brigades, and which almost constantly moved along with them (and thus equipped only with line-of-sight communications). Butch Funk did the same thing. Both Griffith and Funk moved about the battlefield either in ground vehicles or helicopters. Beginning with the night attack on the twenty-sixth Tom Rhame commanded his division in a tank near the front. Don Holder also was up front with a small command group of vehicles as his 2nd

ACR TAC and TOC moved during the day. Though the main CP of the Big Red One began moving north through the breach, the division not only ran away from them, the main never again set up and functioned through the rest of the war. Their reports went to their TAC CP, which had only line-of-sight comms. Meanwhile, most of my commanders directed the fight by radio when they could, but very often, because there was so much coordination involved, they were out of their CPs and up front, commander to commander.

In short, with all of this moving about, the staff officers and NCOs charged with writing things down and reporting to higher HQ could catch only bits and fragments . . . and then only when they themselves were not moving. When the CPs displaced, the staffs missed the part of the fight that went on while they were in transit. If the fight develops fast, the staffs can miss a lot in a short time.

Even today, battle logs are handwritten accounts of unit activities taken down from what the transcriber hears on the radio. These transcribers are normally accurate, but you can't report what you don't hear. In addition, if a radio operator uses a headset, then the transcriber cannot eavesdrop on what the operator's hearing, and so pick up potentially useful information. Finally, there are no electronic recording devices in CPs; and the review and supervision of the transcriber is sometimes haphazard. In other words, it was not a good system and we should get it fixed—but it was the one we were using in Desert Storm.

By the evening of 26 February, my VII Corps main CP in Saudi Arabia was both far out of line-of-sight FM radio range (and thus unable to hear the reports of the fight over the corps FM command net) and far from the sounds and sights we were seeing and hearing ourselves. It was not their fault. I told the CP to stay there, because it was our nerve center, and to break it down, move it more than 100 kilometers, and set it up again would have taken longer than the whole four days of the war.

However, their immobility, combined with our mobility, didn't help the accuracy or timeliness of their reports on the current friendly situation.

The VII Corps SITREP that went to Third Army as of midnight 26 February from my main CP illustrates it:

"2nd ACR attacked in zone to fix elements of the Tawalkana Division. Regiment attacked covering forces of an armored BDE and destroyed enemy T-72s and BMPs vicinity PT4797." Phase Line Smash: "One tank and nine MTLBs were destroyed; 1,300 EPWs were captured. During attacks on 26 Feb, 2nd ACR fought one brigade of the Tawalkana Division and elements of two bde's of the 12 AD, the 46th and 50th Bde's."

Now, considering the circumstances, that is not a bad report, but it is far from complete and scarcely conveys the intensity of the fighting by the 2nd ACR during the Battle of 73 Easting.

In the same SITREP, the 1st AD was reported to have attacked one battalion of the Tawalkana and destroyed more than 30 tanks and 10 to 15 other vehicles, while the 3rd AD was reported to have run into stiff resistance along the 71 north/south grid line, destroyed numerous armored vehicles with direct and indirect fires, and captured 130 EPWs.

In fact, that day the 1st AD destroyed 112 tanks, 82 APCs, 2 artillery pieces, 94 trucks, 2 ADA systems, and captured another 545 EPWs, while the 3rd AD "experienced its heaviest contact of the war and effectively fought both close and deep operations simultaneously. 1st and 2nd Bde engaged forces of the Tawalkana Division along the FLOT, while 2-227 the attack helicopter Bn (AH-64), and 2/6 Cavalry (AH-64), supported by Air Force stealth fighters (F-117A) and A-10s, engaged forces approximately 10–15 kilometers further east." Extracts of their battle logs (some of this was reconstructed at AARs from a number of unit battle logs) showed:

260900: Hundreds of enemy surrendering in trenches at NT815910.
260900: 2nd Brigade engaging MTLBs with close air support in the vicinity of PT690245.
261043: 5 T-72s engaged by CAB (combat aviation brigade).
261610: 4/7 CAV moving across 63 north/south grid, contact with dismounts in trench line; artillery impact PT7310; EPW collection point PU366177; 4/18 INF engaged from bunkers with T-62s at AT698485.
261638: 2nd Brigade, 5/3 ADA taking hostile fire in the vicinity of Phase Line Bullet (just east of Smash).
261702: 3/5 CAV engaging T-72s at PU 722136
261840: 1st Brigade at 713139; damage assessment 23 T-72s, APCs, and trucks. 261927: 4/32 AR reports 1 Bradley hit. 2 KIAs, 3 WIAs; being counterattacked by T-72s.

What these reports indicate is that 3rd AD battles were continuous all day both close and deep. By 2400 they had destroyed upwards of at least two battalions of Iraqi tanks (more than 100 tanks) and other vehicles, and in so doing had cracked the middle of the Tawalkana defense. Their combat was continuous throughout the twenty-sixth into the night and early-morning hours of the twenty-seventh. I knew most of this personally because I often visited with Butch Funk and saw it with my own eyes.

Yet little of the intensity of these and other battles was getting reported to Third Army or CENTCOM. For instance, as the above actions were happening, Colonel Kendall at Third Army reported (accurately reflecting what was known in Riyadh), "At the 1700 hours operational update [26 February], Yeosock announced that the mission was to gain and maintain contact with the RGFC and for the G-3 to ensure that the CENTCOM briefers stressed that ARCENT was still conducting a movement to contact . . . and preparing for a coordinated attack. Just before he departed for the CINC's 1900 hours update, Yeosock talked with General Franks for a situation update. Franks reported that the corps would be moving and fighting all night but that enemy units and logistics bases were being bypassed. He did not know if the 1st Cavalry Division would arrive in time for the battle." We definitely were not in a movement to contact at that time. We were in a series of continuous hasty attacks. From all I have read since the war, it seems that the impression in Riyadh was that the RGFC battle would really start on the twenty-seventh—but in fact we had been in the RGFC attack since noon on the twenty-fifth, and especially since about 0900 on the twenty-sixth, as 3rd AD and 1st AD came on line and I pushed 2nd ACR east.

I did make a short phone call to John Yeosock to give him an accurate description of our maneuvers and to inform him that we were in contact with the RGFC, but I did not go into details about the fighting or the enemy destroyed (I didn't know many of them myself at the time). For that reason, and because other reports were so incomplete at that time, neither CENTCOM nor the Third Army staffs who posted the maps and made up the 1900 briefing for General Schwarzkopf had any details of the 2nd ACR actions at 73 Easting, or of the 1st AD, the 3rd AD, and British actions. Since General Schwarzkopf never called me directly or came out to see for himself, he did not have a complete picture of the VII Corps situation.

I was not to find out how flawed that picture was until much later.

VII CORPS ATTACK

Once I had completed the forecasting and had put the next day's operation into motion, I turned my attention back to our current attack.

You always plan ahead to maintain tempo, but you also have to adjust your forecasted plan—depending on how your current operation works out—so that you can meld the two together and continue relatively smoothly. The two are never a perfect fit. This would be no exception.

Three things were on my mind about the current attack:

First, I wanted to maintain its momentum, yet I also wanted all my commanders to be aware of the rising risk of fratricide as we maneuvered three

U.S. armored divisions abreast to conduct a night attack. I had seen and talked to all the commanders and was confident they would use whatever tactics they thought necessary in their sector. Ron Griffith chose to put all three brigades on line and simultaneously attack both close and deep. Butch Funk, while attacking close and deep at the same time, had two brigades forward and one back, then passed his third brigade forward through a leading brigade to sustain his momentum. Tom Rhame attacked through the 2nd ACR with two brigades forward and one back. Though we monitored the direction of attack of each of the units at the TAC, the units themselves had to make the flank coordination necessary to ensure that no unit strayed or fired across boundaries. It was an enormous task, and it was carried out with the greatest skill and discipline. Although all the commanders made adjustments on their own initiative to ensure that we avoided fratricide, they would not all be successful.

Second, I wanted to pass the 1st INF through the 2nd ACR. The 2nd ACR was skillful in these maneuvers and would take steps to ensure a clean handoff. Their coordination with the 1st INF, and the 1st INF's execution of the maneuver, would be flat well done and a tribute to them all. It was only later that I learned of the initiative at all levels in both units that had made it happen.

The third thing on my mind was our aviation deep attack. I thought there was a good chance we would need two that night. To give us time for them, the first was scheduled to go at 2100, which would make for some complications, since they would be flying out over the 2nd ACR and then returning over the 1st INF. To simplify, we could have waited until the passage of the two units was complete, but that would have eliminated the chance to attack again if it was necessary. It was a risk, but it was a risk worth taking.

The FSCL got in the way of our deep attack—it had been drawn just east of the aviation attack objective of Minden. My air coordination cell informed me F-111s would be attacking the escaping Iraqi forces to the east of the FSCL and along Highway 8. It would have resulted in more damage to Iraqi forces, and fewer Iraqi forces would ultimately have escaped, if we could have adjusted the FSCL, changed that air tasking to move the F-111s to another target, and attacked along Highway 8 with our own Apaches. But making those changes was not possible in the time we had.

By now VII Corps had been attacking for a little more than fifty hours without pause. We had gone about 150 kilometers and our attack was about twenty-four hours ahead of all the prewar projections of movement. Third Army's estimate had had us ready to attack the RGFC at H+74 hours. We were well ahead of that.

DEEP ATTACK

What every commander of an attacking corps tries to do is to fight both close and deep at the same time. The effect is to hit the enemy simultaneously throughout the depths of his formations. His deep forces do not have time to set up a coherent defense to await your fast-closing direct-fire tank and infantry forces. This destroys him physically. These attacks give him so many problems to deal with simultaneously that he cannot handle them. This destroys him mentally as well. The result of this dual breakdown is that his defense starts to lose coherence. Soon you have a disorganized enemy, fixed in position, fighting you in small units without any overall tied-together plan. We were beginning to achieve this effect on the Iraqis on the night of 26 February.

Because the 2nd ACR had found the southern flank of the Tawalkana's three-brigade defense, I thought that if we hit them close at Objective Norfolk and deep at Objective Minden, then we might crack their defense and also prevent more Iraqi troops from escaping from Kuwait.

We assigned the mission to the 11th Aviation Brigade, commanded by Colonel Johnnie Hitt. They had two Apache battalions, 2-229 and 2-6, as well as a lift company of UH-1s and a CH-47* company. Johnnie chose 2-229, commanded by Lieutenant Colonel Roger McCauley, for the mission.

They were to take off from their current location, which was about fifty kilometers behind where we were then fighting, fly over the 2nd ACR, then forward of the line of contact to Objective Minden. Minden was about eighty kilometers deep (or east) from Norfolk, and it was at Minden that we thought the Iraqis had their defense set in depth (Objective Minden was about twenty kilometers in diameter and only imprecisely drawn, based on our best estimate of where Iraqi forces were). Before the attack, McCauley and Lieutenant Colonel Terry Johnson, the 11th Brigade deputy commander, came forward to see me and coordinate personally. Because of the risks of blue on blue, and also because of the passage of 2nd ACR and 1st INF, over which they'd be flying, I told them both to be damn sure they had nailed down their coordination with both units. And stay west of the 20 north/south grid line, Stan Cherrie added. Since that was the current FSCL, east of it was under the control of CENTAF in Riyadh, and F-111s would be attacking targets there. Both of us wished them good luck.

They left at 2100, then had to divert around a tank battle in the vicinity of Objective Norfolk. They arrived in the target area with three companies of six Apaches each, and found some Iraqis attempting to set a defense, but other

---

Chinooks: medium-lift helos for resupply.

units generally moving south to north, apparently trying to escape. It was what they called a target-rich environment, and they hit it hard. They also got return fire from the Iraqis, mostly small arms. For the better part of an hour, they stayed in the target area with their three companies; the spacing of the Apaches varied, but they tried for about 150 meters. Each Apache carried eight Hellfire missiles, and each was constantly firing and destroying Iraqi tanks, infantry carriers, trucks, and air defense vehicles. They let go any Iraqis escaping on foot (after the war, they showed me the gun camera films).

When the attacking battalion returned at 2300, they brought news that caused me some concern. Though they reported that numerous vehicles were destroyed, they also noticed that, further east, Iraqi units continued to move north up Highway 8 from Kuwait City to Basra. They requested to attack at about midnight farther east beyond the FSCL.

That was a tough decision. I wanted to go east all the way to Highway 8. Our Apaches had much more staying power in an engagement area, especially at night, than the fixed-wing air, which would drop a single bomb per pass over the target and then have to leave the target area. My main CP had strongly recommended that we send the second strike east, but when I asked them to try to get it coordinated with Third Army and CENTAF by moving the FSCL east and letting us have Highway 8, the answer was that we couldn't get it done in time. Since none of the decision makers in Riyadh was available at that hour, to request it, and then get it approved and disseminated, would have taken all night and we'd be out of the night attack window.

I could have chosen to go anyway to ignore the boundary, go east, and take the risk that there would be no interference or fratricide from the F-111s attacking Highway 8, or hope that we could tie it together with them on the fly. However, to deliberately cross a boundary and get some of your troops killed by fratricide is a grievous breach of discipline, and in my judgment is cause for disciplinary action. In battle you just cannot have local commanders deciding when or when not to obey boundary restrictions. Another alternative was to try to reach the airborne command-and-control aircraft, and coordinate locally, but it was not clear to me there was one.

Complicating all this was the time and distance between the CPs. We were in the middle of the corps sector at the TAC CP. My deep-attacking planning cell was at the main CP, almost 200 kilometers away. The attack helicopter battalion was 100 kilometers from the main and a good 80 from us. Riyadh was a good 800 kilometers away, or farther than the distance from London to Paris. All of our discussion was over the phone, and it wasn't a conference line, on which everyone could be talking at once, and thus preclude misunderstanding. The people were tired—not the least the aviators. And this time, as they flew forward, they would be passing over the 1st INF Division, which meant that they'd have to coordinate with a different unit in the middle of the night. My gut told me to do it. My head said no. It was not a risk, it was a gamble. If it did not work out, and we had some serious fratricide, then we would never recover from it, and it would be a major distraction from our final attack against the RGFC for the rest of the night and all the next day and the next night.

Besides, if there were that many Iraqis on Highway 8, surely J-STARS or the F-111s also would notice it, and send out some fixed-wing air.

I ordered our Apaches to go back to Minden and as far east as they could, and at 0200 they went back with two companies, A and C, and destroyed more Iraqi vehicles.

Total BDA reported from both attacks was: 53 tanks, 19 APCs, 16 MTLBs, 1 ATC (air-traffic control) tower, 1 ammunition carrier, 1 bunker, and 40 enemy KIA. (I trusted their BDA, since they could see the Hellfires impacting on the vehicles. Once a Hellfire hit something, it was gone.) They had broken the back and the spirit of the Iraqi 10th Armored Division and prevented them from reinforcing the forming RGFC defense. Afterward, many of the 10th Armored abandoned their vehicles and fled on foot. We would destroy their equipment later.

It was an enormously powerful application of the battle-fighting doctrine we had written so long ago—and were now executing in war for the first time.

THE ZONE

At this point late at night, with the sounds of battle close by, my emotions were running high. I wanted to pour it on the Iraqis, just pound them in an unrelenting attack with everything we had. We had the fist where we wanted it and wanted to drive it home. Go for the knockout. Boom. In sports, they call it the killer instinct. I had been in these situations before in Vietnam, only with much smaller units and with much less combat power and fewer complex organizations to maneuver.

I was not alone in these feelings. You could sense the same thing all over the corps. I had already seen it in training, in chats and visits with the soldiers and leaders—seen it in their eyes. Now I was seeing it in combat. It was in the 2nd ACR at 73 Easting. It was in the Apaches' deep strike that night. It was in the Big Red One during their night attack through Objective Norfolk. Later, it was in 1st AD's battles at Medina Ridge and in 3rd AD's battles at Phase Line Bullet. It was in all the cavalry squadrons out front or on the flanks of their divisions. Get the job done. The Army calls it the "warrior spirit," but it is more than that. It's about being a warrior, yes, but also a soldier, which means the disciplined application of force, according to the laws of land warfare and our own values as a people. It goes beyond being a warrior.

And so, as warriors *and* soldiers, we all experienced this go-for-it-and-win feeling. It was nothing personal. But if they wanted a fight, they had come to the right place. There was no holding back.

These intense feelings heightened senses to a new level. They put you in a zone. I cannot explain it, but I have never been so aware of sights and sounds as I have been in combat. You can just sense things you could not before. Maybe it is a function of the physical danger to those for whom you are most responsible, like a parent in a crisis situation with his family. You just know and do things that seem right at the time. You reach into the depths of your memory and recall things from your training, education, study, and experience that were not available to you before. You make patterns out of scraps and pieces of information that you could not make before. Later, when people ask why you did do such-and-so, you answer, "It felt right at the time." There is an uncanny sharp intellectual focus that allows your brain to process information, accept some, reject some, form conclusions, decide, not decide, all in nanoseconds. Napoleon said it was the result of "meditation," of enormous and continuing concentration on an area, off it, then back to it—and then things just appear to you. A certain calmness comes as well, it is all suspended in front of you in your head, the knowledge of what to activate and what not to. You can see it all in your mind's eye. Things go into slow motion; moments seem to last longer than they actually do.

All of these experiences have happened to me in battle, and I have never been able to replicate them anywhere else. I especially felt them when I was out and around the soldiers, sensing their pride and pain. Even though I was not out there in the middle of it, I was close enough and I knew what the soldiers were feeling, because I had been there myself, had been shot at and hit and missed many times. I could feel it all—the emotions, the highs and lows of command and combat.

REFLECTIONS

That night was the most intense of the war, with the most concurrent activities . . . for me as the VII Corps commander . . . for the soldiers in the tanks and Bradleys . . . for the small-unit commanders trying to maintain order in their attack east in the dark . . . for my brigade and division commanders. The largest corps tank force in the history of the U.S. Army was on the attack. There was no time to stop or for summary briefings. I just listened and absorbed it all and used my imagination to picture the battle in my mind's eye.

We had the 1st and 3rd Armored Divisions side by side in contact with the Iraqis on about a seventy-kilometer front, with five brigades attacking, or about 500 tanks and 300 Bradleys. These were supported by twelve battalions of cannon and rocket artillery (close to 300 systems). Coming on line with them on about a thirty-kilometer front in the south was the 1st INF passing through the 2nd ACR. They would attack forward with two tank heavy brigades—or about 230 tanks and more than 100 Bradleys. To their south, the British were attacking with their two brigades, numbering almost 150 tanks and a similar number of Warriors. In all we had literally nine tank heavy brigades on line in a night attack against the Iraqis, plus the Apache attack deep into Minden.

At one point, the noise was so great I thought there was a thunderstorm, grew concerned about the Apaches, and stepped outside the TAC. It was no thunderstorm. It was a JAYHAWK storm of firepower crashing down on the Iraqis. The sky was lit up by tracers big and small, and by the sparkle effect given by the MLRS as they fired off on the ground onto Iraqi positions. The air was filled with the constant roar of exploding artillery and the thump of tank and Bradley cannons. The ground vibrated. It was awesome.

All the while, like all my commanders that night, I had to make quick decisions about this current battle even as I continued to think about the next day's fight. Should we pass the 1st INF at night? Yes. Should we conduct a deep attack with the Apaches? Yes. Should we do a second attack on Minden? Yes. Should we go beyond the FSCL in that second attack to Highway 8? No. There were reports of fire across boundaries and fratricide. Time to call 1st AD and 3rd AD commanders and order them to get their flank coordinated so that it would stop.

Then came the plans for the next battle. If I wanted to maintain the tempo of the attack, I had to issue orders soon, before the current fight was finished. So we drew up the double envelopment, our tentative maneuver scheme for the next day.

Time to give John Yeosock a word picture of what was going on, and to request more maneuver room for the British, and also in the north between us and XVIII Corps (Stan Cherrie had asked for another ten kilometers of space to the north of our sector to ease fitting the 1st CAV into our attack east; he was turned down). Watch the open flank of the 1st AD in the north. Track the progress of the 1st CAV to Lee, then tell them to go to Horse. Figure where to displace the TAC in the morning.

I was enormously proud of the soldiers and leaders in the small-unit actions all over the corps. I knew it was not easy. I had been in battle at night, but never like this, not on this scale, not with almost 1,000 tanks, not with nine brigades on line.

★ After the Big Red One had reported successful passage of lines through the 2nd ACR and the Apaches had returned safely, and after I decided on another attack on Minden, I decided to get some rest—something the soldiers in battle would not get that night.

It was difficult to leave the TAC. I knew we were in the largest corps night attack since World War II, and maybe ever. Before the night was finished, there would be acts of unbelievable heroism by VII Corps soldiers and moments of sheer terror, as units fought their way through Iraqi forces trying both to defend and to get out of the way. Commanders would be tense as they maneuvered their formations to keep them oriented on the enemy and to avoid blue-on-blue, and as they brought their awesome firepower against the Iraqis. Our attack helicopters would range deep, and that would require steady nerves and coordination. A-10s flying night CAS missions would do their best to help, even with their limited night-vision capability.

The Iraqis would try to cope. They'd crank their turrets by hand to keep the tanks cool and thus invisible to the M1A1 night sights. They'd allow attacking U.S. units to pass through, then fire on them from behind creating 360-degree fights, and trying to hit U.S. tanks in their rear grille doors. Some dismounted Iraqi infantry would even try to climb onto U.S. tanks.

Some of our soldiers would be wounded that night.

Some would not see another day.

I knew all that, and felt I should remain awake while it was going on, but the truth was that it was no longer in my hands. The orders had been given, and now it was up to the major unit commanders and their subordinate commanders and the soldiers to execute them. I had made the decision to commit them. All I could do at this point was trust in their leadership, courage, and skill. All were in abundance that night.

I was more convinced than ever that time was running out. At one point, I said to Toby: "I'll bet there will be a cease-fire soon." How soon, I did not know.

The length of a limited-objective conflict is influenced by a lot of factors, most of which I was not privy to as a corps commander. In all of the Arab-Israeli wars, for instance, last-minute tactical actions were undertaken in order to gain ground or positions that could be used to one side's advantage in talks after the war, and stalling allowed eleventh-hour maneuvers.

When the opening shots are fired, the hourglass is turned over. How fast the sand runs from top to bottom is influenced by many factors, and the two chief factors here, at least that I was aware of, were, on the one side, Iraqi resistance, and on the other, our own objectives. On the night of 26–27 February, the Iraqis were still fighting in some coherent defense, and they were capable of brigade and even division-sized actions. Yet I was also aware that their units were beginning to become intermingled, a sure sign that their cohesion was breaking down. We were taking prisoners, but they were not giving up without a fight, as some of their frontline units had done. Some equipment was later found abandoned, but that was because the Iraqis thought they were getting hit from the air (they could not see some of our tanks firing at extended ranges); when attacked from the air, their drill was to abandon their equipment and get in their bunkers.

How much longer would they be able to fight back? I thought another twenty-four to thirty-six hours. Meanwhile, we still had not come in ground contact with either the Medina or Hammurabi Divisions, which meant we definitely had some fighting left.

But the results would be similar. We clearly had the initiative and the firepower. The battles so far had been one-sided, and more one-sided battles would follow. So it was then a matter of how long and at what cost to our troops.

In prewar estimates, I had figured two days to get to the RGFC, four days to destroy them, and two days to consolidate. In fact, we had actually gotten to the RGFC security zone less than twenty-four hours after the launch of our attack—the 2nd ACR action at noon on the twenty-fifth against the 50th Brigade of the 12th Armored Division along Phase Line Smash. And less than twenty-four hours later, on the morning of the twenty-sixth, the 2nd ACR had hit the early defense lines of the Tawalkana. Then 73 Easting had come only a few hours after that, about 150 kilometers from where we had first attacked at 1500 on the twenty-fourth.

At midafternoon, the 3rd AD had begun a major attack against the 29th Brigade and elements of the 9th Brigade of the Tawalkana at what they would call the Battle of Phase Line Bullet (just east of Phase Line Smash).

After they overran the logistics site and HQ of the Iraqi VII Corps at al-Busayyah, the 1st AD turned east and began their attack on other elements of the northern brigade of the Tawalkana, the 29th, and the brigade of the Adnan Division sent south to assist the Tawalkana. The 1st AD also would send their Apaches deep three times to attack repositioning elements of the Medina Division.

Midnight was fifty-seven hours after we had begun at 1500 on the twenty-fourth.

I did not know we had only another thirty-two hours. Neither did anyone else at that point.

So while it was difficult to go rest while the soldiers were still fighting out there, I knew I had to. "Don't worry, General, we trust you." Well, had I fulfilled that trust? To that point I thought I had, but there was more to do. We had to bring this to an end. The troops did not need a tired, fuzzy-thinking

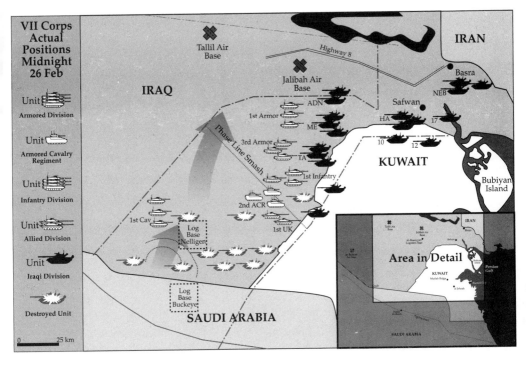

All units were in contact with security and lead tank battalions of the Iraqi forces by midnight on 26 February. Throughout the night, VII Corps divisions fought major armored battles that continued all day on 27 February and into that night.

corps commander the next day when we made our final move. Toby was right. The best thing I could do was get some rest.

I asked Stan to wake me if anything came up, and went to get a few hours' sleep. I think it was sometime past 0100, probably close to 0200. The TAC was still humming and radios were crackling with battle reports. Most of my TAC crew were still at it.

0400 VII Corps TAC CP

It was still dark when I awoke, but by now the sounds of battle to the east had passed us by. Coffee was welcome. You learn to wake up fast in combat—your brain and senses turn up to maximum right away; maybe they never completely turn off.

Time to change stump socks: the last thing I needed was a blister on my stump. It had held up well, though. My enlisted aide, Sergeant First Class

Lance Singson,* had gotten me spare cuff straps in case I needed them, and had brought a spare leg. I never used either, but I was glad to have them. As a student at the National War College, I had broken my leg while running on the streets of Fort McNair doing physical training, and done the same thing later as a member of the J-7 Joint Staff—both times landing as though I'd been cut down by a cornerback on a Saturday afternoon. So a spare leg was good to have. By this time the chemical suits were getting nasty. Though we had had no reports of chemical use by the Iraqis, and had not discovered any chemical munitions, we all had been wearing the suits and sleeping in them for almost three days. The charcoal was coming through and getting all over everything.

Update: Fratricide

On this night, we would have the greatest numbers of blue firing on blue.

It is a fact of war, present in every war we have fought. Who does not remember Stonewall Jackson at Chancellorsville in 1863? The Army chief of ground forces, General Leslie McNair, was killed by blue-on-blue in Normandy in 1944. We certainly had it in Vietnam. In our unit one day, an error with 81-mm mortars brought fire directly onto a unit that had requested fire on the enemy.

The fact of it, though, should not diminish our urgency to eliminate it in the future, however slim the chances. How do we do that? By training the troops, by giving them knowledge of the situations where the probabilities of fratricide are higher, and by simple increased awareness. At the same time, we must not so alarm our troops or leaders that they will become tentative in battle; that would make matters even worse.

In Desert Storm, we tried a few more specialized preventive measures. Some worked better than others. None was foolproof:

Our troops were well trained in identifying enemy equipment, but at ranges in excess of 2,000 meters on a night-vision sight, all you see is a hot spot about the size of one of the letters in this word.

To provide better identification for our vehicles, we tried uniform theater combat markings (which, unfortunately, could be seen only in daytime). And at the last minute, we also got so-called glint tape, which was supposed to be visible through night-vision devices. It did not work. For identification by our own air, we had standard air-ground issue marking panels, but these were not visible from 10,000 feet, where most of our fixed-wing air flew. We tried it by

---

Singson was my aide in 1st AD, in VII Corps in combat, and at TRADOC, and was part of my close family team.

sending Apaches to 10,000 feet; even with optics that were better than the Air Force's, they could not tell friend from foe.

So we did what soldiers and leaders have always done. We relied on discipline, and looked at the risks to various types of tactics in various types of weather, and adjusted accordingly.

In the end, despite all the possibilities for blue-on-blue as the armored formations attacked in close proximity to one another, countless stories emerged about how combat discipline prevented it. Our soldiers and leaders were extraordinarily restrained, and in fact at times that led to severe command tensions in the heat of battle. On many occasions, our troops gave up their range advantage over the Iraqis and closed to ranges where it was possible to make positive ID, even though they were in greater danger from more accurate Iraqi fire. I have already mentioned cases in which units passed Iraqi units, which would then fire on them from behind. When our own units fired back, they occasionally caused inadvertent hits on our own vehicles behind the Iraqis. An enemy force between two friendly units posed similar problems: if one of the friendly units fired and missed, the shot could easily impact on the other friendly unit (that actually happened on the morning of 28 February). Similarly, on the flat desert, rounds traveling at close to a mile a second could easily cross unit boundaries. Finally, if you look through a so-called night sight, it is virtually impossible to tell whether you are seeing an enemy firing at you or a friendly vehicle being hit by enemy fire. We expected our gunners to make that life-or-death judgment in nanoseconds.

In VII Corps during Desert Storm, of the forty-six U.S. soldiers KIA, ten were classified as killed by our own fire. Of the sixteen British KIA, nine were blue-on-blue—the A-10 attack on the Warrior. Other deaths were listed as probable or possible, as they occurred during simultaneous friendly fire and enemy fire, where it was not possible to determine the cause of death. Still, we did our best to find out. A team from AMC (Army Material Command) checked our hit vehicles for uranium residue—a telltale sign that it was from our fire, since the Iraqis did not have that type of ammunition. That team personally briefed me and our commanders.

In every case where there was suspected blue-on-blue in VII Corps, I ordered an investigation. I wanted it done for three reasons: so that commanders could make the proper classification of combat death; so that family members would know what had happened; and finally, so that commanders could make a judgment about *how* it had happened and whether there was justification for punitive action. We were not directed to do this by higher HQ. I just thought it was the right thing to do.

The results of these investigations were all reviewed personally by major unit commanders, by me personally, and by Colonel Walt Huffman, my staff judge advocate, for legal correctness, then they were forwarded to Third Army. It was not until April 1991 (before we left Iraq) that we finished these reviews and forwarded the results. It should not have taken so long to release the information and to tell the next of kin.

None of these thoughts is offered as an excuse, nor are they probably of much comfort to the next of kin. These soldiers died doing what they were ordered to do against an enemy on a battlefield. It does not diminish their status as heroes and soldiers that they died from our own fire or our own munitions. I regret every one of these deaths, just as I regret all the deaths in the corps from every cause.

ACTIONS

During the night of 26–27 February, our attack had gone about forty to sixty kilometers into the Iraqi defense.

BRITISH. The 1st UK had secured Objective Waterloo, and as I had ordered, they were prepared to attack to the northeast behind the Iraqis in front of 1st INF to Objective Denver. They had been impressive in their relentless day-and-night attacks. Since 1200 on 25 February, when they attacked east out of the breach, they had broken the back of Iraqi frontline divisions, primarily by cutting off their heads in the rear; that is, by capturing generals and other senior officers of the Iraqi division leadership who had stayed to fight with their troops. They also had defeated the tactical reserve and prevented Iraqi forces from joining the defense farther north or from interfering with our constant stream of fuel trucks making their way north. I knew I had a decision with the British early that morning. Should I order them north or not? Before I made that decision, I wanted to check the progress of the 1st INF.

1ST INF. The Big Red One had begun passage of lines through the 2nd ACR at about 2200 and finished at 0200. Tom Rhame, Don Holder, and their leaders had done a magnificent job in pulling this off. Eight thousand vehicles of the 1st INF had had to pass through the two thousand of the CAV, and then into battle a few kilometers farther on. The 2nd ACR had established a battle hand-over line and a series of passage points that would let the 1st INF pass through, then give them at least two kilometers before contact with the Iraqis. Lieutenant Colonel Steve Robinette, with Don Holder's approval, had ordered the regiment back that distance earlier in the evening in order to give them that space.

As for the 1st INF: At first Tom Rhame had wanted to pass his first brigade through Don's northern squadron (2nd) and his third brigade through the regiment's southern squadron (1st). This would have allowed Rhame to conduct an envelopment move, with those two brigades attacking the Iraqi defense from the south and north, while leaving the 2nd ACR to keep pressure on the middle. But Don did not like that, as it would leave his middle squadron (3rd) to support by fire, and would thus put that squadron in a possible blue-on-blue situation, where it would be firing into Rhame's two brigades. With so little time to plan, Tom decided that the maneuver was not worth the risk, and he changed to a straight forward passage through all three squadrons on a thirty-kilometer front.

In the north, 1st INF had its 1st Brigade, commanded by Colonel Lon "Bert" Maggart; and in the south, they had the 3rd Brigade, commanded by Colonel Dave Weisman; while the 2nd Brigade, commanded by Colonel Tony Moreno, was then in reserve. Because both 1st and 3rd Brigades had two tank battalions each, plus a Bradley battalion, Tom wanted his tank heavy forces forward. This would put the 1st INF into the fight with 232 tanks in the same thirty-kilometer-wide sector where the 2nd ACR had 123.

Although elements would continue to pass through all night, the passage was almost complete by midnight, and the 1st INF reported it was all clear of the 2nd ACR at 0200. Meanwhile, I had removed the 210th Artillery Brigade (two battalions of 155-mm howitzers and one MLRS battalion) from the 2nd ACR, and used them to reinforce the 1st INF as they passed through (and thereafter until the cease-fire). I also had ordered the 2/1 AH-64 battalion back to their parent 1st AD early on the morning of the twenty-seventh to rejoin them for their main attack in the north.

Let me offer an aside here: One of the ways you influence the outcome of battles and engagements is by weighting the main effort. For a corps commander, the most reusable combat assets are aviation and artillery. Less reusable are ground-maneuver units. These take longer to get from one place to another, and once the battle is joined, they tend to get engaged in actions from which they can't easily be extricated. That's not so with aviation and artillery. So for 2nd ACR's covering force, I had placed an AH-64 battalion with eighteen Apaches from 1st AD, and from corps artillery, a field artillery brigade with two cannon battalions of twenty-four guns each and an MLRS battalion of eighteen launchers. When that 2nd ACR mission was complete, I removed these units from the regiment and put them in the main attack. Likewise, because I thought that Butch needed the combat power in his main attack in the center, I had directed that a battalion of the corps 11th Aviation Brigade, 2/6 CAV, go early on the morning of the twenty-seventh to the 3rd AD. Butch's second attack battalion had been removed in August 1990, when U.S. Army Europe had sent an aviation brigade to support XVIII Corps early on in Desert Shield, and they had never been returned. Likewise, after the breach mission and the shifting of the corps main effort to the enveloping force, I had cut the 42nd and 75th Artillery Brigades from the 1st INF to the 3rd AD and 1st AD respectively. These changes required physical moves and coordination in order to get the radio frequencies set, the maps posted with current situations, the mission orders done, and logistics support arranged. It all took time—but it took less time with aviation and artillery units.

By BMNT, the Big Red One had seized Norfolk (an objective we had placed about thirty kilometers east of Phase Line Smash; we'd anticipated Iraqi second-echelon forces to be located there) and were pressing toward Highway 8, some eighty kilometers east of where they had begun their attack just before midnight.

By now, we had approximate numbers of enemy losses and of our own soldiers killed and wounded. From this, I knew it must have been a hell of a fight, and so was determined to go visit the division right away that morning. Later, I talked to soldiers and commanders of the Division's 1st and 3rd Brigades, and attended a memorial service for the four soldiers killed in action in 1/41 Infantry in 3rd Brigade and heard the details.

Here are some of the specifics of that series of night battles of the 1st INF toward Norfolk:

Colonel Bert Maggart* describes the early scenes this way: "The passage into enemy-held territory was an eerie, almost surreal experience. The night sky was filled with catastrophic explosions, the likes of which I had never seen before. Even the destruction of four T-55 tanks during the breach [on 24–25 February] was nothing compared to the sight that joined our eyes during the transition from friendly to enemy ground. Horrible fires roared from the turrets of Iraqi tanks, with flames shooting high into the night air. At the exact point of passage through the 2nd ACR in the TF 2/34 zone, a T-72 tank that the regiment had destroyed earlier that evening still burned brightly, filling the air with the pungent smell of burning oil, rubber, and flesh."

On 1 March 1991, in a personal talk with Lieutenant Colonel Pat Ritter, commander of TF 1/34 Armor, Pat told me of a close-in action in which Iraqi infantry had climbed onto his tank, only to be shot off by one of his company commanders' tanks.

Soldiers in 2nd Battalion, 34th Armor, commanded by Lieutenant Colonel Greg Fontenot,** referred to the night attack as "Fright Night." If that's what they called it, I can't imagine what the Iraqis called it. Greg Fontenot later

---

*Bert was my executive officer at HQ TRADOC from June 1992 until his promotion to brigadier general in early 1993, when I made him the chief for doctrine.
**Greg later became chief of my strategic planning group at HQ TRADOC, and then went to command a 1st AD brigade in Germany, and then Bosnia. We had lots of time to discuss the actions of his battalion that night.

wrote of his battalion's experience that night: "As Charlie"—Team C—"and Delta passed the command group closing on Bravo's left rear, they encountered infantrymen in spider holes who wanted to fight. . . . At one point, Burns crawled all over his infantry platoon leader for firing on C-66 [Burns's tank] with a Bushmaster [the 25-mm cannon on Bradleys]. The platoon leader calmly replied that he was killing enemy infantry, a fact to which I can attest. . . . In the first hour [about 0130 to 0230], the task force destroyed thirty-five armored vehicles, ten trucks, an unknown number of dismounted infantrymen, and captured nearly one hundred Iraqi troops." The Iraqis did fight back, and Fontenot went on to describe the effect of Iraqi artillery and direct-fire rounds.

Newly commissioned in 1990 out of Southern University, Second Lieutenant Chuck Parker was a tank platoon leader in Company B, 2/34 Armor. He remembers his main task that night as keeping his platoon fixed on the enemy and avoiding blue-on-blue fires. In order to keep his platoon aligned and hammering away at enemy targets, he kept his head out of the turret and used handheld night-vision goggles (NVGs). Without his NVGs, he could not see beyond his tank. Tracers from firing were visible, however, causing alternately bright flashes and darkness, and occasionally washing out his NVGs. The sounds of tank cannon and artillery fire were almost constant. For Lieutenant Parker, the time he and his unit had spent meeting the tough crew and platoon tank-gunnery standards at Fort Riley was well spent. That night they destroyed many Iraqi tanks and other combat vehicles on their way to Norfolk, while in the entire eighty-nine hours of the attack, his platoon did not have a soldier killed or wounded. As part of Company B, they had led the breach force on 24 February with mine-clearing blades on the front of their M1A1s. (The soldiers of Parker's platoon remain close and stay in touch with one another.)

Over on the right in 3rd Brigade (actually 2nd Armored Division Forward, out of Garlstedt in north Germany, sent as the third brigade of the 1st INF), commanded by Colonel Dave Weisman, the engagements and actions were similar.

"The biggest problem was keeping battalions in line, making sure we didn't shoot each other," says Weisman, who was in an M113 behind 2/66 Armor.* And Lieutenant Colonel Jim Hillman, commander of TF 1/41 Infantry, said, ". . . we found ourselves in a 360-degree fight, and that was the hardest part of this whole thing. . . . We were in amongst them [and] spent the rest of the night clearing them, either capturing or killing soldiers in those bunkers."

"We had thermal sights, but unheated targets," said Lieutenant Colonel

---

*Many of these accounts were orginally reported in Army Times. See Bibliography and References.

John Brown, who commanded 2nd Battalion, 66th Armor, that night, refer-ring to the Iraqi practice of leaving tank engines turned off to make them in-visible to our NVGs, while "the Iraqis had daylight sights, but unilluminated targets. Neither of us could particularly see each other." He continued, "We were 'coaxing' [shooting with the M1A1's machine gun] guys running between tanks, running between our tanks and bunkers, as we were moving through. It was really hairy. There were rounds flying all over the place."

Hillman added, "There were burning hulks going up like flares, infantry trying to surrender, infantry trying to hide, infantry trying to fight, infantry getting up on tracked vehicles, either to attack or try to surrender."

Lieutenant Colonel Taylor Jones's 3rd Battalion, 66th Armor, attacked through three Iraqi tank companies, about a battalion in strength. "It just seemed like there was target after target after target," said Captain Tim Ryan, who commanded Company D.

There were casualties and there were heroes and extraordinary courage under fire.

On this night, Command Sergeant Major Conway of 2/66 Armor would crawl up on an Iraqi T-55 tank and drop a grenade in the turret. He was blown off the tank as the tank exploded (he survived). He also led a four-man team to go after an Iraqi RPG team that was threatening the fuel trucks following the attack. Later, Brown's gunner, Staff Sergeant Matthew Sheets, spotted Iraqi RPG teams getting in position to shoot into the rear of advancing 2/66 tanks. "I'm convinced that Sheets saved six tanks," Brown says, "since he killed six Iraqi RPG teams."

In another part of the battle, Captain Lee Wilson was commanding Com-pany B, 1/41 Infantry. While his company was moving to link up with a for-ward unit, the company, and Wilson's own Bradley, came under intense Iraqi RPG and machine-gun fire. U.S. tanks, seeing the battle behind them, fired into the formation. (Through a night sight, remember, RPGs hitting a friendly vehicle look almost like an enemy vehicle firing at you.) Wilson's Bradley was hit, and he was thrown from the Bradley (he survived). Sergeant Joe Dienstag, the Bradley gunner, who was seated next to Wilson in the turret, was un-touched. Private First Class Dennis Skaggs, the driver, whose hands were too numb from the blast to operate the controls that let the ramp down in the back so that the troops could get out, grabbed a sledgehammer and got the ramp open. The troops poured out as the back of the Bradley filled with smoke. Skaggs, a combat lifesaver,* and Dienstag pulled out wounded soldiers,

---

*Combat lifesavers were soldiers with additional medical training, which allowed them to perform emer-gency first aid until medics could arrive. In combat, the first hour of treatment is critical to survival. Com-bat lifesavers in crews saved many lives because they were right there.

and Skaggs immediately began intravenous fluids and pressure bandages. ("This kid was phenomenal," Wilson later said of Skaggs.) The battle continued, with Iraqi small-arms fire all around. Burning vehicles were visible, and you could hear tank and Bradley cannon fire.

For the 3rd Brigade, it was a swirling fight with Iraqi tank and infantry forces that night.

One U.S. Bradley platoon had four soldiers KIA and eighteen wounded. For the entire division, there were six U.S. soldiers KIA that night, and thirty wounded, for VII Corps the largest concentration of casualties in the shortest time in the war.

I constantly bristle at misrepresentations that all the fighting was done at 2,500 meters, or that it looked like the pictures on TV of laser-guided bombs hitting targets from the air. The ground combat was physically tough, often at night or in weather affecting visibility, and at distances measured in a few meters rather than kilometers.

Perhaps, Sfc Jim Sedgwick, a platoon sergeant in 1/41 Infantry, said it best: "We almost lost a platoon, and out of a company element, that's an awful lot of people. . . . Friendly fire, unfriendly, that's not the point. What they did that night was, they took care of their people. They did the best they could in an extraordinary situation. They had a lot of genuine heroes that night. A lot of them."

Sedgwick was a Vietnam veteran.

The attack to seize Objective Norfolk broke the back of the Iraqi defense. More than 300 Iraqi vehicles were destroyed. But it came at a price in dead and wounded. It was a risk. You ask a lot of your soldiers and leaders.

Lieutenant Colonel Jim Hillman said it right: "There was a composure and discipline that reflect a quality of soldier . . . far more than we had a right to expect."

That night is why I always tell people, "It was fast, but it was not easy. Do not equate swiftness with ease." That night, those soldiers wrote new pages in the history of night mounted combat.

3RD AD. By this time, the division had come on line abreast with, first, the 2nd ACR, and then the 1st INF to their south and the 1st AD to their north. I was glad to have the disciplined, well-drilled, and relentless armored force that was the 3rd AD in the middle of the VII Corps attack. You want a steady outfit in the middle. They would keep the flank contact left and right with 1st AD and 1st INF (to keep the corps attack relatively aligned and to prevent shooting across flanks), and they would cut a swath of destruction through the Iraqi RGFC middle.

Since the sector I had given Butch Funk was too narrow to put three brigades on line, Butch had been using two brigades forward (his 1st and 2nd) and one back. By now he had decided to pass his third brigade through his second and leave his first brigade in the south, next to the 1st INF.

Third AD's battle log was full of reports of actions across their front, highlighted late the afternoon before, around 1600, with what they would call the Battle of Phase Line Bullet.

They had been on the move since early the morning before, 26 February, and had been in enemy contact for about twelve straight hours. That morning, they had been my freshest division, but no more. I needed them to sustain the center of our attack east toward Highway 8. The more success they had, the more the Iraqis on either flank would feel threatened.

Late the day before, Funk's two brigades on line were attacking into the center of the Tawalkana's forming defenses. His second brigade, commanded by Colonel Bob Higgins, was in the north, and his first brigade, commanded by Colonel Bill Nash, was in the south, linked with the advancing 2nd ACR.

Nash's three battalions on line had hit the Iraqi security zone at 1630 that afternoon—a twelve-kilometer advancing line of steel. There were many targets, some close, some distant.

First Lieutenant Marty Leners, 1st Platoon leader, Company C, 3/5 Cavalry was the first tank in the 3rd AD to kill a T-72. But for Leners and his gunner, Sergeant Glenn Wilson, it was a tense engagement. Rain and blowing sand made it difficult to use the laser range finder on their M1A1. That meant they had to use battle-sight range (an automatic setting using average expected range) or estimate the range and manually input it into the tank computer. That all takes time. Their problem was that the T-72 saw them and was traversing its turret in their direction, ready to fire. Wilson got a round off, using battle-sight range. It fell short of the T-72. Leners quickly input additional range and Wilson fired a second round, beating the Iraqi tank to the draw and killing it.

Over in Lieutenant Colonel John Kalb's 4/32 Armor, the fighting was at closer quarters. T-72s were closer than 1,000 meters, with Iraqi infantry on board and in bunkers. In a running fight with a T-72 and Iraqi infantry after darkness on 26 February, Kalb's scouts in Bradleys had destroyed the tank and Iraqi infantry, but had lost two soldiers KIA and a Bradley to a fratricide. Early on the morning of the twenty-seventh, Kalb's tank task force had intercepted an Iraqi unit attempting a counterattack, and in less than a minute had destroyed 15 T-72s and 25 other armored vehicles with the massed tank fires of his 43 M1A1s.

To their north, the 2nd Brigade's fights went on all night. Lieutenant Colonel Beaufort "Chuck" Hallman's 4/8 Cavalry, an M1A1 task force, attacked into the heart of the Iraqi defense, which now appeared to be in some depth; and received return fire from the Iraqi's small arms, RPGs, and artillery, in addition to tank and BMP 73-mm fire. Their attack went on for the better part of four hours against a dug-in Iraqi tank/infantry position supported by artillery. Iraqi infantry were in bunkers, and Iraqi tanks and BMPs attempted to use destroyed vehicles as shields. Hallman's tankers relentlessly pressed the attack. By about 0400, the brigade, together with TF 4/18 Infantry, had broken the back of the Iraqi defense, and Funk was preparing to pass Colonel Rob Goff's 3rd Brigade through them to continue the attack.

Artillery supported them all the way. In his notes, Colonel Morrie Boyd of the 42nd Artillery Brigade, supporting Colonel John Michitsch's 3rd AD artillery, writes that the forty-eight 155-mm howitzers of the 3/20 and 2/29 Field Artillery Battalions fired continuously throughout the night, while the eighteen MLRS launchers of 1/27 provided rocket fires against the Iraqi formations. The Iraqis came to refer to these devastating barrages as "iron rain." During the eighty-nine hours of the war, the 42nd Brigade would fire 2,854 155-mm rounds and 555 MLRS rockets in 121 different missions.

By now, Butch Funk was employing his aviation and MLRS deep. With M1A1 tank and Bradley battalions close in, these together made about a twenty- to thirty-kilometer death zone moving east in front of the division. His aviation brigade, commanded by Colonel Mike Burke, had the night before (about 2300) defeated an attempted Iraqi move to get a battalion in between 3rd AD and 1st AD to the north. From five kilometers away, Funk was able to see his Apache battalion engage the Iraqi unit, and in the space of three minutes destroy eight T-72s and nineteen BMPs.

I was glad to hear he had put in a fresh brigade, as that would help sustain the momentum, and I had no other forces to give him except aviation.

Since Butch had used his sole Apache battalion that night and it would be unavailable for part of today, I ordered that 2/6 (commanded by Lieutenant Colonel Terry Branham, an AH-64 battalion from 11th Aviation Brigade) go today to reinforce the 3rd AD (this was non-doctrinal: corps Apaches normally worked deep in the corps sector at night, while division Apaches worked the closer-in fight). I figured Butch needed the combat power to speed his attack east at a high tempo more than I would need it that night in a corps deep attack.

I did not believe the Iraqis expected three armored divisions to hit them at night on line. I wanted to pour it on with everything we had. Time was not only running out in the war, it was running out for some of our units who had had little rest the last few days. I figured we could sustain the current attack tempo for another twenty-four to forty-eight hours, then we would have reached the end of endurance and I would have to begin rotating major units in and out.

Third AD had destroyed hundreds of enemy vehicles and captured many prisoners. Their attack tempo was swift and steady. During their attack, they found the same kinds of prepared positions (including reverse-slope defenses) and positions in depth that the 1st INF and 2nd ACR had found. The Iraqis fought back, and the fights were sharp and brutally lethal. There was depth to the Iraqi defense, either by design or because units were attempting to escape, but the Iraqis were no match for them.

1ST AD. First AD had likewise been attacking all night and were still at it. By now, Ron Griffith had brought his three maneuver brigades up on line and seemed tied in well with 3rd AD to his south. At this point, the division had almost 9,200 vehicles, and almost 2,000 of these were tracked. As they turned east, they soon came into contact with the northern brigade of the Tawalkana defense, which was located about fifty kilometers from where they had made their right turn. Continuing east all night, the division had destroyed the northern brigade of the Tawalkana and the brigade of the Adnan that had moved south into the 1st AD sector from the XVIII Corps sector. Colonel Dan Petrosky's Apaches of the 1st AD aviation brigade and CAS had hit the Iraqis deep in the sector, and they had located a sizable logistics base in the vicinity of their Objective Bonn. They had also discovered the Medina Division moving to protect that base. It was clear that this day the 1st AD would hit the Medina.

They still had an open flank to their north, for the 3rd ACR and 24th Division were about sixty kilometers to their rear, or west, after their ninety-degree turn. The Iraqis had already tried to take advantage of that gap by moving the Adnan brigade south. After meeting the combined artillery and air fires of 1st AD, the RGFC did not try anything like that again. That was the last troop movement south from the northern RGFC infantry divisions.

THOUGHTS

That gap continued to concern me, however, for two reasons. The first had to do with the security of the 1st AD and its vulnerability to attacks from the north, either by ground forces or artillery. The second was that if the Third Army was looking at a coordinated VII Corps/XVIII Corps attack against the RGFC, things would have to happen fast. However, I was not sure the Army maneuver was possible anymore, which meant that we might have to do what we could ourselves in our sector. The time lines we had discussed before the war indicated that Third Army would issue the order for the coordinated attack forty-eight hours prior to execution.

I reviewed our combat-power adjustments I had ordered for the final fights to the Gulf and the destruction of the RFGC:

The 2/1 AH-64 battalion (eighteen Apaches) had gone back to the 1st AD from 2nd ACR, so Ron's ability to attack in depth with Apaches would double. In addition, the 75th Artillery Brigade (24 155-mm howitzers, 12 8-inch howitzers, 9 MLRS, and 9 ATACMS-capable MLRS) also had joined the 1st AD late the day before, and now were firing in support of the division.

A corps AH-64 battalion, 2/6 Cavalry, had joined 3rd AD (also doubling their Apache strength to 36), plus the 42nd Artillery Brigade (48 155-mm howitzers, and 18 MLRS launchers) had rejoined the division and was already supporting their attacks.

The 210th Artillery Brigade (48 155-mm howitzers and 18 MLRS) was now with the 1st INF to add to the fires of its own division artillery.

I made no change with the British.

The 2nd ACR was in Corps reserve, with only its assigned units now, giving it less combat power.

I also had considered the option of a corps deep strike that night with Apaches into Objective Denver, yet at the rate at which the 1st INF was attacking, they might already be there by then. That conclusion led me to retain only one corps attack battalion and to commit the other to that day's fight with 3rd AD.

There were two decisions to be made that day: How to fit the 1st CAV into the fight to destroy the Hammurabi in the north? And what force to commit as the southern arm of our envelopment in the south, the 1st INF or the British? On the one hand, the British were available (they'd finished with the tactical reserve). I figured the Big Red One would still be in the middle of a fight they had begun the night before. If the 1st INF was still slugging their way through Norfolk, the British could get there faster. On the other hand, if the 1st INF had broken through, it meant they were closer, and I would use them. That is what I had to find out.

The main forces of the RGFC, of course, remained up north. From the early reports of the previous night's 1st INF attacks, and after looking at their position on the map, it looked to me as though I could use the Big Red One in the south and keep the British attacking directly east to Highway 8. That would shorten the southern arm by a good eighty to one hundred kilometers.

After an intelligence brief, I determined that I would make those two decisions after seeing for myself, and by visiting both commanders and getting their judgments on the immediate situation in their sectors. I also wanted to get away from the TAC, as they were again going to displace forward to keep up with the fight, which during the night had passed us by. As night turned to day, the sounds of battle had become more distant.

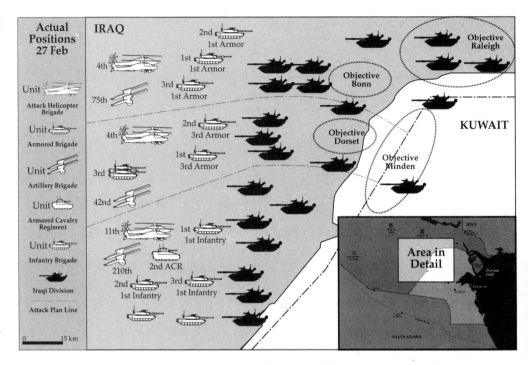

As the VII Corps came into contact with the Republican Guards, attack air and artillery forces struck deep while ground-combat brigades from every direction formed the lethal "fist." The overwhelming combat power generated by this synchronized maneuver stunned the Iraqi units and broke any integrity in their defense.

FLANKS. At this point, we had a poor picture of the situation on both of our flanks—XVIII Corps now to our north and west and the Egyptian Corps to our east. We had a better picture of XVIII Corps. We did know that the 3rd CAV was some distance behind the 1st AD, and would likely not close that gap today. Though our liaison with XVIII Corps had been keeping our main CP advised of other actions of XVIII Corps units, I was focused mainly on what the 24th MECH and 3rd ACR were doing, and whether they also would turn east to attack toward Basra, on our north. We also knew generally from the British that their southern flank was open, as the Egyptians were not yet ready to turn east toward Kuwait City. That did not bother me at all.

We also had a poor picture of what theater air was doing deep to interdict or otherwise isolate the RGFC in the Kuwaiti theater of operations. I had to assume they were interdicting Iraqi forces that were attempting to escape, and isolating the remaining forces in the KTO so that we could close in for the kill. With 1,500-plus sorties a day, I figured they were still very much in the fight. All the RGFC still appeared to be in the KTO that morning.

The previous day and night had been the biggest day of the war for CAS in support of VII Corps. We had used a total of 128 close-air-support strikes. And while we had gotten all that we asked for, that still represented only less than 10 percent of the daily air sorties flown, and we were the main attack.

ENEMY SITUATION. The picture of the Iraqi intent was clear that morning. They continued to use their theater reserve, the RGFC, to form successive lines of defense against our attack. These began with the Tawalkana, then shifted to the Medina, then the Hammurabi. Since some units remained in positions oriented south or southeast, as though we would still attack up the Wadi al Batin, the orientations were somewhat confused. Other units—especially RGFC units—were attempting to orient to the west, now that they had figured out that we were coming from that direction. The Tawalkana continued to set the initial line of defense with whatever forces became available, and because we knew they tended to shift brigades around from one major unit to another without too much difficulty, that doubtless accounted for the reports of unfamiliar units we were getting. Finally, the southern flank of the Tawalkana clearly turned out to be right where the 2nd ACR had said it was, and where the 3rd Brigade of the 1st INF was attacking. It might have accounted for the different type of defense encountered by Dave Weisman's brigade. Their night attack broke the back of that southern brigade (the 37th MECH) and exposed a flank.

At this point early in the morning of 27 February, I still had the corps in a series of hasty attacks, and the enemy still seemed to be capable of brigade-sized defensive sets and local counterattacks. We saw very little evidence that these forces were running away. In my judgment, we were not in any pursuit operation—not yet.

After the war, I directed my G-2, Colonel John Davidson, to attempt to reconstruct the Iraqi plan in our sector from all sources, including captured materiel and prisoners. Although it was done quickly, the report gives a much different picture of Iraqi forces than the one we got from their frontline infantry or from those facing MARCENT near Kuwait City. The document is entitled "The 100-Hour Ground War: How the Iraqi Plan Failed."

Extracts show:

• That the Tawalkana did indeed defend generally along the 65 north & south gridline, with the 12th AD, 37th Brigade in the south. North of that brigade, the 9th, 18th, and 29th Brigades were on line south to north. It was the 9th Brigade and parts of the 18th that the 2nd ACR hit at 73 Easting. "The 9th Armd Bde," the report states, "is amazed that it would be attacked during a rainstorm with blowing sand."

• That the Medina was moving west to establish defensive positions: "Four battalions of the 14th Mech Bde, Medina Division, move in a southwesterly direction to set up a hasty defense in the midst of the theater logistics site. Concurrently, 2nd Armd Bde moves approximately seven kilometers to the northwest to form a defensive line from QU0939 to QU0946. Two unidentified armored brigades depart the south to establish contact between the 14th Mech Bde and 2nd Armd Bde, and provide a coherent defense of the LOCs. These LOCs allow the escape of units from the south to Basra."

• That the Hammurabi Division was assessed to be moving with its nine battalions to defend the Rumaila oil fields, or to take up the defense if the Tawalkana became combat-ineffective.

• That the "mission of Iraqi ground forces," on 27 February, "continues to be a hasty defense in depth to delay the advance of Coalition forces until all forces withdraw from Kuwait, and successfully cross the Euphrates River. The remainder of the Tawalkana MECH Div and the repositioned Medina Armd Div of the RGFC are to block any further penetration of VII Corps forces coming from the west."

Though I did not know all this on the morning of 27 February, I knew enough to determine that we were into a successive series of hastily defended positions, and that the troops we were facing were attempting to fight us, even though up to now the skill level and combat power had been a mismatch.

As soon as it began to get light, we flew the twenty minutes it took to find 1st INF. I wanted to get their assessment and decide early about the attack north.

Either 1st INF or 1 UK.

13

KNOCKOUT

EN ROUTE

A defeated enemy's equipment rushed underneath the helicopter as we flew to link up with the Big Red One. As far as we could see, there were burning vehicles. Tanks without turrets, burning. BMPs burning and overturned. Some equipment obviously hit from the air by LGBs (Laser-Guided Bombs), as the tanks were without turrets and the hulls were almost flattened. Trucks were on fire. Black smoke rose in small columns from burning vehicles littering the sand. Iraqi dead lay on the battlefield. We could see, picking their way through all this, the logistics and support trucks of the 1st INF Division support command, commanded by Colonel Bob Shadley, attempting to keep up the pace to bring needed fuel.

I had seen battle destruction before, but never like this. Visions from World War II newsreels made their way into my head as I searched for something to relate it to. There was brown sand and hundreds of broken and burning Iraqi vehicles all the way to the 1st INF TAC CP.

I was not thinking back—"Don't look back" had been my code ever since I'd decided to have my leg amputated—but if I had been of a mind to, I would have concluded that I had made the right choice to pass the 1st INF through the 2nd ACR to continue the attack the night before.

0630 TAC CP 1st INF DIVISION

We circled before landing. I wanted to get a good look around, and Mark needed to find a spot where he wouldn't hit any destroyed Iraqi vehicles.

After landing, I got out and started toward the M577s of the 1st INF TAC. On the way, I glanced around. There was the TAC, which at that point consisted of two M577s, its extensions stretched out the back, but the sides rolled up now that there was daylight. About a hundred meters away were maybe a hundred Iraqi prisoners guarded by two or three 1st INF MPs. A little farther away were Apaches and scout aircraft from the division's aviation battalion.

My senses told me that, here, at least, the Iraqis were a beaten army.

I took a good look at the prisoners, who avoided my eyes. They were reasonably clothed in military uniforms, but were dirty and unshaven, and were eating MREs our troops had given them. They looked tired, but no more so than the U.S. soldiers guarding them. Unlike our soldiers, though, they were passive, shuffling around, not talking much with one another. They looked defeated.

Around the TAC was more evidence of the destruction that had been brought on by the 1st INF attack the night before. Burning tanks and other vehicles were nearby. If Hollywood had wanted to create a scene of a defeated army, complete with prisoners and destroyed equipment, this is what they would have made it look like. Finally, there were the areas containing unexploded U.S. munitions, mainly artillery DPICM, that the troops had wisely marked off with white engineer tape. The whole war was here in microcosm.

Brigadier General Bill Carter greeted me when I walked into the TAC. He was assistant division commander for maneuver and was running the division TAC. Bill was an experienced infantryman and a decorated Vietnam veteran, and was quick-minded and aggressive. I had gotten to know him well as a tactician when we had run the 1st INF BCTP in March 1990 at Fort Riley. I liked Carter and trusted his judgments.

"Bill, hell of a fight last night," I said. "Saw the destruction on the way over. Give me a SITREP. By the way, where's Tom?"

"It was a tough fight last night. We think we've broken through. Resistance is much less organized than what we ran into last night. Our advance is continuing east toward Denver and Highway 8, per your orders. Not sure what the Iraqis are doing, but they are not in any coherent defenses, and we are taking many prisoners—as you can see. Terrain is slowing us down some. [Just east of where we were, the wadi got deep and wide.] We did have a number of casualties last night. Do not have a final count, but we had about eight KIA and maybe thirty wounded. General Rhame is forward with one of the brigades in a tank. I have him on the radio."

The casualty figure surprised me.

"Get him on the radio," I said.

"DANGER 6, this is DANGER OSCAR"—the TAC CP call sign—"JAY-HAWK 6 is here and wants to talk to you."

"This is DANGER 6."

"This is JAYHAWK 6, give me a SITREP."

"We had a tough fight last night, but we have broken through. I estimate we can get to Denver by dark."

"Roger, DANGER, well done. I saw the wreckage. I want you to press your attack east. Attack to Denver. I'll give details to Bill."

"WILCO."

That was it. The evidence of my senses had been confirmed by Bill Carter's quick summary and now by the judgment of the division commander forward. It was then that I decided (though I was already leaning that way—especially after seeing the destruction on the way out here) to use the 1st INF as our southern envelopment arm, and not the British. Using them would get our southern division where I wanted them more directly and faster, and I would also exploit the success of the Big Red One. The 1st INF was now, technically, in an exploitation-and-pursuit. It had been a long time since a U.S. Army unit had been in that tactical situation. We surely had not practiced that situation in the Cold War, and not much in our training. . . . Well, you must always be prepared for success on the battlefield, and to seize the opportunities opened by an action of one of your subordinate units. I had expected to be in this situation, and now we were ready to exploit it.

Bill Carter had overheard my conversation with Tom, and moments later, he and I and his planners were clustered beside a flat 1:100 000 map off the end of the M577 ramp.

The troops around me looked tired. They had been attacking now since 1500 on the twenty-fourth. They'd had some rest, but not much. The movement forward after the breach had begun at around 0430 on 26 February, and had gone on in blinding sandstorms. They had coordinated, then executed the complex night passage of lines, then fought their way through two Iraqi brigades past Norfolk, and were now heading east. A hell of a series of tactical moves and fights. I was never more proud of any unit than I was of the Big Red One that morning.

But I've been around tired troops, and these troops were tired . . . though clearly not down. They were running on fumes now, but they wanted to finish it. I could imagine what the troops who had fought all night felt like.

As I looked at the map, a piece of blue representing the Persian Gulf was just visible at the far eastern corner of the eastern map sheet. It caught my attention.

"Attack east," I told them. "Go for the blue on the map. That is what is bringing the ships to take us home when this is over. Go for that. Here!" I said, banging on the map. Not too military, but I wanted them—as clearly tired as they were—to have something to seize on to propel them forward another twenty-four hours. As Greg Fontenot was to tell me later, my remark "Go for the blue on the map" got all the way to the battalion commanders, and maybe further.

"Bill," I went on, "now, here is what I am planning for the corps to do." Then I quickly sketched out how the 1st CAV would attack around the 1st AD in the north later that day, while the 1st and 3rd ADs would be the pressure forces continuing to attack due east, and the 1st INF would attack east through Denver across Highway 8 toward the Gulf. At that time, I also planned to bring the 2nd ACR up to the inside of the 1st INF to an Objective Hawk (after the corps's JAYHAWK nickname) that I drew just west of Denver, in order to keep the 3rd AD and 1st INF from running into each other. The British would meanwhile continue due east to Highway 8, just north of Kuwait City.

As soon as I finished my sketch, Bill told me that he had it and they would execute. I then asked him to send a planner along with me back to the corps TAC, where we would quickly finish the graphic control measures.

Before I left the area, I walked over to talk to some of the aviators—scout and attack helo pilots—about what they had seen and done over the last hours. The aviation brigade was commanded by Colonel Jim Mowrey, a smart, aggressive aviator whom I had gotten to know as a war college student at Fort Leavenworth during 1986 and 1987. Jim was not there at the time.

The aviators were clearly tired from flying all night. Again, you could see it in their eyes. They described for me their attack in front of the close fight, during which they had surprised Iraqi units and destroyed numbers of vehicles. The scene they described fit my own visualization. Many Iraqi soldiers, they continued, had soon been running about trying to escape (they had been easily seen on night vision as white or black figures, depending on the mode of the sight). They had chosen not to fire on them, but instead focused their cannon fire on the equipment. I was proud of them. They had never forgotten who they were and what they stood for. I shook their hands, told them well done, and gave them VII Corps coins. Their accounts were more confirmation of a breakthrough.

From what I had seen and heard, combined with earlier intelligence reports, I knew that whatever RGFC remained in our sector were now in a small area north of 1st INF's attack axis and east of 3rd AD and 1st AD. How many, I was not sure.

We now had work to do to get the order out and executed that I had just sketched. The normal time for a complete new corps order is seventy-two hours. Even a change to a basic order (called a FRAGO—short for fragment of an order) usually takes twenty-four hours, as our FRAGPLAN 7 had done. I had given a warning order for this double envelopment the day before. Now I ordered it to be executed later that day and the next.

0715 VII Corps TAC FWD

We flew to our TAC FWD, close to the 3rd AD TAC, about a twenty-minute flight back over the smoking ruins of the better part of two Iraqi brigades. There I linked up with Lieutenant Colonel Dave McKiernan and his crew. They were beat. They had been up most of the night working, moving, keeping up with the battles in the 1st AD and 3rd AD, and keeping us at the TAC informed. By now the main TAC with Stan was displacing forward to this location, or close to it. I was reminded of the reasons why fitness is part of a professional soldier's creed. You have to have something in reserve in times like this.

I needed Dave to understand what I wanted done and to begin making the orders overlays, while I went to lay out my intent face-to-face with the commanders. I sketched out the maneuver for him in the sand and on the map and told him to get to work on it while I went to see Griffith and Funk. I would return at around 1030, I told him, and I wanted an orders group meeting of Tilelli, Holder, and Creighton Abrams at the TAC. If they could get our planners forward from the main CP to help, that would be a bonus. Then I left to go see Butch Funk.

I figured they would have the graphics posted on overlays of acetate ready to pass out by the time I got done with the face-to-face meetings. It would not be easy.

While I was at the TAC, I talked to John Yeosock twice to describe our progress and what I had seen, to go over our double-envelopment scheme of maneuver, and to discuss more maneuver room up north, in order to fit the 1st CAV in without some complex maneuver with the 1st AD. "I'm proud of what the corps is doing," he told me, "and I'll see what I can do to help you."

I have later learned that the day before (26 February), the Third Army G-2, John Stewart, and the G-3, Steve Arnold, had been on their way forward to link up with me to go over final plans for the RGFC destruction. They had gotten as far as King Khalid Military City, then John Yeosock had had to recall them to help him with a crisis with the CINC in Riyadh over our movement rate.

I cannot help but think that the end of the war might have turned out differently if they had been able to continue forward and we could have finalized the VII Corps–XVIII Corps coordinated final attack. As a minimum, I'll bet Steve Arnold would have been able to get our northern boundary changed and notify XVIII Corps about it. That would have allowed us to blitz the 1st CAV forward at about 1100 on the twenty-seventh, when they closed into Horse behind the 1st AD, and to slam into the Hammurabi Division (which was by then retreating). That would have completed the three-for-three heavy division RGFC destruction. It never happened.

0745 3RD AD TAC CP

I linked up with Butch Funk well forward in the 3rd AD's attack zone. With Butch was his aide, plus Brigadier General Gene Blackwell, and his command sergeant major, Joe T. Hill. Blackwell was a long-legged, six-foot-four Clemson graduate from South Carolina, all soldier—a warrior with fighter instincts, who went for the kill. As warriors and soldiers, he and Butch were much alike, but their personalities were very different. Gene was quieter than Butch, and you needed to draw him out. Butch was always explaining and teaching what he wanted done. But they were both very direct when they wanted orders carried out. They were a good team.

Joe T. Hill was a Georgian (with a clipped Georgia accent), a veteran tanker, and a Vietnam vet, who had commanded an M1A1 the four days of the ground war. If you ordered an archetypal CSM out of central casting—a combat-savvy, streetwise, troop-focused veteran tanker—you'd get Joe T. Hill. I had interviewed "Joe T" for the VII Corps CSM job after my CSM had abruptly left in late January, but he had declined. He was honored that I'd thought of him, he told me, but if it was all the same to me, he figured he could do the corps and the 3rd AD more good by staying in 3rd AD, considering they had been last into the theater. Unusual—but Joe T was a real soldier.

I was always glad to see Butch Funk. Butch has a soldier's heart, and I just flat-out trusted him. He also always told me exactly what was on his mind without any hidden agendas, and much of the time, he and I communicated without words. Later, he himself said pretty much the same thing: "I could tell from your voice what you wanted," he told me, "and of course, the shorthand of our common background—and, I daresay, kindred spirits—really helped. I always felt comfortable being candid with you, even though I may not be right. That sort of confidence in one's boss, I have found, is very rare."

He had every reason to feel good about the 3rd AD that morning. In the last twenty-four hours, he had gotten an order from me to turn right ninety degrees, pass around the 2nd ACR, and attack east, destroying the RGFC in his sector. He had coordinated with the 2nd ACR, made his own order, then disseminated it, maneuvered his 8,000-plus vehicle division into two brigades up and one back (from the division wedge they had been in), passed around the 2nd ACR, turned right, linked up the 42nd Artillery Brigade with their division artillery, and fought all day and all night. They were still fighting. He had maneuvered and fought his division about eighty kilometers in twenty-four hours, and had extended the fight a good thirty kilometers ahead of his tank forces with close air and his own attack helos. Early that morning, he had passed his third brigade through his second brigade to maintain the momentum of attack. The 3rd AD had driven the spearhead right through the best the Iraqis had. And they were still doing it.

After I told Butch what I was trying to get done that day, he clearly understood what I was telling him, and he even thought of a few ways the 3rd AD might be able to help. (They looked at an option later that day that I had not considered. It proposed attacking from south to north in front of the 1st AD and behind and into the flank of the Hammurabi, just in case the 1st CAV maneuver did not work. This would have worked if we'd had time.)

As a result, he so paced the tempo of his division attack that day that to the Iraqis they were a relentless, moving, thirty- to forty-kilometer-long-by-thirty-kilometer-wide armored death zone. He gave them no rest. He had them fixed and was now going to finish them. I added an attack helicopter battalion from the 11th Aviation Brigade to the 3rd AD to give them additional fresh combat power and to keep extending their zone deep.

"Butch, give me a SITREP," I said after I explained my intent.

We were leaning over the top of a HMMWV, and he was pointing to a portable map he had unfolded on the hood top. Butch showed me on the map where his units were, explained that he had decided to pass his third brigade through his second brigade, then described the fighting the night before. It had been a series of hasty attacks, he told me, but with stiffening resistance the farther east they went. As they had done elsewhere, the Iraqis had tried reverse-slope defenses, but ground and air reconnaissance and quick-reacting small-unit leaders had overcome this tactical adjustment. They also were running into elements of many divisions, confirming that this was a hasty defense. He even related that at places the 10th Iraqi Armored seemed to have abandoned their equipment and fled.

By now, he went on, he thought 3rd AD had defeated the RGFC in their zone and were into other forces that had been positioned in depth, or were just trying to get out of the theater. But he was clear that 3rd AD was still conducting hasty attacks and were not in any pursuit. Not yet. But soon.

Before I left, he and I shared a few lighter moments. It was a relaxed, yet intensely focused mood we all were in. It was good to loosen up with the welcome Diet Coke Butch handed me, and Joe T. Hill gave me some equipment he had gotten from an abandoned Iraqi bunker. There was an RGFC uniform shirt complete with red shoulder cord, a brand-new Iraqi helmet (which we all signed later and gave to Army Chief Carl Vuono), and a field phone that also looked brand new. And we had a good laugh as Joe T acted out for us (in his Georgia accent) the likely Iraqi conversations as the Spearhead Division slammed into their positions in the middle of the night. . . . It was soldier humor while the battles continued all around us, but also a deeper indicator: We knew by now that the outcome was not in doubt. It was just a matter of how much longer and at what cost.

I left Butch and flew to meet Ron Griffith. Navigation to the 1st AD was always a challenge because of their LORAN, since the rest of the corps mainly used GPS. They weren't trying to be different. They used what we could get. We just did not have enough GPS. As we lifted off from 3rd AD TAC and Mark turned the Blackhawk to head north to find the 1st AD, we could clearly see Spearhead Bradleys and tanks firing at the Iraqis.

0815 1st AD TAC CP

My positive feelings changed abruptly when I saw the 1st AD TAC in the middle of what appeared to be a stopped division. I was quick off the Blackhawk to find out what was going on.

Ron probably could read my mind as he greeted me. "I know you want us to continue the attack," he said, "but I'm just about out of fuel. I figure we have about another two hours, then the division will come to a complete halt. What killed us was the 75th Arty Brigade showed up almost out of fuel, and we had to refuel them." Friction.

"Shit," I said. "Damn it, we just have to keep moving, and I'll get you fuel from somewhere. Just keep attacking like you've been doing."

Very quickly, I went over to the 1st AD comms and called the TAC. "Get hold of Gene Daniel," I told them, "and get some fuel to the 1st AD. Top priority over anything else." I also ordered the 3rd AD to send some fuel to the north to 1st AD.

For a brief time, I was thinking that the worst sin for an armored corps would be to run out of fuel. We had made many logistics arrangements to prevent it, yet we were in danger of it anyway. Stopping because you are out of fuel is a fatal flaw, and to run out of fuel here, on top of the world's greatest supply of oil, was just too much.

The 1st AD had come farther than any other unit in the corps, and out of all the divisions had the most vehicles. They and the corps transportation units had been busting their butts to get to this point. But they were using about 500,000 to 750,000 gallons of fuel a day; and that is a lot of fuel trucks, especially when each one carries 2,500 or 5,000 gallons, and the turnaround time from corps fuel sites was by now twenty-four hours or greater. As an order of magnitude comparison, in Normandy in late August 1944, when there were eighteen divisions in the U.S. Third and First Armies, their total daily fuel consumption had been 850,000 gallons. For eighteen divisions! Ron's 1st AD used almost that much by themselves! It was no small deal.

I was not happy with this situation. It almost cost us. From that day forward, I would tell military and other audiences, "Forget logistics and you lose."

Our choices were really two. One was to stop the division and pass the 1st CAV through to take up the fight, a maneuver that would probably take us the rest of the day and well into the night. The end result: no pressure on the Iraqis for twelve hours or so. The alternative was for Ron to keep attacking and take the risk that the tankers would catch up and he would be able to sustain the momentum. We did not discuss these options. I ordered Ron to keep moving. I was counting on my logisticians.

Meanwhile (though I did not yet know this), the 3rd AD had learned even before I had of the 1st AD fuel situation; as a stopgap measure—on their own initiative, in a superb feat of teamwork—they had sent twenty HEMMT fuelers, each with 2,500 gallons, north to their flank division. This turned out to be the shot in the fuel tanks that 1st AD needed. Later, more fuel caught up, mainly due to the great efforts of the 1st AD logisticians and their ADC for support, Brigadier General Jarrett Robertson, a cavalryman and ex-commander of the 3rd CAV. Jarrett was aware of the situation in 1st AD and had already moved out to keep the momentum going. Likewise, Colonel Chuck Mahan, commander of 7th ASG, the VII Corps logistics unit that was assigned responsibility to support 1st AD and VII Corps units in that part of the battlefield, had gotten a helicopter from Ron and was scouring the desert LOC from 1st AD back to Nelligen for fuel tankers.

In other words, the solution to this mini-crisis had been under way before I got into it. The units and commanders knew my intent, felt a tight teamwork, and had gone ahead and worked the problem and were well on the way to solving it. However, by establishing priorities, I could focus greater awareness of the urgency of the situation at the VII Corps rear and get them into it faster. Delivery of the fuel was the result of "brute force" logistics and a lot of fast-moving, long columns of tankers through the desert. (I later awarded a Bronze Star to Captain Debra Clark of the Arizona National Guard, who had led one of the many such columns forward.)

By late that night, 1st AD got about 100,000 gallons of fuel, but it had been close. The division had certainly been within two hours of running out of fuel.

★   After dealing with that, I got into the back of the TAC M577 with Brigadier General Jay Hendrix, Ron's ADC, for a quick update on the 1st AD situation. Jay Hendrix was an experienced mech infantryman—another one of those mounted unit commanders who could keep five or six things suspended simultaneously in his head, picture the total situation in his mind's eye, and make fast and correct decisions.

Jarrett Robertson was of a similar cut and had an infectious confidence born of competence and experience. He was a superb soldier and a great cavalryman, and he was also a kindred spirit. Later—in June 1991—I chose Jarrett to be VII Corps chief of staff. (Jarrett, along with two other soldiers, was killed in a Blackhawk crash in 1993 in Germany, while serving as Major General and deputy commander of V Corps.)

Just as with 3rd AD, the past twenty-four hours for the 1st AD had been a textbook in maneuvering and fighting an armored division. From my order to Ron late Monday to execute FRAGPLAN 7, the division had done a masterful job. They had attacked and secured al-Busayyah, and had simultaneously gotten together their own plans (complete with intelligence picture) to turn right ninety degrees and attack due east without a halt. As they'd turned east, they'd had two brigades forward and their second brigade to the rear finishing the al-Busayyah fight. Rather than slow the division, Ron had left a task force (6/6 Infantry with Bradleys) and an engineer company at al-Busayyah and pressed on to the east (this turn had caused a big gap to develop between him and the 3rd ACR and 24th INF Division and left his northern flank open). Later that day, he had brought his brigades on line abreast in a sector about forty kilometers wide; and later, the 75th Artillery Brigade had joined the division and had been integrated into the fire planning. They had fought all night, maintaining contact with 3rd AD to their south, and had destroyed the northern brigade of the Tawalkana Division. They'd had two casualties.

Ron was pleased with their actions to date and the tempo of the division. So was I, as long as they kept attacking.

But I was also interested in turning their attention to the maneuver necessary to allow the 1st CAV to attack to their north and east toward Objective Raleigh and the Hammurabi Division. With everything else going on at that time—especially the fuel situation, the continued movement of the division, and the unknown RGFC reaction (they still had three divisions to Ron's north, plus artillery)—I was not sure I had their attention.

Consequently, I stressed to Ron that I wanted him to make room in the north by "necking down" the division zone and allowing the 1st CAV to pass to the north. That was not a precise military order, but the intent to Ron was clear: Make room north in your sector to pass 1st CAV forward toward Objective Raleigh. I left the tactics up to Ron. As far as I was concerned, he could back the second brigade out and continue his attack with two brigades forward, as 3rd AD was doing, or he could attempt to narrow each brigade sector to give them room in the north.

Because of his heavy contact with the Medina and his desire to keep maximum combat power forward, Ron chose the latter. Of the two maneuvers, it was the more difficult; but under the circumstances, it was the right move for continuing the mission I had given him.

As it happened, there was an unresolved question of priorities over Ron's two missions. Specifically, Ron assumed that his continued mission had higher priority than passing 1st CAV forward. I thought both were possible, so I never told him which had higher priority in my mind. As I saw it, whichever tactic Ron selected would leave their adjusted zone about as wide as the one 3rd AD currently had (later my planners drew an adjusted attack axis for 1st

AD that directed them from east to more southeast, opening up room forward of Phase Line Lime for 1st CAV).

In any event, though both Ron and Jay Hendrix told me they understood what I wanted them to do, I left there with the uneasy feeling that Ron was not convinced of his ability to execute while he had the Medina battle going on.

I left to go back to the TAC FWD to brief the order to the other commanders. Now that I had given the double-envelopment order personally to 1st INF, 3rd AD, and 1st AD, it was time to talk to 1st CAV and 2nd ACR, as well as to get the overlays out. The time for them to execute was compressed, but I thought we could do it.

1030 VII Corps Jump TAC

It was a quick fifteen-minute flight back to the jump TAC.

Not only were John Tilelli and Don Holder there waiting, but Dave McKiernan and Ron McConnell had by now drawn the basic maneuver scheme for our double envelopment on an overlay on top of their 1:100 000 map.

It had started to rain slightly. Since we had no shelter there, I asked Ron to lean the four-by-eight-foot plywood map board up against the side of the command M577. We huddled, and I went over the maneuver scheme. It was a good thing they had used permanent marker pens to draw the map overlay, or by the time I got finished it all would have been washed off the map.

I knew I was asking for a lot from these commanders and their units, but it was a simple scheme of maneuver, and I thought we could execute. Tom Rhame and Butch Funk were already doing it, and needed no further orders.

John was an old cavalry friend, had the quickest-reacting division in the theater, and had just broken enemy contact, completed a move through the breach, and raced 250 kilometers in less than twenty-four hours. It had been a magnificent move. My orders to him were simple: Pass north of the 1st AD but just south of the northern border of the corps, attack east toward Objective Raleigh, and destroy the Hammurabi Division. Though I had not planned to give him any additional combat power, I did attempt to have the artillery of 1st AD fire reinforcing fires as 1st CAV moved east beyond 1st AD.

I wanted 1st CAV in the fight that day before dark. John said he could make it happen if 1st AD would give him a lane. I knew he would. John had drilled them to be lightning quick.

The way my planners had figured to provide that lane was by adjusting the direction of attack of the 1st AD and 3rd AD from due east to slightly southeast. With our northern border running exactly east-west, this would open space for 1st CAV's attack. I liked the scheme and thought it would work, but it all depended on 1st AD getting east far enough to make the slight turn that would open the space north of them. Though the place where that would happen was only an estimate, we had to pick a point, since the turn involved not only 1st AD, but 3rd AD to their south.

I ordered Don Holder to follow 1st INF, then to attack north inside them toward Objective Hawk. That way the 2nd ACR would stay between the eastward-advancing 3rd AD and just west of 1st INF. First INF would be attacking generally due east toward the Gulf until they got across Highway 8, where they would turn north. In this way, I thought we would close in behind any Iraqi forces remaining in our sector from the south and from the north, closing the noose around the border between Iraq and Kuwait or just a little to the north around the town of Safwan.

"Roger, I can do it," Don said.

At about 1100, they both left to complete their own planning and to get orders out. We were working in what the Army calls parallel planning in compressed time.

A few others had been with us in our planning group: Chief Warrant Officer Bob Barfield from our corps G-2 section at the main CP; Bob Schmitt, my corps planner and a SAMS graduate (Bob knew what to do in the shorthand language we used and had been part of the quick final planning work since last night); Creighton Abrams; Colonel Carl Ernst, who had come forward from Lucky TAC, the Third Army TAC CP located in King Khalid Military City; and Stan Cherrie.

I told Stan to get in a helicopter with the double-envelopment order and go find the 1st INF so that they would have the graphics and could talk to the 2nd ACR. Meanwhile, Stan also kept the main TAC moving right past us to set up farther east.

From CWO Barfield, I got an updated intelligence read that confirmed what we were seeing on the battlefield: that is, the Iraqis were defending in depth as they retreated toward Basra, while also trying to get as many forces out of the theater as possible. It was not yet clear to me whether they thought we were going for Basra and were trying to defend it (as they had done so strongly in the war with Iran), or whether they were now in full retreat.

Bob Schmitt confirmed that XVIII Corps was still to our west, had not yet turned east, and would not come on line with the corps today. This information intensified my own sense of urgency to complete the envelopment, as it now increasingly appeared that we were the only ones who could close the mission out.

Creighton Abrams continued to have a nose for the fight and the fire-support dimension of the planning that needed to go into it. As of now, he told me, he had no visibility on theater air. By now, the FSCL was being more tightly controlled by CENTCOM, and was out of our hands. Previously, after quick coordination with Third Army when all decision-makers had been available, we had been able to move it at our order; now CENTCOM said they would control it for the rest of the war. That was not welcome news, but a planning factor we had to deal with. I was still under the impression that theater air was attacking targets in front of Basra and sealing off the escape routes over the Euphrates in the XVIII Corps sector.*

Colonel Carl Ernst had been chief of the BCTP team when we had war-gamed early in January, and had stayed in theater at the direction of General Carl Vuono to assist John Yeosock's chief of staff, Brigadier General Bob Frix, who was running Lucky TAC for John at King Khalid Military City. After I showed Carl our past and planned maneuvers, he praised the corps for what we had done, and supported us for what we were about to do to close it. I was glad to hear that, since I figured he was keeping Third Army informed about what we were trying to do. Unfortunately, he had no decision authority to change boundaries, or he would have given us more maneuver room in XVIII Corps sector (who were not yet even anywhere near there).

Though it would probably have been useful to do so, I did not talk directly to Gary Luck at this point, as the comms were not great. A quick meeting might have been possible, but I did not even know where Gary was on the battlefield. If we had managed to link up our comms, we perhaps could have worked out the final maneuver together (absent CENTCOM and Third Army), but we were running out of time, and I really did not even consider calling Gary.

Additionally, our flank contact with XVIII Corps at this forward location was poor, and I did not know where the XVIII Corps liaison officer was or what he was doing. As a point of fact, even if communication with XVIII Corps had been better, in the time I figured we had to get this next battle under way, it would not have been possible to do both the XVIII Corps coordination and

---

*I was informed after the war that the CINC had moved the FSCL out into the Persian Gulf in our sector, and north of Basra and the Euphrates in the XVIII Corps sector. That action took CENTAF out of the isolation attack, since inside the FSCL, CENTAF needed eyes on target to prevent fratricide. However, there were no eyes to be had on the causeways over the Euphrates in the XVIII Corps sector. Brigadier General Steve Arnold and Air Force Brigadier General Buster Glossen had agreed to hit those bridges every four hours to keep them down. When he learned of the FSCL shift, Buster asked the CINC about it, and Schwarzkopf told him he would get back to him. He never did. The result was that theater air was no longer used north of Basra or on the Euphrates bridges. Theater air could not have been used in our sector anyway, as we were out of deep room. But it was in the XVIII Corps and Third Army sector that there was a problem of escaping RGFC units.

planning with Gary and the internal VII Corps work that needed to be done. So I stayed inside the VII Corps and figured we'd do what we could do ourselves. It was a conscious choice.

At about 1330, I left to go see John Tilelli, while Stan Cherrie left with the 1st INF planner to find the Big Red One. I wanted to see the results of John's quick planning, then go forward to 1st AD and personally nail down the final arrangements with them. Everything else was well under way, and all of it would happen. But the critical point was the northern sector of 1st AD. With everyone tired and with time now very compressed, I felt I needed to make that happen myself.

1300 1st CAV TAC CP

We had about a ten-minute flight to the 1st CAV TAC CP, during which we bypassed many Iraqi troops and some units. On our flight, we were at an altitude of about 100 feet and moving fast, when out of the door at a range of maybe 500 meters we could see five Iraqi soldiers holding up their hands as if to surrender. My pilot, CWO Tom Lloyd, asked what he should do. We could not see if they were armed, so we slid the door of the Blackhawk open, circled back toward them to see their intentions, and did a 360-degree turn around them to check them out. They clearly wanted to surrender and probably thought we were an attack helo. Because we had to get to the 1st CAV, and in any case had no room for the five of them, I did not want to land, so when we spotted an artillery unit close by, we went over and told them to police up "our prisoners," and then flew on to the 1st CAV TAC.

As soon as we arrived, John Tilelli briefed me on the passage and attack maneuver he planned toward Objective Raleigh. He was going to lead with his cavalry squadron (1/7 CAV, "Gary Owen"), then follow with one brigade behind the other until they were clear of the 1st AD, where they could then attack to Raleigh with two brigades abreast. His CAV squadron was already on the move. They could make it happen.

While I was at the TAC, I got a call from 1st AD: they were engaged with a brigade of the Medina Division in a large tank fight, and it was going well for the 1st AD. As it turned out, that call was about the Battle of Medina Ridge, our largest individual tank battle of the war.

This was both good news and not so good. The brigade in the fight was Ron's northern brigade, the 2nd, the same one that I had expected would give 1st CAV room to blitz forward. Now that they were in a big fight, I had some questions about how fast they could make room for 1st CAV, which meant that I wanted to go forward to nail this down. I would have liked John to come, too, but he needed to stay to begin moving his division forward, so I had him send his G-3, Lieutenant Colonel Jim Gunlicks, along in John's own UH-1 to meet me at the 1st AD TAC to finish the coordination.

I left to go find Ron.

1330–1400 FLIGHT TO 1ST AD

We headed east.

CWO Tom Lloyd was command pilot on the Blackhawk today. Tom had flown me when I was a division commander in the 1st AD, had gone to Blackhawk transition training, then moved to VII Corps. I trusted Tom just as I did Mark Greenwald. Ever since Vietnam, I had insisted that the pilots of my command aircraft be veteran aviators with both superior flying skills and the judgment to handle tough spots. The kind of flying we did put us in marginal situations from time to time, and I did not want rookies flying us.

Ron had meanwhile moved forward in his HMMWV to a position near the 2nd Brigade's battle with the Medina brigade. When we asked for location, they gave us a LORAN reading. That required Tom to translate in flight the LORAN to GPS. For a time, he and Toby were talking back and forth about it, and when I finally asked if they had the location, the answer was yes.

By then, I was not paying much attention to what was outside, as I was going over our maneuver on the map and thinking about everything else I needed to be doing right then.

A few minutes later, Tom said in a relatively calm voice, "Sir, I think we are over the Iraqi positions. I can see tanks and Bradleys firing this way."

"Well, turn around and let's go back," I said, in about the same tone of voice. But all of a sudden my senses came to life in a hurry. Not much I could do, except hope the Iraqis were so occupied with 1st AD that they did not notice us. I was, however, more concerned about the reaction from our own troops. Up to this point, we had not seen any Iraqi helicopters, but we knew they still had HINDs and other Soviet-made helos in theater, and they still had the capability to use them if they wanted to risk it. We also knew that the best way to disseminate chemical or bio was by aerosol spray from helos, so our troops were on the lookout for HINDs and other Soviet-made helos.

It just so happened that on the pylons on each side of our Blackhawk, the crew had mounted 250-gallon wing tanks that increased our operating range (or time of flight available) for almost an hour. Unfortunately, with those external tanks, if we were flying straight at someone (the normal attack profile of a HIND), we looked almost like a HIND ourselves.

That the Bradleys didn't open up on us as we flew back was a stroke of good luck, more than likely caused by the discipline of the soldiers and the fact that this was day four, and by now our troops no longer looked up.

Ron's crew popped some smoke, and we set down about 200 meters from Ron's HMMWV. As I got out of the Blackhawk, I noticed our own artillery firing outgoing, but I also thought I heard the unmistakable, low-sounding *whu-ump* of incoming. I told Tom to keep the helo running, and if anything got close to the Blackhawk, he was to lift off and meet me later at 1st AD TAC. Then, together with Toby and John MacInerny, I walked over to Ron.

Since Toby and John also had seen the firing, they asked some of the 1st AD troops there what was happening. It was Iraqi fire, they said, but they didn't give it much thought, since they kept firing in the same place. (That meant that the Iraqi fire was what we call "unobserved fire." If they had been able to "observe" what they were hitting, they would have by now shifted it to be more effective.)

"Sir," Ron began, "although the Iraqis continue to fire artillery, we've had a hell of a successful brigade fight here and are just beginning to finish it. I estimate we've destroyed about a brigade of the Medina."

That was great news.

"Terrific. Proud of you and your troops. Keep the heat on the Iraqis." At that point I did not know what an overwhelming victory the Medina Ridge fight had been for 1st AD, and how badly they had hurt the Medina. "What I came to see you about is the passage of the 1st CAV around to your north later this afternoon."

Meanwhile, because our own artillery was firing continually, and this noise was added to the occasional *thunks* of our M1A1 120-mm tank rounds and the normal *thunk, thunk, thunk* three-round burst from the Bradley's 25-mm cannons, Ron and I could barely hear each other over the noise.

"Ron, this is a lousy place to do some future battle planning. Got a suggestion?" I shouted.

"Let's go back to my TAC. It's about five kilometers west of here, right in center sector. I'll drive in my HMMWV and meet you there."

"OK," I said, then went back and got in my waiting Blackhawk and flew the five kilometers to 1st AD TAC CP.

MEDINA RIDGE

First AD's battle at what they called "Medina Ridge" had been the biggest and, as it turned out, the fastest and most one-sided individual battle of the war.

By late morning, Ron had all three division ground brigades on line abreast. The 2nd Brigade, commanded by Colonel Monty Meigs (Monty's great-great-grandfather had been quartermaster general of the Union army for General Grant) had four battalions, but his 6/6 Infantry was still catching up, following their finish of the al-Busayyah fight. The day before, 1st AD had successfully fought off an artillery attack from out of XVIII Corps's sector in the north, and by a combination of artillery and attack helicopters had destroyed a brigade of the Adnan RGFC Division that the Iraqis had repositioned south to thicken their defense.

It was shortly after noon when the 2nd Brigade ran into a reinforced brigade of the Medina.

"The Republican Guards," Ron Griffith said later about 1st AD's battles, "were much more capable forces" than the ones opposite us initially, and the other Iraqi forces in the southern part of Kuwait were "better equipped, trained, fed, led, and disciplined. The battles that were fought out there in the desert were very large battles, and they were not with forces that were running. In fact, they were forces that continued to reinforce and tried with some determination to defend."

Lieutenant Colonel Steve Whitcomb's account of the fight gives a first-hand account of what happened (Whitcomb was commander of 2/70 Armor, consisting of three M1A1 companies and one Bradley company, and one of the three TFs in 2nd Brigade's fight).

"At 1140, brigade began moving forward. While intelligence had not pinpointed enemy locations, we expected the enemy to be twenty to forty kilometers out front.

"Within minutes, as BANDIT's [Company B's] lead platoon was crawling out of a small wadi, the tanks stopped suddenly and backed down to turret defilade. Almost immediately, both BANDIT and ASSASSIN [Company A] reported T-72s and BMPs to their direct front. We confirmed friendly positions and ranges (2,800–3,500 meters). The wadi provided excellent firing positions for the tanks and the task force commenced firing.

"It quickly became obvious that the Iraqis were totally outclassed by our soldiers and equipment. Fire commands were textbook, with only an occasional hint of excitement as a T-72 would explode in a ball of flame. The day had been very gray and overcast and visibility limited to perhaps 1,500 meters. The wind blew sand. Through the haze, one could see muzzle flashes as the enemy tanks attempted to return fire." Steve later told me that it looked to him as though "Hoffman devices"—the training device used to simulate enemy tank fire—"were going off." They were totally ineffective, and as the captured Iraqis would later confirm, they could see us shoot, and watch their comrades explode, but could not identify our vehicles by any means other than their general direction. Our tankers far exceeded their training ranges of 2,200 to 2,400 meters with precise but deadly shots, the longest being 3,650 meters.

"Soon, the horizon was a series of over seventy smoke plumes. In forty-five minutes, the task force's share of the annihilation of the 2nd Brigade of the

Medina Tank Division, Republican Guards, would later be confirmed at 27 T-72 tanks, 8 BMPs, and 6 air defense command-and-control vehicles. . . . In those forty-five minutes, the brigade would destroy 55 T-72s, 6 T-55s, 35 armored personnel carriers, and 5 SA-13 antiaircraft weapons systems."

The enemy "had positioned themselves in an eight-kilometer-long 'fish-hook'-shaped line the day prior and had dug fighting positions for their tanks. They had tied their defense in with what good terrain they found and actually had set up an excellent reverse-slope defense. The enemy was there to fight and knew the importance to the rest of the Iraqi army of their ability to stop us.*

"During the fight, incoming artillery, around several hundred rounds, was received to the left rear of our flank unit, behind us and TF 4/70. The intent of the enemy had been to hit us and force us back into the artillery. . . . The brigade fire-support officer called for counter-battery fire, and within seconds of 'Shot,' the Iraqi guns fell silent. . . .

"In addition, A-10s and Apache attack helicopters, which had been requested earlier, arrived at about 1250 and were able to clean out enemy forces behind the front line of destroyed vehicles. Our soldiers were treated to an aerial display, as repeated runs by the A-10s and engagements by the Apaches' Hellfire missiles silenced any enemy activity. . . .

"It was truly an awesome sight as we passed the still-flaming hulks of the enemy. Explosions continued, even over two hours after the fight, as tank rounds cooked off inside the vehicles, shooting flames skyward. Prisoners were captured, wounded, some seriously, treated and evacuated, and quick examination of the area for intelligence value conducted."

The above account was not merely the story of one battalion, it speaks for the whole division. While Steve Whitcomb's tankers executed the direct-fire fight, the brigade commander, Monty Meigs, ensured maximum combat power forward and used his artillery in direct support and for counterfire. Ron Griffith at the division would see that Monty had all the firepower he could provide, and ensure that the division executed the counterfire, and simultaneously fight in greater depth with A-10s and division Apaches.

This was combined arms—AirLand Battle at division level—working in harmony at each echelon. General George Patton in World War II called it the "musician of Mars." We had the whole VII Corps combined-arms orchestra crashing down on the Iraqis.

This fight also was why Ron Griffith had had his attention drawn to the

---

*When these soldiers surrendered, there was a distinct difference from those prisoners taken earlier, Whitcomb notes. These soldiers were disciplined, had good equipment and uniforms, were well fed, and fought hard till they were killed or surrendered. Those surrendering were in uniform, had weapons, and were under control of their officers. They did not, as advertised, merely fire a few rounds and give up.

situation in front of him, rather than to the problem of finding room for 1st CAV. He needed to bring the full weight of the division to bear, just as he had done at the beginning of Medina Ridge and was continuing to do.

1st AD TAC CP Medina Ridge

The 1st AD TAC CP was not really a CP at all. To keep up with his fast-moving series of battles close and deep, Ron had been moving about the battle area in his HMMWV and a helicopter. While he was doing that, Brigadier General Jay Hendrix had been inside an almost continually moving G-3 M577, directing the close fight.

One M577, with Jay Hendrix inside. I was really pumped up and pleased with what 1st AD was doing in their sector. Clearly they were hitting the Medina hard and were hitting other Iraqi mech and armor units deep. The price of that was an inability to plan, let alone decide on a maneuver to allow 1st CAV to pass to the north. The sight of that lone M577 explained to me the difficulty we were having at the VII Corps TAC getting 1st AD on the radio. It also was a signal to me that getting the 1st CAV in the fight that day would be hard to do.

I met Ron behind the M577. The ramp was up (because of the threat of Iraqi artillery fire), but the ramp door was open. I could hear the crackle of reports over the 1st AD command radio net, as the three brigades attacked on line and the aviation attacked deep. The 2/1 Aviation that I had released from 2nd ACR had by now returned to 1st AD . . . just in time to take up the deep fight from 3/1, whose pilots were by now too fatigued to fly. The full division was committed.

Joining our huddle was Brigadier General Creighton Abrams (there to get the fire support right) and the 1st CAV G-3, Lieutenant Colonel Jim Gunlicks. Also there was the G-3 of the 1st AD, Lieutenant Colonel Tommie Straus.

The discussion went something like this:

"Ron," I said, "I want the 1st CAV to be able to attack east toward Objective Raleigh and destroy the Hammurabi. That means—as we talked about earlier—you need to make room in the north of your sector. I've got Jim Gunlicks here and I want you to get the graphics coordinated between you and 1st CAV. John is moving his division up now and will be ready to pass. I want it done prior to dark."

"Roger, I understand," Ron said. "But it would be a lot easier if we got a boundary adjustment in the north rather than for me to try to make my sector smaller right in the middle of our fight with the Medina. We'll give it our best shot."

"I understand about the boundary, but that will not happen. Get it done by dark. I want to envelop the Iraqis. First CAV is the northern force and the 1st INF is the southern force. Keep pressing your attack."

"WILCO."

I had asked a lot of Ron and the 1st AD. They were in a continuous series of battles stretching out about thirty kilometers in front of the division. His forward units were conducting mostly unplanned meeting engagements. We knew generally that the Iraqis were out there, but final locations were determined only when 1st AD troops slammed into them. That required the continuous focus of the division leadership in case forward brigades ran into an enemy force they could not handle, and they needed reinforcement from division. I had ordered Ron to continue that attack. I had also ordered him to make his sector smaller by slightly changing direction, and at the same time to pass 1st CAV to his north. It was a tough mission.

Though Ron was not enthusiastic about all this, that was irrelevant to me. Sometimes you do not get to choose your missions. You execute. So, as a loyal and skilled commander, and one who had his hands full at the moment, Ron had told me he would do it. Ron's WILCO cemented a lifelong friendship between us.

★ I left and returned to the TAC, which by now had displaced forward and was located just west of where the 2nd ACR had so soundly beaten the Iraqis. I was convinced that within four hours (more or less), Ron and 1st AD would pass 1st CAV through, and we'd have the remaining Iraqis in the bag by late morning the next day. At least in our sector.

1550 VII Corps TAC CP

The TAC was set up in its usual configuration. The site was a bald, sandy hill (more like a knoll or rise in the desert of maybe fifty feet). Around the site were littered many Iraqi armored vehicles, some burning, some smoking, some just demolished from air attacks.

There also were Iraqi dead (I had not seen any when I was flying in). The next day, our VII Corps chaplain, Colonel Dan Davis—a Special Forces Vietnam veteran, and a troop chaplain if ever there was one—supervised the burial of twenty-eight Iraqi dead and sent the locations back through channels to ARCENT. As was the practice in theater, these would later be passed to the Red Cross.

When I got to the TAC, the first thing I wanted to do was get a quick SITREP on the Iraqi situation and see about the progress of the 1st INF. I also wanted to find out if Stan had found Tom Rhame and delivered the graphics.

Next I reviewed the double envelopment. I knew we could do it. Besides, it looked ever more certain that the final maneuver to finish off the RGFC was up to us. From the information I had received from 1st AD, it appeared that the Third Army two-corps maneuver to finish off the RGFC would not work. XVIII Corps was not going to get east fast enough to become the hammer to our anvil that the Third Corps plan envisioned.

Meanwhile, the Iraqi defense was crumbling. Most of their forces in our sector continued to be east of 1st and 3rd AD, right where I had aimed 1st CAV.

John Tilelli reported that 1st CAV was moving up in anticipation of attacking east. Good! His CAV squadron had an action against a bypassed Iraqi unit.

The Big Red One was continuing its attack to the east and would reach Highway 8 by dark. That was great news. On the other hand, there were a couple of things that I thought I'd have to keep an eye on: First, I noticed that their attack was beginning to take a slight turn to the northeast. With 3rd AD attacking due east, then slightly southeast, if 1st INF started to veer northeast, they would eventually run into each other. Second, we were having trouble keeping effective communications with their TAC. From where we were, the distance was causing us to lose line-of-sight FM comms, and we were relying more and more on TACSAT. On top of that, since Tom Rhame was forward in a tank, to be as close to the action as he could get, I no longer had direct voice comms with him. . . . This was, in fact, no big deal, as Tom knew what I wanted done, and if something wasn't clear, Stan was now at their TAC to explain it in person.

I knew the 1st AD situation, as I had just come from there.

The 3rd AD attack was relentless. They had moved farther and faster, and were picking up momentum. They were the Spearhead Division for sure!

Reports of their actions would tell me two things: First, their lead attacking units were telling us of actions around the 83 to 87 north/south grid line. That told us that the division was about to enter Kuwait, which was the 88 grid. By 1700, they were almost ten kilometers inside Kuwait, and closing in on the direction of attack of the 1st INF. The 3rd AD also continued to report that they were attacking and destroying T-72s and BMPs, as well as bunker complexes, but that the Iraqi resistance seemed less and less organized than it had been earlier in the day (these no longer seemed to be brigade actions, but more battalion- and even company-sized).

I was fired up about their success. Was there something I could do to capitalize on it? An option was to take advantage of their forward progress and attack them northeast in front of 1st AD toward the Hammurabi. . . . No, I concluded. Not yet. If we could not get the 1st CAV around to the north of 1st AD, then I would consider that option.

One thing at a time for now. Keep it simple. Everyone was tired: soldiers and leaders were falling asleep in turrets; planners were having short-term memory lapses; so was I. This was not the time to overcomplicate what we were trying to do.

As I've mentioned before, as soldiers and leaders get more tired, you have to "work hard" at simplifying, and must communicate in direct, unambiguous language—even get more dramatic in gesture and language to get people's attention.

Since success in the attack always opens up opportunities, you also have to try to reinforce success where you find it—to seize an opening presented by the initiative of one of your subordinate units.

Recognizing success ("exploitation") and totally finishing the enemy ("pursuit") were skills we had not practiced much in our Cold War training because we had always stressed fighting outnumbered against tough enemies in the Warsaw Pact. The last time the American army had been in an exploitation-and-pursuit had been after the Inchon landing behind the North Koreans in September 1950. Some of my early training and education had been conducted by veterans of both World War II and Korea, and somewhere in the back of my mind, the ability to recognize signs of exploitation-and-pursuit on the battlefield had stuck. I had seen them earlier in the day in the 1st INF. Though I hadn't yet seen them in the 1st and 3rd AD, which were still in hasty attacks and meeting engagements, I knew I soon would.

★ At about 1700, Stan returned. Because Tom Rhame was forward in a tank, Stan had not been able to find him to deliver the order and brief him personally. He had been able to leave the order with the 1st INF TAC CP, however, so that was reassuring. But the lack of comms with Tom, the fact that we hadn't been able to get to him, and the fact that all of us were tired raised my concerns.

A little after 1700, Ron Griffith called.

"JAYHAWK 6, this is IRON 6," he said.

"JAYHAWK 6."

"My 3rd Brigade is in contact and we had some casualties. Cannot execute maneuver to get 1st CAV through in north. Believe it hazards my force to do that while we are in contact."

Damn, I thought. All that work racing around all day to personally tie this together, and now at the last minute we can't do it.

Chance. The unpredictable. It is part of war. My first emotion was anger that it was intervening to screw up our scheme of maneuver, but I let it pass. I had to adapt the plan to the circumstances. There is not much you can do about chance. And if in Ron's judgment they could not do it, then I had to consider options, not act as though chance never happened.

"IRON 6, JAYHAWK 6, confirm you cannot execute maneuver for PEG-ASUS."

"Affirmative. We have contact in 3rd Brigade sector and deep, plus casualties, and cannot execute by dark."

"Wait," I said. I wanted a minute to consider this.

That radio call was the biggest personal tactical disappointment I had ever experienced in my army life, either in training or in war. We had the Iraqis on the run. The Hammurabi was within our reach, and the majority of that division (we still thought) was in our sector. With the double-envelopment maneuver, we would have completed the destruction of at least the heavy forces of the RGFC—our mission. Additionally, it is not often in training or in war that you have an opportunity to execute a double envelopment. It is like a grand-slam home run for the whole unit. The disappointment was not so much personal (though it *was* that) as it was for the entire VII Corps. If we could end this war with an envelopment of Iraqi forces, our troops would have that success to point to for the rest of their lives. It would have been not only mission accomplished, but rather mission accomplished with a bang at the end.

That's what I had in mind. And now this news from Ron. I pushed the anger down and forced myself to consider the options:

First, I could force it. Tell Ron, just do it. You handle your contact, but get it done. I need the 1st CAV in the fight tonight, so we'll bull our way through this. That is sometimes a workable option.

Second, I could adapt tactics; that is, order 1st CAV and 1st AD to make a forward passage of lines, just as the 1st INF had done with the 2nd ACR, rather than have 1st CAV pass to the north. But the 2nd ACR was well practiced in passage of lines and had time to set it up. This would be from a standing cold start, with planning and execution in the dark. Not only was there the risk of fratricide, it would probably take them all night. Besides, in the morning I'd have two exhausted divisions on my hands from all the coordination and passage, and the Iraqis left alone most of the night.

Third, I could absorb the chance by adjusting for time; that is, we could wait until Ron got things under control and then pass the 1st CAV, probably by first light next morning. We had that time, it would involve less risk, and even though we would be giving the Iraqis who weren't in contact with the 1st AD another twelve hours, we would still get the mission done. On the other hand, the RGFC still seemed to be fighting rather than running away (after the Medina Ridge fight experience, it did not look as though the RGFC would be going anywhere soon), and we had theater air to isolate the battlefield and keep them from running.

Fourth, I had to consider Ron's judgment, which I totally trusted. He knew what I wanted to do and had ordered him to do. He knew the significance of attacking east into the Hammurabi. He also knew his current situation. He wanted to finish the fight. I had always trusted the loyalty and judgment of my subordinates. I had never given a mission that I knew was not possible to execute. That principle had never failed me in over thirty-one years, not once in peace and war. Why abandon it now? Besides, we had the next day—or so I thought at the time.

"IRON 6, this is JAYHAWK 6. Roger your situation. I want you to pass PEGASUS at first light tomorrow without fail. Contact him directly and coordinate."

"WILCO."

"PEGASUS 6, JAYHAWK 6, did you monitor my call to IRON 6?"

"Roger, JAYHAWK, understand BMNT to attack east same axis and objective." It was John Tilelli talking; I could hear the disappointment in his voice. They had busted their ass to be in Area Horse by 1100 that day, moving almost 250 kilometers in a little more than twenty-four hours. And now this.

"Affirmative, coordinate directly with IRON for passage."

That was it. We still had time, I thought.

Stan and the troops had heard both ends of this exchange. They made the necessary adjustments.

At 1800, I made my usual call to John Yeosock to give him a SITREP before his 1900 meeting with General Schwarzkopf. I reported that Iraqi resistance was becoming less coherent, and that 1st INF was in pursuit, but that 1st and 3rd ADs were still in hasty attack mode. I then updated him on our double-envelopment maneuver. We needed another twenty-four hours or so, I told him, and it would be all over: by then we would have run out of maneuver room and would have the remaining Iraqi forces surrounded. John agreed with my assessment. Another twenty-four hours was about what we would get, he thought.

I learned after the war that John had already given what was essentially the same message to the CINC on the morning of the twenty-seventh, and that General Schwarzkopf had used that judgment as the basis of a report he had given to General Powell that afternoon.* In that report, General Schwarzkopf stated that he wanted to continue the ground attack one more day to destroy everything to the Persian Gulf.

I was also at that time totally unaware of General Schwarzkopf's briefing the evening of 27 February that has been called "the mother of all briefings," during which the CINC essentially said that the escape door was shut and declared victory.

After that call, Stan, Creighton Abrams, and I went over the next day's operation. We looked at the objectives assigned, the fire-control measures (including placement of the FSCL), and other fire-support and control measures. This was the closest to a war game we could get during our attack—that is, we looked at moves and countermoves by the Iraqis. We figured there was nothing they could do to stop us from our double-envelopment maneuver.

I was satisfied that all of it would work, and by the end of the day—or at the latest by Friday morning—it would all be over, and we would have done what we had come to do. The RGFC would be destroyed, not only in our sector but in the Kuwaiti theater of operations, as XVIII Corps closed in from the north.

Our own actions were to continue to attack in the sector while setting the double envelopment in motion. Yet I also was becoming increasingly focused on ensuring that major corps units did not run into one another, since our success was beginning to run us out of maneuver room.

Here is what I was seeing. The 1st INF was approaching Highway 8, and their axis of advance had them moving northeast rather than the more due east I had ordered earlier. Third AD was into Kuwait and also approaching Highway 8, attacking east-southeast. Looking at the map, it appeared we might have to do something to change their directions or establish a limit of advance, or else they would run into each other. First AD also was approaching Highway 8, to the north of 3rd AD.

I left the TAC and walked outside to clear my head. Not much else I could do right now. We had the corps attacking due east against the RGFC, the 1st CAV committed for a first-light attack, and the 2nd ACR (in reserve) also committed to follow the 1st INF, then attack north inside them to Hawk. I also had my one remaining Apache battalion in our 11th Aviation Brigade in reserve for deep attacks, although that appeared unlikely, given the cramped space deep. I walked around, ate some MREs, then relaxed for a few minutes and smoked a cigar in the small tent the troops had put up for me, about twenty feet from the TAC entrance.

*On the morning of the twenty-seventh, Schwarzkopf asked Yeosock how much more time he needed, and Yeosock answered, "They'll"—the RGFC—"be done for by tomorrow night," 28 February.

At about 1845, when I went back inside the canvas enclosure of the TAC, Stan pointed out to me that the 3rd AD attacks had, in fact, taken them so far east and southeast that if the Big Red One were to keep its current axis of attack, then 3rd AD might run into them. Since all we had to go on was the friendly situation we had posted on our map, this information was not certain enough for me to make a decision to adjust. Figuring how long it takes to get orders out and executed, and wary of map postings not current, I told Stan to confirm the information and, if correct, to give 3rd AD a limit of advance, and to redirect the 1st INF attack farther east (and toward the blue as I had ordered early that morning), then north once they were across Highway 8.

But at 1900, when the call went to the 1st INF Division, it was interpreted as an order to stop. And so they ordered a halt to their movement, and came to a stop sometime later, at around 2200 to 2300 (although unit moves and combat actions continued most of the night).

What I had wanted them to do was to cease their northeast movement and continue due east toward the Gulf. Then, once they were across Highway 8, I wanted them to turn north. They never got the part of the order that told them to resume attacking east.

Meanwhile, their cavalry squadron, by now far forward and out of radio contact with division and the lead or second brigade, knew of my intent from earlier that day and kept attacking east. In the best example of initiative in accordance with the commander's intent that I knew of in the war, Lieutenant Colonel Bob Wilson and the 1st Squadron, 4th Cavalry (known all over the Army as the quarter horse for 1/4 CAV) moved across and cut Highway 8 at around 1900. Afterward, his squadron was inundated with prisoners. His small unit had to handle almost 5,000 of them, which overwhelmed his capability. But by the early evening of 27 February, we had control of Highway 8.

At least that arm of the envelopment was working.

I did not find out until two days later that the 1st INF had interpreted the order from the TAC to stop completely. That was my fault. If an order can be misunderstood, it will be, as the old Army saying goes. After I learned of it, I asked Tom Rhame, "Who the hell ordered you to stop?"

"We thought you did," he said.

"Damn," I said, then explained what I had intended.

G+3 . . . THE REST OF THE THEATER

In the west, on the afternoon of the twenty-seventh, XVIII Corps changed its orientation from north toward the Euphrates to east toward Basra, and then moved to close the by-now-expanding gap with VII Corps. The 3rd ACR, now under operational control of the 24th MECH, was the first XVIII Corps unit to make the turn.

Meanwhile, the airfield at Umm Hajul (which straddled the east-west boundary with VII Corps, a few kilometers north of al-Busayyah, and thirty kilometers south of the more important Iraqi airfield at Jalibah) was converted by elements of the 101st Airborne into FOB (Forward Operating Base) Viper. From this base, 101st Apaches attacked 145 kilometers farther east into what was called EA (Engagement Area) Thomas and shot up with Hellfires, rockets, and chain gun rounds everything that moved between Viper and Thomas. EA Thomas was a kill box directly north of Basra through which ran the highway north that was thought to be a major exit route for Iraqi armor. As it happened, four hours of continuous attack by 101st Apaches destroyed personnel carriers, multiple rocket launchers, antiaircraft guns, trucks, and grounded helicopters, yet no tanks were found to be moving through EA Thomas.

The next morning, the 101st commander, General Peay, planned to air-assault his 1st Brigade into Thomas. If they could get forces on the ground to cut the highway north out of Basra, it was thought they would strangle the last escape route of the Republican Guards. The cease-fire put a stop to this plan.

Meanwhile, the heaviest punch out of XVIII Corps, the 24th MECH, attacked and captured Jalibah airfield, and moved eastward along Highway 8 at about 1300. By 1000, the airfield, which was defended by an Iraqi armored battalion, was secure. The battalion had lost all of its vehicles, and fourteen MiG fighters, abandoned by the Iraqi air force, also were destroyed.

Not far from Jalibah, the division ran into huge logistics and ammunition storage sites; the area just beyond that was defended by scattered elements of RGFC divisions—the al-Faw, the Nebuchadnezzar, and the Hammurabi (the first two were infantry divisions, the last armored). Though Iraqi artillery tried to lay fires down on the rapidly advancing columns, they didn't do any damage. That afternoon, the 24th took more than 1,300 Iraqi ammunition bunkers and captured more than 5,000 Iraqi soldiers.

★ *In Kuwait, the Marines had come close to completing their mission. While Tiger Brigade cut the highway out of Al Jahrah, and the land route north toward Iraq, the 2nd Division had halted on Mutlah Ridge. And at 0600 the morning of the twenty-seventh, elements of the 1st Division made the final assault on the international airport. It wasn't long before they took down the Iraqi colors and raised the U.S. and Kuwaiti flags (the U.S. flag soon came down, for the sake of diplomatic decorum).*

By 0900, Kuwaiti forces, supported by Egyptian armor and other Arab forces, entered Kuwait City.

Coalition forces found a city that had been sacked. Many of its citizens had been tortured (with acid baths, electric drills, and electric prods), killed (dismemberment, shooting, or beating to death were frequent methods), or raped.

Some Iraqi looting had been systematic—a million ounces of gold from the Kuwait Central Bank, jewels from the gem market, marine ferries, shrimp trawlers, baggage-handling equipment, airliners, runway lights, granite facing from skyscrapers, thousands of plastic seats from the university stadium, and grave-digging backhoes, to name a few. Most government and public buildings had been looted and pillaged—many were burned. So too were hotels, department stores, and telephone exchanges. Other looting had been more opportunistic—rugs, drapes, toilets, sinks, light fixtures, lightbulbs, most of the country's cars, buses, and trucks, and books from libraries. The Iraqis sabotaged all but a few of the country's 1,330 oil wells and twenty-six gathering stations. Every day, something approaching 11 million barrels of crude escaped from these broken wells. About half of those 11 million barrels burned up. The rest made vast crude oil lakes. Ships were scuttled, to block channels through the harbor. Water and electrical utilities were sabotaged.

Scattered along the so-called Highway of Death, littered around the ruined—and mostly stolen—cars and trucks, was a partial "inventory" of the loot from Kuwait City—television sets, washing machines, carpets, scuba gear, jewelry.

After the Arabs took the city, the Marines entered. When they did, the Kuwaitis came out like Parisians in August 1944. "God bless Bush!" they cried. "Thank you, U.S.A.! Thank you! Thank you! Thank you!"

★ By evening in Riyadh, momentum was growing in Washington for a ceasefire. And at 2100 (1300 in Washington), General Schwarzkopf gave the live, televised "mother of all briefings" that, in essence, declared victory. Although he allowed that armored battles were still going on, the CINC indicated that he would happily stop fighting if the order came to do that.

He did not have long to wait.

14

CEASE-FIRE

THE NEXT TWELVE HOURS BROUGHT AN END TO THE WAR FOR VII Corps.

On into the night, we continued to fight a series of close battles. Following the decisions to adjust the 1st INF and 3rd AD axes of advance, I continued to focus on making adjustments in these fights in a way that would allow us to complete the double envelopment sometime the next day.

That evening, I got a quick update on the Iraqi units left in our sector and a look at our own situation. From the reports öf the commanders I had visited earlier and from my own observations, it was clear to me that we had the Iraqis on the floor. A short briefing from Bill Eisel, G-2 at the TAC, confirmed it: The Iraqi intent was to continue to defend with what they had while attempting to withdraw their remaining units from the theater over pontoon bridges they were constructing over the Shatt al Arab* and the Euphrates. Since both these areas were outside VII Corps sector, and had been since late on 25 February, there was nothing we could do to stop the units leaving by that route. Meanwhile, the Iraqis we were facing no longer appeared capable of any kind of coordinated defense—battalion-sized actions, but not much more. We estimated that the Hammurabi Division and what was left of the Medina (by this time only a brigade) would defend around the Rumaila oil fields, or our Objective Raleigh (and about thirty kilometers from where the 1st CAV was now). It was still not clear to me how much of the Hammurabi was left in our sector, and whether they were joining the retreat, or were part of the defense. Other Iraqi military options in our sector were extremely limited at this point.

Our own situation was excellent. In the southern part of our sector, the British were racing toward Highway 8, with by now only scattered resistance, and the 1st INF was also in a pursuit, after having cracked through the Iraqi defense the night before and early that morning. Our biggest remaining future fights were going to be in the north, with what remained of the Ham-

*The Shatt al Arab is the river formed north of Basra by the confluence of the Tigris and Euphrates; it flows into the Gulf.

murabi in Objective Raleigh. I figured that with the distance to Raleigh, that fight would take place late the next morning, 28 February, somewhere west of the Rumaila oil fields, and it would be over before the evening—very much like the Medina fight with 1st AD. Thus, I figured that by 1800 the next day, our double envelopment would be complete, and 1st CAV and the 1st INF would have accomplished their linkup somewhere north of Safwan on Highway 8, and we would have trapped the remainder of the Iraqi forces in our sector. By that time, we would have run out of both room to maneuver and Iraqi units to attack.

From there we could always continue north toward Basra, but that would take intervention and new orders from Third Army, and we had none. Nor did we have any new orders for finishing the current fight other than the ones we were trying to execute—i.e., our own double envelopment.

By then, I'd had VII Corps attacking for almost four days straight. Soon we would be at the limit of soldier and leader endurance. But we were not there yet.

I left the TAC and went outside to smoke a cigar.

When I returned at around 2130, Stan had been talking to John Landry at the main. There was talk of a cease-fire in the morning.

Total surprise. It was the second of the two great surprises of the war for me personally. The other was the order to attack early. Both were friendly actions. No warning order, no questions, no real evidence from the battlefield.

Cease-fire! "Who the hell's idea is that?" I wanted to know.

I called John Yeosock right away, and John confirmed the news. "There's talk about a possible 'cessation of offensive operations' effective tomorrow," he told me. "Nothing's definite yet," he added. "But in the light of that development, don't do operations that will unnecessarily cost any more casualties."

I repeated that our situation was a combination of pursuit and hasty attack. Another twenty-four hours or so would finish it. "Why now? Why not give us tomorrow? We have them where we want them. There is less and less organized resistance, but we are not done yet."

John agreed. "I already told the CINC we needed another day," he told me. "But I'll try to get all this clarified." Meanwhile, he directed us to put out a warning order for a possible cessation of offensive operations in the morning.

I was stunned.

But we put out the warning order. None of my commanders came back on the radio to protest stopping.

This was the third set of orders given to the corps that day. First had been the double envelopment. Second had been the adjustment based on Ron Griffith's radio call, our orders to keep 3rd AD and 1st INF from running into each

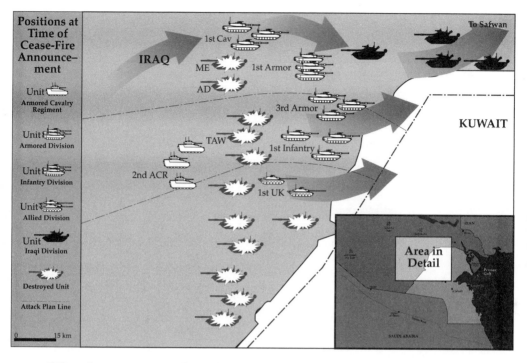

When the corps command post first received word of the anticipated cessation of hostilities, all of the brigades in the corps were in heavy contact with the enemy and the 1st Cavalry Division anticipated action. As the time of the cease-fire changed, units continued to attack forces in Kuwait and Iraq. The 1st INF was heading "toward the blue."

---

other, and the postponement of the 1st CAV attack based on Ron Griffith's late call. Now this. We would issue two more orders before the cease-fire the next day. It was not the kind of battle rhythm pace I liked when issuing orders to an attacking corps of 146,000 soldiers and 50,000 vehicles—in fact, it was the kind of pace that I had been used to when I was a captain with 137 soldiers and fifty vehicles.

As I let it all sink in, many things went through my mind. My initial thoughts were ones of frustration: We had not yet finished the mission. We had the Iraqis on the floor. Let's *finish* it. Run right through the finish line at full speed.

Yet if someone knew something I did not, and if he thought we had reached our strategic goals, I was glad that our troops were done and there would be no more casualties. The corps was tired. In maybe another twenty-four hours,

I would have had to start rotating units in and out to generate some fresh combat power.

I asked myself if I had been forceful enough in painting the local tactical picture to John Yeosock, and decided I had. We had been especially attentive to it since his earlier reports of the CINC's "concerns," and John got reports from not only me directly, but from Colonel Dick Rock and Colonel Carl Ernest, who had been at my 27 February morning planning session. Third Army had as precise a picture of our situation and the enemy's then as at any time in the war. As for CENTCOM, I had no idea what they knew, but I had to assume that it was whatever Third Army knew.

I did not bypass John Yeosock and call General Schwarzkopf directly to protest. I trusted Yeosock. He knew mounted operations and, even though he was in Riyadh, he had a great feel for what still needed to be done tactically in our sector of attack. I had made my case with him and that was it. At the same time, I trusted that the senior leadership knew what they were doing. We were not yet done tactically, but if there were other considerations that made a cease-fire a wise strategic choice, then OK, we would execute.

When I let the TAC know, their reaction was not unlike mine. First, they had questions: "Is this right?" Then, like me, they asked, "Why now?" Then, when the end appeared inevitable, there was a noticeable sign of physical letdown. With the adrenaline gone, the momentum and charged atmosphere of only a few moments earlier went away. I knew it would be like that all over the corps as the word got out.

It is here that human factors come into play in a large combat unit.

By 1800 that evening, I was using the combat power of the corps at full throttle, with maneuvers set in motion that would complete our mission in another twenty-four hours. We had four divisions committed, with a fresh division in the 1st CAV. The troops and commanders, while tired, were still capable of continuing the attacks at a peak level of intensity, stimulated both by the continuation of the attack and the prospects of victory. They were driving on. Yet if ever the momentum got interrupted, it would be hell getting it started again. It is a fact of soldier and unit behavior. When you're operating at close to endurance limits and pushing yourself and your soldiers to stay at that level, you must keep going. Any halt means a precipitous drop in energy level, because the stimulus is removed. Without that stimulus of movement and action, units fall idle very fast, like dropping off a cliff. After that, it is damn near impossible to rouse them to previous levels. I had seen it happen many times in training and in combat in Vietnam.

So when we confirmed the rumors of a cease-fire, the air went out of the balloon. When we put the order out just before midnight, we could just feel the corps attack momentum come to a halt.

VII CORPS ACTIONS

While all this was going on, actions in VII Corps continued.

First INF units had had almost four days of nonstop actions, accompanied by constant adjustment to retain unit integrity—to make sure the right units were in the right combination. These adjustments were especially frequent at night, when the units could easily become separated. One of those units was the 3rd Battalion, 66th Armor, an M1A1 tank battalion in the 2nd Armored Division Forward, which had been one of the two lead brigades in Tom Rhame's night attack toward Objective Norfolk on the previous night. By now they had attacked and moved all day and were approaching Highway 8.

On 27 February, according to an account by Captain Tim Ryan and Captain Bill Rabena, "the afternoon sun was setting as the brigade snaked its way down a valley leading from the Kuwaiti central plateau to the coastal plain, (the troops would call it the "Valley of the Boogers," because of the severely broken terrain and the hidden Iraqis). The dense black smoke from the burning oil wells twenty miles away made it seem several hours later. Captain Tim Ryan, the D Company, 3/66 Armor commander, had just finished issuing orders to his company for yet another brigade night attack when the change of mission from Lieutenant Colonel Jones came over the radio." Because Taylor Jones, the battalion commander, did not want to lose any howitzers to attacks by bypassed Iraqi units known to be still in the area, Jones ordered Ryan to go back to the rear and escort the howitzer batteries of 4/3 Field Artillery battalion forward so that they could safely get in better position to support the attack. Ryan decided to use only two tanks, his and that of Staff Sergeant Stringer, for the mission. "As Ryan and Stringer turned their tanks around for the return trip," after one successful escort, "Staff Sergeant Stringer identified and reported approximately ten dismounted Iraqi soldiers through the tank's thermal sights. The enemy squad was well armed, their light machine guns and rocket-propelled grenades clearly evident at that close range." Ryan wanted to let them surrender and fired warning shots over their heads. "As the tracers from the warning burst of machine-gun fire from Ryan's tank arched through the black sky twenty feet over the enemy's head, a hail of bullets from Stringer's tank slashed through the formation. Several enemy soldiers dropped in their tracks. . . . Meanwhile, the remaining soldiers ran for cover behind a previously unnoticed Iraqi T-62 tank approximately 400 meters away from both Ryan and Stringer." Several minutes passed, as an Iraqi soldier made his way to Stringer's tank to ask for medical care for their wounded. Meanwhile, Ryan's tank loader, Pfc. Berthold, was keeping an eye on the remainder of the Iraqis and the T-62. When he noticed that some of the Iraqi infantry were mounting the tank and others were running away, he alerted his commander, and

Ryan went into action. "Ryan immediately slewed his tank's turret back in the direction of the enemy tank, identified the fleeing enemy through his sights, and squeezed the trigger once again, sending machine-gun bullets through the dark. None of the enemy soldiers was moving when he traversed his turret back to the enemy tank. . . . Before he had come to let the thought sink in, Sgt. Jones [his gunner] reported that the T-62's turret was traversing. . . . Ryan ordered Jones to fire, and the resulting impact of the main gun round on the T-62's turret blew it completely off the hull." Ryan and Stringer would go on to destroy another tank and a BMP and capture an Iraqi infantry squad before they completed their artillery escort mission (at 0230, 28 February). At 0430, they got the mission to resume the attack at 0600 28 February.

First AD had continued their relentless attacks with three brigades abreast. Their combat damage to Iraqi units on into the darkness of 27 February was 186 enemy tanks, 127 personnel carriers of all types, 38 artillery pieces, 5 air defense systems, 118 trucks, and 839 EPWs. For the 1st AD, these attacks had been the heaviest fighting of the four days. One 1st AD soldier, from 4th Battalion, 66th Armor, was killed in action.

By about 2130, the **3rd AD** had reached Phase Line Kiwi and had run out of room. If I continued them east, they would run into the 1st INF. (It was astride Highway 8 that I had redirected 1st INF farther east, so that 3rd AD could continue their attack to Objective Denver.)

Meanwhile, as their two brigades attacked on line toward Kiwi, they'd had continuous combat with Iraqi units. Their 1st Brigade had reported destroying 60 tanks, 13 artillery pieces, and 6 BRDMs (Soviet-built wheeled personnel carriers). At Kiwi, their 3rd Brigade (which had earlier passed through 2nd Brigade) had destroyed three T-72s, three BMPs, and captured over two hundred EPWs. One of the EPWs was an officer, who reported that there were many Iraqi tanks in front of the brigade beyond Kiwi. At a little past 2300, 3rd AD recorded that they had received our corps order to continue the attack to Denver across Highway 8 (made possible by the 1st INF adjustment east).

First CAV had moved east to a position just west of Phase Line Lime, ready to attack east to destroy the Hammurabi after 1st AD cleared a zone of attack. While moving up, their cavalry squadron had destroyed a BMP and a bypassed bunker complex from which Iraqis were firing on them. By 2100, they were set for their attack east. Their written order to attack east was published at 0220 on 28 February, although verbal orders had gone out many hours before.

ORDERS

At 2337, we got the official written order from Third Army that the cessation would take place the next day at 0500, and we put out our own order soon after that. Though we had less than six hours of darkness in which to execute, I was satisfied that there was enough time for the commanders to rein in their ground ops. Meanwhile, we would continue with Apaches forward until 0500, and I called off the operation of the 1st CAV.

I stuck around in the TAC for a little while longer, and when I was satisfied that all the units had received the 0500 cease-fire order, I decided to get some rest. My own adrenaline level had drained away. Gone was the intensity of the previous four days. Gone was the intensity of the previous night. I could feel myself relaxing. I tried to prevent it, but it was hopeless. "Do not let down," I kept saying to myself. I was not successful.

I left sometime at around 0100. While walking to the tent, I told Toby how proud I was of everybody in VII Corps . . . and how severely disappointed I was that I couldn't get the 1st CAV into the fight.

The problem was that, while it was over, I felt a nagging sense of incompletion. In every training exercise I'd ever had as a young officer, we had always tried to end with a successful attack that put us on our objective. Instead, we had ragged edges—and with our final objective clearly within reach.

First Squadron, 7th Cavalry, 1st CAV Division, was within sixty kilometers of Basra; 1st AD Apaches could see the Gulf; 3rd AD was within thirty kilometers of Highway 8 and our Objective Denver; 1st INF was less than twenty kilometers from Safwan. The British were across Highway 8, north of Kuwait City.

0300 28 FEBRUARY

"General Franks, we have new orders from Third Army." It was Toby, jolting me awake.

"What the hell is it now?" I snapped. Although I was waking up quickly, as soldiers learn to do, I was also "shooting the messenger."

As always, Toby was doing the right thing.

"Third Army has ordered a new time for the cessation," he said. "From 0500 to 0800. G-3 thinks you should come over to the TAC."

"OK, thanks, Toby. I'll be right there," I said, getting my head back in the war I'd thought was all but over. Toby left a cup of coffee. I got my leg on in the dark and walked into the bright lights of the TAC.

0315 VII CORPS TAC CP

I called John Yeosock to get clarification, and John confirmed the change. Not only did we have a change of cessation time from 0500 to 0800, he said, but we were to ensure "maximum destruction of enemy equipment." A written order would soon follow. When I reminded him that this was the third set of VII Corps orders that our units would have gotten within the past twelve hours, he told me he did not need any reminding about that. He was well aware that between him and a tank commander, orders had to pass through eight layers of command.

The next order for us was truly puzzling: it was very important for us to get to the crossroads at Safwan, John told me, to prevent any Iraqi units from escaping by that route. Why the Safwan crossroads had suddenly become a high priority escaped me. The 1st INF had already cut Highway 8 south of Safwan, the road leading into that intersection from the Gulf coast was not carrying any significant traffic, and in fact this order was the first time we had been given any geographic objective in the war (it had been a corps decision to seize al-Busayyah). But an order is an order. I said WILCO and called Stan over for a huddle. I had interpreted John's order as one to stop movement through the road junction. The tactics were up to me.

The first thing I wanted to do was make a quick call to the units to change the cease-fire time.

I assumed the time change had been the result of a simple error in converting Zulu time to local time, or a difference of three hours. The use of different times in a single time zone in an operational theater made absolutely no sense to me. I had outlawed the use of anything other than local time use in the corps. We were attacking in one time zone, and I did not want some tired, getting-shot-at soldier having to fool with changing times from Zulu to Charlie or whatever.

But we also had this crossroads business at Safwan to take care of.

Stan circled it on the map hanging in front of us. My first thought was to go after it with the 11th Aviation Brigade. Stan gave them a warning order. With Apaches to interdict traffic, that would get a presence there immediately, and ground troops would follow later. A second look at the map showed that such an attack by corps aviation risked getting in the way of the 1st INF. The Big Red One was not more than twenty to thirty kilometers away from Safwan, which would put the town in the normal deep area for division Apaches to attack. So I said no to the 11th Aviation Brigade option.

I recalled that 1st INF had been attacking on a generally northeast axis before I had ordered the division to go due east until they crossed Highway 8, then north. Now I figured that if they went back to their original attack direction, then they would get to the crossroads. To do that would also mean halting 3rd AD along Phase Line Kiwi, so that they would not now run into the 1st INF. That is what I decided to do.

Just as it was the third change of orders for the corps, it was also the third change of orders for the Big Red One. . . . I could visualize Tom Rhame, forward in his tank, awakened with these orders and wondering if I had gone crazy.

I directed an order go out to all of VII Corps: They were to continue to attack in the same direction and with the same objectives we had been using prior to the early-evening adjustments, they were to continue the attack until 0800 (not 0500), and, until that time, they were to destroy maximum equipment. This order also put the 1st INF back on their earlier line of attack—that is, generally northeast. My assumption was that if our map posting was accurate—if they were indeed twenty to thirty kilometers from Safwan—then the 1st INF would easily get to those crossroads by 0800. I also figured their own Apaches would get there much sooner.

I should have known we would have confusion. Though we did our best to keep things simple, I probably should have realized that I was adding to the confusion simply by transmitting all of these orders. Time was running out.

With the initial cessation order at 2337, the coiled-spring effect had gone out of the corps—after all, soldiers are not machines to be switched on and off at random. Also, big units are harder to move than small units—especially when they have been attacking for the better part of four days. Clausewitz calls this phenomenon the disorganizing effects of victory. That night was the night of maximum friction, all brought on by fatigue, misunderstanding, and miscommunication—the "countless minor incidents," Clausewitz writes—"the kind you can never really foresee" that "combine to lower the level of performance."

Here is one example. We were attacking in one direction at 1800. Units were about to run into each other and were not oriented for the double envelopment. At 1900, an order went out to stop so that we could reorient the corps for the next day's final attack. However, even though orders to resume the attack were sent to all the other divisions, one was not put out to 1st INF—attention to it had gotten lost in all the cease-fire transmissions. Then, to add to the complexity, we got the cease-fire order and tried to go back to the directions that had been in effect before 1800.

At that point, since there was no time for written orders, all of these orders were going out in verbal radio transmissions over both our standard line-of-sight and our SATCOM radio nets. And finally, though the order announcing the 0800 cease-fire was received and acknowledged by each of the major units, I did not speak personally to any of the commanders at that time.

It was now about 0430. All of this activity had taken the better part of an hour. I looked around the TAC. We'd had three mission changes. Fatigue and frustration had overtaken us. What a hell of a way to end this war, I thought.

Sometime later we received the second written order from Third Army that night: an order to a five-division corps to extend by three hours an operation we had expected to end by now. It was totally unrealistic to believe that so large an organization could react that quickly—and in the middle of the night, after four days of battle. Even if everyone in the corps had been listening to the same radio, they would have had trouble executing on such short notice.

As far as I could see, there was nothing more I could do. I was tired, frustrated, and extremely disappointed that we had not been given the time to finish. I felt like the manager of a ball club that had won the World Series in five games, instead of four. We were proud as hell of what we had done, but I wanted that sweep.

Yet, for all that, I still determined that the frustrations would not cast a shadow over the heroic and skillful execution of VII Corps's soldiers and leaders, and for that reason, I said little more about the missed opportunity to bring our mission to its final conclusion. Nor should it cast a shadow today—six years after Desert Storm—over the strategic significance of the victory in the Gulf and the opportunities it has opened for greater peace in the region.

Nevertheless, from the perspective of strategic, operational, and tactical linkage, there are lessons to learn for the future. If students of military history and operations want to learn the major lesson the Gulf War teaches, they should look at the war's end state.

It was a significant challenge, no doubt about it, to orchestrate the end of a campaign of lightning swiftness that had been conducted by a thirty-five-nation coalition in a region of the world with many opportunities and pitfalls. Nonetheless, it seemed that we gave a lot more thought (at least in the theater) to how to get in and get started than how to conclude it. The intellectual focus seemed to be in inverse proportion. The closer we got to the end, the less we focused.

At the end of my briefing on 9 February, Secretary of Defense Dick Cheney asked me, "How will it all end?" The perfect question at the right time—and a question every Secretary of Defense should ask anytime our military is about to be committed to battle. He should keep asking until it is over. Though I gave Secretary Cheney an answer that reflected my sense of how I expected it to end for VII Corps and Third Army, I'm not aware of anyone at any time giving him a picture of the expected end state for the entire theater.

Here, to the best of my knowledge, is the story of how the decision was made that brought us to the actual end state on the battlefield:

In the evening of 27 February, following General Schwarzkopf's "mother of all briefings," General Colin Powell called Schwarzkopf to tell him that the President was thinking of ending the war within a matter of hours, but would defer that decision to the theater commander. General Powell added that he shared the President's view. As far as he could personally tell, it was all over. Yet he too wanted to hear that confirmed by the theater commander.

General Schwarzkopf replied that he would poll his commanders before giving a final judgment.

That poll never got to the tactical battlefield.

In the call back to Powell, General Schwarzkopf confirmed that it was time to end the fighting. After that theater judgment, the Joint Chiefs agreed unanimously that the war had achieved its goals and should stop.

The order went to Third Army, and from Third Army to us.

★ Could we have gone on? Absolutely. Would that have made good tactical sense? From where I was standing, absolutely. Would another twelve hours have destroyed more of Saddam's army? Absolutely (though not much in our sector).

But wars are not fought to make tactical sense. They are fought to gain strategic objectives. When those who are looking at the entire strategic situation, both present and future, say we are at the end, then for the soldiers on the battlefield, that's the end. Sometimes strategic goals have immediate results, such as the liberation of Kuwait. Others take longer to manifest themselves, and are obtained by taking advantage of the new opportunities that arise from the way the tactical outcomes were gained. Now, six years after our victory in Desert Storm, those results are still being played out, and I believe they are mostly positive.

I was not thinking about any of that on the morning of 28 February. I simply trusted those who were making the strategic decisions. That was the difference between the end of this war and of the one in Vietnam. From President Bush to the soldiers in our tanks, it was a matter of trust reunited.

Our VII Corps tactical victories had not taken eighty-nine hours. They had taken almost twenty years.

0630

By now it was approaching daylight; reports of operations were coming in over the radio. These reports were somewhat spotty, however, because our tactical line-of-sight communications were not particularly good at this time. Since we were in their sector, we could talk direct with 3rd AD; we had good line-of-sight comms with 1st CAV; and since 2nd ACR were to our west, they were in direct comms. But because of the range between us and 1st AD, we had difficulty contacting them from time to time; other than SATCOM, we were out of radio contact with 1st INF (because SATCOM was on a different frequency than the other line-of-sight comms, transmissions on one could not be heard on the other).

As for VII Corps main CP, they were by now over 200 kilometers away (about an hour and a half's helo flight). For the past two days, they had been unable to hear tactical radio communications and were thus having difficulty keeping current on the rapidly changing local tactical situation.

Communication with Third Army was in better shape, since Colonel Dick Rock still had his long-haul phone comms directly back there. So I remained confident that John Yeosock's staff had a decent picture—at least of what we knew in the corps TAC.

Though I considered flying east to the 1st INF, I concluded that it would take up the whole time before the 0800 cease-fire, and I wanted to be the one to order it, so I determined to stay at the TAC. Because of the constantly changing orders from Riyadh and the possible mix-up in the corps, I wanted to be next to my most reliable comms during the hours before the cease-fire. After the previous night's rapid changes, I did not know what to expect this morning.

At 0700, John Tilelli called to tell me he was ready to attack if I wanted to exercise that option. It was one hour before the end, with still no room north of 1st AD and no time to get him room. It ripped me up inside. I could picture the 1st CAV, leaning forward in the saddle, as it were. They had deployed in October and had trained to a razor's edge; they had selflessly been the feint and demonstration force that had successfully deceived the Iraqis into believing we were coming up the Wadi al Batin; and finally, they had in a short time come all this way and gotten themselves in a position to attack. I did not want to be the commander to tell them now. It was painful; it's still painful today.

"No," I told John, "we are out of time."

He merely said, "Roger out."

At 0720 a frantic voice was heard over the corps line-of-sight FM radio net: "JAYHAWK, this is THRASHER BLUE 6"—a corps artillery unit, as it turned out—"we are taking incoming friendly fire."

The last thing I wanted was one or more of our soldiers killed or wounded by blue-on-blue this close to a cease-fire. Force protection was much more on my mind than destroying another ten or twenty Iraqi tanks. "Tell them cease fire," I said. The officer closest to the radio ordered, "JAYHAWK, JAYHAWK, this is JAYHAWK OSCAR, cease fire, I say again cease fire." As it turned out, some commanders took it to mean that we were issuing the actual cease-fire order when, in fact, it was only intended to stop the possible blue-on-blue. It was a confusing order, and I should not have let it go out.

The confusion did not end there. We got a reply from everyone, including the 1st INF, whom we had called on SATCOM. A moment later, it occurred to me that the blue-on-blue could not have involved them, since they were not in line-of-sight comms range. "Order the Big Red One to continue the attack," I ordered. The call went out immediately, but I later learned that not all their units got the second call.

Meanwhile, we got a call from 3rd AD explaining that THRASHER BLUE 6 was a corps unit on the other side of the enemy on their (3rd AD's) gun target line. When rounds missed and went over the Iraqis, they impacted in THRASHER BLUE 6's area. I told THRASHER to get the hell out of the way. They had already done that.

At 0740, the order went out to the other units to resume the attack.

★ Just before 0800, the 1st AD reported they had captured the HQ of the Medina Division. That was great news.

I glanced around the TAC. It was full of troops—those from the TAC and those who had come inside to witness the end. Everyone wanted to be in there when the order went out.

I looked at them, their tired faces, their by now grimy uniforms, and I was full of thanks for what they had done. I wished I could shake everyone's hand, give each of them a hug, and tell them all how proud I had been to serve in battle with them.

I watched the GPS Toby had brought into the TAC. It was our most accurate timepiece. At precisely 0800, I got on the radio and told units to cease fire.

First Squadron, 7th Cavalry, 1st CAV Division, was sixty kilometers from Basra (which, of course, was now in XVIII Corps sector) and about twenty kilometers from the Hammurabi. First INF was fifteen kilometers south of Safwan. First and 3rd ADs were twenty-five kilometers from Highway 8, and 1st AD Apaches could see the blue waters of the Gulf. The British were on Highway 8, north of Kuwait City.

It was over.

RESULTS

We had attacked close to 250 kilometers in eighty-nine hours with five divisions, day and night, in sandstorms and rain. It had been an incredible battlefield performance by the soldiers and leaders of VII Corps.

We had accomplished our mission to destroy the RGFC forces in our sec-

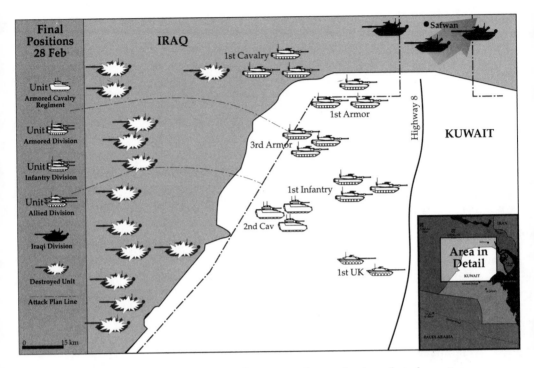

As the time of the cessation of hostilities arrived, most lead combat elements were in Kuwait, with smaller combat units from the 1st Infantry Division and the 1st (UK) Armored reaching across Highway 8. The VII Corps double envelopment did not occur.

tor. The Tawalkana had ceased to exist as a division. The Medina was down to a few battalions, if that. At war's end, we could determine no other RGFC forces (with the possible exception of some scattered units of the Hammurabi) in our sector. Other Iraqi units were either destroyed or combat ineffective, and their equipment would be destroyed later. The better part of eleven Iraqi divisions lay in the wake of the VII Corps attack (including the two RGFC divisions). In those eighty-nine hours, corps units had destroyed 1,350 tanks, 1,224 personnel carriers of all types, 285 artillery pieces, 105 air defense pieces, and 1,229 trucks. And in our rolling attack we had bypassed an amount of equipment equal to that; after the cease-fire we went back and destroyed it. Though we had counted more than 22,000 Iraqi EPWs as captured, the true figure was probably as high as double that, since units lost count.

In the eighty-nine hours, we had fired a total of 55,000 artillery rounds and 10,500 MLRS rockets, and we had also fired twenty-five ATACMs in twenty-one missions. We'd used 348 close-support air strikes, mainly A-10s, and mainly in the daylight.

Kuwait was liberated. The Iraqi army had gone from fourth largest in the world to twenty-second in a little over a month. A coalition of thirty-five nations had quickly formed, had united its forces on the battlefield, and together had achieved impressive results in a short time. Was it perfect? No. But it was a hell of a lot closer to perfect than we had come in anyone's memory or experience. It was a victory of staggering battlefield dimensions.

But it had come at a price. At that point, I thought we had twenty-one soldiers KIA and ninety-seven wounded. That turned out to be grossly inaccurate. The final figure was 46 KIA and 196 U.S. wounded, and 16 British soldiers KIA and 61 wounded. I will never forget them for the rest of my life.

Eleven M1A1s were damaged, and four were destroyed; sixteen Bradleys damaged, and nine destroyed; one Apache damaged, and one destroyed.

I say again: It was fast but it was not easy.

Let no one equate swiftness with ease.

It was a total team effort, as we'd known it would be. I was humbled to have had the privilege to lead such a magnificent armored corps into battle. Their battlefield achievements had come about because of twenty years of rebuilding, and because of their courage and selfless sense of duty. That I had been permitted to return to battle with that Army after we had both been badly wounded was something more than I could ever have dreamed of.

LOGISTICS

The logistics dimension in such a short period of time had been staggering. Modern mounted warfare is fast and lethal, and consumes an enormous amount of supplies. Our logisticians kept the corps constantly sustained, and many entire armies cannot do that. They operate for a while, then pause for days, weeks, or even months, to allow their forces to resupply. That such was not the case with VII Corps was a testament to the skill and hard, brute force work done by VII Corps logisticians in all units.

Fuel and ammunition had been transported by corps soldiers mostly in truck convoys over the trackless desert. Led by junior officers and NCOs with few navigation devices and few radios, the convoys had rolled day and night. They had moved in rain and in driving sandstorms in which it was difficult to see the vehicle in front. They'd come upon bypassed Iraqi units and soldiers and captured them. They'd gone through minefields and our own unexploded munitions. At times, they'd gotten closer to the combat action with their fuel and ammo vehicles than normal practice would dictate.

Here is an account from the 125th Support Battalion, 1st Armored Division, from the day they almost ran out of fuel: "When the convoy [forty-two fuel trucks] arrived at the refuel site [Nelligen] they found that the other two brigades had taken everything and no allocation had been saved. Prior to first light [around 0400] on the twenty-seventh, enough fuel arrived for nineteen HEMMTS. Those fuelers left immediately for our location [about 100 kilometers away] under Major Dunn's control. He raced at speeds of over fifty mph across the desert to get us fuel. One tanker was lost, as it turned upside down when rolling over a ravine. No one was hurt, but we lost 2,500 gallons of fuel. The battalion commander . . . went back to meet them. SPC Spencer [the battalion commander's driver] later recounted topping sixty-five mph as his HMMWV left the ground when hitting even the smallest bump. [Sometime along the way] the second HEMMT convoy drove into a minefield. [One] vehicle ran over one of the mines, and it exploded," damaging the vehicle but not wounding anyone. Later that morning, the convoy reached the 1st Brigade and refueled them with enough to continue the attack on 27 February. "After distributing the newly arrived fuel to the combat battalions, we began movement through the log base [an Iraqi logistics base that the Medina had been defending and 1st AD had overrun]. Everywhere you looked there was total destruction. Ammo pits were burning and exploding, sending shrapnel flying through the air; trucks were overturned and ablaze; trailers full of supplies also were on fire. Moving the BSA through all of this in formation was nearly impossible." (The BSA—brigade support area—was where logistics units supporting 1st Brigade gathered and set up.) "Company-sized units broke into smaller columns and moved through. It took almost all day to re-form the BSA on the eastern side of the complex. As we moved through the area, the BSA captured some 146 EPWs. [And] there was a harrowing moment when one prisoner ran from the holding area to kiss the hand of the soldier who had just thrown him an MRE from his truck. There were no contemptuous victors, only compassionate soldiers."

The 2nd COSCOM work to supply the VII Corps before, during, and after the war had been an extraordinary achievement, one that has to rank in one of the all-time feats of logistics in the history of the U.S. Army. Expanding from a base of fewer than 8,000 soldiers in Germany, the COSCOM had grown before the start of the war to fifty battalion-sized units, in five brigade-sized organizations, with a total of over 26,000 soldiers (an armored division with attachments normally had less than forty battalion organizations). Their operations had begun on 8 November, the moment we were notified to deploy, and they had not stopped until we redeployed. They'd simultaneously deployed themselves, expanded by a factor of almost four, and built an infrastructure in the desert that had kept the corps supplied. It was austere, but it worked.

During the VII Corps eighty-nine-hour war, the COSCOM had moved 2.6 million meals, 6.2 million gallons of diesel fuel, 2.2 million gallons of aviation fuel, and 327 major assemblies, such as tank engines. Every day, they moved 4,900 tons of ammo. To do this, in addition to the transportation assets of each division, they used 1,385 tractor trucks, 608 fuel tankers, 1,604 trailers, and 377 five-ton trucks, organized in 11 petroleum companies, 13 medium truck companies, 8 HET companies, and 4 medium/light truck companies. These transportation assets had been augmented by the CH-47 helos of the 11th Aviation Brigade and by C-130 airlift drops by CENTAF.

Within the COSCOM was the 332nd Medical Brigade, commanded by Brigadier General Mike Strong, a physician from the Reserve component. My VII Corps surgeon, Colonel Bob Griffin, served as Mike's chief of staff and organized the staff of the brigade. They had fifteen hospitals, which provided world-class medical care to our soldiers. They'd arranged the medical support in bands of increasing medical capability, depending on how close you were to the action. In the band closest to the action were the medical assets of the divisions, augmented by five MASHs (mobile army surgical hospitals) from the medical brigade. In the next band were five combat-support hospitals, which augmented the surgical capability of the more forward and mobile MASHs and provided more beds. Back in Saudi, along Tapline Road, were the five evacuation hospitals. Of all our medical facilities, these had the most complete surgical and nursing capabilities, and were used to stabilize patients before evacuation from theater, or to keep patients until they recovered and could return to duty. During the war, the brigade recorded 1,768 admissions and 960 air evacuations. The list of professional medical personnel either called to active duty or already on active duty could fill the pages of a medical *Who's Who.* One hospital commander was a sixty-seven-year-old, physically fit orthopedic surgeon who had begun his service in North Africa as an enlisted soldier with the British in World War II. He wanted to continue to serve, and that he did. Many of our medevac pilots were Vietnam veterans who had stayed in the Reserve component and were proud to answer the call again.

Brigadier General Bob McFarlin and all the logisticians of the 2nd COSCOM, the divisions, and separate corps units were heroes in my book. "Forget logistics and you lose," I have said on many occasions. I might add that one should not forget the logisticians, either. They were magnificent. Nothing got in their way.

OPERATING SYSTEMS

The Army uses the term *battle operating systems* to describe the seven parts of a tactical force that must work in harmony and in the right combination to ensure victory. These are maneuver, fires, logistics, command, mobility and countermobility, air defense, and intelligence.

In Desert Storm, all elements of the VII Corps made these work. Though I have put most of my focus on elements such as maneuver, fires, command, and intelligence, there were many others:

• The engineers of Colonel Sam Raines's 7th Engineer Brigade continually built and maintained thousands of kilometers of MSRs (main supply routes), opened and marked lanes through minefields, built several airfields, and destroyed Iraqi fortifications.

• Colonel Rich Pomager's 14th Military Police Brigade processed over 20,000 prisoners, operated the many EPW compounds, and provided route security on the thousands of kilometers of corps MSRs.

• The corps signal units of Colonel Rich Walsh's 93rd Signal Brigade ensured communications within the VII Corps, as well as with Riyadh and with units processing arriving soldiers and equipment through the ports and airfields. Signal soldiers and MPs operated in small units that often were isolated from their parent unit for extended periods. The successful completion of their mission was a tribute to their small-unit leadership.

• The 7th Personnel Group, commanded by Colonel Jo Rusin, linked our wartime replacement soldiers with equipment, or, where necessary, moved individual replacements forward to units where and when they were needed. She and her staff (together with corps AG Lieutenant Colonel Eugenia Thornton) were meticulous in maintaining accountability and the records of those VII Corps soldiers killed in action, who died as a result of disease and non-battle injury, were wounded in action, and injured as a result of non-battle causes. Later the 7th was timely and thorough in reporting to Third Army the circumstances of soldier deaths caused by fratricide.

• Lieutenant Colonel Larry Dogden's Air Defense TF 8/43 moved with the VII Corps, providing an umbrella from Iraqi tactical missile attack or helicopter attack (CENTAF had earlier established air supremacy against Iraqi fixed-wing attack). At one point I told Larry that his air defense units moved with the same rapid agility as a cavalry unit, the highest compliment I could pay them.

0800–1000 VII Corps TAC

We had some orders to get out.

First, I wanted the corps to understand the rules of engagement; in particular, I wanted them to know they had the right of self-defense. I imagined that many Iraqi units were out of communications and therefore did not know the war was over. Second, we had some minor repositioning to do in order to get into a better and more coherent posture, and some of the commanders might have figured that getting into a more coherent posture would violate the cease-fire. Third, I was concerned about force protection, especially unexploded munitions, which numbered in the tens of thousands all over the battlefield. We'd already had casualties and deaths from these—just getting out of your vehicle in the dark had become hazardous. Fourth, I wanted the corps to stop taking the PSG pills and to get out of the by-now-nasty chemical overgarments we had worn day and night since 24 February.

Fifth, I wanted to meet with the commanders at noon.

1000–1200 Visits

After taking care of these orders, I wanted to get out and around the corps as soon as possible, and personally congratulate as many units and commanders as I could. I began in the north with the 1st AD, to congratulate them on capturing the Medina headquarters.

Ron Griffith had commanded the division with great skill and tenacity, and had been thorough in preparing his soldiers for war. His Old Ironsides team had reflected his thorough, savvy approach to war fighting. He'd drilled them hard. Their intelligence had always been current, and Ron had synchronized his ground maneuver, combat aviation, and artillery masterfully. I always knew that when Ron told me something, it was well considered, and he was what I called an "aware" commander; he always knew the score. I liked having Ron's savvy, street-smart commander wisdom on my team.

Ron went on to four-star rank, and is currently Vice Chief of Staff of the Army, the number-two-ranking general in the Department of the Army.

When Ron Griffith and I met that morning, I shook his hand and told him how proud I was of him and the soldiers and leaders of Old Ironsides.

Ron was elated at the performance of his division, and well he should have been. They had gone farther in their attack than any other of our units. During their attack, they had destroyed the better part of a brigade of the Tawalkana, a brigade of the Adnan, and two-thirds of the Medina, and captured the HQ of that division (by then vacant) and the HQ of the Iraqi VII Corps.

After I left Ron, we flew back toward the TAC. I noticed a tank unit on the ground and told Mark Greenwald to land so that I could talk to some of the soldiers. It was Company B, 1/8 Cavalry, a tank battalion in the 1st CAV. I walked up to a tank and talked to the crew. In a little while, some other soldiers gathered around, then identified themselves and their unit. When I asked what they had done, they told me they had moved all day and night to get there, but had never gotten into the fight. They were not happy about that.

After I explained that the cease-fire had kept them out of the fight, I congratulated them on their magnificent 250-kilometer move from the Ruqi Pocket to where we were now. Then in the sand I sketched out the basic VII Corps attack and the vital role their actions in the Ruqi Pocket had played. After thanking them again for what they had done to help gain the victory, I left to go back to the TAC.

1200 VII Corps TAC CP

The moment I walked into the TAC, John Yeosock called. He wanted us to move corps units around to eliminate pockets of resistance behind us, within our lines, and to do it while staying within the cease-fire rules, which were not to fire unless fired upon or threatened. However, that didn't seem wise to me just then. Moving around put our troops at a disadvantage, I told him, and little was to be gained, since the Iraqis who had not yet heard about the cease-fire could shoot first. John said OK.

At 1220, I met with my five division commanders in the TAC and shook each one's hand. All of us were tired, but elated at our success. We also knew we still had work to do.

"I want to be the first of a long line of people to say well done," I told them. "No matter what is written, said, or shown about what happened out here, the courage of our soldiers in taking the fight to the enemy, day and night, in sandstorms and rain, will be forever stamped in the desert sands of Iraq and Kuwait. I'm not sure where this is going from here, but while it's fresh in our minds, I want to thank the soldiers for their superb performance."

Then I talked about:

• accountability—keeping track of where all our soldiers were, as well as of casualties, and of protection and proper identification of remains;
• safety—especially with unexploded munitions;
• record keeping—to capture what we had done, including battle vignettes and lessons learned for the future;
• awards policy—including awards for valor and guidance on war trophies and souvenirs;
• destruction of Iraqi equipment.

The meeting lasted about an hour, and then the commanders returned to their units.

Soon after that, the first of the media arrived, including a correspondent from AP and another from an Arab news agency. I went over with them what we had done to include what I called our "left hook," thus distinguishing it from what others have erroneously called a "Hail Mary" attack. In football, a Hail Mary play is a last-minute, go-for-broke attempt to score the winning touchdown by throwing a forward pass in the general direction of your opponent's end zone. The game is on the line, you're only a little behind, you have seconds left, so you throw . . . and hope. Our maneuver could not have been further from a Hail Mary. Later, in an interview with Rick Atkinson of the *Washington Post*, I used the terms "closed fist" and "left hook" for our envelopment maneuver. In his story, I noticed later, he used "left hook," and it stuck.

"Was this the best maneuver of your career?" they asked.

I used a remark I had once heard Willie Mays make, after his well-known catch of a long drive from Vic Wertz in the 1954 World Series: "I just make the catches," he said. "I'll let you fellows describe them."

Meanwhile, a few of the staff from the main had come out, and I thanked them all for their work as a team, repeating in more detail what I had told my commanders earlier, then I spent the rest of the day at the TAC with them, going over what needed to be done. There was still an enormous amount to do. We could not let up now (and it was by then seductively easy to let up).

At this point, I thought our future mission was to defend northern Kuwait. I also thought that we might be ordered to leave some equipment at King Khalid Military City in a POMCUS storage configuration. Finally, there was the question of what would happen to VII Corps when we returned to Germany. I had no answer to that yet.

15

DUTY IN IRAQ

0300 1 March 1991

Another early-morning phone call from Riyadh. I was asleep in my small tent at the TAC.

It was John Yeosock. "There will be cease-fire talks tomorrow," he told me when I got to the phone, "and VII Corps will be responsible to set up the site. The CINC," he added, "also wants recommendations about the best place to hold the talks."

"Let me ask around, and I'll get back to you," I answered. My immediate first thought was that the best place would be somewhere out on the battle-field, where the press and the Iraqi brass could see the extent of the damage to the Iraqi army.

I had a quick huddle with the staff at the TAC to get them into it; and I soon had the corps staff at the main CP in on it as well. It would be a huge task to set up in such a short time, and we obviously wanted to do it right.

Though we didn't have a lot of time, we made calls to the units in the corps to find out their views about sites; and the one that I liked best was the Me-dina Division HQ that 1st AD had captured on the last day of the war. It would provide a great backdrop, since it would show the abandoned HQ of one of their no-longer "elite" divisions (we figured that by now we had stripped them of any right to call themselves elite); it was reasonably accessible to the media (I figured we would fly them into the final site); and all around it was destroyed Iraqi army equipment. It would perfectly communicate the magnitude of the defeat of Saddam's army to the world.

★ At about 0400, John called back to ask for our recommendation, and I told him about the Medina Division HQ. John seemed to like that and said he would pass my recommendation to CENTCOM—but he also asked if we had taken the crossroads in Safwan, as specified in the written order we had got-ten the morning of 28 February. I was surprised by the question. I still won-dered why anyone placed any significance on that crossroads, since the remaining RGFC in our sector were in front of 1st and 3rd ADs. But an order is an order, and I believed we had done what we had been supposed to do. I told him we did not have troops there physically, but that we had gotten air there to interdict movement, as I had understood the intent.

He told me that would be a problem. Our written orders had been to seize it, and the CINC thought we had it. Safwan was the site the CINC favored for the talks and he had already tentatively told Washington. I repeated that we did not have it.

John told me the CINC wanted to know why his orders had been disobeyed regarding that crossroads.

I was absolutely stunned.

My first reaction was real anger. I thought about the other war that had ended with my lower leg amputated. Now here in this war I was to have my professional character amputated. I was really disappointed with the CINC. To be accused of disobeying an order is to be accused of a serious breach of discipline, especially in wartime. More than the personal injury, though, was the sudden realization that this had been the first communication from the theater commander to VII Corps after the war. No calls of thanks to the troops. No discussion of casualties. No calls to the locker room, as it were, for the men and women who had made this all possible. That anger burned hot for some time.

I have questioned orders, especially ones I considered stupid, or those to which there might be legal or moral objections. I have argued the wisdom of others and suggested alternatives. I have executed orders I did not like, and for commanders I did not like. But once discussions ended and my commander said, "Here is what I want you to do," never had I willingly or knowingly disobeyed a legal order.

Yet I was also a corps commander of 146,000 U.S. and British troops who had just finished a magnificent operation. I could not let the incident overshadow the great achievements of the troops and my responsibility to them. I also was a subordinate, and my superior officer had requested an explanation. I would do as he requested. Then I would let it pass and get on with the mission. We still had lots to do.

We had interdicted the road junction but not seized it. We had done so with attack helicopters of the 1st INF (they had been there for a number of hours, and I later learned they had observed six vehicles pass through but had not fired because they had gotten the panic cease-fire call at about 0720 on 28 February and had never gotten the order to resume the attack). There had been no intent to disobey orders. I had selected tactics to accomplish what I had interpreted to be the intent of the order.

I had gotten those verbal orders from John at about 0330 on 28 February.

The written order came later that morning. My interpretation of John's verbal orders to me was for us to stop Iraqi movement through that road junction. My selection of tactics was interdiction with air, and the assumption that the 1st INF attack would probably get there by 0800 if they continued on their attack axis. Stan gave the 1st INF the mission to interdict the road junction, which they did. I and everyone else missed the "seize" in the written order. That was my fault.

Any failure of the corps to seize the road junction was my responsibility, but it was not failure based on disobeying an order.

I never heard any more about it, not then and not since. I never mentioned it to any of the other commanders or soldiers, other than in the 1st INF, since they were involved.

I could never understand why the CINC's first reaction would be to accuse John Yeosock and me of disobeying an order.

1 MARCH 1991

Right after first light, I went to visit the 1st INF, who were across Highway 8, just south of the Kuwait-Iraq border. I wanted to tell Tom Rhame what had to be done to get Safwan and to explain that it was now the site of the talks.

On the way, we saw the wreckage of the Iraqi army that had tried to stop them. We had flown over some of the wreckage the morning of the twenty-seventh. Now it went on much farther. Burning equipment, tanks, BMPs, trucks, air defense tracked vehicles, artillery—it was all there. Some isolated pieces of equipment looked brand new and undamaged. Bunkers, trenches, and vehicle revetments were everywhere.

As we crossed over into Kuwait, we saw the oil well fires. They resembled gigantic torches, with bright orange flames reaching from the ground to a height above our flight path. The flames were topped by thick black plumes of smoke, which spread and merged to form a black gray haze over the entire landscape. Close to them, you could hear the loud, roaring sounds of burning gas and oil. It grew visibly darker the farther we flew into Kuwait. It was Dante's Inferno, Armageddon, hell on earth, you pick it. I had never seen anything on this scale before. We quickly counted twenty-seven wells on fire, and there were many times that many. It was an awesome sight . . . and an unconscionable act of material brutality against the assets of another nation. I'm sure the Iraqis thought that if they could not have the oil, then no one else would, either.

Though I wanted to talk to Tom Rhame about Safwan, I first thanked him and his troops for their superb efforts during the war. I had given Tom the most varied combat missions and, in the night passage and attack, the toughest, and they had done what I'd asked with skill and courage. They felt good about it. I could see it in the faces, hear it in the voices of the officers, NCOs, and soldiers I saw and with whom I talked. It was a different unit from the one I had visited on the eve of battle. They were now victorious veterans of mobile armored desert warfare. They would never be the same, and they knew it.

Tom had commanded the Big Red One with skill and courage. Like the rest of us, he was a combat veteran of Vietnam, a veteran of the Cold War, and had had extensive command and staff service in mounted units. I enjoyed being around Tom. He was quick off the mark, never backed away from a challenge, and was always upbeat. He and his division were tough mounted warriors. I had always known it, and now the Iraqis knew it as well.

Tom and I huddled so that he could reconstruct for me the last twelve hours of his war. It was then that I learned that he had not received a specific order to seize Safwan. Then we discussed what we had to do now.

"We have to go get the town and the airfield without getting into a fight," I told him. "Try to seize them without firing a shot, but your troops and commanders always have the right of self-defense."

"WILCO, boss," he answered.

That was not the only guidance Tom got about Safwan that day. He received a lot more—from me, all the way to Riyadh. The anxiety level was up in Riyadh. I guess nobody wanted to tell President Bush that our site for the talks was still in enemy hands. At the same time, I also guess no one wanted to conduct a full assault into Safwan, since that might cause casualties, would attract a lot of attention, and violate our "cessation of offensive operations." So the guidance I gave Tom was to secure the town without a fight. Bluff, threaten, do whatever he had to, but get it. I left the details to him.

Later that day, Tom sent his second brigade, commanded by Colonel Tony Moreno, and the 1/4 Cavalry to get Safwan.

In a superbly skilled use of persuasion supported by force, Tony Moreno quite simply told the Iraqi commander to get the hell out of the way or suffer the results. That threat was credible to the Iraqis. They had already seen what U.S. forces had done to their friends, and Tony had the tanks visible to show he meant business. By late afternoon, they were in Safwan and had the airfield . . . but not before the 1/4 Cav had had to convince an Iraqi RGFC colonel to get out of there, using the same "Moreno" tactics. Moreno's approach had essentially been the same one that President Bush had used to deal with Saddam Hussein in the first place. "Get out of Kuwait, or we are coming in there to throw you out." Saddam had not been convinced, so the Coalition had liberated Kuwait by force. When Tony Moreno used the same threat at Safwan, the Iraqis did not need more convincing. By 1600, they had Safwan, the airfield, and the road junction.

★ Meanwhile, though the mission had to come first, I still had a driving urgency (fueled by the aftermath of Vietnam) to visit the troops and leaders to thank them for all they had done to win this victory. I also wanted to visit the hospitals and especially to talk to as many amputees as I could. I started the process that day . . . as did all my commanders. There would be many visits and many ceremonies, which together would put some kind of closure on all that had happened.

Here is one small example: On the way back to the TAC, we visited with Lieutenant Colonel Pat Ritter and his tankers of the 1/34 Armor and learned from them about the intensity of the 1st INF's fight to take Objective Norfolk on the night of 26 and 27 February.

Pat told me of the tough night passage, the difficulty they had had just navigating, and the enormous discipline shown by the soldiers and leaders to clear fires so that they would not shoot each other. He and his company commanders and NCOs talked about close-in fighting and about the Iraqi infantry with RPGs. He related stories about short-range tank shots of less than 500 meters and about the enemy firing from the rear. He also told of one of his company commanders who had used the machine guns of his tank to kill Iraqi infantry trying to climb on Ritter's tank. As the troops told me about their battles, I felt the emotion and excitement in their voices. When they talked about what they themselves had done, it was in whispered tones, but when they talked about what others had done, their voices grew louder. It had been a tough night for those tankers. Before I left, I told Pat and his troops how proud I was of them.

★ Since I had not yet had a chance to visit 3rd AD, that night I called Butch Funk. He was feeling good about the performance of Spearhead—as well he should have. They had been relentless and had left in their wake the better part of four divisions, including the Tawalkana. Butch had scheduled an AAR with his commanders on top of the captured underground HQ of the 10th Iraqi Armored Division, and I wanted to attend some of that. There was also to be a memorial service in his CAV squadron, and he asked if I would later award his CAV squadron commander the Silver Star. I told him I would be proud to do it.

I also called Cal Waller to get a reading of the CINC on the Safwan issue and the flap over our pace of attack. Cal was always helpful with reading Schwarzkopf, and he was also candid and did not hold anything back.

When I asked him about the uproar and accusations over the Safwan road intersection, Cal explained, as I had guessed, that the problem was that the CINC was embarrassed: Based on what he had been briefed, he had told the President we had the place for the talks. Then he was told we did not have it.

When I asked Cal about the pace-of-attack problem, he told me that the CINC had been upset over that a couple of days before, but now he was pleased about the whole operation.

All right, I thought to myself afterward, they both make sense now, then chalked both of them off to the spur-of-the-moment pressure of command. It even occurred to me that now maybe the CINC regretted he'd raised the Safwan incident at all.

2400 1 March 1991

As of midnight, our VII Corps SITREP to Third Army said this about Iraqi units:

North of us, out of our sector, approximately five battalions remained in the Basra pocket, conducting screening and hasty defensive operations on the southern bank of the Euphrates River. These units were hastily formed battle groups composed of the Medina, Hammurabi, and Adnan Divisions. We also knew that approximately eighteen battalions of five different divisions had successfully withdrawn to the north bank of the Euphrates River and were probably attempting to consolidate before returning to the Baghdad area. We thought the threat to VII Corps in our sector consisted of scattered forces of no larger than company-sized elements who had either been trapped or bypassed, and who might not have gotten the cease-fire word.

2 March 1991

That morning, I got a quick staff update on the enemy and on our own situation.

Though the Iraqis were in disarray, they were rapidly moving units and equipment out of the theater. They were clearly a beaten army and fleeing as fast as they could. Our SITREP the previous night had gotten that accurately.

Except for continuing problems with unexploded munitions, our own situation was good. In the past twenty-four hours, we had suffered our second soldier death due to our own unexploded munitions, and I therefore put out a message to the commanders to reinforce troop protection. Later, throughout all Third Army, we would adopt the saying "Not one more life."

After the briefing, I gave Stan guidance on our occupation duties, and told him to have some alternatives worked out for me when I got back that night.

Next I ordered the formation of a Task Force Demo (a demolition task force) to destroy abandoned and captured Iraqi equipment more rapidly than we'd been able to do up to that time. I also wanted to be briefed on their actions each day hereafter until we left Iraq.

1st INF

That day at 1200 was to be the cease-fire meeting at Safwan. We'd had our people there since late the afternoon before to set up the site. All the equipment had been coming in trucks from King Khalid Military City and theater stocks, but they'd gotten jammed up in the traffic mess created by the destruction just north of Kuwait City. The trucks could not get through. That meant they had to transfer equipment to CH-47 helos and fly it in. The site would be ready at noon, but it would be a primitive setup.

At about 0830, I flew into Safwan and talked to Brigadier General Bill Carter, the senior officer there, and grilled him on all the details of the setup. Tom Rhame joined us as we talked. In the Army, when a commander essentially flyspecks every detail, they call it "getting into the weeds." That was what I was doing . . . and it was different from my usual practice. I usually probe around to determine if an operation has its act together. Once I'm satisfied, I leave the details to the unit that is doing it. On this one, I wanted to go over it all and see how I could help.

As always, things were well organized. At the same time, they let me know there were too many bosses running around giving instructions. I could see that for myself. There were troops from 22nd SUPCOM (Lieutenant General Gus Pagonis's unit), VII Corps HQ, 1st INF, and probably Third Army. Since VII Corps had the mission, I knew I could fix the situation in a heartbeat, and told Carter he was in charge of getting the site ready; he was to take charge and make it happen. It didn't matter what other units were there—as far as I was concerned, they were all in VII Corps territory, and they now belonged to 1st INF, Tom Rhame, and Bill Carter.

After we got the who's-in-charge-here issue straightened out, Bill Carter and the Big Red One took over, and without them—from Moreno taking the site in the first place to Bill organizing it—it would not have happened. But they didn't do it alone. They had a lot of help from Major Dan Nolan, the VII Corps SGS (the secretary of the general staff, the group that works for the corps chief, and that handles all correspondence, information distribution, and protocol), and his crew, plus the troops and equipment from Third Army and 22nd SUPCOM.

They put up a sign that was visible to all those who entered the site: WEL-COME TO IRAQ, COURTESY OF THE BIG RED ONE. That was unit pride working . . . yet it was also a historical fact. I liked that.

While I was there, we got the word that the Iraqis couldn't make it to that day's meeting, so the meeting had been postponed until the next day. We were glad to get twenty-four more hours. The extra time gave the 1st INF more time to prepare the site, and it gave me a chance to continue to visit units.

My first stop was Troop G in 2nd Squadron, 2d ACR, one of the three cavalry troops to make the Battle of 73 Easting so successful. Captain Joe Sartiano gathered the troopers around a tank, and they spoke in whispered tones about what they had done. It is not unusual for those who have seen real combat to talk little about it and almost never in loud locker-room voices or language. This is especially true for those units that have had members wounded or killed in action, as was the case with Troop G.

I almost had to pry stories out of them. They told me about Sergeant Nels Moller, who had been killed in action, and about the heroism of Second Lieutenant Gary Franks and Staff Sergeant Larry Foltz, who when their own vehicle had become inoperative from enemy fire, had crawled through that fire to another vehicle so that they could continue to call artillery on the Iraqis in 73 Easting.

I ended the session by telling them that their actions had found and fixed the RGFC for VII Corps, just as cavalry is supposed to do. Then we had finished the fight they had started with the units that had passed through them. They were now combat veterans and had earned the proud right to wear the 2nd ACR patch on their right shoulder, signifying combat service.

It was when I was about to leave that Staff Sergeant Waylan Lundquist, platoon sergeant of the second (tank) platoon, said that line that I've never forgotten: "Hey, sir, you generals didn't do too bad this time, either."

It was the best compliment a commander could hear. But I also noticed he said "this time"!

My next stop was about thirty minutes south. With Major General Rupert Smith and the British, I found the same attitude as with the U.S. troops: quiet, but pleased and proud with what they had done. Rupert and I compared notes and he confirmed he had been a bit weary of mission changes when, on the twenty-sixth, he did not know if he was to go north to attack in front of the 1st INF, south to clear the zone to the 1st CAV, or due east to Highway 8. Rupert and I laughed about it, but it had not been all that funny then. We also shared a laugh about something else. As radio call signs, we Americans tended to use our unit nicknames to identify ourselves. I called myself JAY-HAWK, Tom Rhame used DANGER, Butch Funk SPEARHEAD, and Ron Griffith IRON. That was strange to the British, and so Rupert had selected SUN RAY as his call sign.

At each visit to the 1st (UK), they assembled a battalion and I was able to tell them thanks from their Yank commander for what they had done and explain how their actions had contributed to our overall success. Working with the British had been a highly successful combined operation: American and British troops together again in the desert, just as in World War II. I would forever see and know the UK differently since I had been privileged to command their soldiers in battle. I hoped the people in the UK would feel the same intense pride in their soldiers and what they had accomplished that we did.

From the 1st (UK), I flew back into Saudi Arabia to visit the soldiers in one of our evacuation hospitals. Fifteen minutes south of the border, we arrived at the 312th Evacuation Hospital and landed on their medevac pad, waving off the medics who rushed out thinking we were bringing in casualties.

We had five such hospitals in VII Corps, in addition to the five MASH and five combat-support hospitals. Each had different capabilities for surgical treatment, trauma, and bed space. Normally, you echelon the MASH forward with divisions, place the CSHs farther back, and keep the larger evac hospitals well in the rear. I wanted to visit our wounded and especially to talk to the amputees.

I was angry to learn that they had no Purple Hearts to award at the hospital. Normally, Purple Hearts are awarded in the hospital, as soldiers are too quickly evacuated from their parent unit to receive them there. A Purple Heart for wounds in combat is a badge of honor for risking your life for your country. I wanted them awarded, and I wanted them now. We got that squared away with a few calls to the right people.

Our wounded soldiers were getting world-class medical care. The staff of our hospitals there would have made any hospital in the U.S.A. proud. Many of the doctors were Vietnam veterans. Our oldest hospital commander had first served as a private soldier in the North Africa campaigns and then, after he had become a doctor, as a surgeon in Korea, Vietnam, and now here.

The troops were hurting from their wounds and full of questions about their fellow soldiers and their unit. I talked to all the amputees in that hospital and tried to share my own experiences with them. I was immensely proud of these young soldiers and those I had visited earlier. They were not from another planet. They were American soldiers who had given it the best they had. All I wanted to do was say thanks, as I remembered my fellow amputees in the ward in Valley Forge so long ago.

I flew in silence most of the hour and fifteen minutes back to the corps TAC 200 kilometers into Iraq.

VII Corps TAC CP Iraq

At about 1830, soon after I got back to the TAC, I got a call from John Yeosock.

"Fred, the CINC wants you to escort him to the talks at Safwan tomorrow," he said.

"Me? You sure about that?" That was a real shocker. The CINC wants me to escort him? I had to get this one straight.

"I'm sure."

"WILCO." I'd be there.

3 MARCH 1991

I was up before first light.

This would be a big day.

Our troops had reported they would be ready when General Schwarzkopf arrived, and I depended on that. After a quick update that told me the situation was otherwise quiet in our part of occupied Iraq, we left at 0715 for Kuwait City and the airport, which by now was back in limited use. The CINC would not arrive before 0930, and it was only a forty-five-minute ride, but I wanted to look around some and to give ourselves plenty of time. Since this was the CINC's first visit north of the Saudi border and to the battlefield, I also wanted to preview what I might show him on our thirty-minute flight from Kuwait City airport to Safwan.

On the way to the airfield, we flew over the so-called Highway of Death, just north of Kuwait City. There was a lot of wreckage there, to be sure, but what impressed me first was not so much the volume of destruction as the great numbers of civilian vehicles in and around the military trucks—the Iraqis had been using them as transportation to haul out their aggressor's loot. I spotted very few combat vehicles. The next thing that struck me was the sheer visual impact of it all. If a target analyst had examined this scene, he would have seen it the way we just had, but if you read about it in a newspaper, you'd likely come to the conclusion that it had been like shooting fish in a barrel—an un-American way to fight a war; and so the sooner ended, the better. If I had known that this was the impression people were getting in Washington, I would have realized at the time that the war would not go on much longer. The impact was too powerful.

I wanted the CINC to get a good look at all of this, and especially at what VII Corps units had done.

Farther north, where the British and 1st INF were across the highway, we had seen combat vehicles, tanks, and BMPs, damaged, abandoned, or destroyed. When we cleared the road later, we had to use both the 1st and 9th Engineer Battalions. Following that cleanup, until the mess on the roads around Kuwait City got cleaned up, we used half the four-lane divided highway for about two weeks as a C-130 strip for resupply. Otherwise, in order to reach the 1st INF, they drove all the way through the desert.

As we made our way toward Kuwait City that morning, we flew by other

burning oil wells. Hundreds were visible. It was fortunate for us that we were west of the oil fields, since the wind generally blew from west to east, and the smoke stayed out over the Gulf (years later on a trip to India, I learned that they had gotten some of the smoke even that far away). On some days, the wind did blow the other way, and it was like night where we were.

(I even asked our doctors about it, but they predicted that the greasy air would not cause any long-term effects for our troops. Breathing the stuff was about the same as breathing big-city smog, they told me.)

We also flew over the destruction in the desert that had been delivered by the 1st INF as they cut a swath through the Iraqis to Highway 8.

Finally, we came to the coast and passed over the elaborate defenses the Iraqis had built to stop the amphibious landing that never came. On the beaches they had laid out complex obstacles: wire entanglements, concrete tetrahedron blocks, steel tangles, and probably mines (although I could not tell that from the air). To prevent helos from landing, they had erected thousands of telephone poles.

On a later visit to Kuwait City, we visited the abandoned Iraqi III Corps HQ (it was this corps that had been meant to defend against the Marine landing). I saw an elaborate twenty-by-thirty-foot terrain board set up, in color, with terrain relief, and a scaled replica of the beach area, complete with overlaid military grid. I could just picture the commander and all his subordinate commanders and staff going over their defense in precise detail. That deception by our Marine and Navy forces afloat essentially tied down a whole Iraqi corps. It was masterful.

Since all of this was on the eastern part of the city, we would not fly over it with the CINC on the way to Safwan.

We landed at Kuwait City International Airport. As you might expect, it looked as if it had been in a war. Hangars were wrecked, their roofs caved in; there were holes in the walls of other buildings; and wrecked Iraqi vehicles. Except for pitted marks here and there, apparently from cluster bomb munitions, the runway itself was not damaged. But we were careful to stay on the runways or taxi aprons and off the grassy areas in between, because there still might be unexploded ordnance in there.

★ At 0930, General Schwarzkopf arrived in a modern civilian Gulfstream jet. It taxied over to our command Blackhawk and stopped, then the CINC came out and down the stairs, and I saluted.

I was a bit uneasy; not only was this a big day, but just the day before he had accused me of disobeying an order; and he had expressed displeasure to John Yeosock at our VII Corps attack tempo early in the war. Despite all that, I was determined to leave the personal stuff out of it and to focus on the day's

mission and show him as much as I could of what we had done out here. I figured the last thing we both needed was for me to be taking up time with personal business between the two of us . . . though if he wanted to talk about it, I was ready and more than willing.

Neither issue came up, not then, not ever, in any of our meetings or correspondence.*

★ For the flight up to Safwan, we had arranged a visible show of force. I had a company of Apaches (from our 2/6 CAV 11th Aviation Brigade) to escort us, three on each side of our Blackhawk. We also had ordered Tom Rhame to do the same at Safwan. We wanted to demonstrate to the Iraqis that we had plenty of combat power left if they had a mind to restart anything. From what I had seen of "Moreno" tactics, the Iraqis respected a credible show of force.

As we took off, I let the CINC know I wouldn't bother him with a lot of chatter, since I knew he had a lot on his mind, and that we would fly lower and slower than usual, so that he would have a chance to look around. The conference site was ready, I added, and described the general setup.

"The Iraqis better not ask for much today," he said, "because I'm not in a charitable mood. I'm not in a position to give them much, and they're not in a position to demand much." From that I concluded that he and Washington had the day's events pretty well figured out. I made no attempt to question him on any of it, since it was none of my business unless the CINC chose to discuss it. He did not.

As we flew over the burning oil wells, he was as shocked as the rest of us by that tragedy. "What would possess a people to do something like that?" he wondered aloud.

Shortly after that, we circled to get a closer look at the "Highway of Death." He had nothing to say. Then we went a little west of Highway 8, so that I could point out the destroyed Iraqi equipment. It stretched as far as we could see, and it impressed him. When we reached it, I pointed out the area of the 1st INF division attack, and explained how they had come out of the west after their night attack and laid waste to the Iraqi army all the way to Highway 8. The scene was the same behind the British and the 1st and 3rd ADs, I added.

He was clearly pleased. "Just like we planned it, Fred," he said.

After the CINC said that, I figured that all the problems and confusions of the previous four days had gone away; and I never expected to hear of them again.

---

*Both issues have been discussed in some detail in General Schwarzkopf's autobiography and in the various histories and commentaries on the war.

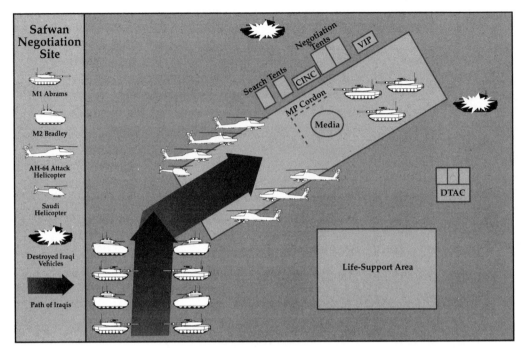

The 1st Infantry Division captured, then arranged the negotiation site at Safwan. When the Iraqi generals rode in U.S. HMMWVs through the cordon of American combat equipment, they saw the might that many of their soldiers had faced in the previous eighty-nine hours.

Safwan 3 March 1991

We landed on the airstrip about 500 feet down from the tents where the meeting would be held, so that we would not blow them away. General Schwarzkopf quickly got off the helicopter. We drew a crowd of maybe a hundred media people, with cameras and microphones at the ready.

To my surprise, there was Gus Pagonis, in complete combat uniform, to greet the CINC. Not Tom Rhame, not Bill Carter, not Tony Moreno. Then, as the cameras rolled, Gus and General Schwarzkopf strolled to the tent area, with Gus carefully explaining the largely VII Corps, mostly 1st INF, setup. I quickly fell in on Gus's left.

I was shocked to see Gus grab the CINC and squire him away. Though 22 SUPCOM had certainly supplied some equipment, this was not a 22 SUP-COM (that is to say, a Gus Pagonis) mission. The Big Red One and VII Corps had taken the site from the Iraqis; they'd organized it and set it up; they'd done the work. VII Corps had fought through the RGFC to get here. First INF had fought all night through Norfolk, and had captured Safwan just the day before. It did not seem right to me. I wanted the spotlight to shine that day on our troops who had fought through more than 250 kilometers of desert and destroyed the better part of eleven divisions to get to this site. I flat missed that one.

★ Under Tom Rhame's orders, Bill Carter and the troops had done a magnificent job. We had our show of force. Meanwhile, the 1st INF had arranged to meet the Iraqi delegation at a designated pickup point. They then put them in our HMMWVs, and drove them on a route that took them through a canyon of M1A1 tanks and Bradleys, spaced about twenty meters apart, with soldiers at their crew positions in full battle dress. The airfield was ringed with tanks and Bradleys, also with soldiers at crew stations (two battalions and the cavalry squadron were there). Apaches and CENTAF A-10s were flying overhead, and an additional Apache company was parked on the airstrip. We wanted to be sure that the Iraqi delegation and any other Iraqi units watching got a firsthand look at our combat power.

There was no way they could have missed the sign WELCOME TO IRAQ, COURTESY OF THE BIG RED ONE proudly displayed in front of three Big Red One M1A1s.

The airfield ran generally southwest-northeast. The strip itself was macadam, about 50 feet wide and 3,500 long. Halfway to the northern end of the strip and on the left were a pair of tents, where MPs would search each member of the cease-fire delegations for weapons. Next to these tents was a separate tent for General Schwarzkopf; in there he could talk to anyone he needed over the secure comms we had set up. Next to his tent were the actual negotiation tents—two standard U.S. Army field tents hooked together. Inside was a standard government conference table, with chairs around it, as well as seating for all the other members of the Coalition who were present that day. On the other side of this arrangement was a VIP tent, where senior Coalition officers could go for short breaks. Directly across the airstrip from the negotiation tent were the three 1st INF M1A1 tanks, with their WELCOME TO IRAQ sign. Next to the tanks was an area for the media, with an MP cordon, to keep it under control.

It had been forty-two hours since 1600 on 1 March, when Tony Moreno and his second brigade, and Bob Wilson and the Quarter Horse (1/4 Cav), had secured the site.

★ General Schwarzkopf seemed very sure of himself as he looked around, chatted briefly with the troops, and waited for the Iraqis to arrive. He knew what he wanted to do. That had been apparent to me on the ride up there in the Blackhawk. One of those he greeted was a senior Saudi general, with a clean Kevlar helmet and goggles on top. This, I learned, was Lieutenant General Khalid, the commander of JFC-E and JFC-N. In large measure, General Khalid had been the real glue in the Arab part of the military coalition.

When the Iraqis rode up in our HMMWVs and got out, they gave him a salute, which General Schwarzkopf returned. Through an interpreter, he explained the setup and the first order of business: they would be searched and would have to surrender any weapons. He would also be searched, he explained. They agreed and that formality was accomplished. General Schwarzkopf then led them into the tent, followed by the Coalition delegation.

When I started to enter, I got stopped at the door by the CENTCOM security troops. My name was not on the CENTCOM list, they told me. "I'm going in, name or no name," I told the MP at the entrance, and in I went.

None of the CENTCOM component commanders, Boomer, Arthur, Horner, or Yeosock, was present at Safwan that day, nor was Gary Luck, though all the Coalition allies were there. I knew some, such as Peter de Billiere of the UK and Saleh Halaby of Egypt, but most I did not.

I found an empty seat in the back by the entrance. Gus Pagonis had a front-row seat, but neither Tom Rhame nor Bill Carter was in there.

It was hot in the tent, and I could hear nothing of what was said at the table; I had a hard time staying awake. General Schwarzkopf seemed to be doing most of the talking, and the Iraqis were very still. They nodded now and then but said little.

It was clear to me what was going on. This was a battlefield meeting of the commanders of the opposing forces, to agree on the separation of forces; later, more detailed strategic-level talks would determine the Iraqi penalty for their aggression against Kuwait.

After about an hour, they took a short break. As the Iraqi generals walked by me, I looked into their eyes. These men had the coldest-looking, most impassive expressions I have ever seen on military officers—Vietnam, Warsaw Pact, NATO, Korea, anywhere.

That day I wrote in my journal, "No compassion in the Iraqis' eyes—none. They are ruthless and we should not let them up before we get what we want. Fear they have mistreated our POWs. We must hold them *accountable* for that. I'd attack to Basra if they did harm POWs."

As they passed, I tried to figure out who these Iraqi officers were. They wore no name tags. Were they RGFC? That did not appear to be so, since they did not wear the red Republican Guards' armbands. Much later, I found out their names: Lieutenant General Salah Abud Mahmud, III Corps commander, and

Lieutenant General Sultan Hashim Ahmad, chief of staff of the Ministry of Defense.

I was also still curious to find out how this event had come about in this particular place. Who had picked the site? Was the site important to the objectives to be achieved? What did we want to accomplish here? Who had decided on the Iraqi level of representation? How much negotiation room did General Schwarzkopf have? Who had decided what he would say?

At the time, I assumed the answers to all these questions had been tied together between State and Defense in Washington, and approved by the President. I did not give it much further thought. Later, I would.

After the break, I stayed outside for a while, since I could not hear what was being said anyway, and talked with Lieutenant Colonel Bob Wilson and Command Sergeant Major Cobb of the 1/4 Cavalry to hear their accounts of the war.

Later, I went back inside and did my best to catch some words, but without any luck. I dozed off from time to time, embarrassed that an obviously historic event, taking place right there in front of me, would not stimulate me more.

General Schwarzkopf seemed to be on top of his game, and I was confident he would do for us what was right. We had done our part.

The talks ended and the tent emptied. They had lasted about an hour and a half.

★ Afterward, General Schwarzkopf and Lieutenant General Khalid held a session with the media, right in front of the Big Red One tanks and their sign. It was skillfully done (I do not recall that Khalid answered any questions), but I was sorry to see that there was no mention of 1st INF or VII Corps, or introductions of any of the soldiers or leaders.

After the press conference, I lost track of General Schwarzkopf for a time, and walked over to talk to some of the soldiers and to tell Tom Rhame and Bill Carter thanks for the great job. While I was talking to them, Toby grabbed me. "General Schwarzkopf wants to see you in his tent," he said.

The CINC wanted me to listen as he reported the results of the talks to General Powell, and also as he gave General Luck his orders, to make sure he did not leave anything out. That way Gary and I would have the same set of orders to implement. (At this point, both Gary and I knew more than our boss, John Yeosock.) I took rapid notes.

Here is a summary of what I wrote:

First was the issue of Iraqi helicopters. At Safwan, the Iraqis made a simple request that they be able to fly from Baghdad to Basra in order to implement the agreement. Since we not only had cut Highway 8 but had also forbidden them any use of military air, they needed some way to get back and forth. No Iraqi helicopters were to be shot down if they had an orange panel on their sides. The helicopter agreement was nothing more than that, and only in that context—a matter of command and control to implement the cease-fire. And that is what General Schwarzkopf agreed to. I do not think he was fooled by the Iraqis that day. He knew exactly what he was doing with that specific request in those circumstances. Later, the Iraqis took advantage of their ability to fly the helos, when they saw we would not do anything about it, and used them to kill their own people. But I think that occurred to them later. That we did nothing then is an entirely different issue.

Then there were a number of other provisions.

There was to be a demilitarized zone two kilometers wide to separate the forces. John Yeosock and Steve Arnold had drawn it on a map used by General Schwarzkopf, and the Iraqis agreed to it.

There were rules of engagement:

- The intent was not to engage if Iraqi forces were trying to get away;
- Vehicles and helos flying an orange panel would not be engaged;
- We were not to get into big battles if all the Iraqi were doing was trying to get out of the theater;
- Bypassed Iraqi units were to be allowed to leave;
- We were to be on weapons hold unless the Iraqis showed clear hostile intent; and
- The Iraqis were not to be allowed to remove ammunition.

General Schwarzkopf also said we would not give up one square inch of Iraqi territory until the permanent cease-fire was signed (and I assumed we got what we wanted). He instructed us to set up a meeting point for radio communications with the Iraqis, and where the two sides could meet to settle any disputes (we subsequently did this at the by-now well-known road junction north of Safwan). General Schwarzkopf emphasized that all forces were to have the right of self-defense. He told me nothing of POW exchanges but I knew that one of his highest priorities was to ensure the safe return of our POWs.

The orders to implement the agreement were now clear to me. General Schwarzkopf had gotten approval from Washington, and Gary and I had what we needed to implement the cease-fire and to remain in Iraq. We would not give an inch until the Iraqis agreed to a permanent cease-fire and to whatever the UN wanted them to do. The CINC was clearly pleased with the way things were going.

(It occurs to me now that it would have been simple on the afternoon of 26 or 27 February for the three of us, plus John Yeosock and Chuck Horner, to have had a similar quick orders group meeting about the end of the war. That way, the CINC could have issued orders about it, and we all would have been clear about their execution.)

I left the tent and waited for the CINC to get ready to leave.

Various members of the media were still talking to soldiers. When my public affairs officer, Lieutenant Colonel Jim Gleisberg, noticed Tom Brokaw of NBC among the correspondents, he asked him if he wanted to talk to the commander of the main attack. He did, so we chatted a short while, and I outlined what VII Corps had done. Since they already had their story for the day, however, it didn't end up in his report.

After we finished, NBC gave the troops a wonderful gift. Because they had not used all their rented satellite time, Brokaw made available what they had left to soldiers so they could call home. The troops quickly lined up. Because of that generosity, I still watch Tom Brokaw's evening news.

RETURN FLIGHT

At about 1430, we got back in the Blackhawk and flew to Kuwait City with the same escort. Once again, it seemed to me that General Schwarzkopf felt good about the day's events. He had apparently gotten all he wanted from the Iraqis, and had his forces positioned in Iraq for any future operations if they were required. If not, we were positioned to leave as soon as a permanent cease-fire had been obtained.

Once more, we looked over destroyed Iraqi equipment. We had bypassed a large quantity of equipment and ammunition during our attack, I told him, and had started to destroy it, but because of the enormous quantities, and because of our lack of EOD personnel,* I was not sure we would get it all done.

"I don't want any Iraqi equipment left in working condition," he told me. "Let me know if you need any more help."

There was not much more talk.

I saluted the CINC as he boarded his C-20 to head back to Riyadh.

It had been a good day. We flew back to the VII Corps TAC CP in Iraq to begin our occupation phase.

OCCUPATION

Later that day, I briefed all the commanders except Tom Rhame, whom I had briefed at Safwan. I used the notes from my session with General Schwarzkopf.

---

*Explosive Ordnance Disposal personnel are soldiers or civilians who are specially trained to deal with explosive munitions.

I did not foresee it then, but we were about to enter a seventy-day occupation period. In this time, we captured and processed more prisoners than we had in the eighty-nine-hour war, and our soldiers and units conducted massive humanitarian work for the indigenous population as well as for refugees and displaced persons. This period ended for VII Corps on 9 May 1991.

In its intensity of concurrent activities, it was not unlike the period before the war. We had to make more command judgments without precedent or guidance than in any period I had ever experienced. It was also a time for emotional reflection, as my commanders and I made it our focus to visit hospitals and memorial services, and to listen to soldiers describe their combat actions, or the selfless actions of their fellow soldiers. It was a time of lessons learned, for the next time. Finally, it was a time of redeployment, and for ceremonies to say thanks and to remember.

IMMEDIATE MISSIONS

There are many things to do after the shooting stops. Despite the urgency everyone feels, you do not just declare a halt, cease firing, and then turn around and go home. The speed with which units can switch from all-ahead full-speed combat to post-combat operations is a matter of both command will and the discipline of soldiers. Our soldiers again proved to be superb.

★ Meanwhile, as I later learned, our national security team at home was more focused on getting the UN resolutions approved than on the meeting at Safwan. They considered it to be a matter of cease-fire arrangements between combatants, nothing more, nothing less, and to be left to the theater commander.

As a result, some senior civilian policy officials in DOD were not even aware that the talks would happen until the last minute, and when they found out, they tried to offer some alternatives to the structure of the talks. But by then General Schwarzkopf had sent the terms he and his HQ had drawn up to the Joint Chiefs, who had approved them, and the meeting was about to be held.

According to an account in Secretary of State James Baker's book, *The Politics of Diplomacy*, on a subsequent visit to Saudi, Baker and Schwarzkopf discussed amending the terms of the talks in light of developments in Iraq. The option was to have a permanent demilitarized zone in Iraq to be monitored by the UN, one perhaps as large as the existing ground under the current no-fly zone. We were already there on the ground and would only have to turn it over to the UN. It was late, however, and a great deal of momentum had been generated by the idea of getting the troops out and getting them home, and so nothing was changed.

The same attitude toward a quick withdrawal pervaded the theater at CENTCOM HQ, except that the CINC had made it perfectly clear that we were not to give up "one square inch of Iraqi territory" until our POWs were returned and the Coalition had what it wanted from a defeated Iraq. Here, at least, we were using the battlefield victory to gain the strategic objectives we wanted.

Meanwhile, Third Army had its hands full. Even before the cease-fire had gone into effect, they had formed a task force (named Task Force Freedom) to rebuild Kuwait, appointed a commander, Major General Bob Frix, and gotten special funds from the Department of the Army (the U.S. Army was appointed executive agent for the job). After the Coalition had kicked out the Iraqis, they rolled into Kuwait City and went to work.

In occupied Iraq, it was a different story.

The demilitarized line and force separation were meant to be short temporary measures, and as a result, there was absolutely no intention in CENT-COM to order us to do anything that would indicate or otherwise cause us to establish what might look like a permanent presence in Iraq. I welcomed that. Along with the rest of my commanders, I was anxious to get our troops out of Iraq and back into Saudi, then home. But things did not work out that way.

This was a strange period for us. We had no formal occupation mission. In fact, since I had initially figured, along with John Yeosock, that the permanent cease-fire would happen about two weeks after the Safwan talks, and then we would leave, we concentrated at first on lessons learned, on the safety and security of our troops, on enforcing the DML (demilitarized line) provisions the CINC had set out, and on destroying Iraqi equipment and ammo as fast as we could. Simple. Mission accomplished.

Then predictions changed. Two weeks became extended to 18–22 March. Then longer. Then I stopped asking. Meanwhile, XVIII Corps was pulling out in accordance with the "first-in, first-out" policy (units were supposed to go home in accordance with their arrival times; we enforced this policy hard in VII Corps). Their withdrawal was completed on 22 March. That meant that we took over the zone previously occupied by both corps, an area about the size of Kentucky. After the XVIII Corps departure, the troops of VII Corps were the only ones left in Iraq.

During this time, we had no orders from Third Army or CENTCOM, other than rules of engagement to enforce the DML. The in-theater intent remained that we should not do anything to suggest permanency. But things in Iraq could not remain the same while everyone waited for the cease-fire. Permanent residents of towns and villages began to appear, as did refugees. Food and water were in short supply. Except for what we could provide, there was no law and order. Likewise, without us, there were no medical facilities.

That made for some difficult choices for us in VII Corps. We could not stand idly by.

Meanwhile, I stayed at our TAC CP in Iraq. I was not leaving as long as we had VII Corps in Iraq.

During those weeks, we spent considerable time going over the battles we had just fought to get it all accurate and to learn for the next time. You must also learn from success.

I directed each unit to conduct an AAR of its unit actions while it was all fresh in everyone's mind and we were still there on the battlefield, which everyone did within two weeks after the end of the war. On 11 March, we did a complete VII Corps AAR at the TAC CP, with all senior commanders in attendance. For that, my TAC crew built a terrain-scaled replica of our attack zone, which included phase lines and markers in the sand for positions of major unit movement. I did eighteen hours of interviews with the VII Corps historian, Major Pete Kindsvatter. My major unit commanders and I attended a Third Army AAR at King Khalid Military City on 12 March, notable for the time differences on unit locations, which further confirmed my suspicions that the map-posting accuracy in Riyadh had been short of the mark and might have accounted for some of the situational misunderstanding. Some CENT-COM times had been as much as twenty-four hours off on the Third Army battle reconstruction. I even found out later that CENTCOM had been in the habit of posting unit locations on the map by the locations of unit command posts, an error of fifty kilometers or more in some cases, since the CPs would sometimes be that far behind.

Both 1st AD and 3rd AD went back over their battle areas to look at what had been destroyed by air and what their units had destroyed. As best as both units could determine, about 15 to 20 percent of the damage had been done by CENTAF; the rest had come from direct-fire systems, artillery, or aviation. Third AD meticulously counted every destroyed tank in its sector and came up with 603. Of that number, fewer than 100 had been by air. In his AAR, Butch Funk confirmed the 9th and 29th Brigades of the Tawalkana in his sector, as well as the 10th and 12th Iraqi Armored Divisions. In some cases the Iraqis had abandoned perfectly functioning pieces of equipment, which we either took back to Germany as display monuments or blew up. First AD methodically reconstructed the Battle of Medina Ridge, locating each Iraqi vehicle by GPS, and recording its orientation vis-à-vis the attacking 1st AD, and what had killed the vehicle. Their statistics of that fight are accurate beyond doubt. I personally spent the better part of an afternoon with Joe Sartiano, H. R. McMaster, and Lieutenant Colonel Mike Kobbe going around the 73 Easting battle step by step.

The previously mentioned booklet, "The 100-Hour War: How the Iraqi

Plan Failed," assembled by a team headed by Lieutenant Colonel Dave Kirk from VII Corps G-2 in a little more than thirty days, and from a variety of sources, remains the most definitive account of what the Iraqis were trying to do in our sector. One Iraqi infantry unit commander said, "You attacked us with the same NATO force that was designed to attack the entire Warsaw Pact, and the entire earth shook." He got all that right, except the part about attacking the Warsaw Pact. An Iraqi brigade commander said, "I stood and looked to the west, and all I could see for as far as one could see were tanks and more tanks; tanks everywhere." One Iraqi general said, after he was captured, "I will never forget the way we were treated. Your soldiers are heroes."

One area where we failed was in capturing the combat in video and still pictures. Since many of our battles were in bad weather, rain, blowing sand, and at night, they would have been difficult to capture on film in any event, but we could have done better. I regret that the video legacy of Desert Storm gives a poor to erroneous impression of the war that the soldiers and Marines fought on land.

We recorded all our lessons learned, as well as made notes for what needed to be improved for the future. We learned that our soldiers, training, organizations, doctrine, and equipment were as able as we had thought they were. It was also a vindication of the Total Army concept that included the Reserve component.

There were also some things we needed to look at for the future of land warfare. I thought Desert Storm represented a transition war (in fact, all wars are transition wars). A lot of the old methods bear repeating in the future, but also some of the new ones. I also thought our possible enemies of the future were watching this war and taking notes. If they ever confronted the United States on a battlefield, they would attempt to stay away from some of our strengths—and take note of our weaknesses. All that meant to me was that we could not stand still and rest on our laurels. We would have to continue to maintain the edge. I filed it all away in my own notes to look at after we had some more time and perspective.

In some of the other actions we started during those days:

• I wanted to get the story told of what the corps soldiers had done in our eighty-nine-hour war, and so made sure there were many interviews with soldiers in the media and in unit publications.
• I had training resume. Not that I had to remind anyone; after the war, commanders instinctively turned to training. We had lots of ammo, plenty of targets still to shoot at, and plenty of real estate. Each unit set up its own target area and began training again. You have to keep your edge. If Saddam had decided to start something again, or if the rules changed, we were ready.

• We continued to destroy the Iraqi equipment we had bypassed in our attack.

We had one ally in all this. When XVIII Corps left, the French left a company-sized aviation unit with us, under my tactical control, and it was of great assistance to us in the western part of our sector. At one point, I asked the French commander when he was going home. "When you do," he answered. "We will stay as long as you need us." That they did. Like the British, they were terrific allies.

DESTRUCTION OF ENEMY EQUIPMENT

This task was vast, and went on from the beginning of the war on 24 February until we left Iraq for good on 9 May. Each unit was given the task of destroying the enemy ammunition and equipment in the area it had been assigned for occupation duties.

Because I was aware that it would require a total corps effort, I directed Task Force Demo to be formed on 2 March, and gave the mission to Colonel Sam Raines's 7th Engineer Brigade. Sam formed a special composite unit, commanded by Lieutenant Colonel Mark E. Vincent from an M577 in the VII Corps TAC CP in Iraq.

At 1500 on 2 March, they briefed me at the TAC on their concept of the operation, and I approved it on the spot. For the next seven weeks, this task force went about destroying Iraqi equipment and munitions and supervising the work done by our divisions, the 2nd ACR, and even the 11th Aviation Brigade in their sectors. It was an enormous effort.

Each day, I got a report on the previous day's destruction. Extensive records were kept of what was destroyed and its GPS location; specific areas were designated, and each day's mission ordered within those areas. Thus, all units knew who was working where, and safety was maintained. In the entire operation, not one U.S. soldier was injured.

In seven weeks, the task force supervised the destruction of equipment equivalent to that of two Iraqi MECH/armor divisions. EOD personnel cleared thousands of unexploded or unexpended munitions, and—in a humanitarian effort—fenced off hazardous areas around populated sites. A total of 6,622 targets were destroyed, worth, we estimated, about $1.2 billion.

The task force did not examine each of the munitions before exploding it, but we were sensitive to the possibility of unexploded Iraqi chemical munitions, and to my knowledge, no one ever detected any release of Iraqi chemical agents. If such agents had in fact been released, the chemical alarms in use with the troops would have detected them. During the time of the mission, no mission-caused illnesses were reported, except for one soldier who got a mustard gas blister on his arm.

We even destroyed an Iraqi gunboat. One day, Tom Rhame called and said, "Boss, we've got an Iraqi gunboat just off the coast by Umm Qasr. We'd like to destroy it."

"Is it occupied?" I asked.

"No."

"Go ahead."

A few 120-mm tank rounds later, the gunboat went to the bottom of the Gulf.

Near Umm Qasr on 10 March, the 1st INF uncovered a huge cache of cruise missiles, Exocets and Silkworms. The unit not only destroyed the concrete facility that housed them, but set off the missiles in a spectacular explosion near the coast (they used remote fusing from five kilometers away).

HUMANITARIAN OPERATIONS

It was in the area of humanitarian operations that we were least prepared, and experienced the most frustrations—and, in the end, the greatest satisfaction—of anything we did in the postwar period.

We were genuinely surprised by the magnitude of this mission.

Immediately after Desert Storm, there were few civilians in the VII Corps sector. The largest towns were Safwan and al-Busayyah. When Moreno and the Big Red One had taken it, Safwan had been largely deserted, while al-Busayyah was now mostly rubble, and completely abandoned. Shortly after the beginning of the XVIII Corps withdrawal on 9 March, and while the talks continued at the UN, a civil war broke out in the south of Iraq, when the Shi'ite Muslims in the region rebelled against the Baghdad regime.

As a direct result of that civil war, and the Iraqi government's indiscriminate and deliberate acts of violence against the civilian population along the Euphrates, a large number of refugees began arriving in the VII Corps sector, starting on about 15 March. Many of these refugees were drawn to Safwan, the only significantly built-up area in U.S.-occupied Iraq, and refugees thought that from there they would have quick access to Kuwait and Saudi Arabia (Safwan was only a few kilometers north of the Kuwaiti border). Soon after the war, however, both of those countries closed their borders to these refugees, and VII Corps faced a growing refugee population.

That meant a real command problem for me, of escalating proportions. I felt we needed to do something.

The day after XVIII Corps moved back to Saudi to begin redeployment, I came to this realization: I am the senior American in occupied Iraq. Orders or not, as American soldiers and according to the laws of land warfare and the Geneva Convention, we have responsibilities in an occupied country. So we acted.

I assembled the VII Corps civil affairs officer and G-5, Colonel Art Hotop, and VII Corps SJA, Colonel Walt Huffman. "Picture this on the day we leave," I told them. "What should we have done as an occupying force in a foreign country up to that time? We will use your determination as the basis for what we will do until we leave." They laid out the normal responsibilities of an occupying force, such as law and order, medical care, the clearance of unexploded ordnance around populated areas, and the provision of emergency food and water.

Though occupation duties had not been part of the mission we had been ordered to execute, for the next seventy days, VII Corps performed them de facto. Afterward, the official VII Corps report to ARCENT, CENTCOM, and the Department of the Army said, "While occupying Iraq, U.S. forces incurred certain legal obligations under international law. VII Corps has aggressively sought to meet these obligations."

For most of us, it was our first experience at occupation duty and large-scale humanitarian assistance.

How did we accomplish it?

We had already divided the occupied area into unit sectors, with each unit responsible for its particular sector—usually where the individual units had ended the war. Thus, 1st INF Division was in Safwan. The remainder of the units, however, were still in the desert, where there was no populated area, and so we shifted them. First we moved the 1st CAV into the area south of the Euphrates that had been vacated by the 24th Division. Next, we put 2nd ACR in the west, and the 1st INF northwest of the 1st CAV along Highway 8. South of them we assigned the entire western sector to the 11th Aviation Brigade, with the French regiment (it was actually battalion sized) under their operational control. When the 1st CAV left, soon after the departure of the XVIII Corps, we assigned the 1st AD to Highway 8 west of Basra. And when 1st INF left to fill the more western area, we assigned the Safwan area to the 3rd AD.

Our work fell into two periods. The first lasted from the beginning of the refugee influx, on about 15 March, to the signing of the UN-sponsored peace treaty, on 12 April. The second lasted from 12 April to 9 May, when all refugees under U.S. protection were settled in a camp in Saudi Arabia.

With the beginning of the refugee movement and the return of the indigenous population, Safwan's population returned to its prewar size of about 11,500. Soon, more than 8,000 refugees arrived, with no place to go, and began to build temporary shelters for themselves on the southern outskirts of town. The other towns of significance along Highway 8 (in what had been the XVIII Corps sector) were ar-Rumaylah and as-Salman, each with about 2,500 people. About 300 people returned to al-Busayyah, but they soon left again.

About 200 kilometers west of the corps TAC, about eighty kilometers north of the Saudi town of Rafha, and just north of the Saudi-Iraq border, the Saudis began a settlement similar to the one in Safwan, which we eventually called Rafha I, after the closest Saudi town. Gathered there were close to 12,000 people, with all the worldly possessions they could bring with them, including automobiles.

While this population and refugee movement was beginning, on 7 March, 1st INF helped to transfer 1,181 Kuwaiti citizens formerly held in Iraq back to Kuwait. During the time up to the cease-fire, we also processed more than 25,000 additional EPWs—Iraqi military who were either escaping the civil war or who otherwise wanted out of Iraq (we stopped this after the signing of the cease-fire agreement on 12 April).

At the corps TAC, I established a special task force to run this operation, consisting of the G-5, Colonel Art Hotop; his deputy, Lieutenant Colonel Nick Marsella; two lawyers, Captains Dan Smith and Jorge Lorenzo; and a logistician, Major Bob Corbett. To command the civil affairs operation, we had Colonel Bob Beahm, commander of the 354th Civil Affairs Brigade out of the Reserve component. Each division commander ran operations in his sector. In Safwan, Butch Funk put Colonel Bill Nash and the 1st Brigade in charge of the town.

Meanwhile, Ron Griffith established a series of checkpoints along Highway 8 leading toward Safwan. At these checkpoints, troops of the 1st AD both screened and assisted Iraqi civilians and others moving through the area. Checkpoint B, about eighty kilometers west of Basra on the way to Baghdad, soon grew into a sizable way point, complete with medical treatment facilities.

On 27 March, I visited Lieutenant Colonel Steve Smith and 1/7 INF, who were manning Checkpoint B and providing medical help. Inside the medical treatment tent, I saw Major Dr. Rodriquez, U.S. Army, obviously dog-tired, but continuing to treat Iraqi civilians (General Powell later awarded him the Humanitarian Service Medal, on our recommendation). He was treating a little two-year-old girl named Nura, who had a gunshot wound in her shoulder, and another little boy, about six or seven, with a wounded leg.

There was an enormous crush of refugees needing medical treatment, brought about by the countless atrocities committed by the Iraqi army upon its civilians. What I saw with my own eyes confirmed reports we had been getting from about 24 March of atrocities in Basra and all over the south—reports of people hanging from lampposts, mass executions, and starvation.

Afterward, I called John Yeosock to tell him, "It's bad enough that this is happening at all. But why are we so slow to react? Let's get observers into the Iraq side of the DML," I went on, "and get the UN to help us with displaced persons."

"I'll see what I can do," John answered.

I then asked my SJA, Colonel Walt Huffman, to start collecting evidence about atrocities from the Iraqi people for whom we were providing care; and Walt had the 1st AD make video- and audiotapes of their firsthand accounts, with their permission. This information was collected according to the rules of evidence, and sent to Third Army a few weeks later. From there it went to CENTCOM and the State Department, for further analysis and use.

★ The 3rd AD ran Safwan. They not only supervised the refugee camp, but essentially reopened the town: they established law and order. They cleared unexploded munitions within the town and to a distance of 500 meters outside it. They opened schools . . . and even got textbooks and school lunches. They reopened medical clinics, using both our own medical supplies and some captured from the Iraqis (one of our first sergeants told me he and his troops particularly enjoyed using Iraqi medical supplies to stock the civilian health clinic in Safwan). According to our doctors, the health treatment we provided to the over 8,000 people in the camp near Safwan dramatically improved the overall health of the refugees there. By the end of April, daily requests for medical assistance were few.

On 22 March, on a visit with Bill Nash and Butch Funk to the Safwan health clinic, I asked CW4 Joe Hatch, the 3rd AD head physician assistant, if I could do anything for them (his assistant was CW2 Ben Beaoui, who spoke Farsi).

"Get us some baby food!" he answered, holding up an infant. "This baby will die soon if we don't get it food and get it treated."

We got them the baby food via C-130s, and the child survived. For his work in that clinic, General Powell awarded Joe the Humanitarian Service Medal.

WITHDRAWAL

At 0230 on 13 April, Toby woke me for another middle-of-the-night phone call from Riyadh. At a little past midnight (our time) of the day before, the peace treaty and the UN resolutions had been signed. This phone call was from ARCENT: the President had ordered us to move the rest of our troops out of Iraq by 19 April. I did not mind being awakened for that call at all.

I had estimated it would take us five days to get out of Iraq, and that was the time we had. We swung into action, with first-in, first-out still my rule.

First out of Iraq had been the 2nd ACR, on 9 April. On the twelfth, we moved the 1st AD, followed on the fifteenth by the 1st INF. By the nineteenth, everyone was out, including all of our own equipment. At each stage, our units had moved into redeployment assembly areas near KKMC, where they had begun the tedious procedures necessary to prepare the vehicles and equipment for shipment back to Germany or the U.S.A.

Since the UN-sponsored treaty included no provision for the protection of the refugees who had fled the Iraqi civil conflict and who (rightly) feared government reprisals, I asked Major General Greindl (the Austrian commander of the UN force) what he planned to do about them. "Since that's not in my orders," he informed me, "I can't do anything."

"General, we have a problem," I said. "We are not leaving until we get this settled. We are not abandoning these people to Iraqi government atrocities."

That same day I told John Yeosock we had a responsibility to ensure the continued protection of the refugees, and he ordered us to protect the refugee sites. In fact, during this period, John constantly went out on a limb for us in order to authorize our humanitarian activities. "Fred, do what you think is right," he told me again and again; and he backed us up.

Meanwhile, on 7 April, we had changed command in 3rd AD. Much to his, and my, disappointment (since he would not be with us for the redeployment and homecoming in Germany), Butch Funk was pulled out of command to become the deputy J-3 on the Joint Chiefs of Staff in Washington. He was replaced by Major General Jerry Rutherford, who had been an ADC in the 1st INF. I assigned to Jerry Rutherford the mission with 3rd AD in Safwan.

In the western part of our sector, 2nd AD (Forward), which I had pulled from the 1st INF, replaced the 11th Aviation Brigade (the French remained). I assigned the protection mission to them.

Under Jerry Rutherford, 3rd AD continued to provide assistance to the refugees at the camp in Safwan and to the inhabitants returning to the town, as well as protection to a second camp just over the Kuwait border that was run by the Red Cross.

Our protection mission put us in an awkward situation, since U.S. troops were no longer supposed to be in Iraq after the treaty went into effect. In order to avoid that, the plan was for the governments of Kuwait and Saudi Arabia to take in the refugees. But that plan did not work; both governments initially refused to take in any Iraqi refugees.

Meanwhile, John Yeosock had been talking to officials in the Saudi government, and on 17 April they committed to building a camp sixty kilometers north of Rafha in Saudi Arabia, just south of the Iraqi border. This timely and compassionate move by the Saudi government was widely reported in Arab regional newspapers, but not, to my knowledge, in the West.

The Saudis then hired a contractor, who told us it would take them sixty to ninety days to build a camp.

"No way," I said. I didn't want us to have to wait around while they took their time to build the camp. "Our engineers will build a temporary camp, if you will agree to build a more permanent one." They agreed, and from 21 to 27 April, our engineers built Rafha II. Our temporary camp was roughly 1.4 kilometers by 1.1 kilometers. Around its perimeter were placed twelve 5,000-gallon water bladders that our engineers kept full. Our engineers (the 588th out of Fort Polk) also placed bottled water and food inside the camp, as well as 250 wooden showers and 250 latrines. These were urgently needed.

In the meantime, we notified Iraqi refugees at both Safwan and Rafha I that we were setting up the temporary camp inside Saudi Arabia, and camp leaders were allowed a visit there. They then had to make a choice: since the U.S. force was leaving soon, they had to make up their minds whether they wanted to stay in Iraq or go to the new camp, with the Saudi government's promise to build a more permanent camp. Most decided to leave. We gave those who chose to stay in Iraq seven days' worth of food and water.

The Kuwaiti government erected a fence around the Red Cross site with the only exit into Kuwait. The government of Iran accepted some 350 refugees a day from this camp flown out of Kuwait City International Airport.

Our VII Corps official report says:

"Movement of refugees from Rafha I to Rafha II began on 28 April. 11,500 refugees were moved, with the final closing of refugees in Rafha II on 8 May. Refugees from Rafha I were allowed to bring automobiles across the Saudi border and park them outside the camp. . . . During the period 28 April to 7 May, a total of 8,430 refugees were flown by USAF C-130 aircraft from Safwan to Rafha," a distance of about 500 kilometers. For all those going to Saudi, our personnel soldiers made new ID cards with photos. It was a masterful operation by both 3rd AD and CENTAF. Likewise, 2nd AD (Forward) did a superb job in moving refugees to Rafha II.

I vividly remember, during the transfer, scenes of U.S. soldiers digging into their own belongings and providing food, blankets, or even Army sweatshirts. As our report puts it, "The individual soldiers' generosity is evidenced by the number of government-issued blankets among the refugees and the U.S. Army sweatshirts hanging from the arms of the children."

The results were staggering: almost 20,000 refugees were resettled. Safwan was reopened as a village, with civil affairs soldiers helping local inhabitants regain self-sufficiency. Total meals of all types distributed during this entire period reached well over a million. Tons of flour, rice, and beans were distributed. Over 1.5 million gallons of water were produced, and close to a million gallons of bulk and bottled water were transported and distributed. Seven hundred cases of baby food were provided. In the hospitals we set up for the Iraqi people, corps doctors, nurses, and medics treated 29,450 Iraqi patients, with 601 of these evacuated to Saudi for further treatment. Many of them were returned and reunited with their families.

Our last message on this operation closed with the words: "The same soldiers and leaders who a short time before had relentlessly attacked and destroyed the Iraqi army in sector turned to and accomplished this humanitarian mission with compassion, discipline, and pride in being American soldiers. Doing both so well is a mark of who we are and what we stand for. JAYHAWK. Franks."

Residual Force

But we were not done.

As the signing of the cease-fire came closer, there began to be talk that we would have to leave a residual force in Kuwait, and I was informed that it was true when Secretary of Defense Cheney visited on 7 May. He told me the Kuwaitis wanted us to stay until the end of the year, but that the President would decide that, and that another force would replace the brigade as soon as possible. He also made it a point to visit the soldiers who would have to stay.

The brigade Jerry Rutherford selected to remain was a composite 1st Brigade commanded by Bill Nash (made up of units from other brigades). Because the decision had come so late, some of the soldiers were on airplanes about to leave, and we had to get them off and take them back to their equipment in Kuwait. It was not a good time for the troops. They had come on no notice, trained hard, won a great victory, done unexpected humanitarian work in and around Safwan—and now this.

I told 3rd AD to pick out a spot for the brigade that had something more than temporary facilities. Bill Nash looked around and recommended a place north of Kuwait City called Doha that had large warehouses for troop shelter and a large hardstand for equipment storage. It also had running water. Jerry Rutherford agreed, and after I took a look, I said that is it, move in.

By this time, CENTCOM HQ had departed the theater and were back in Tampa. John Yeosock departed with ARCENT on 10 May (John had been in-country from the first in August 1990). The CINC left Gus Pagonis in command of CENTCOM forward.

On my last day in-country, 11 May, I flew the 400 kilometers from King Khalid Military City to Kuwait to visit with the soldiers whom I had ordered to stay. I wanted to look them in the eye and explain why. It was not an easy meeting. They were hostile at first and had many questions: Why had they been told at the last minute? What about their families in Germany? Who would tell them? What else after this? How long? I told them we had won a great victory, and that, in the judgment of our government, a residual force was needed to continue to ensure that it lasted. It was a matter of trust. The soldiers accepted it, and said OK, we'll get on with it, it's our duty. It only intensified my sense of urgency to get them home. I told them we'd have them out in thirty to forty-five days, which was going out on a limb, because at that point we did not know who was coming to replace them. I also told them I would personally talk to their families in Germany.

That night I burned up the phone lines with Lieutenant General Denny Reimer in Washington, along with General Gordon Sullivan, to get a replacement force named fast. Sully promised me that he and General Vuono were dedicated to getting the 3rd AD troops out as quickly as possible. Earlier, there had been talk about sending the 199th Light Armored Brigade from Fort Lewis, Washington, but I was against it because they would have to bring their own equipment from Fort Lewis and they would take forever to get there. I had proposed the 11th ACR out of Germany, and General Butch Saint had agreed. They would be here the fastest of any unit, and they were a perfect match for the equipment and the mission.

One of the first things I did when I got back to Germany was to visit the families in Giessen whose military spouses had remained in Kuwait while the rest of the VII Corps had gone home. They were just as hostile as the brigade had been in Kuwait. I could not blame them. Yet all they wanted was some straight information. I identified myself as the one who had made the decision on the brigade of the 3rd AD, and explained the reason. Like their military spouses, they accepted it without question.

Who could ask for anything more of soldiers and their families? I was almost overcome with emotion when I saw how resolute they all were and willing once again to do what they had to do. I promised them their spouses would be home within forty-five days.

They were home in thirty-six.

FULL CIRCLE

It was a time for closure.

VII Corps had many ceremonies, and the individual units had their own.

In early March, as a gesture, all units in the theater were ordered to pick representatives to go home early. Our commanders and command sergeant majors selected soldiers by lot, and on 8 March we assembled them in formation at Al Khubar Village. Our VII Corps band and the troops in their new desert BDUs (we finally got them in time for the troops to wear home!) were all together. It was an emotional day, as all these ceremonies proved to be. This was the first.

General Schwarzkopf attended, as well as Lieutenant General Cal Waller, to say farewell to the soldiers and to tell them thanks. I met General Schwarzkopf that day at the airfield and escorted him all day, including at the formation. Not a word passed about any of the incidents of the war. During the ceremony, he said, "It was a helluva job on the part of VII Corps all the way around. . . . I'm proud of them. The country's proud of them. The world's proud of them. And they should be proud of themselves."

My message was, "No matter what is written, said, or shown about what happened here, your courage, heart, toughness, teamwork, and willingness to take the fight to the enemy without letup in bad weather, day and night, will be forever stamped in these desert sands. . . . You are the best we have. . . . You are all heroes and I am enormously proud of each and every one of you. . . . I have been honored to be in your ranks and privileged to be given the responsibility to lead you in battle."

It was a message I would tell to as many VII Corps soldiers as I could reach, and at each departure ceremony in Saudi, as individual major units of the corps departed.

We arrived home on 12 May to a brief ceremony at the Stuttgart Airport attended by, among others, Ambassador Vernon Walters, SACEUR Commander General Jack Galvin, and Lord Mayor Rommel of Stuttgart. Our arrivals back home in Germany were short on ceremony and long on hugs with spouses, family members, and friends. Denise was waiting for me, as well as Margie, Greg, Jake, and Mickey when we arrived at Kelly Barracks. There was the national anthem, then more band music, and big cheers from the family members on the floor of the gym, who were waving yellow ribbons and U.S. flags. I never hugged and kissed Denise so much as I did at that reunion. Similar scenes went on all over VII Corps and Germany, with "Proud to Be an American" and "From a Distance" by far the most popular songs played.

On 31 May at Kelly Barracks, we had the most emotional ceremony of all. In the small soldier chapel there, amid the stained-glass windows, we paid tribute to the lasting memory of those who had lost their lives in Desert Storm. VII Corps Command Sergeant Major Bob Wilson* and other CSMs read the roll of all the soldiers who had died, one by one. There was neither a sound nor a dry eye. It was a profoundly moving moment, and spurred a vow from us all to remember them that day and every day.

---

*I selected Bob Wilson in late January 1991. We had served together in the Blackhorse in the early 1960s. He was vital to our success in preparing for war and in solving soldier issues. He later put together a pamphlet at TRADOC that outlined senior NCO performance in Panama and Desert Storm.

On 27 June at Kelly Barracks, all units who had been members of the VII Corps Desert Storm team—900 soldiers and commanders, including the British, with their own band, and the French—assembled to honor the corps. Special guests included Ambassador Walters, General Sullivan (the new Army Chief) and General Butch Saint. It was a particularly windy day, with gusts of over forty knots (which perhaps reminded some of the desert winds and sandstorms through which we had fought), but the color guard would not let the flags drop, and their hands had to be pried off the flagstaffs after the formation. We awarded medals to deserving soldiers for valor and humanitarian service, and to civilians and those who had done so much at the VII Corps Base operation in Germany.

General Colin Powell flew over specially to attend the ceremony, and spoke warmly and emotionally to those assembled. In part, he said, "Thank you for your magnificent victory in the Gulf, and I also want to say thank you on behalf of the liberated people of Kuwait and others in the Persian Gulf region whose security you have ensured by your gallantry in action. . . . You have raised the levels of warfare to new heights. You fought a war of complexity and integration that no one has ever seen before. You were at the top of the profession of arms. . . . You have made America proud again. You have made America feel good about herself again. You have made America realize that there is nothing we can't do if we put our hearts to it, if we put our minds to it, and if we put our muscles to the task before us. You have shown that the armed forces of the United States, and especially the JAYHAWK Corps, are the best and brightest of the nation." Following the ceremony, he stayed to greet as many people as possible in the open reception, then flew straight back to Washington. It was another reminder to me of the difference between Desert Storm and Vietnam. General Powell's leadership was one big reason.

In September 1991, Denise and I were invited back to our hometown of Reading, Pennsylvania, for a parade and other ceremonies to honor all Desert Storm veterans from Reading and Berks County. My dad came and sat on the reviewing stand with us, as did the Pennsylvania adjutant general, and a World War II Medal of Honor winner. It was a wonderful event, arranged in part by those who had gone before, our fellow Vietnam veterans who themselves had not had such parades. Following the parade was a large celebration at the Reading Municipal Stadium—the same arena where I had played football and baseball as a boy.

There were other parades as well, in New York and in Washington, as I have written before. They were at once different and the same. For the rest of my life, I will remember the generosity of our fellow citizens to our soldiers who went and did their duty.

In New York, the parade was more intimate. We were closer to the people than on the broader Washington, D.C., streets. Ticker tape fell as we marched through the canyon of office buildings. Looking right and left, all we could see were the faces of America, all ages, all backgrounds, most waving small American flags and smiling and yelling. As we marched proudly down those New York City streets, we reached out and shook hands and said our own thanks to our fellow citizens who had come to honor us so. I only wished all the VII Corps soldiers could have been there (we'd brought only representatives of the units back from Germany).

In Washington, after the 4.2 miles down Constitution Avenue and the enormous outpouring of emotion from our fellow Americans, Denise and I returned to the quiet place—the Vietnam Veterans Memorial. We touched the names and remembered friends, relatives, fellow soldiers who are never forgotten. Never far away. This one was for you, too, the memories of heroes who did what our country had asked and had not had this day.

Now there were more friends. Other members of our Army family. Soldiers of VII Corps talking quietly with their own families, and the next of kin of those who, like before, had not returned. Proud. Confident. Remembering.

It was not like before. Not like after Vietnam.

"Don't worry, General, we trust you." I'll never forget that.

Trust reunited.

16

<center>~~~~~~~~</center>

TRADOC AND THE FUTURE OF LAND WARFARE

"Sir, General Sullivan wants you on the phone," Toby Martinez announced to Fred Franks. General Gordon Sullivan had recently been named to succeed General Carl Vuono as the Army's thirty-second Chief of Staff. He would be sworn in on 21 June. This was not a social call.

At the time, Franks was at a luncheon with General Butch Saint in Heidelberg at USAREUR HQ; Franks excused himself and went to the club manager's office.

"Freddy, Sully," General Sullivan began. "I want you do something for me."

"Name it and it's done."

"I want you to command TRADOC. We have a lot of work to do, and you are the man to get it done for us."

It did not take long to answer. The Army could not have found a better fit for Fred Franks. It would be hard to imagine a job more suited to his talents and experience.

"I am honored and value your confidence. I'll give you the best I've got, and do my best to work your agenda. What about timing?"

"Figure sometime in August. You have to get Senate confirmation. Take some leave and get ready to go to work. We have a lot to do. Downsizing's going to take a lot of attention. We can't get dragged down by that. We have to keep our heads up and looking ahead. Tell Denise, but otherwise keep this to yourself."

"WILCO."

When Franks returned to the table, he tried to keep a poker face. After he told General Saint who had called, Saint seemed in no way curious about the nature of the call (he had been giving Franks advice on future assignments and probably already knew what it was all about).

When he got home and told Denise, she was as excited as he was. They were going home to the U.S.A. She knew TRADOC and what commanding it would mean to Fred, and she was familiar with Fort Monroe in Virginia, which was TRADOC headquarters. It was a good place to live.

After Franks's return from Desert Storm, he and Denise had held many discussions about their future. There were two possibilities: to stay in Germany and inactivate VII Corps in the spring of 1992; or come to Heidelberg to be DCINC in USAREUR (John Shalikashvili, the current DCINC, was about to become assistant to Colin Powell on the Joint Chiefs of Staff). Now there was a third: to go to TRADOC.

TRADOC it was.

SENIOR-LEVEL SELECTION

Congress makes three- and four-star rank available to the military services for specifically authorized positions, and as positions become vacant, the services nominate officers to fill it. Sometimes the Senate holds hearings on the nominee, sometimes it does not. After being confirmed by the Senate, the nominee normally serves in that position for a specified term (most often, two years at a time), and when that term is completed, there are options: the officer can be reappointed to the same position, moved to another job, promoted (requiring another confirmation), or retired. In the U.S. Army, there are twelve four-star generals and forty-two three-star generals in an active force of 495,000. Six of the twelve four-star generals fill command positions in the Joint Command structure (such as CENTCOM commander).

During the process of choosing nominees to fill both three- and four-star nominations, it is common practice for the serving four-star Army generals to make recommendations to the Army Chief. The chief of staff then takes the recommendations under advisement, combines it with his own counsel, and makes his recommendations to the Army Secretary, the senior civilian in the Department of the Army (in order to strictly observe the letter and spirit of civilian control of the military, the final approving authority at each step is the senior civilian in the Executive Branch). Next, the nominations are reviewed by the Chairman of the Joint Chiefs of Staff and approved or rejected by the Secretary of Defense. If the Secretary okays them, they are sent to the President for his approval. Finally, just as he would for any senior executive position, the President offers the nomination to the Senate for confirmation.

For Franks, the principals involved in his selection were Army Chief Gordon Sullivan, Army Secretary Mike Stone (who died in 1995; Stone was a successful businessman, a public servant of long standing who loved the Army), General Colin Powell, and Secretary of Defense Dick Cheney.

Much later, Franks learned from Carl Vuono that it was he who had recommended him to Sullivan. Since Sullivan was about to become chief and needed his own team, however, the choice had to be his.

"I didn't pick you because the Army did not have any alternatives," Vuono added. "I recommended you because—based on your recent experience in Desert Storm, your two previous tours of duty in TRADOC, and your command of Seventh Army Training Command in Germany—you were the best choice for the times TRADOC and the Army were about to enter."

Departure

Leaving VII Corps was not easy. Leaving any command is not easy, but this one was especially hard, since everyone in the corps had been to war together. They had been family on the battlefield, and bonds formed there are forever. Franks went around the corps to say his good-byes, trying as best he could to keep everything as low-key as possible. But at the assembly on the parade-athletic field at Kelly Barracks on 31 July, there was a lot of emotion. "Soldiering with you has been the highlight of my life," Franks told them. "What we have done, we have done as a team. We will miss you all." It had been less than two years since August 1989, when he had taken the VII Corps colors as commander. Together, he and the corps had seen the fall of the Wall and the tearing apart of the Iron Curtain, the end of the Cold War, deployment and victory in the Gulf, and now this. It was a lot to absorb.

After the ceremony, Franks and Denise left Stuttgart.

When Lieutenant General Mike Spigelmire assumed command of VII Corps two weeks later, he had an unpleasant task before him, and in March 1992, in a ceremony in Stuttgart a little more than a year after the biggest armor attack in the history of the U.S. Army, VII Corps was inactivated and its battle colors cased (they are now on permanent display at SAMS at Fort Leavenworth). The Army leadership (with strong dissent from Fred Franks) had decided to keep V Corps as its residual corps in Germany. Frankfurt, not Stuttgart, was to be the headquarters. (Three years later, the V Corps HQ was moved from Frankfurt to Heidelberg. Kelly Barracks, former home of VII Corps, remains open as part of European Command.)

On Tuesday morning, 7 August, at 1000 hours, General Sullivan promoted Franks to four-star general in a small conference room in the Pentagon. The Senate had confirmed him late Friday afternoon. Denise and a few former JAY-HAWKS from VII Corps who worked in the Pentagon were there; and Denise helped General Sullivan pin on the fourth star.

TRADOC

TRADOC was a sizable responsibility.

When TRADOC had been activated as a major U.S. Army command in June 1973, it had been a unique organizational concept, with no precedent in the U.S. Army or in any armies around the world.* As we have seen in previous chapters, TRADOC had two major responsibilities: to be the architect of the future army, and to prepare the army for war.

First, TRADOC determines the requirements for fighting in the future. To accomplish that aim, it makes sure that

• the Army continues to adapt and change to meet future national security demands as part of a joint military team;
• in the future the Army is as relevant and decisive a force as it is in the present;
• growth is coherent; in other words, that doctrine, training, organizational design, leader development, and materiel requirements for the Department of the Army are defined and integrated so that they all come together in time and investment—with particular attention paid to the requirements of individual soldiers to gain combat power.

Second, TRADOC is responsible for training standards across the Army, and it operates the Army's vast training and leader development school system—what Franks likes to call the nation's "Land Warfare University." With over 350,000 students annually; real estate the size of Puerto Rico; a faculty of over 11,000; ROTC and JROTC in close to 1,500 high schools, colleges, and universities throughout America; and with Education Board approval to award master's degrees, this is a university by any measure.

To accomplish these missions, TRADOC has an annual budget of over $2 billion; it has civilian and military manpower levels of close to 60,000; and it operates eighteen major installations (like the rest of the Army, it has been reduced over 30 percent in the past eight years). Each major installation and associated military school or individual training base (Fort Knox, Fort Benning, Fort Sill, Fort Jackson, Fort Leonard Wood, etc.) is commanded by a major general. In addition to the four-star commander, there are two three-star deputies, one** at the HQ at Fort Monroe, Virginia, and one at Fort Leav-

---

*Since 1973, five foreign armies have formed TRADOC-like organizations of their own. The U.S. Marine Corps has established at Quantico a counterpart organization they call MCCDC; in 1996, the USAF established its own doctrine organization within its existing training command; and in 1992, the U.S. Navy located a Navy doctrine center in Norfolk, Virginia (so that it would be near TRADOC).

**This deputy, added in 1995, was not there when Fred Franks commanded TRADOC.

enworth, Kansas, who is also commandant of the Army's Command and General Staff College and supervises all training in TRADOC.

★ As the new Army Chief, Gordon Sullivan saw the coming years as a time of rapid transition for the U.S. Army. The Cold War was over and won. There had been victories in both Panama and the Persian Gulf. There was a clamor for a "peace dividend." Sullivan and Franks were both aware that we had gone through similar periods many times in our history, between World War II and Korea, for example. During such times, in the words of General Colin Powell, we "screwed it up." In July 1990, when speaking to veterans of Task Force Smith, the first U.S. combat unit into Korea in 1950, Army Chief General Carl Vuono had said, "Never again can we allow our soldiers in America's Army to march into battle without the weapons and training essential to their survival and victory." This thought of unpreparedness for the next war haunted Army leaders and propelled a sense of urgency to prevent it. Sullivan's challenge to the Army was "to break the mold," to make the transition different this time.

Most of the transition was physical: the Army had to reduce manpower levels by 30 percent from Cold War levels, with significant reductions in the resources available for modernization and for investments in the future. As a major commander, Fred Franks not only would have to live within these new resource levels, but also look for ways to accomplish the TRADOC mission that were different from what had been done in the past.

But the Army would also have to make the transition from Cold War to post–Cold War in the area of ideas—or doctrine. Like General Vuono before him, Sullivan put great emphasis on keeping the Army trained and ready to fulfill its current responsibilities, while it adapted for the future, and doctrine (as Sullivan put it in a letter to Franks in July 1991) had to be the Army's "engine of change." In other words, the Army had to continue to revise its basic operational manual, the 100-5.

The Army had to continue to be able to adjust and adapt rapidly. This also seemed to be what the nation expected, given the uncertain nature of the new international security scene.

During his four years as Army Chief, Sullivan succeeded in reshaping the Army from twenty-eight active and National Guard divisions to eighteen. Meanwhile, there could be no time-outs from operational commitments. On the contrary, during that same period, the Army saw its operational commitments grow by 300 percent over what they had been during the Cold War. U.S. Army units found themselves in south Florida repairing hurricane damage, in Somalia on humanitarian missions, in Haiti restoring democracy, back in Kuwait to deter Iraqi aggression, and in Bosnia to enforce a peace agreement. At the same time, the Army was withdrawing over 160,000 troops and twice that many families from Europe, and closing over 600 installations overseas. This was a monstrously difficult job. Success was not preordained. In fact, no corporation in America has ever downsized and reorganized as well or as quickly as the U.S. Army had in those few short years.

It was Fred Franks's and TRADOC's job not only to lead the intellectual change in ideas and in doctrine that would ensure that the Army could quickly adapt to the new strategic situation, but to lay the groundwork for the changes needed to meet the requirements of the first two decades of the twenty-first century.

Franks and Gordon Sullivan had several things in common. They had both "grown up right," as General Vuono liked to put it, and that gave them a leg up (an expression Franks uses with a smile) as they worked together. They both had been in tanks and cavalry and had known each other for their entire professional lives. When Franks had commanded the Blackhorse in Fulda, Sullivan had been 3rd AD chief of staff (after commanding a brigade in 3rd AD). They both liked ideas, they liked to conceptualize and brainstorm, and they talked frequently, often long into the night. Now and again, Franks and Sullivan took off together to smoke cigars and fish in the lower Chesapeake in Franks's newly purchased twenty-foot Shamrock boat, the *JAYHAWK*. And each Labor Day weekend, during the three years Franks was at TRADOC, Sullivan and his wife, Gay, assembled a few families at Fort Story so that they might enjoy one another's company and talk Army and national security business.

ENGINE OF CHANGE

Franks had seen for himself that, while it was absolutely necessary, it wasn't easy to stay ahead of the curve. He was reminded of that every day at his own headquarters at Fort Monroe, Virginia. Monroe was the largest stonemasonry fortress in the United States, yet it had been built after the fact—after the British had sailed into the harbor during the War of 1812 and destroyed Hampton.

When Fred Franks assumed command of TRADOC from General John Foss, he knew that he and his team had to be the agents of change, yet he also knew that the prevailing attitude in many places was, "If it ain't broke, don't fix it." The Army had just come off three huge successes in the Cold War, Panama, and the Gulf. Why not leave everything else alone and just get through this downsizing period without breaking the Army?

After the victory in Desert Storm had demonstrated the value of the Air-Land Battle doctrine, Franks was one of the leaders to call attention to that success. Now here he was, moving away from it into new territory.

It's always easier to make physical change in the Army than to change ideas.

Though it might take a lot of work to convert a tank battalion from M60A3 tanks to M1s, you won't encounter much resistance to it.

Changing ideas is harder. "The only thing harder than getting a new idea into a military mind," Liddell-Hart wrote, "is getting the old one out." The great military historian Alfred Thayer Mahan said very close to the same thing about a hundred years ago: "An improvement of weapons is due to the energy of one or two men, while changes in tactics"—that is, in doctrine—"have to overcome the inertia of a conservative class. History shows that it is vain to hope that military men generally will be at pains to do this, but that the one who does will go into battle with great advantage." This is not surprising . . . or even a bad thing. It is a healthy skepticism, if it is kept in balance. You have to expect resistance to ideas that threaten known ways of doing things—and especially if those ways are successful. New ideas are unproven on the battle-field.

At times, new and revolutionary war-fighting ideas have been assimilated rapidly, for example, the U.S. Marine Corps's development of amphibious doctrine in the 1930s; the U.S. Navy's adoption of the aircraft carrier; and the U.S. Army's development of air assault, air mobility, and the use of rotary-wing aviation in firing rockets and antitank munitions.

There have also been blind spots: In the late 1920s and early 1930s, the Army's long attachment to horse cavalry and its policy of tanks in support of infantry held back the development of mechanized warfare. Later, the Navy had its battleship advocates, even in the face of overwhelming evidence that aircraft made battleships obsolete. And the Air Force's strategic bomber theorists still persist in believing that wars can be won from the air alone.

People often dream of a super-weapon that will guarantee victory on the battlefield. Super-weapons make for nice dreams, and sometimes for exciting escapist fiction, but it is only rarely that a revolutionary new technology is needed to win in land battles. Rather, victory usually comes from adapting existing technology to particular advantages on the battlefield. The ways in which you combine that technology and your organizations to fight and to win is another way of saying doctrine. Earlier in the book, we saw that maneuver warfare is dominated more by ideas than by technology. Indeed, in 1940, the French and the Germans had the same technology. They both had airplanes, tanks, self-propelled artillery, and radio. But as Colonel Bob Doughty points out in his book, *Seeds of Disaster*, the Germans got the doctrine right, and the French got it wrong. Their soldiers fought well but their leadership had the wrong war-fighting ideas. It is an instructive period.

Again, the Army is a conservative institution, and you want that. They deal in life-and-death decisions. In no other profession is the penalty for being completely wrong so severe and lasting. The price for failure to prepare is not loss of revenue in the marketplace, it is loss of your most precious resource, your soldiers. That was demonstrated in the American Civil War, when leaders used Napoleonic methods of attack in the face of rifles that were ten times more accurate than when the tactics had been devised. The result: noble failures such as Pickett's charge at Gettysburg. Later, in World War I, leaders continued to use masses of soldiers to gain combat power and failed to win because of machine guns and devastating artillery. The challenge for TRADOC was to prevent something similar to that from happening the next year . . . or in 2003 or 2010.

Ideas lead change. If you want to influence the future, you have to have ideas about the future. In any campaign—in any venture—success begins with a clear vision of where you want to go and what you want to do. In Fred Franks's words: "How you think about the future determines what you think about the future and what you ultimately do about the future." Or, as Gordon Sullivan put it, "The intellectual leads the physical."

That's easier to say than to do. Leading with ideas is damned difficult. It is hard to provide new vision and focus; it is harder still to shake off old paradigms. It's a surprising paradox that the profession that takes on the greatest form of chaos possible—war—is at times so tied to order and fixed paradigms. This doubtless comes from trying to impose order on that battlefield chaos.

Thus, in the Army of 1991, there was something of a tension for some between what was needed to meet present-day training demands and what had to be done to meet the needs of the future. It was a healthy tension, but it was there.

As Franks sees it, organizations change for three reasons:

• they are out in front and want to stay there;
• they are about to be overcome by the competition and have to change in order to stay competitive;
• they have already been overcome, and they must change in order to compete and survive.

The Army was in the first category. Of course, not all periods require modifications. You have to watch out not to bring about change for change's sake . . . or to make them simply in order to leave your imprint on the organization, or to leave a "legacy." That attitude is dangerous. Sometimes the best a senior leader can do is to raise standards of current operating procedures.

And yet, the Army could not ignore the future. How would the next war be fought? Not to be ready was to invite failure, which could take many forms, from the loss of a war (seriously unlikely) to the loss of battles, or worse, humiliating defeats and the unacceptable loss of American lives (seriously possible).

Most often failure is caused by resistance to change in war-fighting ideas, the use of the wrong ideas, or a lack of preparedness—and, as we've seen, preparedness comes through tough performance-oriented training that gives soldiers and units battlefield experience even before combat.

Franks knew that he and TRADOC needed to look hard at all the institutional paradigms to see which ones needed to be transformed, which ones needed to remain, and which ones only needed to be adapted to the new strategic realities. In other words, they didn't want to throw out the baby with the bathwater.

In a sense, it had been easier to reshape the Army in the mid-1970s. There had been a clear threat then. The Army itself had been in bad shape. Army leaders had just witnessed the awesome speed and destruction of the modern battlefield in the 1973 Mideast War. When they looked at the Army's ability to fight and win on that battlefield, they did not like what they'd seen. There had been a clear need for strong action.

The 1990s were vastly different—more like the years between the two world wars. The Army was coming off a great victory. Leaders and military thinkers were discussing new ideas of warfare, but without any urgency. They simply wanted to get the troops home and out of uniform. With no measurable threat, there was little hunger for a large standing military.

Still, Fred Franks found that even though he might have to work hard to overcome resistance, in today's Army, if ideas had merit and if their worth in actual operations or in field trials could be demonstrated, then there would be a chance to make those changes stick.

The Army in the early 1990s was a remarkably adaptive organization. Recent leaders had seen to that. Thus, if point men for change, such as Fred Franks, did not always have their complete attention, it was not so much because they were resistant as that the Army was already handling responsibilities that were close to unmanageable. They just had so much to do in order to take care of the increased commitments, the rapid downsizing, the budget cuts, the massive drawdown in Europe—just to name a few. At the same time, they had to master new ideas, face up to new strategic realities, and look forward into the next century, while simultaneously taking in about 60,000 new recruits annually.

To bring about reform, you have to know the culture with which you are dealing. The Army culture does not so much resist reform as it has to be convinced that it is in the best interests of the entire organization. It wants proof, then it wants broad acceptance by the whole Army. Thus, it is highly suspicious of suggestions advocated by small groups, unless the small groups can eventually bring about that broad acceptance. We have seen the difficulties with the Active Defense FM 100-5 of 1976. Though Active Defense had been the right doctrine for the time, it had been developed by a relatively small group at TRADOC and thus it was initially misunderstood within the Army.

In the Army, you achieve consensus not by following the path of least resistance and compromise, as in a legislative process, but by arguing and debating. You go out there in the Army marketplace of ideas and try to sell your wares . . . and you improve them until you get them right. In the process, you teach them and bring others to accept them.

With these thoughts in mind, Franks and his staff at TRADOC devised their approach to revising the 1986 FM 100-5—the book's last Cold War edition. They consulted as broadly as they could within the Army—for the sake of both the substance of the book, and of its acceptance. They talked the ideas out; they debated them. In that way, they got not only a broad sense of what the Army was thinking, but also good ideas that hadn't occurred to them. By the time the book was published, the ideas were well known, and change had already begun.

IDEAS FOR CHANGE

This was the world the Army faced: The Soviet Union had collapsed, the worldwide communist monolith had crumbled, the Cold War had ended, and the world had entered a new era with a vastly different strategic landscape. A relatively predictable strategic environment was gone. A predominantly forward-deployed military posture was gone. The focus of potential warfare within the confines of a highly developed structure of joint and combined relationships was gone. And gone with that were the operational constraints of the Cold War and its clearly defined potential enemy.

In place of all that was a new strategic landscape, marked by a broader and much different set of conditions, in a more unstable and ambiguous setting. As events since 1989 have demonstrated, we now live in a world that is more complex and uncertain than we ever imagined. "After forty-five years of fighting a dragon, we finally killed it," says R. James Woolsey, former Director of the Central Intelligence Agency, "and now instead, we find ourselves standing in a jungle with a bunch of snakes."

This new strategic era demanded an entirely new security stance for the United States and, in turn, a distinctly different posture for our Army.

As he went around and about the Army, Franks used five categories—warning lights—to define the need for change, which came out of his own battlefield experience and his longtime study and reading of history. They were:

- threats and unknown dangers,
- the national military strategy,
- history and the lessons learned from it,
- the changing nature of warfare, and
- technology.

At times only one indicator may be lit, and that one dimly. At other times, maybe two or three burn. As Fred Franks looked out at the world of the early 1990s, he saw all the indicators burning brightly.

Both Just Cause in Panama and Desert Storm in southwest Asia had set off the lights. Franks calls them "Janus Wars." They had both been fought with twentieth-century tactics, technology, and doctrine, but they both had shown signs of twenty-first-century warfare.

They showed that the United States' competition—whether rogue nations or rogue groups—could quickly acquire and field new technologies and advanced weapons—including weapons of mass destruction—without research-and-development establishments of their own. Even if these weapons were acquired in relatively small numbers, they would give considerable battlefield leverage.

To counter such threats, rather than looking back at twentieth-century industrial-age technologies, the Army had to look ahead to the potential of virtual reality, digitized communications, and other information-age technologies for sharing, retrieving, and transmitting information; they had to talk to futurists about where the world might be heading; and they had to try to make the right decisions about how to put it all together. The last was particularly important. Yet it wasn't the technology itself that they had to examine; rather, they needed to synthesize various disparate pieces—some new, some old—into a new concept for the battlefield. This was not easy, as history has shown.

What were some of the other warning lights?

The Goldwater-Nichols National Security Act of 1986 was one. It changed the way service departments would be involved in operational matters, increased the authority of the regional war-fighting CINCs, and increased and streamlined the war-fighting chain of command. A new national security strategy was published, and a new national military strategy was emerging. Regional conflicts, and even what were then called operations short of war (such as the peacekeeping mission to Bosnia), were replacing the Cold War. Information-age technology was spreading to all parts of the private sector, and there were exciting new possibilities for its application to the military. The days of mobilization of a large standing army to fight the Soviets were over. The U.S. Army was now becoming a smaller army. It now needed to become a force-projection army. It now had to be able to deploy large organizations overseas quickly. In essence, World War II ended in 1989.

The change in size of the Army was dramatic—from a Cold War size of 18 active divisions, 10 National Guard divisions, 5 corps, and 50 percent stationed overseas, to 12 active divisions (later 10), 8 National Guard divisions, 4 corps, and about 80 percent stationed in the U.S.A. The active component strength of the Army dropped from 770,000 during the Cold War to 495,000. In the total active armor force today, there are twenty-eight tank battalions and twelve armored cavalry squadrons. In Desert Storm, VII Corps alone had twenty-two tank battalions and seven armored cavalry squadrons.

In short, battle and operational environments were going to be hard to predict. This meant that the Army had to be able not only to fight and win in several different types of battlefields, but also to accomplish several types of operations other than war. And this in turn meant that the Army's doctrine had to address the issue of the smaller force's versatility. It also meant doing away with the term "AirLand Battle"—not because the concept was no longer useful, but because it suggested the linear battlefield of central Europe. Though such a battlefield might turn out to exist in the future, Army commanders had to be capable of adapting to a very different kind of battlefield.

So this is what they did:

LAND BATTLE

Changes to the land war doctrine fell within four areas: Force Projection, Operations Other Than War, Joint and Combined Operations, and Conduct of the Land Battle.

Force Projection

Because the likelihood that the Army would fight or operate close to garrison locations (as it did in Germany during the Cold War) was about zero, it had to become skilled at quickly putting together tactical teams to fit fast-arising mission requirements that were hard to predict in advance. Then they had to get to where they were going and, depending on the nature of their mission— from fighting their way in to operations other than war—they had to figure out how to place the force on the ground consistent with the way they wanted to conduct the operation (an error in initial disposition, as Moltke said, might not be corrected for an entire campaign). Meanwhile, they had to get early intelligence as rapidly as possible in order to deploy the units. And finally, once there, they had to supply themselves, perhaps half a world away from the U.S.A., or else hundreds or thousands of miles from their garrisons, and sometimes in areas where they wouldn't get local help.

The Army taught itself how to do all that. An entire chapter on force projection was put into the 1993 100-5. Force projection scenarios became the object of study in Army schools. Training programs were begun. Army Chief Sullivan and his principal logistician, Lieutenant General Lee Salomon, began prepositioning Army equipment in key locations around the world, to allow sizable land power to be sent into a region quickly. The recent deployment of a 1st Cavalry Division brigade from Fort Hood to Kuwait has demonstrated that the Army has indeed become a strategic force for the 1990s.

Operations Other Than War
More and more, the Army is finding itself involved in non-war-fighting missions, in operations such as VII Corps's humanitarian relief efforts in southeastern Iraq following Desert Storm; Provide Comfort in northern Iraq; and peacekeeping operations, such as that which the U.S. Army has been performing in the Sinai Desert since 1979. In a world that is no longer bipolar, regional conflicts or crises are sure to demand the peaceful use of U.S. forces.

There is a sharp distinction between the two types of operations: On the one hand, there is war, the deliberate use of force to gain a national or coalition strategic objective. The Army's purpose is to fight and win the nation's wars as part of a joint team, and it trains, equips, and mans itself to do that. In war you want aggressive, tough soldiers and units. That behavior does not always work best in an operation other than war.

On the other hand, military forces can be used to gain objectives by means of (usually) non-combat operations, and (usually) in combination with other elements of national power. Though occasionally some of these operations might involve actual combat, force is not the principal means to the strategic ends. However, the discipline, skills, teamwork, and toughness that come from preparing to fight and win can be used in these operations. (You cannot go the other way. Soldiers and units trained only in skills for operations other than war are not prepared for the rigors of the land battlefield.)

OOTWs, as such operations are called, are not new. The Army has long conducted them—beginning with George Washington's use of the militia to put down the Whiskey Rebellion in Pennsylvania in 1794.

How do you conduct OOTWs?
You need

• a sense of objective: the ability to focus all your efforts on achieving that objective; and the discipline to stay within those parameters;
• unity of effort: all the various military, government, and non-government agencies have to work toward the same goal;

• a sense of legitimacy: the operation must be conducted in such a way that the authority of the local government is reinforced;

• perseverance: OOTWs tend to take much longer to reach objectives than the use of force;

• restraint: you have to stay within specified rules of engagement; and, finally,

• security: you need to protect the force against a variety of threats while it is conducting its operations.

One interesting anomaly that the Army began to notice about OOTWs: while the actual battlefield was becoming less dense with soldiers, these OOTW missions tended to be manpower-intensive. Such a contradiction would lead to tensions, as budget analysts attempted to reduce the Army end strength.

Joint and Combined Operations

Passage of the Goldwater-Nichols legislation in 1986 ensured the preeminence in the U.S. military of joint operations over operations conducted by a single service alone.

Does that mean that Goldwater-Nichols created joint warfare? Far from it. It's been practiced almost from the beginning of the nation's history. World War II saw the largest joint operations in the history of the U.S. military, and the landing at Inchon in Korea was a joint operation masterstroke. Later, however, the long Cold War fixed the services into set patterns of operation. They were ready to fight if that conflict grew hot, but were perhaps not as ready to combine forces to operate quickly in other environments. That changed when Desert One and Grenada inspired a reemphasis on the skillful conduct of joint operations. After that, Desert Storm proved the worth of the new legislation.

Before 1986 little joint doctrine had been published, and actual warfighting doctrine was published by individual services (principally by the Army and, to a lesser extent, by the Marine Corps, since operational doctrine seemed most useful to land forces). The services would then informally meld their doctrines together—essentially with a Cold War scenario in mind—to achieve whatever harmony was appropriate. Starting in 1973, for instance, and lasting into the 1990s, the Army and the USAF had struck up a close working partnership at TRADOC and the AF TAC (Tactical Air Command). The result was the AirLand Battle doctrine. Similar close relationships between the Marines and Army had for years harmonized land battle doctrines—while recognizing the special nature of amphibious warfare.

Yet no body of joint doctrine existed when forces of two or more services were combined to conduct operations. Goldwater-Nichols changed that, but it was General Powell who drove the first real operational joint doctrine, JCS Pub 1, published after Desert Storm, that laid out operating guidelines for joint forces. Soon after that came JCS Pub 3.0, which was a joint version of the Army's FM 100-5.

The June 1993 FM 100-5, written by Fred Franks and his TRADOC team, contained an entire chapter on joint operations, which gave members of the Army the basic outlines of joint operations, joint task force, joint command, unified commands, and command relationships.

Joint operations were clearly not always going to be on the scale of a Desert Storm. In today's more multipolar world, a smaller joint task force would be formed quickly to deal with fast-moving situations in areas such as Somalia, Haiti, or Bosnia. Each would be commanded by a joint task force (JTF)—a headquarters comprised of members of all the services, with component commands of each service reporting to the JTF. Normally, the commander of the JTF would be from the service with the most forces represented, while individual members of the joint task force staff would have to be skilled in working with a joint team. This was a marked change from the Cold War. Learning how to do this—and teach it—required a significant redesign of curricula in the service and joint schools: another provision of the 1986 legislation requiring joint education and joint duty.

★ In a combined—as opposed to a joint—operation, the U.S. military conducts missions with the forces of another nation, either in coalition warfare or coalition operations other than war. In the emerging multipolar world, with U.S. Army forces now smaller than in generations, most future operations will likely be combined.

Combined operations are not new to the U.S. military, either. Without the assistance of the French army and navy, Yorktown would not have happened. And in the twentieth century, combined operations have been the norm rather than the exception. During the Cold War, most combined operations were within the NATO framework . . . or, to a lesser extent, within the framework of the alliance with South Korea. Procedures within those two alliances had long been worked out.

In Desert Storm, the USA put together a political and military coalition of a very different kind—ad hoc, more or less improvised, but highly effective. As Fred Franks and the thinkers at TRADOC looked about the world, they saw that this was likely to be the model for future operations. If so, TRADOC needed to teach the upcoming generation of Army leaders how to do their part in putting such a coalition together, and then operating within it.

Some of the lessons learned in Desert Storm proved applicable:

• Teamwork and trust among members of the coalition team are absolutely essential.

• You have to consider how to combine the forces. Normally, you like to retain a single command; you don't want to break up the allied force and put it with your own. Such a principle governed the use of Pershing's U.S. forces under the French in World War I, and they governed Fred Franks's use of British forces in VII Corps in Desert Storm.

• Forces placed under a single operational command must be employed in accordance with their capabilities and assigned missions with a reasonable chance of success.

• National pride is often at stake . . . and so is mission accomplishment. Assignment of a mission to a subordinate national force that results in failure of the mission or in high casualties has serious consequences for the combined commander and the nations involved.

LAND OPERATIONS: BATTLE DYNAMICS

Land war changes. It will always be changing. In order to make sure that the Army stays ahead of it, and to give it an institutional lens directed at the future, Fred Franks and his team created a concept in 1991 under which all the various ideas about the evolving battlefield could be included. These ideas would then form the basis for experimentation in simulations and in the field. Out of the experimentation would come new insights and discoveries, which in time would lead to changes in the individual ideas. This concept TRADOC called "Battle Dynamics."

There were five central ideas to Battle Dynamics:

BATTLE COMMAND. The battlefield envisioned during the Cold War was almost scripted. After the Cold War, the U.S. Army found itself in a strategic situation where ambiguity ruled. How best to combat ambiguity?

• By reviving the art of command—command in the fluid and constantly changing attack instead of in the defense, which is more orderly and controlled.

• By rapidly applying principles of doctrine to situations that commanders might not be able to predict far in advance.

• By rapidly assessing situations—that is, by rapidly seeing oneself and the enemy and the terrain.

• By focus on the commander, not on the command post. The information and command system would be so constructed that the commander could make decisions and focus combat power from wherever he needed to be on the battlefield. Thus he would be freed from what Fred Franks calls "the tyranny of the command post."

Battle command is decision making. The commander will visualize the present friendly and enemy situations, then the situation that must occur if his mission is to be achieved at least cost to his soldiers, and then devise tactical methods to get from one state to the other (which is what leadership skill is all about). The more completely and accurately a commander can share his pictures of both situations with the rest of his command, the more effectively he can move his organization at a high tempo and focus his own combat power with the combat power available from outside. He will do all this while being with his soldiers, while feeling their pain and pride, and then making the necessary decisions.

BATTLESPACE. In the Cold War, we arrayed our own forces to defend against a powerful force that echeloned itself in depth in order to constantly feed forces into battle and thus maintain momentum. To defend against that threat, the United States laid out geometric lines for its own forces (phase lines, etc.) in order to determine who was responsible for real estate on our side and for carving up the enemy echelons deep in their territory.

That was a special situation against a special enemy. In the future, enemies will look and behave differently, yet we will still want to attack him in depth. To do that may not require the precise geometry of the Cold War battlespace. We may not need forces to be right next to one another. In fact, units will likely operate out of visual range of one another—though they will be in close electronic contact. And battle lines between opposing forces may well be much more amorphous than they are now. Thus, Franks wanted Army commanders to think their way through the tactical problems of the (likely) fluid, free-form, and ambiguous future battlefield without automatically applying Cold War battlespace templates. Since these templates had been so closely associated with the term "AirLand Battle," the Army dropped that term.

DEPTH AND SIMULTANEOUS ATTACK. In the past, there had been a segmented, sequential battlefield model of rear, close, and deep. That model would change and be redefined in future operations. In these operations, we would attack the enemy (or control a situation in operations other than war) simultaneously—not sequentially—throughout the depth of the battlespace.

EARLY ENTRY, LETHALITY, AND SURVIVABILITY. In a fast-moving situation, when a force has to go into an area quickly (called early entry), you want to be able to tailor it so that it goes in with power and protection. Just Cause in Panama was an example of a force so well tailored for that mission that it finished the fight in hours. Similarly, the 10th Mountain Division was rapidly tailored for its Somali mission, and later for Haiti. The Army wants to make a habit of such situations—especially in a world where the likelihood of early-entry missions has increased (and likely to be over a very wide range of situations).

Thus, early-entry forces must be tailorable in a number of ways. They need

- to meet changing conditions and a variety of missions;
- to provide the commander as many options as possible;
- to be able to protect themselves;
- and to have punch, not only close in, but out deep.

In short, they have to be able to win the first battle.

COMBAT SERVICE SUPPORT. In the Cold War, most of the focus was on tactical logistics. Force projection puts a premium on strategic and operational logistics. This new strategic environment will demand rapidly tailorable logistics systems, which must be capable of providing support for joint and combined operations, sometimes over great distances.

Tactical logistics will also continue to be one of the keys to more rapid tempo operations. Anticipation, long a goal of logisticians, will sometimes be aided by what are called telemetry-based logistics. Telemetry on equipment will allow support personnel to know when something is needed before it is needed. Total asset visibility, or the ability to pinpoint supplies worldwide, should help strategic logisticians to provide more precise support in future operations and in more than one operational theater.

BATTLE LABS

Ideas are not enough. The Army is a pragmatic profession. It makes things happen. It gets results for the nation. Army professionals are military practitioners, not military philosophers. As noted, the worth of a new approach has to be demonstrated before Army professionals will change over to it.

During Fred Franks's professional lifetime, he himself was powerfully impressed by the success of air assault and attack helicopter ideas. The pioneers who brought these ideas to the Army banded together in the late 1950s, got senior-level support, some resources for experiments, and by 1963 had a full-scale experimental division going. In 1965, the division was the 1st Cavalry, which fought successfully in Vietnam from 1965 until its departure in 1971. Air assault and attack helicopter pioneers demonstrated the worth of both their war-fighting ideas and their organizational changes, and they supported them either with new technology or with technology that had long been available in the civilian sector.

From this, Franks concluded that the Army needed to do some experimenting. Specifically, it needed an organization to try out new directions in land warfare . . . something like the air assault division experiment in the early 1960s and the series of field experiments known as the Louisiana Maneuvers in the early 1940s, just before World War II.

TRADOC had a major advantage over earlier experimenters—computer-assisted simulations. These simulations, including the new virtual reality simulations, had reached such a level of accuracy that they could replicate the battlefield with great fidelity, which permitted experiments to be performed. This was not only cheaper than running experiments in the field, it also allowed many more repetitions in a given time. When results justified full-scale field experiments, they could then be set up. This approach became the basis for the TRADOC Battlefield Laboratories formed in April 1992. There were five of them, each corresponding to a core idea of Battle Dynamics—a single area where the land battle was changing.*

In the labs, various organizations, not only from within the Army, but from academia, civilian contractors, other services, and the like, came together to work on a common battlefield idea. Such teamwork was unprecedented in the Army.

But there was more to the labs than that.

In fighting, as we have seen, at each echelon (battalion, brigade, division, etc.) you integrate arms—including tanks, infantry, artillery, aviation, and fire support—to get the combined-arms orchestra effect. Franks wanted the same approach in the Battle Labs. There, new technology and ideas were to be integrated at each echelon, rather than vertically by arm.

For example, in the past, the next generation of night-vision equipment might go to Abrams tanks, but not to Bradleys or other members of the

---

The colonels running the day-to-day operations of the labs were key pioneers: Bill Hubbard, Dave Porter, Arnie Canada, John Eberle, Don Kerr, Norm Williamson, Tom Nicholson, Mike Williams, and Mike Dallas.

combined-arms team. That would no longer be the case. Franks also demanded in the Battle Labs that war-fighting experiments be done with what he termed "real soldiers in real units." That way the Army would get normal soldier and leader behavior. He also wanted the experiments done at the NTC or JRTC, the most tactically competitive environments. Both these directives would increase the fidelity of the results.

Battle Labs proved to be such an innovative idea that the Air Force recently announced the formation of six of their own, and the USMC adopted the concept three years ago.

During those days at TRADOC, an excited buzz of activity could be found at Fort Monroe. People were eager; people were brimful of ideas; there was a lot of productive talk . . . there was a glow of energy about the place. Fred Franks used to tell people that he wanted the energy level at Fort Monroe to be so high that when a satellite passed overhead, the fort would glow in the dark like a diamond. Now and again in those days, I would look into my own Maryland night sky south toward Virginia and catch an unusual brightness over Fort Monroe. . . .

FUTURE BATTLEFIELDS

Battlefield technology evolves and develops, as does the nature of threats, tactics, strategy, and doctrine. Yet the military is a hierarchical institution. It needs to be in order to impose some order out of the chaos of battle. The way that order normally is imposed is by adherence to a strict hierarchy of command and by the physical means of control, such as formations, the ability to see others, the assignment of sectors to operate in, and phase lines. When radios came along, units could become more dispersed and still retain a semblance of control, yet adherence to physical means of control continued—and for good reason. There was no better way to bring the team of teams together at the right place at the right time in the right combination relative to the enemy and terrain, and then to fight and win physically.

The outcome of land battles is still decided by physical force. In army versus army, on a given piece of terrain, forces that prevail kill the enemy, destroy his equipment, and capture his soldiers, then control the area. Raw physical courage, physical toughness in all types of terrain and weather, combat discipline, skill with weapons and in units, and leadership in the face of chaos and life-and-death choices are still very much needed. Lethality, survivability, and the tempo of the operation are still measurable quantities that very often determine the physical outcome of the battles and engagements.

Deciding where and when to fight, and at what cost, and where battles and engagements will lead, continue to be the province of what the army has called operational art and strategy. These continue to be influenced by a variety of factors, some physical and some not.

★ TRADOC and the Army have long been very much aware of what other high-performing organizations also have learned—that information not only passes through the normal hierarchical chain of command, it flows in other ways to get quickly where it's needed. In order to take advantage of that fact, the Army needed to structure its own organizations and problem solving so that information flowed in ways that enhanced unit performance. Then the Army had to invest in technologies that promoted it.

Today there's a lot of buzz about winning the information war, as though that in itself wins battles and engagements, as though it were something new. In point of fact, since the early days of warfare, one side has always tried to win the information war over the other. Sun Tzu advised us to see ourselves and see the enemy. The goal of units in combat has always been to know the enemy and to see the terrain, then to decide what to do . . . and to have the skills to do it faster than an enemy. The information age just provides new ways to do it on the battlefield.

That does not mean that the information age is not changing the battle-field. Far from it.

The emergence of information technology, operated by truly high-quality soldiers, is bringing about a revolution in land warfare. In the not-at-all-distant future, commanders will find themselves on a battlefield where all soldiers and weapons platforms will carry sensors. With their help, soldiers will not only know precisely where they are, they will also be able to engage the enemy di-rectly and at the same time to transmit information about the enemy to other platforms that also can engage the enemy. Thus, combat power can be applied simultaneously throughout the depth of the battlespace to confound and stun, then rapidly defeat any enemy.

And that's only the beginning. Other changes may follow:

- telemetry-based logistics;
- broadcast and warrior pull-down intelligence on demand;
- an expanded direct-fire battlespace;
- battle command on the move; and
- rapid tailoring of combat capabilities.

This transformation will have enormous implications for how units are commanded and soldiers are led into battle; for the size and function of staffs;

for the interaction of combat-support organizations in such a high-tempo context; and for interactions among joint partners.

Thus, for example, the trend in land combat has been toward fewer and fewer friendly forces in a given battlespace. They will no longer have to be confined to preset physical control measures. They won't even have to be contiguous to one another. Though massed effects on the enemy will still be possible (and usually without the need to mass physically), dispersal will be the norm, physical mass the exception. If it is necessary to physically mass in order to achieve an intended purpose, you can still do it, and then rapidly disperse again afterward. Such dispersal has the added benefit of increasing survivability probabilities.

In other words, we are moving toward what the British writer Paddy Griffith calls "an empty battlefield"—a battlefield where the trend in direct-contact battle is away from gaining coherence by means of physical mass to gaining it by means of a common picture of the situation, one that is constantly updated and available to all elements in the team of teams.

The U.S. Army vision for the future battlefield has been driven by the following overriding concept: quality soldiers and leaders whose full potential is realized through the application of information-age technologies and by rigorous and relevant training and leader development.

Two recent technical innovations symbolize that vision in a small way.

In September 1992, when the Army took its first M1A2 tank platoon to the National Training Center, Fred Franks and Major General Butch Funk, his old 3rd AD commander in Desert Storm, and at the time the commander of the Armor Center at Fort Knox, visited the NTC in order to see how well the soldiers could handle the rapid display of information while they fought their individual tanks (they did it very well, incidentally, and with initiative). It was the first de facto experiment of the future.

Inside the M1A2 were two revolutionary devices. The first was an independent viewer for the commander. With its addition, both commander and gunner now had sighting systems that could fire and find targets simultaneously. Thus the tank's lethality was almost doubled. As the gunner was engaging one target, the commander was independently finding another, which allowed the gunner to go right to the next.

The second device was even more significant. It looked something like a laptop computer and it was called the Intervehicular Information System (IVIS). IVIS was initially invented so that units would be able to know the location of all vehicles, transmit orders, automatically update logistics information about each tank, and consolidate that information for virtually automatic resupply.

Following the NTC tactical exercise, Franks and Funk huddled with the tank platoon and their platoon sergeant, Sergeant First Class Phil Johndrow, and listened to their experiences. What he learned from the unit was more than just eye-opening.

Navigation was no longer a concern. Nor was the location of other tanks in the unit. The IVIS told them not only their own exact location, but the exact location of each of the other tanks in their unit (there were screens for both drivers and tank commanders). Thus, they did not have to see each other physically in order to keep unit coherence, which meant that they could disperse more. The tank commander only had to give drivers a way point on which to guide, and the drivers did the rest (the driver steers between way points, which are provided automatically from the vehicle commander's screen). Consequently, the commander didn't have to spend as much of his time on navigation as before, which meant he could spend more time fighting the tank. (In Desert Storm only commanders had GPS, and the rest of the unit had to guide on his tank. Moreover, since his GPS was handheld, the vehicle commander constantly had to give course corrections to the driver.)

Before IVIS, all a tank crew knew was what they saw or were told by voice over the radio. They would peak to attention when the tank commander barked out a battle command, then they faded back to an awareness simply of what was available to their immediate senses. Now that the picture of what all the pieces of their unit were doing was available to them, the tank crew were much more able to anticipate platoon tactics and to engage in tactical tasks without being told. Independent action. Their heads were in the situation all the time. Even if another tank in the platoon became a casualty, they were able to continue the mission without missing a beat.

Imagine the power of quality soldiers, in highly trained units, all of whom have a continuing sense of the situation and the direction needed to defeat the enemy. It is the power of information. Further war-fighting experiments at Fort Knox in March 1993, then with battalion tank forces at the NTC in April 1994 by then–Major General Larry Jordan, confirmed the vision.

Some time after that, Franks visited TRADOC's dismounted Battle Lab at Fort Benning, where Major General Jerry White was conducting experiments in advanced night-vision equipment.

The working hypothesis: With an ability to see better, troops can disperse more and, with even fewer soldiers, inflict more damage on the enemy.

Later, troops at the Battle Lab were equipped with a communications link that let them all talk with each other on a common radio net. Soldiers don't like to be out of touch with the others in their team, but they don't need physical contact, as long as they can talk to one another. If they can do that, and if they can see the enemy at ranges greater than those at which the enemy can see them, they will take it from there.

Dispersion: Fewer soldiers in a given battlespace wielding the same lethality against the enemy. That means you don't have to protect so much of your own force.

Power of information: All your troops know what is going on.

But what then? What happens to the hierarchical military command structure? Does it remain the same? Do units remain the same size? Do they need to be as big? Can you expand the leader-to-led ratio while you disperse units, keep them informed, and place fewer troops in a given battlespace? What happens when you horizontally integrate all members of the combined-arms team (tanks, infantry, artillery, engineers, aviation, etc.) the same way you wired that tank platoon? Do you increase the tempo of your operation? Can you bring more lethal fires on the enemy?

By the spring of 1994, results from the Army's Louisiana Maneuvers and TRADOC's Battle Labs, both in TRADOC and at JRTC and the NTC, led to the decision to field an experimental force to explore further issues concerning changes in doctrine and technology investments. Army Chief General Sullivan directed that an experimental unit named Force XXI be established at Fort Hood, Texas, with a goal of a full-brigade war-fighting experiment at the NTC in 1997. The Army had come a long way toward the future since 1991.

As the Army forges into that future, it faces a multitude of questions of ever-growing complexity—but it knows *how* to go about solving them. Fred Franks retired from TRADOC in 1994, but today TRADOC continues to experiment, continues to work on the answers. At TRADOC's Battle Labs, Fort Hood, Fort Knox, the NTC, and JRTC—everywhere, activity flows. The rebirth of the army is not a one-time thing. Thanks to Fred Franks and his colleagues, the generations before and the generations that will follow, the Army is a living, breathing organism. It has seen the twenty-first century—and it welcomes it.

Fred Franks has the last word. . . .

REFLECTIONS

On 5 May 1970, the day I was wounded near Snoul, Cambodia, I could never have predicted the course the next twenty-five years would take—years that ended at a retirement ceremony at Fort Myer, Virginia, after I had completed thirty-five and a half years in the Army.

There is no mystery to what we do as soldiers and as an Army. When called to do so, we fight and win our nation's wars as part of a joint team. We spend a lifetime getting ready to do that. I was no different.

I make no apologies about my pride in our nation, our Army, and our soldiers. From that day in July 1955, when I proudly put on the fatigue shirt with "U.S. Army" over the pocket and took my place in the line with my West Point classmates, I was excited every day to be an American soldier. I loved the Army. I loved soldiering. I loved the cause we served. It is a profession as much about the heart as the mind. There is much passion in what soldiers do. What matters most is the cause we have been privileged to serve and those we've been privileged to serve with.

Someone asked me a few years ago why I wanted to be a soldier. I thought a few seconds before answering. Then I said, "If you like what our country stands for and are willing to fight to protect those ideals, you ought to be a soldier.

"If the sound of the national anthem and the sight of our flag stir something inside you, then you ought to be a soldier.

"If you want to be around a lot of other people who feel the same way about all that as you do, you ought to be a soldier.

"If you like a challenge, are not afraid of hard work, and think you are tough enough to meet the standards on the battlefield, you ought to be a soldier.

"If you and your family are strong enough to endure the many separations, often on a moment's notice, and can live that kind of life, then you ought to be a soldier.

"If the thought that at the end of your life you can say—or have said about you—that you served your country, if that appeals to you and you need no other reward than that, then you ought to be a soldier."

I think of the selfless and total commitment of our men and women and their families. The soldier in Captain Dana Pittard's tank company, who said, "We're family." The troopers of the 1st Squadron, 3rd Cavalry, who in 1975 accepted an amputee Lieutenant Colonel as their commander and who made me feel whole again as a soldier three years out of the amputee ward. The members of the great Blackhorse fist in the Fulda Gap in the early 1980s that we had ready and cocked for the Warsaw Pact.

They are the JAYHAWKS, Blackhorse, Brave Rifles, and Iron Soldiers. They give all they have. Sometimes their lives. They speak in whispered tones, or not at all, about what they have done. They are the best we have in America. I can see their faces and remember their names. They look like America. They are America. Some of them are Cooper, Wiggins, Hallings, Johndrow, Vinson, Hawthorne, Johnson, Bolan, Burkett, Lin-

berg, McVey, Cotton, Williams, Murphy, Butler, Wilson, Woodall, and Paez.

They are my generation of Vietnam veterans and fellow amputees, for whom there were no yellow ribbons or parades, but who did what our country asked and did it so well and at great personal sacrifice. They are our Desert Storm generation, who also did what our country asked and did it so well and at great personal sacrifice. They are America's army. Who would not be proud to serve in the ranks of such Americans and to be called to lead them in battle? "No mission too difficult, no sacrifice too great, duty first," they say in the Big Red One. "Allons"—"let's go"— they say in the Blackhorse. "JAYHAWK" in VII Corps. Iron Soldiers, Spearhead, First Team, Always Ready, Brave Rifles. Values such as selfless service, heroism, sacrifice, honor. Values given real meaning by soldiers' actions in service to our nation on battlefields and at duty posts the world over.

The toughest value has been duty. It demands more and gives less than any value I know. In the mind-numbing cold of a Grafenwohr, Germany, tank range in the pitch blackness, in the lonely outpost of a border OP staring into a dark void across the Iron Curtain, in the daily battles in the jungle while far away, others decide their worth and where they will lead, in the loneliness of a decision to send your soldiers into an all-night tank battle, in the echo of taps in an otherwise still and silent landscape, in all of that, duty calls and you do it: you, and so many who have gone before you in those and sometimes even more demanding circumstances. You are aware of them. You know them from history, but you also know them because you and they are kindred spirits. You hear them talk to you across the centuries. You will not break the faith. You and your generation will do your duty as our country needs it done while you are there, then you will pass the torch to those who follow, those you have helped prepare to take the torch.

Perhaps that is why our Army has proven to be a splendidly resilient institution in service to our nation. The Army's ethic—perhaps mirroring its battlefield behavior—has been to do its duty with a quiet professionalism and competence. It is quite simply service to nation. That is no different now. Yet, as a result, some have missed the enormous and profound transformation in our Army—first from the early 1970s to the late 1980s, and then from that period until now, and then to the challenging threshold we now stand on to the future. Our current Army's identity has been marked by change or growth and informed by ideas thought through by professionals, while simultaneously maintaining standards of performance in the demanding missions our nation expects of us in scenarios as diverse as at any period in our history. There have been substance and depth to our growth, just as there have been demonstrated results in our operations. None of that happens by accident, nor is it preordained. We have described some of that in this book.

I have been privileged to have the sometimes awesome responsibility of commanding soldiers and civilians in peace and in two wars. Battle command is not complicated. To me it has three parts. The first is character: values, such as physical courage, mental courage (the courage to be who you really are), integrity, loyalty and selfless commitment to your mission and your troops. These all make a difference. The second is the competence to know what to do. Soldiers have every right to expect their commanders to know the nuts and bolts of the profession, to know how to make decisions, to outthink the enemy, and to put their units in a position to outfight him. The third is leadership—the skills to motivate and otherwise lead an organization of people to accomplish its mission at least cost to them, and sometimes in directions and in situations where they would rather not go.

I think about what generals do. I was a general for ten and a half years. Many have been generals for far longer than I was. But I have thought about what I did and what might be the essence of generalship, at least for me in this time.

I believe generals get to focus on and solve big problems in peace and war. They must know details and occasionally dip into those, but essentially they must figure out the few deciding issues or battles for their times and conditions and focus their energies on those. These are what I called points of main effort. They cannot be many. You have to decide what they are, and make them stick.

Generals must have an imagination that lets them visualize what needs to be. They must synthesize to create a whole when others cannot see, and then communicate that whole with so much clarity and so much conviction that others will see it, too, and follow it. That is command. That is leadership at the senior levels.

Generals decide where to be bold and where not to be bold.

They must be strong and decisive, yet they must also keep their ego from clouding their judgments. Instead, they must use that ego to stick to doing what is right, even in the face of adversity.

Generals decide where to intervene and where not to intervene.

They decide where to tolerate imperfection and where not to tolerate imperfection.

They must be intensely competitive. They must hate to lose.

They need to demand a climate of dignity and respect, and to know that to lead is also to serve. They can do a lot of good for individuals every day.

They must continue to grow. They must not be complacent.

If they can, they should rest easy in the saddle and have a sense of humor. Smile once in a while.

If generals can remember "Don't worry, General, we trust you," and do their best to fulfill that trust, they will have done their duty.

Finally, there is my own family. Denise, my high school sweetheart and Army wife of now thirty-eight years. My best friend and a woman of great compassion and courage. Margie, our special treasure of a daughter. Our intense love and depth of wisdom about each other and about what is of value born in the Valley Forge crucible.

Now there is Margie's family—her soldier husband, Greg, and our three grandchildren, Jake, Mickey, and Denise.

There is my Dad, who gave me an inscribed clock when I retired: "A boyhood dream becomes a reality. Congratulations, son, on your retirement from a distinguished career of faithful service to the U.S. Army and your country. Love, Dad." My Mom, gone, but never forgotten.

The Army has been like a bigger family for Denise and me. As she is fond of saying, she remembers "new friends, old friends, and forever friends." We had both grown up in West Lawn and West Wyomissing, Pennsylvania, in the 1940s and 1950s, so there were many excellent models for us. Each place we lived we tried to make our hometown. Those we served with became like family. Just like family, there was an intense loyalty in the units. You protected your family. You kept in touch with your family.

Those years after Valley Forge in the Brave Rifles at Fort Bliss, then in the Blackhorse in Fulda from 1982 to 1984, were like magic. Although it was not easy duty, and there were the usual separations and even deaths from accidents and in training, the magic was in the shared pride in being there in proud units. In Fulda, there was even the constant threat of war, as we stared down the 8th Guards Combined Arms Army across the Iron Curtain. But in all that there was emotion, strong bonding, shared duty, proud moments of winning over the adversity of weather, time, or other units in head-to-head competition. All of this forged intensely strong and lasting loyalties. These were units with no pomp or airs of office or even much observed protocol. It was as pure soldiering as you could get, and it was just a hell of a lot of fun for those of us privileged to take part.

It was not all easy. We had our tough times, our time at Valley Forge.

I suspect everyone spends time at a Valley Forge sometime in his or her life. None of us goes looking for trouble, but it finds us all. How we handle it and grow from it is a measure of who we are. We had lots of help. Mostly we had each other. Denise and I and Margie still have each other. We have a steel tempered in fire that will surely be tested again, but that helps us gain perspective on each day and value those many blessings we have and not worry much about what we do not have. And it helps us reach out a hand where we can to those who need it, as we once did, to help them climb out or get up again.

Among my last places to visit while commanding TRADOC and before retirement were Fort Jackson, South Carolina, to see new soldiers in basic training, and Hampton University, Hampton, Virginia, to see ROTC cadets. I wanted to do that last because those soldiers and those cadets represent our future. Our nation is well served by those talented, motivated, selfless young men and women. Truly our Army and our nation will be in great hands if we continue to attract such quality young Americans; if we allow them to grow in a climate of dignity, respect, and challenge; and if we continue to focus on what wins and not compromise on those standards. In that way, we will fulfill our mission to fight and win our nation's wars.

To put the thought another way, and as I have emphasized so strongly, fulfilling our mission comes down to trust. That basic bond of leadership. I had seen the trust fractured in Vietnam. I had seen the trust reunited following Desert Storm. "Don't worry, General, we trust you." Trust us to do what? To stay focused on what wins and on who does it. You train a lifetime to make the few tough decisions you need to make to accomplish the mission at least cost to your soldiers. We expect that of ourselves, our soldiers expect that, and those who send us their sons and daughters expect that. It all comes down to that.

One of the lasting truths about being a soldier is that friendships formed with comrades in arms are the deepest and most enduring. Denise and I were privileged beyond words to have made those friendships.

I was humbled and proud to have been able to serve our nation and "to protect and defend the Constitution of the United States of America" in the United States Army in peace and two wars. That I was permitted to remain on active duty following the amputation of my left leg below the knee, and that I was given every opportunity to serve by Army leaders, by policy, and by my fellow soldiers, has been life's great privilege. My everlasting thanks to this great and noble institution, to our nation which it serves, and to the soldiers in whose ranks I was permitted to serve for thirty-five and a half years.

ACKNOWLEDGMENTS

THERE ARE A GREAT MANY PEOPLE TO ACKNOWLEDGE IN THE PREPARATION of this work, and their sheer number prevents us from recognizing them all in this brief space. I will let Fred Franks speak for both of us here, since there is no need to duplicate his remarks and he expresses them most eloquently. I would be remiss, however, if I did not single out one man. This book would not have been possible without the tireless collaboration, constant encouragement, and extraordinary knowledge and experiences of the "Quiet Lion" himself. It's been a privilege to know you, Fred.

—TOM CLANCY

OVER TWO YEARS AGO, AND WITH MUCH ENCOURAGEMENT FROM members of VII Corps, I found that my friend Tom Clancy thought I had a story worth telling, and he invited me and three fellow commanders from Desert Storm each to do a book on command with him. This is the first of four, and I feel privileged to bat lead-off.

The book is, strictly speaking, not a history book, although it has taken over two years of intense personal research to compile much of the material. Much source material came from interviews and from former JAYHAWKS who volunteered because they wanted the VII Corps story to be told. In doing so, we have attempted to be as historically accurate as possible.

This is a long book, yet even so, much has been left out. One area in which I feel a particular lack is in the story of Vietnam and Cambodia. Editorial decisions did not permit us to go as deeply or as emotionally into that story as I felt was necessary. Because I continue to feel a tight bond with all those who served there, that is left for me to tell in my own voice in another venture. There are other areas. The rebirth of the U.S. Army from the 1970s to the late 1980s is a good-news American story that has many lessons for all government agencies. We only scratched the surface. The actual deployment, then redeployment, to and from Saudi Arabia was an enormous logistics feat and deserves much fuller treatment, especially our deployment from Germany and the role of NATO nations. Actions in Washington by the Department of the Army during Desert Storm are a model of how Goldwater-Nichols 1986 envisioned military service departments working in a crisis, yet we could mention that only in passing. Finally, to show the intensity of the ground war, we included descriptions of some combat actions by VII Corps U.S. and British soldiers and commanders who fought those actions. More of the ground action needs to be told and shown. In other areas we did our best.

The views we have expressed are ours and do not reflect the official policy or position of the Department of the Army, Department of Defense, or the U.S. government.

Tom and I wanted to tell a story of battle command and the good-news story of what our Army and our soldiers have done in service to the nation. It was never our intention to invite controversy. Yet I did get a lot of incoming fire when I was still on active duty, and I was not at liberty to return it. So if anyone is offended, we meant nothing personal. What happened, happened. I believe we are all entitled to our own opinions, but not our own facts. We accept responsibility for facts we used; if we are in error, it is an error of omission and not intended. Quotations are as accurate as I recall them to be or as our notes would indicate. The sense, if not the actual words, I believe to be correct.

I have many to thank for this book.

Let me begin with my immediate family. My wife, Denise, of now almost thirty-eight years. My best friend. An Army wife who always lent an ear to listen and a heart to care. Whose goal in life has always been to make people feel better about themselves. A woman of incredible courage and toughness. Who has been patient with me beyond belief over the two years' work on this book, day after day. I do not have enough of a lifetime left to thank her enough. Our daughter, Margie, who is a mother of three—Jake, Mick, and Denise—and an Army wife. Who has her own brand of courage. Who is also a talented and published author. And who reviewed and helped with the manuscript. To her soldier husband, Lieutenant Colonel Greg Bozek, former Blackhorse, SAMS graduate, and friend, who helped me with my memory of events and with manuscript review.

To Tom Clancy for his friendship and for the opportunity to tell this story with him; who has coached me in my attempts to be a writer; and who challenged me again and again to open up and talk about command to my fellow soldiers and to those who send America's Army their sons and daughters. To the editors at Putnam, most particularly publisher and editor in chief Neil S. Nyren, for advice on book organization, patience with my sometimes military prose in portions of the book, and for listening to my arguments on voice and on relevance of material. To Mr. Tony Koltz, writer in his own right, and daily collaborator, writing counselor, and whose questions drove me to greater depths of thought on command and maneuver warfare. To Mr. Marty Greenberg for advice and counsel. To our agent at William Morris, Robert Gottlieb, who helped me navigate this publishing terrain and get to this objective.

To my parents: Dad, now in his eighties, and Mom, gone now but never forgotten, for getting me and my younger sister, Frances, and brother, Farrell, started right in life. My hometown, West Wyomissing, near Reading, Pennsylvania, a great place to grow up and where the values of duty and teamwork ruled over self, values vital to my own later command beliefs. My uncle, Harry Franks, who taught me and a bunch of kids in hand-me-down jeans (dungarees in those days) a life's lesson in how to compete and win, when we won a county baseball championship in 1950 over a better-uniformed but less-skilled baseball team. That fierce desire to win, gained from sports, was also valuable to me as a commander. Denise's mother, Eva, and her dad, Harry, also gone now but both remembered for their support in our Valley Forge days. The best man at our wedding, my lifelong buddy and high school teammate, Dr. Carl Hassler, whose continuing courage in battling cancer three times in quiet dignity and with steel will reflects the best qualities you could ever find in a person and a friend. He and his wife, Betsy, were there for us in those dark days of our Valley Forge, and have been since.

My bigger family, the United States Army, which let me remain on active duty and continue to serve, despite the loss of my left leg below the knee. Those who helped me do that and gave me encouragement. Those soldiers and leaders in the VII Corps, JAYHAWKS; Blackhorse, 11th Cavalry; Brave Rifles, 3rd Cavalry; 7th Army Training Command; 1st Armored Division, Iron Soldiers; and TRADOC, who asked only that I do my duty as a commander for them and never let me look back. I was inspired by their sense of duty and the intense loyalty born of service in peace and war together. To my many mentors: soldiers, NCOs, and officers who underwrote my mistakes and helped me be a better soldier. Current Army leadership, Secretary of the Army Togo West and Army Chief, General Dennis Reimer.

Those of my fellow soldiers who gave me advice and helped with material.

Colonel (Ret.) Dr. Rick Swain, whose insights on the manuscript and research help were invaluable and whose own book, *Lucky War*, remains the best history with commentary on the Gulf War. Colonel Mark Hertling with manuscript help, battle accounts, maps, reference compilation, and sound cavalryman advice. My VII Corps G-3, Brigadier General Stan Cherrie, who read manuscripts and helped with facts. Some references proved particularly valuable: the Army's *Certain Victory*; archives in the U.S. Army Combined Arms Research Library at Fort Leavenworth and Mr. Harlan Crause; Steve Vogel and his excellent interview series in *Army Times*; and Toby Martinez's and Russ Mulholland's journals and notes.

My JAYHAWK major unit command team from Desert Storm. U.S. division commanders, Butch Funk, Ron Griffith, Tom Rhame, and John Tilelli, who consented to interviews and helped me remember facts and decisions and even read manuscripts. Together with Rupert Smith, they made a talented team of division commanders who led from the front and did all I asked of them and more. Don Holder, who provided the rich source of 2nd ACR materials and who led his fast-hitting "Dragoons" into combat. Bob McFarlin, VII Corps logistician, who provided logistics accounts and whose COSCOM did a remarkable job supplying the corps. VII Corps Command Sergeant Major Bob Wilson, whom I first met in those early 1960s days in the Blackhorse.

My separate brigade commanders in VII Corps: Johnnie Hitt, Rich Pomager, Sam Raines, Jo Rusin, John Smith, and Rich Walsh, who provided perspective and material. Corps artillery commander, Creighton Abrams. Close members of my VII Corps personal staff, Toby Martinez, Violet McInerney, Russ Mulholland, Dave St. Pierre, and Lance Singson. VII Corps Base in Germany: Major General (Ret.) Roger Bean and Brigadier General Jerry Sinn.

What a command team!

There were many others in the Department of the Army and the Defense Department who reviewed manuscripts or who provided their own accounts or information on their part of Desert Storm. Some are cited in the list of references; some here. I regret if we missed anyone.

Logisticians Cary Allen, Jim Chambers, Bob Shadley, and Mike Stafford. Intelligence help from Colonel Keith Alexander, Colonel John Davidson (VII Corps G-2), Brigadier General John Smith, and Major General (Ret.) John Stewart. My great planners, Colonel Tom Goedkoop and Lieutenant Colonel (Ret.) Bob Schmitt, who helped my memory stay accurate. Colonel Mike Kendall, John Yeosock's wartime executive officer and to whom John referred me for accuracy in relating my dealings with him and Third Army. Steve Arnold, G-3 Third Army (and lieutenant general who went on to command Third Army until his recent retirement), who drove the CENTCOM planning work until January 1991, and who devised the Third Army two-corps attack plan. His interview and source material that included perspectives on planning and conduct of the war were invaluable. Brigadier General Jack Mountcastle and Mr. Robert K. Wright at the Center of Military History, U.S. Army. U.S. Army Public Affairs, especially Brigadier General Gil Meyer, Colonel Gene Thornton, Ms. Pamela Carter, Mr. Jim Hill, and Lieutenant Colonel Carl

Kropf in Washington and Colonel George Stinnett at Fort Monroe, Virginia. Army SJA, especially Brigadier General Walt Huffman; and Colonel (Ret. and former VII Corps G-5) Art Hotop. Our VII Corps TAC CP team.

Blackhorse Vietnam veterans: Max Bailey, Brigadier General (Ret.) Grail Brookshire; Commander Sergeant Major (Ret.) Ray Burkett, Command Sergeant Major (Ret.) Don Horn, Miles Sisson, Colonel (Ret.) John Barbeau, Gus Christian, Doug Farfel, Allen Hathaway, Chaplain (Ret.) Larry Hayworth, and John MacClennon; Steve Bourque (whose official history of VII Corps will soon be published); Tom Carhart and his book, *Iron Soldiers*; John Sack and his book, *Company C*; Mr. Art Hughes; Dr. John Romjue; Mr. Charley Cureton; Dr. Susan Canedy; Colonel (Ret.) Skip Bacevich; Colonel (Ret.) Bill Smullen; Mr. Jim Blackwell; Lieutenant Colonel John Scudder; Colonel Mungo S. Melvin (G-3 in 1UK Armoured Division in ODS); Colonel Charles Rogers (battalion commander, Staffords, UK); Ms. Laura Alpher; Colonel Steve Robinette; Colonel John Rosenberger; Colonel (Ret.) Rosie Speed; Chaplain (Ret.) Dan Davis; Colonel Mike Kain; Brigadier General Jerry Sinn; Ms. Sigrid Stanton; Mr. Harold Koehler; Major H. R. McMaster; Major Joe Sartiano; Colonel Greg Fontenot; Colonel Taylor Jones; Major General Rob Goff; Major General Leon LaPorte; Major General Randy House; Sergeant First Class (Ret.) Frederick Wiggans; Mr. Leigh Tallas; Master Sergeant Phil Johndrow; and Major General Tim Sulivan (UK). Members of the media: Peter Copeland (who rode with the 42nd Artillery Brigade); Sam Donaldson for capturing on video on 21 February 1991 the best of America's Army; and James Sterba, who was at Snoul 5 May 1970.

Many others who stopped me on the street, in airports, at ceremonies, at Army posts, and offered help and assistance and encouragement. Their genuine interest and concern that the story of the JAYHAWKS be told kept me at this.

To my Third Army comrades and fellow U.S. corps commanders in Desert Storm, Gary Luck and the soldiers and leaders of XVIII Corps on our west flank and Walt Boomer and the U.S. Marines in the east. Especially my Third Army boss, John Yeosock, for his loyalty and support, and for his selfless performance of duty from August 1990 to May 1991. To the leadership in Germany, General (Ret.) Butch Saint, the mobile armored warrior himself, and General (Ret.) Jack Galvin, for orchestrating the European deployment. To the leadership in Washington. General (Ret.) Carl Vuono, 31st CSA, for his friendship, the opportunity to serve, and leadership in DA during Desert Storm. General (Ret.) Gordon Sullivan, for his friendship and letting me work on change, present and future, at TRADOC. General (Ret.) Colin Powell, who reached out to me when I needed it, and whose decisive force goals reunited trust and are exactly right for America. Secretary of Defense Dick Cheney, for his straightforward focus and genuine integrity we could all feel. President Bush, for his iron will and unwavering determination in seeing our strategy of defeating aggression through to victory.

VII Corps combat actions speak for themselves. Arguably, the armored day-night attack by our combined U.S.-UK VII Corps from A.M. 26 February through P.M. 27 February was the largest concentrated armored attack in history. Was our operation perfect? No, but then most things rarely are. But it was a helluva lot closer to perfect than anything I have ever been associated with in thirty-five and a half years in the Army.

We did all that in VII Corps as a team. We have attempted to mention as many of that team as we could. Of course, it was not possible to mention everyone. But you know who you are. I hope this book makes you prouder of what we did together.

We remember this day and every day those who did not return, and also remember their families. To that end we have formed a VII Corps Desert Storm Veterans Association to honor their memory; provide scholarships for next of kin and soldiers; sustain fellowship and remember the realities of land warfare; and assist those who might need it because of Gulf War–related illnesses or other needs. A portion of proceeds from the sales of this book will be given to that cause, as well as to the Blackhorse Vietnam Veterans Association, whose goals are similar for those who fought in Vietnam.

I had a full and rich life as a soldier. I was helped in that in more ways than I will ever know. My everlasting thanks to our nation, which I was privileged to serve wearing the uniform of the United States Army, and to the magnificent American soldiers in whose ranks I was proud to be through times of peace and two wars. They are proof that America surely is the land of the free and the home of the brave.

—FRED FRANKS

BIBLIOGRAPHY AND REFERENCES

IN ADDITION TO THE HUNDREDS OF HOURS OF INTERVIEWS WITH GENERAL FRANKS, AND dozens of other individuals who played important roles in the Vietnam and Persian Gulf Wars and in the development and rebuilding of the United States Army and its doctrine, we relied on a wide variety of books, articles, monographs, field reports, and newspaper accounts. In addition to those listed in the body of this bibliography, we would especially like to acknowledge interviews with Denise Franks and Marjorie Franks Bozek, along with Margie's book manuscript, *A Soldier's Daughter, A Soldier's Wife* (1992), and her essay "Walks in the Sunshine" (1996). We would also like to thank the large number of brave Army men and women who shared their memories with us, but whose names do not appear below.

Note that a number of the citations were helpful in more than one area, particularly those dealing with military history and doctrine.

MILITARY HISTORY, THEORY, AND DOCTRINE

Books

Brickhill, Paul. *Reach for the Sky*. New York: W. W. Norton and Company, 1954.

Carver, Field Marshal Lord. *The Apostles of Mobility: The Theory and Practice of Armoured Warfare*. New York: Holmes and Meier Publishing, 1979.

Chander, David G. *The Campaigns of Napoleon*. New York: Macmillan Publishing, 1966.

Clausewitz, Carl Von. *On War*. Edited by Michael Howard and Peter Paret. Princeton, N.J.: Princeton University Press, 1976.

Colby, John. *War from the Ground Up: The 90th Division in World War II*. Austin, Tex.: Nortex Press, 1991.

Connell, Evan S. *Son of the Morning Star: Custer and the Little Big Horn*. New York: Harper and Row, 1984.

Donnelly, Tom, and Sean Naylor. *Clash of Titans: The Great Tank Battles*. New York: Berkley Books, 1996.

Doughty, Robert A. *The Seeds of Disaster: The Development of French Army Doctrine, 1919–1939*. Hamden, Conn.: Archon Books, 1985.

Dupuy, Colonel R. Ernest. *The Compact History of the United States Army*. New York: Hawthorn Books, 1956.

Fehrenbach, T. R. *This Kind of War: A Study in Unpreparedness.* New York: The Macmillan Company, 1963.

Fuller, J. F. C. *Generalship: Its Diseases and Their Cure.* Harrisburg, Pa.: Military Services Publishing Company, 1936.

Griffith, Paddy. *Battle Tactics of the Civil War.* New Haven: Yale University Press, 1989.

Guernsey, Alfred H., and Henry M. Alden. *Harper's Pictorial History of the Civil War.* New York: The Fairfax Press, 1866.

Heinl, Colonel (Ret.) Robert Debs, Jr. *Dictionary of Military and Naval Quotations.* Annapolis, Md.: United States Naval Institute, 1966.

Heller, Charles E., and William A. Stofft, ed. *America's First Battles, 1776–1965.* Lawrence: The University Press of Kansas, 1986.

Henderson, George F. R. *Stonewall Jackson and the American Civil War.* Gloucester, Mass.: Peter Smith, 1968.

Ketchum, Richard M. *The American Heritage Picture History of the Civil War.* Narrative by Bruce Catton. New York: Doubleday and Company, 1960.

Ruppenthal, Roland G., ed. *Logistical Support of the Armies, Volume I: May 1941–September 1944.* Washington, D.C.: Center of Military History, 1953.

Shaara, Michael. *The Killer Angels.* New York: Ballantine Books, 1974.

Sherman, William T. *Memoirs of William T. Sherman.* New York: Appleton, 1875.

Slim, Field Marshal the Viscount William. *Defeat into Victory.* New York: David McKay Company, Inc., 1961.

Stackpole, General Edward J. *Chancellorsville: Lee's Greatest Battle.* 2d rev. ed. Harrisburg, Pa.: Stackpole Books, 1988.

Truscott, Lt. Gen. Lucien K., Jr. [1954] 1990. *Command Missions.* Reprint, Novato, Calif.: Presidio Press, 1990.

Weigley, Russell F. *History of the United States Army.* Bloomington: Indiana University Press, 1984.

———. *The American Way of War: A History of United States Military Strategy and Policy.* Bloomington: Indiana University Press, 1973.

Woodward, Admiral Sandy, and Patrick Robinson. *One Hundred Days: The Memoirs of the Falklands Battle Group Commander.* London: HarperCollins Publishers, 1992.

Young, Desmond. *Rommel: The Desert Fox.* New York: William Morrow and Company, 1950.

Government Documents

U.S., Army Materiel Command. *Theater Logistics and the Gulf War,* by Major John J. McGrath and Michael D. Krause. Alexandria, Va.: U.S. Army Materiel Command, 1994.

U.S., Center for Military History. *The U.S. Army's Transition to the All-Volunteer Force, 1968–1974,* by Robert K. Griffith, Jr. Washington, D.C.: U.S., Center for Military History, 1996.

U.S., Combat Studies Institute. *Selected Papers of General William E. DePuy.* Compiled by Colonel Richard M. Swain. Fort Leavenworth, Kans.: U.S. Army Command and General Staff College, 1994.

————. *Studies in Battle Command.* Compiled by the Faculty, Combat Studies Institute. Fort Leavenworth, Kans.: U.S. Army Command and General Staff College, 1995.

U.S., Headquarters, Department of the Army. Field Manual (FM) 100-5: *Operations.* Washington, D.C., 1 July 1976.

U.S., Headquarters, Department of the Army. Field Manual (FM) 100-5: *Operations.* Washington, D.C., 20 August 1982.

————. Field Manual (FM) 100-5: *Operations.* Washington, D.C., 5 May 1986.

U.S., Headquarters, Training and Doctrine Command. TRADOC Pamphlet 525-5: *Force XXI Operations: A Concept for the Evolution of Full-Dimensional Operations for the Strategic Army of the Early Twenty-first Century.* Fort Monroe, Va., 1 August 1994.

U.S., Military History Institute. *Changing an Army: An Oral History of General William E. DePuy,* by Lieutenant Colonel Romie L. Brownlee and Lieutenant Colonel William J. Mullen III. Carlisle Barracks, Pa.: U.S., Military History Institute, 1979.

U.S., Military History Office, United States Army Training and Doctrine Command. *American Army Doctrine for the Post–Cold War,* by John L. Romjue. Fort Monroe, Va.: U.S., Military History Office, 1996.

U.S., Office of the Command Historian, United States Army Training and Doctrine Command. *The Origins and Development of the National Training Center, 1976–1984,* by Anne W. Chapman. Fort Monroe, Va., 1992.

Magazines and Periodicals

DePuy, General William E. "Concepts of Operation: The Heart of Command, The Tool of Doctrine." *Army* (August 1988): 26–40.

Franks, Frederick M., Jr. "Battle Command: A Commander's Perspective." *Military Review* (June 1996): 4–26.

Unpublished Sources

Alexander, Keith. "1st Armored Division's Intelligence Picture of the Battlefield" [n.d.]. Personal notes.

Gorman, Paul F. "The Military Value of Training." Institute for Defense Analysis, Defense Advanced Research Project Agency, Alexandria, Va., December 1990.

————. "The Secret of Future Victories." Institute for Defense Analysis, Defense Advanced Research Project Agency, Alexandria, Va., February 1992.

THE VIETNAM WAR

Books

Dunnigan, James F., and Raymond M. Macedonia. *Getting It Right: American Military Reforms After Vietnam to the Gulf War and Beyond.* New York: William Morrow and Company, 1993.

Nolan, Keith. *Into Cambodia: Spring Campaign, Summer Offensive, 1970.* Novato, Calif.: Presidio Press, 1990.

Palmer, Bruce. *The 25-Year War: America's Military Role in Vietnam.* Lexington: The University Press of Kentucky, 1984.

Sorley, Lewis. *Thunderbolt: General Creighton Abrams and the Army of His Times.* New York: Simon and Schuster, 1992.

Magazines and Periodicals

Sterba, James P. "Scraps of Paper from Vietnam." *New York Times Magazine.* 18 October 1970.

THE PERSIAN GULF WAR

Books

Association of the United States Army. *Personal Perspectives on the Gulf War.* Arlington, Va.: The Institute of Land Warfare, 1993.

Atkinson, Rick. *Crusade: The Untold Story of the Persian Gulf War.* Boston: Houghton-Mifflin Co., 1993.

Bellamy, Christopher. *Expert Witness: A Defence Correspondent's Gulf War, 1990–1991.* London: Brassey's, 1993.

Benson, Nicholas. *Rat's Tales: The Staffordshire Regiment at War in the Gulf.* London: Brassey's, 1993.

Blackwell, James. *Thunder on the Desert: The Strategy and Tactics of the Persian Gulf War.* New York: Bantam Books, 1991.

Blair, Arthur H. *At War in the Gulf: A Chronology.* College Station: Texas A&M University Press, 1992.

Carhart, Tom. *Iron Soldiers: How America's 1st Armored Division Crushed Iraq's Elite Republican Guard.* New York: Pocket Books, 1994.

Gordon, Michael R., and Gen. (Ret.) Bernard E. Trainor. *The Generals' War: The Inside Story of the Conflict in the Gulf.* Boston/New York: Little, Brown Co., 1995.

Kelly, Orr. *King of the Killing Zone: The Story of the M1, America's Super Tank.* New York: W. W. Norton and Company, 1989.

Powell, Colin L. *My American Journey.* New York: Random House, 1995.

Sack, John. *Company C: The Real War in Iraq.* New York: William Morrow and Company, 1995.

Scales, Brigadier General Robert H., and Desert Storm Study Project Group. *Certain Victory: The U.S. Army in the Gulf War.* Washington, D.C.: U.S., Office of the Chief of Staff, United States Army, 1993.

Schwarzkopf, Gen. (Ret.) H. Norman. *It Doesn't Take a Hero: The Autobiography.* New York: Bantam. 1992.

Scott, Harriet Fast, and William F. Scott. *The Soviet Art of War: Doctrine, Strategy and Tactics.* Boulder, Colo.: Westview Press, 1982.

Sullivan, Gordon R. *The Collected Works of the Thirty-second Chief of Staff, United States Army, 1991–1995.* Edited by Lt. Col. Jerry Bolzak. Washington, D.C.: U.S., Office of the Chief of Staff, United States Army, 1995.

Sullivan, Gordon, and Michael Harper. *Hope Is Not a Method*. New York: Random House, 1996.

Swain, Richard M. *"Lucky War": Third Army in Desert Storm*. Fort Leavenworth, Kans.: U.S. Army Command and General Staff College Press, 1994.

U.S. News and World Report. *Triumph Without Victory: The Unreported History of the Persian Gulf War*. New York: Random House. 1992.

Government Documents

United Kingdom. Headquarters Doctrine and Training. *Operation Desert Sabre: The Planning Process and Tactics Employed by 1st Armoured Division in the Liberation of Kuwait 1990–1991*. London, 1993.

U.S., Headquarters, Department of the Army. Field Manual (FM) 100-5: *Operations*. Washington, D.C., 14 June 1993.

U.S., Headquarters, Department of the Army (Public Affairs Staff). CIA *Maps and Publications Released to the Public ("Operation Desert Storm: A Snapshot of the Battlefield" [NTIS PB-94-928102])*. Washington, D.C., January 1995.

U.S., Headquarters, Training and Doctrine Command. TRADOC Pamphlet 525-100-1: *Leadership and Command on the Battlefield, Just Cause and Desert Storm: Brigade, Division, and Corps*. Fort Monroe, Va., 1992.

———. TRADOC Pamphlet 525-100-2: *Leadership and Command on the Battlefield, Just Cause and Desert Storm: Battalion and Company*. Fort Monroe, Va., 1993.

———. TRADOC Pamphlet 525-100-4: *Leadership and Command on the Battlefield, Just Cause and Desert Storm: Noncommissioned Officer Corps*. Fort Monroe, Va., 1994.

U.S., Headquarters, Training and Doctrine Command. TRADOC Pamphlet 525-100-5: *Leadership and Command on the Battlefield, Just Cause and Desert Storm: Family Support*. Fort Monroe, Va., 1994.

U.S., Headquarters, U.S. Marine Corps, History and Museums Division. *U.S. Marines in the Persian Gulf War, 1990–1991: With the 1 Marine Expeditionary Force in Desert Shield and Desert Storm*. Washington, D.C., 1993.

Magazines and Periodicals

Brame, William L. "From Garrison to Desert Offensive in 97 Days." *Army* (February 1992): 28–35.

Cordingley, Brigadier P. A. J. "The Gulf War: Operating With Allies." *RUSI Journal* (April 1992): 17–21.

Donnelly, Michael. "War Diary." *Army Times*, 4 March 1991, 10–36.

Donnelly, Tom. "Courage and Leadership Mark Franks' Career." *Army Times*, 12 December 1994, 1–3.

Fontenot, Gregory. "Fright Night: Task Force 2/34 Armor." *Military Review* (January 1993): 38–52.

Hammerbeck, Brigadier Christopher. "A Desert's Tail." *Tank, The Royal Tank Regiment Journal*, 74, no. 720 (May 1992): 3–15.

Kindsvatter, Lt. Col. Peter S. "VII Corps in the Gulf War: Deployment and Preparation for Desert Storm." *Military Review* (January 1992): 3–16.

————. "VII Corps in the Gulf War: Ground Offensive." *Military Review* (February 1992): 16–37.

————. "VII Corps in the Gulf War: Post-Cease-Fire Operations." *Military Review* (June 1992): 2–19.

Maggart, Lon E. "A Leap of Faith." *Armor* (January-February 1992): 24–32.

Mathews, William. "We Will Set the Time." *Army Times*, 25 February 1991, 60–62

————. "Final Round." *Army Times*, 4 March 1991, 1–6.

Nilsen, David, and Greg Novak. "The 1991 Persian Gulf War: On the Brink of a New World Order." *Command Post Quarterly* (Winter 1994).

————. "The 1991 Persian Gulf War: On the Brink of a New World Order (Part 2)." *Command Post Quarterly* (Spring 1995).

————. "The 1991 Persian Gulf War: On the Brink of a New World Order (Part 3): Modern Equipment Ratings." *Command Post Quarterly* (Summer 1995).

Scicchitano, Paul. "Night Strikes: The Secret War of the 1st Cavalry Division." *Army Times*, 23 September 1991, 8.

Smith, Major General Rupert. "The Gulf War: The Land Battle." *RUSI Journal* (February 1992): 1–5.

Tice, Jim. "Coming Through: The Big Red Raid." *Army Times*, 26 August 1991, 12–21.

Vogel, Steve. "Stand Ready." *Army Times*, 25 February 1991, 59–63.

————. "A Swift Kick: 2 ACR's Taming of the Guard." *Army Times*, 5 August 1991, 1.

————. "Metal Rain." *Army Times*, 16 September 1991, 10.

————. "Hell Night." *Army Times*, 7 October 1991, 5.

————. "Killer Brigade." *Army Times*, 11 November 1991, 11.

————. "Fast and Hard: The Big Red One's Race Through Iraq." *Army Times*, 25 March 1991, 6.

————. "The Tip of the Spear." *Army Times*, 13 January 1992, 8.

Unpublished Sources

Berkheimer, Christopher. 21 December–20 March 1991. Personal journal.

Bourke, Stephen A. *Desert Saber: The VII Corps in the Gulf War.* Atlanta, Ga.: Historical Systems, LLC, 1994.

Boyd, Maj. Gen. Morris J. "Focusing Combat Power—The Role of the FA Brigade." 13 April 1991.

Commander, U.S. Army Central Command (COMUSARCENT). "Consolidated Operations Overlay for Operation Desert Storm." 26 January 1991.

————. "Contingency Plan 1A: Destruction of RGFC (Phase IIID); Positional defense in place template COA 6, 18 1300Z." February 1991.

————. "Contingency Plan: Destruction of RGFC (PHASE IIID); Positional defense in place template COA 6, 24 1900Z." February 1991.

Commander VII Corps. "Situation Report (Combat) #38, Period 232100Z-242100Z." February 1991.

Commander VII Corps. "Situation Report (Combat) #39, Period 242100Z-252100Z." February 1991.

Commander VII Corps. "Situation Report (Combat) #40, Period 252100Z-262100Z." February 1991.

Commander VII Corps. "Situation Report (Combat) #41, Period 262100Z-272100Z." February 1991.

Commander VII Corps. "Situation Report (Combat) #42, Period 272100Z-282100Z." February 1991.

Commander VII Corps. "Situation Report (Combat) #43, Period 282100Z February-012100Z." March 1991.

Command Report, 1st Cavalry Division (First Team). 10 April 1991.

Command Report, 2nd Armored Cavalry Regiment, "Operation Desert Storm 1990–91." 9 April 1991.

Command Report, 207th Military Intelligence Brigade (CEWI), Operation Desert Shield/Desert Storm. 10 April 1991.

Command Report, 2nd Corps Support Command "Operation Desert Storm Battle Chronology." 29 April 1991.

Command Report, 16th Corps Support Group. "Logistics Operations." n.d.

Command Report, 1st Infantry Division (Mechanized). "Division Support Command, Desert Shield/Storm Support Operations." Fort Riley, Kans., 15 January 1992.

1st Infantry Division (Forward). "Desert Shield/Desert Storm After Action Report. VII Corps Debarkation and Onward Movement." 30 May 1991.

Franks, Col. Frederick M. "11th Armored Cavalry Regiment Notes From Command." 1982–1984.

Franks, Lt. Gen. Frederick M. "Desert Battle Command Journals." 1990–91.

———. "VII Corps Command Intent." 10 January 1990.

———. "FY 91 VII Corps Command Training Guidance." 22 May 1990.

G-2, VII Corps Report. "The 100-Hour Ground War: How the Iraqi Plan Failed." 20 May 1994.

Gulf War Collection, Group VII Corps (SSG AAR1-006). "Executive Summary, VII Corps Desert Shield and Desert Storm After Action Report." 29 May 1991.

Gulf War Collection, Group VII Corps (SSG AAR1-007). "Historical Narrative, VII Corps Desert Shield and Desert Storm After Action Report." 29 May 1991.

Gulf War Collection, Group VII Corps (SSG AAR1-008). "Task Organization, VII Corps Desert Shield and Desert Storm After Action Report." 29 May 1991.

Gulf War Collection, Group VII Corps (SSG AAR1-010). "Major Lessons Learned, VII Corps Desert Shield and Desert Storm After Action Report." 29 May 1991.

Gulf War Collection, Group VII Corps (SSG AAR4-002). "1st Infantry Division Desert Campaign After Action Report." April 1991.

Gulf War Collection, Group VII Corps (SSG AAR4-030). "Executive Summary, 1st Armored Division's Participation in Operation Desert Shield and Desert Storm." Report Submitted by Division Chief of Staff, 19 April 1991.

Gulf War Collection, Group VII Corps (SSG AAR4-139). "Executive Summary, 3d Armored Division's Participation in Operation Desert Shield and Desert Storm." Report Submitted by Division G3, April 1991.

Gulf War Collection, Group VII Corps (SSG AAR4-636). "Executive Summary, G-Day to G + 8, 11th Aviation Brigade." 18 March 1991.

"Historical Summary, 125th Support Battalion, 1st Armored Division, Operation Desert Shield and Storm." 5 August 1991.

Hertling, Mark P. "1st Squadron 1st Cavalry Unit After Action Report for Operation Desert Shield/Desert Storm and Operation Blackhawk Aid." 18 April 1991.

Houlighan, Thomas. Unpublished manuscript of Gulf War. 1996.

Kendall, John H. "The Closed Fist: VII Corps Operational Maneuver in Operation Desert Storm." Army War College Monograph, Carlisle Barracks Pennsylvania, 15 March 1994.

———. "Notes From 1 February 1991 Commanders' Huddle Meeting Held at King Khalid Military City." Drafted as a memorandum for record, 1 February 1991.

Klemencic, John, and John Thomson. "Fire Support for the Corps Covering Force: A Desert Storm Perspective." Photocopy, n.d.

Krause, Michael D. "The Battle of 73 Easting, 26 February 1991: A Historical Introduction to a Simulation." A Joint Center of Military History and Defense Advanced Research Projects Agency Project, 24 May 1991.

Martinez, Lieutenant Colonel (Ret.) Toby. "VII Corps Commander's Journal." 11 November 1990–12 May 1991.

Merritt, Daniel A. "The Iron Duke World Tour: A Personal Experience Monograph." Army War College Monograph, Carlisle Barracks Pennsylvania, 31 May 1994.

Michitsch, Maj. Gen. John F. "3d Armored Division Artillery Historical Summary, Operation Desert Shield and Desert Storm." Photocopy, n.d.

Mulholland, Russell. "VII Corps in Operation Desert Storm." Personal journal, 8 November 1990–26 April 1991.

Raines, Sam. "A Commander's Perspective." Photocopy, n.d.

Reischl, Timothy J. "Crossing the Line in the Sand: 4th Battalion, 67th Armor in Southwest Asia." Army War College Monograph, Carlisle Barracks Pennsylvania, 5 April 1993.

Rosenberger, John D. "Personal Notes and Diary, 24–28 February 1991." Photocopy, n.d.

Stafford, Colonel Michael R. "Personal Notes, Thoughts and Recollections Concerning VII Corps Deployment and Actions During Operation Desert Storm and Desert Shield. 23 and 29 November 1994, 5 January 1995, 24 February 1995." Photocopy, n.d.

Thornton, Colonel Eugenia. "Letters Home, 1990–91."

Whitcomb, Roy S. "Personal Experience Monograph of Operation Desert Storm." Army War College Monograph, Carlisle Barracks Pennsylvania, 3 June 1992.

INTERVIEWS, CONVERSATIONS AND PRESENTATIONS

Arnold, Lieutenant General Steve. Personal interview. 7 July 1996.

Bozek, Margie. Personal interview. 6 May 1996.

Cavazos, General (Ret.) Richard. Personal interview. 13 September 1996.

Cosby, Colonel (Ret.) Neil. Personal interview. 23 September 1996.

Franks, Denise. Personal interview. 5 June 1996.

Franks, Lieutenant General Frederick M., Jr. "VII Corps Operation Desert Storm Overview." Presentation to the Secretary of Defense, Riyadh, Saudi Arabia, 9 February 1991.

———. "The 100-Hour War." Presentation to the Staff and Students at the U.S. Army Command and General Staff College, 31 May 1991.

Goedkoop, Colonel Thomas F. Personal interview. 27 March 1992.

Gorman, General (Ret.) Paul F. Personal interview. n.d.

———. "Distributed Tactical Engagement Simulation." Presentation to the NATO Working Group. Brussels, Belgium, 17 November 1992.

———. "Perspectives: Future Training in the Army National Guard." Presentation to Training and Doctrine Command, 22 September 1992.

———. "Preparing the Army for Force XXI." Presentation before the Conference on Army 2010, 31 May 1995.

Gorman, General (Ret.) Paul F., and H. R. McMaster. "The Future of the Armed Services: Training for the 21st Century." Statement before the Senate Armed Services Committee, 21 May 1992.

Griffith, General Ronald. Personal interview. 24 May 1996.

House, Major General Randy. Personal interview. 18 June 1996.

Hughes, Arthur G. Personal interview. 25 April 1996.

Martinez, Lieutenant Colonel (Ret.) Toby. Personal interview. 18 May 1996.

Powell, General (Ret.) Colin. Personal interview. 15 July 1996.

Rhame, Lieutenant General Thomas. Personal interview. 6 June 1996.

Schlesinger, James. Personal interview. 30 November 1995.

VII Corps Desert Storm Veterans in a variety of conversations and recollections.

Starry, General (Ret.) Donn. Personal interview. 23 May 1996.

Sullivan, Major General (UK) T.J. Personal interview. 13 February 1996.

Tilelli, General John. Personal interview. 18 June 1996.

Vuono, General (Ret.) Carl E. Personal interview. 25 July 1996.